METALLIC CARTRIDGE HANDLOADING

PURSUIT OF THE PERFECT CARTRIDGE

At our son's wedding in 2012.

METALLIC CARTRIDGE HANDLOADING

PURSUIT OF THE PERFECT CARTRIDGE

by

M. L. McPherson

SAFARI PRESS

McPherson, M. L.

Second edition

Safari Press

2013, Long Beach, California

ISBN 978-1-57157-371-1

Library of Congress Catalog Card Number: 2011936308

10 9 8 7 6 5 4 3

Printed in the United States of America

Readers wishing to see Safari Press's many fine books on big-game hunting, wingshooting, and sporting firearms should visit our website at www.safaripress.com.

NOTES:

1) Various manufacturers hold copyrights and trademarks on the names of various products mentioned in this manual. Examples include specific descriptive names of most bullets, many propellants, all primers, and many tools. As these designations are in the common parlance of shooters and handloaders, the author has made no effort to identify each such protection specifically. Nevertheless, the reader should understand that the names of such items as are used in this manual are, indeed, protected property.

2) Within this text, the author has used names of components and tools related to handloading with explicit permission.

TABLE OF CONTENTS

McPherson, Internal Ballistics Seminar, 2003, Varmint Hunter's Jamboree: McPherson has given handloading seminars in Arizona, Colorado, and South Dakota. At this seminar, he and By Smalley offered a detailed explanation of what actually happens inside a gun during the period from primer ignition to bullet exit from the muzzle.

McPherson with Jim Lockwood (Master Leathersmith and friend) at 2002 Shootists' Holiday: That year, the Shootists honored McPherson as Shootist of the Year; the following year they honored him as Innovator of the Year "for advancing the shooting sports." The Shootists is a group founded by John Taffin, almost on a lark. During a get-together with friends and acquaintances to do a bit of large-bore revolver shooting, Taffin asked, "Wouldn't it be fun to do this every year?" It certainly is.

ABOUT THE AUTHOR

M. L. (Mic) McPherson has been an avid shooter since age six, when he began wearing out the first of many BB guns. By eight, he had graduated to 22-rimfire rifles and revolvers. For many years thereafter, until the model-rocket bug took hold for a time, he spent every penny he could earn on BBs and rimfire ammunition. Since then, he has worn out several revolvers and many barrels on various rifles.

A seminal event occurred when he was not yet a teenager. Ken Runnestrand, father of Roy (Mic's first lifelong friend), invited Mic to join him and Roy on a trip to a nearby informal shooting area where Ken was testing a rifle he had built. While there, Mic observed hundreds of discarded, empty centerfire cases, including examples of dozens of kinds. He vividly recalls wondering then, and for many years afterward, why so many different kinds of cartridges existed. This fascination ultimately developed into a genuine pursuit revolving around the question: "Does an ideal case design exist?"

Ultimately, this interest led to McPherson's editorship of the acclaimed eighth and ninth editions of *Cartridges of the World,* which he views as among his most significant works. Because he made many thousand editorial improvements and factual corrections in that work, one can appreciate and understand his pride of accomplishment.

He also edited and coauthored *Reloading for Shotgunners, 4th Edition,* which has been a bestseller. In that, he was the first to present shotshell data in an alphanumeric system that any user can easily understand and with which any user can locate any desired load rapidly and without confusion.

As a consultant to Barnes Bullets, he pioneered a spreadsheet analysis method for evaluating loading data, to discover and correct data sheet recording and typographic errors. This approach is invaluable to the industry. Those who use derivatives of this system routinely discover errors that would have otherwise gone to print. For example, application of this technique disclosed eight previously unrecognized errors in the first edition of a reloading manual from a major data source.

Precision Shooting Publications released *Accurizing the Factory Rifle,* his gunsmithing tome, in 2003. It continues to be a bestseller for Precision Shooting Publications, and sales show no sign of slowing. Because many gunsmithing schools now use it as an introductory text, it is bound to achieve the rare status of a perennial bestseller. He has contributed hundreds of articles to magazines such as *Precision Shooting, Varmint Hunter, American Rifleman, Very High Power,* and *Guns.* While these cover many subjects, most at least touch upon handloading.

An avid experimenter, he has visited many ballistic laboratories and has done tests in Norma's, Oehler's, Sierra's, Speer's, Western's, Accurate's, Hodgdon's, and Hornady's labs. Results of his experiments in those facilities answered some important questions and suggested many others.

He attended the prestigious (invitation only) Oehler Research Pressure Testing Seminar. While there, he demonstrated the degree to which charge position matters. This led Oehler to adopt charge-position testing as a standard-load evaluation tool.

McPherson is coholder of four patents on optimized cartridge design. These parametric patents cover the physics behind what represents optimum cartridge design, as measured by ballistic efficiency. These also address the theory and mathematical constructs needed to understand how an optimum cartridge design works. Extensive laboratory testing has proven that the resulting SM^{C} designs deliver maximum performance and barrel life with minimum barrel heating and recoil.

McPherson started handloading at fourteen and has never looked back. Now, having loaded hundreds of thousands of rounds, he is still learning. His philosophy in that regard is very simple: "When you stop learning, you might as well stop living."

This volume represents McPherson's best understanding of what he has learned through these many decades about handloading and internal ballistics. Although various handloading authorities have reviewed this text, McPherson recognizes that some of the interpretations he presents here will surprise some readers because they do not follow conventional wisdom. This is the nature of education—while ignorance is dangerous, a little understanding can be even more dangerous. It is McPherson's fervent hope that all readers will find most of the information and concepts covered within this text to be both informative and useful.

An avid hunter, McPherson has taken a moose in Sweden, dozens of elk and mule deer in Colorado, whitetail in Texas, and many thousands of varmints and predators in various states, including Wyoming, Utah, South Dakota, New Mexico, Nebraska, Montana, Colorado, and Arizona.

Jim Williamson
Friend and fellow handloader, 2010

A 17/23 SMc: Forming cases for this wildcat cartridge requires only the firing of loaded 17 Fireball ammunition. Usable capacity is about midway between the Fireball and the 17 Remington but performance equals the longer 17 Remington due to superior case design. Tested safe loads launch 20-grain bullets at 4,500 fps and 25-grain bullets at 4,100 fps.

Custom Marlin belonging to Tom Knight: Chambered in 17/23 SMc, this unique varmint rifle proves that lever actions can be accurate enough for any hunting purpose.

PREFACE

As I write this, more than a decade has passed since DBI Books published my first loading manual, *Metallic Cartridge Reloading, 3rd Edition (MCR3).* Since then, gunmakers have standardized many useful new chamberings; handloading component manufacturers have introduced many new propellants and bullets; and handloading tool manufacturers have introduced many significant new tools. In *MCR3,* I catered to both advanced handloaders and novice reloaders. My goal here is to update and expand upon the text of *MCR3* by introducing handloaders to newer topics, components, tools, and techniques.

I derived the basis of much of this text from information in my articles published in various magazines *(Precision Shooting, Tactical Shooter, Rifle Shooter, Very High Power,* and the *Single Shot Rifle Journal).* Often, the theme for such text originated with articles I wrote in direct response to queries from serious handloaders and shooters about some specific subject that interested them.

Deliberate repetition occurs within this text and for good reasons:

- To assure that I cover pertinent points whenever I address any particular subject; for example, I cover primer safety several times because, separately, I consider various aspects of primer storage, handling, and usage.
- I often present some basic concept from a somewhat different perspective in an effort to clarify some related point, and I want each such subject to be reasonably self-contained because I do not expect that anyone will study this extensive text thoroughly in any one sitting.

My goal in this work is to present as much information as seems feasible and useful, while attempting to keep each section reasonably self-contained. I trust that those who do read this text cover-to-cover will find sufficient variation in any repeated theme so that such reading will add to their understanding, rather than leading to boredom.

In a data manual that I might eventually write as a companion to this work, I would expect to include data for about 200 cartridges. That will amount to more than 20,000 component and chambering combinations.

In this text, I have assumed that the reader has a certain amount of fundamental background knowledge. However, even the novice should be able to follow these topics and, at the very least, gain an understanding of the advanced techniques that he might employ to improve the quality of his handloaded ammunition. Helping interested handloaders understand the why of important handloading issues is my primary goal. All too many instructive texts offer strident admonitions about the what, where, and how without explaining the why and wherefore. It is my fervent belief that handloaders who understand "why" will be more apt to enjoy the fruits of adhering to safe handloading practices.

To those interested in a more detailed background study of handloading fundamentals, I heartily suggest the latest version of the *Speer Reloading Manual* and the *Hornady Handbook of Cartridge Reloading.* Readers who are particularly interested in the more advanced topics might want to review the *Precision Shooting Reloading Guide.*

My prayer is that this manual will be valuable to handloaders interested in improving their understanding of what they are doing and in knowing how to do that better. While I will picture and discuss specific favorite tools, I do not intend this text as a catalog of handloading tools and components. The World Wide Web now presents a reasonably complete collection of such information and practically all handloading tool and component manufacturers now have more-or-less useful Internet sites. (Handloaders without direct Internet access can easily obtain access at a local library.)

Several subjects covered in this text include some conjecture. These occur as possible explanations of some important aspect of handloading; internal, external, or terminal performance; or some related issue. Conjecture occurs where either I have been unable to find proof of a correct explanation or where no one has yet determined what the correct explanation might be.

Similarly, in some of the more esoteric areas, I have not given a complete explanation simply because doing so would require an entire tome. Some of the subjects I cover in this work are indeed complicated—several such problems fall into the category of what physicists refer to as technically difficult: A problem that would give even the most seasoned theoretical physicist a headache. Obviously, I cannot address every such issue and still offer a book that the general reader would find useful and interesting.

To facilitate visual clarity, within the explanative drawings in this book, I have deliberately exaggerated many features and characteristics. In many drawings, I have exaggerated the scale of certain features, such as neck wall thickness. Also, certain points in this text are applicable only to specialized target rifles and ammunition made specifically for use in those guns.

I list sources for specialized tools, which are not necessarily available from standard outlets, at the end of each chapter and in an appendix.

PERSISTENT (ERRONEOUS) MYTHS

Experienced handloaders all too often pass myths along to novice handloaders. Unfortunately, this has sometimes led to the generational propagation of unsafe handloading practices.

The only thing protecting many (incautious) handloaders from catastrophe is the huge safety margin built into the typical modern gun. I could write an entire book on the subject of just how lucky we are that guns are so strong and are so well designed that when we do manage to destroy one, usually, we can walk away relatively unharmed.

Very good reasons exist for the handloading adage: *Start low and work up carefully.* You should know that any handload that exceeds factory-load ballistics necessarily does so by exceeding factory-load pressure. Whether or not it is safe to use such a load depends upon many factors. Precious few, if any, handloaders outside the ballistics laboratory are competent to make such a judgment call.

Contrary to myth, primer and bullet substitutions often convert a perfectly normal handload into a handload that generates greater pressure than an industry proof load generates! Handloaders have no fundamental way of knowing a priori what the pressure consequences of any component change will be, whence the cautionary adages: *Always treat any loading change as a new load; always refer to a modern manual for data; and always start low and work up to a maximum safe load using due caution.*

Myth: Case design does not matter. Fact: Shorter, fatter cases have significant ballistic advantages. The 6.5mm/60 SM^C (left) has 4 percent less usable capacity than the 6.5mm-284 Norma (right), yet with best loads generating the same peak chamber pressure, the 6.5mm/60 produces more than 100 fps greater velocity. SM^C design features are idealized to maximize performance and barrel life.

When you hear, as I have, an experienced handloader tell a novice, "I always start at the maximum recommended load and work up from there," you should advise that novice to stop listening. It is a myth to suppose that the prolonged good fortune of any experienced handloader will extend to any novice. (If you are that novice, take extra heed.)

One major myth is that handloading is about getting greater velocity (more power). In truth, handloading is about making better ammunition. While better ammunition might be more powerful, generally it is more accurate, has a bullet that is better suited to an intended application, suits some need that no available factory-load fits, is less expensive, etc. Note that more powerful is not included in the above list.

As noted, another myth is the belief that primer choice does not matter. It most assuredly does matter, sometimes dramatically. For example, Accurate Arms once had a customer that loaded commercial 9mm Luger ammunition. During a primer shortage, that company could not obtain the recommended small-pistol magnum primers for those loads, so it substituted standard small-pistol primers. That substitution doubled chamber pressure!

The ballisticians at Accurate Arms once tested all small-size primers. They discovered that the WSPM is the hottest of all in some applications. In the 357 Magnum, they demonstrated that this primer is only appropriate with W296 or H110. In that cartridge, the WSPM significantly, to dramatically, increased pressure with every tested propellant—for example, with BlueDot, pressure increase was about 40 percent; with No. 9, pressure increase was about 20 percent. I

Myth: The 22 Hornet and accuracy are mutually exclusive, especially in a factory gun. This example group, fired from a stock Savage M-40, disproves this myth. This was the first tested load using the Barnes 30-grain Varmint Grenade and Lil'Gun. With further load development, I saw smaller 100-yard groups. The truth: The Hornet can be very accurate but headspace issues commonly cause problems.

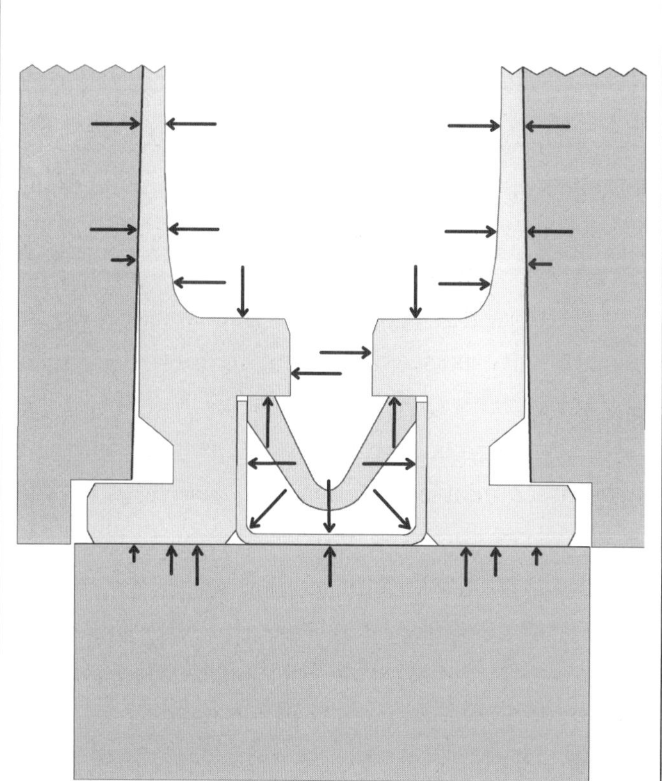

Forces acting upon a case during firing: Fact: Cases stretch during firing. Forces acting upon a cartridge case as a round is fired come from propellant gases—internal—and from the gun—external. Vector force analysis provides a better understanding of what happens. This explains why cases change shape and how cases ultimately fail, whether from excessive pressure or from excessive stretching.

give other examples in the main text. The pertinent point is, we cannot predict the pressure consequences of any primer substitution.

A persistent myth is that all bullets of any given caliber and weight are interchangeable in any given load. Those who believe this one might want to review the tables presented in this text and the data in the Accurate Arms data manual. There, ballistician Bill Falin listed 35 Whelen data for various propellants tested with various 250-grain Spitzer bullets. In that study, maximum loads generating the same pressure required charge adjustments of up to seven grains. With A2015, maximum charge varied by more than 15 percent!

One final myth I want to mention here: "Full-length resizing stretches cases." As explained in chapter 2, resizing only alters case shape; case stretching occurs during firing. The change in case shape often masks the stretching of the case side-wall that occurs during firing—firing often shortens a case because of the increase in case diameter. In many aspects of the handloading process, appearances are deceiving.

Unfortunately, those who do not understand the physics and mechanics of ballistics and handloading have promulgated many such erroneous myths through the printed word. Here, I hope to set the record straight on many such issues.

MYTHS DIE HARD.

STYLE AND OTHER NOTES

1. In an effort to make this text easy to read, I use any nominally masculine pronoun only to represent the reader or a hypothetical character, regardless of sex—I intend no sexism. If this book covered a subject that was more apt to appeal to females, likely I would have used feminine pronouns.
2. Similarly, I sometimes use the kingly "we" to smooth reading, to discuss a hypothetical case involving reader participation, and to keep myself out of the picture, where that is useful.
3. Commonly, I use "we" in instances where the text covers information that was either garnered with the help of another expert in the handloading field or is generally known.
4. I have sometimes used "one" as a pronoun, where "the handloader" or a similar construction might otherwise become repetitious.
5. I use case rather than brass to indicate a cartridge case as this word is more precise; similarly, I often use propellant, or smokeless, rather than smokeless powder (a double misnomer—modern propellant is neither smokeless nor a powder); and, generally, the term loading indicates the handloading process, while the term load represents a cartridge or a particular recipe (particular bullet and overall length, propellant and charge, primer, case, and specific handloading techniques).
6. I have highlighted statements of critical safety importance, or that are otherwise cautionary, in BOLD, SMALL CAPS FONT, and with a gray background.
7. I have used standard abbreviations such as fps for feet per second and ft. lbs. for foot-pounds; I have avoided unusual abbreviations with which a reader might not be familiar; always, before I use any such abbreviation, I define that term.

ACKNOWLEDGMENTS

Without the inspiration, encouragement, and help of family, friends, and acquaintances, this text would never have come to be. I owe a great debt to these folks for their patience, encouragement, and assistance in myriad aspects that led to the creation of this manual: My wife (Peggy), my parents (Bob and Joyce), Winston Meyer, Bob Hodgdon, Bob Bell, Pam Johnson, Norm Nelson, Bill Falin, Allan Jones, Dave Brennan, John Anderson, Ken Howell, Roger Johnston, Randolph Constantine, George Myer, Ken Oehler, Ed Wosika, Hal Swiggett, Steve Artherton, Roger Hazlewood, Finn Aagaard, Bob McCoy, Ken Runnestrand, Christer Larsson, Rick Hartman, Jim Williamson, and Jim Boatright. A sincere thank you to these persons and the many others who have helped. I pray that each of you will find this work worthy of your investment.

The list of companies that provided assistance in the compilation of this text is long, to name but a few of the more important of those: Accurate Arms, Barnes, Forster, Hodgdon, K&M Services, Norma, Nosler, RCBS, Redding, and Sinclair International. Many other companies have helped and I am quite sure that if I tried to credit each of those individually, I would fail to mention several. To the representatives of those unnamed here, please know that your assistance mattered and that I sincerely appreciate it.

A DAY AT THE RANGE WITH FRIENDS

Penny Brewer firing her first group ever from a benchrest. Gun is an almost-finished custom 1894 Marlin built for Tom Knight. Chambering is 17/23 SMc. Tested (fireforming) load was slightly too hot and, therefore, case extraction required a bit of effort. This 26-inch Krieger barrel launched the 20-grain Hornady V-Max at 4,300 fps using 20 grains of H322.

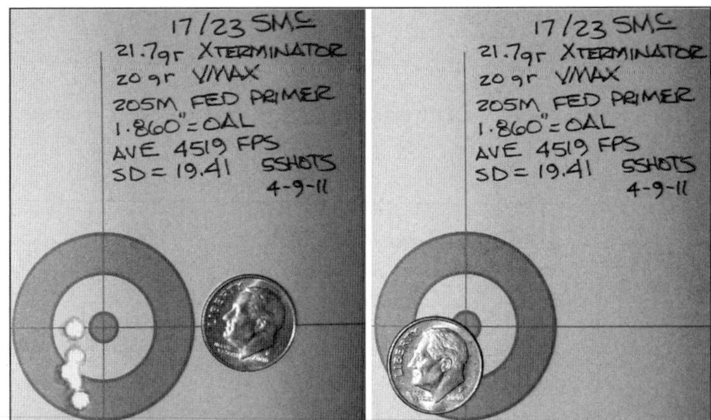

Vertical stringing with 17/23 SMc: Stringing similar to this suggests a load that does not have the needed barrel time for best accuracy with the gun. Often changing the charge 1 or 2 percent or slightly altering the seating depth will alter barrel time enough to produce one-hole groups. Accuracy load development is an important goal for many handloaders, and it is one of the goals addressed in this book.

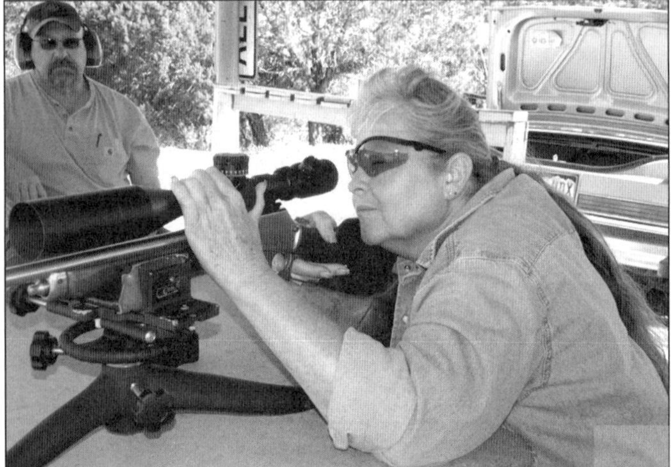

A lever action is not the easiest gun to use on a benchrest. Penny Brewer discovered this method of getting the gun to sit relatively stable, and it worked for her. Her husband, Terry, sits in the background showing the frustration he and I shared that day—we could not shoot a smaller group than Penny did! Note that I have reversed the front rest. This makes it feasible to work the finger lever without unduly disturbing the gun.

Varmint Hunters' Jamboree Balloon-Shoot Targets

Distance (yards)	Number of Balloons	Point Value
106	4	25
246	4	40
365	5	60
492	5	75

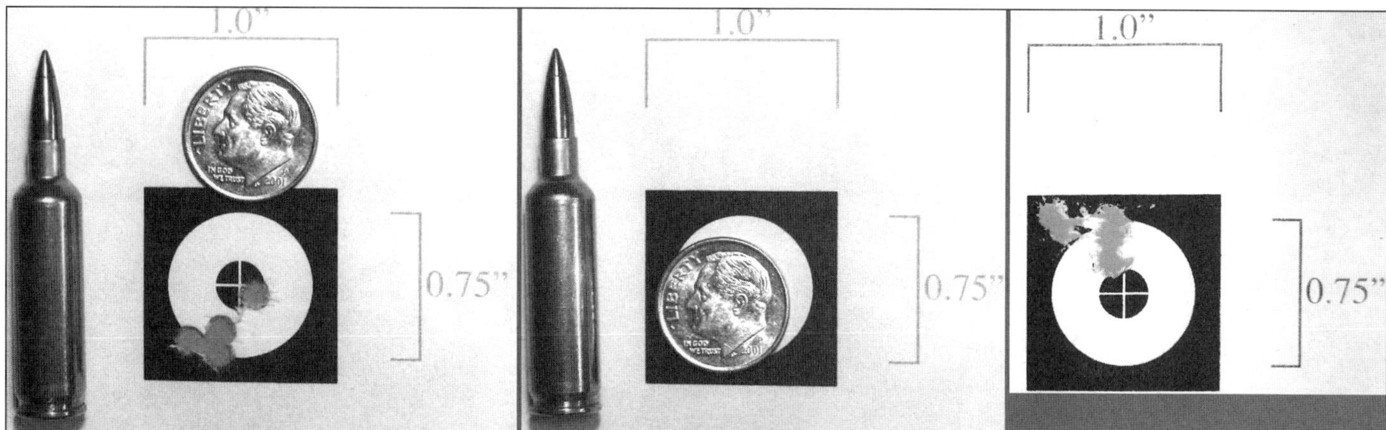

Marlin 1894, 17/23 SMc, 5-shot groups, 100 yards: In the early stages of accuracy load development, Knight found these two loads that are certainly accurate enough for any varminting application for which any 17-caliber gun is suitable.

Terry Brewer testing his lightweight custom 444 Marlin elk rifle as we intended it to be used—offhand. Brewer is one of those "natural" shooters who makes the rest of us jealous—when I practice continuously, I can almost match his skills when he has not fired a gun in years! Life is unfair. With a modified action handling loads up to 2.725 inches in overall length, this gun easily launches the 265-grain Hornady JFP at 2,400 fps with sub-MOA three-shot accuracy. This is a serious rifle for North American game.

Despite the fact that Penny out shot us, we all had a great day at the range. This would never have happened without handloading. For us, this is far more than just a hobby.

After decades of wondering, I figured out why Marlin lever actions are usually so much more accurate than typical Browning-based lever actions. The issue is the lack of lateral receiver rigidity in combination with a locking lug design that almost inevitably places the entire thrust load on one side of the receiver—unless one laps lug engagement to a high degree of precision. Depending upon the gun's design, when the load comes on, the bolt hits only one lug of two-lug guns or only one side of the single lug. That bends the receiver by stretching that side. That forces the barrel to bend sideways, thereby increasing barrel vibration. The same thing occurs in poorly machined two-lug, bolt-action rifles, but in those thrust load is on either the top or bottom, and the barrel is already hanging on the receiver, so the resulting increase in vibration is less significant. Ultimately, because of the solid top, versus the Browning split top, Marlin receivers are far more rigid in the horizontal plane and are, therefore, less sensitive to this effect. This particular Marlin (made after the Remington takeover) had the worst fitted locking lug I have seen. Limited accuracy reflected in this group proves the point. I later significantly improved accuracy of this gun by removing about 5/1000-inch from one side of the lug and lapping the contact areas. (See pictured groups elsewhere.)

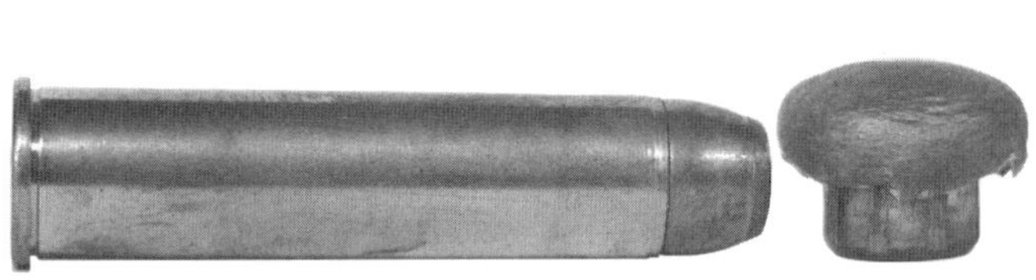

A 50 Alaskan and 450-grain Alaska Bullet Works, bonded-core bullet after firing into saturated telephone book at 1,900 fps: Weight retention was 99% and average expanded diameter 0.84 inch. Performance on a dry telephone book was similarly (and phenomenally!) impressive. Superior components can result in superior handloads.

Left: *475 Linebaugh—400-grain XTP.*
Right: *45-70 Springfield (405-grain Remington JFN loaded long (2.73 inches) for use in a custom modified Marlin)*

The main Jamboree event is the Balloon Shoot. Targets are four-inch balloons held stationary above the ground. Shooters have twenty shots and limited time to break all eighteen targets, which rarely happens. Those who score highest in each relay advance to a shoot-off. In case of a tie in the initial shoot-off, a final shoot-off with ten shots for highest score determines the winner.

This game sounds easy. Many serious world-class Benchrest, NRA Highpower, and F-Class shooters have been tempted into competing. To date, not one of those has made a final shoot-off, let alone won an event. Few return. Many things contribute to the surprising difficulty of the Balloon Shoot:

- Variable wind conditions
- Lack of wind flags
- Unique wind conditions along each target path
- Differences in the lay of the land behind each target on each line. (This makes it hard, or impossible, to correctly judge the needed correction after a miss.)

By using precision handloads in precision rifles, Jamboree competitors often achieve extraordinary accuracy.

The Varmint Hunters' Jamboree in Pierre, South Dakota, in 2007 included the 600-yard Bullseye event: heavy-class, relay one. Winning competitors used precision handloads and properly zeroed guns to shoot the smallest group closest to the target center.

NEVER FORGET: SAFETY IS YOUR RESPONSIBILITY

As in all aspects of the shooting sports, never forget that you are dealing with energetic materials and devices capable of bringing great harm and destruction. Safety is your first priority.

SAFETY, ACCURACY, AND FUNCTIONALITY

CHAPTER 1

Handloading necessarily involves the handling, storage, and usage of potentially dangerous substances and devices. You should always follow all manufacturer warnings and remember that safety is your responsibility. Accuracy of handloads that you develop depends upon the components and tools you use and upon how precisely you use those tools. Functionality of your handloads depends upon your understanding of how the cartridge and gun work and interact, and it depends upon your making sure that the ammunition that you create is properly constructed and that any such ammunition is used only in the specific firearm for which you made it.

In this chapter I highlight some basic aspects of each of these issues. Elsewhere in this text, you will find some of the same information, covered from different perspectives and with more detail, where useful and feasible.

SAFETY—PRIMERS

Few handloaders fully appreciate the potentially dangerous explosiveness of primers. A fact the CEO at a major ammunition company has demonstrated to new employees at the annual company picnic. At 200 yards, he creates two targets. One hides a company coffee cup filled with primers; the other hides two sticks of blasting agent (essentially equivalent to two sticks of dynamite). He then explodes these targets with precisely placed shots from his target rifle.

His question to new employees: "Which was which?" The point is, the answer is not obvious—primers are seriously powerful devices!

Primers definitely deserve your utmost attention toward safe use and handling. Follow all safety precautions listed on primer boxes and those warnings included with all priming tools:

- Always store primers in original containers.
- Never leave unused, unboxed primers unattended.
- Understand that heat, impact, or electric current (a dry-cell battery, for instance) can fire a primer.
- Know that primers in mass are capable of and are quite likely to generate a chain-reaction, mass explosion

Store primers away from any bullet casting activity or any other situation involving significantly elevated temperature—the specter of the consequences of dropping one or more primers into molten lead is best left to the imagination.

SAFETY—PROPELLANT HANDLING

Propellant (powder) is an obvious safety concern for handloaders. Should you ever have the misfortune of igniting a large quantity of any propellant (smokeless, black, or blackpowder substitute) within an enclosed space, you might survive long enough to gain a new respect for what can seem to be such a relatively harmless substance. Furthermore, most, if not all, propellants can detonate, if subjected to a sufficiently brisant shock, e.g., a bullet impact into a propellant canister.

Consider the plight of a fellow handloader who, late in the last century, succeeded in igniting a nearly full and open eight-pound can of RedDot in his handloading-specific outbuilding. He managed to escape. The resulting inferno destroyed the building along with thousands of dollars worth of equipment. Had he hesitated in departure, or had the door opened inwardly, or had it been bolted, he simply would not have survived.

Similarly, a well-known and authoritative handloading expert who also dabbled in gunsmithing somehow managed to discharge a high-powered rifle inside his shop. Unfortunately, he happened to have the gun pointed at an eight-pound keg of smokeless propellant that was located in an adjoining room. That canister was sitting with several others. The resulting detonation (yes, smokeless will detonate, given sufficient motivation) evidently involved at least two eight-pound canisters and essentially destroyed the shop. The only good news is that he probably never knew what happened.

More commonly, we are concerned with the handloading aspects of propellant safety, and rightly so. Inadvertent use of the wrong propellant in a handload is a likely and common source of catastrophic gun failure. Therefore, develop unwavering habits when handling propellant.

NEVER ALLOW TWO TYPES OF PROPELLANT TO BE WITHIN REACH DURING ANY LOADING SESSION. ALWAYS PLACE THE SOURCE CANISTER FOR THE PROPELLANT YOU ARE USING WITHIN HANDY REACH WHILE HANDLOADING. ALWAYS EMPTY THE PROPELLANT MEASURE INTO THE CORRECT CANISTER AFTER EACH LOADING SESSION, AND THEN PUT THAT CANISTER BACK INTO STORAGE.

Failure to observe these rules will, eventually, either result in the direct use of the wrong propellant, by selecting the wrong canister, or the inadvertent use of the wrong propellant, because you had previously introduced unused propellant into the wrong canister.

It took more than thirty years of extensive handloading before I managed to pour unused propellant into the wrong container—a moment of inattention converted almost two pounds of N160 and about four ounces of Rl-22 into expensive, time-released, lawn fertilizer. The good news is that I caught my error before more serious harm occurred.

Always double-check. Be absolutely, positively certain that you are using the intended propellant and the intended charge. A common source of this error is when a handloader refers to loading manual data for the wrong cartridge—for example, 300 Winchester Magnum and 300 Weatherby Magnum data are commonly confused in this manner.

Equally, verify that you have the original container before returning any unused propellant, and avoid storing unused propellant in any device (measure, scale pan, dribbler, etc). If you do temporarily store propellant in any loading tool, always include a label, temporarily attached to that device (masking tape works well for this). This inexpensive insurance is worth the time and effort. (Storage of propellant in a meter hopper is unsafe and it allows ballistic variation because the propellant will either dry out or gain moisture.)

SAFETY—PROPELLANT—CHARGE

Obviously, an excessive propellant charge will generate excessive pressure. This can result in catastrophic case failure and possibly catastrophic gun failure, either of which could injure or kill the shooter or bystanders.

Most commonly this error results from the inadvertent use of the wrong propellant—many distinct products have very similar names. This error represents a fifty-fifty situation. About half the time, use of the wrong propellant will be relatively harmless because said propellant happens to burn slower than the intended propellant. Conversely, when said propellant happens to burn significantly faster than the intended propellant, a dangerous gun failure is likely. Every time you reload, ensure that you are using the propellant that you intend to use, assure yourself that you are not using a charge that exceeds the maximum load listed in modern published data, and make sure that you have demonstrated that said charge is safe in your gun.

SAFETY—BULLET

Besides lead contamination (actually of modest concern), bullet handling has other pitfalls. In certain cartridges, it is possible to seat wrong-diameter bullets. Several pairs of genuine look-alikes exist. These include pairs in the following diameters: 0.224 inch and 0.228 inch; 0.257 inch and 0.264 inch; 0.277 inch and 0.284 inch; and, perhaps others. The combination of oversized bullets loaded into the "correct" cartridges has wrecked guns.

The danger comes from the combination of an oversize bullet with a gun having a relatively loose chamber neck and throat. Given such a situation, the cartridge might chamber without exhibiting any overt sign of the error, despite the fact that chambering has, in fact, squeezed the case neck against the bullet. If so, the case neck cannot freely release the bullet. Such a circumstance delays initial bullet movement. This can lead to the generation of devastating chamber pressure.

Normally, in the above-noted similar-sized pairs, most guns intended for the smaller bullet either will not allow chambering of a cartridge loaded with the too-large bullet or will have enough clearance in the chamber neck so that trapping will not occur. However, if the particular chamber does happen to allow chambering of a cartridge loaded with such an oversize bullet, it is likely that the chamber neck will be sufficiently tight around the case neck as to retard bullet movement from the case. This is a sure road to disaster—and it has happened.

Contrary to intuition, with soft-cored bullets, the swaging that occurs as an oversize bullet enters into the smaller-diameter bore will not normally significantly elevate chamber pressure (if at all). Conversely, firing a monolithic copper or brass bullet or a hard-cored (steel or tungsten carbide) bullet that is just a few thousandths larger than groove diameter is apt to have catastrophic consequences.

Consider the plight of a novice handloader who bought a box of what were supposed to be 0.277-inch diameter bullets. He did not know that someone had been handling bullets from that box and visually similar 0.284-inch diameter bullets from another box and had, thereby, managed to place several 0.284-inch bullets into the 0.277-inch bullet box.

That handloader was using new cases. Evidently, the soft case necks did not give much added resistance to bullet seating when he inserted an errant 0.284-inch bullet. In addition, his particular seating die was loose enough to allow this to happen. Worse, his freebored magnum rifle had a loose enough chamber neck and throat so that, with the particular cases he was using, he was just able to chamber a round holding a 7mm (0.284-inch) bullet. At the shooting range, he evidently either did not notice anything unusual as he closed the bolt on a tight-fitting round or, more likely, he did not recognize that something was badly wrong as he forced the bolt closed. The chamber neck was just tight enough to squeeze the case neck. When he fired the round, the added neck-to-bullet friction retarded initial bullet acceleration; chamber pressure skyrocketed; and, the case failed. This destroyed the gun and terminally ruined his day.

Many guns intended for use with 0.308-inch bullets will allow free chambering of cartridges loaded with 0.311-inch bullets. Often, bolt-closing feel is indistinguishable from what occurs when chambering a cartridge that is loaded with a correct-diameter bullet. While, usually, the chamber neck and throat will have sufficient clearance to allow the bullet to freely move, this might not always be true; potentially dangerous excessive pressure is certainly a possible consequence.

Store bullets in original boxes. A roll of drafting tape is useful for resealing opened bullet boxes and is very inexpensive insurance. Keep bullet boxes segregated, according to diameter. When buying bullets off-the-shelf, insist that the retailer prevents tampering—for some persons, the urge to examine bullets is great. If ever in doubt, measure bullet diameter and weight before use.

SAFETY—CASE

For various reasons, cases in most applications have a limited life span. For example, with repeated reuse, cases can thin near the junction of head (web) and body. Eventually, this will lead to case separation. Such a separation can lead to a monumental gas leak, which can destroy the gun and is not apt to be good for either the shooter or bystanders. The general subject of case life is so important that I cover it separately, in chapter 2.

Other than a worn-out or faulty case, the only common safety issue involves a case with a neck that is long enough to extend, or so that it could extend, into the neck-to-throat chamber transition. This condition can exist after reloading a case many times without trimming (cases often lengthen with use). When this happens, the case mouth can extend into the neck-to-throat chamber transition. In this situation, closing the action, the fall of the striker, or the primer explosion can drive the case forward, sufficiently, to crimp the case mouth solidly into the bullet. At worst, firing such a round can generate gun destroying chamber pressure. At least, such loads will produce dismal accuracy, compared to otherwise identical rounds using cases that fit the chamber properly.

SAFETY—GENERAL HANDLOADING

The list of potential hazards for the handloader is nearly endless. The best approach is to use common sense and to develop a habit of staying as safe as is possible, rather than getting as close to danger as is possible. This is a philosophy advocated eloquently by that dean of pressure measurement, my friend, Ken Oehler (Oehler Ballistics Labs). To paraphrase Oehler: If you really must skate on thin ice (in the figurative sense of handloading to the extreme), instead of handloading, do all other shooters and handloaders a genuine favor by taking up untethered mountain climbing or some other similar sport. Dedicated handloaders neither need nor want the inevitable bad publicity that such handloading will bring.

A comment on pressure and safety: I am still young and enthusiastic enough that I often want to achieve maximum safe performance out of many of my handloads. Although for target work the only meaningful criterion is accuracy, for many loads muzzle velocity is important. For this reason, pressure concerns are paramount.

Creating a handload that surpasses ballistics of a factory load is easy—any nimrod can do it. Simply choose an appropriate propellant and then place enough of that propellant into the case so that the handload generates higher pressure than the corresponding factory load. Certainly, such an accomplishment does not merit a badge of honor.

Despite our desires to the contrary, high-performance handloads often generate greater pressure than factory proof loads generate. Those who routinely handload at such pressure levels definitely are seeing how close they can skate to the thin edge of the ice, rather than seeing how far away from that (unsafe) edge they can remain.

The trick is to develop handloads that surpass factory-load ballistics without increased pressure. This is no mean feat. Please understand that factory ammunition producers have access to every type of propellant that you can buy and many types that you cannot normally obtain. If Black Hills Ammunition—or any other major ammunition producer—so chooses, it can have any quantity of a propellant with any burning rate made up and delivered to its ammunition factory—no problem.

Note that, generally, handloaders cannot duplicate modern increased-performance factory loads, such as those currently offered by Hornady and Federal. Those utilize special propellants that distributors have only recently offered to handloaders, for limited applications.

I do not intend to suggest that the handloader can never exceed factory ballistics without exceeding industry pressure standards. Sometimes this is possible and in certain chamberings, this is quite easily accomplished. Regardless of this, the point is that if you set increased velocity as your primary handloading goal, you are looking toward the wrong goal and you are apt to be disappointed. If you insist upon that result, you are almost certain to increase the potential for something very bad to happen, eventually.

Your goal should always be the creation of ammunition that, when used in your gun, fulfills your ballistic needs better than factory ammunition does. Handloaders can always strive toward this goal without sacrificing the margin of safety—happily, this is also one goal that handloaders can often achieve.

FUNCTIONALITY—AMMUNITION

Contrary to common usage, the terms handloading and reloading are not interchangeable. Technically, handloading is the process of conversion of any case (new or used) and other necessary components into a loaded cartridge; reloading is the process of conversion of a used case and other necessary components into a loaded cartridge. I have chosen to extend these definitions with specific connotations: Ideally, handloading produces the best ammunition possible; ideally, reloading produces functional ammunition. In this book, I concentrate on handloading.

The late Col. Townsend Whelen said, "The only interesting gun is an accurate gun." To paraphrase him, I contend that "The only interesting handload is an accurate handload." Almost any reasonably free person interested in guns can manufacture ammunition. This absorbing and rewarding hobby offers the potential for saving money, increasing shooting opportunities, and so much more.

What separates usable reloads from high-performance handloads is not the respective velocities generated, but, rather, it is how well each load fulfills the intended application while also producing excellent accuracy. In certain applications, other factors are also critical.

An obvious example is hunting ammunition where terminal performance is a major consideration. Regardless of energy or accuracy, if a bullet fails to perform properly upon impact, it might not get the job done. Another example is handgun ammunition, which a person might use in a life-or-death self-defense situation in a dimly lit room, or at night. If the muzzle flash is so bright that the first shot blinds the shooter, that person might be in serious trouble, whether the enraged and charging adversary is a two-legged or a four-legged beast. Similarly, in most applications, functionality is foremost. You must be certain that every round will function perfectly through your gun and that it will do so every time.

A memory from my early years as a hunter involves my cousin, Glen McPherson, pounding the charging handle of his Remington automatic rifle against a handy pine tree. He was alternately trying to force an inadequately resized reload fully into the chamber and then back out of the chamber. This incident would not have burned itself into my memory so vividly had he not been in the middle of a passing herd of elk at the time!

At least one person has been severely mauled after his super reloads failed him in an encounter of the worst kind. In that example, recoil of the high-powered revolver he was using pulled the bullet in one cartridge sufficiently from the case so that the bullet nose protruded from the front of the cylinder and locked up the gun. With his gun reduced to an expensive and awkward club, our hapless hunter bore the brunt of the attack of a wounded grizzly bear, as it came right down on top of him.

He had made a critical and potentially fatal mistake: He had failed to verify that his hunting loads would work every time, and, for that error, he paid a terrible price. His load delivered a good bullet, with plenty of energy to do the job, but, ultimately, it failed the ultimate test—functionality.

No doubt, he had tested that load, almost certainly, when his hands were dry and while using a firm two-handed grip. In that situation, the mass and strength of his hands and arms slowed gun recoil and, thereby, mitigated the force with which the gun pulled back on the cartridges in the cylinder. (The cylinder pulls the case rim rearward during recoil.) Conversely, on the day in question, his situation went from bad to worse:

- An enraged grizzly charged—not good;
- He could not get a solid two-handed grip on the revolver (his only weapon)—bad;
- He placed his first shot badly—very bad;
- As the gun fired, recoil pulled a case sufficiently off a bullet to leave the bullet nose protruding from the cylinder, thereby rendering the gun inoperable—as bad as it gets!

FUNCTIONALITY ISN'T EVERYTHING; IT'S THE ONLY THING!

ACCURACY—AMMUNITION

Generally, it should be possible for any handloader, who is willing to make the effort, to create handloads for any gun that deliver superior accuracy, when compared to typical factory fodder. The Creighton Audette

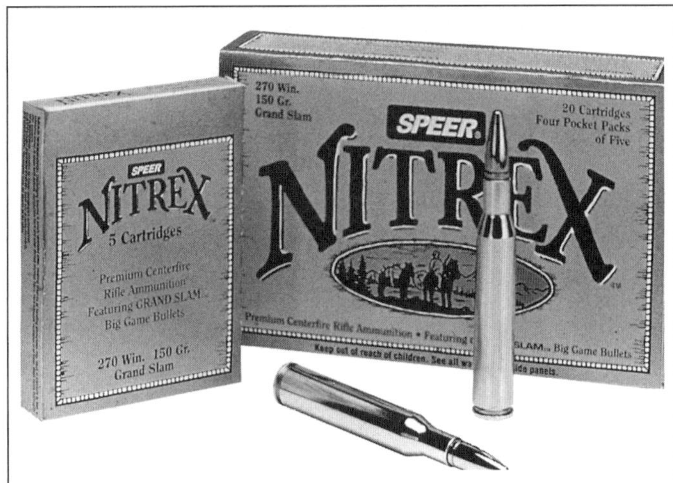

The overall performance of best modern factory ammunition is often hard to beat, even with the most skillfully prepared handloads.

method of accuracy-load development provides a very simple means of developing such an accuracy load, while firing a minimal number of shots. I detail that method in chapter 12.

Improved accuracy is possible with most rifles and many handguns. The reason is easy to understand: Factories must manufacture ammunition with tolerances assuring that every round produced will fit and fire correctly in every commercial gun ever chambered for that cartridge. This is known as universal functionality. Owing to inevitable manufacturing tolerances, cartridges with universal functionality are apt to fit relatively loosely in the chamber of a typical factory gun.

Conversely, handloaders can tailor handloads to fit the chamber closely in any particular gun. Such a close fit can improve bullet-to-bore alignment. This also improves ignition uniformity because the firing pin (striker) does not waste as much energy driving the cartridge to the front of the chamber as it indents the primer. This might also reduce variation of delay between striker release and primer ignition, which might influence barrel vibrations and, therefore, accuracy. In chapter 12, I review the accuracy ramifications associated with the inevitable barrel vibrations associated with firing a shot and how to tune a handload to maximize accuracy.

Better alignment between cartridge (particularly the bullet) and bore is the primary feature separating superior benchrest ammunition used in a benchrest gun from typical factory loads or reloads used in one's trusty hunting rifle. Generally (exceptions always exist), the more closely the cartridges fit the chamber the better the accuracy potential of that particular load is. However, in all ammunition except that used strictly for target shooting, accuracy is subservient to functionality. As noted above, functionality reigns supreme—the most accurate cartridges in the world are useless if those fail to chamber and function properly in the gun at hand.

As far as quality goes, factory producers keep making advances. Performance of the best modern factory ammunition is often superior to performance of the average reload and can be superior to performance of all but the best handloads. Conversely, when I began handloading, it was quite simple to create handloads that surpassed the accuracy of typical factory fodder; this situation has long since changed. If you want to beat the Big Boys, you had better know what you are doing and you had better concentrate on doing that well. One of my goals with this book is to help you know how to reload safely and how to handload well so that you can create ammunition that delivers excellent reliability and accuracy when you use it in the intended firearm.

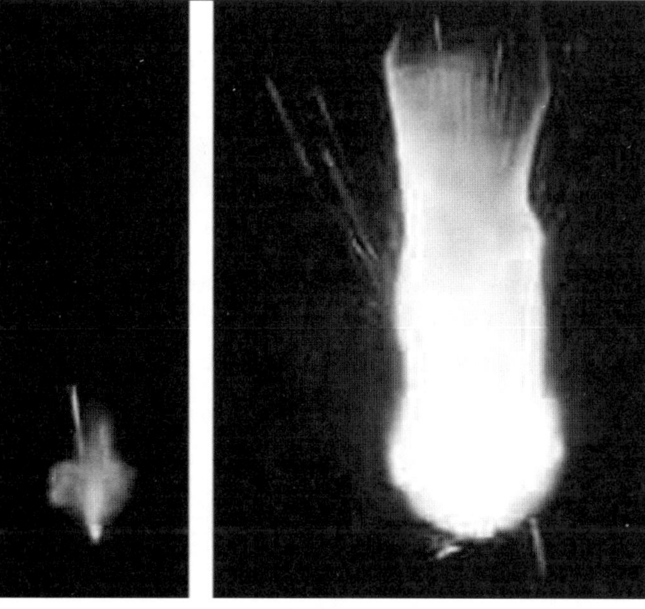

Variation in primer energy and heat is rather significant. I created these images from different primer flashes using identical focal length, lens, exposure, and development.

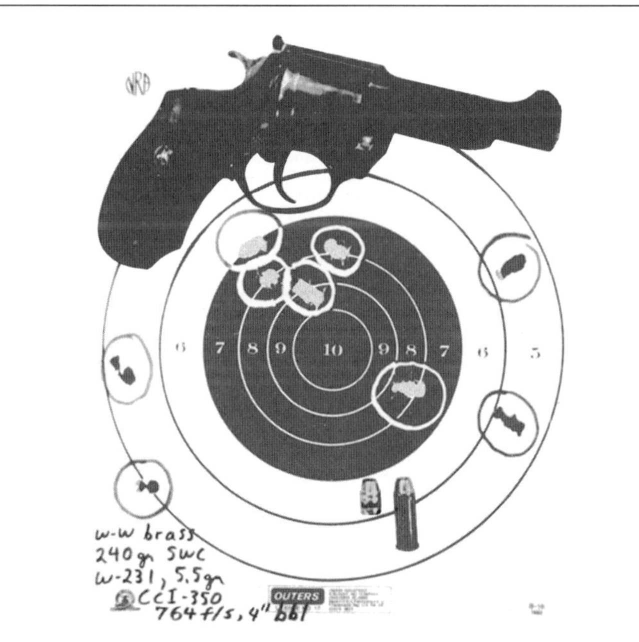

Sometimes a modest change in load parameters can make all the difference. Velocity was insufficient to stabilize a 215-grain SWC (above). Increasing propellant charge ½ grain increased velocity sufficiently to stabilize that bullet fully. Result: 2.1-inch, 25-yard, five-shot group fired offhand from pictured Charter Arms Target Bulldog (below).

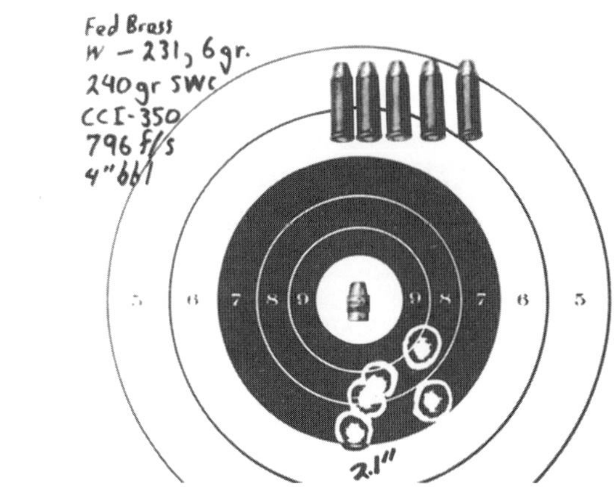

BENCHREST TESTING IS THE DEFINITIVE METHOD FOR DEVELOPING ACCURATE LOADS

Regardless of the scope used, quality rests and a rigid bench are critical to achieving maximum benchrest accuracy. In the field, the Tower Stool Company Hench Bench and companion stool provide an easily transportable, durable, and affordable system. These almost instantly fold into compact packages. The Midway front rest and Bald Eagle rear bag complete my field system. Whatever field system you use, keep the basics in mind: steady, simple, and portable. The Leupold VX-7L was right at home on this amazingly accurate Savage M-40.

Testing the CZ 527 American, 22 Hornet: I was in the process of firing groups with every factory load I could get to test. My friend, Tom Taggart, had finished testing loads in his 30-30 Ackley Improved Marlin and was observing the amazing accuracy of this fine rifle. When I did my part, three tested factory loads produced 5-shot, 100-yard groups smaller than 1 MOA, on centers. Later testing with selected handloads showed ½-MOA accuracy. Secrets to exceptional Hornet accuracy include the use of the Lee Collet die, the use of small pistol primers, and the use of a properly chambered gun so that headspace is not excessive. This was formerly common with guns made in the USA, whereas most European-made guns are chambered with very precise headspace and give great accuracy and case life.

THE CARTRIDGE CASE

CHAPTER 2

Introduction

Cartridge cases have two functions:

- Containment of components necessary to make a cartridge work, and
- Sealing the gun chamber against the high-pressure gases that are generated when the cartridge fires.

In shotgun shells, paper and plastic have proven adequate to these tasks; in other sporting cartridges, brass, aluminum, and steel are the materials of choice, but manufacturers have also made one-time-use plastic cases.

Generally, although it is possible to reload steel and aluminum cases, equipment and safety considerations necessitate the use of brass cases. Cartridge brass alloy contains 70 percent copper and 30 percent zinc, with minimal nonmetal impurities (such as sulfur), or other metals (such as manganese or lead).

Cartridge case manufacture requires very large machines, precision dies, and other expensive tooling. Most producers buy preformed cups of the correct diameter and thickness, as needed to form particular cases (larger cases require larger, heavier cups). Very massive die-punch machines produce these cups from sheets of cartridge brass.

Manufacturers use a series of draw-press operations to lengthen the cup progressively while thinning the sidewalls. Generally, the longer the case, the more drawing steps are required. Also, most rifle cases require partial annealing during these drawing operations. Final forming steps include stamping the case head to produce the final form and to emboss the headstamp; forming a pocket in the head to accept a primer; and punching the flash hole, from the primer pocket through to the case body. Next come sizing to final form, trimming to length, and cutting the rim to final dimensions. Finally, manufacturers anneal the case neck and shoulder to soften these excessively work-hardened areas. Considering market price, dimensional uniformity, and functionality, the brass cartridge case is a miracle of modern manufacturing.

Basic tool design and construction techniques used in making the common brass case have changed very little since the late 1800s. Although quality varies, all brass cases are similar. Cartridge brass has several advantages over other materials:

- High ductility (easy to manufacture);
- High lubricity (minimizes frictional wear of tools and gun chambers);
- Corrosion resistance (minimizes storage concerns);
- Work-hardening (allows potential use of usefully high chamber pressure);
- Heat annealing (allows softening of case neck and body to facilitate loading and chamber sealing);
- Relatively inexpensive (reduces ammunition cost); and
- Correct physical characteristics when compared to the steel of chamber and action (accommodates easy extraction of any case fired with a load that generates normal pressure).

To prevent corrosion in leather cartridge loops or to enhance appearance, manufacturers sometimes nickel-plate brass cases; nickel plating serves no other purpose. In some applications, such plating can lead to increased chamber pressure because it can significantly increase bullet-to-neck friction.

VibraShine makes some of the finest vibratory cleaners offered to handloaders.

I have one batch of nickel-plated 45-70 cases that came to me as weeks-old, factory-loaded ammunition. Upon firing, the mouth split on most of those. Often, the acid bath pickling, used to clean cases before plating, causes embrittlement of the case walls (through corrosion along crystal boundaries), which is what happened to those 45-70 cases.

Next, I will cover inspection of brass cartridge cases for possible problems. Our handloading concerns involve safety, functionality, and accuracy.

INSPECTION—NEW AND USED CASES—GENERAL CONSIDERATIONS

Consider cleaning dirty or tarnished cases before inspection. Clean cases are easier to examine. Shiny cases add to pride of production and ownership. Furthermore, clean cases are less apt to damage reloading dies or a gun chamber.

Perform a cursory case examination before initial use and after each subsequent use. Look for structural

Generally, handloaders are wise to avoid nickel-plated cases for use in rifle cartridges; conversely, these cases can be quite beneficial when used in revolver cartridges. It is prudent to reduce charges a few percent whenever substituting nickel-plated cases in an established load.

Through experience, I have come to believe that most of us would be better off if we avoided nickel-plated rifle cases as we would avoid the plague. However, if you process such cases carefully (particularly critical is proper inside case neck deburring of new cases), if you use plenty of a superior case sizing lubricant, and if you are puritanical about cleaning each case before resizing, you might not have trouble working with nickel-plated rifle cases—maybe.

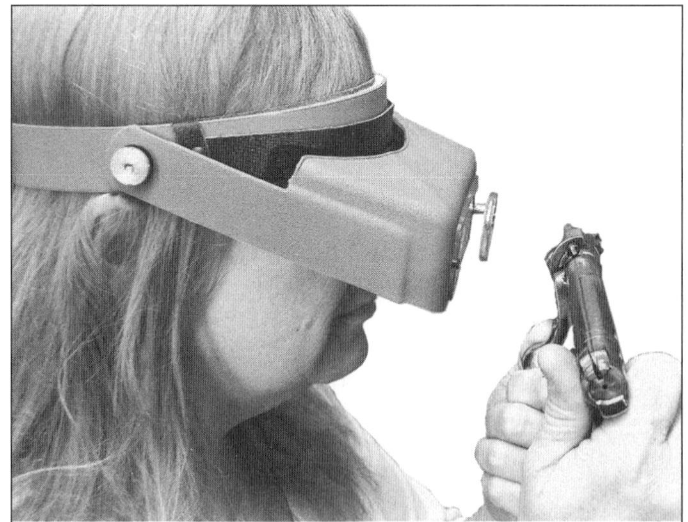
The Opti-Visor, available from Brownells, provides significant magnification and allows aging eyes to accommodate (focus) on objects close to the eye. This tool is useful for various inspections during handloading and bullet casting; it eases examination and provides a magnified image with hands-free usage, as my wife, Peggy, demonstrates here.

problems, either manufacturing flaws or problems that could have developed through usage. These include cracks, splits, visible case head deformation, and appearance changes in the head area. (These latter can indicate underlying problems, such as use in a previous load that generated excessive pressure.)

Whenever you work with any new batch of cases, you must take the time to make a reasonable inspection. This is true whether the cases are factory fresh or come from some other source. For this examination, find an area with good light. A loupe or magnifying glass can be very helpful.

Many pundits have advised against using cases of unknown history. For those unwilling or unable to perform the hardness test described hereafter, that is very good advice. The surest approach is to use only factory-new cases or cases from factory ammunition that you have fired or that you have watched someone else fire. However, if you study cases carefully for defects, I believe that you can safely reuse most range brass.

It is critical to test head hardness of any case of unknown history; although rare, cases can be exposed to sufficient heating to anneal (soften) the case head without exhibiting any significant visual evidence—I have had bad personal experience in this regard.

As a young man, out of practical necessity, I scavenged every case I could find. I once found a 270 Winchester case that showed signs of long-term exposure; it was uniformly and heavily tarnished, but otherwise it appeared to have been perfectly normal. I reloaded that case using my standard varmint recipe (56.5 grains H414, CCI-250, Hornady 110 JHP), a load that had proven to be quite mild and phenomenally accurate in my rifle.

When I fired that round, several bad things happened. Fortunately, I was shooting the unusually strong and safe Model-760 Remington Pump. The soft case head simply swelled to fill the available space. In doing so, it enlarged sufficiently so that the primer could no longer seal the primer pocket against chamber pressure. The result was the release of a tremendous amount of high-pressure gas into, and then from, the action. The nylon ejection-port cover violently ejected from the rifle (it might still be in orbit!). The action locked shut.

I took the rifle home and separated the barrel assembly from the receiver. I was then able to open the bolt and pull the gun apart. I cleaned it and took it to my local gunsmith for an inspection, replacement of the departed nylon piece, and reassembly.

That event cost me five dollars and a bit of inconvenience, but I learned a valuable lesson: the importance of not using cases of unknown heritage, at least not until after verifying case head hardness. Considering what might have happened, that was a very inexpensive lesson.

Evidently, that case had been subjected to a fire—perhaps simply a weed or a brush fire. Then, continued exposure had tarnished it sufficiently to erase any visual evidence of that fire. Had I simply done a hardness test on the case head, I would have known that it was dangerously soft.

Hardness testers are available but are very expensive. These can easily do a proper job of testing case head hardness. However, the handloader can adequately judge case-head hardness by comparing a suspect case to a case of known adequate hardness. Here's what to do:

Simply press the edge of the rim of a case that you know is in good condition against the flat part of the head of the questionable case. Then, while maintaining as much pressure as you can muster by hand, slide the cases against each other. If doing so creates a significant gouge in the tested case, assume that it is unsafe to use for any load—destroy and discard any such case.

With unprimed cases, observe the flash hole; if it is not properly centered, destroy and discard the case—this will save the inconvenience of a broken

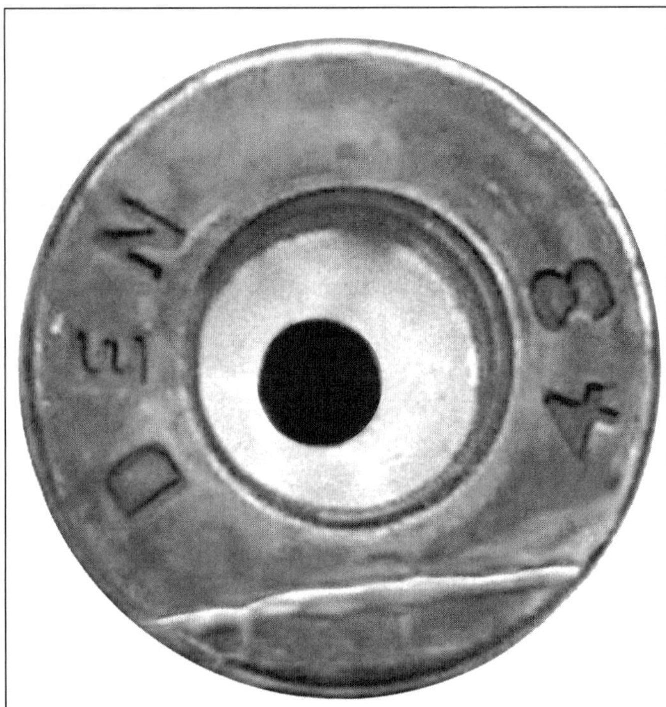

A normal case head easily scratches an unusually soft case head; note bright scratch across head (near bottom in this view). Such deformation proves that this case is unsafe for any use—destroy and discard any such case. Flash holes that are significantly off center (such as this one) are rare. While this condition might or might not limit accuracy, it can certainly lead to a destroyed decapping pin. Therefore, destroy and discard any case where the flash hole is visibly off center.

decapping pin, at the very least. Also, note that some experts conjecture that off-center flash holes might be detrimental to accuracy. As this condition is so rare, seldom does a sufficient reason exist to use any case that has such a flaw.

WHY CASES STRETCH—INCIPIENT SEPARATIONS AND EXCESSIVE LENGTH

Consider the typical bottlenecked case: Many experienced handloaders do not understand what causes case stretching. Historically, some pundits have attributed this to full-length resizing and to the use of hot handloads; actually, stretching is a consequence of excessive headspace. In rear-locking action types, the amount of stretching can also reflect the amount of chamber pressure used in the previous firing. Excessive headspace can be created either during case sizing or at the beginning of the firing process. The striker (firing pin) impact and primer blast shove the case forward in the chamber. These forces can also drive the case shoulder rearward. This will shorten the case body and lengthen the case neck.

Subsequently, as the charge burns, chamber pressure builds. As this happens, the case body expands into contact with the chamber at all portions forward of the solid case head (web). The resulting case-to-chamber bonding locks the hollow portion of the case body to the chamber walls. Thus bonded, the case cannot slide backward in the chamber. Finally, when the force of chamber pressure pushing on the inside of the case head exceeds the strength of the case walls, the case body yields and stretches along a zone near the point where the solid web meets the pressure-bonded case wall. Subsequently, the case head moves backward until it contacts the supporting bolt face. With the case body locked in place and with the case head moving backward, is it any wonder that the case stretches and thins near the junction of the solid web and hollow body?

Thereafter, as chamber pressure continues to build, the force pushing back on the inside of the case head is transferred to the bolt. This compresses the bolt, locking lugs, and lug supporting area of the receiver. Simultaneously, chamber pressure stretches the chamber and receiver walls. Elastic stretching and compression within the receiver and chamber stores considerable energy. Greater chamber pressure (force) results in greater elastic compression and stretching. (This is a precisely linear relationship—doubling force doubles elastic deformation but quadruples stored elastic energy.)

As the bullet accelerates down the bore and then escapes from the bore, chamber pressure plummets. The

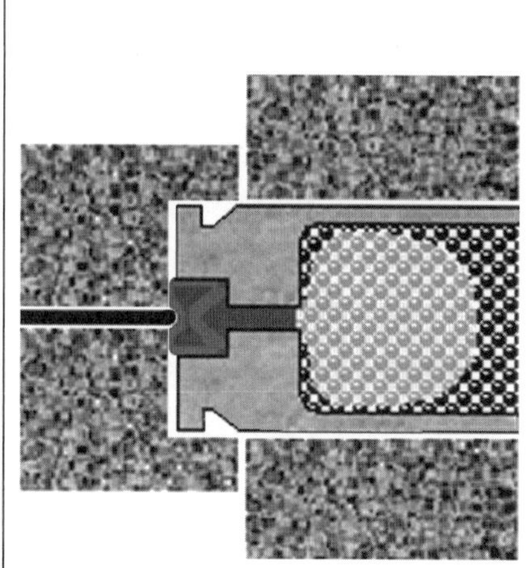

After striker hits primer, before pressure swells case, primer backed out of case.

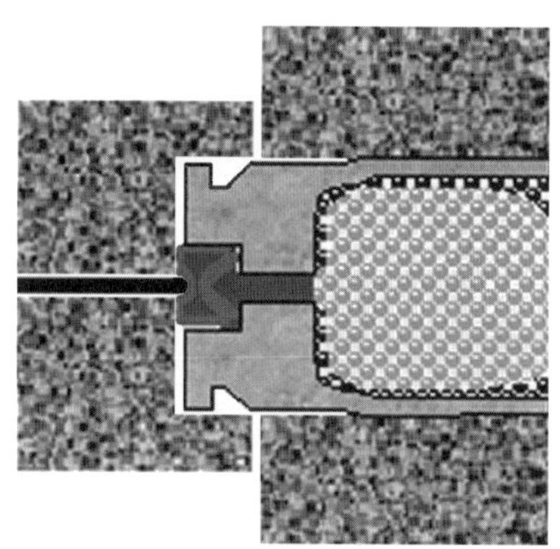

After pressure swells and bonds case body to chamber, before case stretches.

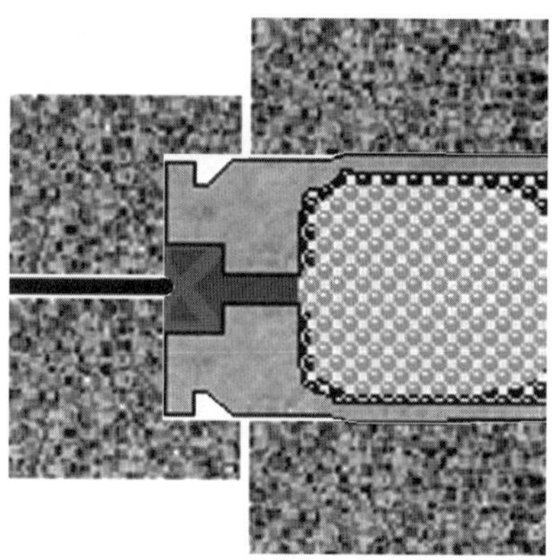

After chamber pressure forces case head against bolt, body stretched and thinned.

stored elastic energy in the bolt, receiver, and chamber are thereby released. Consequently, the bolt hammers the case head forward while the chamber shoulder hammers the case shoulder backward. At the same time, the stretched chamber shrinks back to normal diameter and can slightly reduce case body diameter.

Beyond this (partial) case resizing mechanism, the case continues to shrink elastically. Normally, this latter mechanism assures easy extraction of the fired case because it shortens the case body and reduces case body diameter sufficiently so that the case will freely fit inside the chamber (this is a good result). On bottlenecked cases, this hammering process lengthens the case neck (this is a bad result).

When subjected to excessive chamber pressure, the case head will begin to deform and the case can stretch so much in length and in diameter that the subsequent hammering will not resize the case sufficiently. The subsequent elastic case shrinkage will be insufficient to leave the case free in the chamber; moreover, the hammering can wedge a tapered case in the chamber—such a case will not extract freely. With loads generating progressively greater chamber pressure, degree of extraction difficulty will be progressively greater.

Often, the case is the same length after firing as it was before firing—or the case might even be a bit shorter after firing. After resizing, the case is longer because resizing reduces the case-body diameter. The handloader might believe that resizing had stretched the case; however, this is illusory.

What happens is that the pertinent permanent change in case dimensions occurs during firing but the related increase in case diameter masks that alteration. When the handloader resizes the case so that the body is at its prefiring diameter, the case gets longer. Resizing changes the shape of the case. Resizing does not actually stretch the case. The case simply gets smaller in diameter while increasing in length. A parallel situation, represented by the associated sketch illustrates what actually happens. (See page 14.)

Case resizing is analogous to squeezing opposite corners of an open-ended box. It is easy to change the shape so that the box becomes narrower and taller, but this action does not stretch the box. Neither does resizing stretch a cartridge case—the case gets narrower and longer. Any stretching that does occur, occurs during firing, but often remains hidden until the case is returned to its prefiring diameter.

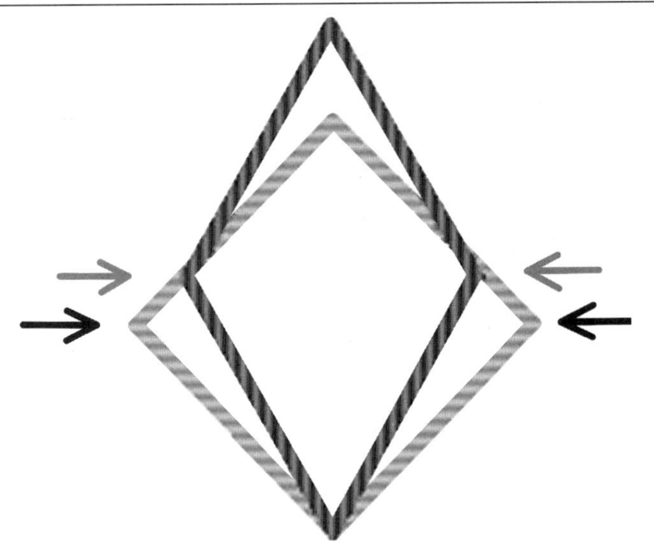

Squeezing opposite corners of an open-ended box does not stretch it; squeezing only changes its shape. This is analogous to what happens when one resizes a case. First, the die reduces body diameter, which lengthens the case body. Then, near the end of the sizing operation, the case shoulder hits the die shoulder; thereafter, as the shellholder drives the case farther into the die, the die shoulder necessarily forces the case shoulder rearward, thus lengthening the case neck.

When compared to a bottlenecked case with a narrow sloping shoulder, a case with a wider and sharper shoulder will exhibit less stretching. When used in high-pressure loads the latter design will also extract more easily.

RESIZING ALTERS CASE SHAPE; RESIZING DOES NOT STRETCH A CASE; FIRING STRETCHES A CASE.

CASE STRETCHING—BOTTLENECKED CASE DESIGN

Comparing otherwise similar cases, the wider and sharper the shoulder, the less any given striker impact and primer explosion will move the shoulder. Shoulder movement increases functional headspace. Increased headspace results in increased stretching.

Similarly, the hammering that occurs as chamber pressure plummets will not drive the case as far into the chamber. Hence, such a case will be wedged less tightly (or not at all) into the chamber. Modern bottlenecked case designs, with little body taper and relatively sharp shoulders are, therefore, quite desirable.

Formerly, some pundits interpreted the combination of easier extraction with reduced case stretching as an indication that improved case designs placed less stress on the action. The previous explanation should make it clear that any such theory is baseless. Case head thrust depends upon several factors whereas case wall taper and case shoulder angle make absolutely no difference whatsoever.

The tiny, thin-walled 22 Hornet is the worst-case example. With the chamber cut in the common manner, the primer blast drives the case forward until the initially unsupported case rim abuts the chamber rim cut. Because, inexplicably, the chamber rim cut is usually deeper than it should be and the case rim is thinner than it should be, the firing process hammers the case far forward. Subsequently, chamber pressure first bonds the case walls to the chamber and then pushes the head back, stretching the case body. In many Hornet-chambered guns, case life is very limited; cases often separate after only one or two loading and firing cycles. For these same reasons, Hornet accuracy is often dismal.

The simple expedient of rechambering to 22 K-Hornet or 22 Ackley Hornet (designs with wider and sharper shoulders) often solves both case life and accuracy problems. However, if manufacturers would simply stay close to minimum and maximum dimensional specifications for chamber and case design (respectively), the standard Hornet would work just as well as the K-Hornet—because the rim would properly support the case in the chamber. Alas, this often does not happen in the United States, as it does in Europe where serious shooters hold the Hornet in high regard.

Action flexing and resulting case stretching is more pronounced in rear-locking guns, but, to varying

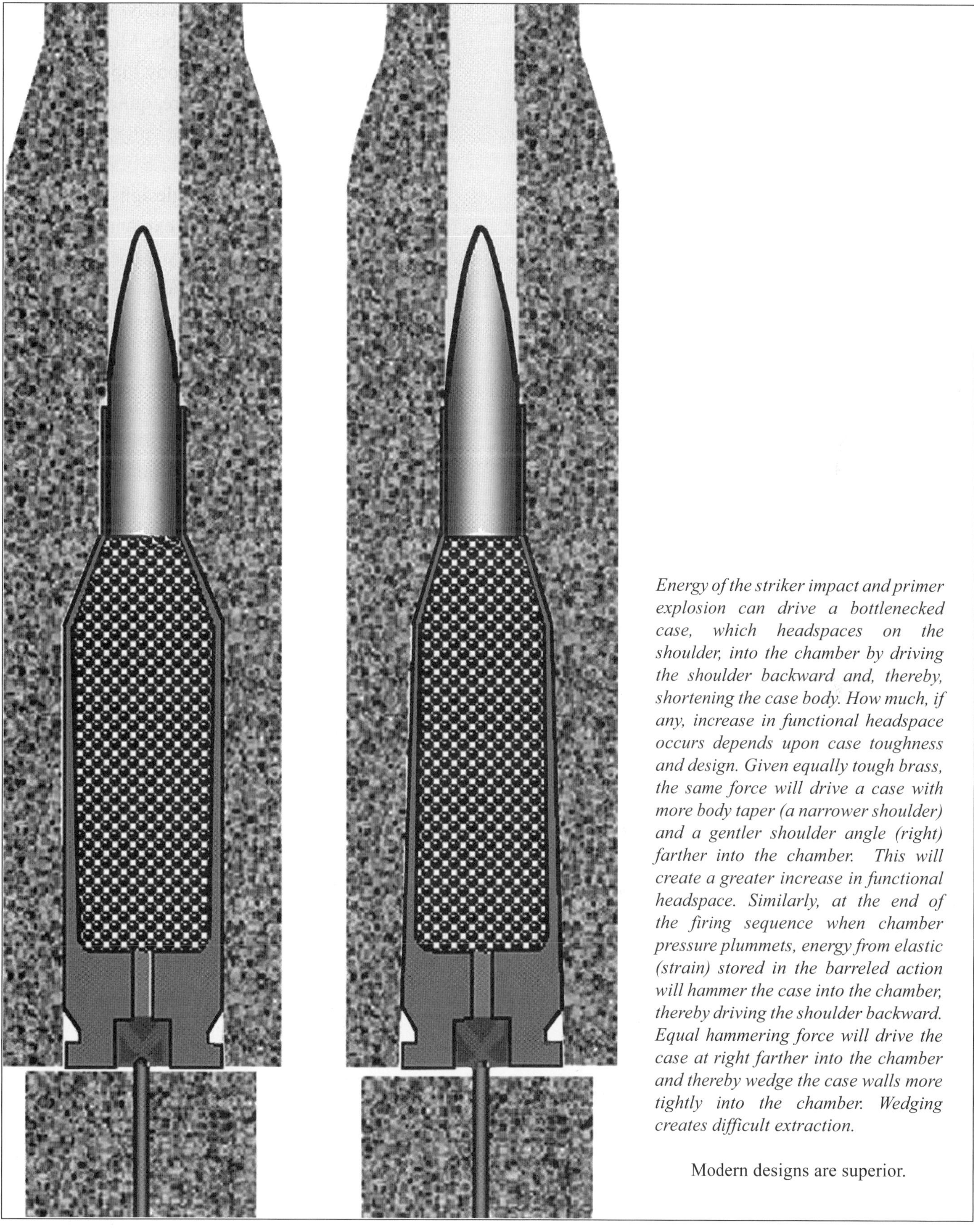

Energy of the striker impact and primer explosion can drive a bottlenecked case, which headspaces on the shoulder, into the chamber by driving the shoulder backward and, thereby, shortening the case body. How much, if any, increase in functional headspace occurs depends upon case toughness and design. Given equally tough brass, the same force will drive a case with more body taper (a narrower shoulder) and a gentler shoulder angle (right) farther into the chamber. This will create a greater increase in functional headspace. Similarly, at the end of the firing sequence when chamber pressure plummets, energy from elastic (strain) stored in the barreled action will hammer the case into the chamber, thereby driving the shoulder backward. Equal hammering force will drive the case at right farther into the chamber and thereby wedge the case walls more tightly into the chamber. Wedging creates difficult extraction.

Modern designs are superior.

degrees, this occurs in all action types. Increasing peak chamber pressure or case-head diameter increases action stressing. (A larger case head pushes against a larger area of the bolt, and, therefore, with any given pressure it exerts more force—force equals stress.) Similarly, increasing the duration of chamber pressure increases action flexing. Therefore, even when peak chamber pressure and case head diameter are unchanged, a case with a longer body (greater capacity) can stress the action more than a shorter case does because the larger charge of slower-burning propellant will apply greater pressure for a longer period. Physicists refer to this sort of thing as an inertial effect.

Inertial effects are a chief reason the copper crusher pressure measuring method is incapable of indicating anything resembling actual peak chamber pressure. Modern conformal transducer methods do much better at this, but inertial bias also limits accuracy of these systems; it is impossible to account for inertial effects fully. Actually, no feasible pressure measuring system can eliminate such influences because it is fundamentally impossible to quantify any dynamic system with exactitude.

CASE STRETCHING—GUN DESIGN

Conversely, in rear-locking guns, the unusually rapid pressure rise associated with a cartridge such as the 454 Casull (a relatively small charge of a relatively fast-burning propellant that generates unusually high peak chamber pressure) can lead to action battering. This battering occurs because the case head drives the bolt rearward so fast that the bolt acts as a hammer when it hits the locking lugs.

Also, not all front-locking actions are equally rigid. However, regardless of action type or case design, excepting cases used in low-pressure loads, all normally resized rifle cases stretch with every firing. Eventually such cases become unsafe for further use—these are subject to separation near the web-to-body junction during subsequent firing. Handloaders must watch for signs of excessive stretching or incipient separation.

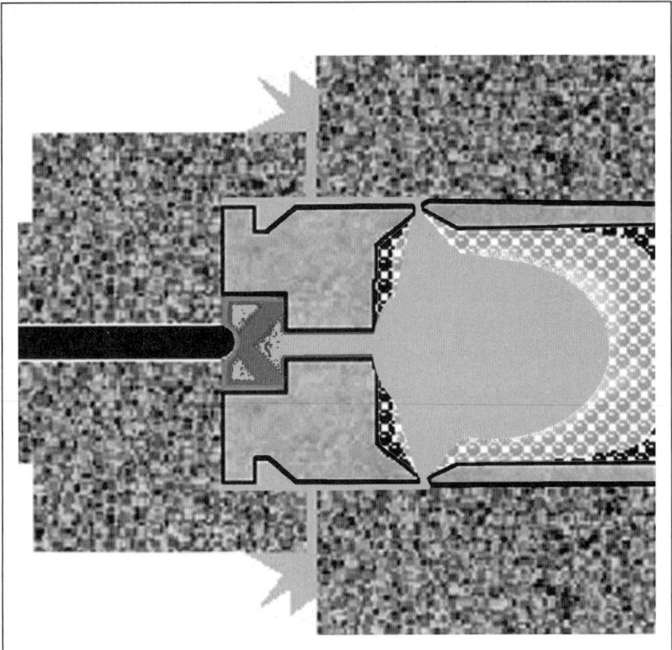

High-pressure loads can stretch a case near the base of the body. This can lead to case separation and dangerous gas leakage.

CASE SEPARATION WITHOUT LENGTHENING

It is possible that asymmetric internal case stress could create a situation where a case that stretched only slightly at the web-to-body junction during firing might not lengthen at all. This can happen when the case walls slightly thicken with each firing and reloading cycle. Therefore, lack of evident stretching does not equate to lack of thinning at the web-to-body junction.

This is common in cylindrical cases—at each firing, the body wall gets slightly thicker everywhere except the zone where stretching occurs and that zone gets progressively thinner, with the inevitable result of eventual separation—despite the fact that it was never necessary to trim the case to keep it at the same length.

Left-to-right: Partial separation (visible on polished case); significant thinning (shown in cross section); nearly complete separation (visible crack); bright band (highly tarnished case). A visible bright band, usually near web, indicates excessive case body thinning. Such a case is apt to separate on next usage, with potentially dangerous consequences.

We also see this when using the wonderful RCBS X resizing die with bottlenecked cases. This die can eliminate the need to trim a case but the case is still thinning near the base! Periodically, inspect all cases for thinning (usually) near the web-to-body junction, as I explain next.

Examine the case body for evidence of excessive case stretching. A bright ring around the case head, just forward of the solid portion of the web, is evidence of significant stretching. Any suggestion of a crack in the case body necessitates case destruction. Reuse of such a case will create an unsafe cartridge.

Using an RCBS Case Gauge to check case wall thinning. Note bright ring around base of this badly stretched case. In this instance, the ring is highlighted to an unusual degree because this case was significantly tarnished.

DESTROY AND DISCARD CASES HAVING SIGNIFICANT BODY WALL THINNING NEAR THE HEAD.

The RCBS Case Gauge gives useful relative measurements of case-wall thickness. With this tool, handloaders can accurately assess case thinning near the junction of the hollow body and solid web. When thinning has reduced case wall thickness in that area to less than about the thickness just forward of the thinnest section in that area, destroy and discard the case.

If you have fired and reloaded every case in the batch the same number of times using similar loads and loading practices, the best practice is to destroy and discard the entire lot. If, on the other hand, variations in usage have occurred, it is likely that many cases in that lot will continue to give safe service for several more, perhaps many more, loading and firing cycles. In the latter instance, the best practice is to pay progressively greater attention to cases after each firing to avoid using any case that is too thin near the web.

CASE NECK LENGTH—SAFETY

Measure case length after assuring that the case body is sound. The caliper is my favorite tool for this task.

Many handy tools exist for doing this, but the caliper is so useful for so many handloading tasks that every handloader should own one. You need no other tool for measuring case length. However, for those who just want to keep things simple, a dedicated case gauge is a handy device that eliminates the need to ever measure length—if the case fits, it is within standard specification length.

RCBS and others offer affordable calipers. Modern electronic units that feature automatic power off (after a period of disuse) are wonderful tools; design of these units minimizes the potential for error, due to misreading the scale, or of damage resulting from misuse, abuse, or misadventure.

A CASE NECK THAT IS UNNECESSARILY SHORTER THAN THE CHAMBER NECK CAN REDUCE THE ACCURACY POTENTIAL OF ANY CARTRIDGE. CONVERSELY, A CASE NECK THAT IS TOO LONG FOR THE CHAMBER NECK CAN RESULT IN A WRECKED GUN, WITH INJURY OR DEATH TO THE SHOOTER AND BYSTANDERS.

All reputable data manuals should list maximum nominal case length in the data section for each cartridge. Theoretically, before reloading, you should trim cases that are longer than the listed Maximum Case Length. I cover a general exception to this rule later in this chapter under "Case Neck Length—Matching to Chamber."

Case length is a critical safety issue. When chambered, an over-length case can extend into the tapered transition between the chamber neck and throat. If that should occur, closing the action can crimp the case mouth into the bullet. Many actions have significant camming force so that a shooter might not feel this happening, or the shooter might attribute the resulting resistance to the action closing or to some other cause. Obviously, any resistance to the action closing should raise a bright-red, mental-warning flag. Unless the shooter is certain that the cause is innocuous, he should not fire the round.

A worst-case scenario exists. A too-long case can chamber freely. This can happen when the mouth of a chambered case just reaches the front of the chamber neck. In this instance, dangerous crimping would occur if the striker impact or the primer blast drove the case farther into the chamber, which is apt to happen. Firing such a round can lead to a gun-destroying pressure excursion. After resizing, trim all too-long case necks, as necessary, to provide chamber clearance.

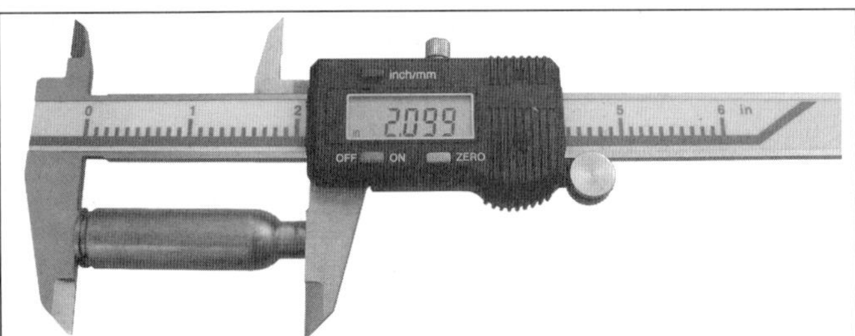

An RCBS Electronic Digital Caliper is affordable, durable, and dependable. With careful and practiced usage, measurement accuracy is 5/10,000 inch. Newer versions of this basic caliper turn off after a period of disuse; and battery life is very long. These tools measure in mm or inch and allow zeroing at any specific opening, which is most useful for comparing variation between similar items.

CASE CRACKS

Carefully examine cases for cracks. The Opti-Visor is a valuable aid. Destroy and discard any case with any crack. Body cracks can lead to catastrophic gas leaks. Neck cracks can destroy the potential for accuracy and can lead to inadequate bullet containment. This latter effect concerns functionality and could lead to any of several unsafe conditions. Examples include:

- Unchambering such a round (without firing) could leave the bullet lodged in the barrel, spilling propellant in the action and chamber and, thereby, rendering the gun temporarily inoperable. (Cleaning such a gun in the field is difficult, at best.)
- Conversely, the bullet could move into the case during chambering — this could result in elevated and unsafe chamber pressure, when the round is fired.
- Finally, the bullet could move into or out of the case while in the magazine. This alters overall cartridge length—an over- or under-length cartridge can increase pressure or jam a gun.

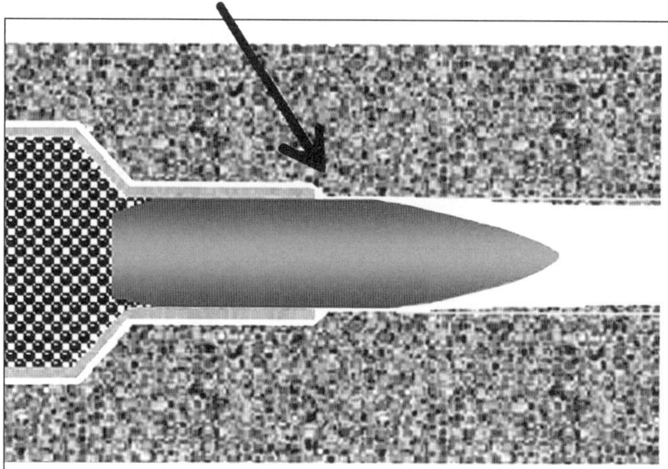

Neck of chambered case touches, or almost touches, end of chamber. Note clearance between case shoulder and chamber shoulder.

Too long case neck, worst-case scenario: Case mouth clears chamber-neck shoulder until striker impact and primer explosion drive the case deeper into the chamber.

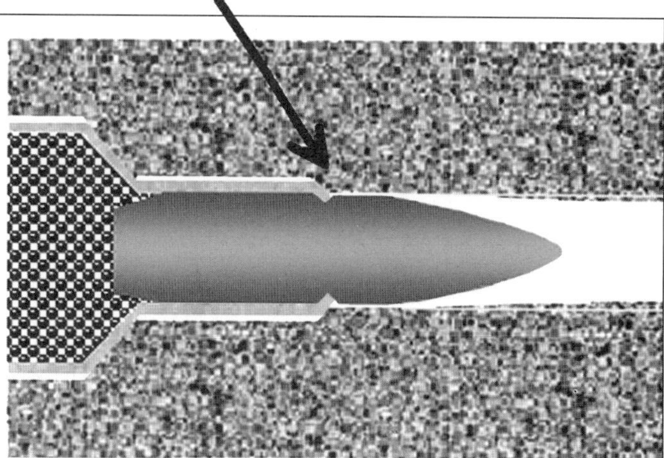

Striker impact and primer explosion drive case forward. This can also set case shoulder back, thereby lengthening case neck. Shoulder now touches.

Neck solidly crimped into bullet. This locks bullet in case, and as chamber pressure builds, bullet cannot freely move—it must swage past crimped-in case mouth. This retards bullet acceleration and can lead to gun-destroying chamber pressure.

SIGNS OF EXCESSIVE PRESSURE ON CASE

Manufacturers have designed most modern rifles and chamberings to work at relatively high pressure—near the limit of the feasible strength for work-hardened case brass. In these combinations, excessive loads can damage the case. Therefore, examination of cases after firing is critical—to look for signs of use with a load that generates excessive pressure. When the cartridge fires, the case is the only thing standing between you and the significant volume of hot gases at enormous pressure inside the gun chamber; hence, changes in fired case appearance suggesting that any particular load might exceed safe and prudent pressure levels are certainly worth noting.

This important step can help keep you out of trouble. Should anything seem out of the ordinary when you fire a shot (e.g., unusually heavy recoil) or when you extract a fired case (e.g., difficult extraction), carefully examine the case, the action, and the bore interior before firing another shot.

With previously fired cases, check the case head for obvious signs of excessive pressure, softness, or headspace issues. Excessive functional headspace is surprisingly common. One such sign is unusual appearance of the fired primer, which I cover in chapter 7.

Another more universal and useful pressure indicator is case head appearance. If the case head reflects any features of the bolt face—typically bright spots or lines on the headstamp area—be concerned. Any case showing such a sign has probably been subjected to excessive pressure. To clarify this fact, consider that cases from industry proof cartridges (using cases from standard production lots) do not show any objective evidence of excessive pressure. If case head deformation is significant, destroy and discard the case.

Conversely, while rare, case heads that are unusually soft can show marking and deformation with normal loads. In that instance, such marks do not necessarily indicate a ruined case or a dangerous load, but those cases and that load recipe do warrant further monitoring, as when seating the next primer.

Examples of case cracks: Cracks can occur anywhere along body of case; see the chapter entitled "Interesting Pictures" for more examples. These cases cracked at time of firing. Cracks in cartridge necks are common after long-term storage of loads with improperly annealed necks and in handloads using cases that have been reloaded many times without annealing. Destroy and discard any cracked case.

If the primer seats without any resistance, destroy and discard that case. The load was too hot for that case. At the very least, it is necessary to reduce the propellant charge for loads used in cases from the same production lot. At the worst, such a load might well be unsafe for use in cases of any brand or production lot. I cover this aspect in detail in chapter 13.

While comparatively soft cases are rare, two manufacturers (Norma and Federal) have sometimes produced cases with heads that are somewhat softer than those made by most other manufacturers (Norma has resolved manufacturing issues behind this former problem). Some pundits have claimed that heads on military cases can sometimes be softer than the heads on commercial cases. (Also, some writers have reported that some military cases are heavier—less capacity—than commercial cases.)

Firing a normal load in a case with a relatively soft head can cause modest head deformation. Usually, such firing will work-harden the case head sufficiently so that further marking and deformation will not occur—so long as subsequent reloadings do not create loads that generate pressure that significantly exceed the pressure of a factory load.

If, after firing an established load in a new batch of cases, you notice any case head marks, back down

Cracks can occur anywhere along hollow case body. Usually, such cracks occur during firing, but these can also occur during resizing, bullet seating, or storage. Using any cracked case is unsafe—destroy such cases. Case at left was produced during WWII. Wartime exigencies might explain this unusual failure.

5 percent on the charge—any load that leaves any visible marks on the case head is too hot for use in that case. If you cannot live with that, try to find a harder batch of cases for your top loads.

Meanwhile, never forget this salient fact: That piece of brass is the only thing standing between you and certain disaster; when you see it reacting to a load by exhibiting permanent head deformation, you are seeing solid proof that the load is pushing that case right up against the ragged edge of what it will tolerate—pressure generated by such a load is pushing such a case very close to the point of complete failure. For the shooter, consequences of case-head failure range between unpleasant and fatal.

You might have fired such loads thousands of times without incident. If so, that fact only suggests that you are long past due for an accident. Is it actually appropriate to call such an incident an accident? This is akin to rolling dice with life and limb on the line; sooner or later, you will shoot craps.

This case shows ample evidence of a prior usage with a load that generated dangerously excessive pressure—likely exceeding 80,000 psi. Primer pocket will no longer hold a primer—this case is ruined. More critically, the load that caused this deformation came very close to generating enough pressure to cause the case head to rupture, which could have destroyed the gun with the potential to injure or kill the shooter and bystanders.

This 243 case shows a very good example of excess pressure forcing case material into the ejector plunger hole in the bolt face (area at left).

When firing any case a second (or perhaps third time) with the same full-power load, measurable case head expansion is an indication that a load is simply too hot. Generally, such loads will soon open the primer pockets sufficiently so that primers will no longer seat solidly. Until that happens, unless the handloader bothers to measure the case-head diameter, both before and after shooting any given case, this sign of excess pressure can easily go unnoticed. Hence, if you have any questions about the safety of your loads, it is a good idea to observe the case-head diameter. A blade micrometer with accuracy to 0.0001 inch is most valuable here.

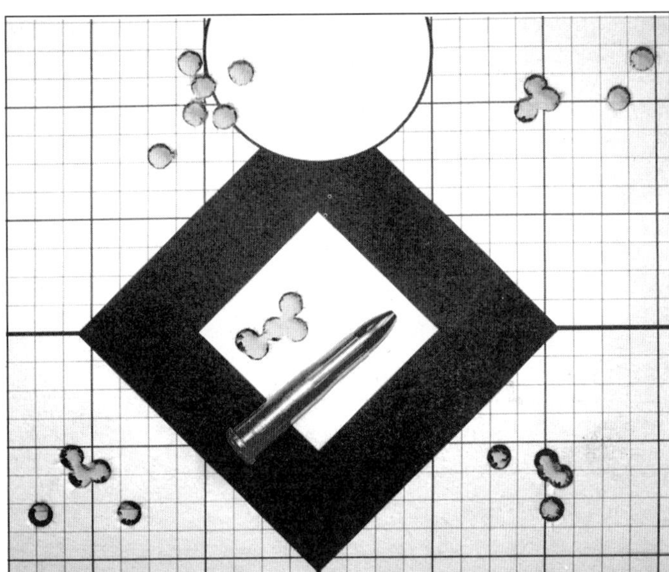

Case preparation and maintenance are important considerations when developing an accuracy load. Case-to-case variations will limit accuracy results. Best practice is to keep all cases in the same condition with regard to length and number of times used.

The most accurate measurement of case-head expansion is immediately forward of the rim, but measurement across the rim will usually suffice and is far easier to take. I cover this technique in detail in chapter 13.

CASE PREPARATION—GENERAL CONSIDERATIONS

Any of various steps, which I cover in chapters 3 and 4, can increase the value of new or used cases. The goal of those steps is to make all cases in any batch as similar as is feasible. Some steps are necessary to assure that reused cases produce safe and functionally sound handloads. Other steps improve accuracy and reduce shot-to-shot velocity variation.

In those chapters, I cover various aspects of case preparation procedures, from the most mundane (e.g., trimming to uniform length), to the most esoteric (e.g., outside neck turning). Which of those steps are important to you will depend upon what you intend to do with the ammunition. However, an understanding of each of those procedures can be beneficial, regardless of your goals.

Assuming that you have purchased new cases or that you are working with once-fired cases, you should consider several steps in your quest to produce superior handloads. Base your decision to perform any of these steps upon an analysis of the goals and potential benefits that each operation might garner.

None of these steps will harm the accuracy or functionality of your handloads, so I recommend that you perform as many as you feel comfortable doing. Of the steps considered in chapters 3 and 4, only trimming to length and neck turning involve safety issues. These steps are necessary to provide adequate neck-to-chamber clearance.

Several such steps require preliminary case sizing. For example, neck sizing is helpful before trimming a case to length using a lathe-type tool or the Lee Trimming tool. Neck sizing is also required for neck outside turning or inside reaming. (The latter is an obsolete technique that I do not recommend.) Obviously, flash-hole deburring and primer pocket uniforming require preliminary case depriming.

CASE CLEANING

Before working with cases, cleaning is worthwhile, to remove grit and debris. A fine method is to place cases in a vibratory tumbler with a corncob or walnut-hull media I often clean cases for several hours, but if the cases are not too dirty, thirty minutes will suffice. It does not matter how you clean cases, but it is important that the cases you use are sufficiently clean to not scratch the die. Hard particles can become embedded in the case and can thereby scratch the die or the gun chamber. This is particularly critical when working with nickel-plated cases.

Several companies offer additives for tumbler media. By far, the best I have found is Champion's Brand. This product is a mixture of fine mineral abrasives. These are relatively harmless to steel but vigorously attack tarnish on brass. A tiny amount goes a long way—for most serious handloaders, an eight-ounce tub more than likely represents a lifetime supply. While removing tarnish and any traces of lubricant, this product also polishes cases and leaves a beautiful finish. Normal cleaning and polishing time is usually two hours or less.

Similarly, after sizing lubricated cases, it is important to remove sizing lubricant. You can easily remove some types of lube from cases by wiping the case with a clean, dry rag. Other types of lubricant are difficult to remove; vibratory tumbling in a corncob media is the best method of removing sticky lubes—addition of a bit of water to dampen the media often helps. Rubbing alcohol is the ideal solvent for this purpose.

FULL-LENGTH CASE SIZING—LUBRICATING

Before each reloading, you should full-length resize cases used in most hunting, plinking, and self-defense applications. Some target-shooting applications do not require full-length resizing, and you can often achieve better accuracy by sizing only the case neck. Straight-walled pistol and revolver cases are easiest to resize, particularly when using carbide or similar dies, which require no lubrication. For these, all that is necessary is to run the cleaned cases through the die. Because lubrication is unnecessary, it is also unnecessary to clean such cases after sizing with such a die. Conversely, tapered and bottlenecked cases require lubrication before sizing and clean up after sizing.

As one pulls a case out of the resizing die, the decapping rod usually expands the case neck. Therefore, lubrication of neck interior (to ease neck expansion) can be either necessary or useful (depending upon tools used and neck condition). New cases might not require neck lubrication; however, the more times one reloads a case, the harder the neck gets. Eventually, either neck interior lubrication or neck annealing will become necessary.

Avoid using more than a trace of wet lube inside the case neck, as excessive lube will lead to difficulties when you pour propellant into the case. Granules will stick to the lube and, thus, slow or stop the charge from entering the case. In addition, excessive wet lubricant will contaminate some portion of the charge. It is better, therefore, to use a tiny amount of dry lubricant. White mica, graphite, and molybdenum-disulfide are good choices—the latter is my favorite.

An easy way to do this is to use an appropriate size brass brush wrapped full of fine steel wool. Periodically dip this brush into the dry lube. Passing the brush into, and back out of, the case neck will deposit a fine film of dry lube that will provide ideal lubrication to ease the neck expansion operation.

The handloader can lubricate the case exterior using various products and methods. Regardless of the lubing method and lubricant used, avoid getting excessive lubricant on the case neck or shoulder. Excessive lube on these parts will lead to hydraulic dents in the case shoulder because the sizing die traps and concentrates lube that was on the neck and shoulder onto the shoulder. If you observe dents on resized cases, use less lube (especially in that area).

Formerly, my favorite case lubes were lanolin based. These have several advantages:

- Sufficient lubricity for most tasks
- A tiny amount does the job
- Easy to apply
- Easier to remove
- Cleans cases during removal
- Innocuous to handle and to use
- Inexpensive

I have a new favorite, Royal Case and Die Lube, from SharpShoot-R, Inc. This product has all the advantages of lanolin but with greater lubricity and it smells good! Royal Lube comes in a small plastic tub that costs a few dollars. One tub will lubricate far more than ten thousand rifle cases. Simply press and slide a fingertip against the paste surface to transfer a tiny dab onto your finger. A volume about equal to a typical pinhead is sufficient.

Starting near the base of the case, spin and slide the case body between your fingertip and thumb. Proceed with this rotating and sliding motion while moving toward the case mouth. In about one second, you can thereby distribute a thin lubricant film sufficiently over the case body and neck to assure uniform resizing.

SharpShoot-R also offers the same product in an aerosol spray, diluted with a quick evaporating and harmless solvent. The contents of one bottle will lubricate thousands of cases. That company is considering offering a pump spray version, which I would prefer, owing to economy and precise dispensing and application.

A dedicated shoebox lid stored in a clean area is a handy adjunct to spray-on lubes. Lay cases from the working group in the lid (enough cases to cover most of the available space). While slowly passing the bottle about one foot above the cases, apply enough lube to wet the exposed surfaces and no more—when visible case surfaces are just barely wetted, application is sufficient. Then, gently shake the lid endwise, to roll the cases. Allow the cases to rest for a few seconds. This allows the fluid to distribute over the case surfaces, as the solvent evaporates. In a few seconds, the cases are ready to resize.

With a bit of care during application, just enough lube will migrate into the case necks to add the necessary lubricity without danger of propellant contamination. The secret is to not spray directly into or toward the case mouths.

Royal Lube and lanolin remove easily, either through vibratory tumbling in an untreated (clean) corncob media or by twisting the sized cases inside a clean rag. Removing these lubes also removes dirt and some tarnish.

Whatever system and chemical you use, your goal is to get enough lubricant on the cases to assure correct resizing and, thereafter, to fully remove the lubricant from resized cases. Inadequate lubrication can lead to a torn case rim with a case stuck in the resizing die (various manufacturers offer stuck case removal tools—believe me, it is far better to never need one).

A lubricated case will pick up grit and can thereby scratch the gun chamber. Moreover, firing a lubricated

VibraShine, Dillon, Midway, Lyman, and others all offer vibratory tumblers, which are most useful for case cleaning.

Hornady offers an entire line of case care products. For many decades, I used Unique Case Lube (lower right).

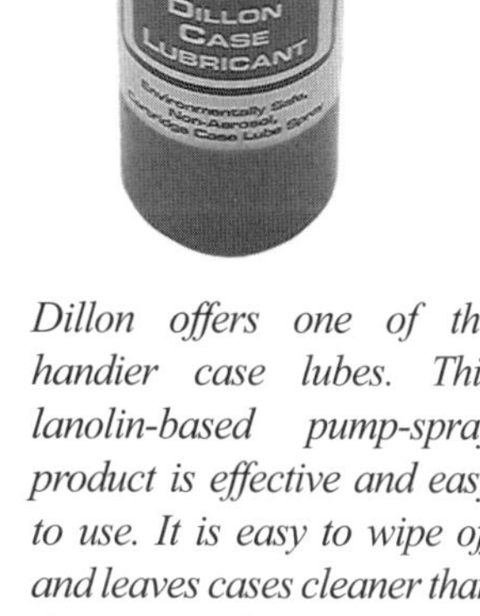

Dillon offers one of the handier case lubes. This lanolin-based pump-spray product is effective and easy to use. It is easy to wipe off and leaves cases cleaner than they were before lubricating.

SharpShoot-R Inc. offers both a paste and an aerosol version of Royal Case and Die Lube. I have compared every case lube now marketed, and this is the one I prefer.

case significantly increases total case thrust against the bolt and, therefore, increases action stressing. This will decrease action life and, in extreme instances (when using loads that generate far too much pressure), it could permanently deform the action and, thereby, increase headspace.

CASE LUBRICATION—ACCURACY

Tests have proven that failure to provide uniform lubrication on bottlenecked cases will result in variations in case body (headspace) length of resized cases of several thousandths of an inch. Such functional headspace variations can destroy accuracy.

Owing to increased endwise friction between case and die, the shoulder of an inadequately lubed case will not push against the die shoulder as hard as will the shoulder of a well-lubed case. During the last increment of resizing, the degree of end-to-end elastic compression of the case body, therefore, depends upon the degree of lubrication. As you begin to remove a poorly lubed case from the sizing die, the case can elastically lengthen more than a properly lubed case will lengthen.

As with all things in handloading and shooting, uniformity is paramount. Uniform case lubrication is key to uniform case resizing and to accuracy.

FULL-LENGTH SIZING DIE—ADJUSTMENT

Adjusting the body of a tungsten carbide, or similar, sizing die so that it will touch the shellholder when the ram is fully raised could result in a broken die or broken carbide insert. Adjust such dies about one turn from touching the fully raised shellholder.

By adjusting such a die progressively farther away from the shellholder, you can leave the base of the case body partially unsized. With careful adjustment, you can size the base of the cases so that each freely enters in the chamber while still nearly fitting it; hence, the bases of the cases center better in the chamber. The seated bullet will expand the case neck to nearly fit the chamber. Hence, both ends of the cases will better center in the chamber and the bullets will center on, and align with, the bore axis. This technique can improve accuracy.

For full-length sizing of bottlenecked cases, the only correct way to adjust the die (to achieve the most consistent full-length resizing) is to make sure that the fully raised ram always causes the top of the shellholder to abut solidly against the die body. If, when resizing a case, you do not feel the shellholder abut against the die, adjust the die body deeper into the press. I cover how to adjust the functional headspace of bottlenecked cases correctly in chapter 5.

Placing an O-ring under the locking ring on the die body allows the die to tilt, as might be necessary, to align correctly with the shellholder. This method is of sufficient value that I prefer Lee Locking Rings, which have built-in O-rings and offer the added advantage that adjusting how far the die body threads into the press requires no tools.

When using the Lee Locking Ring or an interposed O-ring with a conventional locking ring, the simple expedient of marking the top of the press and the die body with a permanent marker allows die changes with precise settings and without ever needing to use any tool.

When using Lee Lock Rings, remember to turn the die by the lock ring until it is loose in the press, so the locking ring does not turn on the die body; otherwise, you will lose the desired adjustment setting.

DECAPPING STEM ADJUSTMENT

Correctly adjusting the decapping rod is a simple but critical matter. Normally, the decapping pin should protrude no farther than about one-eighth inch from the die base. If it does not protrude sufficiently, it will fail to drive the primer free of the case. If it protrudes too far, the decapping stem will hit the case web before you have driven the case fully into the resizing die. In this instance, when using a conventional resizing die, driving the case farther into the die (to complete the resizing operation) will destroy the decapping rod.

On such dies, place an O-ring between the decapping rod lock-nut and the die body (or rod carrier nut). This allows for tool-free adjustment and allows the decapping rod to wiggle, which might be necessary to center the expander in the case neck. This technique reduces the risk of bending the case shoulder during neck expansion.

The Lee Precision decapping rod system uses a frictioning collet to lock the decapping rod in place. In this system, if you adjust the rod too low in the die, a subsequent full-length sizing operation will harmlessly force the rod upward through the collet.

An added advantage of the Lee system is that it provides a built-in, stuck-case remover. Should you tear the rim from a case leaving the case stuck in the sizing die—which most often results from inadequate lubrication, especially with nickel-plated rifle cases—all that you need to do to drive the case from the die is to loosen the collet slightly and then to hammer on the decapping rod. Simply brilliant.

Placing O-rings between die body and decapping rod carrier and between carrier and locking nut affords easy decapping stem adjustment, while allowing expander and decapping pin to align with case. This can prevent a broken decapping pin and reduces the potential for the expander to bend the case shoulder, thereby bending the neck out of alignment with the case body.

One potential disadvantage of the collet-style stem is misalignment. Necessarily, proper collet tightening locks and locates the decapping stem solidly within the die body. If the manufacturer erred in the concentricity of the die or collet, the decapping stem will not center in the case neck; this could bend the case shoulder during neck expansion. However, in practice, this has not proven to be a significant issue because die makers that use this system control die straightness quite well.

Another advantage of the Lee Die Decapping Rod system is that adjustment is simple. Merely adjust the decapping rod so that it sticks out of the die body significantly, tighten the locking nut securely, and full-length resize a case. The case web will force the decapping rod upward through the collet lock. This makes it impossible to damage the decapping rod through improper adjustment (too far down), which is not true with any other brand of die.

An easy method of adjusting a threaded decapping stem is to raise it so that it is obviously too high in the die, then full-length resize a case. Make sure that the shellholder solidly abuts the die base. Then screw the stem downward until the primer comes free of the case. Continue to screw the decapping stem down until the decapping rod hits the case head. Finally, screw the decapping stem up, about two turns, and lock it in place (or apply enough friction with the locking nut on the added O-ring) to assure that stem adjustment does not change.

The Lee Locking Ring is a superior invention. It allows easy hand adjustment of dies but will hold the die setting during die changes (loosen and tighten die by turning lock ring), and it allows die body to align with axis of press. Interposing an O-ring between a conventional locking ring and press duplicates the latter benefit when using conventional locking rings.

Redding standard (conventional) Full-Length Sizing Die. (Decapping pin protrusion is minimum in this example.)

I discuss in chapter 5 a useful decapping rod improvement whereby the tinkerer can locate the expander higher on the decapping rod.

SPECIAL DIES—NECK BUSHING

Die manufacturers offer various types of sizing dies that use interchangeable neck bushings. These allow precise control of degree of neck sizing.

Consider what happens when using a conventional die to size a case neck. If the case has an unusually thin neck, the die must still apply sufficient sizing so that the neck will subsequently hold the bullet. Variations in neck wall thickness, from lot-to-lot and from brand to brand, often exceed 0.002 of an inch. Hence, a die that sizes the thinnest necked cases small enough to hold a bullet will size the thickest necked cases more than 0.004 of an inch smaller than is necessary. Hence, to allow for proper bullet seating on thick-necked cases, the expander ball must enlarge the case neck at least 0.004 inch. For this reason, the resizing operation excessively expands most case necks.

One solution is to use a sizing die designed with interchangeable bushings and a bushing that sizes the neck just right. Bushings are available in various sizes (in one-thousandth-inch increments), and some manufacturers offer these with low-friction coatings, such as TiN (titanium nitride), which eliminates the need for case neck lubrication.

Redding, RCBS, and Forster, offer full-length neck-bushing dies. These are similar to conventional sizing dies but have several advantages: First, these are ideal for use with neck-turned cases (necks are usually a bit thinner than average and of uniform, concentric thickness); second, these provide easier sizing and longer case neck life with any given batch of cases—the ideal bushing sizes the neck sufficiently so that the expander ball is just slightly larger than the neck as that comes out of the bushing.

Redding offers neck-bushing dies that have a micrometer top. (See page 29.) This feature allows easy and precise adjustment of the length of case neck that you resize. With these dies, you can leave a specific amount of the base of the neck unsized. This technique can improve case centering of the chambered round and can, therefore, improve accuracy. Generally, leaving about 0.020 inch of the neck unsized will not cause any chambering difficulty or result in a significant reduction in bullet-to-neck friction (bullet pull).

Redding offers a carbide expander for these dies that provides consistent neck-to-bullet friction for cases that do not have uniform neck thickness. This is also a potentially useful adjunct when working with neck-uniformed cases because it assures that the re-sized case neck has no dents.

Lee Precision (and some Hornady) dies use a collet to align and lock the decapping rod in place. A significant bonus of this design on Lee dies is that the decapping rod doubles as a stuck-case remover—simply loosen the collet and hammer on the decapping rod.

SPECIAL DIES—SMALL-BASE SIZING

Small-base, full-length sizing dies were invented in response to a perceived need when handloading for semiautomatic rifles. If you happen to be shooting such a rifle, you might find that use of this style of die improves cartridge functionality. While many pundits have recommended using small-base dies for any loads intended for use in any non-bolt-action rifle, I have never seen any need or advantage to this. Generally, it is my opinion that small-base dies would never have been invented if gun and die manufacturers had kept the various manufacturing tolerances a bit closer to nominal specifications.

Lee Precision studied this question and chose not to offer small-base dies. Lee and most other modern dies work for all guns with standard chambers.

Lee Collet Die: This die decaps the case and resizes only the neck. This approach offers many advantages: It cannot bend the case shoulder; degree of neck sizing is easily adjustable by altering diameter of decapping rod; and no lube is ever needed because the case does not move relative to the sizing body. This is one of my favorite dies for applications where full-length sizing is not needed.

The Redding Competition Neck Bushing Die features micrometer adjustment for length of neck that is sized. Redding offers both hardened steel and TiN-plated (titanium nitride) bushings. The spring-loaded, sliding body centers and supports the case for precise neck sizing, without any chance of bending the case shoulder. Redding also offers a carbide expander for this die. This will remove dents from the neck and provide uniform (minimal) neck sizing of unturned necks.

Regardless of action type, you should consider having the gun inspected by a competent gunsmith if you experience chambering difficulties while using cases that you have resized along the full length of the case (full-length resized) and when both chamber and ammunition are reasonably clean. Likely, something is wrong with the chamber; if not, you should be able to solve the problem by using small-base dies.

I would prefer not to have to add the word competent in the above statement. However, most serious gun aficionados have seen enough examples of incompetent gunsmithing to know that all that is required for a person to practice this art is a shingle, a nail, and a single-action revolver—the latter to use as a makeshift hammer. Incompetence is all too common.

Note: One die maker was pressured to offer small-base 223 Remington dies, so it compared many standard and small-base 223 sizing dies from other manufacturers. It found that often, the small-base, full-length sizing die left sized cases larger than the standard full-length sizing die did. Never assume anything.

Full-length die adjustment technique for neck sizing of significantly tapered cases. Adjust full-length die about two turns from touching fully raised shellholder. This method will not work for most modern bottlenecked case designs because limited taper of such cases will result in some case-body sizing, which will drive the case shoulder forward; such a partially sized case will not freely chamber.

SIZING DIE—INADEQUATE SIZING

Rarely, a particular resizing die and shellholder set will fail to shorten the body of a bottlenecked case sufficiently to allow free chambering of the resized case in a particular gun. When this occurs, the best solution depends upon the cause.

Begin by measuring and recording the length of both die body and shellholder, for reference. If you know that the shellholder and die combination works when sizing cases for use in other guns, likely that particular gun chamber is on the short side. If so, the best solution is to modify a separate shellholder that you will dedicate for use only with that gun. Carefully grind the top surface to shorten the shellholder. This modified shellholder will allow you to drive the case farther into the resizing die and thereby shorten the body more than normal.

Conversely, if you test the die with several standard shellholders and if the resulting resized cases chamber tightly or not at all in several rifles, likely the die is faulty—the manufacturer has cut the chamber in such a die too deeply. In this instance, the best solution is to shorten the die body.

One method of modifying either the die or the shellholder is to grind on the tool by working it against the flat surface of a coarse sharpening stone. While doing so, continuously rotate the tool between your fingers so that you do not remove more material from one area (side) than from another. The end of the tool should remain square with the body of the tool. Periodically measure the length of the modified tool. When you have reduced tool length by about 0.002 inch, resize a few cases. Make sure that the shellholder solidly abuts the ram, and check the cases to assure free chambering. Repeat this process until resized cases freely chamber.

Permanently mark any shellholder that you have modified so that you will not inadvertently use it for any other purpose.

PRESS—CONSISTENT OPERATION

As with all handloading operations, it is always important to operate the press in a similar manner each time. This is particularly true when resizing bottlenecked cases.

All else being equal, if you run one case into the press very slowly and you run a second case into the press as fast as you can, sized-case shoulder placement of those two cases is almost certain to be different. This difference is not apt to be obvious, but it is apt to exist, and because any such variations are detrimental to accuracy, consistent press operation is a worthwhile goal.

PARTIAL CASE SIZING—NECK SIZING

What type of die we use for resizing the case can depend upon the shooting activity. For target and varmint loads, we often use a different type of die for resizing our cases. Usually we will want to use the full-length die if it is necessary to maintain easy cartridge chambering. In addition, we will use that die for all loads used for hunting large or dangerous game—dependability is paramount in such loads. However, for target and varmint work, we prefer other, more precise, case sizing methods.

For some chamberings (e.g., 22-250), the handloader can often use a standard full-length sizing die by simply screwing it back about two turns from the normal full-length resizing setting. When using this technique, screw the die out sufficiently to assure that case body resizing is minimal.

Sometimes, depending upon case taper and the relationship between chamber and die body diameter, this adjustment will partially resize the case body. Significant body sizing will force the case shoulder forward and subsequent chambering will be either difficult or impossible. In that situation, when feasible, turn the die out progressively until the partially resized case chambers freely. In some instances (such as with Ackley-Improved case designs, or where difference between body diameter in the gun and die is excessive), this method will not work. If so, a dedicated neck-sizing die is required.

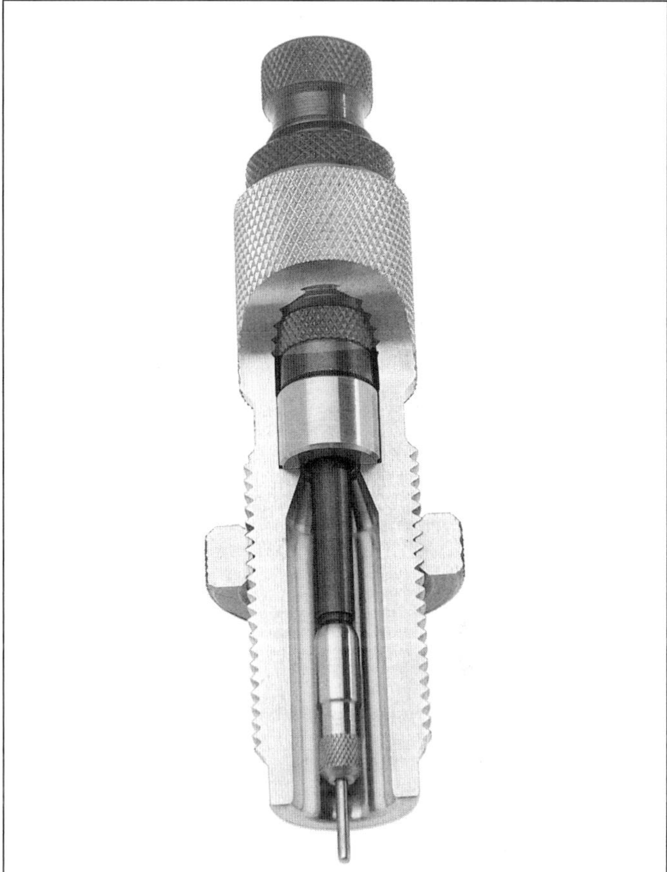

Redding offers two styles of neck bushing dies. The first is the Type-S, which only sizes the case neck, according to bushing diameter. The second is the Type-S Full, which combines precise neck sizing with full-length resizing. Redding also offers a carbide-bushing expander kit for its neck-bushing dies. This is quite useful for ironing out any neck dents with minimum effort and minimum potential to bend the case neck.

Various manufacturers sell such dies for use in most common rifle chamberings. These work the same way as standard full-length sizing dies but only resize the case neck. Just as is true with full-length sizing dies, standard neck sizing dies work the case neck more than is necessary. This shortens case life. Therefore, a preferred option is a neck-size-only bushing die or the Lee Collet die.

With such a die, the handloader adjusts neck tension by bushing selection and, thereby, minimizes neck working during case resizing—one does not have to size the neck of the average case smaller than is necessary, only to then expand it back up, as happens with a standard sizing die. Therefore, use of a neck-bushing die can significantly increase case life.

With a standard die that you have not screwed far enough into the press to fully resize the case, the sizing operation sizes only a portion of the case neck; with a neck-sizing die, you can get the same result in the same way. Usually, for target loads, resizing the entire case neck is unnecessary to achieve adequate neck tension for functionality and accuracy.

Leaving a portion of the base of the neck unsized generally improves accuracy because this, as fired, portion of the neck will fit and center in the chamber neck and will therefore center the bullet in the throat. Because the base of the neck-sized case will closely fit the chamber of the gun in which it was fired, both ends of the case will be piloted (held on-center), so the chambered cartridge should give the bullet a superior degree of alignment with the bore.

Many manufacturers offer dies that perform only specific sizing operations. Forster offers a bushing shoulder-bump die and Redding offers a neck-size-only die. The latter has a spring-loaded sliding section that centers and supports the case body before neck sizing occurs. Interchangeable bushings are available. These require no lubrication. These are the ultimate (conventional style) neck-sizing dies.

To use bushing dies to best effect, case necks must be of uniform hardness and consistent thickness, i.e., turned precisely. Normally, because handloaders can match bushing diameter to case neck thickness and bullet diameter, subsequent neck expansion is not required. However, Redding offers a carbide expander-button kit that might provide the best of both worlds. This allows the handloader to size the neck, just slightly smaller than is necessary, and to automatically expand it back to the proper size for bullet seating. This combination dispenses with the necessity of neck turning. When using neck-turned cases, this combination still provides optimum results (for example, it will remove dings and dents from case necks).

With any die using interchangeable neck sizing inserts, handloaders can adjust bullet pull. If you have worked up a good load using one of these dies, try experimenting with both smaller and larger bushings. See what happens to the resulting groups. Sometimes, a minor adjustment in bullet pull can result in a large accuracy improvement. As with all other load development variables, the only way to find out is to experiment.

A phenomenally useful tool is the Lee Collet die. Properly adjusted, this die does nothing but decap the case and squeeze the case neck, just enough so that it will hold a bullet adequately for normal cartridge handling. Slight changes in adjustment of the Lee Collet Die body and reduction of mandrel diameter will alter resulting neck-to-bullet tension.

This die has several advantages. First, because lubrication is not required, it eliminates concerns about proper case lubrication and subsequent cleaning. Second, it leaves the case body unaltered; assuming the gun chamber is square and true, cases neck-sized in the Collet Die will perfectly align with and center in the gun chamber—particularly if you measure the curvature of the cases, mark those and insert the round into the chamber in the same orientation each time. Third, this system works the case the least of any die. As the collet squeezes the neck, the die holds the neck perfectly square to the case body and no other force is transferred to the case, hence, it is impossible for the case shoulder to bend.

It is possible to straighten a bent case shoulder by using the Collet die. Lee recommends sizing the neck, withdrawing the case from the die, rotating the case through one-half turn, and sizing the neck a second time. Contrary to what some folks believe, Lee makes some very fine handloading tools; this die is a prime example of a genuinely fine product.

SPECIAL DIES AND SPECIAL TOOLS CAN MAKE THE DIFFERENCE IN AN ACCURACY LOAD

Benchrest shooters usually use custom (hand) sizing dies chambered to resize the case only sufficiently for it to freely rechamber in the same gun. Usually, hand dies work in an arbor-style press. Hand dies work identically to screw-in neck bushing dies. For conventional handloads used in conventional guns, hand dies offer no obvious advantage over conventional neck-sizing dies.

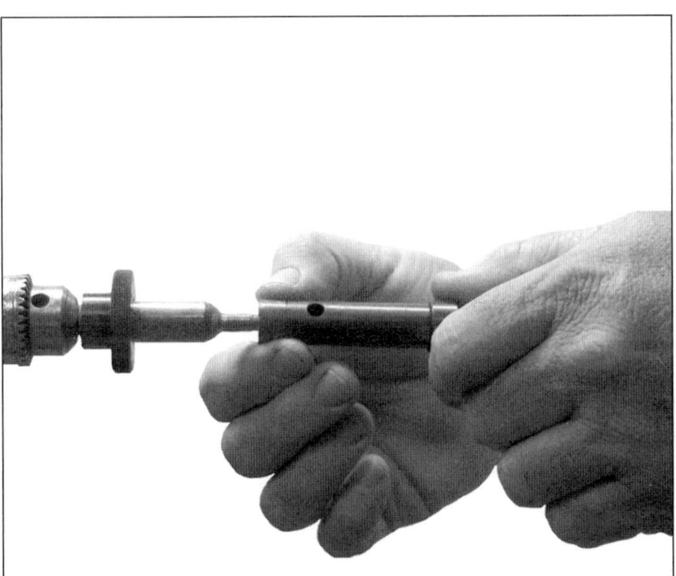

Lee 3-Jaw Chuck is very handy and useful for case alteration and related tasks. It chucks into a vised hand drill (or a drill press). A quick turn of knurled nut opens or closes three jaws into rim cut on case and then screws a support rod against the case head, thereby locking case in place and adding friction to prevent slippage. Shown here with Superior Shooting Systems, Ballistic Meplat Uniformer (BMU) in use—the BMU removes burs and deformations from tips of hollowpoint match bullets. (Tipped bullets are setting records in many events.)

Unlike the situation when I started my handloading career (1967), we now have myriad superior loading dies for use in conventional reloading presses. Represented here are various premium dies from RCBS, Redding, and Forster. Each of these has a specific purpose and can allow the handloader to produce superior ammunition with less effort. I routinely use and appreciate the fine dies now offered by these manufacturers. I also appreciate and use several premium dies from Hornady and Lee Precision. Particular favorites of mine include the Lee Collet neck-sizing die and the Lee Factory Crimp Rifle Die. Each has unique advantages for many applications. My favorite seating die when I load hundreds of cartridges at one time and for anything involving bullets smaller than heavy 6mm is the RCBS Gold Medal Seating die. I use the fine Hornady seating die for many wildcat rifle applications.

SPECIAL TOOLS FROM K&M

This is a K&M outside neck turning tool fitted with dial indicator and auxiliary comfort handle. Any adjustment of the cutter depth is via a thread-in thread system. This allows precise and repeatable adjustments with precision closer than 1/100,000 inch, which suffices for any need.

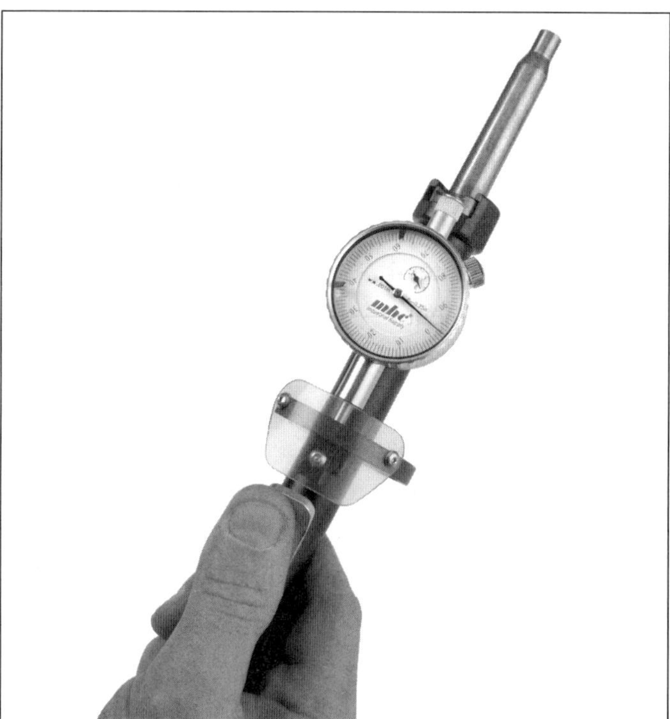

This K&M premium primer seating tool measures primer height and primer pocket depth, allowing the handloader to seat any primer in any case with a precise preload (3/1000 inch is a common recommendation).

The K&M shellholder is versatile; it uses Lee AutoPrime shellholders to fit practically any case.

Redding offers this handy tool to allow precise measurement of case-neck thickness.

MAINTAINING THE CARTRIDGE CASE

CHAPTER 3

INTRODUCTION

In this chapter, I cover basic case maintenance operations. In chapter 4, I cover advanced maintenance and improvement operations that you might want to consider as a means of improving the overall functionality, quality, and accuracy of your handloads.

Depending upon load pressure and fit and design of the case-resizing die, loading and firing of cartridge cases change various case dimensions and case characteristics by varying amounts.

In order to continue to reuse a cartridge case safely, it might eventually be necessary to trim it to length. In order to continue to use a cartridge case as long as possible, it will eventually be necessary to anneal the case neck. The following will increase case stretching:

- Use in a rear-locking action
- Case design with limited headspace control
- Loading to higher pressure
- Unnecessary degree of full-length case resizing

The following will increase work hardening of the case neck:

- Firing in a relatively loose chamber (most factory chambers)
- Excessive neck resizing (most standard resizing dies)
- Bellmouthing and crimping

CASE MAINTENANCE— TRIMMING TO PROPER LENGTH

Most rifle cases and some handgun cases lengthen with each use. The amount of lengthening in any given instance depends upon a plethora of gun, cartridge, and load characteristics. To assure proper chamber clearance and to maintain uniform cartridge performance, handloaders must periodically trim case necks to achieve and maintain proper and uniform case length.

We have three basic systems for case-length maintenance. First is the file-type trim die. Various manufacturers make these inexpensive, hardened dies. File trim dies are available for many case types.

To use this tool, simply screw the trim die into a standard reloading press and run a lubed case all the way into the die—assure that the shellholder touches the die. Then file off any protruding portion of the case

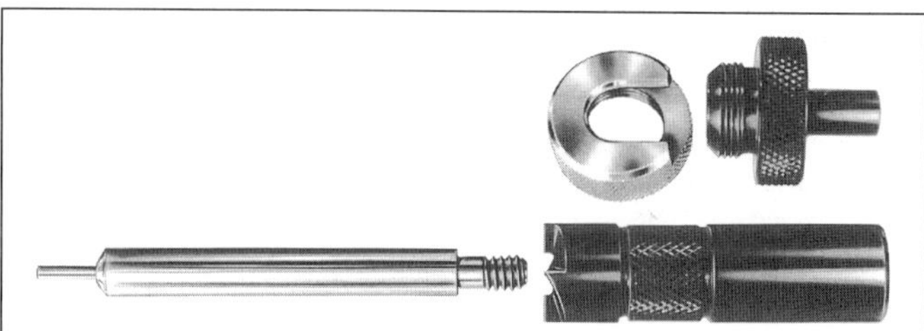

Lee Precision offers this splendid case trimming system. Advantages include affordability and ease of use. Although it is possible to use this tool to turn cases by hand, using an optional power drill is the superior method. The only disadvantage is that this system does not allow unique adjustment of trimmed case length.

This Redding TR-1400 case trimmer is ready to use: While hand powered, this is a fine choice for low-volume loading or for those with plenty of time for case trimming.

neck and debur the neck interior. This process is simple but tedious, slow, and messy (brass shavings), and it can be hard on the file if you apply too much downward force against the die.

The second system involves a lathe-type tool. Because these devices are useful for several handloading operations, such a tool represents a good investment for the serious handloader. Many manufacturers list these tools. Some offer manual and power-driven models. If you intend to work with large batches of cases, consider a power model.

To trim cases using a manual lathe-type tool, install the proper case-neck pilot and the necessary shellholder or collet. (Some tools use a conventional shellholder and lock the case by pushing it forward in the shellholder.) As required, adjust the tool so that it will trim the case to the proper length; then tighten the length-controlling adjustment screw. Using a lathe-type tool, applying moderate endwise pressure and turning the crank handle several turns is usually sufficient to properly trim any standard case.

Most manual trimmers easily do a good job, but all are somewhat time consuming. The RCBS Pro Power Case Trimmer is a favorite power-driven alternative. Among lathe-type case trimmers, this is one of the simplest, quickest, and easiest to operate. It offers quick shellholder changes and even quicker shell changes. It allows indexed one-thousandth-inch incremental changes in trimmed case length. RCBS and Forster offer combination cutters. These provide simultaneous length trimming with precise inside and outside neck deburring. This accessory attachment is

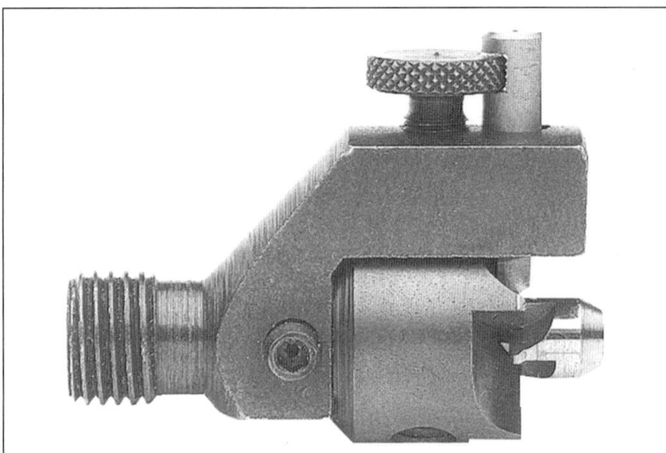

The RCBS 3-way cutter, Trim Mate accessory, combines case trimming with precisely adjustable inside and outside deburring. Forster now has a similar unit for its tool, but with a carbide cutter, it is even better!

An RCBS Trim Pro Power Case Trimmer eases and speeds case trimming operations. Trim length is adjustable with indexed 1/1000-inch precision. This is the fastest and most versatile lathe-type, case-trimming tool.

Redding file-type trim die. Install die in press, run case fully into die, and file any protruding portion of neck away using a medium mill-bastard file. After inside mouth deburring, case is ready to reload.

a significant time saver and affords very precise and uniform deburring.

Because many rifle cases require trimming after only a few uses, the cutter is apt to see considerable use and will eventually require sharpening. When the cutter no longer removes excess brass easily and quickly, consider replacing it. Most manufacturers charge a nominal sharpening fee; some provide this service gratis. Moreover, most manufacturers offer spare cutters at a modest price. By keeping a spare cutter on hand, you can return a dulled unit for resharpening, while suffering no interruption of tool availability.

Regardless of the advantages of a lathe-type tool, my favorite system for rapidly and easily trimming a large number of cases to standard length is the Lee Precision Case Trimmer. This tool is simple, affordable, and practically foolproof.

To use the Lee case trimming tool, simply chuck a standard Lee case-trimming shellholder, or Lee 3-Jaw Chuck (page 54), into your drill press or a vised hand drill and tighten the sized and deprimed case into that chuck. Start the drill and push the proper cutter head into the case mouth. When the built-in cutter stop passes through the flash hole and abuts against the shellholder base, cutting stops and the tool will have trimmed the case to the standard trim-to length for that cartridge case. This process takes only seconds.

Because all Lee cutter units are cartridge specific, the handloader never needs to measure anything. To some users, this is a significant advantage. This characteristic also eliminates one potential source of error—maladjustment.

CASE MOUTH—CHAMFERING

Once you have reduced all cases to the recommended trim-to length or to the proven maximum chamber length minus 0.015 inch—explained in chapter 4—you must debur the case mouths, both inside and outside. Seating bullets into cases with burs inside the case mouth will damage the bullets and degrade accuracy. In addition, burs can interfere with bullet seating and proper crimping. This step is particularly important for shooters using molybdenum-disulfide plated bullets or nickel-plated cases. Refer to chapter 10.

Bullet damage resulting from seating into a rough case neck is quite common. After trimming and deburring, the best protection against destroying the potential for accuracy is to run the case neck over a spinning, one-caliber-smaller, brass brush wrapped with enough four-aught steel wool to provide a snug fit in the case neck. Attach the brush into a hand drill and clamp it into a vice, lock the drill on at full speed, and run the trimmed and deburred case necks over the brush.

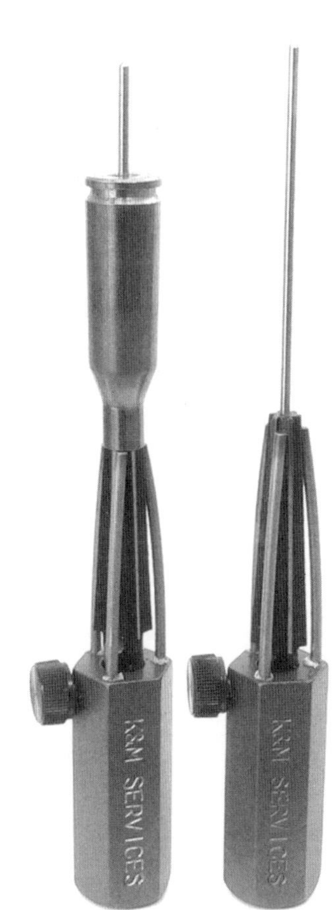

K&M offers the ultimate tool for inside case-mouth deburring: This tool cuts at a 4-degree angle and thereby removes any wire edge created during neck trimming or standard deburring. Travel is limited, so inside deburring is always applied equally to all cases. Standard models cover cases from 17 to 33 caliber. The spring wire pin helps maintain case alignment, so chamfering is more nearly perfectly concentric. As a final polishing step, using a smaller-caliber, bronze bore brush wrapped in 4-0 steel wool is beneficial.

I chuck the wrapped brush into a hand drill that is secured in a vise and run each case neck over the turning brush—when using moly-plated bullets, this step is critical.

Exterior case mouth burs can interfere with chambering and can increase chamber pressure. New cases often have surprisingly rough mouths. It is best to debur new cases before the first loading.

The typical deburring tool is a simple, hand-operated, two-ended, 60-degree reamer (30 degrees on each side). These tools are widely marketed and available. It's been my experience that Lee Precision makes the most compact deburring tool. Any such quality tool will last most handloaders a lifetime.

During case-neck deburring, the goal is to remove burs and to bevel, ever so slightly, the case mouth interior. However, inside deburring cutters often leave a wire of brass rolled into the case neck at the bottom extent of the tapered cut. This is analogous to the wire edge that forms when sharpening a cutting blade. Removal of this wire edge is critical for best handloading results. K&M makes a handy tool that precisely deburs without forming such a wire edge.

The standard model works only with 22- through 30-caliber cases but K&M offers models for both smaller- and larger-caliber cases. The 4-degree, controlled-depth, beveled cut provided is quite precise. After using this K&M tool on a case, I prefer to polish the neck interior with a spinning bore brush wrapped in extra-fine steel wool, as noted above.

In addition, handloaders can use one leg of the outside deburring end of a standard tool, or a small knife blade, to remove the aforementioned wire edge. Insert the cutting edge into the case neck and hold the edge almost parallel with the neck. Then, while pressing the blade lightly against the neck interior, give the case a quick turn through one rotation. Learning how to perform this simple, albeit delicate, operation consistently is important.

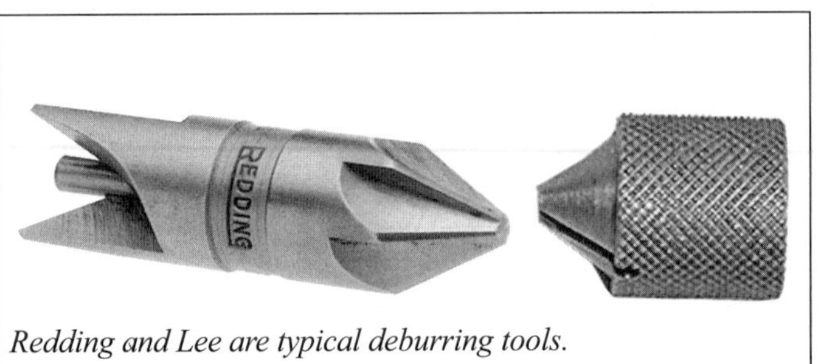

Redding and Lee are typical deburring tools.

CASE NECK—ANNEALING

Regardless of the annealing method you use, water is essential. Not because quick cooling (quenching) softens the brass (it does not) but because rapid cooling prevents the case head from getting too hot through the transfer of heat from the case neck to the case head. Should you somehow manage to heat the head of a cartridge case above about 400 degrees F, the brass will soften. Thus softened, the case head loses any ability to control chamber pressure.

Upon use with any normal load, the head of such a case would expand uselessly. Depending upon gun design, the case head might rupture. Even if the case head did not rupture, such extreme expansion is apt to open the primer pocket sufficiently to break the seal between the primer cup and the primer pocket. This will allow high-pressure propellant gases to escape from the case. This could destroy the gun and perhaps injure or kill the shooter and bystanders. Use extreme caution.

Having noted previously the importance of consistent case-neck tension, this is a good place to suggest methods and explain reasons for adjusting case-neck tension. Each loading and firing cycle work-hardens the case neck. This happens, regardless of type of sizing dies used, but standard full-length and neck-sizing dies generate the most neck hardening. Even in benchrest-style cartridges fired in very closely chambered guns and resized in special dies (at a minimum), reloading involves sizing the neck down several thousandths of an inch and firing expands the neck several thousandths of an inch. Cases used in typical chambers and reloaded with typical dies experience considerably more squeezing and swelling

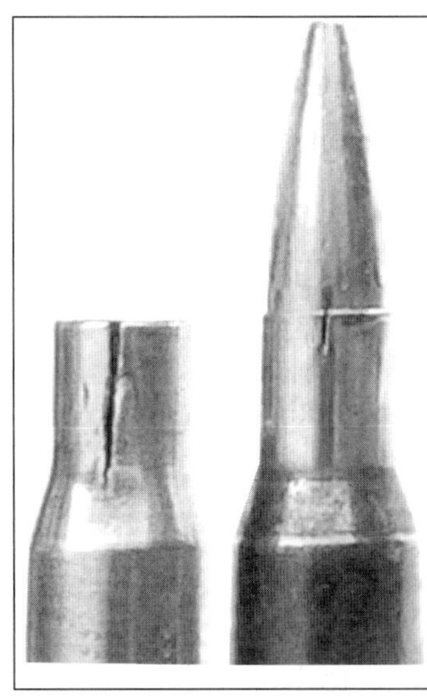

Necks of excessively worked or aged cases commonly split, either at time of firing or simply during long-term storage (usually with bullet seated). Even tiny cracks (example on right) will alter ballistics and reduce accuracy. The best practice is to destroy any such cases and cartridges.

during each shooting and reloading cycle—typically, about six thousandths of an inch. (This causes the necks to harden more than three times as fast.) As necks harden, cartridge performance changes, and, eventually, necks will begin to split.

There exists no guarantee that all necks in any given group of cases will work-harden at the same rate or that all portions of any particular case neck will work-harden equally. Therefore, differences in bullet pull will accumulate. Because the case neck undergoes more working than any other portion of the case during both the shooting and reloading cycles, it work-hardens faster than any other portion of the case. Without periodic annealing, it will eventually crack—usually splitting along the length of the neck. Also, necks of both loaded rounds and even empty cases spontaneously crack with age.

Progressively hardened case necks make case sizing and bullet seating progressively more difficult. Ultimately, the accumulation of variations in case-to-case neck tension, which is the inevitable result of working a group of cases through many shooting and reloading cycles, leads to increasing variations in bullet pull. Usually, these variations increase both shot-to-shot velocity variations and group size.

Assuming the same loading practices, as the neck hardens, bullet pull increases. This retards bullet release. This progressive additional delay in bullet movement progressively increases both chamber pressure and muzzle velocity. This, in turn, alters both barrel time (alters accuracy and point of impact) and external ballistics. Obviously, best accuracy and case-to-case variation in neck tension are mutually exclusive.

Here, case neck annealing comes to the rescue. This process can equalize case-to-case neck tension and prolong case life. If case body thinning is insignificant and if the primer pocket remains tight, periodic neck annealing can extend case life, indefinitely—blackpowder and Schuetzen shooters sometimes reuse cases hundreds of times.

Hornady offers a very handy, fast, accurate, and consistent system for neck annealing. Tempilaq® is only needed for testing with the first few cases. After that, a practiced technique, while counting seconds, will produce precisely uniform annealing. This system requires a stable propane bottle, a hand drill, and a water container (to cool annealed case—to prevent heat from soaking into case head and ruining case).

After reloading a batch of cases, perhaps ten times, the handloader should consider either annealing the necks or discarding the cases. Those who have done considerable preparation on a batch of cases will have a significant incentive to anneal rather than discard cases with too-hard necks. Annealing softens brass and, thereby, prevents neck splitting; for the same reason, it is essential that annealing not occur at or near the case head. Neck annealing eases the chore of full-length resizing. When properly done, case-neck annealing also minimizes shot-to-shot variations in bullet pull.

The most popular low-budget method of case-neck annealing is to stand unprimed cases in a bath of water that reaches about halfway up the case body. With the cases so positioned, apply the flame from a propane torch to each case neck until it glows dull red in a dimly lit room. As soon as the color looks right (brighter red indicates higher temperature and therefore increased annealing and a softer resulting neck), gently tip the case over into the water, by pushing the tip of the torch against the case shoulder. (Cases tipped into the bath are thereby marked as having already been annealed.)

The trouble with this annealing method is that it relies upon the handloader to do a good job of repeating the heating rate, duration, and maximum temperature (color) on each case neck. Each of these variables is critical to total annealing. With practice and a good eye, the typical handloader can accomplish this process with reasonable consistency, but this process is not easy.

This method is also apt to result in differential annealing because it is very difficult to spread the heating uniformly around the case neck. Given the high rate of thermal conduction in brass, this difference is slight but it still exists. Hence, I prefer other techniques.

A much better method involves your trusty bullet-casting lead pot—if you have one. If you are interested in annealing case necks, this method is so good that I recommend buying an inexpensive lead pot (as offered by Lee Precision), a thermometer, and enough lead alloy to fill the pot, just for this purpose.

Position the lead pot on a standard workbench and locate a large bucket of water within reach but well below the bench top. Fill the pot with bullet metal alloy, turn it on, and set the thermostat at the highest temperature setting. However, to assure that the melt never exceeds 850 degrees F, a trustworthy lead thermometer is most valuable here. (Lead alloys heated significantly above 850 degrees F can produce significant quantities of invisible, odorless, and toxic vapor.) Add a thin layer (1/10 inch is sufficient) of fresh plain and unscented, clay-based, kitty litter over the top of the alloy to shield your case-holding hand from radiant heat and to retard oxidation of the melt.

Never attempt this method on new cases because lead can bond (solder) to clean brass. Unless the neck is tarnished or carbon coated, it is best to apply a graphite dusting to the neck and shoulder area of the case, inside and out, before beginning. Run a graphite-saturated cotton bore swab into and out of the neck and spin the neck exterior between a graphite-coated finger and thumb or thoroughly blacken the neck area using a candle flame. Never leave any conventional case lubricant on the case neck. This can act as an oxygen scavenger and can thereby promote soldering; it works as a flux.

Never anneal primed cases! Should the primer pop due to heating, the results could be rather nasty. First, the cup will eject from the case with potentially lethal velocity; second, if the case neck were still submerged in the melt, the primer blast would spray molten alloy through the surrounding space, making occupancy of that region most unpleasant!

After the lead comes to temperature, hold a decapped case by the head, located between your index and middle fingers and your thumb. It is important that you do not wear a glove—the thin layer of kitty litter assures that the only significant heat that you feel will be heat that the case body conducts. Turn the case until the mouth is pointing straight downward. Quickly insert the case mouth into the molten lead. Fully submerge the case neck and, perhaps, a specific portion of the case shoulder.

It is important to insert the same amount of each case (of each batch) into the lead. Hold the case, thusly, until the case head becomes too hot to hold comfortably. Immediately remove the case from the molten lead and gently drop it into the water bath. Be cautious not to splash water into the lead pot or get water on your hand, which might then drip into the lead pot—water and molten lead make a very bad, albeit very temporary, combination because the water turns to steam and explosively expands and can thereby spray molten lead haphazardly into the surrounding area.

Empirical evidence suggests that use of propellants with tin added (such as A8700) can embrittle case necks (perhaps only with low-pressure loads). (Tin scavenges copper from the bore and case.) Annealing does not solve neck embrittlement.

Hornady now offers a wonderfully effective and simple tool for neck annealing. This consists of an aluminum case holder that chucks into a hand drill. As with the water-bath method, this system requires a propane torch for heat, but it has the advantage of spinning the case during annealing.

When using this tool, lightly clamp the torch in a bench vise. Chuck the tool into a drill, lock the drill on, adjust the speed to about 500-rpm (near the middle of adjustment range of a typical hand drill), and drop a case into the open end of the spinning tool. While keeping the tool pointed slightly upward, bring the case mouth into the torch flame so that the flame envelops the entire case neck and, perhaps, part of the case shoulder. Consistency matters—use the same hold for each case.

As soon as the case neck glows dull red in a dimly lit room, it is sufficiently annealed. Further heating will only soften the case body and potentially the case head. As heat migrates into the case body, the mass of the aluminum holder shields the case body from direct heating and absorbs heat, which mitigates case-body heating. However, the best practice is to minimize case heating. Therefore, as soon as the neck begins to glow at the desired color, quickly point the drill downward and drop the case into a pail of water on the floor. Then insert another case and repeat the operation.

Counting seconds while heating the neck of each case will improve case-to-case consistency. Hence, while doing the first case, count the seconds required to achieve a dull-red glow, then use the same heating time for all subsequent cases. This helps because visual perception changes. After each ten or so cases, use a misting spray bottle to spray water onto the spinning tool, as necessary, to cool it to near room temperature. Let the tool fully dry before proceeding with the next case.

Neck annealing does require a bit of time and skill but it offers the opportunity to establish virtually identical case-to-case neck tension and it can significantly extend case life. Considering all the other work you might have done in producing uniform cases, this small effort promises significant rewards.

One final note on annealing: In many instances, conversion of one type of case to work in a different chamber requires considerable working of the brass. This can leave the case neck, shoulder, and upper body areas too hard for proper functioning or for good case life. Case neck annealing after finishing the conversion, and sometimes as an intermediate step, solves this problem.

With some propellants in some cases, as the neck gets harder you will progressively see more propellant residue on the outside of the neck of the fired case. Several other things exacerbate this condition, and these include freeboring (Weatherby), increased case capacity, thicker neck, use of slower propellant, and use of a ball-type propellant.

BENCH TESTING TERRY BREWER'S CUSTOM LIGHTWEIGHT 444 MARLIN

Due to the two-piece stock, bench testing lever-action rifles requires consistent bag placement and hold. When possible, cheek weld must be consistent. When I am testing traditional lever-action guns, the bag positioning and hold shown here usually prove to give the best results. With my stronger hand I pull the gun hard into my shoulder. With my weaker hand, I pull gently down and back but with a tight grip. To prevent the gun from jumping out of the front rest, this latter is particularly important with hard-kicking guns.

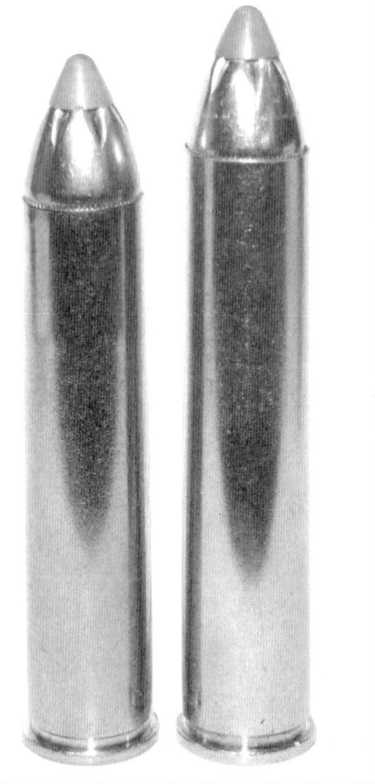

Modifications to the 444 Marlin allow use of the 265-grain FTX Hornady bullet without resorting to case shortening (as Hornady does for its factory load—on left). This improves accuracy potential because bullet-to-rifling jump is significantly reduced, and it allows custom handloads that generate about 100 fps greater velocity due to the significant increase in usable case capacity.

IMPROVING THE CARTRIDGE CASE

CHAPTER 4

INTRODUCTION

In chapter 3, I covered basic necessary case maintenance procedures that the handloader should or must follow in order to continue to reuse cases. In this chapter, I cover advanced case maintenance, case modifications, and case sorting.

One purpose of this chapter is to help you decide how you can improve your handloads and when you might want to do so. By applying these modifications and procedures, you can improve case quality and uniformity and, therefore, the accuracy of any resulting cartridges. You might find some or all of these processes either useful or unnecessary in any or all of your handloading.

I address these modifications approximately in order of ease and importance. However, depending upon case type and quality and your desires, you might choose to address these in some other order.

FLASH HOLE DEBURRING AND UNIFORMING

Consistent propagation of primer flash into the propellant chamber is critical to consistent propellant ignition; therefore, uniforming and deburring of the flash hole is critical to maximizing shot-to-shot ignition uniformity. Ignition uniformity is critical to uniform velocity and maximum accuracy. We achieve flash-hole uniformity by using a flash-hole uniforming and deburring tool; this is a once-per-case alteration.

RCBS offers this handy flash-hole deburring tool. K&M and others offer similar tools.

Manufacturers create the flash hole by piercing (burnishing) a hole from the bottom of the primer pocket through the case web, into the propellant chamber. They use a special hardened-steel punch. This operation creates rough brass burs where the flash hole breaks through into the case interior. These burs interfere with the uniform and consistent propagation of the primer-flash into the propellant charge. This characteristic of unaltered cases decreases round-to-round ignition uniformity, and, therefore, it reduces accuracy.

Flash-hole uniforming tools simultaneously drill the flash hole to a uniform diameter while creating a beveled flash-hole exit. Some tools stop cutting when a gauge impinges the flat interior floor of the case body (which is technically the forward end of the case web).

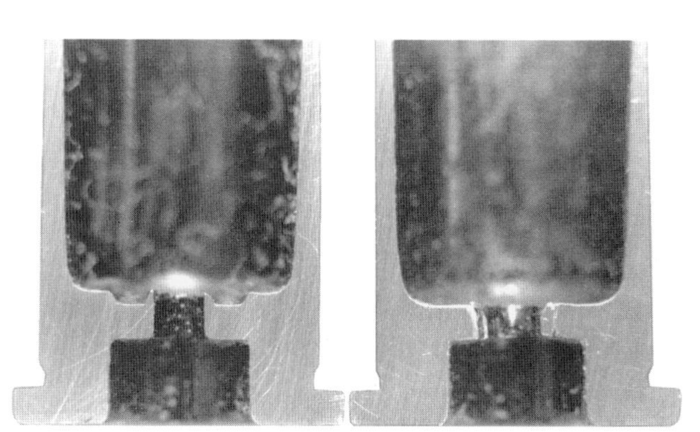

Different case brands have different interior conformations. Most brands have significant burs where the flash hole enters the case body (left). Use of a flash hole deburring tool improves case-to-case uniformity (right).

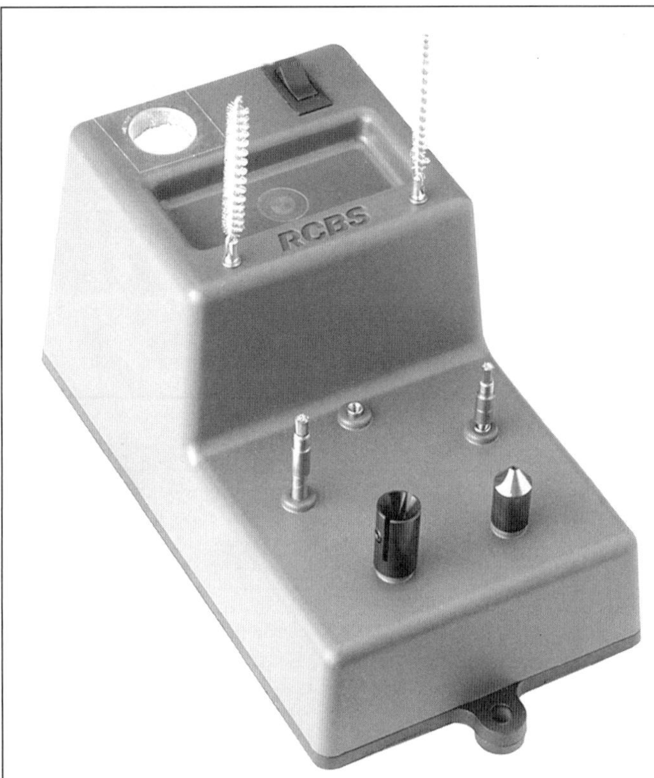

The RCBS Trim Mate is an unusually handy tool. RCBS offers various accessories, such as these shown here, along with primer pocket uniforming cutters. On the upper left is powdered mica for lubrication of case neck interior. The center (left and right) contains nylon brushes for cleaning necks. On the bottom are powered points: (clockwise from top) unused (as shown), large primer pocket brush, inside neck chamfering, outside neck chamfering, small primer pocket brush. Many other tools are available for use in these powered locations.

RCBS Trim Mate with modified K&M flash hole deburring tool (center) and K&M 4-degree inside neck chamfering tool (right foreground and out of focus in this view). (Debris on top of working area of tool is brass from various cutting operations.)

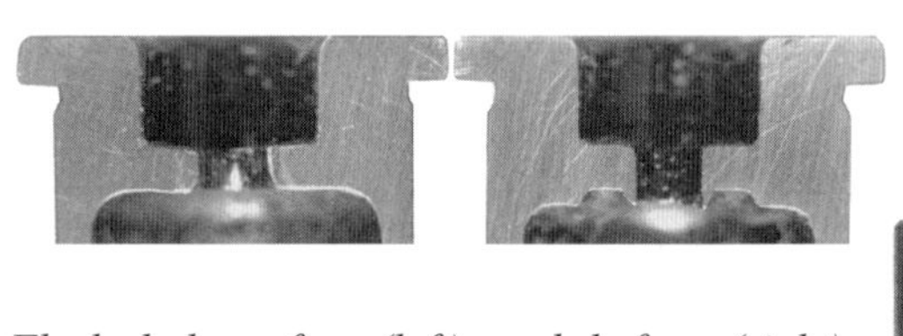

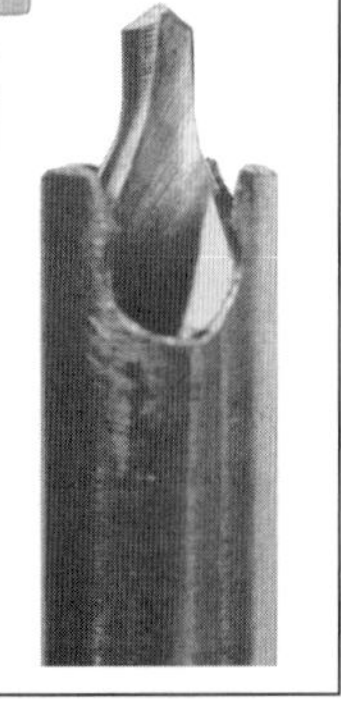

Flash holes after (left) and before (right) deburring. Close-up view of modified K&M Flash Hole Deburring Tool. Cutaway sections of collar allow cuttings to fall clear of tool during use in this orientation (as when modified to work as a tool on the RCBS Trim Mate).

With quality cases from any given production lot, case-web thickness (and, therefore, flash-hole length) is reasonably uniform; conversely, significant lot-to-lot and brand-to-brand variation in web thickness does exist. While testing has proven that flash-hole length is far less critical than are diameter and configuration of the exit bevel, flash-hole length does matter. Therefore, the best practice is to segregate cases according to production lot.

When using any of these tools, you should frequently clear cuttings from the tool; you can also expect limited tool life. Here you have a hardened steel cutter working against brass that, during case production, has been work-hardened to the maximum feasible extent. Creation of the flash hole reworks (and further hardens) adjacent brass; hence, the burs around the flash hole are the hardest part of any case, by a significant margin.

However, as this is a once-per-case operation, these tools will last most shooters a very long time. The

K&M tool that I currently use has processed more than 15,000 cases and is still going strong, although it no longer cuts as easily as it once did—imagine that.

Many of these tools can be power driven. This reduces labor and is very helpful when processing a large batch of cases. However, be certain that you do not turn the tool too fast. Midway in the speed range of most variable-speed $^{3}/_{8}$-inch drills is about right (near 500 rpm). Power screwdrivers turn far too slowly for ideal results.

Running the tool too fast will heat the cutting edge sufficiently to reduce tool life. Also, by design, these tools work best when the cutting end points downward, at least slightly. With this orientation, cuttings tend to fall clear; otherwise, those can jam the cutting face. This orientation also makes it easier to keep debris cleaned out of tool recesses.

It is feasible to modify the K&M Flash Hole Uniformer and Deburring tool to work on the RCBS Trim Mate—another practically indispensable tool. Necessary modifications include threading the driven end of the K&M tool to fit the Trim Mate and adding a spring to push the centering flange into the case neck. Because the Trim Mate orients the tool vertically, a further modification is necessary to prevent cuttings from jamming the cutter tip sleeve. This involves drilling holes in the sleeve and doing a bit of filing. This forms channels that allow the cuttings to fall free of the cutting head during use.

A tool that chucks into a vise-mounted hand drill is ideal. With the drill set to run at about 500 rpm (about midway between the fastest and slowest speed adjustment on a typical $^{3}/_{8}$-inch drill), the cutting process is perceptible and the job goes very quickly. However, the Trim Mate is particularly handy because it places the neck deburring tools and primer pocket tools (and, as described above, the K&M flash-hole uniforming tool) in one location. These tools are then handy and ready to use during case preparation, if need be. It is hard to argue with the advantages provided by the RCBS Trim Mate. If you are serious about accuracy, you are likely to find this tool to be most worthwhile.

Case Improvement—Primer Pocket Uniforming

Nominal Primer Pocket Dimensions (Inch)

Type	Diameter	Depth
Small (All)	0.175	≈0.120
Large, Pistol	0.210	≈0.120
Large, Rifle	0.210	≈0.126

Having gotten this far along the path, I will now consider why it might be important to machine primer pockets to a uniform depth with a square bottom. The most obvious reason is to facilitate primer seating to a uniform depth and, thereby, to improve ignition uniformity. This makes sense, even if field data does demonstrate that this step usually garners little, if any, improvement in ballistic uniformity. This operation does make it easier to seat primers consistently, and that can certainly add to one's confidence.

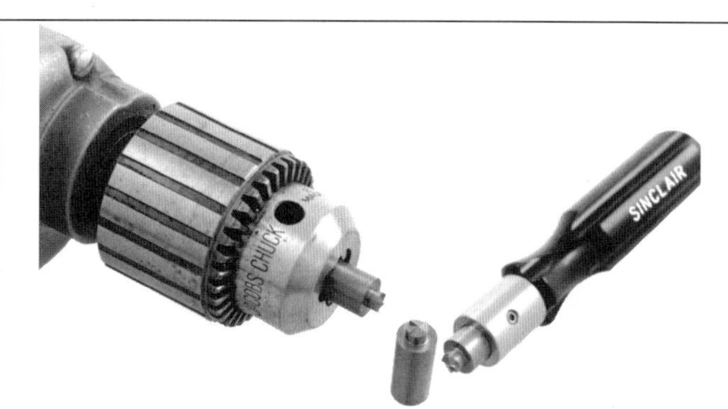

Sinclair primer Pocket Uniforming Tool: set up for power-driven use (left); freestanding (middle); in auxiliary handle for hand use (right). K&M and other manufacturers offer similar tools. Although most can be operated by hand, the fastest method involves a vised hand drill.

Many things in handloading and shooting contain a significant element of the self-fulfilling prophecy: If a shooter does not expect a particular combination to shoot well, he might not give it a fair chance when at the range. This can happen without his ever realizing that his perceptions and his preconceived notions will influence his performance, and that his performance can dramatically influence how well the combination performs. Myriad carefully controlled scientific studies have absolutely proven that results always depend upon expectations.

A little-studied aspect of accuracy is conformation of the flash-hole entrance from the primer pocket. Squaring and uniforming the primer pocket floor will certainly improve uniformity of this area within any group of cases. If you watch the primer pocket uniforming operation proceed, you can see why this is so. Production of standard flash holes always creates

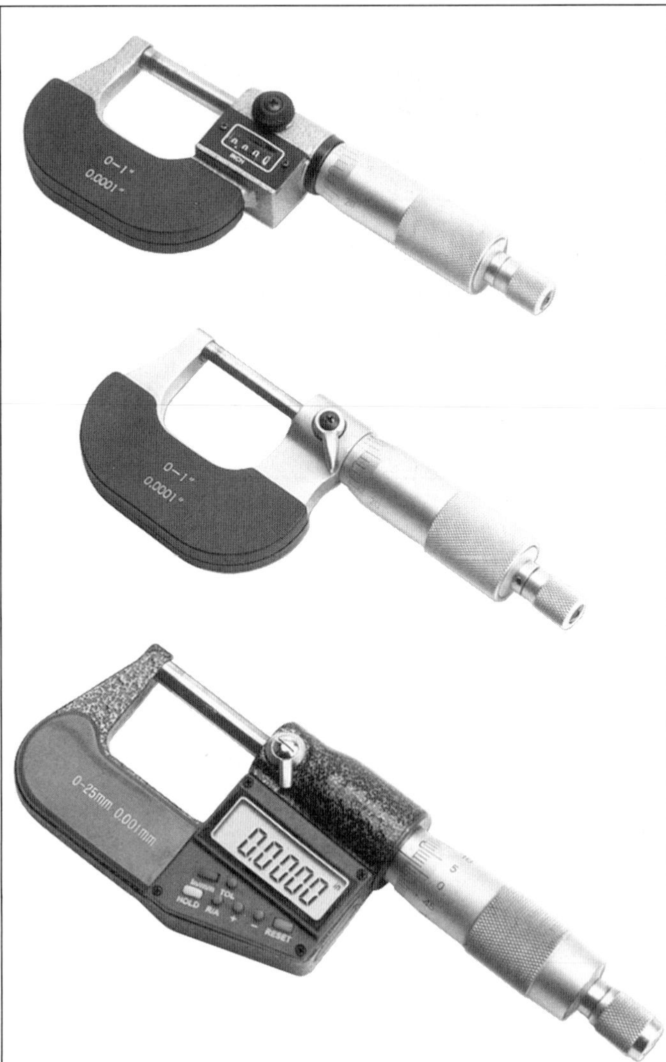

RCBS micrometer options: Each is a perfectly fine tool that will deliver measured accuracy beyond one's needs during any handloading operation. Accuracy with any micrometer depends upon careful and consistent usage, proper handling, and suitable storage.

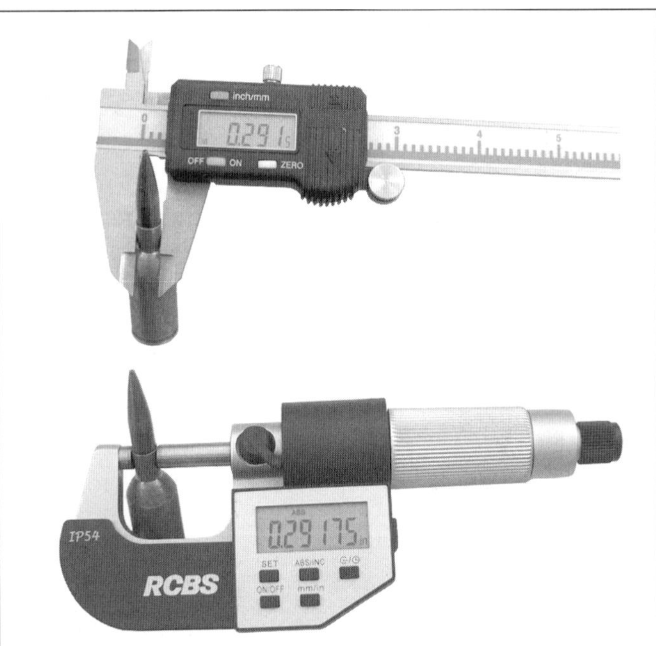

Precise measurements are not always necessary. A digital caliper (top) often provides adequate accuracy; micrometer (bottom) is ideal when the handloader needs to know a precise measurement. In this instance, a difference in accuracy is 2½ ten-thousandths inch, not enough to matter here but useful in other instances, such as when observing case-head expansion.

some degree of beveling on the entrance side. The amount of beveling and the exact distance from the case head to flash hole entrance varies from case to case and around the perimeter of each flash hole.

Squaring the primer-pocket bottom provides a consistent floor against which the primer anvil will seat. This condition reduces variations in primer response to the striker blow. Although this might not be manifest as a reduction of shot-to-shot velocity

A restful day at the range testing various loads or firing tiny groups with a proven load is very useful toward honing one's shooting skills. Knowing precisely what a super-accurate gun and load will do is a two-edged sword: This adds considerably to the shooter's confidence, but it leaves him few options for explaining a miss! For the target shooter, this is where it all pays off. Serious varmint hunters and big-game hunters will also use bench testing to determine accuracy of their carefully concocted handloads. Without bench testing using a good scope, a good rest, and good technique, the handloader can never know how accurate any given load will be in any given gun.

variation, it could still reduce shot-to-shot variation in ignition lag time—that period between the instant that the falling striker first touches the primer and the onset of propellant ignition—and it could reduce shot-to-shot variations in gun vibration. For these reasons, this step should improve accuracy.

Finally, in rare instances, primer pockets are actually too shallow (handloaders who often see pockets that seem to be too shallow are very likely simply failing to properly seat the primer. Refer to chapter 7. While this is unlikely, you might encounter a combination of cases and primers where it is practically impossible to seat the primers sufficiently deeply so that the primer faces are below flush with the case heads. In such combinations, seating the primer so that the face is correctly below flush can damage or destroy the primer. The high quality of most modern primers and cases renders this possibility truly ephemeral, but, years ago I found such a combination—tall primers and short pockets—and so have others. My friend, Ed Wosika, discovered this situation with cases and primers of recent manufacture.

In any case, primer-pocket uniforming is a complex issue. Some advise doing this for every case during every reloading cycle. Others suggest that it is of no value whatsoever to nontarget shooters and of precious little (if any) value to most target shooters. I suspect that reality lies somewhere in the middle. Likely, this step is always of some accuracy value to any handloader, and, as noted, it does have the advantage of easing the task of uniformly seating primers. Perhaps most importantly, this operation also affords the fastest and simplest way to completely clean primer residues from primer pockets—whether or not doing that is ever of any ballistic value remains an unanswered question.

For what it might be worth, I have decided that this extra step is worthwhile for most of my rifle loads, regardless of intended usage. After using such a tool to cut the pocket to full depth, it almost instantly removes 100 percent of the primer residue from the pocket during the next loading cycle—this is no small advantage to my ease of mind. Given my longstanding decision to clean such residues from all cases routinely before reloading, this step is worthwhile to me—recall the significant issue of the self-fulfilling prophecy.

The initial cut offers the benefit of disclosing a primer pocket that is off center or is significantly out of square with the case head. Either condition is extremely rare and is cause to discard the case or to relegate it to gauging use. Equally, this operation will identify any case with an unusually deep or shallow pocket.

A wide variation in primer-pocket depth in cases from one production lot suggests that overall quality might be less than normal—this calls for extra scrutiny of other aspects of case quality. However, of itself, such variation is insufficient cause to remove cases from your best-load group. After all, this step is intended to square the bottoms of primer pockets and to cut those all to a uniform, acceptable depth. You should probably relegate any cases with pockets that are so deep that the cutter will not completely cut a flat floor in the pocket to your plinking load or gauging application.

Several companies offer primer pocket uniformers made of tungsten carbide. Some are adjustable, whereas others feature a proper and fixed depth of cut. Three sizes are available: large rifle, large pistol, and small (rifle and pistol)—never use a large rifle uniformer on traditional pistol cases. (The 500 S&W is an exception, for it uses rifle primers.) Because these tools will be cutting through primer residues that often contain glass and aluminum oxide, which are considerably harder than hardened steel, and then into the hardest portion of the case, carbide cutters are preferable. K&M, Sinclair International Inc., RCBS, and others, offer useful tools.

Unless you have a specific need and access to the proper tools, and an understanding of how to do this job, I cannot recommend adjusting the cutting depth on such a tool. Normally, you should leave the factory-set cutting depth alone.

On adjustable models, before each use, check to make sure that the cutter-locking set screw has remained tight. With the vibrations and heat generated by long-term use, this screw can work loose. I have had this happen. This occurrence requires resetting the cutter depth and retightening the set screw. Because this cutter is best set with accuracy near +/– 0.0005 inch, this is a difficult task.

Without proper tools and gauging equipment, the only way to do this is to use a properly cut primer pocket as a gauge—this method is not particularly precise. Extend the cutter from the tool somewhat beyond the proper setting; tighten the set screw so that only moderate pressure is required to push the cutter into the tool; and then insert the cutter into a properly cut primer pocket until the main body of the tool abuts against the case head. In so doing, the cutter will first reach the bottom of the primer pocket and will then slide into the tool. When the main body of the tool comes to rest against the case head, it should just touch the bottom of the primer pocket. Then, without moving the tool or the case, tighten the set screw. If properly done, the cutter will just touch against the bottom of the gauging primer pocket and will only slightly cut into that surface when you apply considerable pressure. Best bet: Keep the set screw tight. Applying Loctite to the set screw threads is a good idea.

The manufacturers have designed many of these tools for use with a power drill. If you use this time-and-effort-saving method, do not run the drill faster than about 1,000 rpm (near full-speed with a typical 3/8-inch drill). Running the tool about 600 rpm is a better choice. This will allow you to feel what is going on and will prevent excessive heat from possibly damaging the tool. Note, also, that running the tool too slowly is poor practice—this leads to cutter chatter. Find a speed that discourages chatter and thereby produces a smooth cut on the primer-pocket floor. Determine this by the sound and feel during cutting and by appearance of the finished primer pocket.

Tools designed to make primer pockets uniform will not increase primer-pocket diameter. If the tool will not enter the pocket freely, the pocket diameter will be on the small side, which is apt to cause problems during primer seating. Conversely, if the cutter is obviously loose in the pocket, the pocket might be too loose to hold a primer properly.

> IN ANY DISCIPLINE, QUALITY PRACTICE IS WHAT SEPARATES ADEQUATE FROM PROFICIENT; THE AMOUNT OF QUALITY PRACTICE IS WHAT SEPARATES THE PROFICIENT FROM THE EXPERT.

CASE IMPROVEMENT—NECK TURNING AND NECK REAMING

Outside neck turning is a simple, albeit precise, operation that offers significant advantages for best accuracy. This process requires expensive tools, considerable skill, and plenty of patience. As with trimming case-neck length, this step requires full-length case sizing as a preliminary operation. For several reasons, reaming the inside of the neck or removing material from the outside of the neck can be either beneficial for accuracy or necessary for safety and functionality.

If, for whatever reason, the neck of the chambered case is too thick to allow clearance for free bullet release, the handloader must thin the case neck before loading the case. Do not overlook gun-to-gun chamber variations. Cartridges with very tight neck-to-chamber tolerances in one gun might be too tight in another gun

Fine example of a properly turned case neck: Note that the entire visible surface is bright and shiny and that turning has progressed just slightly into shoulder area of the case. This case is ready for use in a tight-necked chamber. Turning an entire batch of quality cases to this level of precision can improve accuracy, even when using a gun with a standard chamber.

Nonconcentric Case Neck

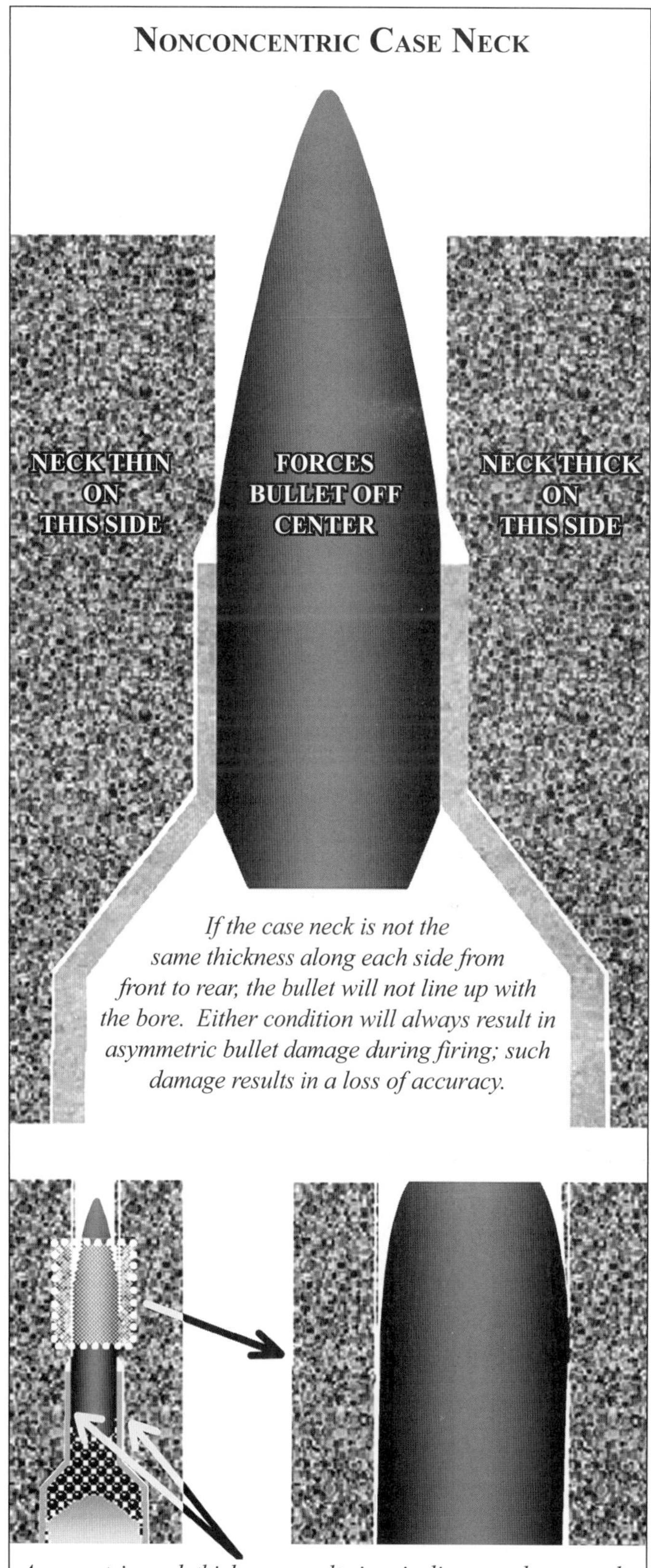

If the case neck is not the same thickness along each side from front to rear, the bullet will not line up with the bore. Either condition will always result in asymmetric bullet damage during firing; such damage results in a loss of accuracy.

Asymmetric neck thickness results in misalignment between the bullet and the bore. Firing the cartridge will deform the bullet asymmetrically.

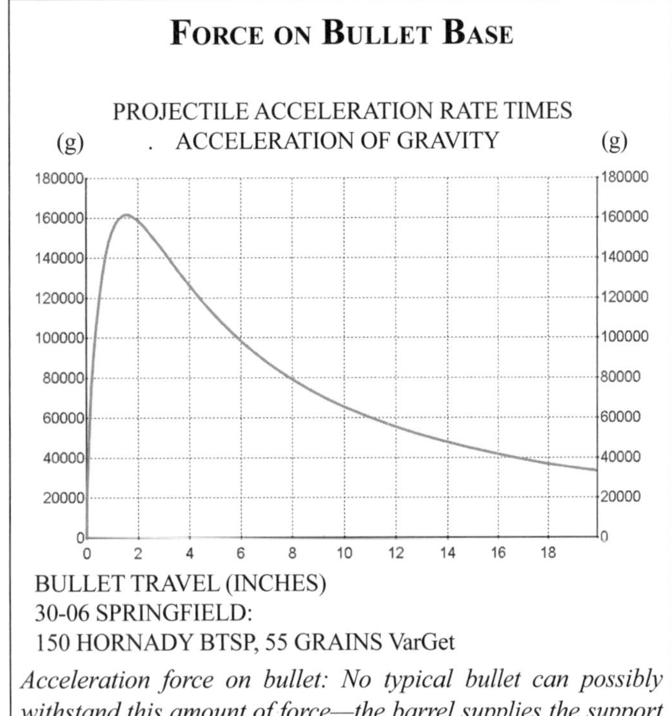

Acceleration force on bullet: No typical bullet can possibly withstand this amount of force—the barrel supplies the support needed to prevent the bullet from swelling indefinitely.

BULLETS SWELL INTO THE AVAILABLE SPACE.

of the same nominal chambering. A too-tight neck can prevent free cartridge chambering, which can lead to increased pressure and decreased accuracy.

In general, inconsistencies in neck thickness translate into inconsistencies in alignment between bullet and bore, which can lead to bullet deformations when the chamber pressure forces the bullet into the bore. Bullet deformation causes imbalance and imbalance causes inaccuracy. I address this concept in more detail later in this chapter, under "Case Indexing—General Considerations."

Too-thick case necks can result from case forming operations used to modify a case for use in a shorter chamber—for example, conversion of 30-06 Springfield cases to work in an 8mm Mauser. Another cause of too-thick case necks is necking down a given case to a significantly smaller caliber. For example, making 243 Winchester cases from 308 Winchester cases can sometimes result in excessively thick necks.

In addition, case stretching can result in excessive thickness at the base of the neck. As the firing process stretches a case (at a point near the junction of the web and body) and as resizing the case moves the shoulder back (to shorten the body and thereby maintain free case chambering), brass that was originally located at the forward end of the shoulder moves into the rear end of the neck. If the shoulder was thicker than the neck, this will result in thickening at the base of the neck. In unaltered cases, relative brass thickness in these areas depends upon variable manufacturing characteristics; in cases where the handloader has thinned the neck, by outside turning or inside reaming, the case shoulder will often be significantly thicker than the neck.

One solution to a too-thick case neck is inside reaming, which is done after sizing the entire outside of the neck, to the case shoulder, to a specific diameter. Reaming is accomplished easily with any lathe-type case-trimming tool that is equipped with the proper reaming attachment. As a matter of accuracy potential, inside reaming has two significant disadvantages. First, this process is not particularly precise, with regard to finished neck concentricity or thickness—i.e., thickness uniformity of the reamed neck, both from

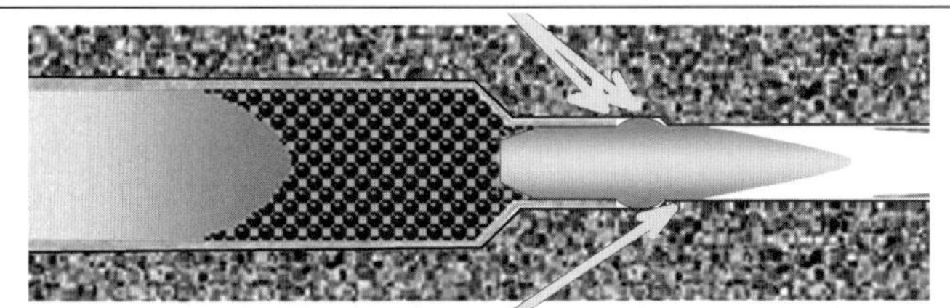

When the case neck is significantly shorter than the chamber, bridging strength within the bullet cannot support the bullet against acceleration force.

Front of chamber neck swages swelled bullet to fit bore. Swelling and subsequent swaging is not apt to occur with perfect symmetry; hence, this deformation is almost certain to result in an imbalanced bullet. As discussed in text, this is one reason why it is advantageous to leave case necks as long as is safely feasible.

end-to-end and around the perimeter, is imperfect. Second, inside reaming destroys the uniform and precise character of the surface of the case neck interior that the case drawing operation produces. Hence, reaming can increase case-to-case variations in bullet pull. For these reasons, few, if any, competitive shooters now use this method.

Outside-neck turning is the method of choice in any effort to add uniformity and accuracy potential to any ammunition through improvement of case neck uniformity. Although, in many guns, this process might be of limited value, it cannot hurt. I recommend it for any situation where increased accuracy might be beneficial. From my perspective, this seems to cover the gambit of shooting.

Outside turning of case necks, combined with the proper necking operation, offers the possibility of precisely matching neck-to-bullet tension from one round to the next. If the case necks are not uniform in thickness around the circumference, along the length, and from one case to another, how can we hope to achieve uniform bullet pull (the force required to push bullet from case)? Cartridges with varying bullet pull are notoriously inaccurate.

However, the most commonly noted reason for outside-neck turning is to improve bullet-to-bore alignment. Assuming a straight case body and neck, when the case neck is concentric and the case properly centers in the chamber (as occurs when using a neck-sized case), the bullet will center in and align with the bore axis. Generally, compared to a loose-fitting cartridge where the bullet neither centers in nor aligns with the bore, this situation can dramatically improve accuracy.

This is the main area where benchrest guns and loads excel. Benchrest ammunition and benchrest gun chambers are consistent and precise. Tolerances are so tight that benchrest ammunition is gun specific. (Use of such small clearances and precise tolerances in mass-produced rifles and ammunition is infeasible but serious handloaders can create cases that come close to this level of fit in a typical rifle, as I describe elsewhere in this text.)

Some pundits have argued that excessive neck turning is generally ill advised. Some folks have suggested adjusting the tool so that the cutter trims only about 60 percent of the neck area, as evidenced by exposure of bright new brass.

At least one author has expressed a belief that deeper cutting increases case neck working in subsequent loading and firing cycles. At first consideration, this seems reasonable because a thinner case neck must expand farther before the chamber neck confines it. However, for those using conventional sizing dies, this is a meaningless consequence.

Consider the action of a conventional sizing die on a case neck. The die first sizes the outside diameter sufficiently so that the inside diameter will be smaller than needed to properly hold a bullet. The expander then expands the neck to a proper, uniform inside diameter for proper bullet seating. These two steps are necessary because of the inevitable variation in neck thickness on unaltered cases.

On the sizing stroke, the sizing die returns all case necks to a specific outside diameter. Therefore, for cases fired in any given chamber, the amount that the die sizes the neck is identical for both a thick and a thin neck. However, the expander does not expand a thinner neck as much. The result is a wash:

- A thicker neck expands less in the chamber, but it expands more in the die;
- A thinner neck expands more in the chamber, but it expands less in the die.

Hence, when using conventional sizing dies, total neck modification with each firing and reloading cycle is identical, regardless of the neck-wall thickness.

Slightly thinner neck walls can lead to truer cases. During the resizing operation, compared to a thicker neck, a thinner neck expands with less resistance and the expander does not have to enlarge the neck as much. For these reasons, pulling the expander of a conventional resizing die through a thinner neck requires less force. Because the expander is not pulling as hard on the case neck during the expansion phase, the case shoulder is less apt to bend.

If thickness variation exists around the case neck, it will almost certainly extend to the case shoulder. Hence, if the case shoulder permanently deforms during the neck expansion operation, it will almost certainly bend asymmetrically. When this happens, the case neck will no longer align with the case body. A thinner case neck can reduce the incidence and degree of shoulder bending that leads to what we observe as bent case necks.

Despite all this, for reasons of functionality and sufficient case-neck tension, never cut case necks thinner than is necessary to achieve case-to-case uniformity, neck concentricity, and proper neck-to-chamber clearance (at least 0.001 inch annular–0.002 inch total).

A subtle reason to avoid unnecessary case-neck thinning is that doing so increases bullet deformation that can occur as the bullet expands to fill the neck portion of the chamber, in response to acceleration. As pressure builds, force on the bullet base rapidly exceeds internal bullet strength. In most loads, long before the bullet has moved fully out of the case and into the supporting chamber leade, it will have expanded to fill the available space; the greater this expansion, the greater the disruption to bullet integrity, concentricity, and balance. This is an important reason that benchrest guns have unusually tight-fitting chamber necks.

Similarly, a uniformly thick (concentric) neck is less apt to result in asymmetric bullet deformation during obturation. Hence, compared to a thicker, nonconcentric neck, a thinner neck will result in greater bullet deformation, but that deformation is not as apt to degrade potential bullet accuracy as significantly. This is one reason that uniforming neck thickness can improve accuracy. As noted, uniform neck thickness also contributes to uniform neck tension, which is also critical to accuracy.

For these reasons, adjust cutting depth on the neck turning tool so that almost all case necks from any given lot show at least some cutting on almost every portion. At least 90 percent, and preferably closer to 100 percent, of the neck exterior should be bright and shiny. With such a cutter setting, any tiny areas that were not touched will be only about 0.0001 inch thinner than the remaining portion of the neck. Such tiny variations are not apt to degrade accuracy measurably. In any group of cases, cull those few that show evidence of significantly thinner necks and set those aside for nondemanding uses.

Permanently marking substandard cases is a useful step. One method is to use Birchwood Casey Brass Black to mark the case permanently by applying this liquid to the case head sufficiently to darken the rim cut and headstamp area. This creates a permanent visual distinction that allows easy recognition. Another method is to create a notch in the case rim using a small triangular file.

Unless you have a specific need to do so, never thin case necks more than is necessary to achieve uniform thickness and sufficient neck-to-chamber clearance. Exceptions, where additional thinning is required, include situations where you use cases in a tightly chambered target rifle or when you are converting otherwise similar but longer cases—e.g., 30-06 Springfield cases for use in an 8mm Mauser chamber.

THINNING CONVERSION CASE NECKS AND NECKS ON CASES USED IN TIGHT NECK CHAMBERS

Reduce neck thickness until case neck outside diameter, with a seated bullet of proper diameter, is no less than 0.002 inch smaller than chamber neck diameter. Generally, in conventional guns, 0.003 inch difference is preferable. In blackpowder loads, about 0.005 inch difference is preferable. When using cases with such a tight fit, maintain a constant vigil to keep both rifle chamber and cartridges clean. Benchrest shooters loading ammunition for a specific gun sometimes use tighter tolerances. Obviously, a tighter fit requires greater caution and precision during handloading and shooting. To verify chamber dimensions to this level of accuracy, you will need one of the following:

- Cellophane tape (each type has a specific thickness: Scotch brand is 0.002 inch thick; some bargain brands are closer to 0.0015 inch thick)
- Chambering dimensions (based upon reamer specifications)
- An accurate chamber casting (Brownells offers Cerrosafe for this purpose)

Cerrosafe is easy to use and can provide an accurately dimensioned chamber casting—but only if you follow the directions carefully. If you intend to work with such close tolerances, this is a good place to start.

To determine approximate neck-to-chamber clearance using cellophane tape, begin with an unprimed, uncharged case that you have full-length resized. Seat a bullet deeply enough so that the beginning of the ogive is at least 0.030 inch below the case mouth. Apply one complete wrap of Scotch brand tape around the case neck—trim this tape, as necessary, so that only one layer covers only the neck area. If this dummy round chambers freely, then annular neck clearance between case and chamber exceeds 0.002 inch. This is adequate clearance for most smokeless-propellant applications.

If this dummy will not chamber freely, remove the tape wrap, then apply a strip that only covers one side of the case neck (about one-sixth of the way around)—trim this tape, as necessary, so that it only covers one linear strip and only along the neck. If the dummy round still will not freely chamber, total neck clearance is too tight for any standard application in any standard gun.

If the one-sixth-wrapped round freely chambers, repeat this process with a wrap of tape around one-quarter of the neck. If the dummy no longer freely chambers, total clearance is about 0.002 inch, which is acceptable for use with carefully prepared target cartridges and, perhaps, for varminting cartridges. Repeat this process with tape wrapped about one-third of the way around the neck. If the dummy will not freely chamber, total clearance is about 0.003 inch, and neck clearance is nearly ideal for precise cartridges used in a factory-chambered rifle.

The partial-wrap method above assumes that the diameter of the case body near the shoulder is at least 0.004 inch smaller than chamber diameter at that location and that the bullet is seated deeply enough so that no portion extending forward of the case mouth is within 0.004 inch of the chamber throat diameter. Conventional full-length resizing dies usually provide the necessary case body clearance, but custom dies might not do so. If in doubt, test the case shoulder using a similar tape wrap to make sure that the case can tip sufficiently in the chamber in order to allow the cartridge neck to enter the chamber neck. If not, find another method to assure adequate neck clearance.

One method is to thin the neck progressively, reseat a bullet, and attempt to chamber that dummy until the round will freely chamber and then to thin the neck even more, as needed for the intended application.

The K&M outside neck turning tool has the degree of accuracy and adjustment precision to make this task easy and to assure precise results. Some neck turning tools are far less precise with regard to adjustment precision. K&M achieves this degree of precision through use of a thread-in-thread micrometer adjustment system.

OUTSIDE NECK TURNING TOOLS—LATHE TYPE

Several makers offer outside neck turning attachments for lathe-type case trimming tools. Forster's and RCBS's case trimmers feature mechanisms to control cutter feed rate during the turning operation.

To use the Forster unit, the handloader must have sufficient dexterity to turn two things at the same time and to do so at the proper rates. Nevertheless, this tool has advantages. For example, the collet-type shell-holder provides precise case alignment (which could result in improved neck concentricity) after outside-neck turning.

Conversely, the RCBS system is far easier to use. With this unit, spindle turning rate controls cutter feed rate; this assures proper feed rate. With this tool, which is simple to set up and use, it is easy to do a proper job of neck turning. This system includes a pilot that will ream out any high spots from inside the neck, before the outside cutter goes to work. This can be advantageous. Refer to "Neck Turning—Dreaded Doughnut" in this chapter. The manual RCBS Trim Pro can also be adapted for power drive, for faster results, which can matter to those doing large batches of cases.

With a lathe-type tool, the distance the cutter progresses along the case neck is independent of case body length or case neck length. Hence, to minimize variation in case body length, it is necessary to resize all cases before neck turning; however, trimming case necks to uniform length before outside turning (or inside reaming) is not necessary.

The biggest problem with these tools is, perhaps, the limited rigidity of the cutting head, which limits precision of concentricity of the turned neck. While such a tool can do an acceptable job of outside neck turning, for applications where the handloader desires the utmost in precision, a better system exists.

OUTSIDE NECK TURNING TOOLS—DEDICATED

Handheld, dedicated outside-neck-turning tools can turn a case neck to an impressive degree of precision in both thickness and concentricity. Some of these tools allow a repeatable neck-wall-thickness adjustment with almost incredible precision. The K&M tool is easily, accurately, and repeatedly adjustable to a specific neck wall thickness far closer than 0.0001 inch, at any desired value.

For precision handloads, outside turning tools are reasonably affordable. These are necessary for the most serious of target loads. These tools are adjustable to work with cases of most popular target sizes, and most such tools will work with any case through 35-caliber. Forster and K&M offer units that will work with cases up to 50-caliber.

To use these tools, start with properly sized cases—full-length sizing is advisable. Because the cutting depth of these tools is determined by the length of the case neck, it is necessary to first resize the cases and then trim them to uniform length. If case body length is constant and neck length varies, or if case body length varies and overall case length is constant, then, when the indexing surface of the tool reaches the end of the case neck, the cutter will be in different locations on different cases. On cases with longer necks, it will not have reached the case shoulder; on cases with shorter necks, it will have cut too far into the case shoulder.

Next, run the preturning mandrel through the case neck to open the neck so that the cutter pilot guide will fit snugly. This fit should provide modest friction. If the pilot is too tight to turn in the neck without using too much force or if the tool heats significantly, turned necks

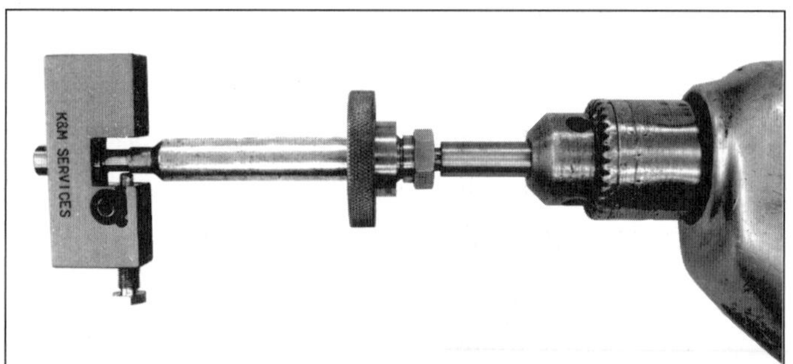

Left-to-right: K&M neck turning tool; Lee, 3-jaw chuck; vised 3/8-inch drill. This system and these tools allow for rapid, precise, and easy outside neck turning. A final polish with four-aught steel wool removes any burs and improves appearance.

will not be as uniform in thickness. Neck annealing will usually solve this problem. Refer to chapter 3.

If neck annealing does not help, you will need a modestly larger mandrel; conversely, if the pilot is not snug in the neck, you will need a smaller mandrel. K&M offers preturning mandrels that are a specific percentage larger than the guide pilot for use with normal cases. K&M offers slightly smaller and slightly larger mandrels to account for variations in neck wall thickness and hardness that will result in a variation in the case neck spring-back as one withdraws the preturning mandrel.

Precise inside neck sizing prior to using these tools is critical to getting quality results. Working with either a too-tight or a too-loose neck guarantees poor results. If the cutter pilot is loose, then the cutter can cut any amount of material from the case neck—the neck can remain thicker in some areas and thinner in others.

If the cutter pilot is too tight, then the cutting operation will be difficult, and it will unnecessarily stress the tool, which will lead to asymmetry of the turned neck. Ideally, use a preturning mandrel that provides some, but only slight, interference between pilot and neck.

Lightly lubricate either the neck interior or the mandrel—use only enough lube to get the job done. Imperial Die Wax and Hornady Unique Case Lube are good products for this purpose; however, SharpShoot-R Royal Lube works even better. A good method of applying just a trace of such a lube to the neck interior is to wet a brass bore brush with the lube and pass that into each case neck before turning the neck. With a bit of practice you can learn just how much lube is necessary and, thereby, avoid using either too much lube (which contaminates the neck interior and is hard to remove) or too little lube (which makes the turning operation difficult and can lead to galling, which transfers brass from case to mandrel).

Adjusting the tool, to achieve uniform case neck thickness, is the easy part of this operation; simply keep closing the cutter toward the pilot until it touches most of the case neck on most of the cases in the working batch.

ALWAYS USE A MANDREL THAT LEAVES JUST A LITTLE FRICTION BETWEEN THE TURNER PILOT AND CASE NECK.

The K&M neck expanding mandrel includes an adjustable screw. When properly adjusted, the screw hits the case web before the case mouth hits the shoulder of the mandrel.

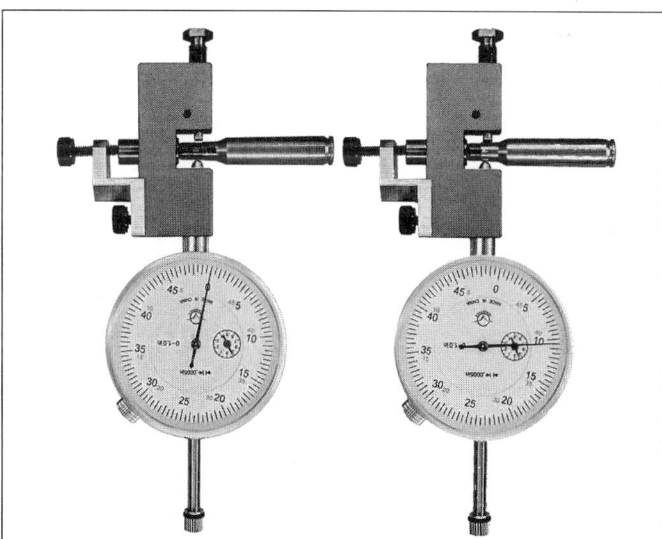

The various features on this top-of-the-line K&M outside neck turning tool include: a dial indicator that shows turned neck thickness; as with all K&M models, adjustment precision is closer than one ten-thousandth inch, for turned neck wall thickness; thumbscrew behind cutter (at left in these views) allows precise adjustment of cutting length along case neck.

Outside neck turning produces a bright, shiny surface. This bright surface shows exactly what is happening and where.

All hand-held, neck-turning tools provide some means of allowing the user to adjust and lock-in the neck length that the cutter will turn. This adjustment

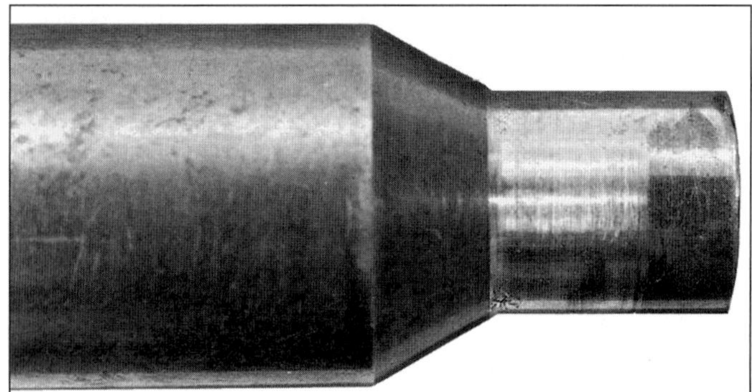

Natural tarnish on case neck, before outside turning, makes it easy to see where cutter has removed material and where it has not done so—obvious, even in this black and white photo.

is critical. Cutting too far into the case shoulder will destroy the case. Not cutting far enough into the shoulder can create a condition that is more damaging to accuracy than not turning the case neck at all. This is true because failure to trim the entire length of the case neck can exacerbate misalignment between the chambered bullet and the bore axis.

With most of these tools, adjusting the cutting length is difficult, at best; conversely, the premium K&M tool includes a screw-adjustable depth stop that simplifies this adjustment. This tool also includes a dial indicator that reports thickness of the turned case neck.

In all instances, cut the entire length of the neck until the cutter just bumps into the case shoulder around the entire circumference. To get this length perfect, you should use a loupe, to examine the area where the cutting ends. The fresh shiny cut surface should extend just slightly up the case shoulder and it should do so completely around the circumference. On case necks that were far from concentric, the distance that this cut extends up the case shoulder will vary considerably from the thin side to the thick side of the case; this is normal.

One can use these tools by hand; however, a variable-speed power drill eases this chore (a drill press will work similarly but is not as handy to use). For use with a drill, the K&M tool is particularly handy because the shellholder easily inserts into the drill chuck. However, I prefer to use the universal-fit Lee 3-Jaw Chuck (page 54) for holding cases. (Note: this Lee tool is equally useful for other case modification and maintenance operations.)

Clamp a power hand drill in a bench vise and chuck the shellholder in the drill. Adjust the drill speed to apply only enough power to keep the drill turning when it is working on the thickest portion of the neck.

With energy supplied by a power tool, you can concentrate on advancing the cutter at a slow and constant rate, but first you must get the tool properly adjusted. Follow the instructions provided by the manufacturer. Each system has unique idiosyncrasies, and, as these are precision tools of the first order, it is necessary to learn to adjust and properly use each specific tool. Instructions provided are generally adequate—study those. When you have established the length-of-cut and amount of thinning required, lock those adjustments.

Insert the pilot into the case neck, start spinning the case at a slow speed, and, ever so slowly, advance cutter until the case mouth bottoms against stop—better to advance slower than is necessary than to advance too quickly. Then, with case still spinning, slowly withdraw the cutter.

Final polishing of the cut surface, using extra-fine steel wool (four-aught/0000) is worthwhile. Simply leave the case spinning and clamp the case neck between the layers of steel wool held between your thumb and forefinger, just long enough to polish away the high spots—no

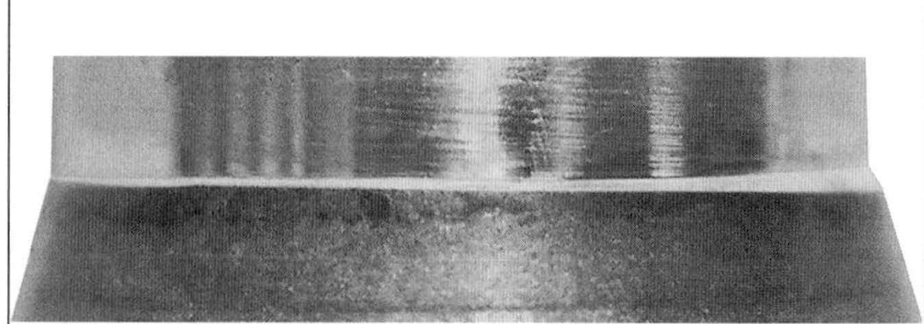

Properly turned neck: One side was significantly thicker (right in this view). Here we can see this because the cutter reached farther onto the shoulder on the right side (as viewed here).

longer. Apply moderate pressure for about one second. This leaves the case neck exterior picture perfect.

A CAUTIONARY NOTE

IF IMPROVING ACCURACY IS YOUR REASON FOR TURNING CASE NECKS AND IF YOU ARE CONSIDERING SKIMPING ON EFFORT, DO NOT BOTHER WITH NECK TURNING; RESULTS WILL BE WORSE THAN DOING NOTHING AT ALL. YOU CAN COUNT ON THAT.

NECK TURNING—DREADED DOUGHNUT

Consider a resized bottlenecked cartridge case: Owing to support provided to the case neck by the case shoulder, inside neck diameter at the neck-to-shoulder junction will always be slightly smaller than inside diameter along remainder of case neck. Included sketches demonstrate this situation.

A similar problem occurs in cases after outside neck turning. Serious shooters (benchresters and the like) refer to this case neck condition as the dreaded doughnut. Outside neck turning exacerbates this condition because turning enough length of the neck exterior to reach to the base of the neck interior would ruin the case. The associated sketch (page 59) shows why this is true; turning the neck exterior to the full depth of the neck interior creates an entirely too thin section of the case wall at the neck-to-shoulder junction. The degree of this influence depends upon case shoulder angle and thickness, angle of the leading edge of the cutter, and vagaries of case design, but it is always a factor of some importance.

As the sketches on pages 58 and 59 show, after turning the outside of a neck, a constriction practically always exists at the base of the neck interior. Conventional outside neck turning cannot resolve this problem.

K&M offers an outside neck turning tool that includes a specially designed fluted carbide pilot designed to remove this potentially detrimental feature without significantly harming the surface finish of the remaining portion of the neck interior. Handloaders who intend to turn the outside of a case neck should give this precision tool due consideration.

A potentially significant problem can occur when any doughnut or hump exists after outside neck turning. Seating a bullet so that the shank extends to, or below, the base of the case neck will result in a corresponding increase in the outside neck diameter on the thick portion of the case neck. Through case deformation, this will also increase diameter of the case at and immediately behind the shoulder. Both conditions are potentially detrimental to optimum accuracy.

Leaving a doughnut has two additional potentially negative influences that result from the swelling at the case shoulder. First, it requires sizing the case body a bit smaller than would otherwise be necessary (or full-length resizing after fewer shots).

Second, this makes it impossible for the entire case body to fit equally within the chamber walls. While the case body is solidly located and supported at the shoulder, the case will not be so solidly supported toward the base—this can allow the case to tip out of alignment with the chamber (relative to the bore axis), which is detrimental to accuracy. Because the resulting shoulder swelling cannot be perfectly symmetrical, this influence cannot contribute to consistent cartridge centering and orientation within the chamber.

The former situation results in a tighter chamber-to-neck fit toward the base of the neck. Except for tightly chambered target rifles, it is unlikely that this condition would cause any safety problem because neck-to-chamber clearances in sporting guns are typically relatively large. However, in a tightly chambered target rifle, that is not the situation. Such guns normally have only about one-thousandth inch radial (annular) neck-to-chamber clearance. The resulting case neck swelling created by bullet seating could, therefore, create interference between cartridge and chamber. These guns have sufficient camming force to allow a shooter

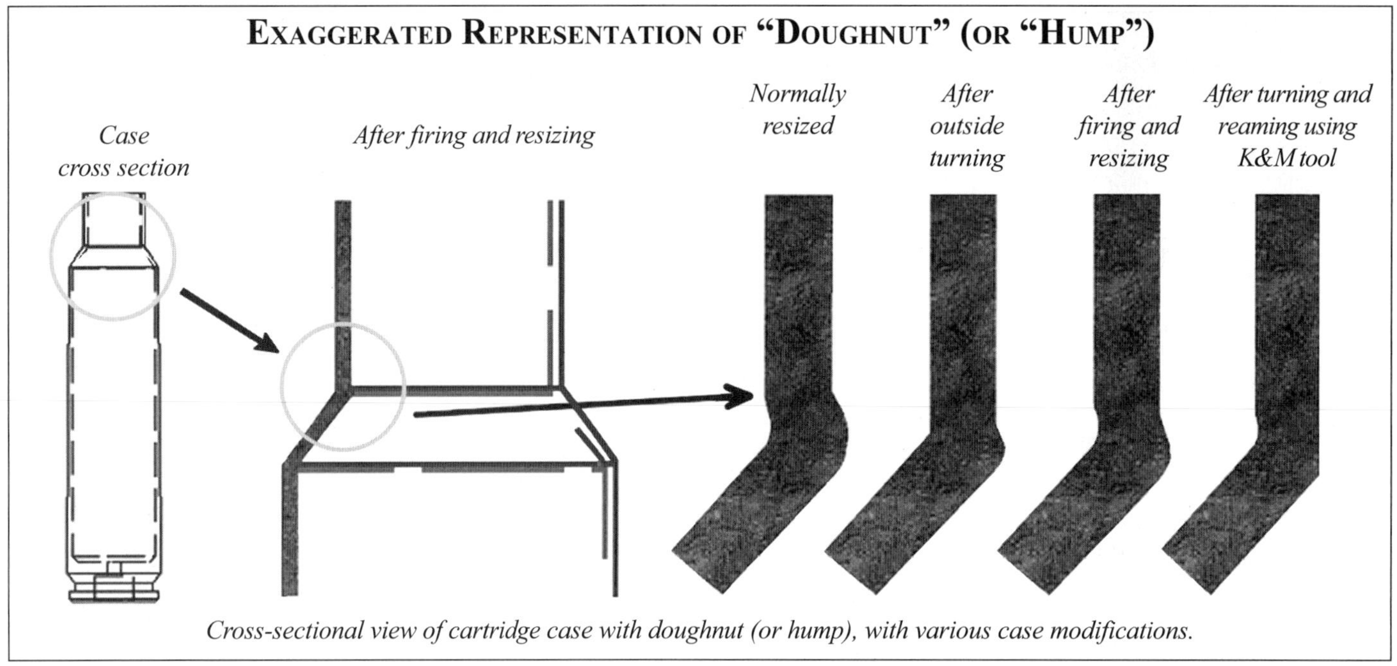

Cross-sectional view of cartridge case with doughnut (or hump), with various case modifications.

to easily close the bolt upon such a round; doing so will crimp the case into the bullet shank. That condition can lead to dangerous chamber pressure and it cannot contribute to shot-to-shot consistency (accuracy).

To assure free cartridge chambering with maximum consistency, it is necessary to either turn case necks somewhat thinner than would otherwise be necessary or to eliminate the dreaded doughnut. Regardless of the type of gun or cartridge, the latter is the best solution and is easily accomplished using the K&M doughnut removal pilot in the K&M tool.

Therefore, as the associated sketch above demonstrates, we can imagine several very good reasons to remove the doughnut and, thereby, relieve the hump. Ideally, doing this could allow us to keep a slightly thicker case neck and to maintain a closer case-to-chamber fit with superior case-to-chamber alignment, thereby, keeping the chambered bullet more nearly centered on and aligned with the bore axis. During firing, as the bullet begins to move from the case, improved bullet-to-bore alignment will reduce asymmetric bullet deformation. Therefore, it seems likely that, if we can accurately remove this neck constriction, we should be able to produce superior cases, which are always the basis of the most accurate handloads.

To reiterate, outside neck turning is preferable to inside neck reaming, except that inside reaming of the dreaded doughnut (and nothing else) is beneficial. The main issue in the latter regard is finish and character of the interior surface of the case neck (particularly with regard to consistent case-to-bullet friction and fouling properties).

Consistent bullet pull is a critical accuracy issue. While I do not claim to know that inside reaming is automatically detrimental to accuracy, significant practical, empirical, and theoretical evidence seems to suggest that it is. Therefore, if we are to remove the doughnut and hump by inside reaming (I know of no other method), we must do so with minimal scarring in the remaining neck interior. For this, the K&M tool is ideal.

CASE SORTING— GENERAL CONSIDERATIONS

After performing any initial case preparation steps that you deem necessary or useful, as an advanced handloader, you can perform additional sorting steps, to determine case quality and to classify cases by:

- Weight
- Concentricity (wall thickness uniformity)
- Straightness of body
- Alignment of neck and body

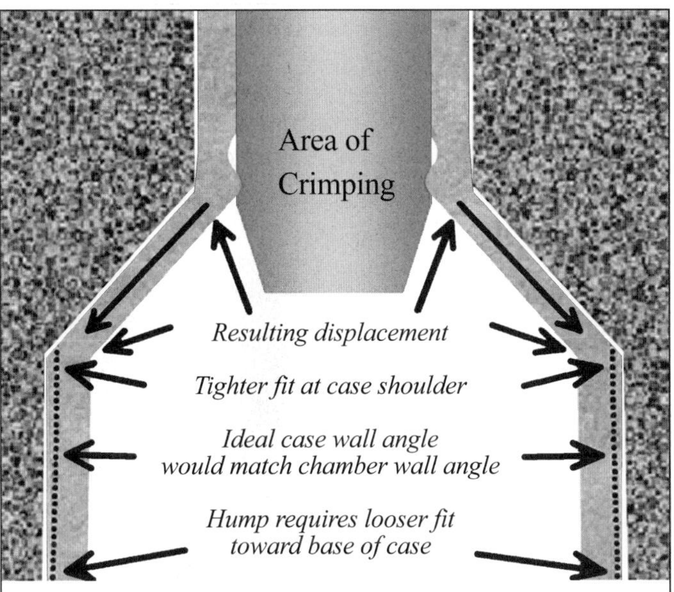

Case thickness and deformations are exaggerated to show areas where case neck crimps into bullet shank and area where deformation pushes neck away from bullet.

Close-up view of fluted-carbide pilot for K&M, outside neck-turner: This pilot is designed to remove dreaded doughnut without significantly scarring remainder of neck interior. Because carbide has a much lower coefficient of friction than steel does, this pilot eases the effort in neck turning. This pilot removes doughnut as it passes portion of neck where hump existed, so turning effort remains modest.

Ideal turning length

Turned too deeply

Trying to eliminate the doughnut by turning a greater length of the case neck excessively thins the case shoulder. Outside neck turning requires careful attention to detail, such as pilot adjustment, to control how deeply cutter progresses along case neck.

Cross-sectional view of a well-used 6 PPC case: Note bright band where K&M tool removed the dreaded doughnut. This provides dramatic evidence of just how necessary this step can be and of how precisely the K&M doughnut remover works. (It completely and perfectly removed this detrimental feature without touching the rest of the neck interior.) This neck had been outside turned before it was used at a National Championship Benchrest meet, but the K&M Doughnut remover had not been used.

Separating cases into weight groups can minimize shot-to-shot velocity variations that would otherwise result from differences in internal case volume (size of initial boiler room). The most serious of shooters will deem this step useful for application to their most serious of cartridges.

Using only the most concentric cases will improve alignment between bullet and bore, which will improve accuracy. Again, this step is most applicable to serious target cartridges used in quality target rifles.

Checking cases for straightness and marking the direction of the bend in the case body allows indexed chambering (feasible in target shooting and varminting situations), which can enhance accuracy. These methods will also identify a bent case shoulder, which indicates a round that is unlikely to demonstrate good accuracy. Refer to "Case Indexing—General Considerations" in this chapter.

These tests will also identify overall quality of cases from any given production lot: typical, unusually good, or unusually bad. For this reason, it is often useful to test a handful of cases from any given batch, just to determine if cases from that batch are potentially capable of delivering unusually good results or, conversely, if those might best be relegated to your plinking-use-only category.

CASE SORTING—BY WEIGHT

As are many other shooting-related components, cartridge cases are an industrial marvel. Considering the combined costs of raw material, manufacturing, handling, transportation, etc., it seems miraculous that retailers can sell cases of incredible precision and utility for pennies apiece. That this is true is a tribute to economies of scale and to efficient manufacturing processes.

The general high quality of run-of-the-mill cases is a tribute to manufacturing technology. The mass of any given case is often consistent to better than plus-or-minus 1 percent of the average mass of cases in that production lot. When we consider the manufacturing variables that can contribute to case-weight variations, such consistency is rather impressive. However, those shooting at longer ranges (where uniform muzzle velocity is critical to accuracy) will benefit from sorting cases to a greater degree of weight precision.

Serious shooters often sort cases weighing about 100 grains into categories of one-grain increments—plus or minus one-half grain. Serious competitors often sort to plus-or-minus 0.2-grain precision.

Our concern with weight variation centers on our belief, which is generally correct, that weight variation directly reflects a variation in internal case volume (initial boiler-room capacity). Despite having otherwise identical load parameters, when loaded and fired, cartridges with varying internal capacity will manifest pressure and velocity differences. The former results in variations in barrel time, which reduces potential accuracy; the latter creates vertical stringing at long range.

In cases from the same production lot, some tiny portion of case-weight variation results from external case differences—such as rim and case-head dimensional variations. However, when considering quality cases, external variations are inconsequential. Hence, same-lot cases of similar weight will have similar internal volume (usable capacity). Even when considering cases from different lots and of different makes, external dimensions are reasonably similar; hence, differences in case weight reflect differences in internal capacity. As noted, case capacity directly influences chamber pressure and velocity; hence, case weight is an important accuracy consideration, especially for cartridges that you might use to shoot at targets beyond about 600 yards.

We have no particularly accurate means by which to measure effective internal case volume precisely. We could load and fire our new cases, weigh each fired case with the fired primer in place, fill the case with water, and reweigh it. Although such testing would obviously be time consuming, it could be the perfect solution because we would be measuring only internal case volume of a chamber-fitting case, and, with a good scale and with good technique, we could measure that value very accurately. Unfortunately, this approach suffers from several fundamental problems.

First, all cases are elastic. This means that, as produced, every case comes out of the forming die a bit larger than the die; equally, when fired, it will (usually) come out of a gun a bit smaller than the chamber. If all cases in any particular group were equally elastic, this would be of no consequence, but, alas, even in brand-new cases springiness varies. For instance, the variations in case-wall thickness that we are hoping to discover are apt to influence the amount of sidewall and shoulder spring-back of any given case. As a result, our proposed system of measuring case volume would not work very well.

A second problem is that it is rather difficult to remove all the air from the case when filling it with water. We could use an effective wetting agent (as are available for photographic solutions), but this is a messy system and it requires thorough case drying. Nevertheless, if such a system allowed us to precisely determine case volume, it would, no doubt, be worth the effort, at least for the most dedicated target shooters. However, because it does not and cannot give perfect results, those who have tried this method have not found it to be worthwhile.

Therefore, for practical purposes, weighing cases is our best means of estimating usable capacity. Now, the question is, how best to do this? This is an area where mental preparation and considerable forethought are very helpful.

Before preparing any batch of cases, each handloader must decide the degree of precision to which he wants to separate those cases. Handloaders must also decide which advanced preparation steps they will want to incorporate into any given lot of cases, and they must accomplish all of those steps before separating any particular batch into weight groups.

Let us consider a hypothetical example. You have just installed a custom Krieger barrel on your Savage Model-12, short-action, single-shot rifle. You chambered this barrel for the 6.5-284 Norma but with a custom tight-neck chamber so that you can neck turn cases to achieve precise fit and concentricity. Moreover, it was chambered with a long throat so that you can use heavy match bullets without seating the bullets too deeply.

Your interests for this gun include both long-range varmint shooting and big-game hunting. Most shooters would argue that taking extraordinary accuracy steps is unnecessary for big-game hunting purposes; however, for varmint hunting applications you, reasonably, want to wring out the last measure of accuracy that you feasibly can get.

Figuring that you can do considerable varmint shooting on a good weekend, you plan to buy several hundred, high-quality Norma cases, in bulk, at a good price. This seems a reasonable plan. The main advantage of a bulk purchase is that it gives you a large batch of cases manufactured in the same production lot. Such cases are more likely to be similar in dimensions and performance. This way, once you have worked up your loads, you can be sure that all your cases will give similar results. If you had used cases from several manufacturing lots, you might have to change the charge weight to maintain similar velocity, pressure, and barrel time because of (potential) significant lot-to-lot case weight variations. Also, some hard-to-measure variables that can alter internal ballistics (for example web-to-body transition shape) will be more similar within cases from the same production lot.

While breaking in the barrel, you use one box of Black Hills factory Match loads and are impressed with the accuracy of this load and gun. You suspect that the gun has potential as a real shooter. Evidently, it is worthy of your efforts in accurizing and precision loading. You decide to glass bed the action and do all the other little things that can improve accuracy potential. The list of projects you contemplate includes lapping the locking lugs and tweaking the Accu-Trigger to minimize let-off. (On a factory barrel, you might include firelapping.) You might cryogenically treat (controlled-rate deep freezing) the barreled action to reduce internal stress in the steel, which might increase barrel life.

In my book, *Accurizing the Factory Rifle,* you will find a detailed analysis of each of these steps and many others. That book is available from Brownells.

Having decided to go the extra mile with this fine rifle, it now makes sense to contemplate how far along the extreme accuracy road you are willing to travel with your handloads.

As with a custom rifle, you can improve accuracy with a box-stock hunting rifle by using precise handloads. However, no amount of load tinkering will cure accuracy problems in a gun. Think of it this way: Half the intrinsic accuracy is in the load; the other half is in the gun. The most accurate rifle in the world will not shoot lousy ammo into world-class groups, and the most accurate ammunition in the world will not shoot into world-class groups when fired from a faulty or poorly made rifle. This was a philosophy expounded by my late friend, Roger Johnston. The more I consider it, the more I realize just how significant his simple observation was—partition your time, efforts, and expenditures so that you can most easily get the most from any given combination of rifle and ammunition.

MTM offers some of the easiest to use handloading blocks. Here, temporary labeling with masking tape indicates cases of widely differing weights, but this method is also useful for locating cases that have been weighed into specific weight ranges (see text)—the first step toward sorting cases by weight.

Dimples are a useful and permanent way to mark cases to indicate weight grouping.

In our example, you have time to do the work and you decide to buy the tools needed to turn the case necks, make the primer pockets and flash holes uniform, and measure cases for concentricity and straightness. Of course, regardless of any other steps that you might take, you will need some means of trimming cases to length and deburring case necks after trimming. You buy those specialty handloading tools that you do not already own and, perhaps, two hundred same-lot cases. Now what do you do?

Begin by running the cases through a full-length resizing die, verifying (or creating) uniform length, deburring necks, and polishing case mouths. Often, you will find dented case mouths, as occurs during final polishing, shipping, and handling; moreover, the standard mouth interior opening will never be polished adequately for best results, particularly when using bullets that are plated with molybdenum-disulfide.

Assuming that you intend further case preparation, the following steps are worthwhile:

- Turn the case necks and remove the dreaded doughnut.
- Make the primer pockets uniform.
- Debur and make the primer flash holes uniform.

(While primer-pocket uniforming is less valuable than is flash-hole deburring, pocket uniforming can create an entrance bur on the flash hole; hence, if you do make the primer pockets uniform, it is best to debur flash holes last.)

Depending upon the number of cases involved and tools available, facing this work might be daunting. Most handloaders find it easier to proceed in steps. When you have fully prepped all cases, it is time to sort those by weight. You must now decide to what degree of weight uniformity you want to sort cases.

For a 6.5-284, even when fitted with such a high-quality barrel, plus-or-minus one-half grain weight increments seems amply sufficient. If you were dealing with a typical factory rifle and barrel, plus-or-minus one-grain increments would likely be sufficient. In the big magnums, plus-or-minus two grains generally provides sufficient consistency. This decision depends upon several things: the accuracy potential of the gun and your handloads; your shooting skills; how much time and energy you want to spend sorting and marking cases; and, the uniformity of that particular batch of cases. Ultimately, you must make this decision.

As noted, uniformity of cases in the particular lot could influence your decision. You really do not want to end up with an excessive number of weight groupings any more than you want to have excessive weight variation within any given grouping. Before making any decision on group boundaries, as a preliminary step randomly select a handful of cases and weigh those to get an idea of expected weight variation within that batch of cases.

You might find it useful to establish permanent weight groups for any given case type. For example, I have established 202 grains +/– ½ grain as standard for Norma 6.5-284 cases for all my target cartridges. To minimize velocity variation, I adjust the charge used in cases falling outside this weight range. I cover that in chapter 9.

If, for example, maximum weight variation in twenty randomly sampled cases was close to +/– ½ percent of average case weight, you might want to buy more cases from the same lot because those are evidently unusually consistent. If that were the situation, you might want to sort into +/– ¼ percent weight groupings because that would be reasonably convenient. Conversely, if maximum weight variation in such a sample exceeds (about) +/– 1½ percent you might want to try a different case brand or production lot, as it is unlikely that such cases will be of generally high quality to justify further effort for accuracy loads. (These percentages are arbitrary; generally, some case types are more consistent and others are less consistent. This often has something to do with how hard the manufacturer tries—for example, 30-30 cases are not apt to be as consistent as 22-250 cases are.)

The type of handloading scale you use is an issue here. Availability of an electronic digital scale monumentally reduces the effort involved in sorting cases by weight.

CASE SORTING—BEAM SCALE

You can use a beam scale to sort cases into weight groups, but this method is ponderously slow. Either you must adjust the scale to get the weight of each case the first time through (a procedure that is monumentally time consuming and practically certain to lead to adjustment or recording errors), or you must weigh each case many times (similarly time consuming and error prone).

When using a beam scale (a method that, thank goodness, I no longer endure), the easiest method involves determining weight boundaries before starting. First, set the scale at the lightest weight for the heaviest group. Then, sort all cases into two groups, heavier and lighter than that weight.

Having separated all cases thusly, set the scale to the bottom weight of the next-lighter group. All remaining cases from the lighter group that are heavier than this setting become members of the next-to-heaviest group. Repeat this procedure to sort all cases into groups based upon weight range.

Finally, reweigh all cases in the heavier group (to find any that are heavicr than the upper weight boundary for that group); then, reweigh all members of the lightest group (to find any that are lighter than the lower weight boundary of that group). Mark any such cases (rare exceptions, we pray) as gauging dummies or for use only during preliminary load development. This process is simple, boring, and wrought with opportunities for human error—and, I suspect, we are all human.

Redding beam balance scale: This precision instrument is easy to set up and easy to use. As with most such balances, this scale will provide accuracy closer than 1/10-grain (1/70,000 pound), which is adequate for any handloading purpose.

CASE SORTING—ELECTRONIC SCALE

Conversely, consider using an electronic digital scale (such as the RCBS Charge Master scale). With such a scale, weighing each case to the nearest tenth-grain takes only a few seconds. Case weighing becomes the easiest of all case sorting and preparation tasks. Prepare several loading blocks and mark sections with labeled masking tape so that you are certain to sort each case properly into the correct tenth-grain-weight-increment grouping—grouping comes next.

After you have segregated all cases into 1/10-grain weight groups, look at what you have. Unless you have chosen to establish permanent standard-weight groupings, you can now choose grouping boundaries that give the largest number of cases in one group. You

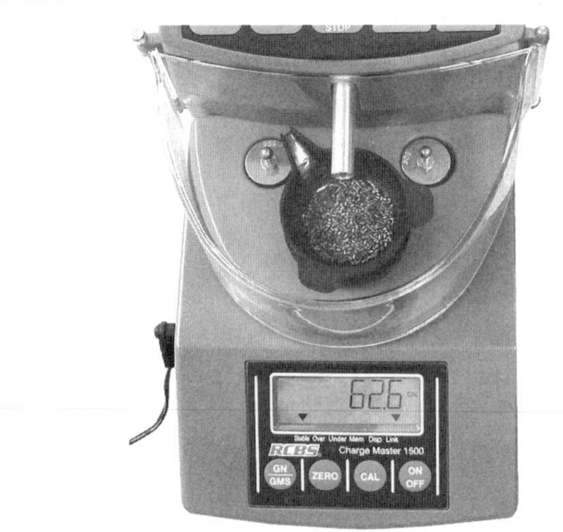

The RCBS Charge Master Scale is, perhaps, the finest electronic scale now available to the hobby handloader. It is shown here attached to a Charge Master Electronic Propellant Dispenser (scale offered individually). Note plastic shield that eliminates air motion on pan: Tiny wind motions (such as one's breath) will prevent accurate measurements with any handloading scale.

might then choose to relegate the (few) heaviest and lightest cases for use during die adjustment, gauging, and initial load development work. If case weight distribution matches what mathematicians refer to as a normal distribution, most will be in the middleweight groups. In this situation, it would make sense to choose group boundaries that would create the largest number of cases within one group. If the number of cases in each group is similar, you might choose to use larger grouping boundaries. This will leave more cases in each group—more practical but less precise. This decision is yours.

CASE SORTING—MARKING AND OTHER CONSIDERATIONS

Next, decide how to go about marking or segregating grouped cases to keep the cases permanently identifiable. This latter consideration is why I prefer permanently marking each case, compared to simply sorting cases into different ammunition boxes. Handloaders who use the latter system must maintain eternal vigilance to prevent the inadvertent remixing of carefully sorted cases—good luck. Experience has proven that I cannot rely on simple segregation, so I mark cases.

Various systems of permanent case marking are feasible. An electric stenciling tool allows precise scribing, a tiny set of number stamps allows code embossing, and a spring-loaded staking tool allows punching a dimple. A staking tool costs only a few dollars and allows the application of a coded dimple in about one second.

A coded indentation, located somewhere on the headstamp area of each case head, allows the handloader to specify enough weight groups for any need. One coding method involves a single dimple placed before or after the numerical portion of the headstamp, in the name code letters, or in other areas. In this way, with only one mark, the handloader can easily and distinctly designate at least five weight groups.

I prefer to note the codes on the label associated with the handload and to include the case weight group in the "Case Make" area of the label. The important thing is to establish a code system with which you are comfortable and to keep sufficient records to keep track of what you have done; otherwise, several years later you might forget.

As a final identifying method, it is worthwhile to note somewhere on the handload label the manufacturing lot number (if available) and the case-preparation steps you have performed on that group of cases. For example, you might write: "Midway, lot purchase, 1993, fully prepped."

For use in the most serious of shooting situations, some shooters advocate selecting only cases from the middleweight group or groups while other shooters prefer other techniques. I suggest that you weigh all cases you intend to use for serious shooting and carefully consider your goals before deciding which approach you will take.

My choice for big-game-hunting loads is to use almost all cases—excepting only the lightest and heaviest few. As I cover in the following chapter, I simply adjust the propellant charge, where feasible, to compensate for capacity (weight) variations. However, I do not intermix cartridges using cases from different weight groups during any shooting session—all cartridges in the magazine and in reserve are from the same weight group.

With this approach, I know that my cartridges are going to be as consistent as is reasonably feasible. That knowledge adds to my confidence. That confidence inevitably improves my performance behind the stock. See self-fulfilling prophecy on page 46 for a discussion of this critical reality.

As noted before, variations in case weight result in variations in cartridge performance. Heavier cases have less boiler room, and so, with otherwise identical loads, they create cartridges that generate greater chamber pressure and higher muzzle velocity. In chapter 9, you will find a detailed analysis and a table listing necessary charge corrections, to approximately account for differences in case weight (capacity).

CASE INDEXING—GENERAL CONSIDERATIONS

In recent decades, manufacturers have improved the quality of most jacketed bullets to the point where concentricity is no longer a significant consideration for most shooters under most conditions. We are concerned here with another factor that can upset bullet balance.

With conventional bullets, if, for any reason, the chambered bullet does not center on and align with the bore, the violent acceleration resulting from the explosive force of propellant combustion will lead to asymmetric bullet deformation, as the bullet hits and enters into the rifling. Such deformation will ruin bullet balance and aerodynamic symmetry about the longitudinal axis.

For example, in the relatively mundane 30-06 Springfield, a typical 150-grain cartridge will accelerate the bullet to about 70 fps before it has traveled 50/1000 inch, and to about 150 fps before it has traveled 100/1000 inch. In a standard rifle, with a standard length cartridge, we could expect such a bullet to hit the rifling when it is already traveling faster than 100 fps.

The side of the bullet that first hits the rifling will tend to slow, while the other side will have no such restraint. When the combined force on the bullet from sudden impact with the rifling and continued acceleration exceed bullet strength, an off-center or out-of-square rifling impact will generate asymmetric bullet deformation. (See associated drawing below.) Such deformation compromises bullet balance and aerodynamics.

Conventional sporting bullets achieve accuracy through a gyroscopic force imparted by the spin imposed upon the bullet by the rifling. Imbalanced bullets are inaccurate, and the more imbalanced they are the more inaccurate they are. We can identify two common causes of bullet-to-bore misalignment that lead to bullet imbalance:

- Nonconcentric case necks
- Bent cartridges (body, shoulder, or both)

I covered neck concentricity earlier in this chapter, under "Case Improvement—Neck Turning and Neck Reaming." I will now consider the bent cartridge case. Because bent ammunition can ruin a group or a shot, serious target competitors, varmint hunters, and those (rare) big-game hunters possessing the skills required to take shots at longer distances can benefit from case indexing—measuring cases and cartridges for straightness and marking accordingly.

While producers continue to improve jacketed bullet quality, no bullet is perfect. As many experienced shooters know, bullet quality is a fundamental component of the intrinsic accuracy of any cartridge. Hence, before considering case indexing I will reflect upon what separates an accurate bullet from an inaccurate bullet.

In an out-of-balance bullet (nonconcentric jacket, or firing-related asymmetric deformation), the center of rotational mass (about which it will freely rotate after leaving the bore) will not coincide with the geometric axis—the bore axis. Bullet rotation will introduce a tiny corresponding barrel motion. This motion superimposes upon the other barrel motions associated with firing the gun. This cumulative barrel motion will degrade accuracy because the muzzle will have a random, nonconsistent position as the bullet exits.

More importantly, as the bullet exits, it is no longer constrained to rotate around the geometric axis and

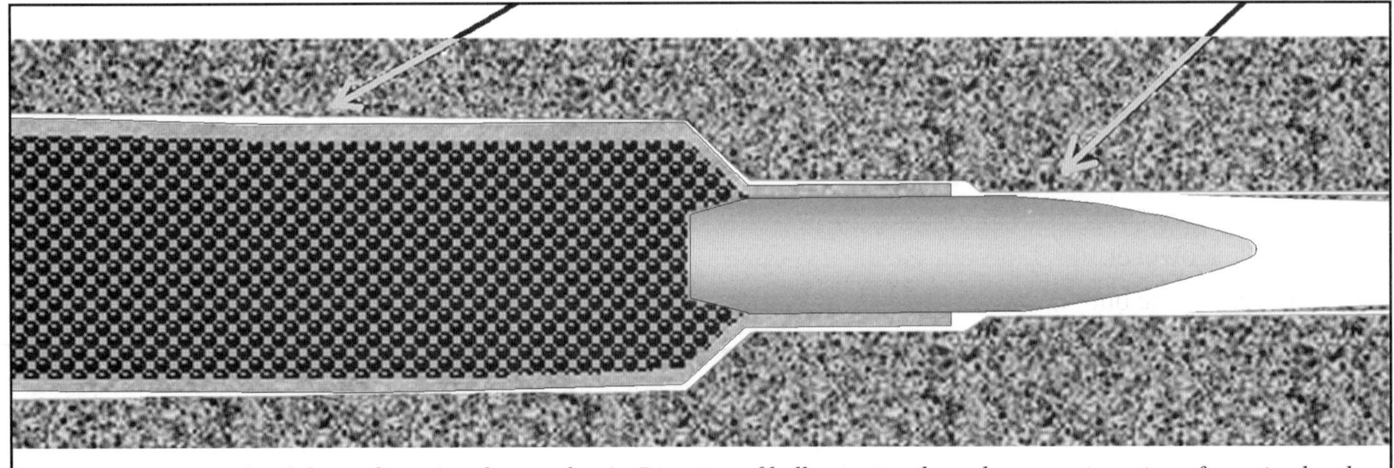

Bent case represented with low side up (can be anywhere). Direction of bullet tipping depends upon orientation of case in chamber. Bullet tips up (in this example).

will begin to rotate around the center of mass. This transition dramatically degrades accuracy.

What happens when this transition occurs is complicated and most pundits have inadequately understood this process and the consequences. Many texts have presented an erroneous explanation. Here I offer an accurate, if incomplete, analysis.

The simplest way to see why an out-of-balance bullet results in poor accuracy is to consider what necessarily happens as such a bullet exits the muzzle. Keep the following facts in mind:

- No two bullets will be deformed or imbalanced identically.
- No two bullets will be deformed or imbalanced with the same relative orientation as the bullet comes free of the bore.
- At some instant, as the amount of bullet shank that remains engaged in the rifling decreases, lateral torque generated by the out-of-balance rotation will exceed the strength of the engaged portion of the bullet shank.
- At that instant, the bullet nose will begin to pivot (move sideways), as necessary, so the bullet can begin to rotate about the longitudinal axis of balance.

This longitudinal rotation necessarily forces the bullet to acquire an average sideways velocity because, as the bullet begins to turn into alignment with the balance axis, the muzzle solidly holds the base of the bullet shank. If the bullet were free when rotation occurred, it would simply turn about the center of gravity to align to the balance axis and no sideways (lateral) velocity would result. However, the bullet is not free. Hence, the entire front of the bullet must move sideways as the base remains essentially stationary (in the lateral sense); thereby, the bullet always acquires lateral motion.

This motion adds to the lateral motion and muzzle pointing error associated with barrel vibrations. The cumulate effect of these motions will be randomly oriented because each bullet will have a random, unique, orientation and the resulting sideways push will reflect that random orientation.

In his 1909 book, *The Bullet's Flight,* Dr. Mann described, correctly and well, the motion of a bullet in flight. Subsequently, until Jim Boatright's recent work, everyone else seems to have gotten it wrong.

We do not need to go into a complicated discussion of gyroscopic stability. Simply put, when an out-of-balance bullet exits the bore, it acquires a lateral velocity; this lateral velocity is superimposed upon its forward velocity.

Because this lateral velocity is relatively slow, seldom more than several inches per second, it decreases very slowly throughout ballistic flight. For practical purposes, it is essentially a constant. Therefore, if the bullet were not rapidly losing forward velocity, this source of inaccuracy would result in a constant MOA (minute of angle) divergence, regardless of target distance. However, in reality, the bullet is losing forward velocity rapidly and lateral velocity slowly; therefore, this divergence grows, in approximate inverse proportion to remaining forward velocity.

I believe that another source of intrinsic inaccuracy exists. A steering push results from the coning angle of the bullet as the axis of rotation yaws around the parabolic axis of flight. The magnitude of yaw varies throughout ballistic flight at a constant rate, but the bullet is slowing, so the bullet acquires an overall lateral push, which cannot be zero. So, because of the initial lateral push (at the muzzle) and the push resulting from yaw, generally the farther we shoot, the larger the MOA of the resulting group.

Now that we understand why asymmetric bullets are inaccurate, we need to understand how bullets can become asymmetric. The random insertion of bent cartridges into a chamber will result in random bullet tipping—up, down, left, right, and anywhere in between. Now let us consider what happens when we launch such a tipped bullet into the barrel. As the bullet

Pay Attention to the Entire System

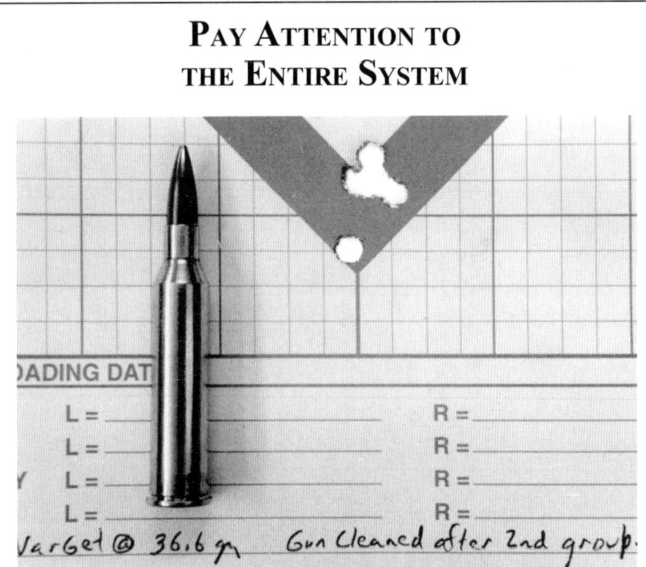

I included this photograph for one salient reason—I worked diligently to get this gun to shoot consistently good groups. Occasionally, I would get a tiny group; often, I would get a tiny group with one flier (as shown here); usually, I would get one tiny two-shot group and one tiny three-shot group separated by about one-half inch. After analyzing several targets, I realized that centers of the two groups were always separated by a similar distance and in a similar orientation. The externally adjustable scope mount, which allowed the scope to recoil against a spring, was damaged; often, the scope would not return to the proper location between shots. After a simple repair, the gun consistently shot good loads into a tiny one-hole group.

hits the rifling, if it can deform asymmetrically it will do so. The degree of this deformation depends upon:

- Degree of misalignment
- Variables of bullet design and toughness
- Rifling leade design (the leade is the area of the throat that tapers from groove diameter—with zero-depth rifling, to bore diameter—with full-depth rifling)
- Bullet velocity at the leade
- Acceleration force acting upon the bullet when it hits and as it passes through the leade

This depends upon:

- Propellant burning characteristics
- Charge mass

How far, and in which direction, any given bullet hits from the nominal group center depends upon:

- Degree of asymmetric deformation that occurs during firing
- Which direction the bullet was tipped in the chamber
- Where any unusual barrel vibrations leave the muzzle pointing
- Which direction the muzzle is moving at the instant the bullet exits the bore

Obviously, we would prefer to eliminate these variables; however, this is impossible. Realistically, we can always control these variables, to some degree.

One thing we can measure is direction and degree of bullet tipping. Formerly, the standard means of testing for bent cases was to fire cartridges. Target shooters assumed that accurate rounds suggested good, straight cases. Conversely, they assumed that an unexplained flier indicated a crooked case. Formerly, benchrest shooters loaded up a large batch of cases and began test firing; when a cartridge generated an unexplained flier, they discarded the case. Using that method, random variables sometimes led the shooter to keep a bad case and often led him to discard a good case.

Whatever else you might do to improve the accuracy of groups you produce, never forget that quality practice to improve your ability to shoot good groups is equally important. Tiny groups result from quality ammunition fired from a quality gun by a skilled shooter. And no, you are not apt to just naturally be a great shot simply because you are a red-blooded American male.

We now have a better way. Bersin, RCBS, and Sinclair International offer tools designed to simplify case concentricity testing and cartridge straightness testing. Before loading cases, handloaders can measure the potential for case bending. Equally, handloaders can measure cartridge straightness. Further, the serious shooter can identify and mark all bent or potentially bent cases and segregate those into groups, depending upon case concentricity (quality) and degree and direction of bending. By segregating cases accordingly and by then chambering bent cases in the same orientation, target shooters can significantly reduce variables that reduce accuracy.

Several of these tools allow measurement of relative case-wall thickness along the case body. For example, the RCBS tool includes a probe that the user can adjust to align with and touch the tip of the dial indicator. With this setting and the dial indicator zeroed, interposing the case wall will then provide an approximate thickness reading. More importantly, as the user rotates the case between the probes, this setup provides a relative thickness reading. By testing the circumference at a location approximately midway between shoulder and web, it is possible to determine relative case quality (in terms of concentricity) and to predict relative degree of bending that will occur up on firing.

Unfired cases are usually straight. However, upon firing, most cases will bend somewhat. As noted previously, it is easy to determine the bending propensity of any new case by measuring case-wall concentricity. Normally, cases stretch more on the thin side, so the thin side will become the high side. A greater difference in thickness between thin and thick sides results in greater differential stretching, which results in greater case bending, which results in a greater diminution of accuracy potential.

To measure case bending, place the fired case or loaded cartridge in a supporting fixture and, while rolling the case, measure runout—difference from straightness. The RCBS tool features a pair of adjustable

An RCBS Case Master Gauge Tool provides many important case measurements. Here it is set up to measure total runout. (With this setup, as one rolls the case in the vee-notches, the indicator shows the totality of shoulder and body bending.)

V-blocks. Position these blocks near the case head and shoulder. Sinclair's concentricity tool has a different but functionally similar design.

As you roll the case, note the high side. Once you have determined the high side, use a permanent ink marker to add a tick mark along the high side. Add a number to indicate the amount of runout (difference from high side to low side), in thousandths of an inch.

In all instances, follow the instructions provided by the manufacturer and take the time to do a good job. The quality of the data you gather will either make this effort worthwhile or make this a waste of your time.

When using the RCBS case gauge to measure bent cartridge necks, place the cartridge on the V-blocks and locate the dial indicator about midway along the bullet ogive. (Ogive, pronounced: ō′jīv: is that portion of the bullet between the cylindrical shank and the tip.) Then slowly roll the case. Unless the case neck is bent (actually it is the case shoulder that gets bent), the bullet tip should be bent in the opposite sense as

Most who have worked with the Hornet would consider this phenomenal accuracy. Use of quality tools and components, extra effort in case preparation, and careful loading can pay off. This five-shot, 100-yard, 22 Hornet group was, indeed, the best fired from the Meacham 1885, reproduction Low-Wall using this load; however, this and several other combinations routinely produced groups on centers that were far smaller than one-half inch. Small changes in load variables made significant differences in accuracy.

the case body is bent—high side of bullet should be opposite to high side of case; if not, the case shoulder is also bent. Often, shoulder bending occurs during bullet seating. I address this problem in chapter 11.

The Bersin tool only measures total bullet runout. It does not distinguish between a bent case body and a bent case shoulder. However, it does allow the user to measure and to eliminate bullet runout in one easy operation. For this reason, this is the premier tool of this type.

Sizing a case in a badly bent sizing die could bend the case differently every time. Otherwise, owing to brass elasticity, once established by firing, the high side of the case persists. Marking bent cases to facilitate chambering of loaded rounds with the bullets consistently tipped in the same direction is likely to improve accuracy.

A technique that works in many non-bolt-action and some bolt-action guns is to mark the high side of the case by filing a small notch in the case rim, or by some other means. This index mark becomes a permanent identifier. The shooter can chamber indexed cartridges in a consistent orientation, relative to the bend in the case. The handloader can refine this technique further by separating bent cases into groups reflecting the respective degree of bending, which is (usually) a reflection of the degree of differential case-wall thickness, which is a reflection of overall case quality, and is apt to manifest in the degree of delivered accuracy. This technique is applicable and useful to almost any kind of cartridge used for almost any kind of shooting.

The RCBS tool has other useful features and is a worthwhile addition to any loading bench. For example, it allows the handloader to measure case body thinning at the web-to-body junction. The older version of this tool included a handy, if slow to use, case-head-diameter measuring system and a means of measuring rim thickness on 22 rimfire cases. (Consistent rim thickness is critical to rimfire accuracy.)

CASE CONVERSION—FIREFORMING

Fireforming is the process of altering an existing case shape to fit a chamber with a different shape. Fireforming is usually necessary when making wildcat cases. Other types of case conversions are possible. Fireforming uses the pressure of firing to expand the case to fill a larger chamber.

Perhaps the best way to explain this process is to consider an example. Imagine that you own a rifle that was originally chambered in 257 Roberts and that you have had it rechambered to 257 Ackley Improved. One method of forming cases to fit the new chamber is to simply fire full-power 257 Roberts cartridges in the gun—fireforming. Regardless of what you might read elsewhere, best results with fireforming always occur when using full-pressure loads. One common consequence of the fireforming process is that the case neck gets shorter—as the case stretches to fill the shoulder and body area of the chamber, it pulls the case neck rearward. Interestingly, fireforming loads are often amazingly accurate.

An advantageous alternative approach involves no bullet. Needed supplies include conversion cases, Bullseye, pistol primers (Remington 1½s or 2½s are best), a hand-decapping tool and a hammer, a hand-priming tool, a Lee propellant dipper set, and a propellant funnel. Either new cases or cases that have had the neck and shoulder annealed work best.

Prime a test case and choose a Lee dipper that will hold a charge of Bullseye that fills about 40 percent of the case. Transfer the charge into the case. After informing the range master and other shooters of what you are doing, carefully chamber the case and fire the round while holding the gun with the muzzle pointing significantly upward. (Safety is an issue here. Hearing and eye protection are necessary because the shot will be very loud. Caution is necessary because a significant fireball will result.)

Extract the case and examine the primer. Some rifles will pierce the cup of a pistol primer; if this happens, use a mild rifle primer (RWS 5341 or CCI-200). Then examine the case shoulder. Usually, it will not have formed properly—typically, the shoulder will not have sharp corners and the body might not be full diameter. Decap and reprime the case. Choose the next-larger Lee dipper and use that to charge the case. Repeat this firing, examining, and retesting process until you find the smallest charge that results in very sharp angles on the case shoulder; then use a dipper that delivers 10 percent more propellant.

This method wastes no bullets, does minimum barrel damage, and provides one big advantage. With a bit of tinkering with dies, it is easy to create a converted case with a neck that is longer than the chamber neck. So, after fireforming, you can trim the neck to correctly fit the chamber. With the standard fireforming procedure (using a bullet), the neck will always end up far shorter than would be ideal. Refer to "Matching Length of Neck to Chamber."

The Bersin Tool allows a shooter to measure easily, quickly, and accurately how straight the overall cartridge is. As a bonus, it also allows a shooter to straighten a cartridge very precisely and to do so in a matter of seconds. Long-range target shooters are setting new records with ammunition straightened using this tool.

CASE CONVERSION—REFORMING

Although this is outside the realm of typical case preparation operations, case forming has several potentially significant advantages. Sometimes, handloaders can use case forming to produce cases that are otherwise unavailable—to use an old or rare gun; cases offering superior accuracy potential—as with a standard (loose) chamber in a factory gun; or cases having other advantages.

Left to right: Norma 7mm Mauser cases showing various steps during conversion to 243 Ackley Improved with neck length adjusted to have only 15/1000-inch clearance to end of chamber neck. Fireforming shown here is a method using no bullet (discussed in text).

Over the past several decades, I have done considerable research in this area, toward the goal of improving accuracy and to be able to use a gun for which factory-made cases no longer existed.

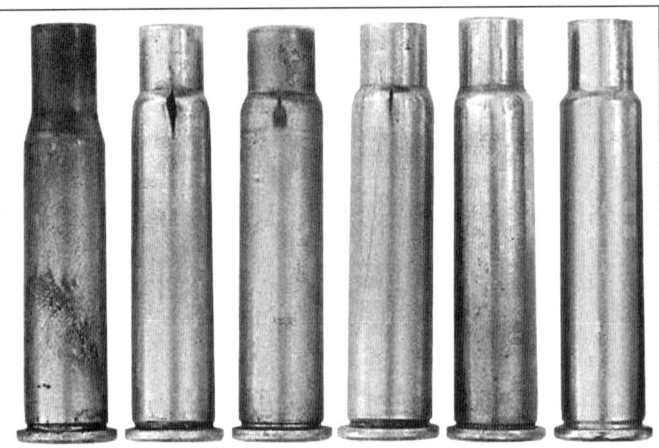

Examples of 30-30 cases after an attempt to fireform into 30-30 Ackley Improved configuration. When fireforming cases to fit an improved chamber, always use full-power loads; the maximum recommended charge for the same component combination when used in a standard chamber is usually the best choice. Failure to use a heavy enough load always results in case failures or unsatisfactory case forming. Cases, from left to right, with loads generating increasing pressure: failed to seal chamber, essentially unaltered; expanded slightly, large crack at shoulder; almost fills chamber, small crack at shoulder; similar result; case held but not fully expanded; case held and fits chamber perfectly. As pressure generated by the fireforming load increases, case straightness and concentricity increase.

A simple-to-accomplish example is conversion of Norma 7mm Mauser cases for use in a factory-chambered 6mm Remington rifle. Converting these thicker-necked 7mm cases to 6mm creates a situation where, even in a relatively loose-necked 6mm chamber, it will be necessary to turn the case neck to achieve adequate neck-to-chamber clearance. In this way, the handloader can create cases with concentric necks that also closely fit a factory chamber. This creates a chambering situation that is similar to what we would obtain when using standard cases in a tight-necked, custom-chambered rifle. Many similar conversions are feasible, given a few special tools and a bit of skill and imagination.

For example, a tinkering handloader can form 308 Winchester cases from 30-06 Springfield cases. With proper neck turning, he could create cases with a benchrest fit in any standard 308 chamber. We can accomplish many such conversions using nothing more complicated than the correct progression of sizing dies, which we might well already own. However, we must sequester any such ammunition to prevent possible use in any gun where adequate neck-to-chamber clearance might not exist.

Consider converting the 7x57mm Mauser to 6mm Remington. Depending upon how many steps proved necessary to avoid case damage, we might first size the case neck down by running it fully into a 257 Roberts seating die; then, we could switch to the 257 full-length sizing die, and, finally, to the 6mm sizing die. Once we had sized the case in the 6mm die, we would expand the neck as necessary to use a neck turning tool. We would then proceed to outside-turn the neck to a uniform, albeit greater-than-typical, thickness. We would then seat a bullet and measure neck clearance. Refer to "Case Improvement—Neck Turning and Neck Reaming" in this chapter. To assure sufficient clearance, generally, we should adjust neck thickness to achieve a minimum of 0.002 inch total neck-to-chamber clearance.

A similar conversion of excellent Norma-made 7mm Mauser cases to fit a 7-08 Remington chamber allows creation of a tight-neck case fit and a neck length that correctly matches the chamber. Refer to, "Case Neck Length—Matching to Chamber" in this chapter.

Certain conversions are infeasible without proper forming dies. In some instances, it might not be possible to come up with a simple conversion that would offer thicker case necks. However, if you are serious about maximizing the accuracy potential of your stock-chambered rifle, you might want to consider this approach, where it is feasible. Various manufacturers offer myriad case-conversion-forming dies that will ease this task.

Sometimes, during (and usually after) such radical case conversion, it is a good idea to anneal the work-hardened case necks. For details on various annealing processes refer to chapter 3.

Note that safely reforming rimless bottlenecked cases to shorten the neck (and move the shoulder forward) can be tricky. The best approach is to neck the case up by several calibers and then run it into the desired full-length sizing die. The false shoulder thus created will hold headspace during subsequent fireforming.

CASE NECK LENGTH—MATCHING TO CHAMBER

Variations in chamber neck length are rather significant and, generally, the chamber neck is unnecessarily long. In many guns, it is completely safe to use much longer cases than is suggested by the maximum case length listing in any data manual. To test for this situation, purchase a proper chamber length gauge, as available from Sinclair International, Inc. This affordable tool shows exactly how long a case can grow and still be safely used in a specific gun.

FOR SAFETY, ALWAYS MAINTAIN A MINIMUM 0.015-INCH CLEARANCE BETWEEN THE CASE MOUTH AND THE BEGINNING OF THE TRANSITION BETWEEN THE CHAMBER AND THE THROAT.

I have measured chambers where the maximum safe case length is fully 0.050 inch greater than the listed maximum case length. In such instances, longer case necks can improve accuracy because, as demonstrated in the associated drawing below, an

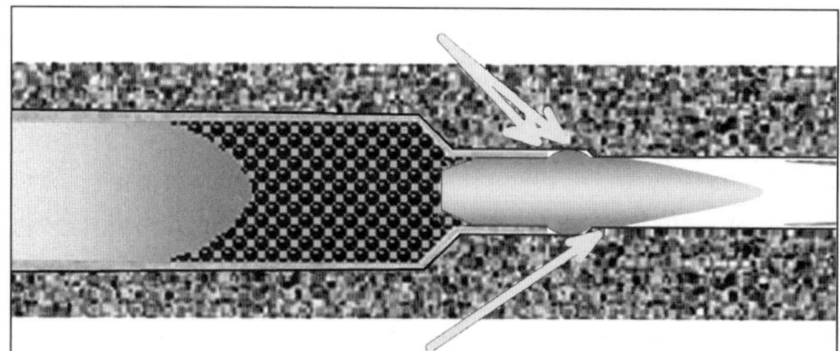

If the case neck is significantly shorter than the chamber neck and acceleration force exceeds internal bullet strength, the bullet will obturate into gap.

As the deformed bullet passes into the leade, it will necessarily be swaged smaller to fit the bore. This swelling and swaging will inevitably damage the bullet and reduce accuracy.

excessive gap between the end of the case neck and the beginning of the chamber leade can result in excessive bullet deformation during acceleration through that gap. Any such deformation inevitably degrades bullet concentricity and balance and, therefore, is detrimental to accuracy.

Moreover, most handloaders prefer to avoid spending time trimming case necks unnecessarily short. So, it can be useful to know how long case necks can actually be for safe use in any given gun and then to allow the necks to grow to approach that length before trimming.

The caveat: The handloader must provide the necessary safeguards to assure that any deliberately "over-length" cases will never be used in any gun other than one in which such cases are proven to fit safely. Such an occurrence can result in a too-long neck situation and, as noted previously, that situation can result in a major disaster. Please refer to "Case Neck Length—Safety" in this chapter.

NEVER USE CARTRIDGES THAT WERE MADE TO FIT CLOSELY INTO A SPECIFIC CHAMBER IN ANY OTHER CHAMBER.

SOURCES FOR SPECIALTY TOOLS REFERENCED IN THIS CHAPTER:

BERSIN GmbH
30 St. Jakobs-Strasse, CH-4002
Basel, Switzerland
WWW.BERSIN.INFO OR BERSIN@BERSIN.INFO

Champion's brand case cleaner and polish
www.championbrands.com
K&M Precision Shooting Products LLC
6852 Lakeshore Drive
West Olive, Michigan 49460
616-399-7894, www.kmshooting.com

SharpShoot-R Inc.
Box 171
Paola, KS 66071
Telephone: 785-883-4444
e-mail: getinfo@sharpshootr.com
www.sharpshootr.com

Sinclair International
2330 Wayne Haven Street
Fort Wayne, IN 46803 (800-717-8211)

Superior Shooting Systems
800 N. Second Street
Canadian, Texas 79014 (806-323-9483)

HOW FAR WILL A BULLET TRAVEL?

The following table is worth considering as a matter of safety when at the range or in the hunting field. I generated this table as an adjunct to a range safety evaluation done at the request of the Fifty Caliber Shooters Association. These data represent the approximate results of firing each bullet at sea level across a flat, level plain at the angle of departure that will result in maximum horizontal bullet travel. The software used in this evaluation is exceedingly accurate for such studies.

Note that many of the listed spitzer loads that are launched significantly faster than about 2,000 fps, and especially those with relatively light bullets, in any given caliber, and most of those smaller than about 30-caliber, will usually not maintain normal stability beyond the distance where the velocity of the bullet falls below the speed of sound. Usually, such bullets will begin to exhibit a periodic yaw that reaches sufficient magnitude so that it reduces effective BC to about one-half. This situation will usually hold until the bullet reaches terminal distance. Such bullets will demonstrate a significant reduction in ranging, terminal velocity, and terminal energy. However, any given bullet might, for some reason, defy this aerodynamic consequence and might, therefore, achieve the maximum (worst-case-scenario) values presented here.

Note also that expert authorities on such matters have determined that any bullet carrying more than about twenty foot-pounds of energy can inflict a potentially fatal wound to an adult human. Bullets with far less energy can do so given certain points of impact, where the brain, spine, or some other vital organ or blood vessel has inadequate protection. Children and infants are far more vulnerable.

Terminal Ranging Data: Current and Feasible Factory Ammunition

Cartridge	Bullet Type, Weight, and B.C.			Approximate: Muzzle Velocity and Maximum Range (FPS)	(Range in Yards)	Angle of Fire°	Terminal Velocity and Energy (FPS)	(Foot Pounds)
223 Remington	V-Max	40	0.200	3710	2845	30	259	6
	V-max	55	0.255	3160	3260	31	260	8
	V-Max	60	0.265	3020	3330	31	295	12
	A-Max	75	0.390	2820	4300	33	350	20
	VLD	80	0.490	2750	4790	33	390	27
6mm Remington	V-Max	58	0.275	3600	3540	31	300	12
	A-Max	105	0.500	2800	5030	33	390	35
308 Winchester	V-Max	110	0.280	3175	3510	31	300	22
	V-Max	155	0.460	2785	4710	33	380	50
	HPBT	168	0.462	2675	4680	33	380	54
	HPBT	190	0.533	2500	5050	34	400	68
300 Winchester Magnum	V-Max	155	0.460	3200	4930	32	380	50
	HPBT	168	0.462	3100	4900	32	380	54
	HPBT	190	0.533	2950	5320	33	405	69
	HPBT	240	0.711	2625	6040	34	450	108
338 Lapua Magnum	SBT	250	0.565	3050	5550	33	415	96
	Match	275	0.780	2850	6650	34	480	140
	HPBT	300	0.768	2800	6460	34	470	147
	HPBT	400	1.024	2450	7460	35	530	249
416 Weatherby Magnum	HPBT	300	0.465	3100	4920	32	380	96
	HPBT	350	0.540	2875	5300	33	405	127
	HPBT	400	0.620	2700	5700	34	430	164
50 BMG	Speer	647	0.700	3000	6300	33	455	297
	Barnes	750	1.070	2800	7680	34	530	468
	A-Max	750	1.050	2800	7840	34	540	486
	Barnes	800	1.095	2700	7960	34	545	528

These data represent maximum ranging potential for typical sea-level conditions. Most high-velocity bullets will not actually travel this far nor carry this much energy at terminal range because most such bullets will lose stability when velocity falls below the speed of sound. These data assume the worst-case scenario: when the bullet does not lose stability. Nevertheless, obviously, any fired bullet is always dangerous; most of these carry potentially life-threatening energy at any distance. We can never be too cautious.

CASE FAILURES OF VARIOUS TYPES

Left-to-right: 30-30, partial separation; dissected 30-30, showing thinning near web; 8mm Mauser, evidently fired in a 270 Winchester chamber!; tarnished 280 Remington, showing stretching (bright ring). (Folks can be phenomenally ingenuous at forcing the wrong ammunition into a gun and making it fire, and the number who get away with this sort of thing is amazing.)

LOADING THE CARTRIDGE CASE

CHAPTER 5

INTRODUCTION

Reloading includes one major aspect not necessarily found in handloading: Those alterations of a previously used case that are necessary to prepare it to accept a new primer and bullet (some of these steps are, or might be also, necessary or helpful when loading a new, unused, case). Here, I will further explore advanced case preparation and loading steps that handloaders can take to assure that their reloads deliver the superior performance that warrants the moniker handloads. These include steps intended to increase accuracy, case life, cartridge dependability, and safety.

With each reloading, cases require some sort of resizing—at the very minimum, enough neck sizing to hold a bullet in place during handling (the noted exception is certain blackpowder target cartridges used immediately after loading and requiring no sizing of any kind). Cases used in most types of loads require periodic full-length resizing. This keeps the case body short enough, and small enough in diameter, to assure easy chambering. After many cycles of reloading and firing, case necks harden sufficiently so that annealing becomes necessary to restore proper functioning and prevent splitting. Annealing thereby extends case life. I covered each of these subjects in chapter 3.

Generally, decapping (removing the used primer) occurs during resizing—others have noted that very few primers work properly the second time. Also, attempting to seat a primer on top of a used primer is both fruitless and dangerous—the resulting crushing can detonate the live primer.

It is often advantageous to adjust headspace by altering the full-length sizing operation; this can reduce case stretching and improve cartridge-to-chamber fit and, therefore, accuracy. Partial case resizing is an important method of improving accuracy. While case neck annealing can be an important case preparation step, more often, it is associated with repeated case reloading. Refer to chapter 3.

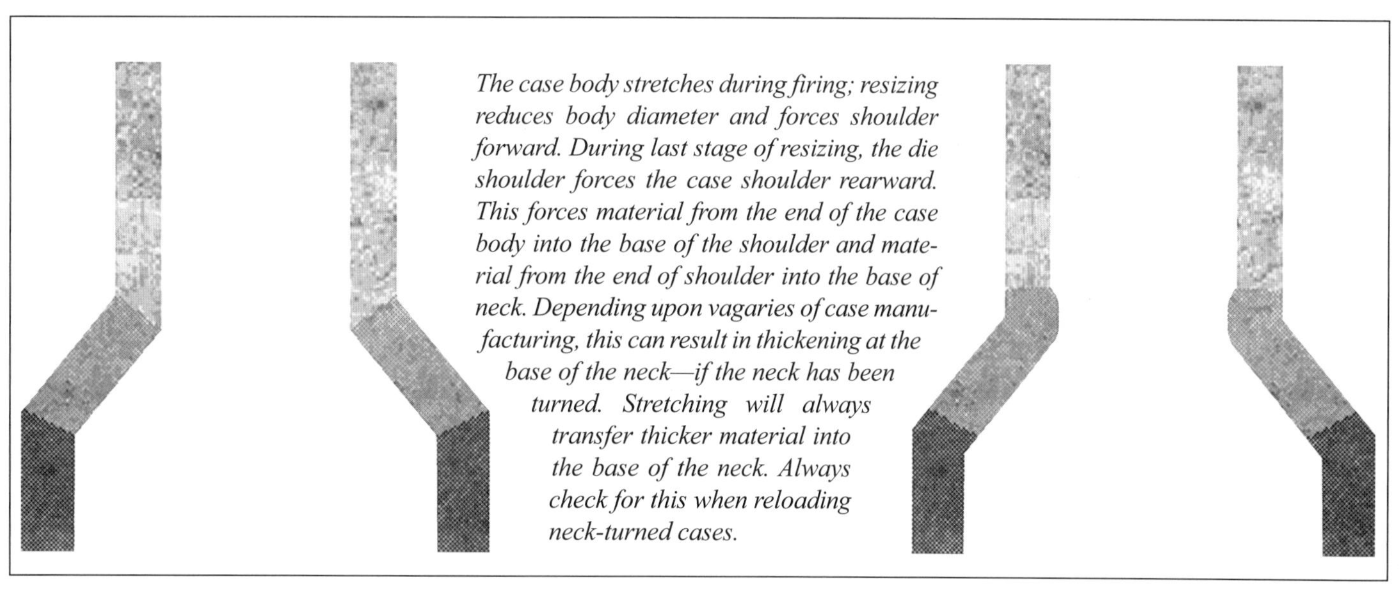

The case body stretches during firing; resizing reduces body diameter and forces shoulder forward. During last stage of resizing, the die shoulder forces the case shoulder rearward. This forces material from the end of the case body into the base of the shoulder and material from the end of shoulder into the base of neck. Depending upon vagaries of case manufacturing, this can result in thickening at the base of the neck—if the neck has been turned. Stretching will always transfer thicker material into the base of the neck. Always check for this when reloading neck-turned cases.

After one, or a few, normal full-length resizing operations, most bottlenecked cases require trimming to maintain acceptable case length. I describe the following operation in chapter 3: "Case Maintenance—Trimming to Proper Length." After each trimming operation, cases that initially were neck-turned might again require neck turning, and we analyze that operation in chapter 4: "Case Improvement—Neck Turning and Neck Reaming" and in the associated section on "Neck Turning—Dreaded Doughnut." For handloads where the bullet shank extends completely to the bottom of the case neck, neck-turned cases that significantly stretch with each firing will require neck turning after each resizing. See sketch on page 77.

As the case stretches, what had been shoulder material adjacent to the case neck moves forward to become material that makes up the back end of the neck. The transfer of material into the neck might require outside turning to achieve proper thickness and concentricity; otherwise, if the base of the seated bullet shank extends into this unturned portion of the neck, the bullet will sit crookedly in the chamber and the case neck might lack sufficient clearance to properly release the bullet. Both conditions compromise accuracy; the latter condition creates an unsafe situation. In loads where the bullet shank does not protrude completely to the rear of the case neck, handloaders can postpone additional neck turning. However, when the seated bullet shank approaches the thicker portion of the neck (near the shoulder), neck turning becomes necessary.

UNDERSTANDING HEADSPACE

Headspace is the single dimensional cartridge characteristic of greatest concern to handloaders. Headspace describes potential endwise movement of a chambered cartridge case. For our purposes, I will define headspace as the distance a chambered cartridge can (freely) move forward and backward. Lacking some amount of positive headspace, it would be difficult or impossible to chamber the cartridge and lock the action. However, if headspace is excessive, a chambered cartridge might not fire, or, upon firing, the case might separate. Either result could have devastating consequences. Obviously, headspace is a critical characteristic of any cartridge and gun combination. The important consideration here is how each case design controls headspace.

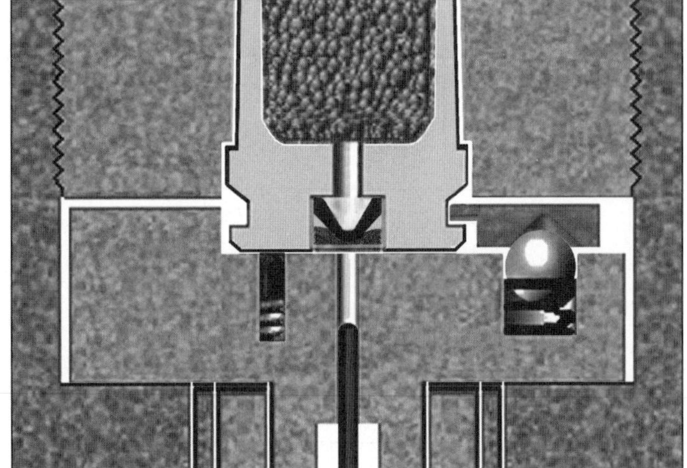
With belted and rimmed cases, headspace control nominally relies upon the belt (or rim) and corresponding chamber recess (or flat) area at back of chamber.

A bullet seated out far enough to impinge against the rifling when the round is chambered can impede the forward movement of the cartridge. This has been suggested for certain fireforming operations (case alterations) where the case is not otherwise properly headspaced. However, this is not a dependable headspacing method because either the striker impact or the force of the primer explosion is apt to drive the case forward onto the bullet, regardless of neck tension, and thereby create a potentially unsafe headspace situation. For this reason, I cannot recommend long bullet seating as the only means of controlling headspace during fireforming.

For this discussion, I will consider the belted-magnum case as a rimmed type (which it is). By design, rimmed (and belted) cartridges normally headspace on the rim. On most bottlenecked-belted cases, producers

Case body stretching leads to case separations, as represented here. Excessive body shortening during resizing effectively increases headspace. This leads to excessive stretching and shortens case life.

are supposed to control rim thickness to between 0.212 and 0.220 inch. Gun manufacturers are supposed to control depth of the rim cut in the gun chamber to between 0.220 and 0.225 inch. Hence, when chambered in a maximum chamber, a minimum case will have 0.015 inch headspace. This is entirely too much headspace to provide best accuracy and good case life. Worst yet, either or both of these dimensions can vary from these nominal values, i.e., thin rims and deep chamber rim cuts do occur; hence, actual functional headspace sometimes (often?) exceeds 0.015 inch.

The situation is similar with conventional rimmed cases. I have measured rim thickness on hundreds of rimmed cases. Norma cases always have a rim thickness very close to SAAMI maximum specification. Conversely, U.S. made cases often have rims that are between about 0.004 to about 0.006 inch thinner than the SAAMI minimum specification. Typically, when using U.S. made cases, guns chambered for rimmed cases will have about 0.012-inch headspace, often more.

Factory conventional bottlenecked cartridges might well have similar headspace. After firing, normal full-length resizing (using a standard die and shellholder) typically reduces headspace to a more reasonable 0.006 inch after firing.

Handloaders can measure effective headspace accurately by using any of several sophisticated (relatively expensive) tools, addressed later. Meanwhile, in most guns, and with most case designs, we can get a reasonably accurate headspace measurement by applying layers of inexpensive cellophane tape to the case head. Trim each layer so that it does not protrude past the bevel at the perimeter of the flat portion of the case head.

Cellophane tape thickness is extremely uniform and, depending upon maker and type, is always a specific thickness. For example, Scotch Brand tape is 0.002-inch thick. Apply one layer over the head of a fully resized case and attempt to chamber that case and fully close the bolt. If the bolt closes freely, apply a second layer and test again. Repeat this process until the bolt will not freely close. Then remove the stack of tape and measure the thickness, using a micrometer. We can characterize measured functional-headspace as follows:

- Greater than about 0.025 inch, potentially very dangerous—can cause a case separation upon firing (even on a new case)
- 0.015 to about 0.025 inch, excessive—case life will be only a few loading and firing cycles
- 0.008 to about 0.015 inch, excessive—will significantly reduce case life
- 0.005 to 0.008 inch, typical—will reduce case life
- 0.003 to 0.005 inch, unusually tight—promotes long case life and accuracy
- <0.003 inch, might cause chambering difficulties—not recommended for anything other than target or varminting use.

In rimmed bottlenecked cases, the handloader can easily eliminate excessive headspace by moving headspace control to the case shoulder, which is generally preferable for best accuracy and case life. As I will cover in the following sections, when using conventional dies, the only worthwhile, repeatable, and precise method of adjusting headspace depends upon the use of Redding Competition Shellholders, which increase minimum separation between the base of the case and the base of the sizing die during case resizing. By using the appropriate Competition shellholder, the handloader can create ammunition with reduced and uniform headspace in any given gun. However, such ammunition will not necessarily properly fit any other gun. I cover this later in this chapter, under "Headspace—Competition Shellholders."

In rimless and semirimmed, straight or tapered case designs (e.g., 45 ACP, 9mm Luger, 38 Super Auto, 30-carbine, etc.), case length controls headspace—the case mouth abuts a shoulder at the end of the chamber. Obviously, in these guns, case length is critical. Trimming any such case more than about 0.005-inch shorter than maximum design length compromises both headspace and functionality. Similarly, never apply a roll crimp to any case designed to headspace on the case mouth. For crimping, use a taper-crimp die. These generate only a modest taper at the case mouth so that crimping does not reduce the case mouth diameter more than about 0.005 inch. Hence, because the case mouth of these cases is always at least 0.010-inch thick, a taper-crimp die cannot reduce the case-mouth diameter below the chamber-shoulder diameter.

In all other case designs, the headspace is controlled on the case shoulder. This class includes most rifle chamberings. As with rimmed or belted bottlenecked cases, the handloader can adjust shoulder placement by choosing the correct shellholder from the Redding Competition set, as required by the specific combination of sizing die and gun chamber.

ADJUSTING HEADSPACE— AN OLD WIVES' TALE?

You might have read or heard that you can effectively alter headspace of a bottlenecked case by simply adjusting the full-length sizing die so that it does not touch the fully raised shellholder. This is an interesting theory, and it is certainly true that this will increase the body length of a resized case.

However, tests prove that this method simply does not work well. Unless the shellholder solidly abuts the sizing die, inevitable variations in press stretching—resulting from variations in case lubrication and hardness and operator technique—always result in increased case-to-case variation in headspace length. Cases with varying amounts of headspace are certain to produce inconsistent (inaccurate) cartridges. The degree of case-to-case variation depends upon case and press rigidity.

During full-length resizing with a typical press, potential press flexing easily exceeds 0.015 inch. The degree of flexing depends entirely upon case-sizing resistance, which varies from case to case. Specifically, the amount of press flexing (stretching) depends upon the stress associated with resizing each case; this, in turn, depends upon case body thickness and hardness, degree and quality of lubrication, operator technique (how fast one forces the case into the die), and who knows what else. The important fact is that the resizing stress on the press will never be identical from one case to the next.

For this reason, when the shellholder reaches the top of the ram stroke and if it does not abut the die base solidly, the case-body length in any batch of resized cases will vary, and the case-to-case functional headspace will differ. This situation cannot contribute to accuracy. Commonly, case-to-case headspace variation will exceed 0.002 inch.

As a nascent handloader in the 1970s, I tested this technique with loads for my 270 Winchester chambered Remington, Model-760 (pump-action) rifle. Compared to cartridges created with the die solidly abutting the shellholder, cartridges produced with the resizing die screwed back slightly produced groups that were fully twice as large.

Consistency is the key. Having a loose case-to-chamber fit is not ideal for accuracy; however, that situation is far superior to having some cases generate a very tight fit, other cases provide a very loose fit, and all other cases fitting somewhere between those extremes. Such a situation is bound to occur when the shellholder does not solidly abut the die.

Those who have never handloaded for any rifle other than a bolt-action might never have noticed this accuracy-limiting problem. The bolt-action camming system can mask case-to-case headspace variation and mitigate the loss of accuracy, but the problem still exists, and it is always detrimental to accuracy. However, I suspect that with the smallest and weakest cases (such as the Hornet) this might not matter when using a heavy-duty press.

Using Redding Competition Shellholders and a bit of fitting, as I cover later in this chapter under "Headspace—Competition Shellholders," you can precisely adjust full-length sizing to give so little functional headspace that case trimming will never be needed (quite useful for match-grade rifles).

HEADSPACE—FULL-LENGTH SIZING

When considering the manufacture of guns and ammunition, headspace has a specific definition and we always measure it in a specific way. However, for handloaders (functional), headspace is quite different, this is merely the distance that a chambered cartridge can move fore and aft when the action is fully closed. This latter is the intended connotation in most of the themes in this manual.

As noted previously, with many belted or rimmed bottlenecked cases, handloaders obtain best accuracy and case life when using case resizing tools that shift headspace control to the case shoulder. Whenever referring to any bottlenecked case, I will henceforth refer to case head-to-shoulder length as the case headspace datum, regardless of case type or nominal headspacing design.

Before performing various uniforming steps, as noted in chapters 3 and 4, we assumed initial full-length case sizing. Full-length sizing is a good idea regardless of case source. Unless the handloader is working with factory-load cases fired in the gun for which he is handloading, full-length resizing is a necessary step before he can properly accomplish any other processing steps. Full-length resizing assures that all cases will chamber easily. (By forcing the bolt closed on a too-long case, shooters have damaged bolt-action rifles—the resulting stress can gall the locking surfaces.) Understanding this, we should consider what else standard full-length case resizing could do.

For starters, full-length resizing almost certainly creates a case with some degree of unnecessary functional headspace. Excessive headspace shortens case life, usually reduces accuracy, and usually results in case stretching (which necessitates periodic trimming). Full-length resizing assures that the case will fit in any like-chambered gun by reducing the case-body diameter and length so that the case is smaller than the chamber. Moreover, normal resizing excessively works the case neck, first making it smaller than necessary, and then enlarging it to accept a bullet properly. This two-step process eases the bullet seating while assuring adequate bullet pull (neck-to-bullet tension). For ammunition used for big-game hunting or for self-defense, this is as

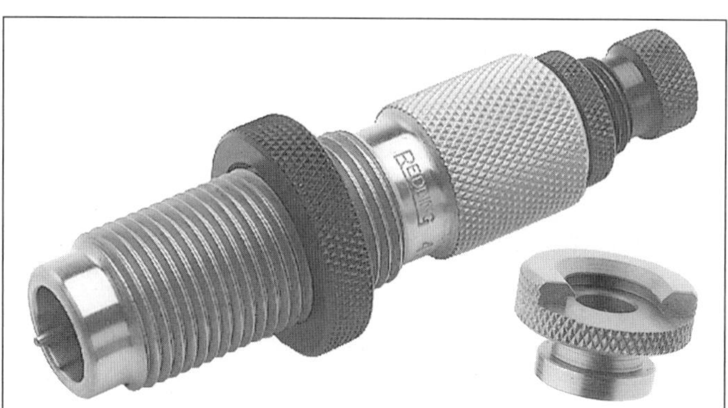

When used with standard shellholders, full-length sizing dies usually resize cases to give about 6/1000-inch headspace in a sporting chamber—variation is significant.

it should be. Conversely, for most target and varminting ammunition, and to some extent for big-game hunting ammunition, we can do better. Three main subjects come to mind:

- Die and shellholder adjustment, for optimal headspace control
- Die alignment, for optimal case concentricity
- Consistent case lubrication, to minimize and equalize case resizing friction. (Proper lubrication minimizes variation in press and die flexing and, thus, improves headspace uniformity within a group of resized cases.)

Theoretically, producers design and build shellholders and full-length sizing dies to maintain proper headspace automatically.

A proper full-length sizing die adjustment requires that the handloader thread the die into the press far enough so that the shellholder makes very solid contact with the base of the die while resizing the case.

This is all fine and good, providing the existence of ideal dimensioning of die, shellholder, and rifle chamber. However, even if the various producers do meet the headspacing criteria, generally, this procedure still introduces an unnecessary amount of headspace. Producers intend this result.

Ample headspace assures that all full-length resized cases will fit into all guns chambered for that cartridge. Typically, producers try to create a situation where full-length resizing sets the case shoulder back between about 0.002 inch and about 0.006 inch farther than would be necessary for the case to precisely fit a chamber that had been cut to match minimum SAAMI headspace specification. This provides for assurance of easy chambering of resized cases in any correctly chambered gun.

However, should your gun have an unusually short chamber, one that is only 0.002-inch longer than the SAAMI minimum specification (most factory chambers are actually close to maximum length), you will be loading cases with at least 0.004-inch headspace. In truth, built-in tolerances more often add up to about 0.006 inch. This is not dangerous, but it can shorten case life and result in the need for more frequent case trimming, and it might limit potential accuracy of the resulting cartridges.

Often, the situation is much worse with bottlenecked versions of belted-magnum cases. Nominally, the headspace of a belted case is determined by the front of the case belt, which is nothing more than a wide rim with an extractor groove cut near the aft end. For this reason, manufacturers have played notoriously fast and loose with body length dimensions of bottlenecked-belted-magnum cases and chambers. Commonly, manufacturers have cut the chamber base-to-shoulder length on the long side and the sizing die base-to-shoulder length on the short side. In a typical rifle, it is not unusual for the shoulder of a normally full-length, resized-belted-magnum case to be an astounding 0.030-inch short of touching the chamber shoulder.

Recall that case manufacturers often make the belt too short and that gun manufacturers often cut the chamber belt recess too deep so that headspace is commonly near a whopping 0.015 inch. This seems odd, considering the chamber pressures normally employed in such numbers, which are among the highest pressures used in commercial cartridges.

Because the belt controls headspace, excess clearance between shoulders of case and chamber does not necessarily create an imminent safety problem. Upon firing, chamber pressure simply shoves the case shoulder forward until it hits the chamber shoulder. This fireforming process is not, in itself, dangerous. Unfortunately, this action also generally shoves the case walls somewhat forward. Hence, commonly, firing the round stretches and thins the case body. This is very similar to what the handloader would see if the case had stretched because of excess headspace, except that this thinning often occurs much farther forward on the case body.

This characteristic combines with the commonly greater-than-necessary headspace to cause a tremendous amount of case body stretching. Hence, when using conventional loading techniques and tools, cases used in belted-magnum-chambered rifles often separate after the third or fourth reloading. My friend, Allan Jones (formerly of Speer) told of a coworker who purchased a factory rifle and matching ammunition to go elk hunting. At the range, the hapless hunter found that every round fired created a partial case separation. Such a situation represents a recipe for disaster. (Interestingly, the rifle, chambering, and ammunition all shared the same company name.)

Fortunately, this general problem is easy to solve. When working with belted-magnum-bottlenecked or rimmed-bottlenecked cases, it is both easy and desirable to move headspace control to the case shoulder. This alteration generally improves accuracy, it always improves case life, it can eliminate the need to trim cases, and it certainly increases the safety factor. Whether belted, rebated, rimmed, or rimless, it is generally advantageous to minimize headspace in all cartridges intended for use in a specific gun. Useful minimum headspace depends upon the application:

- Dangerous-game hunting, >0.006 inch;
- Big-game hunting, 0.004 to 0.006 inch;
- Varminting, 0.002 to 0.004 inch;
- Target rifles used in rapid-fire events, about 0.003 inch
- Benchrest target rifles, less than 0.002 inch (often practically zero!)

Assuming that your shellholder and die are initially square and true, stoning the top of the shellholder and the bottom of the sizing die to a smooth finish using a very fine and flat sharpening stone is a worthwhile alteration. Only remove burs or high spots, nothing more, else you will be increasing the functional headspace of resized cases. The goal is to remove possible high spots generated by operations such as stamping a number on the shellholder. This finishing touch will eliminate bending stresses that will tend to tip the die as the shellholder abuts the die. In addition, it will reduce variability resulting from where the die happens to stop turning when you screw it into the press, and upon specific shellholder orientation. Consistency counts.

ADJUSTING HEADSPACE—REDDING COMPETITION SHELLHOLDERS

Redding Competition Shellholders come in sets, which are available in most common case sizes. Shellholders in each competition set are individually marked with the basic Redding number (indicating the case family that each shellholder in the set fits) with an additional marking indicating shellholder length. In the standard set of five, these markings are +.002, +.004, +.006, +.008, and +.010. These marks specify the additional thickness (in thousandths of an inch), of each shellholder, beyond the industry standard thickness (0.125 inch for most applications). This thickness (0.125 inch plus the additional amount specified [e.g., 0.008 inch]) represents the distance from the recessed face of the shellholder (where the case head rests) to the top surface of the shellholder. Increasing this dimension prevents the shellholder from driving the case as deeply into the resizing die and, thereby, results in a greater case body length after full-length resizing. This, in turn, reduces functional headspace.

Redding also offers noncataloged individual custom shellholders with increased thickness. These include belted-magnum shellholders, up to at least +0.030-inch thickness. When working with a gun and die combination that is far out of specification, such a shellholder is a worthwhile investment.

Selecting the correct shellholder from the Competition set is a simple matter. Begin with a batch

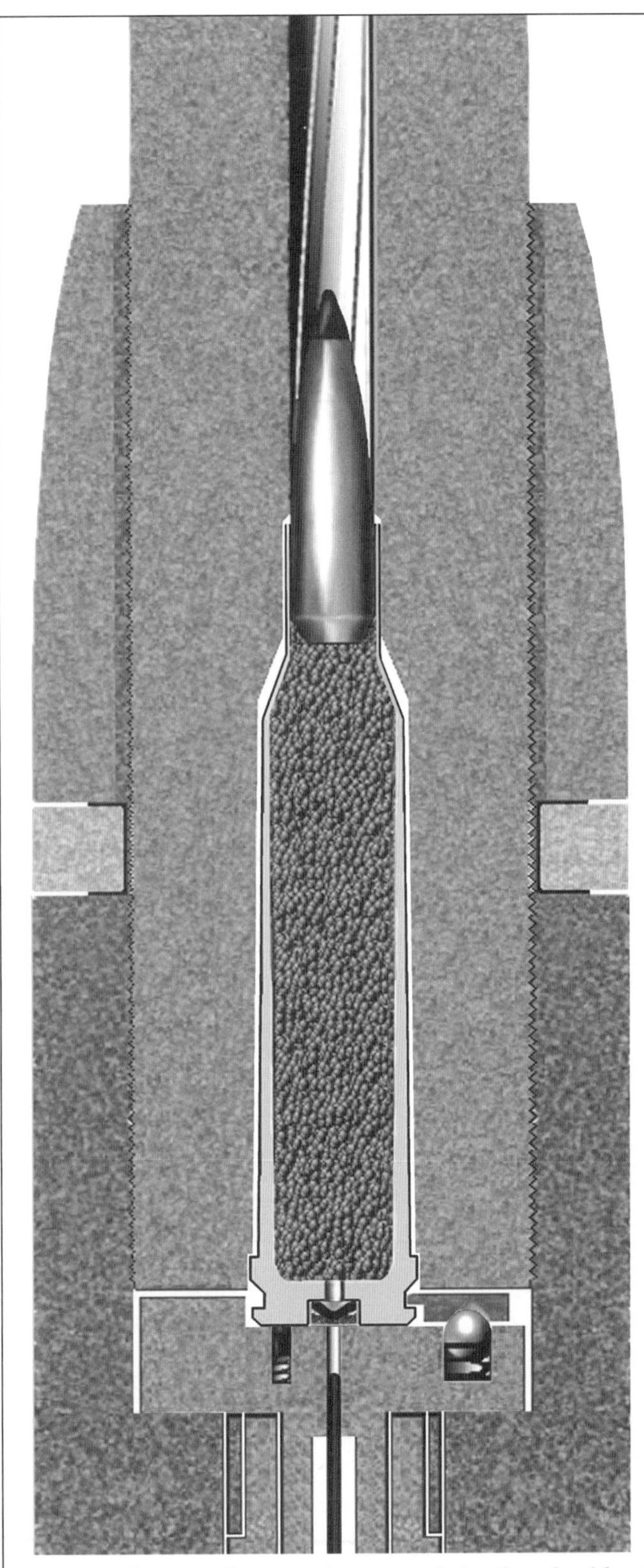

Excessive clearance between the case and chamber shoulder is common in belted-bottlenecked chamberings. Often, clearance is sufficient to lead to case separations after only a few uses of the case. Moving the headspace control to the case shoulder usually improves accuracy and case life.

of fired cases from normal full-power cartridges that have been fired in the intended rifle. Carefully clean and lubricate each fired case. Install the +.010 shellholder in the press. Adjust the full-length sizing die so that when you fully raise the ram, the shellholder abuts the die base very solidly. Correct adjustment is such that when you resize a case, the shellholder still abuts the die solidly, despite the strain from case sizing. If it does not, you must turn the die farther into the press.

Size a case and wipe it free of lube. Then attempt to chamber it. Normally (unless the die is very short or the chamber is very long, which often happens with belted-magnum cases but rarely otherwise), the body of the resized case will be too long to allow the bolt to close freely. Very possibly, you can force the bolt closed but that is not the point; the bolt should close freely. If the bolt does close freely, you have found the correct shellholder, or at least the best fit within the standard Competition

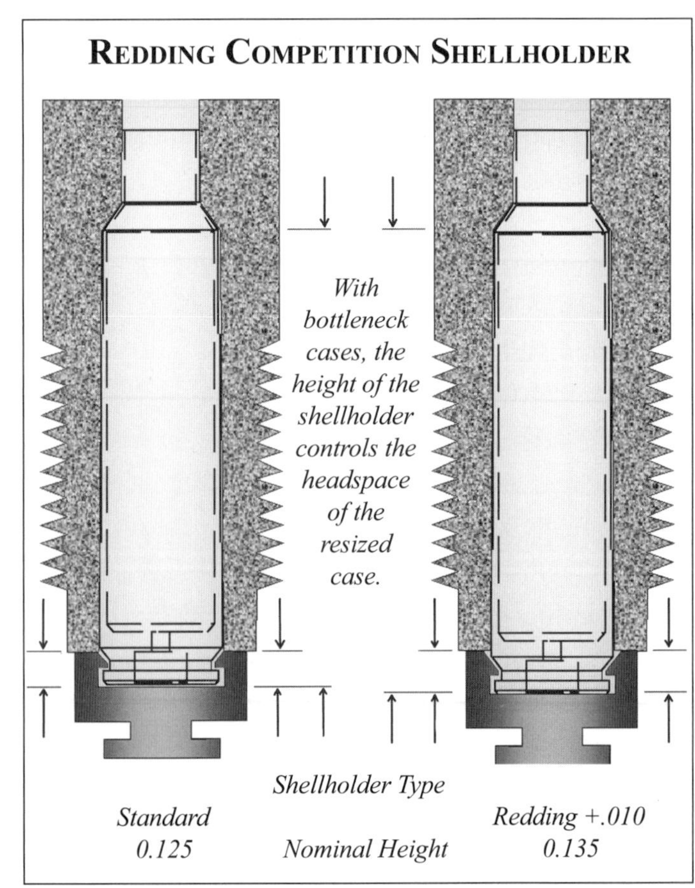

set—with that resizing die, the +.010 shellholder is the best you can do for that rifle. (Redding can and often will make thicker shellholders, to customer specification—do not be shy and do be patient, these shellholders are produced on an as-can basis.)

More likely, the bolt will not freely close on the +.010-resized case. If so, lubricate the same case, install the +.008 shellholder and, again, fully resize the case. Clean lubricant from the case and try to chamber it. If the case freely chambers, the +.008 shellholder provides some clearance. If the case will not freely chamber, repeat this sequence. (Test and, if necessary, size using the next shorter shellholder from the set.) Continue until you find the shellholder that provides free chambering. Then, using the same shellholder, resize several more fired cases and test those for free chambering.

It could occur that some resized cases will chamber freely and others will not. In that situation, you should opt for the next-shorter shellholder. Also, it could occur that, to maintain free chambering of all cases, different cases (or the same cases after cycling through repeated reloading and firing cycles) might require use of the next-shorter shellholder. When this occurs, either switch to the next-shorter shellholder or anneal the case neck and shoulder area—the latter is usually a better solution. (It is also feasible to shorten the almost-short-enough shellholder to achieve an ideal fit.)

When considering accuracy and functionality, free chambering is particularly critical. Hence, it is much better to resize all cases 0.002-inch shorter than necessary rather than to have some that are slightly snug in the chamber with others that are a loose fit in the chamber. When in doubt, always use the next shorter shellholder from the set.

Keep in mind that the above suggestions, toward minimizing functional headspace, are not appropriate for ammunition that anyone might use in dangerous-game hunting situations. When an enraged grizzly charges from the brush at twenty yards, any potential reduction in case life or accuracy resulting from having a few-thousandths-inch extra headspace is a meaningless price when balanced against the added security of assured functionality.

Redding offers a handy shellholder box. This is particularly useful for storing Competition Shellholder sets, as illustrated here.

Once you have established the correct Competition shellholder for a given combination of gun and die, create a permanent record to indicate which die and shellholder set works best for that rifle. One method is to use an electric carbide scribe to write on top of the full-length resizing die, for example:

"Rem—7600 + .006 CS"

Note: The common spring-loaded, plunger-type ejector can make it difficult, perhaps impossible, to feel the exact point of free case chambering. Such an ejector pushes the case away from the bolt face. Likely, you will feel the ejector spring tension instead of the case fit. To do this operation <u>precisely</u> in a rifle with that ejection system, you might need to temporarily remove the plunger. Although this is neither a simple nor an easy task, most reasonably skilled gun-tinkerers *can do this with only a vise, a properly sized punch, and a small ball peen hammer. As you remove the assembly pin, beware of potentially ejected parts and be careful not to lose parts.*

Before reassembling the bolt, you might consider slightly shortening the extractor-plunger spring. This spring is usually far stronger than is necessary for most applications. However, if you might use this gun while hunting dangerous game, this latter step is ill advised because it might impair rapid and dependable case ejection. On the other hand, some competitive shooters believe that a shorter, weaker spring that still provides positive ejection is beneficial because, compared to the full power spring such a spring reduces canting force on the chambered case and closed bolt, factors that are detrimental to accuracy.

When correctly set up, the Redding Instant Indicator precisely compares headspace of fired and resized cases with extreme comparative precision. With the right accessories, this tool has many other uses, such as measuring effective shellholder height and relative bullet-to-rifling jump.

Redding offers the Instant Indicator, a handy tool that, among other uses, measures case headspace, before and after resizing. This makes it quite simple to precisely determine amount of case shoulder setback resulting from use of any given die and shellholder. RCBS offers the Precision Mic (pronounced mike, as in micrometer), which also does this job.

FULL LENGTH SIZING— KEEPING IT SIMPLE

If matching sized case headspace to chamber headspace (as described in the preceding sections) seems to be too much work, simply adjust the die until the standard shellholder hits it solidly when you fully raise the ram while resizing a case. This approach is likely to shorten case life and to reduce accuracy potential, slightly, but it will size every case as identically as is feasible and it will assure that all cases will fit any normal gun. Experts have long since proven that accuracy is far more dependent upon round-to-round consistency than it is upon an unusually close case-to-chamber fit.

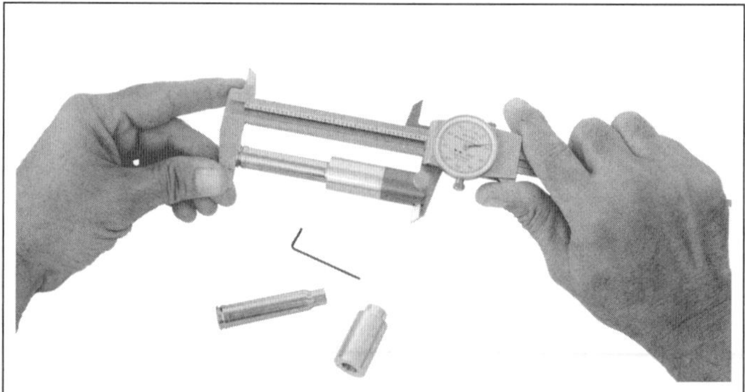

Stoney Point Headspace Tool is handy, compact, and convenient. When used with a digital caliper, it provides a comparison of headspace before and after resizing, and does so in a matter of seconds.

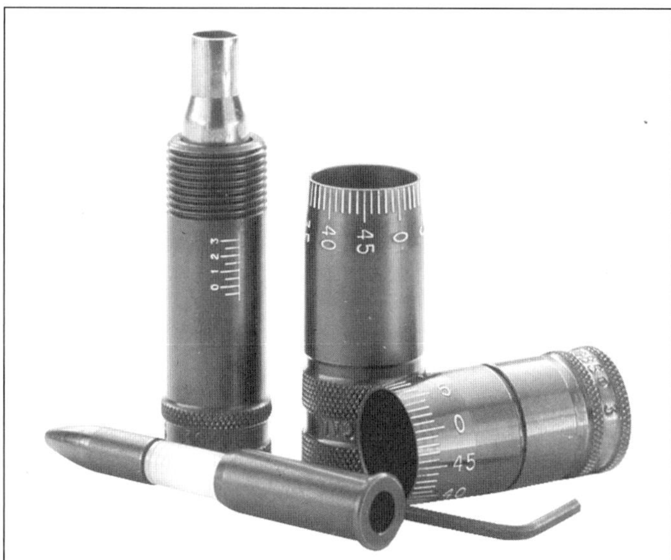

RCBS Precision Mic provides accurate, functional headspace measurements of fired and resized cases. When selecting the correct Redding Competition Shellholder, this is a useful alternative to the trial-and-error approach.

IMPROVING DIE-TO-PRESS ALIGNMENT

It is useful to install a rubber O-ring between the press and the die lock ring. This provides a springy platform and might allow the die to achieve better alignment with the shellholder, thereby minimizing the possibility of bending the case head out of square with the case body. Such O-rings are readily available at hardware stores. Choose one with significant thickness and a diameter that produces a friction fit around the die body. As an alternative, use Lee Locking Rings, which incorporate such an O-ring and are otherwise quite desirable.

NECK TENSION (BULLET PULL)—GENERAL CONSIDERATIONS

It is important to recognize that, for most types of ammunition (perhaps with the single exception of benchrest ammunition that competitors load immediately prior to use), we practically always obtain maximum accuracy when using maximum neck tension. Increasing neck tension is always beneficial, so long as doing so does not result in bullet distortion during seating (due to insufficient bullet hardness) or case shoulder bending (due either to misalignment between bullet and case during seating or to asymmetric case shoulder strength).

Consider a novice NRA Highpower competitor who had an accuracy problem related to neck tension. He had been using a load that routinely generated near minute-of-angle (MOA) accuracy. However, he wanted to increase the number of shots he could fire without barrel cleaning, so he switched to molybdenum-disulfide plated bullets. Thereafter, he was hard-pressed to keep his shots inside three MOA. (When properly applied to a bullet, molybdenum-disulfide significantly reduces friction between bullet and case neck and, therefore, reduces the force needed to move the bullet.)

A recommended change to a milder primer shrank his groups to less than one inch. Then, by reducing neck expander diameter from 0.307-inch to 0.305-inch, he solved the root problem (insufficient bullet pull) and he began to shoot the smallest groups of his life—neck tension matters! See "Altering Expander—Diameter."

Fundamentally, the hot primer (great brisance—explosive force) of his original load did not cause this accuracy problem. The problem was the varying and inadequate bullet pull (round-to-round bullet pull can never be identical). With a plated bullet, in some rounds, the blast from the hot primer moved the bullet into the rifling and, in other rounds, neck tension held the bullet in place until charge combustion generated sufficient force to dislodge the bullet. Such round-to-round variation produced significantly differing muzzle velocity and barrel time. These differences limited accuracy of that load.

Because smokeless propellant is a progressive burning substance, round-to-round variations in chamber pressure at the instant when the bullet begins to move lead to continuing variations in pressure, as the bullet accelerates through the bore. Because greater pressure (force on base of bullet) causes the bullet to accelerate faster, those bullets where neck tension delays initial movement longer will reach the muzzle sooner and with greater velocity, and conversely.

Round-to-round variations in bullet pull always result in inconsistent shot-to-shot barrel times and muzzle velocities—shot-to-shot variations in barrel vibrations and velocity always degrade accuracy potential. Reducing round-to-round variation in bullet pull is, therefore, always beneficial.

NECK TENSION—HARD BULLETS

An important characteristic of accuracy and dependability for all standard ammunition is degree and consistency of bullet pull. Bullet pull is a technical term indicating the force required to move the bullet from the case, as necessary to overcome friction generated by the interference fit between the bullet and the elastic case, along with the bonding that occurs between case and bullet. For hunting and self-defense ammunition, bullet pull is a paramount consideration because it relates directly to cartridge durability and dependability—functionality. For maximizing accuracy with all types of target ammunition, consistent bullet pull is equally critical.

Especially in dies made before about 1990, the expander might be too large to give best results. While the expanders in most full-length resizing dies do an acceptable job of assuring adequate case-neck tension when using conventional bullets, reducing expander diameter can lead to the production of superior ammunition, especially when using friction-proofed bullets.

Some pistol loads using relatively slow-burning ball propellants benefit markedly from maximizing neck tension. In some instances, reducing expander diameter by up to 0.003 inch is quite beneficial. Moreover, in revolver loads generating significant recoil (anything similar to a full-power 41 Magnum, or heavier), it is practically impossible to achieve too much bullet pull—considering the importance of preventing bullets from moving out of cases, in response to recoil, and thereby jamming the gun, all the bullet pull you can get is just barely enough! Similarly, a reduction in expander diameter is desirable when producing rifle ammunition used for hunting of dangerous game. As noted, generally, so long as doing so does not result in bullet damage or in case shoulder bending during bullet seating, increasing bullet pull is always beneficial.

Decreasing inside diameter (ID) of the resized case neck by reducing expander diameter usually increases the force required to move the seated bullet. This adds to ammunition rigidity against mishandling or recoil influences in the magazine (or cylinder). However, for very complicated reasons (that I will not address in this tome), beyond some point, further reduction in sized-neck ID is of no value and can actually degrade cartridge quality.

A similar approach is useful when using a neck-bushing sizing die. Remember that case necks tend to spring back (often more than one-thousandth inch) and therefore get smaller as the expander passes out of the neck; conversely, case necks tend to enlarge a similar amount when removed from the constricting bushing. Amount of spring back depends upon neck diameter and brass hardness. Only experimentation can demonstrate the exact amount of spring back that will occur in any given case and, hence, optimum expander or bushing diameter. Refer to the following table, for recommended minimum expander and neck bushing diameters.

NECK TENSION—SOFT BULLETS

It is important to recognize that, when using unusually soft bullets, inside diameter of the resized case neck should not be more than a few ten-thousandths-inch smaller than bullet diameter. Seating soft lead bullets, such as the bullets used in black-powder and most Cowboy Action Shooting loads, into conventionally sized cases easily swages (reduces) bullet diameter to match case neck interior diameter. Seating such a bullet into a significantly

Suggested Approximate Expander and Bushing Diameters: Various Bullet Types and Sizes

<table>
<tr><th colspan="11">Bullet Diameter in Calibers (1/100 inch)</th></tr>
<tr><td><20</td><td>20–23</td><td>23–26</td><td>26–29</td><td>29–32</td><td>32–35</td><td>35–38</td><td>38–41</td><td>41–44</td><td>44–47</td><td>>47</td></tr>
<tr><td colspan="11">Best Expander (left) and Neck Bushing (right) Diameter Equals: Multiply 0.001-inch by the appropriate following value: Subtract that result from bullet diameter</td></tr>
<tr><td colspan="11">Soft Bullets (swaged lead)</td></tr>
<tr><td><⅛ | ¾</td><td>⅛ | 1</td><td><¼ | 1⅛</td><td>¼ | 1⅜</td><td><⅜ | 1½</td><td><⅜ | 1⅝</td><td><½ | 1⅞</td><td>½ | 2⅛</td><td><⅝ | 2¼</td><td>⅝ | 2½</td><td><¾ | 2⅝</td></tr>
<tr><td colspan="11">Soft Cast Bullets</td></tr>
<tr><td>>⅜ | 1⅛</td><td>½ | 1⅛</td><td><⅝ | 1½</td><td>>⅝ | 1¾</td><td>¾ | 2</td><td><⅞ | 2⅛</td><td>>⅞ | 2⅜</td><td>1 | 2⅝</td><td><1⅛ | 2¾</td><td>>1⅛ | 3</td><td>1¼ | 3¼</td></tr>
<tr><td colspan="11">Medium Cast and Soft Jacketed Bullets</td></tr>
<tr><td>⅝ | 1⅜</td><td>¾ | 1⅝</td><td>⅞ | 1⅞</td><td>1 | 2⅛</td><td>1⅛ | 2⅜</td><td>1¼ | 2⅝</td><td>1⅜ | 2⅞</td><td>1½ | 3⅛</td><td>1⅝ | 3⅜</td><td>1¾ | 3⅝</td><td>1⅞ | 3⅞</td></tr>
<tr><td colspan="11">Hard Cast and Conventional Jacketed Bullets</td></tr>
<tr><td>¾ | 1½</td><td>1 | 1⅞</td><td>1⅛ | 2⅛</td><td>1⅜ | 2¼</td><td>1½ | 2¾</td><td>1⅝ | 3</td><td>1⅞ | 3⅜</td><td>2 | 3⅝</td><td>2⅛ | 3⅞</td><td>2⅜ | 4¼</td><td>2½ | 4½</td></tr>
</table>

smaller case neck can seriously damage the bullet and thereby reduce accuracy potential.

When loading unusually soft bullets, the best cartridges always result from using fully annealed case necks. I covered annealing in chapter 3. Similarly, I cover the ideal degree of crimping and crimp style in chapter 11. Generally, the softer the bullet, the lighter the crimp that is beneficial.

Progressively harder bullets tolerate a progressively greater (tighter) interference fit without damage. However, as noted in the previous section, a maximum useful difference exists. When you might use bullets of widely varying hardness, in any particular caliber, it is worthwhile to have expanders of different diameters (three is usually sufficient), so you can match expander diameter to bullet hardness, in order to achieve maximum feasible bullet pull without bullet or case damage; with neck bushing dies, usually, three bushings is sufficient to accommodate most bullet types. Forster offers ex-panders in half-thousandth-inch increments for its line of dies (20-, 22-, 24-, 26-, and 30-caliber).

NECK TENSION—MEASURING

LoadForce-2000 from Recreational Software allows the handloader to measure resistance to bullet seating in real time. This sophisticated tool works with a strain gauge within the reloading press and can connect to a personal computer, to give a real-time force curve representing what happens during the bullet seating process. This unit will also work as a stand-alone device but, when used in that mode, it provides only the maximum force value.

This system removes all guesswork—so long as bullet seating does not bend the case shoulder or deform the bullet—the expander (or bushing) diameter that produces the highest readings during bullet seating is ideal for those cases and bullets.

ALTERING EXPANDER—POLISHING

A useful minimum alteration for most steel neck-expanders is polishing. With most types of sizing dies, you can accomplish this operation easily. Remove decapper and expander stem from die body and chuck that into a vised hand drill. With the drill locked on at the highest speed, fold a piece of 600-grit (or finer) sandpaper over the expander. Apply moderate pressure for a few minutes, as needed, to polish the expander to a mirror finish. Many newer expanders (e.g., Forster) do not need this step.

ALTERING EXPANDER—DIAMETER

As noted in the previous sections, when using conventional jacketed and hard-cast bullets, reducing the expander diameter can be beneficial. Refer to the table on page 89 as a guide toward determining the most likely useful diameter. Measure before and during polishing using a micrometer with 0.0001-inch accuracy. If you are loading ammunition for a heavy-kicking revolver or if you intend to use friction-proofed bullets in rifle cartridges (as with moly-plating), reducing the expander diameter is particularly critical—as noted above.

Altering hard-surfaced-plated expanders (TiN—Titanium Nitride—is a common type) is infeasible. Although you can grind through the hard surface using a diamond-impregnated cutting tool, the underlying material is often too soft to expand the case necks without galling. On the other hand, it is quite feasible, and relatively easy, to contour and decrease the diameter of hardened-steel or tungsten-carbide expanders using conventional corundum paper, for the former, and a grinding tool made with diamond, for the latter.

For hardened-steel neck expanders, chuck the expander stem into a vised drill. Then, with the drill running at full speed, begin with 220-grit corundum paper and sand until expander diameter is about one thousandth inch larger than desired. Then switch to 320-grit paper and continue sanding until diameter is about 0.0005-inch larger than desired. Then proceed with progressively finer-grit paper (to at least 600) to polish the expander surface and to attain the final desired expander diameter.

For tungsten carbide expanders, use a very-fine (polishing) diamond-impregnated, knife-sharpening tool. The technique is similar to that used with conventional hardened steel expanders. However, because tungsten carbide expanders float on the decapping stem, it is necessary to affix the ball to the stem first in order to center it and prevent it from freely turning. This can require a bit of skill and tinkering but it is feasible.

A convenient method is to clamp the stem with the decapping end vertically up. Apply a dab of quick-setting epoxy to the stem near the shoulder that supports the expander. Slide the expander onto the stem and over the epoxy and allow the epoxy a few minutes to cure. After the diameter alteration, mild heating of the expander stem with a propane torch or a hot-air gun will soften the epoxy for removal.

Left to right: Carbide expander, RCBS decapping pin-nut with expander, and replacement decapping nut.

ALTERING EXPANDER—LOCATION (HEIGHT)

Forster and Lee are the only companies that offer conventional reloading dies with the expander placed where it should be—very near the top of the body portion of the die. On other makes of bottleneck-case dies, where possible to do so, a useful expander stem alteration is to raise the expander so that case neck expansion begins as you are withdrawing the case neck from the necking portion of the die. Generally, this requires the purchase of a few spare parts and a bit of tinkering on the stem, but it is certainly worthwhile.

The combination of the original stem and the carbide-expander conversion kit (as are available from various manufacturers) includes enough parts to do this job. The process includes reducing the diameter of and threading a portion of the expander stem so that the floating expander can slide farther up the stem. As shown in the associated pictures, threading the expander stem allows installation of a smaller nut that supports the new expander (usually, one can modify an old expander to do this job). The end of the threaded section limits upward travel of the carbide expander and the replacement fixture retains the decapping pin.

The only difficulty with this modification is getting the measurement correct so that the expander is not too high in the die—positioning must provide clearance so that the case neck is not bound between the expander and the neck-sizing portion of die. On the other hand,

Converting the RCBS decapping rod to use a raised carbide expander: This requires extending existing threads farther up rod. These are standard threads, and all hobby tap-and-die sets include the needed die.

Left to right: An unaltered RCBS expander; unaltered RCBS expander stem; and altered stem. Top-to-bottom: Hornady carbide expander; modified RCBS decapping-pin nut (original expander can be modified for this purpose); and modified original expander (diameter reduced). The threading distance is critical. The goal is to raise the expander far enough up the stem so that expansion begins as soon as the neck is being pulled out of the necking portion of the die. If you move the expander too far up the stem, the expander will interfere with the case neck freely entering the necking portion of the die.

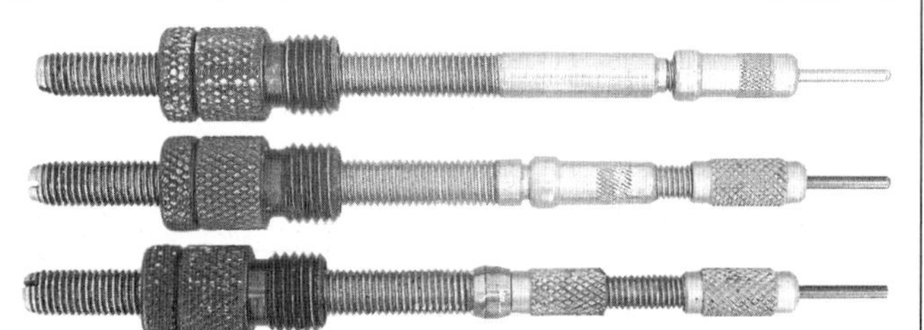

Top to bottom: Standard RCBS expander; modified RCBS raised expander for 30-30-length cases; tungsten carbide expander raised for 30-06-length cases.

Placing an O-ring between decapping stem lock nut and die body allows the rod to freely center in die. This reduces the potential for a broken decapping pin or a bent case shoulder.

the higher you can position the expander without causing interference, the better. Ideally, the top of the expander should be just below the bottom of the case neck when the case is fully inserted into the die.

This system provides several benefits. First, it can dramatically reduce the force required to pull the expander through the case neck because expansion occurs during that portion of the press handle swing with the greatest mechanical leverage. Second, because it is so much slicker than steel, the use of a tungsten carbide expander will dramatically reduce friction during neck expansion. Third, with a properly modified and adjusted expander, the case neck still comes free from the necking portion of the die when neck expansion begins. As such, the neck expansion process simply cannot bend the case shoulder, as can otherwise happen.

Modifying a standard expander rod to use a raised carbide expander is certainly worth the effort. When using such an expander, it is never necessary to lubricate the neck interior. Friction is so low and mechanical advantage is so great that you probably will not feel neck expansion occurring.

WHEN USING DIES WITH A COLLET-LOCKED DECAPPING STEM THAT IS MODIFIED TO RAISE THE EXPANDER, BE EXTREMELY CAUTIOUS TO TIGHTEN THE COLLET ADEQUATELY SO THAT THE STEM WILL NOT MOVE DURING NORMAL DIE USAGE. FAILURE TO DO SO WILL RESULT IN RUINED CASES IF THE STEM MOVES UPWARD BECAUSE THE RAISED EXPANDER WILL INTERFERE WITH CASE-NECK SIZING.

ALTERING EXPANDER—IMPROVING ALIGNMENT

When reassembling the expander onto the decapper stem on a die other than the Hornady or Lee, install a snug-fitting, rubber O-ring between the locking nut and the body of sizing die. This allows the stem to center in the die and to align with the case neck, which minimizes the potential for the expander to bend the case neck. In addition, this allows the stem to freely wobble, as is necessary to enter a slightly off-center flash hole, which minimizes the potential for decapping pin breakage.

SOURCE FOR SPECIALTY TOOLS REFERENCED IN THIS CHAPTER:

Recreational Software Inc
1343 Navajo Drive
Cottonwood, AZ 86323
www.shootingsoftware.com
Telephone: 928-634-8028

Always adjust cartridge overall length to leave sufficient clearance between the bullet tip and the front of the magazine—30/1000 inch is a reasonable minimum.

Inexplicably, in some guns such as the Remington Pump and semiauto, the magazine will accept and function perfectly with a cartridge that is too long to eject from the gun! The devil is in the details. This Barnes XBT, 280 Remington load proved unusually accurate in this Remington Pump. Everything seemed perfect, except that a loaded round would not eject! A minor, simple, receiver modification solved this problem.

A Forster Ultra die set includes several advanced features. A raised expander is useful in easing sizing effort and is far less apt to bend a case neck as the handloader pulls the case from the die. This seating die is similar in many respects to the Redding Competition seating die.

Redding Micrometer Die heads include a "Zero-Set" feature that is useful as a reference for bullet-seating depth or for neck-sizing length (depending upon type of die).

Cracked case necks can be subtle or obvious and can happen during loading (example at right), storage (example at left), or firing (most common). Case inspection is important.

Radical case forming alterations, such as those necessary to form SMC cases from much longer cases, can work-harden the case sufficiently to lead to a shoulder split during fireforming.

The 250 Ackley Improved (left) is a far superior design to the original 250 Savage (right). Increase in usable case capacity is significant but Improved design is also more efficient (more unignited propellant is trapped inside the chamber so less follows the bullet into the barrel). Note the shorter neck, typical result of fireforming standard cases to fit an Improved chamber. Note also that the end of the shoulder is lower on an Improved case; Ackley designed his Improved chambers so that chambering standard cases requires a crush fit.

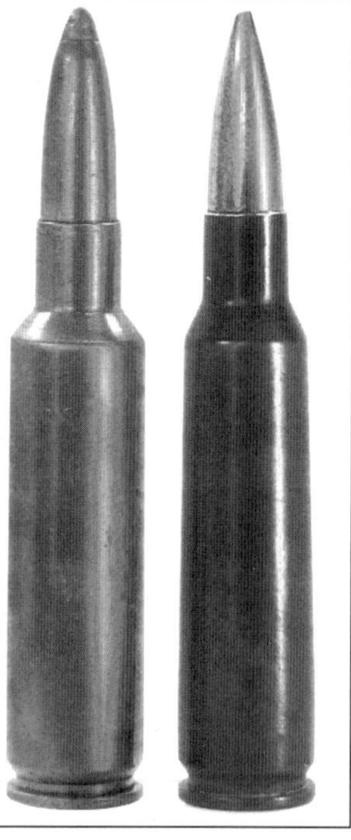

Chambering and firing the wrong cartridge can be dangerous: Left to right, 32 ACP, 32 ACP case (after firing in a 380 ACP), 380 ACP case. Such a case rupture can damage or destroy the gun and can injure the shooter and bystanders.

PRIMERS

CHAPTER 6

INTRODUCTION

We have two basic primer types for reloadable cases, Boxer and Berdan. Other than requiring a special depriming tool, the Berdan system represents no significant problem.

I have chronographed many types of third-world, military-surplus, Berdan-primed ammunition; such ammunition is routinely far more consistent than any but the very best Boxer-primed ammunition. Despite this evidence that the Berdan system has the ballistic advantage, U.S. handloaders rarely reload Berdan-primed cases.

At times, RWS has cataloged and exported various Berdan primers to the United States. But, obtaining any RWS primer here—Berdan or Boxer—has always been difficult. If more handloaders expressed a serious interest in reloading Berdan cases, such primers might be more readily available. Be that as it may, our concern here is the proper use and safe handling of Boxer primers (safety issues apply equally to Berdan primers).

The four basic sizes of Boxer primers in current handloader use for metallic-cartridge loading include:

- Small rifle and small pistol
- Large pistol
- Large rifle
- 50 BMG

The cup diameter of all primer sizes is nominally several thousandths-inch larger than the corresponding primer pocket; this provides an interference fit that seals the pocket. The diameter of primer pockets designed for both small rifle and small pistol primers is nominally 0.175 inch. Diameter of primer pockets designed for both large pistol and large rifle primers is nominally 0.210 inch. Diameter of primer pocket in the 50 BMG case is 0.3165 inch—50 BMG primers are extremely powerful and have no other handloading application.

Small pistol and small rifle primers are dimensionally interchangeable. Large rifle primers are about 0.006-inch taller than large pistol primers and primer pockets made for large rifle primers are, therefore, deeper than those made for large pistol primers. Normally, large rifle primers will not seat correctly into pistol cases; however, many rifle loads respond particularly well to the use of pistol primers. (Most non-bolt-action guns working at less than about 45,000 psi fall within this class.)

Rifle and pistol primer cups and pellets differ. Usually, rifle primers have a heavier pellet (to deliver more energy) and a thicker cup (to withstand greater pressure). Generally, conventional handgun cartridges use relatively small quantities of easily ignited propellants, so a relatively weak primer blast is adequate; conversely, rifle cartridges often use relatively large quantities of hard-to-ignite propellants, so a relatively strong primer is needed. Many handguns often deliver a

This primer seems to show that the load generated excessive pressure; however, pressure was normal. Headspace was excessive (causes excessive flattening) and the fit of the firing pin was poor (results in blanking).

Above, tested 22 Hornet loads. I tried each of these bullets with ten likely propellants. Before beginning that regimen, I tested one bullet with three propellants and nine primers. In my Savage M-40, the evaluation demonstrated that the WSP (extruded and flake propellants) and Federal 100 (ball-type propellants) gave, by far, the best ballistic uniformity. Often, without any other load development, these two primers gave the best accuracy, example below left. Different primers in otherwise identical loads usually give different accuracy, as below.

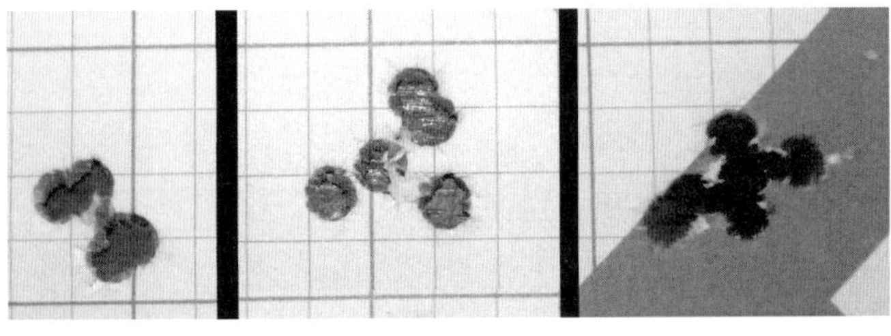

Various rifle primers: Significant variations in anvil design exist. Some have foil (top); others have no foil (bottom left). Performance is equally varied from brand to brand and between standard and magnum.

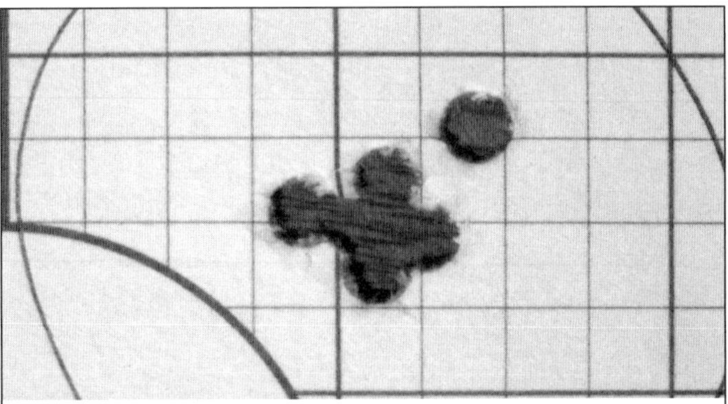

When testing loads, you must have the ability and confidence to call a flier when you are reasonably certain that something other than intrinsic accuracy fouled the shot. In this instance, I knew the instant the gun fired that I had goofed.

relatively mild striker blow, so, to assure proper ignition, a thin cup is needed; conversely, rifle cartridges often work at very high pressures, so a thick cup is needed—in most rifles, striker energy is sufficient to result in proper ignition despite the relatively thick cup.

The CCI-350 (large pistol magnum) is an exception. CCI designed this primer specifically to properly ignite H110 (W296), which is a common magnum pistol propellant that is unusually difficult to ignite. So, the 350 is unusually powerful—more so than all but the two hottest rifle primers.

Because pistol primers have softer and thinner cups, generally, these should not be used either in rifle cartridges that generate more than about 45,000 psi peak chamber pressure or where the firing pin does not properly fit the corresponding hole in the bolt face. Too-high chamber pressure or a poorly fitting firing pin can result in blanked (pierced) primers. However, use of pistol primers can provide superior results in various relatively low-pressure rifle loads—often, ballistic uniformity is far better than with rifle primers. This is true, particularly, in lever-action rifles where striker energy is modest—striker impact energy relates to primer ignition energy, and relatively light impacts tend to result in both lower velocity and greater ballistic variation.

Small rifle primers will fit pistol cases. However, such use is generally ill advised as this can lead to ignition failures resulting from inadequate striker energy—thicker cups require a harder strike, which might not be available in a typical handgun. The hotter blast can create extremely high pressures with some pistol propellants. (Accurate Arms tested several handgun cartridge loads where primer substitutions

Types and Sizes of Boxer Primers Now Sold for Metallic Cartridges: Commonly or Sometimes Available in the United States

Make	Size	Type	Comments
		Small Pistol	
CCI	500 | 550	Std. | Mag.	
Fede	100 | 200	Std. | Mag.	Ignites with relatively light impact
Fiocchi	100	Standard	
Remington	1½ | 5½	Std. | Mag.	Low brisance, high heat | 5½ for 357 Magnum
RWS	4031 | 4047	Std. | Mag.	
Winchester	WSP | WSPM	Std. | Mag.	
		Small Rifle	
CCI	400 & BR4 450 & 41	Std. & Match Mag.& Mil-Spec	Same pellet Same pellet
Federal	205 & 205M	Std. & Match	Same pellet, 205M most used primer in Benchrest
Fiocchi	200	Standard	
Remington	6½ | 7½	Std. | Mag.	7½ Magnum is Benchrest rated
RWS	4033	Standard	Low brisance, high heat
Winchester	WSR	—	Rated for all applications
		Large Pistol	
CCI	300 | 350	Std. | Mag.	350 Mag. is hotter than most Large Rifle Mag,
Federal	150 | 155	Std. | Mag.	Ignite with relatively light impact
Fiocchi	150	—	
Remington	2½	Standard	Mildest Large Pistol primer | low brisance, high heat
RWS	5337	—	Low brisance, high heat
Winchester	WLP	—	Rated for all applications
		Large Rifle	
CCI	200 & BR2 250 & 34	Std. & Match Mag. & Mil-Spec	Same pellet Same pellet
Federal	210 & 210M 215 & 215M 216	Std. & Match Mag. & Match Super Mag.	Same pellet | 210M widely used target Same pellet, second hottest Large Rifle Needed but not marketed!
Fiocchi	210	Std.	
Remington	9½ | 9½M	Std. | Mag..	Hard cup | High heat, low brisance
RWS	5341 | 5333	Std. | Mag	Mildest Large Rifle primer: low brisance, high heat Magnum very hot
Winchester	WLR | WLRM	Std. | Mag.	WLR similar to 215 | WLRM hottest available primer
		50 BMG	
CCI | RWS	35 | 8212	—	No other application

Note: Federal Gold Medal (GM) primers use the same materials as the corresponding Federal Match primers, but Federal uses higher quality standards for these top-of-the-line primers. Similarly, both CCI Benchrest and Federal Match primers are produced at a higher standard of quality than are the corresponding standard primers. Generally, where a load recipe specifies a particular primer, the only assuredly safe course is to use that primer, exclusively.

led to devastating pressures.) The 454 Casull and 500 S&W Magnum are exceptions; in full-power loads, the former uses small rifle primers, the latter uses large rifle primers.

Generally, magnum primers deliver a hotter and more voluminous flame. The design purpose of magnum primers is to ignite large charges of slow-burning propellants (which are difficult to ignite, due to a relatively heavy deterrent application), even when used under adverse weather conditions (cold temperatures). Usually, the use of magnum primers in standard loads increases pressure and, often, degrades accuracy, but the result of any primer substitution is generally unpredictable.

As counterintuitive as this might be, in some types of loads, substitution of a nominally hotter primer results in a reduction of pressure and velocity. What is more confounding is that, sometimes, such a substitution results in a load that generates lower velocity but higher peak pressure. Commonly, in any particular load, any primer substitution can increase or decrease velocity, increase or decrease pressure, and improve or degrade ballistic uniformity—any one of these changes can be bad. Rarely, such a substitution will result in no change in one or more of these characteristics. Any ballistician who has done this sort of testing will attest that any person who expresses a belief that the results of any particular primer substitution are predictable, a priori, has positively demonstrated one thing: He does not know what he is talking about.

Generally, propellants toward the extreme ends of the burning rate range are most sensitive to primer substitutions. For example, substitution of a hotter primer in a load using a fast-burning, porous-based, propellant is apt to increase pressure monumentally; equally, substitution of a milder primer in a load using any of the slowest propellants can lead to a misfire, a squib, or a detonation. Each of these handloading errors has resulted in destroyed guns.

The only thing that we can say with any degree of certainty is that, usually, primer substitutions will alter ballistics somewhat and that, sometimes, such substitutions will alter ballistics significantly. The only completely safe course is to stick with the specified primer. However, in our search for improved accuracy, inevitably, we (handloaders) will substitute primers. Hereby, I wish to admonish one and all to do so only with a good understanding of how to read pressure signs and with due caution—when testing a different primer in any load, start low and work the load up again, every time. Failure to follow this advice is certain to lead to trouble.

Several makers offer premium primers (Match or Benchrest) using the same nominal pellet as a similar conventional primer. Ballistically, primers within these pairs are interchangeable. The manufacture of premium primers involves the use of more stringent quality control standards and other techniques that improve precision.

CCI Mil-Spec primers are useful for semiautomatic guns and have other applications. Excepting superior quality control and one minor design difference, these are equivalent in every way to the corresponding CCI Magnum Rifle primer. CCI holds anvil and cup heights to closer tolerances and the anvil is slightly blunter. Therefore, compared to CCI conventional primers, Mil-Spec primers are easier to seat correctly and are dramatically less sensitive to an unusually light striker impact. These modest changes reduce the potential for a slam fire by a factor exceeding one million. (A slam fire can occur when inertia carries the firing pin into the primer and when the action closes very rapidly, as can occur in a semiautomatic gun when dropping the bolt on an already chambered round.)

The 250 anvil is significantly taller than the 34 anvil. This difference and improved control of 34 cup and anvil height are key factors in the reduced sensitivity to a light striker impact of the 34. These same differences apply to the corresponding small rifle primer pair—450 and 41.

PRIMERS—HANDLING SAFETY

As odd as this might seem, people often find ways to unintentionally set off one or more primers. Stories abound of handloaders, and others, managing to explode primers en mass. Sometimes, these incidents involve the Lee Auto-Prime or an automatic primer feed using a tube of stacked primers and, sometimes, other tools and situations. I have met one person who lost fingers this way.

Often, one can abuse a primer unmercifully without incident. Various obvious abuses include:

- Seating a primer sideways and crushing it to fit completely within the primer pocket
- Dropping primers on a concrete floor
- Stepping on loose primers on a hard floor while wearing a hard-soled shoe
- Pounding on a column of primers (in an automatic primer feed tube)
- Dropping a hand-held priming tool full of primers onto a concrete floor
- Trying to seat two primers into one primer pocket
- Carrying cartridges in a pocket with an unprotected 9-volt (or other) dry-cell battery
- Overheating primers
- Dropping objects onto primers (single or packaged)

Handloaders can treat primers with all manner of disrespect, but, sooner or later, such abusive events will result in the unintentional ignition of one or more primers. If that unintended ignition happens to occur within a large group of primers, the resulting explosion can be devastating. Errant ignition of a single primer can result in a severe wound.

One handloader had a primer cup driven completely through his finger, breaking the bone on the way. Had that cup hit him in the eye it might well have killed him. Handle primers with respect and follow all safety precautions provided by primer and priming tool manufacturers. Always wear safety glasses when handling primers.

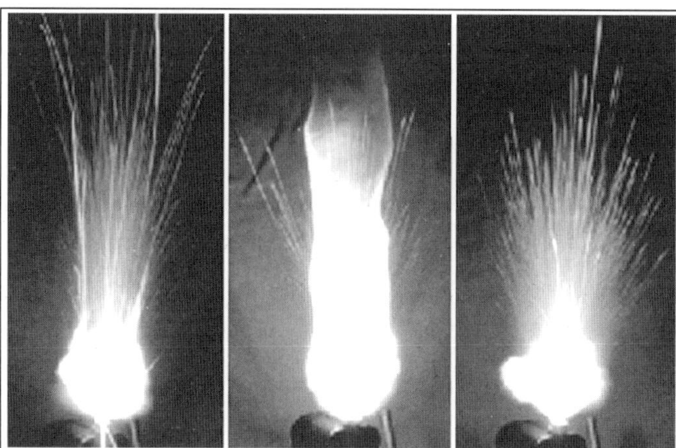

Unconfined large magnum primer plumes, left-to-right: Remington (9½M), Winchester (WLRM), and Alcan (LRM). Primers seated in the case head with the case body removed and both primer pockets and flash holes deburred and made uniform. Pictures taken in a dark room with an open shutter. The area of each picture is about 8x16 inches. Visible differences are indicative of various tested primers—the mildest appearing large-rifle primer (not pictured) produced a flame that was about one-tenth the volume that the Remington 9½M primer produced. The flame from the mildest large pistol primer (not pictured) occupied about one-half that volume.

I have seated hundreds of thousands of primers; these have included myriad examples of practically every brand and kind in all manner of cases using all manner of tools and loaded to every feasible degree of precision. I admit, freely, that all too often I have made mistakes when handling primers. Occasionally, I have partially seated a primer that was sideways in the primer pocket—especially when trying to use a poor-quality automatic primer feed or an automatic primer feed system that was badly designed or was poorly adjusted.

Occasionally, I have decapped cases with live primers seated normally, sideways or backward—but I have tried to use extreme caution and have taken prudent and appropriate safety precautions when doing any of these things. I have dropped primers on a hard floor—but I make an effort to keep such dropped primers cleaned up, and, routinely, I keep a rubber mat under my work area. I suspect that I might have stepped on a primer or two in these many decades of handloading—but I try, deliberately, not to wear shoes with hard soles, or with nails in the heels, while handloading. In all my misadventures of this nature, excepting one glaring incident, I have never popped a primer that I did not intend to pop. However, no doubt, caution and some good luck have prevented that from happening more often.

That one exception is impossible to explain fully, but it involved a moment of inattention. The result was painful but did no permanent harm other than to my ego. I was decapping a live primer from a 38 Special case (I forget why). I was using a Lee hand-decapping tool, which is a one-quarter-inch-diameter rod that is four inches long with a decapping pin in one end and a knurled gripping section just below the other end. One is supposed to hit the stem top with a hammer.

The Forster spring-clamping puller is the fastest pulling method. However, it damages the tip of most bullets (as each subsequent bullet pushes the previous one free), and it scars the bullet shank.

To tear down a large number of cartridges without damaging the bullets, the collet-style (clamping) bullet puller is a better choice. Forster (shown), Hornady (fastest design), and RCBS all offer such a puller.

However, Lee never intended that anyone use this tool for decapping cases with live primers. To make matters worse, I could not find the base, which has a hole where the primer can drop out and which holds the case centered, preventing trapping of the primer in the case.

My poor solution was to locate the case over the slightly opened jaws of a bench vise. I adjusted the vise so that the jaws would support each edge of the case head but with a sufficient gap to allow the primer to freely pass from the bottom of the case and fall between the jaws. Good theory; bad execution.

Something distracted me. I looked up as I swung the hammer to produce a deliberately light blow on the decapping rod (I intended to hit the rod several times, as needed, to drive the primer free of the case, slowly and gently). As I swung the hammer, the case slipped backward. When the hammer hit the rod, the primer was fully over one jaw of the vice. Consequently, the hammer blow crushed the pellet as it drove the anvil into the cup. SURPRISE! The pellet exploded.

Now, consider the situation: The decapping rod pin practically sealed the flash hole, leaving almost zero room for generated gases to escape, via that avenue; and, the primer sealed the primer pocket perfectly, as it is designed to do, so no gas venting existed there either. So, what happened?

Pellet combustion generated greater than 40,000 psi within the primer pocket, creating about 1,000 pounds of upward force on the case. Hence, because the primer could not move, the case accelerated upward until it cleared the primer cup and thereby vented the gas. By that time, the case had accelerated to considerable speed. Of course, the case did not stop when the primer came free; it continued traveling up the decapping stem until it hit the support rod. It then drove the entire rod upward, between my tightly clenched thumb and finger, until that hit the hammer, which it then knocked upward, violently. The open case mouth hit my thumb and finger with sufficient force to cut me practically to the bone. And that was a standard small pistol primer, one of the least powerful of all types.

Please, make every effort to treat primers with the respect these energetic little packages deserve. If you handle and store primers properly, it is most unlikely that you will ever suffer any primer-related mishap. If you do not treat primers properly, you are equally unlikely to escape such a potential catastrophe forever. Many once-careless handloaders can attest to this fact. Serious injuries have occurred. Be careful and use caution.

This is a good place to warn against one potential hazard that is not necessarily obvious: Let us assume that you have just completed seating a bullet in a cartridge and you notice, belatedly, that you failed to properly seat the primer. "No problem," you surmise, "I will simply run the case back through my priming tool." Please avoid doing so.

You now have a loaded round, complete with propellant and bullet. There could well be a reason the primer did not seat properly the first time. Propellant granules might also have infiltrated into the primer pocket—most ball-type propellants can easily pass through a flash hole. Both factors are good reasons to suspect that attempting to reseat the primer could cause it to pop. If that happens, you are quite certain to have problems. The case, almost certainly, will rupture, expelling burning and unignited propellant granules at unpleasant velocity; in addition, pieces of the ruptured case could tear free to puncture and penetrate any nearby object. The best practice is to pull the bullet, dump the charge, and start over.

About the only scenario that could be worse would be in a press system where the handloader inserts a loaded cartridge in a die, either open ended or closed ended, during primer reseating (such as could happen when trying to reseat a primer using the Lee LoadMaster Press). In that combination, you have all the ingredients for either a gun or a bomb, which you are trying to set off. Again, this is not a theory; it has happened.

In one instance, a handloader was working with a solid shellholder while seating bullets. Evidently, one particular case had a high primer. As he was seating the bullet in that case and as the ram reached full travel, the shellholder reseated the primer, which then fired (who knows why?)! By some miracle, the seating die held. Inertia and geometry saved the handloader from having the handle of the press driven through his hand. Ejected portions of the ruptured case missed him and the violent gas jetting missed his face. This totaled the die and press, but the handloader escaped serious injury. Nevertheless, just try to imagine what might have happened if he had been using a weaker press. This is one reason never to use any shellholder that lacks a hole through the center.

PRIMERS—STORAGE SAFETY

Always store primers in original containers and on a low and secure shelf. Never store large quantities of primers in any rigid container. Even a few dozen primers in a sealed, rigid container represent a recipe for an explosion, with potentially lethal consequences.

Never store primers close to propellant (particularly blackpowder). An isolated primer explosion is one thing, but an event that leads to ignition of a propellant magazine is something else entirely—a destroyed cabinet and damaged wall, compared to a destroyed building.

Never store primers on a high shelf or where a heavy object can fall onto the primer containers. Consider the fate of one delivery truck and driver. When found, the smoldering truck remains were unrecognizable—little more than the mangled frame and drive train, associated with scattered debris covering many hundreds of feet in an area behind where the chassis came to rest. Interestingly, according to the driver's invoice, he had 50,000 primers and a heavy blacksmith anvil undelivered when the incident occurred. Why that driver might have placed the anvil on a shelf and the primers on the floor below such a heavy object will, forever, remain a tragic mystery.

PRIMERS—QUALITY

Modern primers are a manufacturing miracle, perhaps second only to the 22 Long Rifle rimfire cartridge—the electronics industry has nothing on the ammunition industry. Production sophistication, typical quality, and retail pricing boggle the mind. Consider this question: When was the last time you had a primer fail to function properly and the malfunction was not your fault?

Employees at Black Hills Ammunition visually inspect every primer used. CEO Jeff Hoffman reports that about one in every 200,000 primers coming in the door is, in some way, faulty. These faults include:

- Deformed cup
- Cocked anvil
- Missing anvil
- Two anvils
- No pellet
- No foil
- Foil out of place

Of these faults, all but the last two are either apt to, or are certain to, result in a primer that will not function properly to ignite the propellant charge.

According to Black Hills (the only major ammunition producer that examines every primer it uses), a similarly tiny percentage of faulty primers exists in every brand. Approximately 1 in 500,000 primers is sufficiently faulty as to lead to a certain misfire.

Because handloaders report a significantly higher percentage of misfires in otherwise complete cartridges—some report one misfire in about every 5,000 handloaded cartridges—we know that about 999 out of 1,000 primer-related misfires result from something other than a faulty primer. Likely causes for primer-related misfires include:

- Manufacturing error (probably far less than one in one thousand)
- Contamination of primer pellet with some type of penetrating oil or other chemical (depends entirely upon degree of improper handling and storage)
- Failure to seat primer cup to bottom of primer pocket (very common)
- A too-light striker, or firing pin, fall (rare in stock guns but common in highly tuned guns such as those used in Cowboy Action games)
- Excessive cartridge headspace

PRIMERS—PRODUCTION

Here I will describe primer production at one particular facility. Other manufacturers are likely to use different specific techniques and methodologies. My purpose here is not to describe every possible production method in detail but, rather, to give handloaders an idea of what the basic process is.

A typical primer line produces cups and anvils six at a time, in parallel—at each step: six separate tool heads process these pieces, six at a time. These presses punch and then form cups and anvils from brass sheets. Through a series of stamping steps, the machines process each punched-out piece until that article reaches the desired configuration. These steps can include annealing and plating or other modifying operations. Precise control of thickness, composition, and hardness of the brass sheet stock are fundamental to finished product quality.

Primer pellets are composed of an energetic mixture of various chemicals having several significant properties. It must be possible to handle this mixture during various manufacturing steps with essentially complete safety. For this reason, all producers create, handle, and form the primer pellet mix in a dampened state—the texture is similar to peanut butter but this material is not particularly sticky. The finished product must exhibit long-term stability and resistance to chemical action or degradation by atmospheric humidity.

The pellet must have sufficient physical integrity to tolerate stresses of handling, assembly, and anvil reseating (as one seats the primer into the case). For this reason, all mixes contain some percentage of binding and plasticizing agents. Mixes also contain some substance or combination of substances that will render the dried pellet sensitive to a crushing blow, whereby ignition will occur. In most modern primers, this characteristic derives from inclusion of a percentage of either lead styphnate or basic lead styphnate, with entrained gases. Technically these chemicals are contact-sensitive high explosives.

In conventional primers, the almost instantaneous compression of inevitably entrained air and volatile gases from the mix (at a microscopic scale) generates ignition in response to striker impact. Compression heats these tiny gas pockets (adiabatic heating) to thousands of degrees. In far less than one-thousandth second, these hot gas bubbles heat and, thereby, ignite adjacent material.

In addition, the primer pellet must contain chemicals that will generate sufficient heat to ignite a propellant charge adequately and consistently. For this reason, most primer mixes contain admixtures of fuel and oxidizer. Compared to mixes using only lead styphnate for energy, for any given total energy release, mixes containing separate fuel and oxidizer components produce a less brisant (less shattering) blast and more total heat—the energy is released in a gentler manner. Generally, this is beneficial.

To create pellets, a skilled operator uses a squeegee-type tool to spread the pellet dough over a steel plate. This plate has many rows and columns of essentially identical cylindrical holes through it. Such a die plate might have 100 columns of 100 rows (10,000 holes). By using various skillful techniques, an operator can produce charges of almost precisely identical mass into each hole on each plate. A magnetic transport system then lifts this plate and moves it to a machine where pins drive the individual pellets into semifinished primer cups.

Rows of formed cups pass under the plate and ram punches drive the pellets from the plate and into the cups. In some systems, another device positions a foil sheet (paper or layered paper with aluminum) between the pellet and the punches. This creates a foil disk that interposes the ram and pellet and, thereby, prevents the moist pellet from sticking to the ram. Newer, and generally superior, techniques make it possible to dispense with this uniformity-degrading foil.

Once the pins have driven the pellet and foil (if used) into each cup, another device inserts the anvil. Then, a punch drives each anvil and cup assembly through a die. This sizes the cup correctly to create a friction fit in the primer pocket of the intended case. Some makers size the cup after anvil insertion.

Universally, the last manufacturing step in primer production is drying. The manufacturer stores semifinished primers in a dry, warm room to remove excess pellet moisture. As it dries, the pellet becomes progressively more rigid and sensitive and is, therefore, rendered useful, albeit less safe to handle or (more correctly) less safe to mishandle.

Interestingly, a primer is not actually ready to function normally until it is correctly seated into a primer pocket. Proper primer seating during the loading process necessarily reseats the anvil. This correctly compresses the pellet for safe and proper functioning and thereby finishes the primer.

Manufacturers produce and distribute primers for our pleasure. Everyone involved profits. And, we can buy these little industrial marvels for less than the cost of a stick of gum. To me, the quality and relatively low cost of primers is utterly amazing.

As covered previously in "Primer—Quality," few properly handled primers fail to function correctly because manufacturers monitor every component of every primer in every production batch continuously throughout the production process. A final quality-control step involves testing random samples for sensitivity, dimensional quality, and functionality. Manufacturers seldom produce bad primers, and the shipping of bad primers is an ephemerally rare occurrence, but, as noted above, this occasionally and inevitably does happen.

PRIMERS—PELLET COMBUSTION

The primer pellet is, in itself, a minor miracle. It starts life as a group of relatively harmless chemicals; most are solids in a powdered form. The sensitizing energetic ingredient of modern primers is usually either lead styphnate or basic lead styphnate (a chemical derivation of the same impact-sensitive substance). Various other components include additional fuels, oxidizers, and binders. At least one formulation that has been used is a mixture of chemicals, none of which will individually explode or even burn. Formerly, most compositions included abraders, such as very fine particles of aluminum or glass.

Abraders act to cut through the difficult-to-ignite surface of deterrent-treated propellant granules, thereby facilitating ignition. Some types of abraders (aluminum) become incandescent and, thereby, additionally promote rapid ignition of heavily deterred granules by direct heating. Since about 1980, inclusion of abraders has fallen from favor as producers have perfected gas-generating mixtures with superior effectiveness. Comparatively, hot gases penetrate farther into the charge and promote faster granule ignition with greater shot-to-shot uniformity through condensation heating of the entire granule surface, rather than point-of-contact heating, as with particles.

The addition of fuels and oxidizers increases total heat generation without increasing primer brisance, as would happen if one simply used a heavier charge of lead styphnate. (Brisance is an explosive, shattering, force.) Binders act to glue the pellet together during manufacture, seating, striker impact, and inchoate combustion.

Each company has a proprietary formulation for each primer it produces and each formulation has particular advantages. Further, specific primer types use different amounts and mixes of priming compound chemicals. The handloader who suspects that one primer brand and type will work well for all shooting needs across a wide spectrum of loads is liable to be very disappointed.

The pellet contains both fuel and oxidizer; hence combustion occurs without any need for outside fuel or oxidizer. Strictly speaking, modern primers do not detonate. The pellet burns particularly rapidly through self-combustion—it deflagrates, rather than detonates.

Technically, a detonation is a chemical reaction where propagation of the boundary between the unaltered product and the reacting product exceeds the speed that a shock wave would travel through the reacting substance (the speed of sound in that substance). Conversely, deflagration is a chemical reaction where propagation of the boundary between the unaltered product and the reacting product is slower than the speed that a shock wave travels through the reacting substance.

A little reflection will suggest the effective difference between these two reaction modes. If one could view either reaction at a large enough scale, and in slow enough motion, to see what was happening, one would see distinct features and results. In a detonation, any areas beyond the propagating explosion front would remain completely unaffected until the reaction front arrived. Thereafter, that material would simultaneously compress and begin chemically reacting, and, hence, essentially 100 percent of the material would react, in-place.

Conversely, in a deflagration, shock waves and associated physical disruptions would influence areas beyond the propagating reaction front. Sometime thereafter—when the propagating reaction front arrived—those areas would begin to chemically react. As a result, the reaction could blow entire significant chunks of the material away from the reacting mass before those began to react. This is of critical internal-ballistic importance to what happens in a cartridge—pyrotechnic material that flows through the flash hole and into the propellant column is still reacting and is, therefore, still generating energetic (hot) gases.

As a practical matter, detonations are more efficient at converting available material into reaction products because all the intimately associated material will normally fully react. Also, because detonation reactions propagate faster compared to deflagration reactions, detonations generally create a faster, more brisant energy release.

Effectively, because the reaction blows unburned portions of a deflagrating pellet away from the reacting mass, vagaries of confinement have a profound influence upon efficiency. Increased confinement speeds and increases conversion of reactants into reaction by-products and energy. For this reason, controlling primer-pocket depth and flash-hole geometry improves ballistic uniformity.

This might explain why benchrest shooters have found that smaller flash holes often increase consistency of their best loads. By increasing containment, a smaller flash hole decreases precombustion disruption of the primer pellet, thereby increasing both total energy release and primer-to-primer reaction consistency. (Another advantage of a smaller flash hole might be the generation of a longer-lasting pyrotechnic plume but with less effective brisance and, therefore, less chance of prematurely dislodging the bullet.)

PRIMERS—PERFORMANCE

Since about 1980, manufacturers have made great strides toward improving overall primer quality and consistency. One area of improvement that is immediately obvious is dimensional control and beveling of the outside open end of the cup. For example, CCI primers manufactured after 1989 are far more consistent in size; for this reason, these primers are generally far easier to seat correctly than older CCI primers are.

Generally, manufacturers have been striving toward primers that can deliver improved ballistic uniformity. So, in recent decades, several manufacturers have changed formulation of the priming mix for various primer types.

Producers that have designed new formulations have worked to keep the old and new versions ballistically interchangeable, within feasible limits. However, should you have an old load that used an old primer and that was right against the edge of the safety envelope, you might keep the following bit of common sense logic well in mind:

SIMILAR IS NOT IDENTICAL: TREAT ANY CHANGE TO A SIGNIFICANTLY NEWER PRIMER JUST AS IF IT WERE A CHANGE TO A DIFFERENT BRAND OR TYPE OF PRIMER. REDUCE THE CHARGE AND DEVELOP THE LOAD ALL OVER AGAIN.

You can set up your own tests of visual and energy differences among primer makes and types, but no such test can suggest, with any particular degree of certainty, the ballistic consequences of changing primers for any given new load combination. A milder appearing primer can generate greater pressure with certain propellants or bullets. Paradoxically, in many load combinations, a primer that is actually milder, as proven by every quantitative measure, often generates greater pressure and vice versa.

This can occur because the pyrotechnic blast from a hotter primer can dislodge the bullet, driving it from the case and against, or into, the rifling before any effective propellant ignition occurs; with a larger initial boiler room, the load then generates less pressure than it would have generated if the primer blast had not moved the bullet (or if it had not moved it as far or as fast), as occurs with a milder primer. Therefore, a milder primer CAN INDEED generate greater pressure. The classic example is the 44 Magnum loaded with H110; in almost any normal load, substitution of any other pistol primer for the unusually hot CCI-350 routinely increases resulting chamber pressure.

This is one area where no one can outguess the load and the gun. If you believe that you can, trust me, a surprise awaits you. It is always best to stay with the specific primer usage recommendation. If, for any reason, you

Primer Substitution Study
Tests Conducted at the Accurate Arms Ballistics Laboratory: 30-06 Springfield, Match Prepped Cases, Sierra 168 Mk at 3.300-Inch OAL.

Part I: 58.0 Grains A4350

Primer		Pressure			Velocity			Difference from Lowest	
Make & Number	Mfg. Date	PSI	Extreme Spread	Std. Dev.	FPS	Spread	Std. Dev.	Pressure	Velocity
Win-WLRM	**1995**	**63,900**	**2,700**	**1,100**	**2951**	**30**	**11**	**20.3%**	**4.4%**
Win-WLR	1995	61,600	2,600	1,200	2926	23	10	16.0%	3.5%
Fed-215	1970s	61,400	5,000	2,000	2927	43	16	15.6%	3.5%
Fed-210	1970s	61,100	2,000	900	2932	21	9	15.1%	3.7%
Alcan LRM	1970s	60,900	3,800	1,400	2906	33	13	14.7%	2.8%
CCI-350	1992	59,400	1,700	700	2905	23	9	11.9%	2.8%
Fed-215	1995	59,400	3,200	1,300	2908	50	19	11.9%	2.9%
Fed-210	1995	59,000	4,700	1,800	2901	52	20	11.1%	2.6%
Alcan LR	1970s	58,900	3,200	1,500	2925	54	22	10.9%	3.5%
Rem-9½M	1995	58,900	6,000	2,200	2896	64	22	10.9%	2.4%
Rem-9½M	1970s	58,800	3,000	1,300	2904	39	14	10.7%	2.7%
Rem-9½	1970s	58,500	1,600	700	2897	23	10	10.2%	2.5%
Fed-210M	1995	58,100	2,700	1,200	2892	35	14	9.4%	2.3%
CCI-250	1995	57,700	1,100	400	2882	9	4	8.7%	1.9%
CCI-200	1974	57,500	4,800	1,900	2874	77	29	8.3%	1.7%
CCI-BR2	1995	57,300	3,700	1,500	2886	39	18	7.9%	2.1%
CCI-250	1979	57,000	1,400	600	2872	31	12	7.3%	1.6%
Rem-9½	1995	56,300	1,500	600	2867	12	4	6.0%	1.4%
CCI-200	1995	55,100	3,200	1,100	2858	36	14	3.8%	1.1%
Win-WLP	1995	55,000	2,600	1,300	2859	46	19	3.6%	1.1%
RWS-LR	1994	54,900	1,700	600	2850	30	11	3.4%	0.8%
CCI-200	1980	54,500	2,600	1,000	2855	30	12	2.6%	1.0%
Fed-155	1990s	54,400	1,400	600	2853	13	4	2.4%	0.9%
Fed-150	1990s	53,600	2,100	900	2839	31	12	0.9%	0.4%
CCI-300	1994	53,400	1,800	700	2831	29	10	0.6%	0.1%
Rem-2½	**1994**	**53,100**	**1,200**	**600**	**2827**	**20**	**9**	**0.0%**	**0.0%**

PART II: 53.0 GRAINS A2700

PRIMER		PRESSURE			VELOCITY			DIFFERENCE FROM LOWEST	
MAKE & NUMBER	MFG. DATE	PSI	EXTREME SPREAD	STD. DEV.	FPS	SPREAD	STD. DEV.	PRESSURE	VELOCITY
Win-WLRM	**1995**	**59,200**	**1,900**	**800**	**2790**	**24**	**9**	**13.0%**	**2.8%**
Fed-210	1995	57,800	3,500	1,500	2778	42	16	10.3%	2.4%
Rem-9½M	1995	57,500	5,400	2,300	2771	52	24	9.7%	2.1%
Fed-215	1995	57,300	2,600	1,000	2770	32	12	9.4%	2.1%
CCI-350	1992	56,900	1,700	600	2765	20	7	8.6%	1.9%
Win-WLR	1995	56,100	2,800	1,100	2764	38	14	7.1%	1.8%
Fed-210M	1995	55,900	2,500	1,000	2764	13	5	6.7%	1.8%
Rem-9½	1995	54,500	1,900	800	2740	20	10	4.0%	1.0%
CCI-BR2	1995	54,400	2,800	1,100	2741	42	15	3.8%	1.0%
Fed-155	1990s	53,400	1,600	700	2734	17	7	1.9%	0.7%
CCI-250	1994	53,200	1,300	500	2715	20	8	1.5%	0.0%
Rem-2½	1994	53,100	2,300	1,000	2730	25	9	1.3%	0.6%
RWS-LR	1994	53,100	4,600	1,800	2722	59	23	1.3%	0.3%
Fed-150	1990s	52,900	1,700	600	2727	26	10	1.0%	0.3%
Win-WLP	1995	52,700	3,400	1,300	2719	50	18	0.6%	0.5%
CCI-200	**1995**	**52,500**	**2,800**	**1,300**	**2708**	**68**	**27**	**0.2%**	**-0.2%**
CCI-300	1994	52,400	1,000	600	2714	14	8	0.0%	0.0%

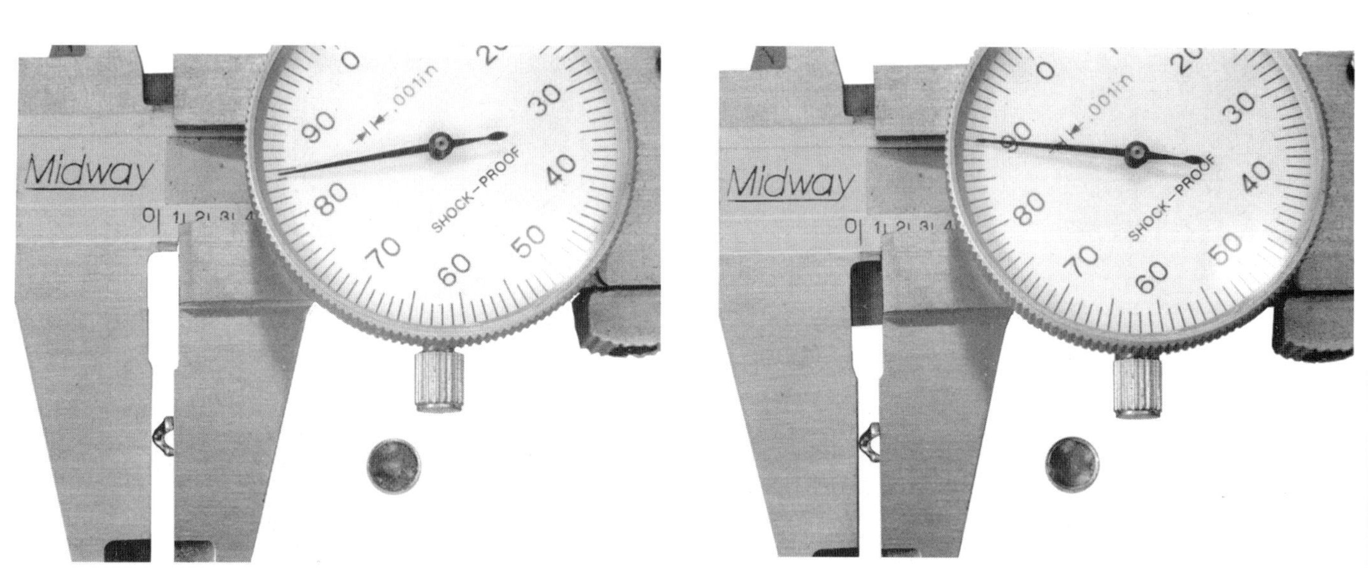

CCI Mil-Spec primers differ from corresponding CCI Magnum Rifle primers only in design and precision of the cup and anvil. The Mil-Spec anvil (above left) is shorter and less pointed than the CCI-250 anvil (above right). Also, the cup and anvil heights are more closely constrained in the Mil-Spec primers. These differences apply to both large- and small-rifle types. Many handloaders have found CCI Mil-Spec primers to be unusually consistent and to produce superior results when used as a substitute for the corresponding CCI Magnum Rifle primer.

Part III: 44.5 Grains A2015

Primer		Pressure			Velocity			Difference from Lowest	
Make & Number	Mfg. Date	psi	Extreme Spread	Std. Dev.	fps	Spread	Std. Dev.	Pressure	Velocity
Win-WLRM	**1995**	**63,000**	**6,100**	**2,500**	**2759**	**31**	**11**	**10.1%**	**1.1%**
Fed-215	1995	61,700	2,400	1,100	2752	23	9	7.9%	0.9%
Fed-210	1995	61,400	4,500	1,900	2756	29	13	7.3%	1.0%
CCI-350	1992	60,300	5,000	2,300	2749	36	16	5.4%	0.8%
CCI-BR2	1995	59,600	3,700	1,400	2745	30	10	4.2%	0.6%
Rem-9½	1995	59,300	3,900	1,500	2741	41	16	3.7%	0.5%
Fed-210M	1995	59,000	5,500	2,200	2736	49	17	3.1%	0.3%
Win-WLR	1995	58,900	4,100	1,700	2737	41	16	3.0%	0.3%
RWS-LR	1994	58,700	3,500	1,600	2733	37	16	2.6%	0.2%
Fed-150	1990s	58,600	2,500	900	2747	13	5	2.4%	0.7%
CCI-200	1995	58,600	3,100	1,200	2743	29	10	2.4%	0.5%
Win-WLP	1995	58,100	2,200	900	2730	17	7	1.6%	0.1%
CCI-250	1994	57,900	1,700	700	2732	21	8	1.2%	0.1%
CCI-300	1994	57,800	1,500	600	2743	4	1	1.0%	0.5%
Rem-9½M	1995	57,700	1,900	700	2731	20	7	0.9%	0.1%
Fed-155	1990s	57,600	2,100	800	2731	19	7	0.7%	0.1%
Rem-2½	**1994**	**57,200**	**2,000**	**900**	**2728**	**18**	**7**	**0.0%**	**0.0%**

Highest velocity and lowest velocity loads highlighted in bold font; highest pressure and lowest pressure loads highlighted in italic font.

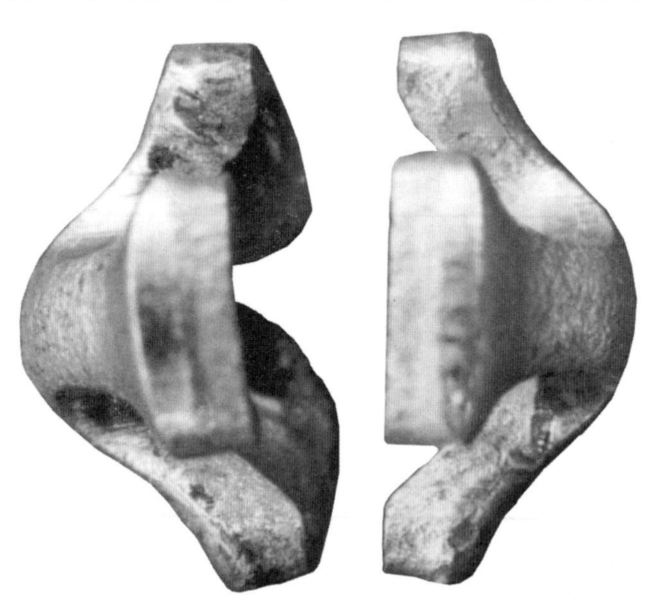

The CCI-250 anvil (left) is more pointed than the CCI-34 anvil (right). This subtle difference is critical.

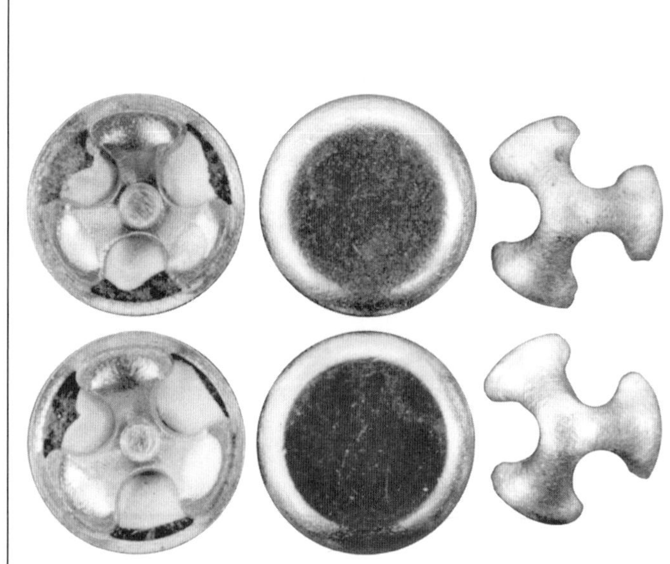

The CCI-34 (top) and CCI-250 (bottom) use identical pellets: The cup and anvil differences are difficult to see in these views at this scale.

Primer Power Study
Distance (Inches) That Primer Drove Swaged-Lead Bullet from Unsized 45 Colt Case

Make & Number	Average Distance	Standard Deviation	Lot Number
Fed-150	0.932	0.037	2BY093
Win-WLP	0.970	0.046	HHL399G
Fed-155	1.017	0.057	2CH117
CCI 300	1.032	0.046	H18Z
Fed-GM150M	1.048	0.088	2BY323
RWS 5341	1.071	0.024	—
Rem-2½	1.091	0.050	406
CCI 200	1.095	0.119	G25A
CCI BR2	1.155	0.133	D13A

Make & Number	Average Distance	Standard Deviation	Lot Number
CCI 250	1.287	0.132	K13Z
Win-WLR	1.318	0.063	HHL228G
Fed-210M	1.324	0.159	2CY117
CCI 350	1.379	0.116	K11W
Rem-9½	1.430	0.129	849
Fed-215	1.431	0.164	2BH271
Rem-9½M	1.480	0.056	2376
Fed-210	1.525	0.013	2BY241
Win-WLRM	1.830	0.145	HLM093G

Tested in a Freedom Arms revolver: unsized case, zero neck tension, and no propellant. The case retained enough crimp to allow finger seating of Hornady Cowboy bullets to cannelure.

switch primer types, remember that you are dealing with a new load. Work up the load all over again. The safety aspect of this is critical; the accuracy aspect is important, especially with rifles. A change of components, deliberate or inadvertent, will change the load. The result is often a reduction in accuracy of an optimized load because the mean exit point of bullets from the load might change from near the end of the vibrational muzzle swing to nearer the midpoint. Refer to chapter 12. This can occur even if muzzle velocity is virtually unchanged.

Within the sphere of target-rifle competition, no single facet of load development has been analyzed more thoroughly than has primer selection. The consensus is that the only way a handloader can determine which primer works best is through development with a specific gun and load. After the handloader has settled upon a basic load that delivers good accuracy, primer substitutions can show accuracy advantages. Before proceeding along this path, please study and keep in mind the associated proof that primer substitutions can dramatically alter pressure—use extreme caution in any such testing.

For most varmint and target cartridges, nonmagnum primers are likely to offer best accuracy. However, in some instances, this might not be true and, even within the sphere of nonmagnum primers, the handloader has many options. First, four primer brands are commonly stocked in any good handloading supply store and customers can sometimes special order other brands. Then, the option to use premium-quality primers exists (Match or Benchrest). Not to mention the possibility of using pistol primers in relatively low-pressure cartridges used in relatively small rifle cases (usually in non-bolt-action types), plus the option of using pistol primers for cast bullet cartridges used in almost any rifle.

In the former instance, the softer primer cup compensates for the relatively low striker energy so often exhibited by non-bolt-action guns. However, avoid the use of pistol primers in medium- to high-pressure rifle cartridges and in guns with an unusually heavy striker impact or having a particularly loose-fitting striker. The former can lead to holes in the primer cups with associated gas leakage; the latter can lead to blanked (pierced) primers with attendant gas leakage. Where feasible, a standard pistol primer will often work better than any rifle primer in any load not exceeding factory 30-30 pressure levels (about 45,000 psi) that uses a relatively fast propellant—the CCI 300 and Federal 150 often work splendidly.

PRIMERS—PREMIUM

CCI achieves production of its superior Benchrest primers through several special steps. First, output of one of each of the six simultaneous production lines that produce primer cups is diverted so that all primers from that lot of Benchrest primers are as dimensionally identical as is feasible—every cup in that lot is produced using the same respective set of tools (anvil uniformity is so precise that it is not an issue). Second, the operator who has shown the ability to create the most consistent pellets during the previous month wins the right to make benchrest primer pellets (and a significant pay bonus). Finally, CCI uses a dedicated production line to install pellets, foil, and anvils, and to finish processing Benchrest primers—the keyword is consistency.

Perhaps surprisingly, primers marketed for benchrest or match applications might offer a particularly large consistency advantage when used in non-bolt-action guns. In these action types, striker energy is often comparatively low; also, striker energy can be relatively inconsistent. These primers can provide significant improvements in shot-to-shot uniformity in such a gun. I have proven this. So, although it might seem odd to spend extra money on cartridges destined for use in a rifle of moderate accuracy potential, doing so can be extraordinarily worthwhile. Such primers are always worth considering in one's best accuracy loads for use in any gun.

Amazing 223 slam-fire example (right): How this case held when the primer ignited with so much of the case wall unsupported is a mystery. Very likely, had this case ruptured, serious gun damage and injury to shooter, and possibly to bystanders, would have occurred. Most likely, the use of the CCI Mil-Spec primer would have prevented this slam fire.

PRIMERS—CCI MIL-SPEC

For handloaders working with gas-operated semiautomatic rifles, CCI Mil-Spec primers offer a significant safety advantage (see the introduction to this chapter). CCI intends these primers for loads using ball-type propellants; therefore, CCI only offers these with the magnum primer pellet. Hence, loads using easily ignited propellants might show increased pressure when ignited by these primers. The added safety margin against a slam fire well offsets that factor but, should testing prove an increase in muzzle velocity, it is certainly prudent to apply a commensurate charge reduction.

Perhaps because CCI makes these primers on its newest machines and with increased attention to dimensional uniformity, many advanced handloaders have reported superior accuracy when using these primers in bolt-action rifle cartridges. Because these primers use the same primer pellet as the corresponding CCI Magnum Rifle primer, CCI Mil-Spec primers are worth considering in any load specifying use of the CCI magnum rifle primer, and these are a direct substitution in such an application.

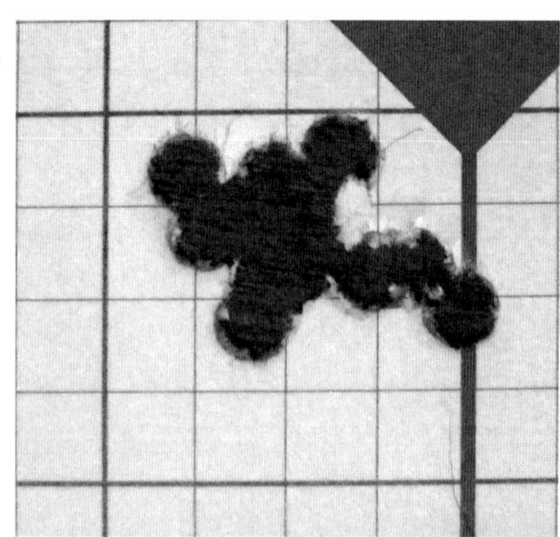

Finding a Hornet load that shoots this accurately (20 shots!) is rare. The Hornet is perhaps the single most sensitive cartridge to primer choice.

SEATING AND READING PRIMERS

CHAPTER 7

INTRODUCTION

A review of the previous chapter, particularly the discussions on primer safety, will suggest that pressing a primer into the primer pocket of a case has ramifications going far beyond the mechanical process involved. Safety issues loom—both handling and usage—but beyond that are the accuracy ramifications associated with choice of primer type and correct primer seating. In this chapter, I will address these aspects in some detail.

PRIMERS—SEATING

Among precision handloaders, opinions on primer seating vary. These seem to run the gamut from "It doesn't make a lick of difference how you seat a primer so long as you are reasonably consistent; seat it below flush, and don't crush the cup," to "You absolutely must be sure that you preload the priming pellet exactly three-thousandths inch (or some other specific distance) on each and every primer." Every opinion between these two extremes is well represented.

For what it might be worth, most target shooters agree that so long as the tool used seats the primers reasonably squarely and allows the operator to feel what is happening as the primer bottoms in the primer pocket, it will do the job. The handloader must practice reasonable care in seating all primers sufficiently deeply and consistently in the primer pockets. We even have good evidence to suggest that applying varying amounts of excess pressure after fully seating the primer harms ballistic uniformity little, if any; however, some action types, specific action designs, and even specific guns have proven to be unusually sensitive in this regard.

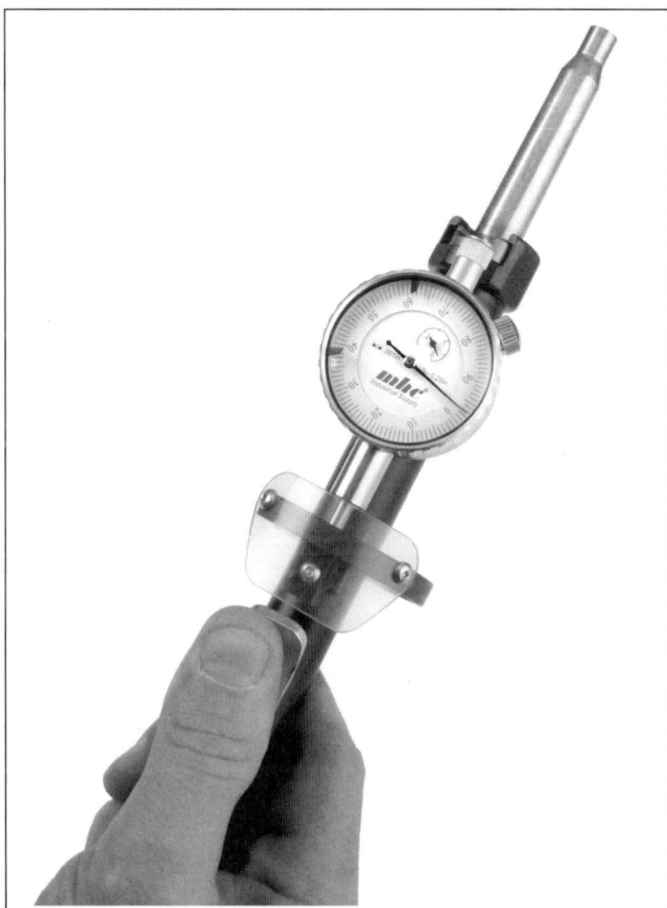

This K&M handheld priming tool is the most sophisticated of its kind. This tool allows handloaders to measure primer pocket depth and primer height and then to seat every primer to a specific amount of pellet preload (3/1000 inch is suggested for primers used in benchrest loads).

If you simply must have perfection, K&M makes a tool that allows precision seating of every primer to achieve exactly the same pellet preload, regardless of any vagaries in primer pocket depth or primer height.

This tool is expensive and comparatively slow to use. Furthermore, for accurate results, the handloader must square and clean the primer pocket of each case before using this tool. However, this tool does allow

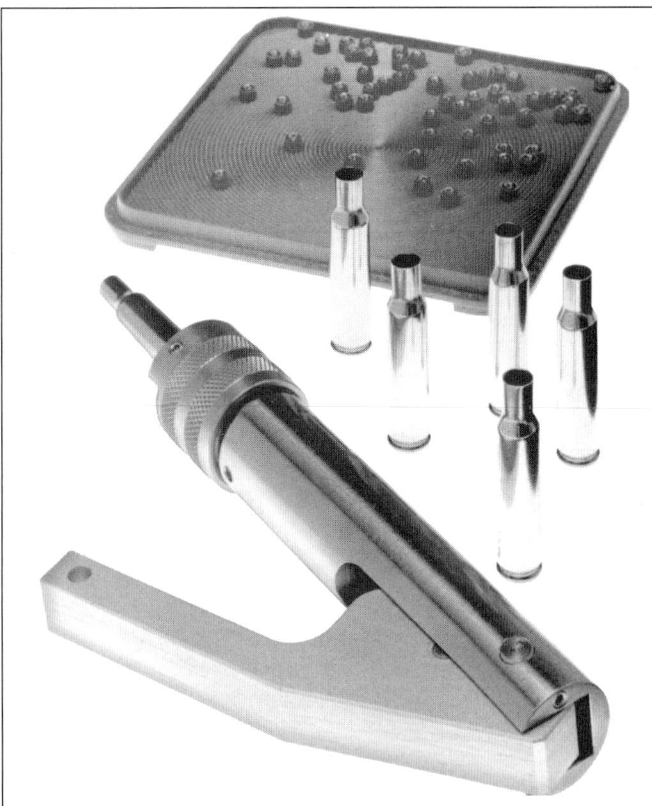

Sinclair (pictured) and K&M offer premium handheld primer-seating tools that offer exquisite feel. These are appropriate when loading a small number of critical cartridges—common during benchrest matches.

primer seating with precise consistency beyond all evident need of perfection, and it does offer exquisite feel during primer seating.

Both K&M and Sinclair International offer similar tools lacking the dial indicator. These tools allow accurate control of seating depth because each affords precise tactile feedback as the primer anvil impinges the bottom of the primer pocket.

Lee specifically proscribes use of Federal, RWS, Remington, or Fiocchi primers in its original Auto-Prime tool and the primer feeding systems used in its various progressive presses—use only CCI and Winchester primers with these. Lee periodically retests primer types, and, as formulations and processes change, other brands might prove to be safe for use in these tools—check the literature that came with your Lee tool and telephone Lee Precision for the latest information. The Auto-Prime XR resolves this limitation.

Proscribed primer brands are potentially unsafe in the noted Lee tools because of the potential for a mass detonation. In those tools, should an operator detonate one primer, as can happen when he carelessly crushes a primer by trying to seat it into a primer pocket that already contains a primer, that detonation subjects other primers in the tray to both shock and an incandescent flash. If this shock and flash can ignite a second primer, then most, or all, primers in the tray, perhaps one hundred, will very likely detonate en masse. Such an occurrence could have lethal consequences.

Lee has tested all available primer brands and types with its standard Auto-Prime tool located inside an explosion-proof box. Excepting CCI and Winchester, when the primer that is being seated is forced to detonate (experimentally by heating), all brands produce an unacceptable number of mass explosions.

By comparing Federal and CCI primers, we can gain some understanding of why brands vary in this regard. Federal primers do not have a foil cover over the primer pellet. An energetic combustible celluloid paint replaces the foil. That sealant ignites extremely easily at low temperature and burns quickly. For the intended

The original Lee Auto-Prime should only be used with CCI and Winchester primers. The newer XR version is significantly improved and is safe with all primer brands and types.

application, these are beneficial characteristics; among other things, these attributes help reduce combustion residues. However, use of this type of pellet sealant renders these primers comparatively easy to ignite through exposure of the open front of the cup to the flash from an adjacent primer.

Conversely, CCI and Winchester (and other primer brands) have a paper foil that substantially covers the pellet face. This foil deters inadvertent pellet ignition because it is only moderately combustible and it has a relatively high kindling temperature—with CCI and Winchester primers, the short-duration flash from an adjacent primer is unlikely to either ignite or penetrate through this paper, as is necessary to ignite the underlying pellet. Even when the paper does not fully cover the pellet face, the exposed paper absorbs heat and shock energy, so the pellet is not nearly as apt to ignite.

Compared to seating primers using a handheld priming tool, using a press-mounted priming tool is generally neither as fast nor as precise. The exception is the built-in primer seating system in the Forster Co-Ax press, which is marvelous. RCBS has also done a superior job with the APS system in the Pro-2000 press; this system provides acceptable feel during primer seating and it never malfunctions.

MTM and other manufacturers offer primer flipper trays. These are handy, particularly when filling primer tubes.

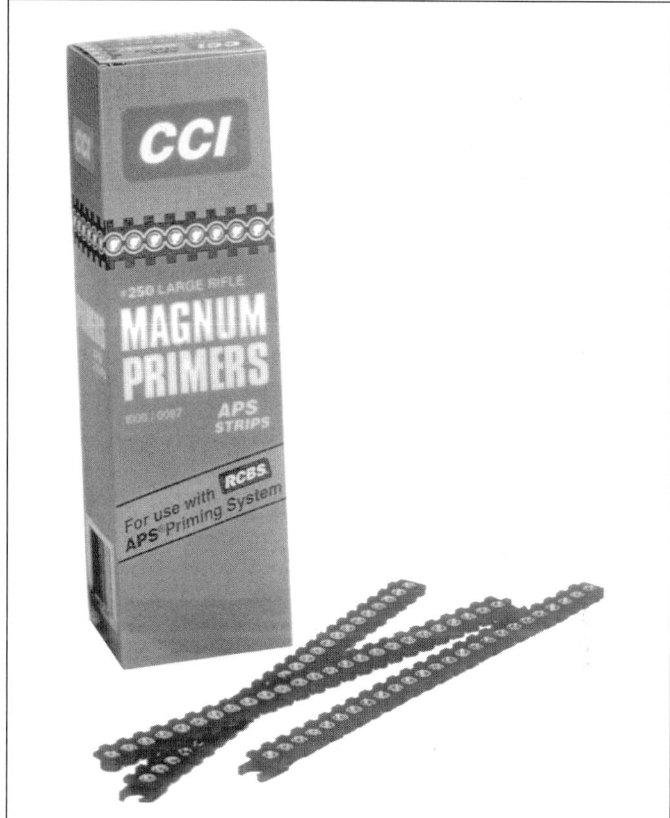

CCI offers primers packaged in APS strips. Federal might follow suit. This is a superior system for handling and installing primers.

Owing to the geometry involved, conventional press-mounted primer seating systems provide very little mechanical advantage and, therefore, the operator must use significant force, and he, therefore, does not have a good feel for what is happening as the primer bottoms into the primer pocket.

When loading with any progressive press, unless you decap cases and clean primer pockets ahead of time, you cannot conveniently remove primer pocket residue. While such residue does not generally degrade quality of the resulting cartridges, some handloaders prefer to remove it, as a matter of habit. I am in this group.

PRIMERS—APS SYSTEM

RCBS and CCI have teamed to offer special primer packaging and three related priming tools, all under the APS banner. (RCBS reports that APS does not necessarily stand for anything—Automated Priming System seems reasonable to me.) This system combines plastic strips containing primers, located in tight holes at fixed intervals, with a positive feed mechanism. As factory loaded, these strips are color-coded, to identify primers by type.

The RCBS APS system is the ultimate method for handling primers (you do not have to!) and for seating primers. RCBS also adapted this system to its Pro-2000 press. Refer to chapter 17.

This system includes a tool that allows handloaders to fill the reusable APS strips quickly and easily with any brand of primer (this patented system is several times faster than manually filling primer tubes). This system is so good that we can only hope that other press manufacturers will see fit to incorporate it into their progressive units.

The RCBS handheld APS priming tool is one of the best such tools. It features a universal shellholder that works for everything from 22 Hornet to 45-70 Springfield and easily converts for left-hand use, as shown here.

The handheld APS unit has a one-size-fits-all shellholder, and it takes only a few seconds to change seating stems as necessary to switch between primer sizes. I am so fond of this tool that I own two: one set-up for large primers and one set-up for small primers. This saves me the few seconds that it takes to change out the priming ram stem.

APS strips hold twenty-five primers. These strips clip together and automatically ratchet through APS priming machines. This guarantees that this system is the fastest and most convenient on the market. The handheld unit easily converts for proper right- or left-hand use, which is most appreciated by sinistral users. The only noted drawback is that the handheld unit is a bit short on leverage; hence, seating large quantities of primers in one session (more than about 100) can become tiring. For this reason, inclusion of a padded-rubber grip would be helpful.

RCBS offers three versions of the APS tool—press-mounted, bench-mounted, and handheld. Each type is useful and has specific advantages. The press-mounted tool provides sufficient leverage so that a child could properly seat hundreds of primers without tiring. The bench-mounted tool is almost as easy to use and has the advantage of being always ready to use—handy.

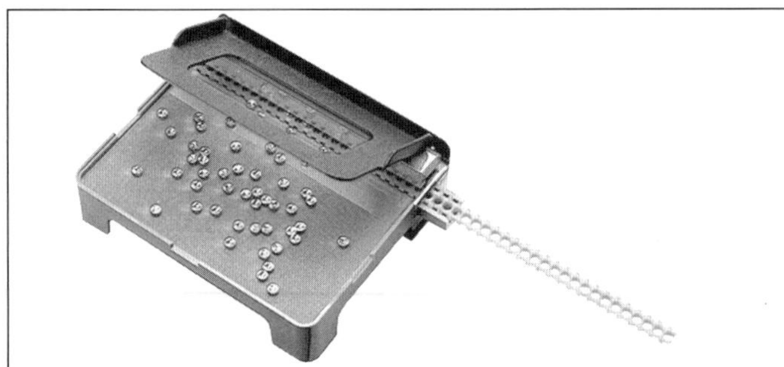

With this APS accessory, the handloader can insert 200 primers into eight APS strips in about one minute! These strips work with any brand of primer.

Those who intend to hunt dangerous game are well advised to use a sealant on both primer-to-case joint and bullet-to-case joint. Just wipe a dab of sealant on these joints of finished cartridge, wait a few seconds, and carefully remove any excess.

The handheld unit is portable and convenient, but, as noted, it can be tiring to use when priming a large number of cases.

PRIMERS—SEALING

Ammunition that you might use in areas of extreme weather conditions, and, especially, where atmospheric humidity is unusually high, is subject to ballistic alteration by infiltration of moisture into both primer and propellant. By the simple expedient of sealing both the primer pocket and the case neck, handloaders can eliminate this problem.

A more serious concern, for most of us, is the possibility of penetrating oil reaching the primer pellet by infiltrating between the case and primer. This sort of contamination can lead to duds, squibs, and hangfires. In a dangerous-game hunting or self-defense situation, any such outcome could have personally lethal consequences. Perhaps the worst eventuality is a squib cartridge that leaves a bullet stuck in the barrel. This renders the gun worse than useless. In the heat of battle, one might chamber and fire a second round. With a bullet stuck in the barrel, a violent and potentially dangerous barrel burst is most likely.

George and Roy's primer sealant can completely prevent this problem. Providing that primers are not contaminated before seating and that cases and bullets are free of oil, a simple application of this product creates a loaded round that is highly resistant to infiltration and contamination by water (either from humidity or as a liquid), penetrating oil, and most other common chemicals (in either liquid or vapor form). When making ammunition that is potentially subject to questionable handling practices, this is certainly a worthwhile step.

PRIMERS—PRESSURE SIGNS

Excessive headspace is common in traditional lever-action rifles—the typical culprit is a too thin case rim. (U.S. producers have routinely and incessantly insisted on making case rims that are significantly thinner than the industry specified minimum thickness, which suggests the question, "Why bother to have a specification?") An excessively heavy striker blow can drive a rimless bottlenecked case into the chamber by moving the case shoulder. This creates functional headspace at the instant of firing. Similarly, full-length resizing can excessively shorten the body of a bottlenecked case. Refer to chapter 5.

When firing a low- to moderate-pressure cartridge in a gun with excessive functional headspace, the primer cup initially backs out of the case until it hits the bolt. If the case body bonds to the chamber and does not stretch, the primer will protrude from the fired case to the extent that functional headspace allows. Conversely, if the case body stretches, as the case head moves toward the bolt face, it will reseat the primer. Sometimes, when this happens, the unsupported portion of the cup will swell. This creates an excessively flattened primer—some ballisticians have referred to this as a "nailed" primer. To some extent, this mechanism creates a situation in high-pressure cartridges where greater headspace (within the normal range) results in a flatter primer despite identical chamber pressure.

These examples represent an entire suite of complications to anyone reliably "reading" pressure by looking at fired primers. Each round used a different brand of primer, and these loads generated very similar pressure. Note the variation in primer flattening, marking, and partial blanking. Flattening of primer at lower right suggests excessive pressure; deep dimple and small flat area of primer at upper left suggest mild pressure; modest flattening and partial blanking of the other two primers simultaneously suggests high and low pressure!

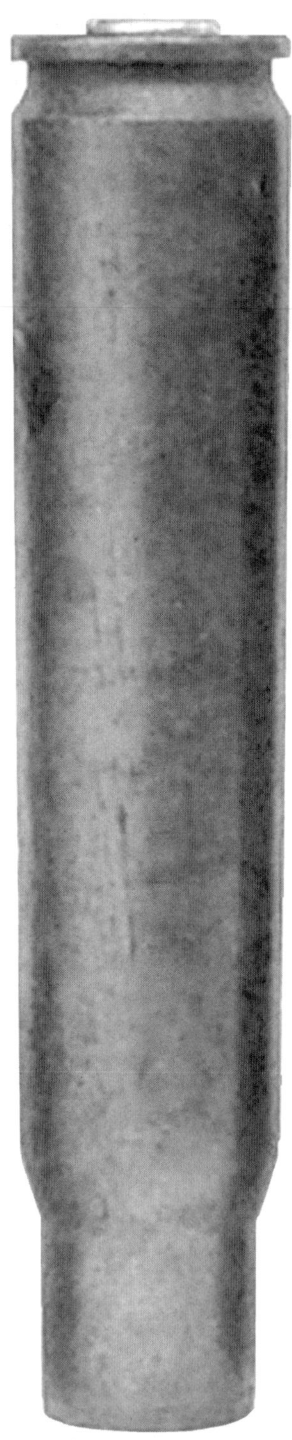

This view shows a 8mm Mauser case that has been fired in an unusually long chamber. This represents about 15/1000-inch headspace. Many 30-30 and similar rifles show similarly excessive headspace. As with this particular 8mm Mauser load, many factory 30-30 and similar loads do not generate enough pressure to stretch the case to fit the chamber, and, therefore, primer protrusion mirrors headspace. In loads generating significantly higher pressure or when the chamber or case is lubricated, the primer is reseated as the case head moves rearward, which masks this potential headspace indication. Most normal loads usually generate sufficient pressure to reseat the primer.

Keeping in mind the complications associated with variations in headspace, general primer appearance is a pressure indicator in relatively high-pressure cartridges. All else being equal, greater chamber pressure results in a larger flattened area on the primer face. However, no one can consistently use primer appearance as a means of assuredly monitoring peak chamber pressure. Besides headspace sensitivity, other pitfalls exist.

First, primer cup thickness and hardness varies from lot-to-lot and from brand-to-brand, and primer cups harden with aging (worked brass age hardens). With any given chamber pressure, the size of the flattened area on the face of the fired primer depends upon primer cup hardness and thickness.

Because primer cup hardness, cup thickness, and gun characteristics all control cup flattening in response to

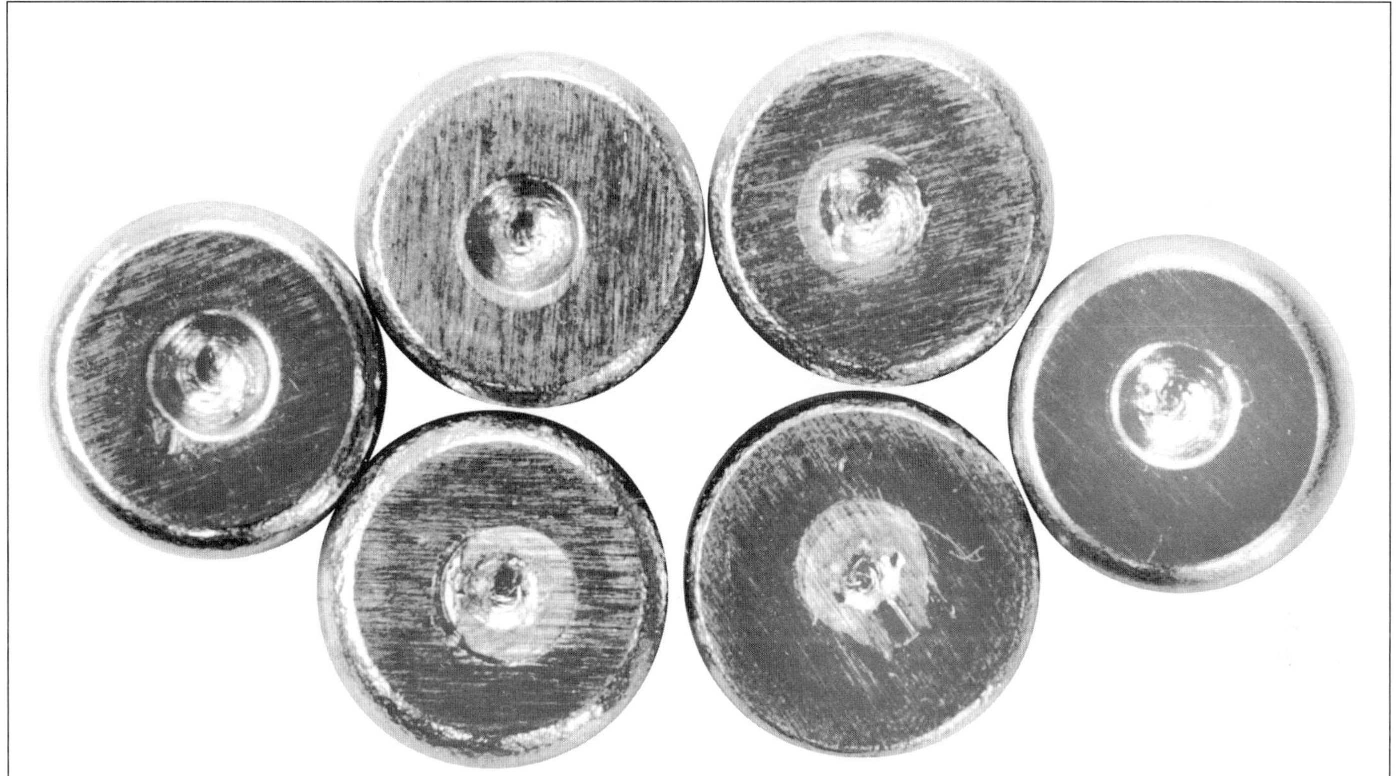

These are various brands and types of small (rifle and pistol) primers from otherwise identical 22 Hornet loads. The 1885 low-wall rifle used had a light hammer and striker and was, therefore, sensitive to cup strength. Partial blanking, which resulted in softer and thinner cups (center), created brass cuttings that would eventually jam the striker hole sufficiently to result in misfires. (In some guns, a blanked primer can release significant, potentially dangerous, gas into the shooter's face.)

any given level of chamber pressure, it is fundamentally impossible to judge pressure accurately by looking at primer flattening. When we realize that no two primers are identical and that, with any given load and in any given gun, every brand, type, production lot, and age of primer will show a different amount of flattening, this method of reading pressure retains very little appeal; nevertheless, it has some value.

Second, in many cartridges, safe and sensible pressures do not create any primer flattening. Examples include most revolver and pistol cartridges and normal loads for many older rifle chamberings.

Third, partial blanking (protrusion of cup material into the firing pin hole in the bolt—often incorrectly referred to as cratering) or blanking (piercing of the cup by extrusion into the firing pin hole in the bolt—often incorrectly referred to as piercing) is dependent upon striker-to-bolt fit, chamber pressure, and striker characteristics. Often, a very mild load can completely blank a primer when fired in a gun with a loose striker-to-bolt fit or with an unusually light striker; conversely, a patently dangerous overload with the same primer might not show any evidence of primer blanking when fired in a gun with a heavy, properly fitted striker.

Fourth, a weak striker spring can contribute to this problem. In most guns, a bit of gunsmithing easily corrects this problem. And, usually, it is advisable to correct this problem because low striker energy always results in poor ballistic uniformity and accuracy, even if blanking or partial blanking does not occur.

Of itself, the existence of a primer-to-case gas leak (as evidenced by a smoky ring around the primer) proves nothing. During case manufacture, primer pockets sometimes acquire longitudinal scratches along the

This excessively flattened primer represents a perfect example of the primer "nailing" that can occur when a cartridge has significantly excessive headspace.

Note the complete absence of evident case-head deformation or engravement of bolt features into the primer face. Also note that one area of the primer cup actually protrudes past the outside edge of the entrance radius of the primer pocket (near bottom, in this view). If chamber pressure had been anywhere nearly as high as this degree of primer flattening suggests, the case head would be monumentally deformed (more likely it would have completely failed), and both the primer and case head would mirror bolt-face machining imperfections.

cylindrical perimeter walls. Those scratches can allow insignificant gas leakage that will, nevertheless, leave a small amount of smoky residue on the case head. I have an entire batch of such cases that came to me as factory-loaded ammunition.

Conversely, intense overloads that open case heads until the primers fall out of the case often do not generate any gas leakage. This is because the force acting to expand the primer pocket is also acting to expand the primer cup and, thereby, keep it solidly pushed against the primer pocket wall.

The bottom line on primer appearance is this: Unless you are completely familiar with the load, gun, and primer used, never suspect that any visible characteristic of a fired primer will allow you to make a precise pressure judgment. Yes, you can make observations, and, yes, those observations might be valuable, but this is an inexact art, at best.

SOURCE FOR SPECIALTY PRODUCT REFERENCED IN THIS CHAPTER:

George and Roy's
2950 NW 29th
Portland, OR 97210
800-553-3022

PROPELLANT

CHAPTER 8

INTRODUCTION

Here, I will consider the history and manufacture of various propellant types (blackpowder, bulk smokeless propellant, smokeless propellant, and blackpowder substitutes). Some of these are now available to handloaders. Each propellant has characteristics that determine how it functions and, therefore, its proper usage.

PROPELLANT—SAFETY

Again, we must consider safety issues. It is all-too-easy for handloaders to become complacent about storing, handling, and using propellant. Your safety, and that of others, depends upon doing each of these with respect and attention to detail. Adhere to the following:

- Never allow more than one type of propellant to be on the loading bench and within reach of your loading position during any loading session.
- Never allow any kind of propellant to come into contact with any significant heat source (where temperature might exceed about 300 degrees F), even for an instant. Examples include sparks, open flame, hot lead, an electric heating element, etc.
- Whenever possible either store smokeless propellants at room temperature or under refrigeration—the cooler the better.
- Never use a vacuum cleaner or any other type of electrically driven cleaning tool to clean up spilled propellant—ignition can result.
- Never use any propellant of uncertain origin or condition.
- Always follow all recommended propellant handling safety precautions, copies of which are available from all major distributors.
- Follow all precautions printed on the container.
- Always store unused propellant in the original container.

BEFORE PROCEEDING WITH ANY HANDLOADING, ALWAYS DOUBLE-CHECK TO ASSURE THAT YOU ARE USING THE PROPELLANT THAT YOU INTEND TO USE AND THAT THE PROPELLANT THAT YOU ARE ABOUT TO USE IS THE ONE THAT THE LOADING DATA SOURCE REQUIRES FOR THE INTENDED LOAD. IT IS AMAZING HOW OFTEN EXPERIENCED HANDLOADERS MANAGE TO DO OTHERWISE.

I have personally examined the remains of three rifles that a veteran handloader had thoroughly destroyed because he failed to follow these obviously critical mandates. In one instance, the handloader managed to use one propellant when he believed he was using a different propellant. In another instance, the handloader managed to confuse two propellants, believing that one was the other because the names were too similar. In both of those instances, the propellant used burned many times faster than the suggested propellant for the load.

I am aware of all too many instances where a novice handloader was too lazy to buy and use a loading manual and, therefore, relied upon information from some other source—a fellow shooter, the Internet, or otherwise. All too often, such a shooter gets the recipe wrong and therefore ends up using the wrong propellant with disastrous consequences.

On one occasion, as a nascent handloader, I had to pull the bullets from twenty rounds of my meticulously prepared 244 Remington ammunition. I discovered, while cleaning up (after I thought I was finished) that I had not set the scale at the weight I had intended to set it at. Each round contained precisely five grains less than the intended charge. Always properly zero the scale before each use and double-check to make sure that you have correctly adjusted the scale (or measure). Carefully wrong is just as dangerous as haphazardly wrong.

ALWAYS VERIFY THAT THE CHARGE YOU ARE USING IS THE CHARGE THAT YOU INTEND TO USE.

Always store propellants in a safe place. Cool storage conditions are ideal; cold is better. Store propellants in original containers. Always read and heed label warnings.

With correct storage, shelf life of properly made smokeless propellant is many decades and can exceed one century. However, poorly made smokeless propellant can contain a significant percentage of residual acids, which can dramatically reduce shelf life, particularly with storage at elevated temperature (anything significantly above about 80 degrees F). Even when such a propellant is stored properly, it can deteriorate. Such deterioration generates heat, additional acid, and acidic fumes.

Once such deterioration begins, the progression of deterioration will accelerate by autocatalysis. In the worst-case scenario, the process of deterioration can lead to autocombustion. Two of my acquaintances have observed this happen.

In 1966, Norm Nelson opened the door and looked into his garage. He had stored a three-year-old can of 4320 on a window sill, where the sun periodically shone onto the can and, thereby, warmed the propellant. As he looked into the garage, red fumes began to spew from that sealed can. This caught his attention. Very soon, the cap blew off the can, profuse red fumes erupted, and, seconds later, the propellant ignited.

Periodically check smokeless propellant by opening the can and smelling the contents—THE SNIFF TEST. Existence of any harsh, sharp, or acidic odor is cause for concern. When such an odor exists, discard the propellant, as suggested by the manufacturer.

While autodeterioration is rare in modern propellants, handloaders have reported it in some lots manufactured since about 1975. Hence, it is advisable to check all propellants periodically with the simple sniff test.

PROPELLANT—BLACKPOWDER

Smokeless propellant is a relatively new invention. My friend, David Livingston, is a blackpowder enthusiast. He proclaims, "Smokeless propellant is a passing fad; it will never last."

Conversely, blackpowder has been around for a very long time. Although the origin of blackpowder is lost in history, we do know that it was the first substance used effectively for propelling objects from a tube—the crude barrel of a crude gun.

In the Middle Ages, alchemists tested various formulations related to fulminate of mercury for use as cannon fodder; all were entirely too violent. Much later came energetic nitrations of cellulose, guanidine, and ammonia. Experimenters also tested various compositions combining these substances with diverse organic materials. These compositions represented an effort to mitigate the energy release rate of these chemical compounds. More recently, chemists have tested several other substances, some of which have found some application. Those noted within this section are the most important.

What was the first use of a propellant in the military context? In the thirteenth century, armies of the Middle East (Greek & Muslim) used a crude mixture of potassium nitrate and pine pitch (or petroleum) to power rockets. Evidently, these formulations were less than a booming success. No doubt, the unpredictable nature of those mixtures was a major limiting factor. Even if the combatants did use these devices primarily for psychological influence, the result more often than not represented a two-edged sword—rocketry and gunnery crews need to have at least a modicum of faith that the weapons they are using will bring destruction upon the enemy and not upon themselves.

Blackpowder was the first substance adapted for use as a propellant, in the modern sense. The best evidence suggests that Chinese were the first to discover this physical mixture of potassium nitrate [KNO_3], elemental sulfur [S], and charcoal (elemental carbon [C] with an imprecise admixture of various hydrocarbons). Certainly, the Chinese knew of blackpowder by as early as the eighth century BC. In 1242 AD (two millennia later!) in an anagram, the European Roger Bacon, described the product. His intention, evidently, was to veil his discovery, as if that might somehow delay others from discovering and using blackpowder for potentially nefarious purposes—historically, such misdirection has seldom been of much value.

The first known recorded European mention of blackpowder was in 848 AD. In a treatise called *Liber Ignium (The Book of Fire),* by Marcus Graecus, almost four centuries earlier than Bacon's widely credited 1242 anagram. Therefore, truly, it seems that it must have been useless for Bacon to veil his information.

It is likely that several Europeans discovered blackpowder about the same time. Most likely, several experimenters independently discovered the propellant properties of blackpowder—chemistry students are still doing so. Although, as noted, the Chinese knew of blackpowder for many centuries BC, there exists no proof that they were either first or unique in that discovery. It is also likely that Bacon, or others, deduced this mixture, based upon hearsay, without ever seeing it used in firecrackers or as a novelty compound.

Vagaries of uncertain history have shrouded all such information. What is a bit more certain is that Bacon was among the first to have realized the potential for military application and, specifically, the potential for the destructive use of blackpowder. Interestingly, owing to military secrecy, we do know that we will never know much about the first use of blackpowder as a propellant. Sometime after 1242, someone adapted some type of tube to make a gun by inserting blackpowder and a projectile; we will never know who that was, where it happened, or the date (references and claims vary widely). We do not even know the effectiveness of that gun.

Experimenters hollowed out logs to create the earliest barrels. These were too weak to withstand substantial charges of properly prepared blackpowder, even without any projectile inserted. That weakness led to the introduction of the steel-banded wooden structure. Artisans fashioned these in direct replication of the well-established banded water barrel and, hence, the modern name *barrel.*

Typical Blackpowder Formulations: Various Eras (Parts by Weight)

Source	Era (circa)	Salt-Peter	Charcoal	Sulfur
Marcus Graecus	1700s	66²/₃	22²/₉	11¹/₉
		69²/₉	23¹/₉	7²/₃
Roger Bacon	1252	37½	31¼	31¼
Arderne (sample)	1350	66²/₃	22²/₉	11¹/₉
Whitehorne	1560	50	33¹/₃	16²/₃
Bruxelles studies	1560	75	15⅝	9⅜
British Govt.	1635	75	12½	12½
Bishop Watson	1781	75	15	10
Typical Modern	1990	75	15	10

For various reasons, powder makers neither established nor followed exact formulations for the most energetic form of blackpowder until centuries later. One problem was that the raw ingredients were routinely of unknown and variable purity. Another reason was that each craftsman kept his favorite recipe as a trade secret. A final factor is that different applications required formulations generating differing amounts of energy. Across a wide range, adjusting percentage of each ingredient serves to change combustion rate and total energy production. Owing to the limited strength of barrels, increasing energy was not beneficial until several centuries after blackpowder had come into wide use as a propellant.

What those early makers strove to realize was a product that generated the maximum performance the gun barrel could withstand. A greater charge of a slower, less efficient product could often produce greater projectile distance without busting the gun—distance mattered a great deal; the amount of propellant used mattered very little. Generally, we follow a similar path today, even with our most modern smokeless cartridges and guns—to limit generated pressure, producers slow the combustion of smokeless propellants for most applications; to improve performance, we use bigger cases that hold larger charges of relatively slower-burning propellants.

Original blackpowder formulations were simply loose physical mixtures of powders—whence the name, powder. These powders would not remain properly mixed during handling—gunners had to use the mixture of powders without significant transport, which would rapidly separate the component particles. Moreover, owing to the extremely hygroscopic nature of potassium nitrate (saltpeter), powder makers most often mixed blackpowder on the battlefield immediately before use. This added a complicating and interesting specter to battle; for the first time, participants found themselves concentrating on protecting their own turf.

Very early, producers discovered that coating loose granules with graphite significantly reduced moisture absorption. Some evidence suggests that producers might have standardized this approach as early as the late thirteenth century. However, the advantages offered by graphite were of little value when cannoneers typically used powder within minutes of preparation.

Alchemists and other experimenters soon discovered the process of saltpeter purification through recrystallization. This provided a material of consistent and significantly increased purity (energy potential). However, again, typical guns of that era simply could not withstand the pressure generated by such powders—for hundreds of years thereafter, for most applications, cannoneers preferred to use the original product.

By 1450, most manufacturers had adopted a more-or-less standard blackpowder composition, by weight:

- 50 parts potassium nitrate (saltpeter [KNO_3]);
- 25 parts sulfur [S];
- 25 parts charcoal (carbon [C], with a significant percentage of hydrocarbons).

Makers pulverized these into powders and mixed those dry. The manufacturer named the resulting product serpentine powder. The carbon is responsible for the black half of the modern name.

If cannoneers used either a too heavy projectile or an excessive charge, serpentine would develop enough pressure to destroy the gun. Therefore, despite the relatively poor energy yield, serpentine powder was sufficient for the task at hand; there existed little demand for a formulation that either contained more energy or that burned faster.

Before 1400, progressive advances in metallurgy had rendered barrels that could effectively utilize something more powerful than serpentine. Gunners and battle strategists recognized that a more powerful propellant would allow increased range, which is of monumental importance. (I will return to this.) Thus began the race to perfect blackpowder.

Perfection of modern corn blackpowder occurred about 1450, in Nuremberg. This came a century after initial investigations in France. Production of corn powder begins with a paste formed of the three dry ingredients, plus water. In that era, application of crushing blows from large hammers, or the grinding action provided by rolling large stone wheels over a stone base (the preferred modern method), provided the energy necessary to process the paste.

As the resulting mixed paste—which (ideally) contains only minute and thoroughly intermixed particles—dries, it produces a layer of cake where the three ingredients are in intimate physical contact. The producer controls constituent particle size through altering grinding and mixing time. As mixing continues, constituent particles are ground progressively finer. Mixes with finer constituent particles burn progressively faster and cleaner, thereby producing more energy and less fouling. This improves efficiency, which increases potential velocity.

As the wet cake of slurry dries, saltpeter crystallizes out in a way that binds the mix together (as a glue), preserving the even mixture that the three components had in the paste form. After partial drying, the producer manipulates the resulting sheets to break the material into small pieces, called corn—this name derives from the general size and shape of the resulting particles (corn is the European term for various cereal grains).

In the most advanced production facilities, the final step was the application of a graphite glaze to the corned powder. Producers applied this glazing immediately after drying, polishing, and sieving. Graphite glazing represented a significant improvement and offered several benefits. First, it reduced the tendency of granules to absorb atmospheric humidity. Second, it reduced the tendency for production of static electric charges to occur during interparticle mixing—such as could occur during handling, transportation, or loading. Third, it improved granule flow characteristics. Finally, it reduced the tendency of propellant granules to form large cakes while in storage. Excepting this final factor, graphite glazing provides the same benefits in modern smokeless propellants.

Owing to the intimate intercrystalline physical contact produced, wet mixing imparts corn powder with an entirely different burning characteristic when compared to serpentine powder. Corn powder burns at least twice as fast. This creates a significant indirect benefit. With corn powder, back venting (gas venting through the touchhole) wastes almost none of the combustion force. Conversely, back venting considerably reduces serpentine powder performance. When used in a weight-for-weight replacement, corned powder produces one-third greater projectile energy than does serpentine powder. Moreover, corned powder leaves far less residue and requires less careful ramming. (The buildup of static electric charges often resulted in ignition of serpentine powder during loading.)

Comparison of Blackpowder Energy Production (Parts by Weight)

Powder Type	Strength Factor	Composition		
		Saltpeter	Sulfur	Charcoal
Bacon's	41 1/5%	37½	31¼	31¼
Serpentine	57%	50	25	25
Corned	75%	50	25	25
Modern	100%	75	10	15

Despite the benefits of corned powder, for many decades serpentine powder retained a stronghold for use in weaker barrels. Employment of corned powder in small arms began in England long before 1560. However, higher cost and excessive energy continued to limit use of corned powder in early ordnance—the big guns.

Contrary to common intuition, blackpowder does not detonate—it burns. Deflagration is the correct term—deflagration is defined as unusually rapid self-combustion, without the need for added fuel or oxidizer. Blackpowder will burn in a vacuum, as will smokeless propellant.

Blackpowder is a progressive-burning substance. Near room temperature, increasing temperature by about 10 degrees C (18 degrees F) doubles combustion rate. In a blackpowder propellant charge, combustion temperature easily exceeds 2,000 degrees C (3,600 degrees F), so combustion progresses extremely rapidly. In a typical cartridge, complete charge combustion occurs in less than one-thousandth second. Combustion of a comparable charge burned freely in the atmosphere takes several-tenths of one second. (Modern smokeless propellants are far more progressive—a small, unconfined pile takes several seconds to burn.)

The fact that blackpowder burns, rather than detonates, has been proven in the laboratory and is easily observed by examining performance of progressively smaller granulations in otherwise identical loads. All else being equal, progressively smaller granules produce progressively greater chamber pressure and muzzle velocity. In effect, granules ignite and burn inward from the surface until combustion is complete. Within the granule-size range of commercially available blackpowders, the smaller the granules, the greater the initial combustion surface area and the greater the overall combustion rate.

Any significant deviation from the typical modern blackpowder formula reduces both combustion rate and effective energy yield. This reduces performance in firearm applications. However, such alternative formulations are in common use for other applications.

Napoleon's chemists found the ultimate advancement in blackpowder propellant. They discovered that incorporation of end-to-end holes through hexagonal granules was extremely beneficial for cannon powder. Perforations allowed the use of much larger granules. Upon ignition, these initially generated gas comparatively slowly. However, as these burned, the rate of energy release and gas generation either remained constant (one perforation) or increased (multiple perforations).

Under constant confining pressure, a solid granule burns with a degressive response curve—as combustion progresses energy generation diminishes because surface area decreases. A single-perforation granule burns with a flat response curve—as combustion progresses, energy generation remains constant. A multiperforation granule burns with a progressive response curve—as combustion progresses, energy generation increases.

When comparing ideal granule sizes of solid and perforated granules and maximum safe charges, the latter maintained higher pressure behind the projectile as they moved down the barrel. This resulted in much higher muzzle velocity.

This was a major factor in Napoleon's military success. His cannoneers could establish an artillery line that was absolutely out of the range of the opposition's cannon and then proceed with an annihilating barrage from a position of essentially total safety. The result literally was not a fair fight. The same scheme (granule perforation) is used today in the most effective smokeless propellants—velocity has always been king, which is why we prefer guns to arrows, spears, knives, rocks, and fists.

PROPELLANT—BLACKPOWDER ALTERNATIVE MIXTURES

Cocoapowder, also known as brownpowder, was an improved type of blackpowder. Cocoapowder was blackpowder with a higher percentage of saltpeter, less or no sulfur, and brown charcoal.

Saltpeter content was higher than in standard blackpowder, up to 80 percent versus 75 percent. This increased the amount of oxidizer in the mix, which improved combustion. This increased combustion efficiency. This reduced particulates and increased energy.

The role of sulfur in the combustion of blackpowder is very difficult to define. Sulfur is something of a catalyst and something of a plastic carrier that promotes intimate contact of active particles while also rapidly conducting heat. Having said that, no one has proven any actual catalytic properties; nevertheless, the fact that sulfur speeds combustion would seem to suggest that some such activity actually does exist. In any case, in these formulations sulfur has two deleterious properties. First, it generates acids that destroy steel: more sulfur, more acid . . . more acid, more damage. Second, these acid-forming reactions consume energy, which reduces ballistic potential.

Partial combustion of rye straw produces brown charcoal. Brown charcoal includes a relatively high percentage of various hydrocarbons. This gives brown charcoal significant plasticity. This reduces, or eliminates, the need for sulfur. Cocoapowder contains about 17.6 percent to about 20 percent brown charcoal.

Reducing sulfur content slows combustion. This allows the use of a heavier charge to achieve the same peak pressure. With more total energy and more gas produced, chamber pressure stays higher longer. Therefore, total bullet acceleration force is greater. Therefore, bullet velocity is greater.

Compared to typical charcoal, the increased hydrocarbon content of partially burned rye straw is the secret to these propellants. Brown charcoal is sufficiently plastic to supplant the primary role of sulfur. Brown charcoal flows easily, achieving intimate contact between the carbon (fuel) that it contains and the saltpeter (oxidizer).

However, in gunnery applications brownpowder was more difficult to ignite compared to blackpowder. Also, these products were more apt to ignite under the process of vigorous shaking or stirring. These propellants saw application in the Spanish-American War (1898) with impressive effect. However, upon cessation of hostilities, all unused stocks were destroyed because of their well-recognized extreme volatility. Smokeless powder was then eclipsing almost all blackpowder derivatives, owing to its superior potential as a propellant; hence, the Spanish American War represents the last military use of brownpowder.

Before moving beyond blackpowder, I must mention two other related compounds that achieved some measure of importance. In 1885, a Hamburg resident named Gäns obtained a patent for an energetic propellant powder that came into use under the name amidpulver (*pulver* means powder in German). His original formulation contained 40 percent to 45 percent saltpeter [KNO_3] with 35 percent to 38 percent ammonium nitrate [$NH4NO_3$] and 14 percent to 22 percent charcoal [C].

Later changes in composition improved the propellant properties of amidpulver. Chiefly this

Typical Brownpowder Compositions (Parts by Weight)

Country	Saltpeter	Brown Charcoal	Sulfur
England	79	18	3
	$77^2/_5$	$17^3/_5$	5
Germany	78	19	3
	80	20	0
France	78	19	3

resulted from a reduction of saltpeter [KNO_3]. The improved version typically contained 14 percent KNO_3, 37 percent NH_4NO_3, and 49 percent charcoal. Experimenters also tested similar mixtures containing a small percentage of aromatic nitrogen compounds (generally explosives related to picric acid or to trinitrotoluene—TNT).

These substances had significant advantages, compared to blackpowder. Amidpulver creates no muzzle flash. Equally important, the small amount of bluish smoke produced dissipates very rapidly. The absence of any visible flash and the production of only a limited amount of quickly dissipating smoke make it possible for cannoneers to maintain a clear field of fire and to shoot at night without compromising their location. Amidpulver also has a comparatively low combustion temperature. This suggests low barrel erosion and corrosion rates, both of which are significant artillery considerations.

A similar propellant, ammonpulver, was used extensively during World War I. Ammonpulver is composed of 80 percent to 90 percent NH_4NO_3 (ammonium nitrate) with charcoal making up the remainder. Ammonpulver has several interesting characteristics. In an unconfined burn, flame temperature reaches only about 900 degrees C. Ballistic performance is very similar to double-base smokeless propellants containing about one-third nitroglycerin (by weight)—which is startling performance for any physical mixture.

The manufacture of ammonpulver is inexpensive and simple. Ammonpulver produces great power, zero muzzle flash, and zero smoke. These factors are significant positive attributes. It is insensitive to shock and friction but it is more difficult to ignite than blackpowder. As a propellant, it requires a strong igniter charge, but in most applications that is easy to provide.

When using ammonpulver as a cannon propellant, designers usually create a single, cartridge-fitting, perforated granule. Minor modifications to this basic geometry allow for the precise control of burn rate.

A serious drawback is that ammonpulver is highly hygroscopic; hence, it is necessary to hermetically seal both bulk propellant packaging and loaded ammunition. Worse, ammonpulver does not tolerate wide ambient temperature swings. In granules containing any significant moisture, freezing will generate ice crystals that can disrupt the granules and thereby dramatically increase the surface area and the relative burn rate. Worse, at 32.1 degrees C (89.8 degrees F), ammonium nitrate [NH_4NO_3] undergoes a state transition; hence, when the temperature of ammonpulver exceeds 89.8 degrees F, the ammonium nitrate spontaneously recrystallizes from the low-temperature (rhombohedral) form into the high-temperature (monoclinic) form. This change in crystalline shape crumbles the granule. Firing a cartridge containing such a pulverized charge is almost certain to result in a burst gun.

Because both amidpulver and ammonpulver are simple physical mixtures of an oxidizer and a fuel, most ballisticians classify these substances with other blackpowder-related propellants. Excepting the newest blackpowder substitutes, these are the only such substances showing significant potential as propellants.

Typical Bulk Propellant Compositions (Parts by Weight)

NC	N in NC	KNO_3	$BaNO_3$	Starch	Paraffin	Diphenylamine
84	$13^{15}/_{100}$	7½	7½	0	0	1
87	$12^{9}/_{10}$	6	2	0	4	1
89	$12^{9}/_{10}$	6	3	1	0	1

PROPELLANT—EARLY NITROGEN BASED

Before 1900 and simultaneously with the discovery of dramatically stronger steel formulations, smokeless substances were gaining popularity as propellants. The value of smokeless propellant is easy to understand if we consider the consequences of blackpowder combustion—the by-products include heat, gas, and particulates. Blackpowder produces sufficient heat to suggest impressive ballistic potential. However, even the most efficient combustion of the best grade of blackpowder converts more than 50 percent of the charge into particulates.

This characteristic dramatically limits blackpowder efficiency. The relatively heavy and therefore docile particles cannot effectively accelerate a bullet and accelerating these particles consumes considerable energy. Because combustion converts practically 100 percent of smokeless propellant into gas (relatively light molecules), a charge of smokeless propellant that generates the same total heat and peak pressure will impart about twice the projectile energy, and will do so while producing very little smoke or corrosive barrel fouling.

In 1864, Captain Schultze of the Prussian artillery produced what was evidently the first successful smokeless propellant. This followed the 1846 discovery of nitrocellulose (NC) by Christian Friedrich Schönbein, a German Swiss; it took some time for experimenters to find a way to tame nitrocellulose for safe use in guns. Captain Schultze's product was a bulk smokeless propellant based upon saltpeter-impregnated sawdust. His process was quite sophisticated. It was, however, worthwhile. It resulted in a volume-for-volume, low-fouling substitute for blackpowder, hence the bulk name. On a volume-for-volume basis, bulk propellant and blackpowder are essentially ballistically interchangeable.

Compared to blackpowder, this product had many of the clean-burning advantages of modern smokeless propellants, and no significant handicaps. This and similarly working products (organic mixtures containing nitrocotton and chemically related compounds) continued in use for the better part of one century. Nevertheless, these were of limited value because the newer, stronger steels could take advantage of propellants that produced more energy. The advent of carbon and nickel steels in the 1880s brought the final push toward propellants that were more energetic and ballistically controllable.

PROPELLANT—CORDITE

Cordite is of great historic significance. It carried the British Empire through two world wars. This British invention was based upon modifications of the original Ballistite formulation, which contained camphor. Cordite is an unlikely seeming blend of guncotton, nitroglycerin, and mineral jelly (now known as petroleum jelly).

The original composition was 37 percent guncotton, an amazing 58 percent nitroglycerin, and 5 percent mineral jelly. Owing to the high nitroglycerin content, that formulation caused excessive barrel erosion. A modified composition, containing 65 percent guncotton, 30 percent nitroglycerin, and 5 percent mineral jelly proved superior—performance was essentially the same but with far less erosion.

The designers believed that the mineral jelly would lubricate the barrel. However, because cordite combustion chemically destroys the mineral jelly, that component could not function as believed. However, mineral jelly does act as a very efficient stabilizer because it effectively absorbs any excess acidic nitrates out of the guncotton.

Cordite also found wide application in rocketry. It was safe to cast cordite into simple shapes or to machine it into complex shapes.

Military and commercial ammunition loaders controlled the burn rate through the proper choice of

Composition of Various Cellulose Nitrates

Name	Comments	Chemical Formula	% Nitrogen	Density
Cellulose Hexanitrate	Chief component	$(C_{12}H_{14}N_6O_{22})_x$	14.1417	1.66
Cellulose Pentanitrate	Insoluble component	$(C_{12}H_{15}N_5O_{20})_x$	12.7502	1.66
Cellulose Tetranitrate	Constituent of collodion	$(C_{12}H_{16}N_4O_{18})_x$	11.1103	1.66
Cellulose Trinitrate	Constituent of collodion	$(C_{12}H_{17}N_3O_{16})_x$	9.1491	1.66

an individual cord diameter for each application. In most rifle and artillery applications, producers cut cords to fit the propellant chamber of the finished cartridge precisely (length behind bullet and forward of solid case web); in most revolver and automatic pistol applications, the charge consisted of relatively short pieces of cord. Because the maker charged bottlenecked cases before forming the shoulder and neck, this method created no difficulty in making rifle ammunition. However, compared to modern tubular propellants, charging finished cases with cordite was tedious, at best. Handloaders found that using cordite in bottlenecked cases required insertion of the correct number of strands, one at a time, which was problematic.

NITROCELLULOSE—BASICS

In 1884, the French physicist, Paul Vieille, invented a dense colloid *poudre* B, which stood for *poudre blanch*—powder white; as opposed to *poudre* N, which stood for *poudre noire*—powder black (blackpowder). The French army and navy immediately adopted Vieille's product.

The foundation of *poudre* B and all typical smokeless propellants is nitrocellulose (NC, guncotton). Production of colloidal nitrocellulose begins with the chemical and physical action of concentrated nitric and sulfuric acids (respectively) on simple cellulose fibers, which can come from cotton, wood (that has been treated with sodium hydroxide), or any of many other sources.

Nitric acid reacts with the cellulose fibers to produce nitrocellulose and water. The water inhibits further reaction. Sulfuric acid (a strongly hygroscopic substance) removes the water. This allows the reaction to continue to completion. Sulfuric acid has no other function in this reaction.

Various physical and chemical manipulations during the nitrating process control the percentages of the various forms of nitrated cellulose in the finished product. Some types of cellulose nitrate are fully soluble in a mixture of ether and ethyl alcohol; other types are not. All modern guncotton contains an admixture of the insoluble fraction, which acts as reinforcing fibers in the finished product—in the same manner that glass fibers reinforce epoxy resin in fiberglass compounds.

Each type of NC contains a unique percentage of nitrogen. The higher the nitrogen content the more energetic the propellant. Hence, formulations with differing percentages of each component have different energy. Similarly, unintentional variations in nitrogen component percentages result in variations in energy content and, hence, performance variations in the finished product.

NITROCELLULOSE—DENSITY MODIFICATION

The addition of potassium nitrate (KNO_3) to colloidal nitrocellulose (NC) allows producers to make porous-based smokeless propellant. Sufficient kneading of the mixture evenly distributes the microscopic KNO_3 crystals throughout the colloidal guncotton. Later, added water leaches the KNO_3 into solution. Thorough rinsing of the resulting mix removes essentially all KNO_3. The resulting product is shot full of (microscopic) porosity, hence the porous-base designation.

NITROCELLULOSE—ENERGY MODIFICATION

Manufacturers can add nitroglycerine (NG) [(O_2N-OCH_2CH (ONO_2) CH_2ONO_2, density 1.59] to nitrocellulose (NC) to create a smokeless propellant with greater energy. In such double-base propellants colloidal NC adsorbs NG. (See page 131.) Alfred Bernhard Nobel (benefactor of the Nobel Prize) invented this process in 1888. Nobel patented his new product under the name Ballistite. The original formulation included camphor, which he later omitted (with superior results).

It is interesting to note that NG-impregnated NC has a higher bulk density than pure NC despite the relatively lower bulk density of NG. This is similar to mixing one pint of pure water with one pint of pure ethyl alcohol; one does not get two pints of moonshine but somewhat less. Water molecules tend to fill empty spaces between alcohol molecules, and conversely. Similarly, areas of the NG molecules fill voids within and between the NC molecules. Generally, increasing the percentage of NG progressively increases density of double-base propellants.

It seems almost miraculous that any process can incorporate NG into NC with extreme safety; nevertheless, this is exactly the situation. Producers use a compatible solvent to dissolve the NG. The resulting suspension is no more dangerous to handle than is gasoline. Physical mixing of this solution into colloidal NC facilitates adsorption (page 131) of NG into the colloidal paste. Thereafter, detonation requires intense shock, which never occurs in normal handling or use. (However, firing a high-velocity rifle bullet into a can of smokeless propellant, especially any double-base type, is ill advised—the propellant is apt to detonate, with explosive consequences.)

Admixtures of NG, up to about 16 percent, are particularly safe to handle. Common propellants often exceed this percentage (Bullseye contains a whopping 40 percent NG!) and require special handling precautions during manufacture. Nevertheless, the manufacture of these products is routine and occurs with an amazing degree of safety.

VihtaVuori cooks NG into otherwise finished tubular NC granules. VihtaVuori suggests that this process can result in a situation where maximum NG concentration occurs at a controlled depth from the granule surfaces. These propellants are the famous N5xx VihtaVuori numbers (now including N530, N540, N550, N560, and N570).

In such granules, initial rate of energy release is similar to that of similar conventional granules. Then, as the burn front reaches the zone containing a higher concentration of NG, the rate of energy release increases. By design, this zone is adjacent to, and within, the granule core. By the nature of internal ballistics, it is easy to get pressure to rise rapidly at the beginning of combustion; it is progressively more difficult to keep the pressure high as the bullet accelerates, and (thereby) enlarges the combustion chamber progressively more rapidly. Effectively, N5xx propellants tend to stretch the peak of the pressure curve so that after the pressure peaks, the pressure does not drop as quickly. (Compared to conventional propellants, the granule cores burn hotter and, thereby, keep the gas hotter—hotter gas equals higher pressure.)

However, it remains a mystery how any such gradation can persist in opposition to the inexorable osmotic pressure that should work, continuously, to drive the NG concentration toward uniformity throughout the granule—NG is a fluid and, therefore, is positively subject to osmotic pressure. This being the case, proper storage of N5xx propellants is probably particularly critical (as cool as possible). Moreover, it seems likely that, for best results, one should use these within a few years of manufacture. Regardless of this consideration, history has shown that these are safe; the concern is that delivered velocity could degrade as the propellant ages; however, testing has proven that developed pressure is essentially unaffected by normal aging.

Compared to single-based propellants, double-based propellants are less susceptible to spontaneous hydration because NG already somewhat fills many of the crystalline interstices of the NC. Depending upon storage and environmental conditions, moisture content of single-based propellants can vary considerably. Hydration alters density significantly, and it can alter effective burning rate very significantly—increasing moisture content slows burn rate, sometimes dramatically. Double-based propellants are much less sensitive in this regard.

NG also stabilizes NC. It prevents residual acid from touching the NC because it wets the NC better than the acid does. See next section.

Triple-base propellants are less important for small arms applications. Along with other advantages, the addition of nitroguanidine produces a propellant that creates no muzzle flash. However, such granules are relatively fragile and are, therefore, less tolerant of improper handling. For application to artillery, pentaerythritol tetranitrate (PETN) is also useful; PETN significantly increases energy yield. Nevertheless, for various reasons, triple-base propellants have yet to find any meaningful application in small arms, which is too bad.

KEEP PROPELLANTS IN ORIGINAL CONTAINER AND KEEP THAT CONTAINER SEALED TIGHTLY.

NITROCELLULOSE—STABILIZERS

Producers blend about 1 percent of a chemical stabilizer (such as diphenylamine) into the colloidal nitrocellulose (NC) suspension. Stabilizers work by displacing residual acid. Effectively, these chemicals wet guncotton (NC) better than acid does and, thereby, prevent residual acid from retaining physical contact with NC molecules—if the acid cannot touch the NC, it cannot attack it. When residual acid does attack smokeless propellant, an autocatalytic reaction results in degradation with progressive energy loss. If the acid content is unusually high, as degradation proceeds the reaction rate will progressively increase and auto combustion will eventually occur.

Properly made modern propellants are essentially free from any such degradation. With proper storage (as cool as is feasible), the shelf life of properly manufactured smokeless propellant is usually many, many decades. Because we cannot assume that manufacturers will always properly produce every batch of propellant, it is certainly prudent to check each can periodically with the smell test—the somewhat sweet solvent smell is obviously different from the acrid smell of nitric acid that is coincident with degradation.

The autocatalytic degradation of smokeless propellant generates nitric acid and heat. Because nitric acid is the active ingredient in this reaction, it will inevitably accelerate once the reaction rate exceeds a certain threshold until spontaneous combustion occurs. This has happened with disastrous results. Periodically check all smokeless propellant with the sniff test.

NITROCELLULOSE— FOULING SUPPRESSANTS

Smokeless propellant often includes small percentages of several other substances. Formerly, producers added lead stearate or lead oxide, which combined with gilding metal fouling and stripped that from the bore. These chemicals work extremely well. Tin oxide, the modern substitute, has the same effect but, unfortunately, it is not nearly as efficacious. Some formulations contain additives that act as abraders (which physically strip gilding metal fouling from the bore).

NITROCELLULOSE—BURN RATE CONTROL

Manufacturers slow the combustion rate of finished granules through the surface application of various inert chemicals. Typical deterrent chemicals, which adsorb (defined below) into granule surfaces, include the following: centralite, potassium sulfate, dibutyl phthalate, cryolite, and several proprietary substances.

These work by reducing the temperature of gas produced during the initial stages of granule combustion. This reduces burn rate (lower temperature) and initial gas generation rate, which slows pressure buildup and which allows the projectile to move farther down the bore before chamber pressure peaks. As the granule burns, deeper layers are exposed; those contain less deterrent and therefore burn hotter and with the release of more energy—the granules burn progressively faster through about 50 percent of combustion. Deterrent modification allows substantially increased muzzle velocities at any given limiting pressure level. (Consider the battlefield advantage the increased velocity potential offered by perforated hexagonal blackpowder granules gave Napoleon.)

NITROCELLULOSE—FLASH SUPPRESSION

Muzzle flash is an important self-defense and military consideration. A bright muzzle flash can temporarily blind a shooter and disclose his location, particularly when he is firing at dusk or in the dark. Application of certain salts onto granule surfaces reddens, dims, and reduces the size of the fireball produced as the bullet clears the muzzle. Porous-based propellants respond particularly well to application of a flash suppressant. However, flash suppressing substances increase barrel fouling, erosion, and corrosion, and reduce ballistic performance.

Muzzle flash is often misunderstood. This flash is not the completion of the burning of propellant granules; rather, it is the explosion of highly reduced (oxygen-starved) combustion gases after those gases have turbulently mixed with the oxygen-rich air outside the bore of the gun. As the propellant gas supersonically enters the atmosphere, turbulent mixing can heat it sufficiently so that when it has incorporated sufficient oxygen it will detonate. This detonation occurs almost instantly and increases the noise of the shot. And, it does not always occur.

NITROCELLULOSE—GRAPHITE GLAZING

The application of a graphite coating (glazing), generally between one part per thousand and five parts per thousand (by weight), provides the finishing touch for granules of smokeless propellant. Graphite glazing is necessary to eliminate the potential buildup of static electricity among moving granules. Such a static charge could cause a spark of sufficient magnitude to ignite the charge. This coating also facilitates propellant flow through measuring and dispensing devices. Finally, this coating slightly slows combustion.

Producers sometimes make minor adjustments to the burn rate by slightly altering the amount of graphite used. Graphite has a natural affinity for smokeless propellant, so it stays in place quite well. Note that ADI (maker of Hodgdon Extreme Brand propellants) evidently uses an alternative means of static suppression—microscopic examination of granules reveals little, if any, graphite.

ADSORPTION VERSUS ABSORPTION

Adsorption differs from absorption in the sense of physical versus chemical wicking (osmosis). Water is absorbed into a sponge, we can remove it by physical means (squeezing, for example); conversely, when one chemical is adsorbed into another chemical (as with deterrents in smokeless propellant), chemical affinity binds the two substances. While no chemical reaction occurs, no physical means will suffice to separate such materials. The effective difference is similar to comparing latex and oil-based finishes applied to wood. While latex paints can be scraped (physically removed) from wood, oil-based finishes impregnate the wood and are, thereby, intimately bonded into surface layers; similarly, (molecular solid) deterrents applied to propellant granules are impregnated into surface layers at the molecular level.

Having had five editors of my books who were too lazy to use a dictionary and who changed the correct usage of *adsorbed* to the incorrect usage of *absorbed*, perhaps I am overly sensitive about this distinction.

SMOKELESS PROPELLANT—MODERN PRODUCTION

Safety is a serious consideration when dealing with many tons of such a volatile and highly energetic material. However, safety in smokeless propellant production is readily achievable for two basic reasons. First, in almost all production stages, the product is comparatively safe to handle—if ignited, it will burn, surprisingly slowly, until completion of solvent combustion. Second, producers can remotely control most production stages through monitoring and automation.

Those manufacturers that produce tubular propellant granules extrude nitrocellulose dough through a die plate. The size of the holes in the die plate controls the finished granule diameter. The granule length is determined in subsequent cutting operations.

Those manufacturers that produce spherical propellant granules add specific amounts of various solvents to nitrocellulose dough and then agitate the resulting coloidal suspension. Increasing the percentage of solvent added to the propellant dough creates smaller granules in the resulting agitated suspension. Proprietary variations in the solvent-mixture recipe, temperature, container design, and agitation energy are all potentially useful toward producing granules of any desired size. It is not particularly critical that all granules come out exactly the same size because the manufacturer sorts the granules into useful fractions containing only similarly sized granules before further processing occurs.

Manufacturers can produce flake-type propellant granules by any of three processes. The first method involves rolling the dough into thin sheets and cutting those sheets into pieces—this was once very popular in Europe. The second method is to cut extruded tubes into very short pieces. The third method is to flatten the spherical granules significantly. The former two methods allow creation of flakes that spontaneously crinkle as the solvent evaporates, giving the propellant a much lower packing density and higher compressibility, which is very useful in shotshell loads. Despite the fragile appearance, finished smokeless flakes are durable and mechanically tough.

Consider the production of a typical tubular propellant. The action of a hydraulic press expresses the stiff jelly through a steel plate having myriad nominally identical perforations. In propellants designed for small arms applications, a central needle extends from behind the plate (the working side) into each opening. These pins create a centered perforation in each extruded tube. Because the product still contains about 30 percent solvent, handling is quite safe.

After further evaporation reduces solvent content to about 15 percent, a machine cuts these strands into tubes of a specific length. (Intermediate solvent evaporation is necessary to prevent collapse of the central perforation during cutting. A sophisticated belt-and-blade system chops the strands into granules of specific length. Sieving assures that the finished product will contain only granules of the proper size and dimensional uniformity. Further solvent evaporation, through the action of low-humidity warm air, removes essentially all solvent.

Chemical granule treatment imparts a carefully controlled deterrent concentration into the granule surfaces—manufacturers do this by boiling granules in a water solution containing specific concentrations of one or more deterrent chemicals for a specific time. After this, manufacturers adjust moisture content into equilibrium with air at about 60 percent relative humidity and near normal room temperature. Finally, the application of a graphite glaze produces finished granules.

Glazing limits hygroscopic tendency, improves granule flow characteristics, and reduces the hazard of static discharge (which otherwise could result in an inadvertent ignition, as with blackpowder granules). In some instances, producers manipulate the amount of graphite glazing to alter product burn rate slightly. A thicker graphite glaze will progressively retard initial combustion.

It is important to understand that the quality of smokeless propellant rests entirely in production details—no magic exists here. What separates also-ran smokeless propellants from top-of-the-line smokeless is practically all explained in these two simple phrases: Proper production control and raw material quality.

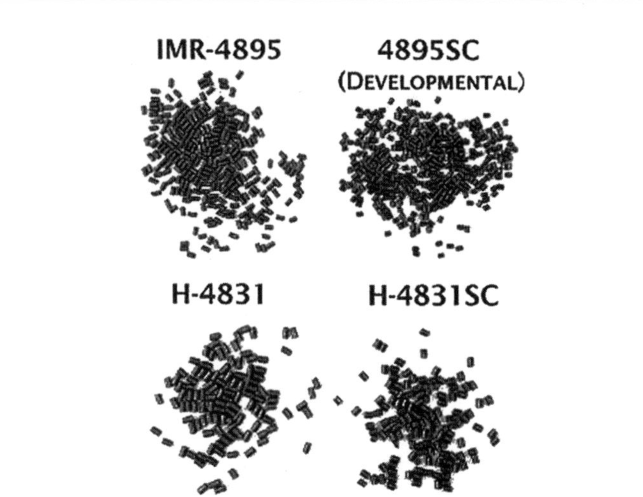

These tubular granules demonstrate ongoing research toward perfection of smokeless propellant. In many instances, tubular powders for sporting purposes do not meter consistently. The Short-Cut approach addresses this limitation. Another limitation is sensitivity to ambient temperature; Hodgdon has addressed this with its Extreme line of tubular propellants as exemplified by VarGet, which is very similar in general appearance to H4831SC. (VarGet granules are slightly smaller.)

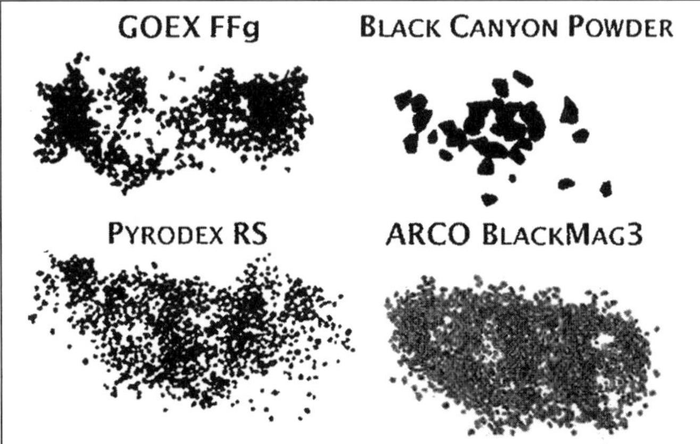

Blackpowder and substitutes are widely used in sporting applications. GOEX offers a complete sporting line, as represented by FFg, shown here. GOEX also offers a cartridge grade, intended for use in long Sharps cartridges such as the 45-120 and 50-140 when using heavy bullets. Pyrodex is the standard to which all blackpowder substitutes compare. It duplicates blackpowder performance with less fouling and reduced corrosion. Several recent substitutes are now obsolete; newer substitutes are gaining favor.

Control of the effective burn rate of the granules in any one batch of modern smokeless propellant results from manipulation of deterrent coatings, granule size and shape, porosity, and the number and size of perforations (if any). Manufacturers also manipulate effective overall burn rate of any given propellant type by blending granules from various batches.

As noted with blackpowder, multiperforation tubular granules can achieve a significant ballistic advantage. Unfortunately, producers have heretofore resisted production of such granules in propellants suitable for use in small arms, which is too bad.

For this reason, artillery has an advantage. In those applications, it is feasible to use essentially undeterred extruded granules of very large size and having as many as seventeen perforations. During combustion, multiperforation tubular granules produce hot gas (energy) at a progressively increasing rate—as the diameter (surface area) of the outside gets smaller, the diameter (surface area) of each perforation gets larger; hence, the total burning surface area increases until the perforations coalesce. Therefore, multiperforation granules have significant progressivity; hence, as the projectile accelerates (progressively enlarging the boiler room), the propellant produces energy progressively faster. This characteristic allows the use of relatively large charges to obtain an essentially flat pressure curve during much of the time the projectile is in the bore. Granules of this design can generate much greater muzzle energy than is possible using the very best single-perforation propellants. (The price of this performance is monumental recoil—owing to the relatively massive propellant charge and unusually short barrel life—for the same reason.)

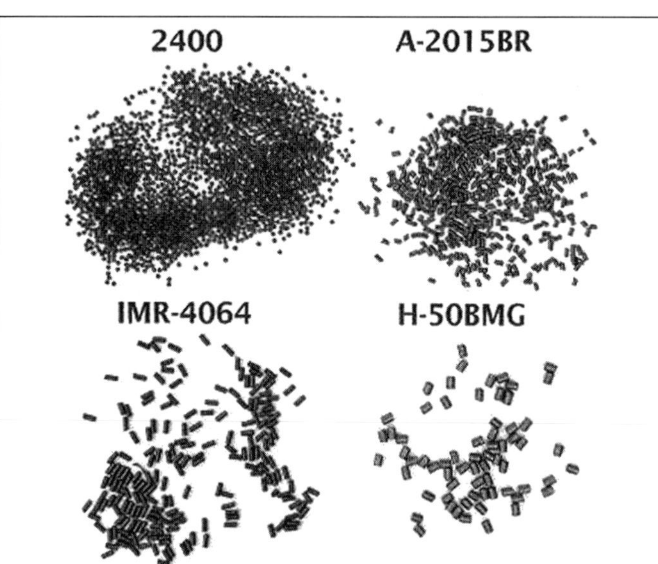

A representative sampling of sporting tubular powders covering a wide range of burning rates (fastest shown here is about ten times faster burning than slowest): Alliant 2400 is a very fine granulated extruded propellant (one could equally well define these granules as thick flakes) and is useful in magnum handguns and small-rifle cases. Accurate 2015 is well proportioned and finely granulated, meters quite uniformly, and is useful in relatively small-rifle cases. IMR-4064 is very long granulated, meters poorly, but is useful in medium-capacity rifle cases. Hodgdon H-50BMG is short granulated, meters consistently, and is useful only in relatively large capacity cases.

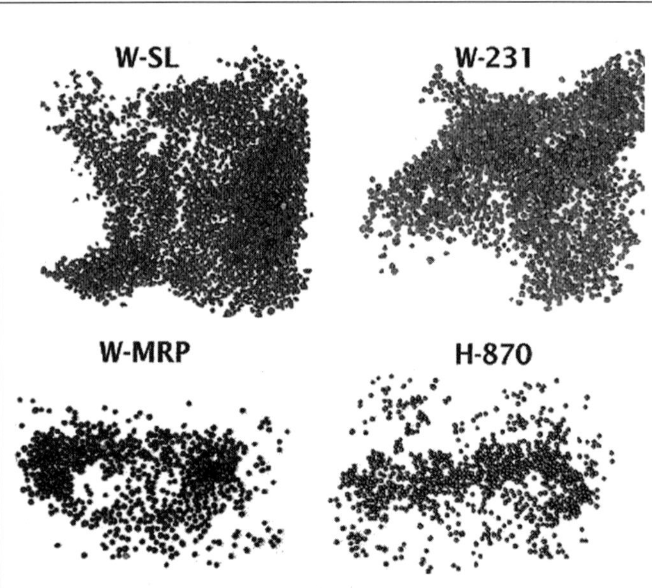

Olin Industries invented ball powder. It has marketed this propellant under the Winchester banner, through surplus sales, and through the Hodgdon Powder Company. Many Winchester-brand propellants have recently become obsolete. Winchester Super-Lite (WSL) is a porous, flattened, double-based (34 percent NG) powder with a packing density of about 0.765. W-231 is similar in form but with less nitroglycerin (22.5 percent), with a packing density of about 0.70. Winchester-MRP is double-based (13.5 percent NG), with typically slightly flattened granules. H-870 (obsolete) contains about 10 percent nitroglycerin; these granules are typically quite spherical; packing density is about 0.965. (Performance of the H-870 replacement, US 869, not shown, is similar.)

During combustion, untreated, single-perforation tubular granules produce hot gas (energy) at a relatively constant rate—as the granule diameter gets smaller, the perforation diameter gets larger; hence, gas release remains constant throughout granule combustion. Incorporation of deterrents into granule surfaces garners significant progressivity at the cost of increased fouling. Nevertheless, the pressure curve can never remain near the peak anywhere nearly as long as it can with ideal multiperforation granules.

Ball propellants cannot incorporate perforations. Because a sphere naturally burns degressively—the more of the granule that burns, the less surface area it has and the more slowly it produces hot gas (energy)—ball powder makers rely solely upon adsorption of the deterrent to achieve progressivity. One advantage of ball propellants is that they allow a somewhat increased loading density—generally, these granules pack better than extruded granules do and usually have a higher intrinsic specific density (due to incorporation of nitroglycerin). Often, it is possible to use a heavier charge of a slower-burning ball type, compared to any tubular type. With relatively significant nitroglycerin content and sophisticated, multiapplication, deterrent technology, ball propellants designed for small-arms cartridges produce equal or superior ballistics compared to the best currently available tubular propellants.

On the other side are porous-based propellants. Usually, designers of porous propellants look to achieve two goals: high compressibility and increased burning rate. Compressibility is essential for proper shotshell loading. This provides for accommodation of various packing schemes within the propellant and shot charges. This also allows for substantial variations in charge and shot volume without requiring use of a different casing or shot container. The increased burning rate accommodates shotshell and light pistol loads, where gas from a small charge pushes on a comparatively light bullet of large diameter. Granulation of nonporous propellants to accommodate these applications would result in a material of very fine particle size, which would be correspondingly difficult and dangerous to manufacture and to handle. The porous-base approach solves both problems.

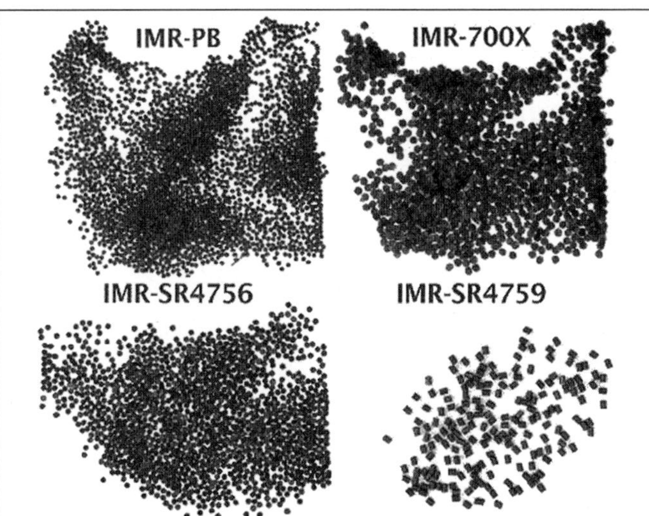

Porous base propellants are available in a wide variety of burn rates, chemistry, and configurations, as represented by these IMR offerings. Described as a flake type, 700X is double-based (29 percent nitroglycerin) and is among the fastest burning and least dense of sporting powders, with a packing density near 0.5. Also a flake type, the single-base PB, although considerably slower, is still among the fastest and least dense of smokeless propellants, with a packing density of about 0.55. Described as either a thick flake or a short tube, single-based SR4756 is a slow shotshell powder with a packing density of about 0.61. An interesting tubular propellant, single-based SR4759 is among the fastest burning of rifle propellants and has a packing density of about 0.675.

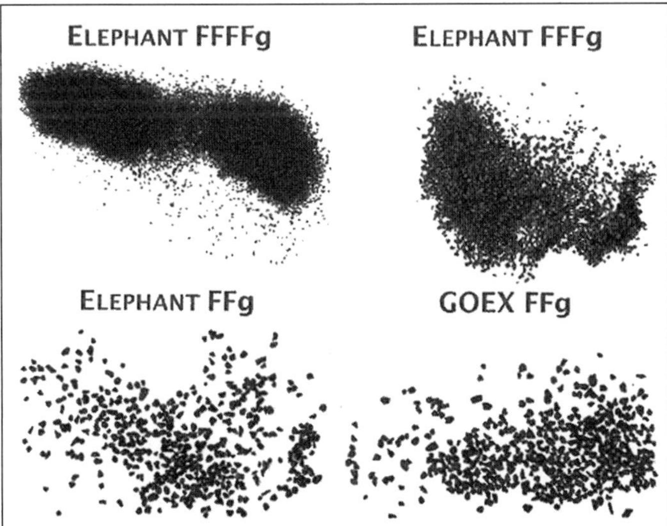

These representative blackpowders are now available for sporting purposes. Elephant also offers FFFFFg (5Fg) granulation. That product looks more like dust than blackpowder! Some suggest that a flash-pan mixture using about 30 percent of 5Fg mixed with 4Fg can improve flintlock performance. Elephant and GOEX do not use the same formulation—ballistics differ significantly. Typically, 4Fg is used only for flintlock ignition; however, with light bullets it works quite well in the Ruger Old Army revolver, for it delivers relatively clean burns with good ballistics. Normally, 3Fg is used in guns to about 50-caliber, although it is useful in larger muzzleloading guns with lighter charges where it produces improved ballistic uniformity. For guns from 50-caliber to about 60-caliber, 2Fg is preferred. Shotguns can use Fg grade even though Fg is nominally a small cannon-grade granulation and is most useful in salute cannons.

Common porous propellants have bulk densities as low as about 0.4, compared to about 0.85 to about

1.035 for nonporous propellants. Reduction in packing density results, partly, from the crinkling of the flake-type granules that occurs during solvent evaporation. However, inherent porosity is the primary method of reducing density. Porous propellants also accommodate novel applications of flash suppressants, which can coat cavities in this type of propellant. Typically, compression of porous propellants, to about one-half unconfined volume, requires little force and will not disrupt individual granules, deter ignition, or significantly alter combustion rate.

RedDot is a fast flake, shotshell propellant that has far less density and energy than Bullseye. This makes it an ideal choice for midrange or target loads in revolver and pistol cartridges because, with a charge that produces normal pressure, it does a better job of filling the available space. GreenDot and Nitro-100 are similar in appearance and application. Clays and Solo-1000, while similar in appearance, are single-based propellants and are, therefore, far cleaner burning. Both offer the same advantages as RedDot for these types of loads and have become favorites of mine and of many others who have ventured away from traditional handgun propellants. Alliant now offers a single-based number (American Select) with similar application but data are limited.

SMOKELESS PROPELLANT—ADVANTAGES AND DISADVANTAGES—BALL TYPE

Olin Corporation invented Ball Powder propellant in the 1940s. Ball propellant granules are ellipsoids (more-or-less spheres). As with any propellant, granule size and amount of deterrent in surface layers are the primary burn rate controls. Producers often adjust ball-propellant burn rate by somewhat flattening some or all granules in any given propellant mix—flattening increases surface area and, thereby, burn rate.

Significant granule flattening also significantly increases progressivity—the relative increase in burn rate (gas and energy release) during progress of combustion as deterred surface layers burn away. This is true because, as the surface layers burn away, the surface area of a flattened sphere decreases far more slowly than that of a true sphere.

Consider, for example, a flattened granule (a spheroid) that is ten times as large in diameter as it is thick. Assuming a constant burn rate to a first approximation and when the flat sides have burned halfway through the granule (and therefore touch, meaning that the granule is 100 percent consumed), combustion into the edges will only have reduced the granule diameter by 20 percent. Hence, as the last vestige of the granule burns, surface area will still be about two-thirds of initial surface area.

VihtaVuori N310 is the fastest propellant now offered to the handloader. It is extremely easy to ignite and unusually clean burning. It is particularly useful in low-power loads of all types. Charge-position velocity influences are minimal, but the potential for dangerous, potentially gun-destroying, multiple charges looms—be extremely cautious when using this and similar numbers.

Conversely, as the last fragment of a true sphere burns, surface area approaches zero.

As noted earlier, compared to tubular propellants, ball-type propellants have several advantages. Generally, due to the necessary inclusion of a greater percentage of inert chemicals (deterrents), ball propellants produce lower flame temperatures. This can extend barrel life. Generally, ball propellants have a greater packing density. This is partly due to shape and is partly due to increased intrinsic density (compared to pure nitrocellulose). Hence, in any given application, compared to tubular propellants, handloaders can often use a slightly heavier charge of a slightly more energetic and slightly slower-burning ball propellant.

For this reason, handloaders can sometimes achieve greater velocity using a ball propellant. In addition, these propellants have superior metering characteristics. Similarly, use of a ball propellant monumentally speeds and eases loading of rifle ammunition because metered charges are uniform enough for any application. Factory ammunition producers often prefer ball propellants for all these reasons.

Conversely, traditional ball propellants exhibit two noteworthy disadvantages. Owing to the necessary inclusion of a greater percentage of inert deterrent chemicals, propellant-related barrel fouling is significantly greater. For this reason, those target shooters who must shoot many dozens of shots without cleaning the barrel seldom find ball propellant loads that work well. Note that ball propellants offered by Western Powder Company, under the Ramshot banner, use deterrent chemicals that generate less fouling. For this reason, these are relatively clean burning and have found some applications with target shooters.

Modern propellants are available in a wide range of granulation forms and sizes as these representative rifle numbers suggest.

The second problem with traditional ball propellants is sensitivity to ambient temperature—as temperature changes, pressure and velocity also change. Usually, any smokeless propellant will generate more pressure when used at higher temperature. However, the precise temperature-to-pressure relationship is generally unpredictable. Exceptions do exist, as discussed in the following section. Some types of ball propellant are unusually sensitive to ambient temperature changes—W748 is a glaring example. Ramshot claims that

Bullseye is an old standby. This relatively dense flake propellant contains 40 percent nitroglycerin. Power Pistol is identical in all ways except that a portion of the flakes are deterrent modified, so burning rate is significantly slower. Very high NG content renders relatively high velocity in appropriate loadings.

its rifle numbers are less temperature sensitive than are some older ball types.

SMOKELESS PROPELLANT—ADVANTAGES AND DISADVANTAGES—TUBULAR TYPE

Tubular propellants have long been the most common type available to, and used by, those folks who are handloading rifle ammunition. In modern varieties, granule length and diameter are often similar. In some older varieties, granule length was significantly greater than diameter—the best examples are IMR3031 and IMR4064, where length is nearly three times diameter.

As with ball propellants, slower-burning formulations usually use larger granules. However, because extruded propellants require a relatively lower percentage of deterrent, producers have more leeway in granule size; therefore, granulation size is less indicative of burn rate than it is with ball-type propellants.

Generally, due to a relatively low deterrent concentration, extruded propellants are relatively clean burning. Target shooters who routinely fire extended shot strings without the opportunity to clean the gun appreciate this characteristic—NRA Highpower competitors, for example.

Similarly, compared to ball types, extruded types tend to exhibit less sensitivity to ambient temperature. At least part of this results from the relative reduction in deterrents, which progressively impede ignition at progressively lower temperatures. However, there is more to this story.

Extruded propellants made by Australian Defense Industries (ADI) are unique. (ADI produces Hodgdon extruded propellants marketed under the Extreme banner.) ADI propellants are unusually clean burning, partly because of the almost complete elimination of graphite glazing—I suspect that ADI has incorporated an energetic conductive polymer into the mixture or that it coats such a polymer onto the finished granules. Whatever the case, these granules lack significant graphite glazing. This characteristic might reduce temperature sensitivity through promotion of quick ignition across a wide temperature range.

Moreover, Extreme propellant granules incorporate a fundamental primary means of reducing temperature-related performance variation (in general, practically eliminating it). Across a wide ambient range (from somewhat below 0 degree F to well above 100 degrees F), temperature only minimally influences velocity and pressure. ADI accomplishes this extremely desirable goal through precise control of size, number, and depth of microfractures that naturally occur on granule surfaces as solvents evaporate out of the granules during the final stages of manufacture.

Nitrocellulose is plastic (deformable). As with any plastic material, the degree of plasticity is a function of temperature—the colder the material, the harder and less plastic it is. When a propellant granule is colder, it is more rigid. Therefore, in response to any given force, the surface does not deform as readily. So, as pressure increases upon a granule (as the charge burns), the colder the granule core is, the longer the microfractures in the surface remain open. So, when a colder granule begins to burn, combustion can extend deeper into those fractures. This has the consequence of increasing the burning surface area in a colder granule. Through precise manufacturing manipulation, ADI can adjust microfractures on granule surfaces so as to, almost, eliminate dependence of burn rate on ambient temperature.

The singular and obvious disadvantage of using extruded granules is difficult and imprecise metering. When using large-granule extruded numbers, shooters interested in long-range accuracy necessarily must weigh individual charges. As I covered elsewhere, getting the most accuracy out of weighed charges requires careful and consistent charge dumping. Refer to chapter 9.

Charges that the handloader has precisely weighed and has then haphazardly dumped into cases are apt to generate greater shot-to-shot velocity variation than dumped charges of the same propellant having several-tenths-grain weight variation—the granule-packing scheme is critically important to ballistic uniformity. Refer to chapter 9.

Contrary to intuition, the granule-packing scheme established as case charging occurs is extremely robust, even if the charge is not compressed. Generally, short of a precise and deliberate act of energetic vibratory settling, the granules do not reorient. Therefore, during normal transportation, handling, and use, the packing scheme established during case charging remains functionally intact.

SMOKELESS PROPELLANT—ADVANTAGES AND DISADVANTAGES—FLAKE TYPE

These propellants are easy to produce and exhibit desirable burn rates for use in many shotshell and handgun loads. Manufacturers can manipulate production to create finished flakes that are crinkled. Such flakes exhibit a combination of significant compressibility and low natural packing density. The former is critical to modern shotshell loading practices, and the latter is beneficial in many handgun-type loads because it reduces charge-position effects. Refer to "Smokeless Propellant—Charge Position" in this chapter.

Typical flake propellants are, however, particularly sensitive to handling with regard to packing density. When fully settled, such propellants often have about 25 percent greater packing density than when not settled; with certain types, this differential can reach 40 percent. Therefore, when using a flake propellant, it is particularly important that the handloader maintain consistent loading practices so that the propellant measure will consistently drop charges of similar and intended mass.

These propellants include very short tubular granules where the diameter is significantly greater than length. Another production method involves rolling ball granules through rollers to create essentially flat flakes. A generally obsolete method involves the creation of large thin propellant sheets and the cutting of those sheets into roughly square flakes.

SMOKELESS PROPELLANT—ADVANTAGES AND DISADVANTAGES—POROUS TYPE

In addition, manufacturers produce both ball and extruded propellants in porous-based form. During manufacture, water leaches the potassium nitrate (which had been thoroughly intermixed into the nitrocellulose dough) out of the granules. Depending upon how much potassium nitrate was included, a specific percentage of granule mass is, thereby, removed, leaving voids in the nitrocellulose. Increasing porosity has the following influences on smokeless propellant:

- Decreases density
- Increases compressibility
- Increases burn rate

Decreasing density is beneficial where a small charge of a fast burning propellant is desirable, such as in target 38 Special cartridges. Low-density propellants fill more of the available space and, therefore, provide improved ballistic uniformity through decreased sensitivity to charge position. Refer to "Smokeless Propellant—Charge Position" in this chapter. These also improve ignition. Refer to "Smokeless Propellant—Cowboy Action" in this chapter.

Increased compressibility is most desirable in shotshell loads, where differing loads must all fit in a shell of a specific size and yet exhibit some degree of propellant compression. Increased burn rate is beneficial as this eliminates the need to create propellants with unusually fine granulations as would otherwise be needed to achieve particularly rapid burn rates—such

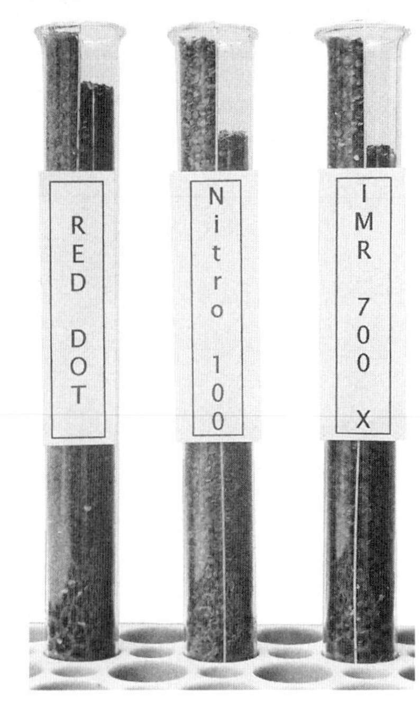

Different types of propellants show markedly different degrees of potential settling. Here rigid card paper separates the two sides. I dumped propellant into both sides of each tube, full to the top. I then vibrated the tube until the propellant stopped settling. Then, for visual clarity, I refilled one side. This simple experiment demonstrates why it is so critical that handloaders practice consistent operation of loading equipment. It is OK for the propellant to settle so long as settling is consistent and the meter is adjusted to drop the desired charge mass. That can only happen when the handloader practices and delivers consistent operations.

propellants are difficult to manufacture and to use. Porous-based propellants are also particularly amenable to the inclusion of effective flash suppressants.

Generally, we cannot use porous-based propellants for maximum-velocity loads. Moreover, porous-based flake propellants are particularly sensitive to handling with regard to packing density. When fully settled, such propellants can have a phenomenal 40 percent greater packing density than when loosely packed. Therefore, when using such a propellant, it is critically important that the handloader maintain consistent loading practices so that the propellant measure will consistently drop charges of similar and correct mass.

SMOKELESS PROPELLANT—VARIETY

Unlike the situation as recently as about 1985, modern handloaders have a dazzling array of propellants from which to choose. Where formerly many potential loads were limited to one or a few good propellant choices (a few noted examples had no good choice!), handloaders now find several (usually many) useful propellants for almost any application. This is both a boon and a burden. It is wonderful to have a choice of several propellants that will work properly in the cartridge and load under consideration. However, having too many good choices can equally be daunting for the novice and experienced handloader alike, particularly when working with an unfamiliar cartridge.

In this chapter, I will try to offer reasonable guidelines to mitigate this situation. However, it is not my intention to suggest that you should only try the propellants that I propose here in any given application. Perish the thought!

Recently, several European manufacturers have attempted to establish distribution of about thirty potentially useful propellants in the United States, although with limited success. Nevertheless, currently, we have far more than one hundred smokeless propellant types that are more-or-less readily available. Certainly, this is sufficient variety for most any handloading application.

SMOKELESS PROPELLANT—RELATIVE BURNING RATE

Various physical and chemical characteristics of smokeless propellant granules are the primary means of controlling absolute burn rate. Absolute burn rate describes how fast any given granule burns at any given pressure (temperature). Conversely, relative burn rate depends upon the combination of absolute burn rate, incremental confining pressure, and the rate of incremental combustion-chamber expansion. The latter factors are generally more critical in controlling relative burn rate. This explains why we can consider the same propellant as fast-burning in one application and as slow-burning in another application.

For example, when used in a 44 Magnum with a 240-grain bullet, IMR4227 is among the slowest of useful propellants. Conversely, when used in a 30-30 with a 150-grain bullet, IMR4227 is among the fastest of useful propellants.

In this 44 Magnum load, 23 grains is a somewhat compressed charge that generates about 36,000 psi. In the 30-30 load, 23 grains only fills about two-thirds of the available space but still generates about 36,000 psi. The difference is in this 44 Magnum load that the bullet offers less resistance to the burning gases. With the same pressure applied, the 44 Magnum bullet accelerates faster because it has a lower ratio of weight to cross-sectional area; therefore, in response to any given chamber pressure, combustion chamber volume increases faster in the 44 Magnum, and, hence, it requires a relatively greater charge (as a percentage of case filled) to achieve the same peak pressure.

Now, compare the 44 Magnum to the 444 Marlin. These cartridges have similar SAAMI maximum pressure specifications and use identical bullets. The difference is case length and, hence, usable capacity—the 444 Marlin holds almost exactly twice as much propellant.

In the 44 Magnum, Accurate No. 9 is one of the better propellants—21.3 grains accelerates a 240-grain jacketed bullet to 1,625 fps from a 20-inch barrel while generating 40,000 CUP. In the 444 Marlin, Accurate 2230 is one of the better propellants—54.2 grains accelerates a 240-grain jacketed bullet to 2181 fps while generating 40,000 CUP. Accurate No. 9 is entirely too fast to produce useful loads in the 444 Marlin; conversely, 2230 is entirely too slow to produce useful loads in the 44 Magnum. In this example, the only difference is usable case capacity (initial boiler-room volume).

As an extreme example, consider the 9mm Luger and the 35 Remington. These 35-caliber cartridges work at very similar pressures. Propellants that are entirely too slow for use in the tiny 9mm case (11.4 grains of usable capacity with a 100-grain bullet) are entirely too fast for use in any normal 35 Remington load (44.0 grains of usable capacity with a 200-grain bullet). Conversely, the fastest useful 35 Remington propellants are entirely too slow for use in 9mm Luger loads.

The point of importance here is that many variables—bore diameter, usable pressure, bullet weight, and case capacity—influence the perceived burning rate of any propellant in any given application. Propellants that are relatively slow numbers in one application can be dangerously fast when used in another application. When it comes to smokeless propellant, fast versus slow is an entirely relative concept.

When compared in controlled, closed bomb tests, the difference in absolute burn rate between the fastest and the slowest handloader propellants is about twelve times. This fact has no value to the handloader except as a safety flag.

USING THE WRONG PROPELLANT CAN GENERATE GUN-DESTROYING PRESSURES AND COULD LEAD TO LOSS OF LIFE OR LIMB.

I have included relative burn rate tables in this text. Assigning order in any such table is fraught with difficulty. When used in different applications, propellants do not always burn with the same relative speed even when used at similar pressures. In any given pair, the slower propellant in one application might well be the faster propellant in another application. Relative speed can also vary as a function of peak chamber pressure. In any given pair, the faster propellant when used at one peak chamber pressure can be the slower propellant when used at another peak chamber pressure. And, if that were not enough complication, chamber design and bullet mass will also influence the effective burn rate; for example, in SM^{C} cartridges, the burn rate variation is less than in conventional cartridges.

Nominal Relative Burn Rates of Selected Propellants (Based upon Predicted Performance, in Terms of Charge Required to Achieve a Specific Pressure in a Given Application—Slowest to Fastest)

CHARGE REQUIRED TO ACHIEVE A SPECIFIC PRESSURE			
Heaviest Charge	IMR4350	Accurate 2495	Ramshot True Blue
VihtaVuori 20N29	Hodgdon H414	IMR3031	Winchester 540
Accurate 8700	Accurate 2700	Hodgdon Benchmark	VihtaVuori N105
Hodgdon H870	Ramshot Big Game	Ramshot X-Terminator	Winchester WAP
Hodgdon H50BMG	Hodgdon H380	VihtaVuori N133	Ramshot Silhouette
VihtaVuori 24N41	VihtaVuori N150	Hodgdon H322	Alliant Power Pistol
Ramshot Magnum	Norma 203	Accurate 2015	VihtaVuori 3N37
VihtaVuori N170	VihtaVuori N540	VihtaVuori N130	Alliant Herco
Hodgdon Retumbo	Hodgdon BL-C2	Alliant Reloader 10	VihtaVuori N350
Hodgdon H1000	IMR4320	Norma 200	Ramshot Zip
Alliant Reloader 25	Norma 203B	Accurate 1680	Winchester 231
VihtaVuori N165	Alliant Reloader 15	Hodgdon H4198	Hodgdon HP 38
Norma MRP	Accurate 2520	IMR4198	VihtaVuori N340
Winchester WXR	Accurate 4064	VihtaVuori N120	Alliant Unique
Alliant Reloder 22	Winchester 748	Alliant Reloader 7	Accurate Solo 1250
Hodgdon H4831SC	Norma 202	IMR4227	Hodgdon Universal
VihtaVuori N560	IMR4895	H110 (W296)	VihtaVuori N330
IMR7828	Ramshot TAC	Hodgdon H4227	Norma R1
Accurate 3100	Hodgdon VarGet	Accurate 5744	Accurate Solo 1000
VihtaVuori N160	IMR4064	Accurate Solo 4100	Accurate No. 2
Norma 204	Hodgdon H335	Ramshot Enforcer	Alliant GreenDot
Alliant Reloader 19	VihtaVuori N140	VihtaVuori N110	Alliant Bullseye
Ramshot Hunter	Accurate 2460	Accurate No. 9	Hodgdon Clays
IMR4831	VihtaVuori N135	Alliant 2400	VihtaVuori N320
Hodgdon H4350	Norma 201	Norma R123	Alliant RedDot
Winchester 760	Accurate 2230	Alliant BlueDot	Accurate Nitro 100
Accurate 4350	Hodgdon H4895	Accurate No. 7	VihtaVuori N310
VihtaVuori N550	Alliant Reloader 12	Accurate No. 5	**Lightest Charge**

Nominal Relative Burn Rates of Selected Propellants (Based upon Predicted Performance, in Terms of Charge Required to Achieve a Specific Velocity in a Given Application—Heaviest to Lightest Charge)

CHARGE REQUIRED TO ACHIEVE A SPECIFIC VELOCITY			
Heaviest Charge	IMR4350	Hodgdon H4895	VihtaVuori N105
VihtaVuori 20N29	Accurate 2700	Accurate 2015	Ramshot True Blue
Accurate 8700	Hodgdon H414	Ramshot X-Terminator	Winchester 540
Hodgdon H870	Norma 203	Hodgdon Benchmark	VihtaVuori 3N37
Hodgdon H50BMG	Accurate 4064	Hodgdon H322	Winchester WAP
VihtaVuori 24N41	VihtaVuori N150	VihtaVuori N133	Ramshot Silhouette
Ramshot Magnum	Ramshot Big Game	Norma 200	VihtaVuori N350
VihtaVuori N170	Accurate 2520	VihtaVuori N130	Alliant Power Pistol
Hodgdon Retumbo	Accurate 2495	Alliant RI-10	Alliant Herco
Hodgdon H1000	Hodgdon BL-C2	Accurate 1680	Ramshot Zip
VihtaVuori N165	Norma 203B	Hodgdon H4198	Winchester 231
Accurate 3100	VihtaVuori N540	VihtaVuori N120	Hodgdon HP 38
Alliant RI-25	Alliant RI-15	Alliant RI-7	VihtaVuori N340
Norma MRP	Accurate 2460	IMR4198	Accurate Solo-1250
Winchester WXR	IMR4320	IMR4227	VihtaVuori N330
Hodgdon H4831SC	Winchester 748	Hodgdon H110	Norma R1
Alliant R-22	Norma 202	Winchester 296	Accurate No. 2
IMR7828	VihtaVuori N135	Hodgdon H4227	Hodgdon Universal
VihtaVuori N560	Accurate 2230	Accurate 5744	Alliant Unique
Norma 204	VihtaVuori N140	Accurate Solo-4100	VihtaVuori N320
VihtaVuori N160	IMR4064	Ramshot Enforcer	Accurate Solo-1000
Accurate XMR4350	Norma 201	VihtaVuori N110	Hodgdon Clays
IMR4831	Hodgdon H335	Accurate No. 9	Alliant GreenDot
Alliant RI-19	IMR4895	Norma R123	VihtaVuori N310
Hodgdon H4350	Ramshot TAC	Alliant 2400	Alliant RedDot
Winchester 760	Hodgdon VarGet	Alliant BlueDot	Accurate Nitro-100
VihtaVuori N550	IMR3031	Accurate No. 7	Alliant Bullseye
Hodgdon H380	Alliant RI-12	Accurate No. 5	**Lightest charge**

The range of propellant burning rates needed in these representative 22-caliber cartridges is about six times—the ideal 22 Short rimfire propellant burns about six times faster than the ideal 220-Swift propellant burns. "Super Magnum" rifle cartridges require propellants that burn about half as fast as the ideal Swift propellant.

SMOKELESS PROPELLANT—CHARGE POSITION

Whenever the charge does not fill the usable portion of the case (volume under bullet), the charge distribution within the case will influence ballistics, often significantly. In some combinations and in many applications, this difference is inconsequential; in other instances, this can be monumentally important. Because this fact is so nearly universally unfamiliar to experienced shooters, a few examples are worth noting.

When we handle and fire a gun normally (oriented nearly level), the charge distribution will be more-or-less even along the bottom (side) of the case—I will refer to this as the normal situation. However, the

These cutaway 38-40 WCF cartridges each contain 5.0 grains of Bullseye, a perfectly normal charge, and a standard 180-grain bullet. In this combination, the position of the charge alters ballistics by 50 fps. In one tested factory 38-40 load, the charge-position variance was 186 fps!

A fine 44 Magnum midrange load uses 7½ grains of Solo-1000, Remington 2½ primer, Starline cases, and any typical commercial-cast 240-grain bullet. With the bullet seated normally, as shown, the charge position is significantly variable with the result that velocity also varies significantly (about 30 fps—depending upon where the charge happens to settle). The simple expedient of seating the bullet deeper (to roll crimp lightly over driving band) and using 7.0 grains of Solo-1000 (charge recommended for 44 Special loads with this bullet at the same length) reduces velocity variation to about 10 fps!

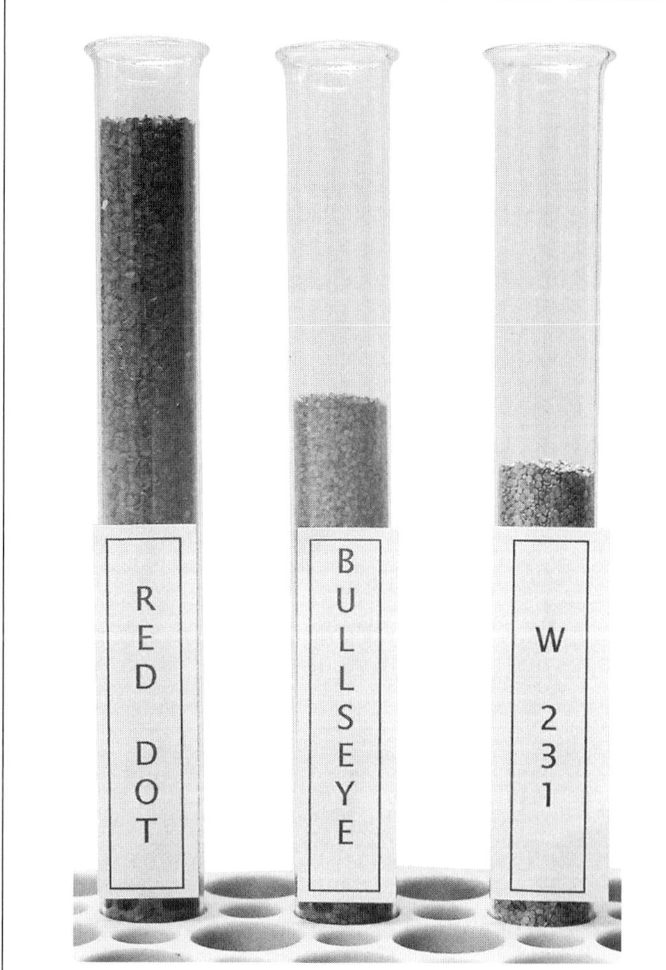

These test tubes contain equal mass as dumped charges. Generally, in midrange pistol and revolver loadings, similar charges of each produce similar velocity. Obviously, when the charge position is an issue, propellant choice matters!

charge does not always distribute so evenly, and this is where the problem arises.

I have tested factory 38-40 ammunition that produced an average velocity that was 180 fps faster when the charge rested near the primer, compared to when the charge rested near the bullet. That, however, was fantastically good consistency when compared to one handload I concocted for the same gun. When fired normally, muzzle velocity was about 900 fps, ballistic uniformity was acceptable, and accuracy was good.

Then I tested that load for charge-position effects. With the charge against the primer, muzzle velocity exceeded 1,100 fps; conversely, with the charge against the bullet, muzzle velocity was less than 300 fps. When I fired the gun while it was pointing down at a 45-degree angle, I could watch the bullet and the following fused chunk of unignited propellant travel from muzzle to ground—velocity might have been 100 fps. Depending solely upon charge position, this combination could generate either an overpressure load or a bullet-in-bore squib.

Consider one highly successful IPSC husband and wife team that used a single gun for competition. He loaded all their ammunition. He had to use different loads for his and for hers because when she shot the pistol, recoil left the propellant resting differently in the chambered case as compared to when he shot the gun. Evidently, when she shot the gun, the charge tended to settle toward the bullet end; when he shot the gun, the charge tended to settle toward the primer end because, in order to achieve the required velocity to qualify as a Major round, he had to use one-tenth grain more propellant in her ammunition. (Physiological differences between the two shooters—how much the gun recoiled—could not account for more than a minor fraction of the difference in measured velocity.)

Mr. Ken Oehler, of Oehler Ballistics Labs, loaded a batch of primed Remington 38 Special cases with a charge of Unique that occupied about 70 percent of the available space under the Speer 110 JHP bullet. His pressure test gun was a 10-inch T/C Contender fitted with a strain gage and connected to the Oehler Model-43 Personal Ballistics Lab.

With the charge settled against the bullet (as much as was feasible), these cartridges averaged 1,110 fps with an average peak pressure of 15,000 psi—perfectly normal 38 Special numbers. Cartridges from the same batch fired with the propellant settled against the primer (to the extent feasible) produced an average velocity of 1,393 fps with an average pressure of 26,100 psi—which is only a hair's breadth from the mean average pressure of Industry Standard 38 Special +P Proof loads (27,000 psi).

Those who doubt this result are welcome to get proper equipment and try this test themselves. Call Oehler Research. They will be happy to set you up with the tools you need to learn just how much difference charge position can make.

The charge-position effect explains why it is so difficult to achieve consistent velocity with cartridges such as midrange 44 Magnums. Using any conventional propellant, the charge does not nearly fill the case; with normal handling it is apt, therefore, to settle in different locations in each subsequent round. Hodgdon Trail Boss solves this problem because it is so bulky that normal charges entirely fill available propellant space in typical handgun cartridges.

SAAMI and CIP both specify precise cartridge handling during ballistics testing. The purpose of these practices it to orient the charge the same way in every cartridge before chambering and firing. This represents the implicit recognition that charge-position effects can be quite significant. My experience suggests that this is true in nearly all cartridges where seating the bullet does not compress the charge.

Randolph Constantine, master NRA Highpower competitor and author of the bible on NRA Highpower shooting, *Modern Highpower Competition* (Precision Shooting Publications), reports that in one of his tested rifle-load combinations, the charge filled about 95 percent of available space, and yet charge position proved to have a significant ballistic influence. With that load, if he handled the gun to bias the charge toward the bullet, he would get a ½-inch, 100-yard group. If he then handled the gun to bias the charge toward the primer, he would still get a ½-inch, 100-yard group. The mean velocity and ballistic uniformity for the shots making up each group were statistically similar. However, the centers of these groups were 1½ inches apart! This occurred because barrel time was significantly different for each situation.

Charge position always matters!

SMOKELESS PROPELLANT— BEST FOR INTENDED PURPOSE— GENERAL CONSIDERATIONS

In choosing likely propellants for your handloading requirements, consider and compare your needs. If you intend to shoot competitively, visit with other competitors using similar cartridges. Certainly, a propellant that they use will be a good place to start—such information is available through such publications as *Precision Shooting Magazine.* Those interested only in hunting cartridges might have different choices. For self-defense purposes—whether intended for use against two- or four-legged vermin—an entirely different selection criterion might come into play. Refer to "Smokeless Propellant—Self Defense" in this chapter. For some applications, economy is an important consideration; often, propellant prices vary, and buying in quantity can be worthwhile (many makers offer propellants in larger containers at considerably less cost, per pound).

SMOKELESS PROPELLANT— TARGET CARTRIDGES— GENERAL CONSIDERATIONS

I will start this discussion with formal target shooting. Here, several separate criteria muddy the water. First, I will consider traditional handgun events, where mild recoil, consistent velocity, clean-burning characteristics, and (in some events) maximum feasible energy are all considerations.

Typically, handloaders produce ammunition for handgun target shooting using progressive presses. These systems measure and dump propellant charges automatically into sized and primed cases. Despite this automation, consistent operator technique can add measurably to uniformity of resulting cartridges—practice consistent press operation. Segregate cartridges produced at the beginning of each batch and those produced during and immediately after any interruptions from those produced during steady-state production conditions. Use such interrupted-procedure cartridges for fouling, plinking, and informal practice.

Conversely, handloaders usually produce ammunition for target rifle competition using a single-stage, conventional press or an arbor press. However, nothing prevents a careful handloader from producing top-quality rifle ammunition using a progressive press. The Hornady L-n-L Auto Progressive and the RCBS Pro-2000 come to mind as likely candidates. As with many progressive presses, these units offer the option of separate propellant charging. For some types of competition, handloaders carefully weigh propellant charges. Whereas, for other types of competition, they measure charges as precisely as they feasibly can. Most progressive presses are amenable to propellant charging via either method. Regardless of the system used, the operator's skill, patience, attention to detail, and the consistency of the press operation are all critical to the production of top-quality ammunition.

One other point to consider is the fact that some small-granulated propellants can migrate through the flash hole and infiltrate into available spaces in the primer pocket. To minimize this, it is advisable to keep all ammunition, from any batch, oriented with the bullet pointing downward during handling and transportation. This is particularly important when using (finely granulated) propellants that might infiltrate the flash hole—many ball type and the finest extruded propellants fit within this category.

To test for this potentiality easily, pour a small quantity of the propellant in question into an unprimed case. If granules freely fall through the flash hole or if gently shaking the case results in granules passing through the flash hole, then the propellant is likely to infiltrate the flash hole in loaded rounds.

If you do not make an effort to handle, store, and transport cartridges loaded with any such propellant with the bullet down, possible infiltration of the propellant into the flash hole will alter ballistic uniformity with an inevitable degradation of overall accuracy. This can happen because each cartridge can have a unique number of granules within the flash hole and around the primer anvil. When that situation exists, the strength and duration of the primer ignition pulse as that enters into the main body of the case will depend upon how many granules have infiltrated the flash hole and upon how those granules are packed therein.

With highly compressed charges, this is not an issue because seating the bullet will lock the granules solidly in place so that granule movement (or charge settling) cannot normally occur. Also, with larger-granulated propellants (those proven not to easily pass through the flash hole), this is not a consideration. However, to limit the chance of anything entering the flash hole, transporting and storing all ammunition in a bullet-down orientation is good practice. MTM ammo boxes with a separate internal tray facilitate this while protecting the bullet tip.

SMOKELESS PROPELLANT—COWBOY ACTION

For standard targets, bullets fired in this game have a specific and somewhat unusual requirement for low velocity—maximum velocity cannot exceed 900 fps. Practically, winning competitors routinely prefer to use cartridges launching the lightest feasible bullet at the lowest feasible velocity (often slower than 700 fps!). This combination results in unusually low pressures, and it places monumental strain on the functionality of traditional smokeless propellants.

Generally, such loads entail potential problems. First is the specter of a multiple charge. When using traditional propellants, room often exists for several charges. Use extreme care to avoid this gun-destroying and potentially dangerous eventuality.

A DOUBLE CHARGE GENERATES QUADRUPLE PRESSURE; A TRIPLE CHARGE GENERATES MORE THAN SIX TIMES THE INTENDED PRESSURE, NO MATTER HOW MILD THE INTENDED LOAD! A DOUBLE CHARGE IS APT TO DESTROY THE GUN; A TRIPLE CHARGE IS CERTAIN TO DO SO!

Second, is the reality of the squib cartridge. This is common in this game. It occurs when the primer does not ignite the charge properly because too much primer energy is wasted moving the bullet and charge and in heating the exposed case walls. Some of the charge might ignite, but as the bullet moves, the chamber volume increases dramatically and, therefore, temperature plummets. Granules that did not ignite soon enough will never ignite, and if too few granules initially ignite, gas generation would be insufficient to keep the bullet moving.

In this sport, winning requires firing multiple shots as rapidly as is feasible. Hence, while the competitor might hear and feel the squib, he or she might find it physiologically impossible to not fire another shot behind it. This happens very commonly and results in bulged and destroyed barrels at least, or destroyed guns with attendant hazards at worst.

Two things are helpful. First, increase the neck tension; to limit or prevent bullet movement due to the impulse from the primer blast—if the primer blast does move the bullet, this will occur before any charge burning occurs. Second, use a primer that generates more heat (heat ignites granules) with less brisance (what can move a bullet); the Remington 1½ (small) and 2½ (large) pistol primers are ideal here and are highly recommended. However, most competitors strive to modify their guns to have the lightest-possible hammer fall with the goal of speeding and easing gun manipulation. For this reason, they prefer Federal primers, which are usually the easiest primers to ignite. Hence, increasing neck tension and using a particularly easy-to-ignite propellant are critical. However, with the unusually low pressures used in these cartridges, it is also necessary to use very soft bullets, and soft bullets do not tolerate high neck tension. This is a classic quandary. As I often point out, "It is always something, it is usually two things, and it is often three things!"

Those tempted to use magnum primers in an effort to mitigate squibbing potential are very often disappointed. Doing so is counterproductive because the more powerful primer simply dislodges the bullet a greater distance and, thereby, increases boiler room volume more. This cools the gas even more, thereby exacerbating the potential for squibbing. This simply does not work.

Among traditional propellants, N310 is ideal for this application. Clays and Solo-1000 are also good, as are several older numbers and new shot-shell numbers from Alliant called E3 and American Select. These share the combination of rapid and easy ignition with relatively low packing-density and clean-burning characteristics. The former characteristics reduce sensitivity to charge position and reduce the potential for squibbing; the latter is obviously beneficial toward proper gun functioning with extensive shooting. While these are good choices, we now have a far safer option.

About 1995, I began incessantly pestering every propellant producer for a truly low-density, low-energy smokeless propellant. In 2005, Hodgdon answered this call, after no small expense in development (on the order of $250,000) with a propellant it named Trail Boss. While the burning rates of Trail Boss and Unique are similar, Trail Boss has significantly less energy and is far bulkier. Any given mass of Trail Boss takes up about twice as much space as does any previously available smokeless propellant. Hence, in the revolver and short rifle cartridges most commonly used in the Cowboy Action game, a full case of Trail Boss will not generate excessive pressure; moreover, a slightly compressed charge will generate desirable velocity; finally, squibs are practically impossible because the easily ignited charge fills, or nearly fills, the case.

Trail Boss deserves an entire book; I certainly cannot do it justice here. But, then, I am prejudiced—after all, it was my idea.

For long-range Cowboy Action side matches using rifles, 4198 or similar propellants are likely choices. However, for those interested in duplicating ballistics (velocity and pressure) of most original blackpowder rifle cartridges, 5744 is unmatched, as explained in the following section.

SMOKELESS PROPELLANT—COWBOY ACTION—DUPLICATING BLACKPOWDER BALLISTICS

I will consider two classes of cartridges in this category. These are cartridges using:

- Cylindrical or nearly cylindrical cases shorter than about 1½ inches
- All other cases

For the former category, Hodgdon Trail Boss is the premier choice. In average-length cartridges within this class when bullet seating slightly compresses the charge, ballistics will approximate a full charge of blackpowder. For shorter cases within this class, it will be necessary to compress the charge somewhat more. For longer cases within this class, a charge that almost fills the available space will do the job.

Chronographing will tell the tale. As necessary, you can adjust the charge between filling about 90 percent of the usable space to about 10 percent compression (under the seated bullet). When velocity matches the original blackpowder load, pressure will also be similar to the blackpowder load.

Remington pistol primers are the best choice. The best alternatives are Federal and CCI standard pistol. When feasible, use a mild pistol primer with this propellant, even when loading a rifle case.

For longer cases, no smokeless propellant currently exists that will fill the case while developing blackpowder pressure and velocity—Trail Boss is just marginally too fast for this application. Hence, it is necessary to use a charge that does not fill the available space. Just as with most other propellants, this leads to significant deleterious charge-position effects. Refer to "Smokeless Propellant—Charge Position" in this chapter. Propellants that work well in these applications include BlueDot, 4759, 4227, 4198, 2400, and many others. However, none of those has proven to be as versatile as Accurate 5744.

Accurate 5744 is a relatively low-density, double-based, extruded propellant. Generally, double-base propellants tend to ignite somewhat faster than single-based numbers and hence are less apt to create a squib. Accurate 5744 is composed of relatively large, lightly deterred granules; therefore, it is particularly easy to ignite. Evidently, for these reasons, loads using 5744 are only modestly sensitive to charge position.

One particularly intriguing characteristic of 5744 is that handloaders can develop a load safely for practically any blackpowder rifle cartridge using a case that is longer than about 1½ inches and with any bullet of reasonably normal mass. The process is conceptually simple:

- Using an unsized case with a spent primer in place, mark outside of fired case to indicate where bullet base will be in the loaded round.
- Measure and record case weight.
- Fill case with water up to the level where the bullet base will be located in loaded round.
- Measure and record weight of case plus water.

- Subtract weight of empty case from weight of case partially filled with water (to obtain usable case capacity, in grains of water).
- Multiply usable capacity in grains of water by 0.45 to obtain a starting charge of 5744 for that case, bullet, and overall cartridge length.

Generally, chronographing will demonstrate that such a charge produces less velocity than the original blackpowder load—it will also generate significantly less pressure. In addition, such a load will usually leave a significant number of unburned propellant granules in both the case and the barrel.

Testing with incremental charge increases of one grain, or less, will soon demonstrate a load that practically duplicates velocity of a blackpowder load. Conveniently, such a load also approximately duplicates blackpowder load pressure.

Usually, such loads work well with commercial and home cast bullets that are not particularly hard. Generally, for best accuracy, Brinell hardness of cast bullets used in such rifle loads should be between about 12 and about 15. When using such bullets, the goal is accuracy—it's not to duplicate original-load velocity precisely; hence, we use incremental load development to find the most accurate load that does not lead the barrel and where handload velocity does not significantly exceed original load velocity. Generally, by quirk of fate, such a load is the lowest charge where few, if any, unburned granules remain in the case and bore.

For all such loads, whether with 5744 or with some other similar propellant, the preferred primer is the Remington 2½ because that primer provides the most heat with the least brisance. Testing at Accurate Arms has demonstrated superior results when using the Remington 2½ with 5744. Second choices are Federal 150 and CCI 300, which are similarly mild. If piercing occurs with pistol primers, the Remington 9½ is the best optional choice.

Hodgdon Clays is one of many clean-burning, single-based shotshell propellants that are proven performers in target handgun loads.

SMOKELESS PROPELLANT—BULLSEYE HANDGUN

Traditional handgun target shooters use cartridges and loads with low-to-moderate case capacity, e.g., 38 Special WC, 45 Automatic, and similar chamberings. This is most beneficial because it is much easier to develop good, consistent smokeless loads with small capacity cases, especially when working at low pressures. Customary propellants for these types of loads are those that are similar to Alliant Bullseye; usually, such propellants are fast burning, relatively low density, flake, and double-based; examples include Bullseye, Red Dot, Green Dot, Nitro-100, No. 2, HP 38, and W231. Newer offerings that have utility include American Select, Clays, N310, N320, Solo-1000, ZIP, and similar propellants.

In choosing a propellant for such loads, look for a combination that both nearly fills available propellant space and generates the needed velocity within safe pressure limits. When looking at combinations that do not nearly fill the available propellant space, double-base propellants might be preferable. These tend to be less sensitive to charge position. Additionally, in any load of any type, where the propellant does not substantially fill the available propellant space, pay critical attention to how you handle the gun between shots—charge-position effects can be significant. Refer to "Smokeless Propellant—Charge Position" in this chapter.

In addition, it is important to note that some of the best loads used in Bullseye Target shooting and in other handgun events use so little propellant that a double charge easily fits under the bullet. Take every precaution to guard against this gun-destroying and patently dangerous eventuality.

DOUBLING THE CHARGE INCREASES CHAMBER PRESSURE ABOUT FOUR TIMES AND IS ALMOST CERTAIN TO LEAD TO A DESTROYED GUN OR SOMETHING FAR WORSE—INJURY OR DEATH.

SMOKELESS PROPELLANT—SILHOUETTE PISTOL

Silhouette pistol shooters generally use magnum revolver cartridges, relatively small-capacity rifle cartridges chambered in one-hand guns, or wildcats that resemble small-capacity rifle cartridges. Most magnum revolver cartridges work best with propellants with performance that is similar to Accurate No. 9. Examples include N110, W296 (H110), 2400, 4227, Enforcer, and A1680. With small rifle or rifle-type cartridges fired from short barrels, often these same propellants will work quite well. For small rifle cartridges, other good choices include IMR4227, SR4759, H4198, IMR4198, Rl-7, R1-10, N130, N133, H322, Rl-10, and BenchMark.

Ramshot Enforcer is a high-performance ball-type propellant that delivers unusually high velocity in many applications. It is particularly well suited to various magnum revolver chamberings and is useful to those looking to achieve good velocity with minimum recoil. Its performance is similar to that of Power Pistol and BlueDot.

In some applications, slower propellants might offer greater velocity potential but, generally, at the expense of a significant increase in recoil and muzzle blast. In this game, most competitors strive to minimize recoil because the cumulative effect of recoil is bound to eventually degrade one's Match performance (after firing many shots).

SMOKELESS PROPELLANT—ACTION PISTOL (IPSC)

Action Pistol shooters have some of the same requirements as traditional handgun Bullseye shooters, including the need for consistent velocity and clean-

Alliant Power Pistol is one of the best propellants for pistol loads. It is quite versatile, and, in many combinations it delivers more energy than any other propellant. It is also a fine choice for midrange revolver loads.

shooting loads. However, these folks sacrifice mild recoil to achieve the required power level. This means that IPPC (International Practical Pistol Confederation) competitors usually use slower propellants where the charge nearly fills the available space or is somewhat compressed and generates significantly higher pressures, compared to loads typically used by Bullseye target shooters.

Each of these characteristics makes it easier to achieve ballistic uniformity. Charge-position effects are less of a concern but can still be an issue. Refer to "Smokeless Propellant—Charge Position" in this chapter. Also, smokeless propellants burn cleaner and more consistently when loaded at relatively high pressure, as is common with loads used in this sport. Many propellants have potential application in Action Pistol cartridges. Those similar in burning rate to Accurate No. 7 are popular. Examples include Enforcer, True Blue, Power-Pistol, No. 7, BlueDot, HS6, AutoComp, N340, N350, 3N37, Universal Clays, and Unique.

If the charge in the load that you settle upon fails to fill the available space substantially, pay critical attention to gun handling because charge position matters even when the charge nearly fills the available space.

Many Benchrest competitors and those who compete in similar events use VihtaVuori propellants.

SMOKELESS PROPELLANT—BENCHREST RIFLE

Chamberings used in various target rifle events run the gamut from those using relatively small cases to those using relatively huge cases, such as the newest super-magnums. First, I will consider traditional benchrest competition. Here, accuracy is the only criterion. Benchrest shooters will forgo anything to achieve any improvement in absolute accuracy. Current traditional benchrest cartridges tend to be of small capacity and to work at very high pressures. The use of such small cases sacrifices velocity potential for a measure of increased consistency. Another thing traditional benchrest shooters can give up is fouling control. In some games, they clean the bore after firing eleven or twelve shots—one or two fouler shots plus ten shots for the record; in other games, they fire six or seven shots—one or two fouler shots plus five for the record.

Propellants that winning competitors have used successfully or that show promise in benchrest competition include H322, N133, A2015, Rl-7, Rl-10, TAC, IMR4198, H4198, N130, and BenchMark. Recently, VihtaVuori propellants have dominated in traditional Benchrest matches.

Considering the nature of this game, no propellant is out of the question. While the following is a slight exaggeration, it should make the point: If Pyrodex or Cannon Grade blackpowder shot the smallest groups, rest assured you would see plenty of smoke at benchrest events. In reality, velocity does matter because the shooter can do nothing about wind changes that occur after the bullet leaves the muzzle and before it reaches the target; hence, time of flight is important. Competitors, therefore, will strive for reasonably high velocity.

With continued reductions in benchrest case capacities, progressively faster propellants will come into play. Again, if the propellant and charge combination that you happen to settle upon does not completely fill the available propellant space, pay particular attention to gun handling to maintain consistent shot-to-shot charge position. Refer to "Smokeless Propellant—Charge Position" in this chapter.

Most traditional benchresters use a measure to dump charges directly into the cartridge case. For this reason, there exists little to review concerning possible variations in case charging technique. Uniformity of charge mass and charge packing scheme are determined by operator technique with the powder measure and by the characteristics of the measure and by how that tool happens to interact with the propellant used.

Conversely, long-range benchrest shooters usually weigh charges because they often use propellants that will not meter with sufficient accuracy for such use. Here, the handloader must make every effort to ensure consistent case charging. If the resultant load results in a highly compressed charge, swirl charging is particularly beneficial. Refer to chapter 9.

The question of how much handling it might take to randomize the as-dumped propellant packing scheme in any load (where bullet seating does not significantly compress the charge) remains unanswered. However, I can report that, despite significant cartridge vibration, rotation, and the shaking associated with transportation and handling, the as-dumped packing scheme can be an amazingly persistent characteristic. Nevertheless, to make sure of maximum round-to-round consistency, make every effort to handle all non-compressed-charge loads as similarly as possible. Ammo boxes are particularly useful here and storing rounds with the bullet down is probably beneficial.

SMOKELESS PROPELLANT—HUNTER BENCH

Cartridges used in this specialized game are 6mm or larger caliber and cannot have less than 46 grains of case capacity (grains of water to case mouth—equal to the 30-30 Winchester case). Due to the relatively short-range shooting of this game, relatively lightweight bullets are preferred—usually custom match bullets of about 110- to 150 grains (in 30-caliber). These restrictions limit useful propellant choices. (This game is still evolving and longer-range events are now common.)

Propellants that winning competitors have used, or that show promise, in the Hunter Bench game include H322, A2015, H4198, IMR4198, Rl-7, Rl-10, N130, N133, N135, IMR4895, H4895, TAC, W748, A2495, and X-Terminator.

If the propellant and charge combination that you happen to settle upon does not fill the available propellant space completely, pay particular attention to gun handling to maintain consistent shot-to-shot charge position. Refer to "Smokeless Propellant—Charge Position" in this chapter.

Many competitors measure and dump charges directly into the cartridge case. For this reason, there exists little to review concerning possible variations in case charging technique. Uniformity of charge mass and charge packing scheme are determined by operator skill with the powder measure and by the characteristics of the measure and how that tool happens to interact with the particular propellant used.

If you are weighing charges, make every effort to be consistent during case charging. If the resultant load features a highly compressed charge, swirl charging is particularly beneficial. Refer to chapter 9.

SMOKELESS PROPELLANT—NRA HIGHPOWER

Long-range competitors have a different set of considerations and an entirely different perspective. First, they are concerned with finding a load that will shoot small groups consistently over a long string of shots and without the necessity of barrel cleaning. Second, they are much more concerned about maximizing velocity,

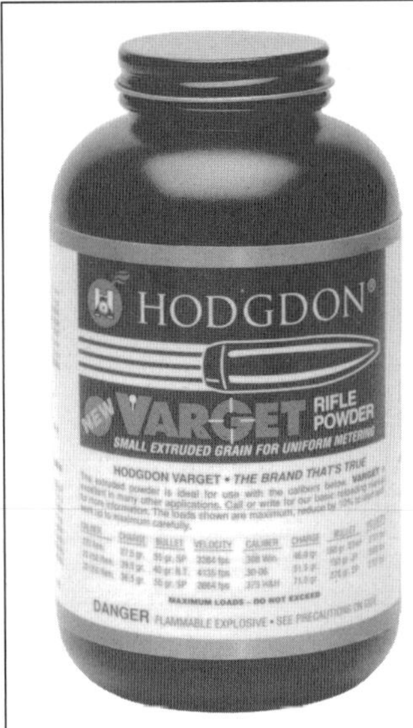

VarGet and all other Hodgdon Extreme propellants are comparatively insensitive to temperature variation. This is a critical consideration for competitors (and some hunters) who must load match-grade ammunition without knowing the conditions that will exist when those loads are used. VarGet is a fine 308 Winchester propellant. It has proven to be ideal for such loads used in NRA Highpower competition. It is Hodgdon's top seller.

minimizing extreme velocity spread, and minimizing wind deflection (chiefly through use of a highly efficient bullet and, in some events, through use of a chambering that will launch such a bullet at relatively high velocity). These issues begin to take precedence when one is target shooting beyond about five hundred yards. Finally, because these competitors do a passel of shooting in any good season, they look for combinations that can offer any possibility of extending barrel life.

For these reasons, NRA Highpower competitors look for propellants that minimize bore fouling and bore wear while providing a consistent, high-velocity load and without any individual shot falling outside the narrowest possible velocity window. Curiously, this is one area where normal statistical analysis does not give the most useful information.

Normally, we can say that the standard deviation of velocity, a measure of the expected (velocity) variation around the mean (average) velocity of shots with a given load, is the most useful measure of the consistency of a load. However, in long-range, bullseye target shooting where scoring rings are concentric circles and where errors in wind deflection estimations are inevitable, this is not the situation. Here, the most important measure of ballistic consistency is extreme velocity spread. For example, a load where testing of a large sample showed an extreme spread of 30 fps with a standard deviation of 11 fps would be less desirable than a load where testing of the same number of shots generated an extreme spread of 22 fps with a standard deviation of 14 fps.

For bullets fired across long distances, modest changes in muzzle velocity result in large changes in drop and in wind deflection. Because the target is a group of concentric circles, when the complication of windage correction errors is added into the equation, the shooter is more apt to make a higher score with a load that will keep all shots closer to the vertical center—the scoring circles are wider there—even if, on average, those shots fall somewhat farther above or below the center.

If long-range target shooting is your game, look for a propellant that can deliver shot after shot within the narrowest possible velocity window.Forget the standard deviation of velocity. Concentrate on minimizing extreme velocity spread—otherwise, count on it; those rare velocity fliers will cost you points. (Interested readers should consider *Modern Highpower Competi-*

While it showed good promise for many magnum and similar applications, Winchester Magnum Rifle was only offered for about one year! If you find that some new propellant happens to shine in some application, consider stocking up, for that product might similarly and unexpectedly disappear from the market.

tion by Randolph Constantine, available from Precision Shooting Publications.)

Generally, the extended shot strings involved in this game require relatively clean-burning propellants. Historically, traditional IMR numbers, especially 4895, 4064, and 4350, have prevailed. These are still a good place to start. Newer numbers with great promise include VarGet and other Hodgdon Extreme propellants, N140, N150, N160, N165, Rl-19, and Rl-22. Several new Ramshot propellants, including Big Game, Hunter, and Magnum might be worth considering.

SMOKELESS PROPELLANT—HUNTING CARTRIDGES—GENERAL CONSIDERATIONS

Hunters have different criteria when compared to formal target shooters. Generally, hunters are more concerned with trajectory and delivered energy than with any other factor. I, like many other nimrods, simply try to find the propellant that safely delivers the highest velocity while achieving some perceived necessary level of accuracy—my personal minimum accuracy criterion for normal big-game hunting use is consistent 1½ minute of angle (MOA), 300-yard, three-shot groups.

Barrel fouling, extended shot string accuracy, component costs, and equipment costs are inconsequential to big-game hunters; however, these often are critical considerations to varmint hunters.

SMOKELESS PROPELLANT—BIG GAME

Rifle hunting involves two main categories. I will start with big-game hunting. Opinions vary concerning what a propellant should do in a hunting cartridge. I contend that only two issues regarding propellant choice matter when one is looking through the sights at a big-game target:

- Delivered energy
- Muzzle energy and bullet efficiency (BC)
- Potential shot placement
- External ballistics and accuracy

Delivered energy is simple enough: All other things being equal, the load that safely generates the highest muzzle velocity with any given bullet is the best choice. Similarly, that load will shoot the flattest and will otherwise have the external ballistics edge.

Regarding accuracy for a big-game-hunting cartridge—rifle or pistol—the hunter should judge

When a hunter gets a chance at a trophy (as my brother, Stan, did back in 1965), he certainly wants to use a propellant that dependably delivers accuracy and power.

Bench time in cold weather is a fine preamble to a successful hunting season. Here, my son, Jody, is testing 338 Lapua Magnum loads, and I am recording the data. MRP2 proved ideal.

accuracy based upon the first shot from a cold barrel and, perhaps, one or two additional shots. I prefer a compilation of data from many three-shot groups, each starting with a cool barrel, as a superior measure of accuracy potential of a hunting rifle and load combination.

Most important is that the first shot goes where the shooter intends. Should a pulled shot or an intervening twig prevent that first shot from doing the intended job, then one or two follow-up shots can be important, but it is ever so unlikely that accuracy after the third shot will matter to a big-game hunter. Measuring accuracy of a hunting rifle using more than three shots makes little sense. It is better to fire many three-shot groups, each starting with a clean, cold barrel and to fire those groups under differing atmospheric conditions. Then, similarly, fire three-shot groups from a fouled barrel. Fire three-shot groups at 100 yards and then at 300 yards. But always fire three-shot groups.

When you find a propellant that can deliver good velocity with a load that always keeps three-shot groups near one-MOA (minute of angle), even at 300 yards, and that will keep the group centered near where it should be, with the specific sight setting used, you have found an ideal propellant.

No one can predict what propellant will give the best performance in any hunting gun using any particular bullet and with any given load variables. Nevertheless, some loading manuals list suggestions associated with specific load data—loads that had proved accurate in a tested rifle.

However, unless your gun happens to match the tested gun, it seems unlikely that the same load will be your most accurate combination. Generally, look for a load developing good velocity with a safe charge that either fills, or nearly fills, the available charge space or that is somewhat compressed during bullet seating (which is generally desirable).

Again, pay attention to how you introduce charges into cases. Consistency is the keyword. If you happen upon a good load that leaves considerable unused space under the seated bullet, an eventuality that is unlikely (except in certain magnum chamberings), pay particular attention to gun handling. Strive to locate the propellant in the same position in the case before each shot.

Consider ongoing propellant availability. For example, Winchester MRP (Magnum Rifle Powder) was a promising propellant that performed well in many magnum chamberings. However, before anyone had developed data for more than a few applications, Winchester dropped MRP—marketing issues prevailed. The marketers never gave this product a chance. Keep this in mind: If you find a new propellant that seems to be indispensably perfect for your needs, you had better stock up; it might not be around the next time you go shopping.

Left to right: A 204 Ruger, 5mm/35 SMC, and 22-250. Regardless of chambering, the goals for varmint ammunition are usually similar. These include acceptable accuracy (Minute of Prairie Rat), maximum velocity, and minimum cost. Using a less-expensive propellant might allow budgeting for plastic-tipped bullets (as shown here). These bullets extend useful range at least 10 percent and are, therefore, worthwhile.

SMOKELESS PROPELLANT—VARMINT

Varmint hunters are working in an area that is functionally somewhere between benchrest and NRA Highpower. If all goes well, varminters will see extended shot strings without pausing for barrel cleaning (or cooling!), so they will be looking for a propellant that minimizes fouling. In addition, they will be doing both short-range and long-range shooting, and they will be taking shots at unknown distances. For these reasons, muzzle velocity will be particularly important. Generally, they also care about barrel life because they hope to fire hundreds of rounds during any given outing.

Absolute accuracy is important but varmint hunters do not really care if their pet load throws an occasional flier. So long as the vast majority of shots are similar in velocity and shoot to the same point of aim, the load will do the job. The point is that varmint shooting, by its very nature, will inevitably include a considerable number of missed shots. Varmint hunters will view anything that increases the number of good shots in any string or that decreases barrel fouling as beneficial. Nevertheless, they will always prefer a load that is usually more accurate, or that delivers a flatter trajectory and, therefore, gives less wind deflection.

Several newer propellants show great promise here. The Hodgdon Extreme propellants VarGet, BenchMark, and H322 are obvious choices; the granules have little (if any) graphite coating and, therefore, generate considerably less fouling than do many other propellants. These propellants also show considerably less sensitivity to temperature variations, which can be an important consideration to the varmint hunter—temperature commonly varies by more than 40 degrees F during any given outing.

Brass is an efficient heat conductor, and smokeless propellant is an efficient insulator. Hence, unless one leaves a round chambered for many minutes, the temperature of the surrounding chamber is of little consequence to ballistic performance. What matters is the temperature under which the ammunition is stored during the hours prior to use.

Ramshot X-Terminator, TAC, Big Game, and Hunter (all ball propellants using unique deterrent chemistry) combine potentially reduced barrel heating with relatively clean burning and splendid shot-to-shot uniformity. Other ball-type propellants also burn cooler and might, thereby, extend barrel life; however, most of these tend to generate more barrel fouling and are usually more sensitive to temperature. Evidently, VihtaVuori propellants (all extruded) use very clean raw materials because these are unusually clean burning.

Ball-type propellants, and some smaller-granulation tubular propellants (e.g., H4198SC, H322, N130, N133, and BenchMark), have another significant advantage—loading ease. These are particularly amenable to use in a conventional measure. When the fortunate varminter might need several thousand rounds for an extended outing, this is a significant consideration.

Be that as it may, most varmint hunters look first at velocity and then at accuracy. Before testing any other propellants, the handloader should test the accuracy obtained using the propellant offering the highest velocity because when shooting at unknown distances, the load giving the flattest trajectory gives the best odds of making good hits. Even when using a rangefinder, trajectory matters because conditions vary, ranged distance does not always correspond to actual target distance (the device can pick up the wrong reflection), and it is not always convenient to range each new target.

All else being equal, if two propellants offer similar velocity, the one that generates the lowest standard velocity deviation is preferable. If two propellants offer similar velocity and accuracy, the one that generates the least fouling is preferable. If two propellants offer similar velocity, accuracy, and cleanliness, the one that costs less or that burns cooler (ball types)—i.e., minimizes overall shooting costs (for ammunition and for replacement barrels)—is preferable.

SMOKELESS PROPELLANT—SELF-DEFENSE

Propellant choice for self-defense loads is completely straightforward. First, we need to realize that true self-defense situations, whether involving two- or four-legged vermin, almost always happen at extremely close distance—seven feet is an oft'-quoted figure for encounters with the two-legged variety. Accuracy is not an issue; neither is ammunition cost, decibels produced by muzzle blast, or myriad other considerations that might matter in other types of shooting.

Recoil might be an issue. Necessarily, under the constraints of a life-or-death situation, the shooter must be capable of properly handling the recoil generated by the load and gun. Therefore, remember that in large handgun cartridges and in most rifle-type cartridges propellant jetting adds considerably to recoil. As an example, when firing a 180-grain 44 Magnum bullet at 1,500 fps from a revolver—certainly an effective self-defense combination—a load using Bullseye produces an astonishing 48 percent less recoil than a load using H110. A load generating less recoil is always and obviously advantageous in any situation where one or more quickly delivered follow-up shots might save your life.

On one occasion, a Kodiak Island cattle rancher used a 22 Short Rimfire against an enraged, charging Kodiak bear at 15 feet; this resulted in an instant, one-shot kill! However, this here pilgrim—yours truly—

would still prefer a howitzer, thank you very much. Rest assured that if the 29-grain slug had not centered the eye socket and hit at exactly the needed angle, that shooter would never have reported the incident.

If recoil is unmanageable, consider using a lighter charge of a faster propellant, a lighter bullet, or deliberately reducing velocity. If you do the latter, you have reduced potential delivered energy, which suggests that a commensurate increase in precision of shot placement is necessary. Note that I did not write "accuracy." The two are distinct concepts.

When the target is only a few feet away, almost any gun and load will have all the intrinsic accuracy necessary to place a shot within a hair's breadth of where the gun is pointed. On the other hand, in a life-or-death situation, very few shooters will have the necessary control to keep shot placement within a one-foot circle.

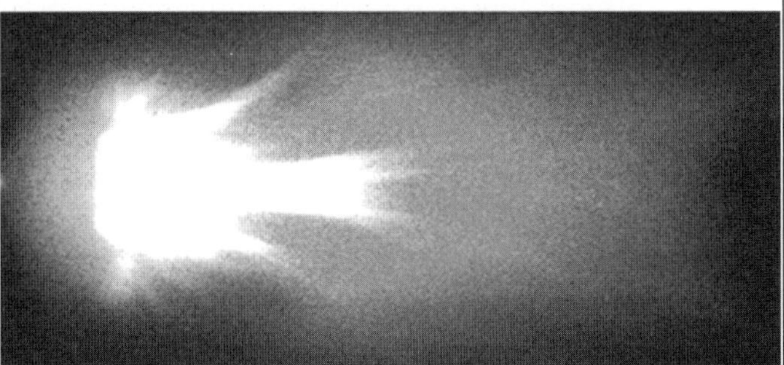

Top: Speer Gold Dot self-defense ammunition, which uses a flash suppressed propellant. Bottom: A similarly marketed load from another manufacturer that does not bother to use a flash-suppressed propellant, which is true of many manufacturers. When fired in a dark room—as might well happen when your life is on the line—the difference is blindingly obvious.

No matter what gun you hold, in such a situation shot placement is your first priority. However, if you have deliberately chosen a less-powerful chambering or a reduced-power load to increase your control, you had better concentrate just that much harder upon training to achieve proper shot placement. This is easier said than done when the adrenaline rush hits and your higher brain functions literally turn off and you go into the autopilot mode—if you have not properly trained sufficiently to produce effective and accurate muscle-memory of the required motions you will likely die.

Even when you use factory ammo for your concealed-carry gun (see the following comments under liability), it is useful to develop a handload that performs similarly. Once you have settled upon a factory load, your next goal is to develop an inexpensive handload that shoots to the same point of aim and that gives comparable recoil so that you can occasionally practice with a load that mimics the factory load without the high cost. This is how winning shooters assure themselves of automatically achieving correct shot placement, regardless of the level of stress.

When you use a handload that mimics recoil and point of impact of a factory load for correct training practice, that training can provide a realistic-and-affordable surrogate for a real-world encounter (practice makes permanent; perfect practice makes perfect). In most revolvers, one can create such a practice load using relatively hard commercially cast bullets or homemade cast bullets with gas checks. In a semiautomatic pistol, a plated or jacketed round-nose bullet might serve best.

In choosing the best propellant for self-defense loads, we must consider several issues. First, as all but a few of the most powerful conventional hand-

On a dark night, Andy Tuttle demonstrated the muzzle flash from an H110, 460 S&W load fired in a revolver. Imagine yourself in a self-defense situation using a load that generated this amount of flash! Propellant choice matters.

guns offer truly limited stopping power, handloaders should always look at velocity first. In a semiautomatic pistol, the best choice is the propellant that safely delivers the highest velocity with a load that dependably cycles the gun.

The next consideration is how cleanly the propellant burns. With loads used in revolvers and semiautomatic pistols, unburned propellant and propellant residue can be important considerations, especially if one should be so fortunate as to achieve some sort of barricade in an extended shooting situation. Even for the average outdoorsman where dangerous game is the main concern, this is still an issue because so few of us spend the time we should in properly cleaning our guns.

For self-defense, house-gun loads, muzzle flash is a major concern. The difference in muzzle flash amongst otherwise similarly performing propellants is nothing less than startling. Test your load in the dark and find out if the flash produced is tolerable. If not, test other propellants that perform similarly until you find one that does not generate a blinding flash. Manufacturers produce propellants with special additives to minimize flash. Some factory ammunition producers, such as Speer, use flash-suppressed propellants when loading law enforcement and other self-defense-type ammunition. These propellants are also available to handloaders but, unfortunately (perhaps due to liability concerns), we must discover which propellants qualify by testing.

PROPELLANT CHOICE IS CRITICAL IN SELF-DEFENSE LOADS.

NECESSARY AND UNFORTUNATE COMMENTS ON LIABILITY

Some pundits have advocated never using handloads in traditional self-defense applications. I have two personal comments. The first regards intrinsic liability. If you cannot produce ammunition of the highest quality using only the best available components, then do not use handloads for self-defense. Performance and effectiveness of your best load might equal but will never exceed performance of the best factory ammunition, such as Speer offers in its Gold Dot line.

Second, explicitly, your only purposes for producing self-defense ammunition are convenience and to save money—you are a handloader, after all. While you might be able to produce cartridges that generate greater energy than any available factory load (very unlikely, particularly when we consider the high-performance ammunition offered by Cor-Bon and Speer), it is unlikely that such a cartridge will actually perform better than a factory cartridge. The reason for this paradox stems from modern expanding-bullet technology; manufacturers design such bullets to perform best at a specific velocity. Factory loads produce the required velocity to optimize bullet performance. Driving such a bullet faster is most apt to actually degrade terminal performance and, hence, effectiveness.

Some have made the argument that no one should ever use handloads in a self-defense handgun owing to civil liability concerns: "The defendant used handloads because she wanted to create more powerful, deadly ammunition." While this might be a real concern in some jurisdictions, I would argue that this intelligent, informed counterargument, "I never fire factory ammunition and I always strive to duplicate factory performance with my handloads, as my chronographed data will demonstrate" should suffice to defeat that spurious argument.

SMOKELESS PROPELLANT—PLINKING CARTRIDGES—GENERAL CONSIDERATIONS

One reason many shooters begin handloading is to save money or to do more shooting on a limited budget. (The latter is usually the situation, even if we actually believed that we intended to save money, while doing the same amount of shooting; usually, we end up doing more shooting, which is not a bad thing.) In this respect, component cost is an issue. In the previous analysis, we have ignored this consideration, respecting the common sense of individual shooters to choose what they can afford. Here, I mention this only because plinking loads offer handloaders a unique opportunity to dispose of small quantities of unused propellants, or to use inexpensive surplus propellants in unusual applications.

Formerly, the classic example of the latter situation involved H870 and A8700. In many instances, handloaders could concoct a perfectly good low- to moderate-velocity rifle load using either of those propellants. A representative example is the 30-06 Springfield with heavy cast bullets. Simply dump about 60 grains of either propellant into the case and seat a bullet. The resulting load will generate about 2,000 fps. Generally, accuracy and consistency are surprisingly good. Pressure is appropriate for hard-cast bullets. Where data are available, testing has shown that these propellants are surprisingly adaptable for similar loads in a wide variety of chamberings.

Here, an exception to a rule crops up: In this type of load and with this type of propellant, one can usually improve ballistic uniformity by using either WLRM or Fed-215 primers. Generally, these primers are safe for use with such slow-burning propellants.

Because these propellants were so much less expensive formerly when compared to other rifle propellants, one could produce plinking loads on a budget, despite the need to use a relatively heavy charge. The one unavoidable cost of this approach was unusually heavy propellant fouling. One possible disadvantage is that some versions of these propellants might cause case neck embrittlement when used in this type of load.

Similarly, the handloader can realize considerable savings by using a very small charge of a fast-burning propellant for a low-velocity practice cartridge.

SMOKELESS PROPELLANT—TABLES

The following information is generally useful for comparison purposes. I have not included all currently offered smokeless propellants, and some listed propellants are now obsolete.

Inexplicably, Hodgdon has asked that I redact some propellant property data for the propellants that it now controls (Winchester, IMR, and Hodgdon). Therefore, if you are interested in knowing more about the composition of these particular numbers, you will either need to refer to the 16th edition of *Handloader's Digest,* or obtain the Material Safety Data Sheet (MSDS) on that product.

Smokeless Propellants — General Information

Name	Granule Shape	Ng %	Packing Density g/cc	Suggested Primers	Primary Uses (cartridge loading—faster types used in shotshells)	Notes and Exceptional Applications
Accurate (now under Western Powder)						
A2	S	17	0.635	P (S)	Light to moderate pistol	Wide application
A5	S	17	0.975	P (S)	Moderate pistol	
A7	S	11	0.985	P (S/M)	9mm Luger, 10mm	
A9	S	11	0.950	P (M)	Magnum pistol, 30 Carbine	Reduced muzzle flash
A4100	S	10	0.950	P (M)	Magnum pistol, 410	
A5744	T	21	0.920	1½, 2½	Rifle blackpowder loads	Excellent, see text
A1680	S	10½	0.980	M	454 Casull and Small Rifle	
A2015	S	0	0.890	R (S/M)	Medium capacity rifle	Benchrest
A2230	S	11½	0.985	R (S/M)	223, medium capacity rifle	
A2460	S	11	0.985	R (S/M)	Medium capacity rifle	Benchrest
A2495	T	0	0.913	R (S/M)	Medium capacity rifle	Superior with Cast
A2520	S	10½	0.985	R (S/M)	Medium capacity rifle	Garand, M14
A4064	T	0	0.919	R (S/M)	Medium capacity rifle	
A2700	S	11	0.955	R (S/M)	Medium to large rifle	22-250. heavy bullets
A4350	T	0	0.922	R (S/M)	Large and Magnum rifle	Excellent in Wby.
A3100	T	0	0.920	LR (S/M)	Large and Magnum rifle	
MagPro	S	12	0.985	LR (M)	Large and Magnum rifle	Can give high velocity
A8700	S	10	0.960	215	Magnum rifle and 50 BMG	Discontinued
Alliant						
E3	F	—	—	P (S)	Light pistol	
RedDot	F	20	0.480	P (S)	Light pistol	
Promo	F	20	0.480	P (S)	Light pistol	Inexpensive
ClayDot	F	—	—	P (S)	Light pistol	
Bullseye	F	40	0.620	P (S)	Light to medium pistol	Versatile, 45 ACP
Am. Select	F	0		P (S)	Light to medium pistol	Versatile
GreenDot	F	20	0.515		Light to medium pistol	
2028	F	—	—	P (S)	Light to medium pistol	
Unique	F	20	0.610	P (S)	Med. to heavy pistol, cast-bullet	Wide application
Power Pistol	F	40	0.620	P (S)	IPSC	High energy
Herco	F	20	0.570	P (S)	Medium pistol	
Steel	F	—	—	P (S)	Medium to heavy pistol	
BlueDot	F	20	0.780	P (S)	Medium to heavy pistol	bullets in Magnums
ProReach	S	—	—	P (M)	Heavy pistol	High Energy
2400	T	15	0.870	P (S/M)	Heavy and magnum pistol	An old standby
410	S	Pr	—	P (S/M)	Heavy and magnum pistol	
PP-300-MP	S	P	0.970	P (M)	Magnum pistol	High Energy
RI-7	T	7	0.890	R (S)	Medium capacity rifle	444 & 30-30, light bullets

Smokeless Propellants — General Information

NAME	Granule Shape	Ng %	Packing Density g/cc	Suggested Primers	Primary Uses (cartridge loading—faster types used in shotshells)	Notes and Exceptional Applications
RI-10	T	Pr	—	R (S/M)	Medium capacity rifle	30-30, 444, 45-70
PP-Varmint	S	Pr	—	R (M)	Typical varmint cartridges	High Energy
RI-12	T	7	1.000	R (S)	Medium capacity rifle	
RI-15	T	Pr	0.920	R (S)	Medium capacity rifle	
PP-200-MR	S	Pr	—	R (M)	Medium capacity rifle	High Energy
RI-17	T	Pr	—	R (S/M)	Med. to large capacity rifle	
PP-3000-LR	S	Pr	—	LRM	Med. to large capacity rifle	High Energy
RI-19	T	Pr	0.890	R (S/M)	Large and magnum rifle	
RI-22	T	Pr	0.890	LR (S/M)	Large and magnum rifle	
PP-4000-MR	S	Pr	—	LRM	Large and magnum rifle	High Energy
RI-25	T	Pr	0.89	LRM	Large and magnum rifle	
Hodgdon (Pr = proprietary information)						
TiteWad	S	Pr	—	P	Target pistol	
Clays	F	Pr	0.475	P (S)	Target pistol	Clean target pistol
TiteGroup	S	Pr	—	P	Target pistol	
International	F	Pr	0.525	P (S)	Pistol	
HP-38	S	Pr	0.635	P (S)	Light to medium pistol	Wide application
Universal	F	Pr	0.650	P (S)	Pistol	
HS6	S	Pr	0.945	P (S)	Medium to heavy pistol	Heavy loads, small cases
LongShot	S	Pr	—	P	Target pistol	
HS7	S	Pr	0.990	P (S)	Heavy pistol	Discontinued
H110	S	Pr	0.975	P (M)	Mag. pistol, 30 carbine, 410	Same as W296
Lil'Gun	S	Pr	0.960	P (M)	Magnum pistol, small rifle	22 hornet and Mag.
H4227	T	0	0.870	S	Cast-bullet pistol and rifle	
H4198	T	0	0.850	R (S)	Excellent cast-bullet rifle	444, 45-70, 458,
H4198SC	T	0	0.870	R (S)	Excellent cast-bullet rifle	Discontinued
H322	T	0	0.920	R (S)	Medium capacity rifle	Wide application
BenchMark	T	0	0.960	R (S)	Medium capacity rifle	Meters well
H335	S	Pr	1.035	R (M)	Medium to large rifle	Densest propellant
H4895	T	0	0.920	R (S)	Versatile Rifle	Cast & reduced loads
VarGet	T	0	0.950	R (S)	Wide application	308 Win. Match
BL-C(2)	S	Pr	1.035	R (M)	Medium to large rifle	Densest propellant
H380	S	Pr	0.967	R (M)	Medium to large rifle	22-250
H414	S	Pr	0.995	R (M)	Large rifle	270 and 30-06
H4350	T	0	0.910	R (S/M)	Large and magnum rifle	Short Cut Granules
Hybrid 100V	CS	Pr	—	R (M)	Large and magnum rifle	High Energy
H4350SC	T	0	0.930	R (S/M)	Large and magnum rifle	Discontinued
H450	T	Pr	0.990	LR (M)	Large and magnum rifle	Unique applications
H4831	T	0	0.930	LR (S/M)	Large and magnum rifle	Target 270 Win
H4831SC	T	0	0.960	LR (S/M)	Large and magnum rifle	Improved metering

Smokeless Propellants — General Information

Name	Granule Shape	Ng %	Packing Density g/cc	Suggested Primers	Primary Uses (cartridge loading—faster types used in shotshells)	Notes and Exceptional Applications
H1000	T	0	0.955	215/LRM	Magnum rifle	7mm Rem
Retumbo	T	0	0.935	215/LRM	Magnum rifle	Very large cases
H570	T	0	0.945	LRM/215	Magnum rifle and 50 BMG	Discontinued
US869	S	Pr	0.960	LRM/215	Magnum rifle and 50 BMG	Good metering
H870	S	Pr	0.965	215	Magnum rifle and 50 BMG	Discontinued
H50BMG	T	0	0.935	35	50 BMG	
H5010	T	0	0.910	35	50 BMG	Discontinued
IMR (Pr = proprietary information)						
700X	F	Pr	0.500	P (S)	Light pistol	
Trail Boss	P/S	Pr	—	P (S)	Low velocity revolver	Cowboy Action
PB	P/F	0	0.555	P (S)	Light pistol	
7625	F	0	0.640	P (S)	Pistol	
800X	F	Pr	—	—	Light pistol	
4756	F	0	0.610	P (S)	Light pistol	Std. Primers only!
4759	T	0	0.675	S	Heavy pistol, cast rifle	Clean
IMR4227	T	0	0.870	S	Cast pistol and rifle	Minimizes leading
IMR4198	T	0	0.850	R (S)	Excellent cast-bullet rifle	444, 45-70, 458
IMR4895	T	0	0.920	R (S)	Cast bullets and reduced loads	Works across wide range
IMR3031	T	0	0.880	R (S)	Medium capacity rifle	
IMR4064	T	0	0.905	R (S)	Medium capacity rifle	30-30, Swift
IMR4320	T	0	0.935	R (S)	Medium to large rifle	Heavy bullets Whelen, -06
IMR4007SSC	T	0	—	R (S)	Medium to large rifle	Apt to replace 4320
IMR4350	T	0	0.910	R (S/M)	Large and magnum rifle	Excellent in Wby.
IMR4831	T	0	0.925	LR (S/M)	Large and magnum rifle	Not = H4831!
IMR7828	T	0	0.915	LRM/215	Large and magnum rifle	7mm Rem Mag
IMR7828SSC	T	0	0.960	LRM/215	Large and magnum rifle	Short magnums
Norma (Pr = proprietary information)						
R-1	F	Pr	—	P (S)	Target pistol	Discontinued
R-123	F	Pr	—	P (S/M)	Heavy and magnum pistol	Discontinued
N200	T	Pr	—	R (S)	Small capacity rifle	
N201	T	Pr	—	R (S)	Medium capacity rifle	
N202	T	Pr	—	R (S)	Small to medium rifle	
N203	T	Pr	—	R (S/M)	Small to medium rifle	Discontinued
N203B	T	Pr	—	R (S/M)	Small to medium rifle	
URP	T	Pr	0.895	R (S/M)	Medium rifle	
N204	T	Pr	0.99	R (S/M)	Large and magnum rifle	
MRP	T	Pr	0.99	LR (S/M)	Large and magnum rifle	Ideal in 6.5-284 Norma
N205	T	Pr	1.00	LR (S/M)	Large and magnum rifle	Lot-to-lot variations
MRP2	T	Pr	0.99	—	Large and magnum rifle	Ideal in 338 Lapua

Smokeless Propellants — General Information

NAME	Granule Shape	NG %	Packing Density g/cc	Suggested Primers	Primary Uses (cartridge loading—faster types used in shotshells)	Notes and Exceptional Applications
Ramshot						
Competition	S	23	0.510	P (S)	Bullseye target	
Zip	S	20	0.800	P (S)	Bullseye target	
Silhouette	S	14	0.800	P (M)	IPSC target	
True Blue	S	20	0.975	P (M)	IPSC target	
Enforcer	S	10	0.950	P (M)	IPSC, magnum pistol	45 Auto
X-Terminator	S	10	0.975	R (M)	223 and similar	Unusually Clean
TAC	S	10	0.985	R (M)	223, 308 and similar	Unusually Clean
Big Game	S	10	0.975	R (M)	Medium rifle	Unusually Clean
Hunter	S	10	0.970	R (M)	Medium to large rifle	Swift, heavy bullets
Magnum	S	9½	0.985	LRM/215	Magnum rifle	Excellent Accuracy
Scott (Now Under Accurate, which is now owned by Western)						
Red Diamond	D	22	—	P (S)	Light pistol	Announced, never offered
S1000	F	0	0.515	P (S)	Light to medium pistol	Unusually clean
Nitro-100	F	23	0.510	P (S)	Light pistol	
S453	S	13	0.555	P (S)	Light pistol	Discontinued
Royal S	F	0	—	P (S)	Light to medium pistol	Discontinued
Pearl	F	0	—	P (S)	Medium pistol	Discontinued
S1250	F	0	0.515	P (S)	Medium pistol	
S1500	F	0	—	P (S/M)	Medium to heavy pistol	Discontinued
S4197	T	0	0.850	R (S)	Excellent cast-bullet rifle	Discontinued
S3032	T	0	0.880	R (S)	Medium capacity rifle	Discontinued
S322	T	0	0.92	R (S)	Medium capacity rifle	Discontinued
S4065	T	0	0.905	R (S)	Medium capacity rifle	Discontinued
S4351	T	0	0.910	R (S/M)	Large rifle	Discontinued
S4831	T	0	0.930	LR (S/M)	Large and magnum rifle	Discontinued
VihtaVuori						
N310	P/C	0	0.450	P (S)	Target pistol	Wide application
N312	P	0	0.435	P (S)	Special blank propellant	Not currently available
3N17	P/C	0	0.520	P (S)	22 Rimfire	
N318	P/F	0	0.430	—		
N319	P/F	0	0.430	—		
N320	P/C	0	0.500	P (S)	Light to medium pistol	Wide application
N321	P/F	0	0.450	—	Shotgun	Not Currently Available
N322	P/F	0	0.430	—		
N32C	P/C	0	0.350	P (S)	Light to medium pistol	Cowboy Action
N324	P/F	0	0.470	—		Not currently available
N325	P/F	0	0.520	—		
N326	P/F	0	0.520	—		
N328	P/F	0	0.500	—		
N330	P/C	0	0.580	P (S)	Light to medium pistol	
N331	P/C	0	0.680	P (S)	9mm Luger, light to medium	Not currently available

Smokeless Propellants — General Information

Name	Granule Shape	NG %	Packing Density g/cc	Suggested Primers	Primary Uses (cartridge loading—faster types used in shotshells)	Notes and Exceptional Applications
N338	P/C	0	0.540	—	Blanks	
N340	P/C	0	0.560	P (S)	Medium to heavy pistol	Wide application
N342	P/C	0	0.560	P (S)		Not currently available
N344	P/F	0	0.520	—		
N347	P/F	0	0.540	—		
3N36	P/C	0	0.500	P (S)	22 Rimfire	
3N37	P/C	0	0.640	P (S)	High Vel. 22 Rimfire, pistol	
N350	P/C	0	0.570	P (S)	Medium to heavy pistol	
3N38	P/C	0	0.640	P (S)	Light to medium pistol	Wide application
N105	T	0	0.680	P (S/M)	Heavy and magnum pistol	Hornet
N110	T	0	0.760	P (S/M)	Heavy and magnum pistol	Hornet
N120	T	0	0.820	R (S)	Light bullets, varmint loads	Limited application
N125	T	0	0.850	R (S)	7.62x39mm	Not available now
N130	T	0	0.850	R (S)	Factory 22 and 6mm PPC	Benchrest rifle
N530	T	15	0.900	R (S)	5.56mm NATO	
N132	T	0	0.860	R (S)	5.56mm NATO tracer	Not available now
N133	T	0	0.860	R (S)	222, 223 & 45-70	
N134	T	0	0.860	R (S)	7.62mm NATO tracer	Not available now
N135	T	0	0.860	R (S)	308 Win., medium rifle	
N140	T	0	0.860	R (S)	Medium to large rifle	
N540	T	15	0.900	R (S)	Medium to large rifle	
N150	T	0	0.850	M (S/M)	Large rifle	
N550	T	15	0.900	M (S/M)	Large rifle	
N160	T	0	0.900	R (M)	Large and magnum rifle	
N560	T	15	0.900	R (M)	Large and magnum rifle	
N165	T	0	0.900	LR (M)	Large and magnum rifle	
N170	T	0	0.900	215	Magnum rifle and 50 BMG	
N570	T	20	0.900	LRM/215	Magnum rifle	
24N41	T	0	—	35	Super Mag., 50 BMG	
20N29	T	0	0.900	LRM/215	50 BMG	
24N64	T	0	—	35	20mm	
Winchester (Pr = proprietary information)						
WAA Lite	S	Pr	—	P (S)	Light pistol	
230	S	Pr	0.715	P (S)	Light pistol	Discontinued
452AA	S	Pr	0.555	P (S)	Light pistol	
Super Hand.	S	Pr	—	P (S)	Light pistol	
231	S	Pr	0.700	P (S)	Light to medium pistol	Wide application
WST	S	Pr	0.535	P (S)	Target pistol	45 ACP target
WSL	S	Pr	0.765	P (S)	Target pistol	Discontinued
473AA	S	Pr	0.665	—		Discontinued
WAP	S	Pr	—	P (S)	Pistol	Discontinued

Smokeless Propellants — General Information

NAME	Granule Shape	Ng %	Packing Density g/cc	Suggested Primers	Primary Uses (cartridge loading — faster types used in shotshells)	Notes and Exceptional Applications
Auto Comp	S	Pr	—	P (S)	Pistol	Wide Application
WSF	S	Pr	0.770	P (S)	Medium pistol	
540	S	Pr	0.950	P (S)	Pistol	Discontinued
571	S	Pr	0.955	P (M)		Discontinued
630	S	Pr	0.965	P (M)	Heavy pistol	Discontinued
296	S	Pr	0.975	P (M)	Magnum pistol, 30 Carbine, 410	Same as H110
680	S	Pr	0.950	M	454 Casull and small rifle	Discontinued
748	S	Pr	0.995	R (S/M)	Medium to large rifle	458, 30-30, 35 Whelen
760	S	Pr	1.000	R (S/M)	Large rifle	Accurate in 270 and -06
S780	S	Pr	1.015	LR (M)	Large and magnum rifle	
785	S	Pr	1.015	LR (M)	Large and magnum rifle	Discontinued
WXM	T	Pr	—	LR (M)	Large and magnum rifle	Discontinued
WMR	S	Pr	1.000	LR (M)	Large and magnum rifle	Discontinued

U.S. Optics (shown), Leupold, Nightforce, and a few other brands shine when it comes to overall quality. Unfortunately, I could not obtain representative scopes from all makers for testing in the studies reflected in tables located elsewhere in this text. The U.S. military was purchasing many top-end scopes when I did that work.

MEASURED PACKING DENSITY: HANDGUN PROPELLANTS IN REPRESENTATIVE HANDGUN CASES

Name			Measured Density: One-Inch High Circular Column Filled as Specified									Percentage Volume Reduction			
	Granule Shape	Listed Density	0.357-inch diameter As Dump	0.357-inch diameter 6-inch Drop Tube	0.357-inch diameter Max	0.410-inch diameter As Dump	0.410-inch diameter 6-inch Drop Tube	0.410-inch diameter Max	0.452-inch diameter As Dump	0.452-inch diameter 6-inch Drop Tube	0.452-inch diameter Max	810 psi Immediate	810 psi Relaxed	3320 psi Immediate	3320 psi Relaxed
ACCURATE ARMS															
N-100	F	—	0.445	0.497	0.550	0.477	0.509	0.543	0.493	0.521	0.533	54.3	53	—	—
No. 2 Imp	B	—	0.650	0.658	0.695	0.663	0.676	0.707	0.677	0.691	0.715	13.1	8	33.7	28
S1000	F	—	0.450	0.486	0.497	0.469	0.489	0.497	0.465	0.483	0.488	34.3	23	52.3	45
Scot-D	F	—	0.460	0.470	0.501	0.483	0.509	0.531	0.472	0.517	0.528	29.4	15	48.1	40
453	B	0.555	0.624	0.656	0.658	0.631	0.656	0.690	0.634	0.660	0.686	14.8	8	37.8	33
A5	B	0.950	0.893	0.897	0.920	0.861	0.943	0.955	0.875	0.943	0.974	19.6	10	34.3	28
A7	B	0.985	0.457	1.006	1.047	0.969	1.037	1.063	0.965	1.019	1.064	7.7	2	17.3	8
A9	B	0.975	0.931	0.950	0.987	0.937	0.963	0.986	0.946	0.967	0.988	8.5	2	18.6	10
A1680	B	0.950	0.976	1.009	1.047	0.972	1.026	1.060	0.979	1.038	1.061	7.5	2	17.7	10
ALLIANT															
Bullseye	F	0.620	0.607	0.609	0.658	0.605	0.656	0.707	0.608	0.667	0.689	44.9	43	—	—
RedDot	F	0.480	0.400	0.447	0.467	0.409	0.455	0.477	0.417	0.474	0.485	54.9	50	—	—
GreenDot	F	0.515	0.434	0.486	0.520	0.469	0.517	0.528	0.488	0.514	0.533	50.6	46	—	—
Unique	F	0.610	0.497	0.542	0.568	0.514	0.554	0.565	0.542	0.578	0.587	43.4	43	—	—
Herco	F	0.570	0.482	0.538	0.550	0.503	0.545	0.562	0.505	0.564	0.571	41.9	35	—	—
BlueDot	F	0.780	0.665	0.755	0.759	0.707	0.744	0.766	0.708	0.764	0.783	25.4	15	44.0	40
2400	F	0.870	0.837	0.871	0.901	0.844	0.898	0.909	0.842	0.901	0.910	17.1	13	34.1	30
HODGDON															
Clays	F	0.475	0.407	0.464	0.475	0.449	0.486	0.494	0.451	0.498	0.503	39.0	35	—	—
HP-38	B	0.635	0.639	0.725	0.748	0.687	0.724	0.735	0.693	0.731	0.757	27.4	20	45.3	40
International	F	0.525	0.479	0.538	0.557	0.506	0.548	0.554	0.509	0.554	0.559	36.4	30	—	—
Universal	F	0.650	0.591	0.624	0.658	0.608	0.670	0.682	0.618	0.672	0.684	23.6	15	41.9	36
HS6	F	0.945	0.893	0.957	1.002	0.901	0.952	0.997	0.903	0.974	1.004	12.3	5	27.0	18
HS7	B	0.990	0.897	0.972	1.021	0.937	0.947	1.031	0.915	1.000	1.040	12.3	5	24.4	20
4227	B	0.870	0.811	0.879	0.897	0.827	0.889	0.898	0.837	.0899	0.908	11.8	6	24.0	15
H110	B	0.975	0.987	1.034	1.084	0.994	1.054	1.088	0.995	1.057	1.090	6.8	1	17.7	5
IMR															
PB	F	0.555	0.512	0.583	0.607	0.537	0.594	0.611	0.535	0.594	0.614	20.1	13	41.5	33
700X	F	0.500	0.471	0.523	0.583	0.483	0.528	0.585	0.488	0.554	0.583	56.0	48	—	—
800X	F	—	0.572	0.647	0.692	0.594	0.653	0.705	0.587	0.660	0.712	49.8	45	—	—
SR4756	F	0.610	0.587	0.665	0.684	0.611	0.670	0.682	0.606	0.670	0.679	18.6	8	38.1	25
4227	T	0.870	0.852	0.879	0.931	0.869	0.946	0.955	0.875	0.934	0.946	10.6	4	21.5	10

Measured Packing Density: Handgun Propellants in Representative Handgun Cases

Name	Granule Shape	Listed Density	0.357-inch diameter: As Dump	0.357-inch diameter: 6-inch Drop Tube	0.357-inch diameter: Max	0.410-inch diameter: As Dump	0.410-inch diameter: 6-inch Drop Tube	0.410-inch diameter: Max	0.452-inch diameter: As Dump	0.452-inch diameter: 6-inch Drop Tube	0.452-inch diameter: Max	810 psi Immediate	810 psi Relaxed	3320 psi Immediate	3320 psi Relaxed
			Measured Density: One-Inch High Circular Column Filled as Specified									Percentage Volume Reduction			
Winchester															
WST	B	0.535	0.516	0.564	0.602	0.545	0.574	0.619	0.542	0.580	0.620	26.4	18	47.1	40
WSL	B	0.765	0.680	0.781	0.826	0.722	0.770	0.815	0.712	0.776	0.815	36.0	34	—	—
231	B	0.700	0.645	0.714	0.748	0.690	0.724	0.756	0.691	0.733	0.750	28.4	20	45.5	40
WSF	B	0.770	0.707	0.781	0.821	0.736	0.770	0.824	0.731	0.792	0.833	32.3	30	46.0	40
WAP	B	—	0.800	0.841	0.875	0.815	0.855	0.889	0.811	0.856	0.882	12.8	2	28.0	15
540	B	0.950	0.893	0.961	0.998	0.920	0.972	1.009	0.920	0.995	1.017	14.5	4	29.2	20
571	B	0.955	0.905	0.968	1.021	0.929	0.991	1.020	0.941	1.007	1.031	14.1	4	28.4	19
296	B	0.975	0.964	1.024	1.054	0.983	1.045	1.068	0.982	1.054	1.073	8.2	1	18.3	5

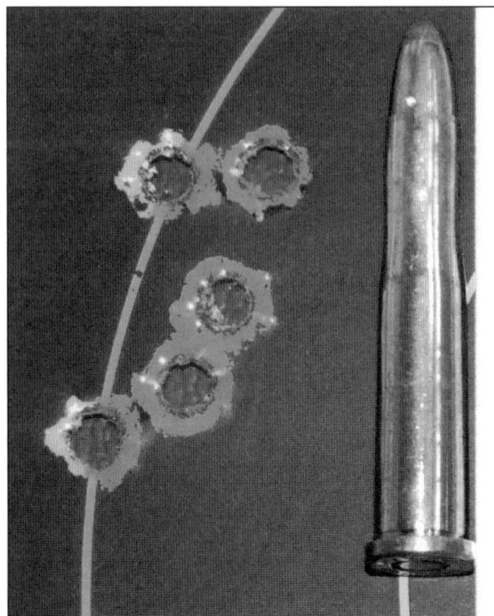

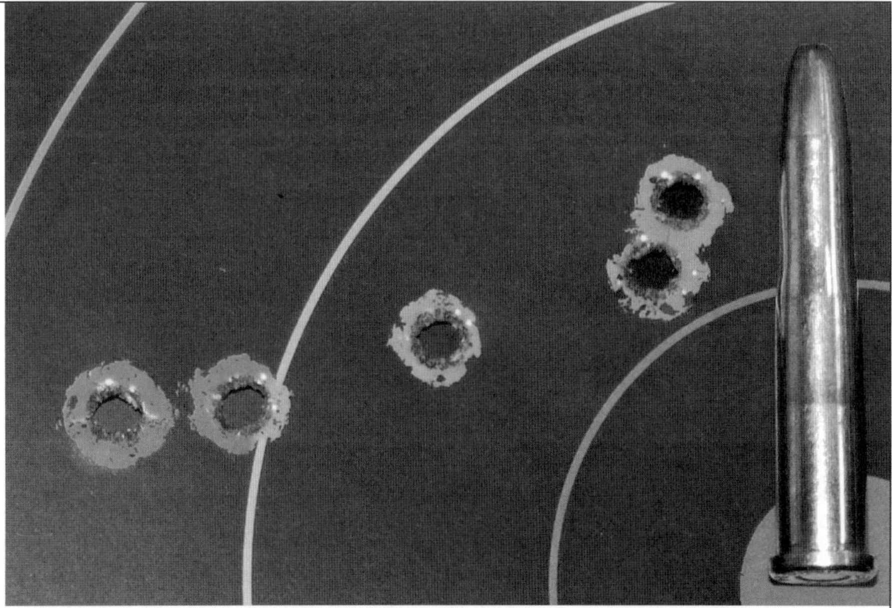

A 22 Hornet factory-load comparison: These two loads offer a fine example of the value of testing different components. We tested every factory load available in the Savage M-40 and the CZ-527. While the Winchester SP load had a huge edge over the Winchester HP load (as shown here), just the opposite was true with Remington ammunition. Handloaders see the same thing—some components just do not work while others do. With the best factory loads, the Savage would typically produce ¾-inch, 5-shot, 100-yard groups; the CZ shot closer to ½ inch. With the best handloads, both routinely shot under ½ inch. H-110 worked particularly well in both guns. Several other propellants gave good results, and several tested numbers (including one that has long been touted as a go-to choice for Hornet loads) consistently produced dismally disappointing accuracy. Without testing all likely propellants, finding an accurate load would have been a matter of pure chance.

Measured Packing Density: Rifle Propellants in Representative Rifle Cases

Name			Measured Density: Rifle Case Filled as Described									Percentage Volume Reduction			
			As Dump	6-inch Drop Tube	Max	As Dump	6-inch Drop Tube	Max	As Dump	6-inch Drop Tube	Max	810 psi		3320 psi	
	Granule Shape	Listed Density	222 Remington			308 Winchester			7mm Remington Magnum			Immediate	Relaxed	Immediate	Relaxed
Accurate Arms															
1680	B	0.950	0.998	1.030	1.058	0.984	1.026	1.054	0.986	1.041	1.053	6.4	1.5	17.0	7.5
2230	B	—	0.998	1.041	1.062	1.011	1.047	1.065	1.022	1.058	1.071	8.1	2.0	20.7	8.5
2460	B	0.975	0.928	0.965	0.991	0.928	0.965	0.977	0.943	0.978	0.993	8.3	3.0	21.2	12.0
A2495	T	—	0.839	0.871	0.885	0.876	0.910	0.913	0.887	0.918	0.929	9.4	2.0	20.9	10.5
2520	B	0.970	0.945	0.988	1.012	0.963	1.009	1.023	0.968	1.025	1.029	7.7	1.5	20.0	12.0
2700	B	0.960	0.938	0.963	0.988	0.954	0.982	1.002	0.956	1.004	1.018	8.2	1.5	20.2	10.0
4350	T	0.950	0.850	0.878	0.896	0.888	0.916	0.929	0.905	0.925	0.938	10.4	4.0	22.9	12.0
3100	T	0.945	0.853	0.896	0.903	0.893	0.921	0.930	0.915	0.935	0.942	8.8	2.5	20.2	9.0
8700	B	0.960	0.924	0.977	1.019	0.942	1.002	1.035	0.958	1.006	1.041	7.8	2.0	20.4	10.0
Alliant															
2400	F	0.870	0.846	0.878	0.910	0.846	0.890	0.933	0.854	0.909	0.936	16.3	9.0	32.5	26.0
7	T	0.890	0.843	0.899	0.917	0.879	0.923	0.937	0.889	0.935	0.950	10.5	3.0	22.9	14.0
12	T	1.000	0.889	0.928	0.956	0.916	0.960	0.977	0.940	0.979	0.991	9.5	2.0	21.2	10.5
15	T	0.920	0.867	0.913	0.935	0.911	0.951	0.956	0.920	0.949	0.959	10.6	5.0	22.3	12.0
19	T	0.890	0.864	0.903	0.917	0.895	0.940	0.951	0.920	0.945	0.957	13.3	7.0	26.5	17.5
22	T	0.890	0.871	0.896	0.928	0.907	0.940	0.947	0.923	0.946	0.959	13.0	7.5	25.9	18.0
Hodgdon															
4227	T	0.870	0.818	0.871	0.882	0.837	0.876	0.890	0.843	0.887	0.898	11.8	6.0	24.0	15.0
110	B	0.975	0.995	1.027	1.069	1.009	1.046	1.084	1.006	1.058	1.090	6.8	1.0	17.7	5.0
4198	T	0.880	0.776	0.814	0.822	0.807	0.844	0.849	0.820	0.847	0.854	10.8	2.5	24.1	10.0
H4198SC	T	—	0.850	0.896	0.906	0.890	0.923	0.930	0.892	0.933	0.946	9.5	2.5	20.3	10.0
322	T	—	0.885	0.917	0.931	0.897	0.942	0.953	0.906	0.959	0.968	9.4	3.0	18.6	8.0
BL-C2	B	1.035	0.991	1.041	1.065	1.016	1.056	1.081	1.020	1.064	1.084	6.5	1.5	16.3	6.0
335	B	1.035	0.991	1.037	1.058	1.005	1.035	1.070	1.011	1.055	1.076	6.3	1.5	15.7	5.5
4895	T	0.920	0.878	0.913	0.924	0.898	0.942	0.947	0.913	0.949	0.959	9.5	3.5	19.1	10.5
380	B	0.967	0.917	0.952	0.981	0.944	0.974	1.007	0.951	0.981	1.008	6.9	1.5	17.4	5.5
414	B	0.995	0.935	0.988	1.027	0.951	1.004	1.040	0.957	1.018	1.049	6.8	1.5	17.0	7.0
H4350SC	T	—	0.899	0.935	0.945	0.926	0.963	0.969	0.940	0.982	0.988	8.9	3.0	20.2	10.0
450	B	0.990	0.928	0.963	0.981	0.944	0.981	1.002	0.947	1.001	1.014	7.9	1.5	19.0	8.5
4831	T	0.930	0.892	0.913	0.928	0.930	0.953	0.964	0.945	0.964	0.974	8.6	2.0	20.0	9.0
H4831SC	T	—	0.906	0.928	0.945	0.940	0.958	0.976	0.952	0.982	0.992	9.0	2.5	19.7	9.5
1000	T	—	0.889	0.942	0.952	0.937	0.965	0.981	0.947	0.985	0.992	8.8	3.0	19.2	10.0
570	T	—	0.857	0.899	0.917	0.912	0.939	0.947	0.927	0.959	0.972	8.2	1.5	19.5	7.5
870	B	0.965	0.942	0.984	0.998	0.958	1.005	1.023	0.964	1.020	1.030	9.8	2.0	18.6	6.5

Measured Packing Density: Rifle Propellants in Representative Rifle Cases

Name	Granule Shape	Listed Density	Measured Density: Rifle Case Filled as Described									Percentage Volume Reduction			
			222 Remington			308 Winchester			7mm Remington Magnum			810 psi		3320 psi	
			As Dump	6-inch Drop Tube	Max	As Dump	6-inch Drop Tube	Max	As Dump	6-inch Drop Tube	Max	Immediate	Relaxed	Immediate	Relaxed
IMR															
4227	T	0.870	0.860	0.910	0.928	0.883	0.940	0.942	0.884	0.946	0.961	10.6	4.0	21.5	10.0
4198	T	0.850	0.793	0.832	0.850	0.833	0.874	0.884	0.844	0.884	0.891	10.6	2.5	23.6	11.5
3031	T	0.880	0.814	0.860	0.885	0.853	0.893	0.902	0.858	0.894	0.904	10.2	2.5	23.9	12.5
4895	T	0.920	0.882	0.924	0.942	0.907	0.949	0.961	0.929	0.965	0.972	8.8	2.5	19.6	9.0
4064	T	0.905	0.829	0.871	0.885	0.872	0.905	0.920	0.885	0.923	0.930	9.9	3.0	22.3	10.5
4320	T	0.935	0.903	0.942	0.952	0.923	0.974	0.981	0.942	0.979	0.992	8.3	2.0	18.5	8.0
4350	T	0.910	0.853	0.885	0.899	0.890	0.930	0.942	0.910	0.932	0.949	9.3	2.5	21.1	13.0
4831	T	0.930	0.864	0.889	0.910	0.898	0.926	0.939	0.917	0.946	0.958	8.8	2.5	20.0	8.0
7828	T	—	0.857	0.896	0.913	0.900	0.937	0.953	0.913	0.953	0.964	9.8	4.0	20.8	10.0
Norma															
205	T	—	0.928	0.975	0.995	0.975	1.012	1.018	0.981	1.025	1.034	9.3	3.0	20.2	8.0
VihtaVuori															
133	T	0.88	0.853	0.896	0.927	0.883	0.923	0.944	0.887	0.930	0.950	9.1	2.0	18.8	8.0
140	T	0.92	0.867	0.919	0.935	0.902	0.951	0.972	0.924	0.961	0.975	9.3	2.0	19.2	8.0
150	T	0.91	0.860	0.882	0.920	0.902	0.940	0.956	0.915	0.943	0.954	8.6	2.0	18.5	6.0
160	T	0.94	0.885	0.935	0.952	0.919	0.961	0.972	0.939	0.971	0.984	8.8	2.0	19.0	7.0
170	T	—	0.896	0.935	0.953	0.939	0.977	0.991	0.961	0.985	0.995	8.6	2.0	19.0	7.0
24N64	T	0.84	0.818	0.867	0.889	0.882	0.905	0.918	0.895	0.905	0.924	9.0	2.0	20.1	7.0
Winchester															
296	B	0.975	0.963	0.991	1.062	0.984	1.026	1.068	0.985	1.023	1.069	8.2	1.0	18.3	5.0
748	B	0.995	0.956	0.984	1.051	0.975	1.019	1.067	0.972	1.044	1.074	7.1	1.5	17.2	8.0
760	B	1.000	0.931	0.984	1.035	0.944	0.995	1.044	0.963	1.000	1.044	7.3	1.5	17.8	7.5
WMR	B	—	0.889	0.942	0.988	0.921	0.965	0.998	0.926	0.970	1.011	7.6	2.0	18.7	9.5

GRANULE SHAPE KEY:

B = spherical
T = tubular (single perforation)
F = flake
P/C = porous, cylindrical
P/F = porous, flake
CS = cylindrical with round ends
P/S = porous, special shape to minimize density

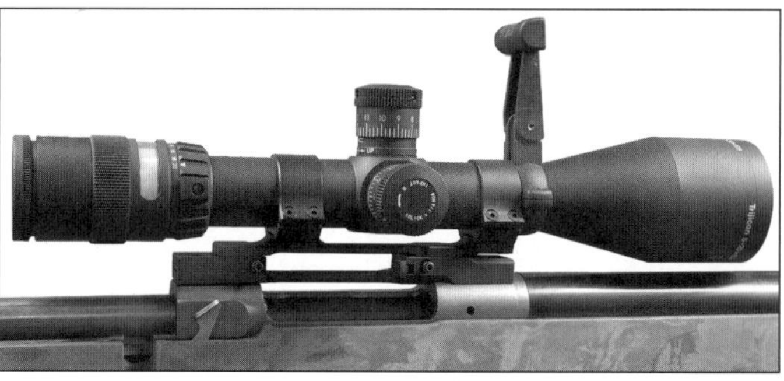

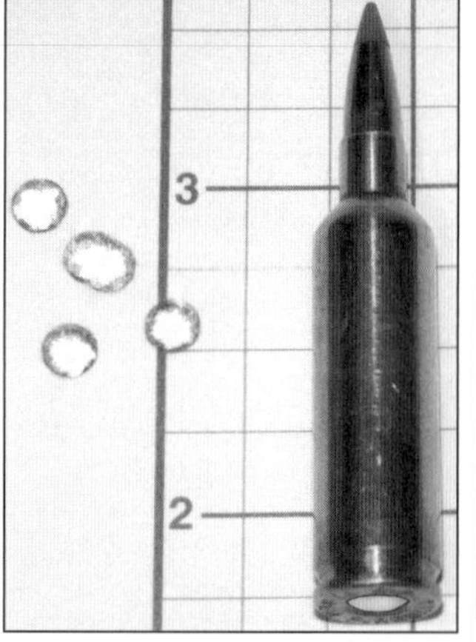

Above left: Bill Falin giving the Savage M40 (22 Hornet) a workout. On this day, we managed with my best handloads several 5-shot, 100-yard groups smaller than ½ inch. We also tested Deb Falin's CZ, which shot similarly with most loads.

Above right: The Trijicon TR-23, 5–20X scope proved to have phenomenally good resolution. We compared various high-end scopes at the Friends of Billy Dixon Range (see picture below). The TR-23 proved to have, by a significant margin, the highest resolution. We could see where the bullet had blown paint off the steel targets, and we could see the shape of the dark spot left behind—we were seeing details of the shape of a paint chip smaller than one inch across and 1,538 yards away.

Right: A 5-shot, 100-yard group reproduced life size. Jim Williamson fired this group from his custom M12 Savage, 17/23 SMC. Williamson was then a nervous novice at the bench. After he fired this group, I sat down and fired three, 5-shot ragged-one-hole groups. I was using the right bag technique and I was having a particularly good day. (With practice, Williamson is improving his bench-testing skills.)

Below: Using my son's custom M12 Savage chambered in 300 Jody (300 WSM with Ackley case taper and hemispherical shoulder), Bob Boyle (left) and I each fired one, 3-shot group at this steel target located 1,538 yards distant. The horizontal spread reflects variable wind (it takes very little wind to move a bullet many inches at this distance. Of course, Boyle out shot me. The spread of his group was right at 12 inches—sub-MOA accuracy at ⅞ mile!

CHARGING THE CASE

CHAPTER 9

INTRODUCTION

In 1967, as a nascent handloader, I was baffled when I tried to install the suggested charge of IMR 4064 into sized and primed 30-30 cases, for use with Sierra's 150-grain 30-30 bullet. When I poured the charge into the case, it simply would not fit. That experience led to a lifelong fascination with the various aspects of charging cases.

Many handloaders seem oblivious to the possibility that the skill and technique used in charging cases can make any difference. Many years ago, through evident confusion, one handloading pundit demonstrated complete ignorance in this area when he explicitly stated that Hercules proscribed the use of compressed charges of its rifle propellants, which was an unfounded claim—Hercules did recognize that charges near 100 percent loading density could be inaccurate. Other writers have expressed similar doubts about the advisability and safety of using compressed charges. Perhaps for this reason and likely because it seems that it might be dangerous to compress smokeless propellant, many handloaders are loath to do so, which is too bad—compressed charges are perfectly safe and make great loads, often some of the very best.

This is just one aspect of case charging that many handloaders understand poorly. Other areas of confusion include the relative importance of consistent charging technique versus the use of charges with identical mass and the importance of consistent charge positioning within the case when using a load where the charge does not fill the available space. Here I hope to clarify these aspects, and others.

LOADING PROPELLANT—CHARGE SELECTION

After settling upon a few propellants to try, the next step is conceptually simple: Discover the best charge to use. Here, it is particularly worthwhile to keep meticulous records. Functionality is always critical but, in most situations, the primary goal of charge tinkering during load development is to maximize accuracy.

However, in semiautomatic guns, functionality has precedence—does the cartridge cycle the action sharply, smoothly, and consistently. Similarly, with cast bullets, one goal is to minimize barrel leading, which also happens to be a prerequisite to good accuracy—a load that generates either too much or too little pressure will lead the bore, with attendant and rapidly progressive accuracy degradation.

MEASURING CHARGES—QUICK MEASURE

Compared to any other measure, the Quick Measure (QM) works through a unique principle. It is capable of accurately and rapidly dispensing any charge of any propellant. Compared to conventional measures, the QM is easier to learn to use properly and is in many ways a superior invention. However, the biggest advantage is that the QM will accurately dispense charges of large-granulated extruded propellants with a degree of consistency that we cannot obtain with conventional measures. The QM system naturally drops charges with consistent mass; then the dispensed charges consistently funnel into the case with a consistent packing scheme—each of these consistencies is critical to accuracy.

The QM use is simple. Install the special funnel over the case neck and position the funnel and case under the measure—a special button in the funnel seals the QM metering reservoir—lift the case and funnel. This actuates the measure and thereby fills the reservoir with a charge. Then lower the funnel. This releases the charge. Wait for the charge to funnel into the case, move the funnel to the next case, and repeat the process.

MEASURING CHARGES—CONVENTIONAL MEASURES

Competitors in traditional benchrest and most pistol disciplines measure propellant charges. Most benchrest competitors do quite well at maintaining uniform charges by using a proper and consistent technique to operate the powder measure. Several companies offer particularly precise propellant measures to benchrest

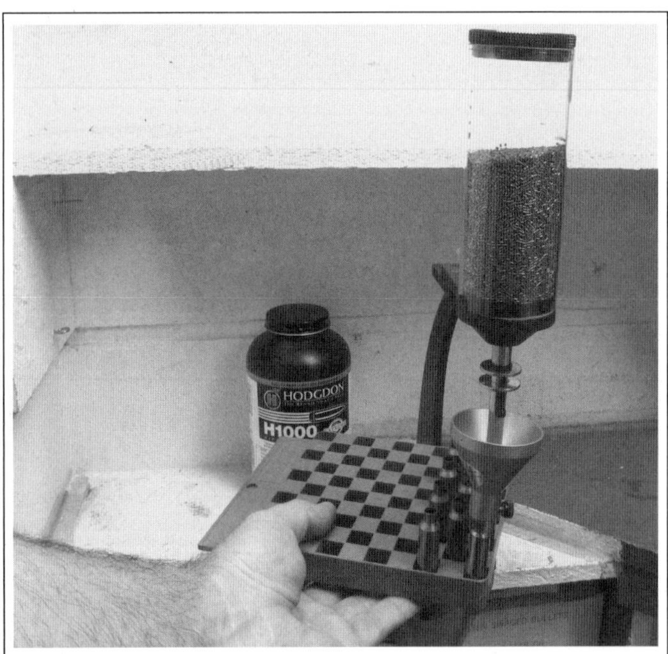

The Quick Measure (QM) represents a new paradigm in dropping charges. With very little practice, the average handloader can learn to use the QM. With this tool, it is easy to meter charges of any large-granulated propellant with precision that exceeds the needs of almost any application. Often, the QM is faster and easier to use than any conventional measure.

The Redding BR-30 is a precision tool, one of the best conventional measures on the market. A baffle in the hopper keeps the propellant column similarly settled. A zero-backlash micrometer provides repeatable, calibrated settings. A handy stand and clamp allows for an easy, portable setup. This makes it easy to use the BR-30 at the range.

shooters. These are all adjustable in click increments. Redding offers the BR-30, which does a splendid job of metering relatively small charges—up to about 30 grains of most rifle propellants. For larger charges, the Hornady measure is my favorite.

To use a traditional measure properly, the handloader must develop a precise technique and then practice to perfect and maintain that technique during every loading session. Further, the technique that works best with one propellant might not work best with any other propellant. Fortunately, with ball and small- to medium-granulated propellants, one simple technique works well. I will describe that method later.

Begin by filling the hopper with the propellant of choice. Then repeatedly tap the side of the hopper lightly with an open hand (only sufficiently vigorously to settle the charge column). This uniformly settles the propellant in the hopper—which might not help, but it cannot hurt. Then dump about five charges into a scale pan. Return that propellant to the container. This eliminates any unusual packing that might have occurred near the base of the column during hopper filling.

MTM offers this handy Handloader's Log. This, or a similar system, is a wonderful adjunct to target shooting and record keeping. Whatever method you use, record all loads—and fill out and attach labels to each box of ammunition.

MEASURING CHARGES—DOUBLE TAP METHOD

According to the manufacturer's instructions, adjust the metering rod to drop the desired charge. For smaller charges, I prefer to drop ten charges into a scale pan, weigh that, and divide by ten. For larger charges, I drop five and divide by five. Then, I always drop and weigh at least three individual charges, just to be assured that the charge-to-charge variation is acceptably small.

One suggested method to drop consistent charges is to use a steady, deliberate, and repeatable motion. Move the handle until the measuring cavity fills and the handle stops. Move the handle the other way about one inch, reverse the motion, and return the handle to the stop. This repeated motion should settle the charge in the measuring cavity, thereby providing a more uniformly packed volume and hence a more uniform mass of propellant in the subsequently dispensed charge. Hold a case under the discharge funnel. Move the handle the other way until it stops. This action dumps the metered charge into the case. Again, start the handle back. Move it about one inch and then reverse it until the handle again hits the stop. This motion helps settle that part of the propellant that is in the hopper and directly over the drum. This prepares a more consistent charge to fill the measuring cavity the next time. Repeat this process until you have charged all cases in your working batch.

MTM Compact loading trays are versatile, handy, and convenient, especially when loading batches of ammunition while using a measure to drop charges.

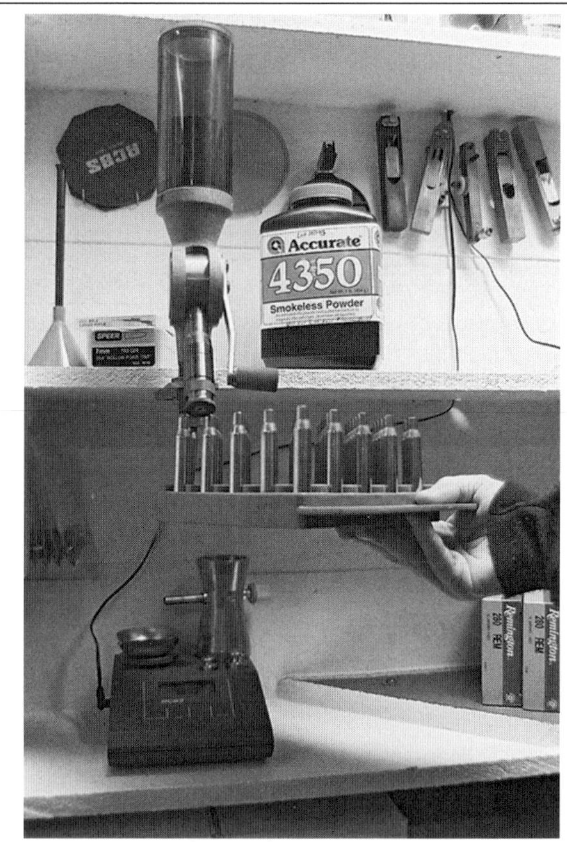

Dumping charges into cases in a tray is fast and convenient. Even a relatively large-granulated extruded propellant such as A4350 will meter with sufficient precision for most applications—key is to use a consistent technique.

MEASURING CHARGES—TWO-FINGER METHOD

I have found that with ball-type and small-granulated extruded propellants, reversing the handle motion at each end of the stroke is of no value. Using any conventional measure, I can drop charge after charge of any ball propellant with weight variations smaller than I can demonstrate on any high-quality beam scale.

My method is to raise and drop the handle consistently at a moderate speed, solidly bumping the drum against the stops at both ends of the travel. I add a twist: I trap the handle between my index and middle fingers, about halfway along the handle and about halfway along each finger. I just let the drum rotate naturally. This method seems to help me obtain consistent charges.

MEASURING CHARGES—OPTIMIZING

Try several methods. Use the technique that proves to work best for you. For short-range target shooting (under three hundred yards), especially where handloaders can use finer-granulated and shorter-cut tubular propellants, dropping charges from a measure rather than weighing charges is always the preferred method for best accuracy.

If you want to use a conventional measure with a larger-granulated tubular propellant, you will have to drop a few dozen charges using your best technique to verify the level of consistency that you can obtain. You might or might not find that you can obtain the needed load-to-load charge consistency.

For informal target shooting and varmint hunting and if the nominal load is not pushing too closely toward maximum pressure, handloaders can afford an occasional charge that misses the desired mass by a few parts per thousand. For paper punching at moderate distances, the same is likely true; any such charge variation is not apt to matter enough to tell. However, for long-range, formal target shooting, even slight charge-weight errors can introduce velocity variations that will make enough difference in bullet drop and windage error to ruin a group. This is critical, particularly, at six hundred yards and beyond. Only you can determine the needed degree of precision for your cartridges.

A traditional measure will not meter consistent charges of relatively large-granule tubular propellants, regardless of the charging technique used. Nevertheless, through consistency, ammunition manufacturers minimize the load-to-load variation to an amazing degree. Pull the bullets from several factory cartridges that are loaded with tubular propellant and weigh the charges; you are apt to be surprised at the charge-mass consistency among those meter-charged loads.

WEIGHING CHARGES—BALANCE SCALES

Most long-range target shooters and many big-game hunters who take shots at longer distances will weigh their propellant charges but usually not because they enjoy this process! Reasons for using this approach vary.

Some handloading hunters do not own a powder measure. Many use tubular propellants that do not meter accurately. Some might not have practiced enough with a measure to be confident in their ability to drop consistent charges, even when using ball propellants. Where a shooter might only fire a few rounds a year when hunting, weighing charges is a minor inconvenience.

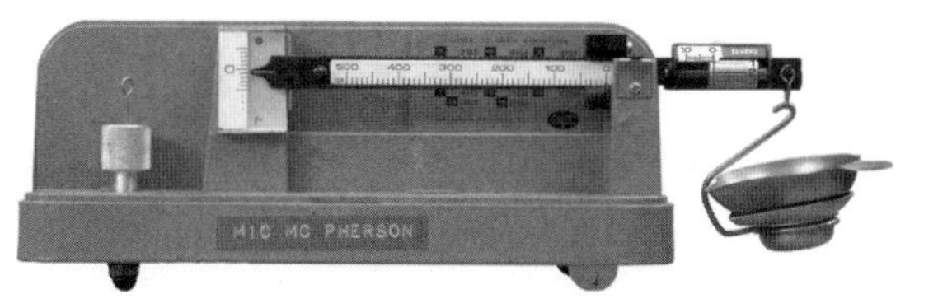

I acquired this Ohaus 10-10 Reloading Scale about 1980 and have used it extensively. It is my favorite handloading balance scale. Accuracy is +/- 1/10 grain (1/70,000 pound). Most handloading tool manufacturers offer similarly useful balance scales, and all are similarly accurate. (Most handloaders find that magnetically dampened scales, such as this one, are faster and easier to use.)

RCBS offers a comprehensive set of calibration weights. When properly cared for and used, these will assure the handloader greater scale precision than is ever needed.

The situation is different for long-range target competitors. In this game, the propellant producing the most accurate extended shot strings is usually one of the coarsely granulated tubular types. These simply will not meter with sufficient consistency to achieve the ballistic uniformity required for accurate shooting at well beyond five hundred yards.

With a quality beam balance or digital electronic scale, it is easy to weigh charges of any propellant repeatedly and consistently to an error of less than plus-or-minus one-tenth of a grain. Carefully zero the scale and use calibration weights to verify accuracy: Always practice proper scale-usage techniques.

In all instances, with any scale of any type, always keep it isolated from air currents. (Open windows, doors, and air ducts cause handloaders no end of grief in this regard.) Do not breathe over or toward the scale or pan as you weigh a charge or as you zero the beam. After adjusting any beam scale, lightly tap the pointer end of beam downward so that all weights are properly settled into the selected grooves. Then verify that the actual scale setting is the intended scale setting.

A COMMON CAUSE OF DAMAGED GUNS IS THE RESULT OF A HANDLOADER SETTING A BALANCE SCALE AT A DIFFERENT MASS SETTING THAN THE INTENDED SETTING!

WEIGHING CHARGES—ELECTRONIC SCALES

The electronic RCBS Range Master Dispenser and Charge Master Scale system does not require any significant warm-up. In this regard, these units are unique. After turning on any other electronic scale, wait until it has fully warmed, perhaps fifteen minutes, and then calibrate it. (The best practice is to never turn the scale off except during extended periods of nonuse.)

With very little effort, anyone using a quality handloader's electronic scale should be able to weigh charges with more precision than is necessary for any type of shooting.

WEIGHING CHARGES—PROPELLANT TRICKLERS

Shorter-cut granules and several of the smaller-granulated tubular propellants measure reasonably consistently. However, I do not trust any conventional measure to meter weights of any but the finest-granulation tubular numbers as consistently as I can achieve using a scale. When using a scale, a propellant trickler can speed and ease this process, considerably.

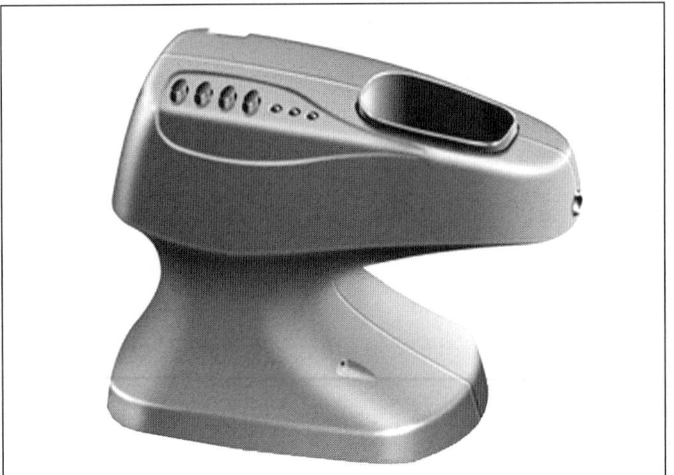

RCBS offers a very handy propellant trickler. Some brands interfere with electronic scales, so verify before buying.

WEIGHING CHARGES—ELECTRONIC DISPENSERS

Several companies offer automatic electronic charge dispensers. Without a doubt, the best I have tested is the RCBS Charge Master (CM). The CM combines a superior scale, a vastly superior propellant-metering unit, and monumentally improved programming. It is also very fast to set up and to use. When situated in a room where the temperature remains reasonably constant, it is ready to use less than ten seconds after you turn it on.

Charge dispensing is fast. The CM routinely meters sixty grains of extruded propellant in less than twenty seconds. For those who charge cases and seat bullets individually, this is generally fast enough to allow continuous operation—by the time you have charged the case, seated the bullet, and placed the

The dispensing system of the Charge Master has many handy features. Among these is a memory system that allows a user to store 30 loads with information on cartridge, bullet and weight, and powder and charge (only two of relevant displays from one memory set are represented here—powder and cartridge). After depressing correct two keys, related load data cycles through display. After selecting desired combination, the handloader can fill the hopper with the specified propellant and proceed to dispense specified charges. For safety, the CM keeps track of the number of charges dispensed. The newest version of the CM has a larger display with seven digits. It also automatically dispenses a new charge, each time the pan is returned to the scale. Although it will work, this unit is inappropriate for metering finely granulated propellants (a careful handloader can meter such propellants almost perfectly through a typical measure, which is a much faster method).

The RCBS Charge Master hopper holds more than one pound of typical rifle propellant. Dispensing is both fast and accurate. Both a tone and a large lighted readout indicate when the machine has doled out the correct charge.

finished round in an ammo box, the CM will have finished dispensing the next charge.

Unlike any previous similar system, the accuracy of the dispensed charge weight is usually adequate for all applications. When metering large-granulated extruded rifle propellants (for which such a device is most needed), charge-to-charge mass consistency is often within plus-or-minus one granule from the specified mass (this represents several times the advertised precision of plus-or-minus one-tenth grain). However, because of the shape the granule and the size of some propellants, this unit will often dispense 0.1 to 0.2 grains more than the specified charge.

The CM has only one power cord for both the powder measure and the scale. Handloaders can use the CM electronic scale as a freestanding unit. It plugs into the measure and, thereby, delivers power and establishes a communications link with that unit.

Turn on the unit, fill the hopper, set the desired charge mass, and dispense. CM programming is sufficiently sophisticated to determine, on the fly, how fast the CM is dispensing the particular propellant. With this information, the CM automatically compensates the dispensing rate so that it accurately dispenses the desired charge as rapidly as is feasible.

Finally a computer-controlled system that actually works! Imagine if the computer software I used to create this text were similarly efficient and dependable!

The CM includes a handy memory function. This feature allows the handloader to enter specific charges of specific propellant types and to describe specific loads. Once programmed and upon recall of any particular memorized load, the CM sequentially displays abbreviations for caliber, bullet weight, propellant type, and charge weight. This is very handy as a memory aid, if nothing else, but this also automatically readies this machine to dispense the specified charge for the particular selected load.

Another handy feature is that the CM keeps track of the number of charges dispensed in any

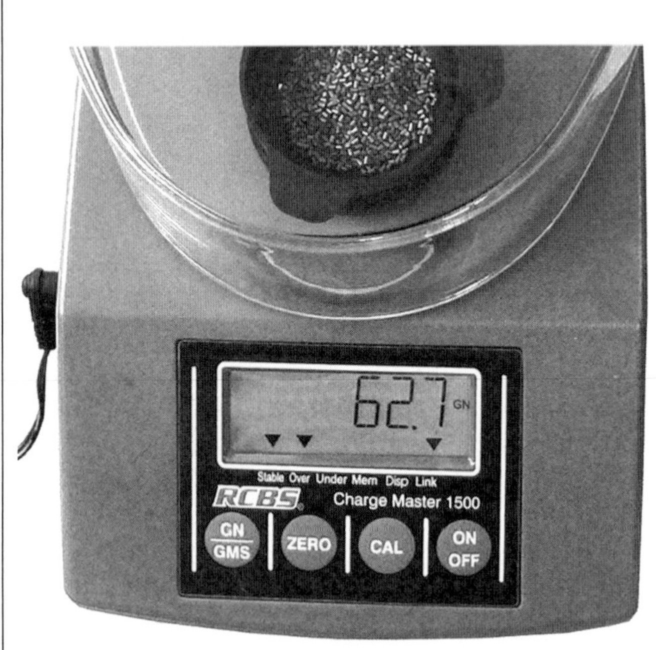

The RCBS Charge Master is almost foolproof. Here, the readout indicates that the charge dispensed exceeds the specified amount (arrow above OVER*). (I created this condition artificially for this picture: In normal use, this rarely happens with most propellants.)*

given loading session. If, at the end of a session, the number of loaded rounds and the number of dispensed charges does not tally, you have a problem. The likely possibilities are a cartridge with no propellant or a cartridge with a double charge. Neither one is a good thing.

The metering unit also includes a specially designed valve and drain that allows the handloader to remove all propellant granules from the reservoir easily. I offer this handy hint—after having left the drain valve in the open position once: The open side of this valve on my CM is now painted a bright fingernail-polish red as a visual-warning indicator.

In order to dispense a new charge after returning the pan to the scale, the original CM required that the user press the DISP button. At my request, RCBS changed this. With new units, each time you return the pan to the scale the machine automatically dispenses a new charge and continues to do so until you press the CANCEL button.

As an example of CM performance, consider the following test results:

- 60-grain BenchMark (extruded, finely granulated)—15 seconds
- 60-grain Retumbo (extruded, moderately coarsely granulated)—16½ seconds
- 120-grain H50BMG (extruded, very coarsely granulated)—25 seconds

RCBS reports that about 99.7 percent of the time the CM meters precisely the specified charge, within the accuracy of readout resolution. (R1-25 is an exception.) Programming is sufficiently sophisticated so that the unit never stops with less than the specified mass in the pan. Conversely, despite the most delicate of dispensing tube tweaking, a logjam at the mouth of the tube will result in several granules dropping into the pan when only one was needed. For this reason, very rarely the CM will stop after dispensing at least one-tenth grain more than the specified charge. When this occurs, a distinctive warning tone sounds and an arrow indicates OVER.

The CM turns itself off when not in use and start-up includes a self-test. The CM scale features a handy hinged pan cover to eliminate problems from air movement. Both dispenser and scale have adjustable leveling feet. The illuminated display is large enough to accommodate aging eyes.

AVOIDING SLIGHTLY-COMPRESSED CHARGES

This is an important consideration for any cartridges used in any type of shooting. Avoid combinations that result in a slight charge compression during bullet seating. The problem is that some percentage of such charges might spontaneously settle differently during case charging or might settle during or after bullet seating—the latter would result, most likely, from strong vibrations during transportation or shock when in the magazine, as when another round is fired. When this happens, one will find that the two situations thus produced—those loads with the charge loosely packed and, therefore, compressed, and those loads with the charge densely packed and, therefore, uncompressed—will usually shoot to unique points of impact and will usually generate unique average velocities. Many decades ago, the folks at Hercules studied this phenomenon in some detail—it is a significant accuracy consideration.

In cartridges where the charge is significantly compressed, granules are locked together so tightly that spontaneous settling cannot occur; conversely, if the load you are using might result in a packing density near 100 percent, use a settling technique so that all charges are settled, and, hence, none are compressed. This will protect the consistency and accuracy of the resulting cartridges. Refer to the following section.

Pictured are equal-weight charges of H-570 in identical 7mm Remington Magnum cases. On the left is charge dumped into a case via swirl charging; right, charge was dumped into a case by the conventional method. With care, swirl-charging can increase the charge density by about 6 percent with extruded propellants and about 8 percent with ball-type propellants.

SWIRL CHARGING—CONSISTENTLY INSTALLING DUMPED CHARGES

Achieving maximum ballistic uniformity and charge density requires special care when charging the case. Many pundits have ignored this critical subject. Assume that you have finalized the development of a load that exhibits great accuracy and ballistic uniformity; however, it uses a compressed charge. Such loads are common. The only thing unique about a compressed-charge load is that seating the bullet will positively lock in the granule packing scheme. It is a very good thing when each charge has essentially the same packing scheme, but that only happens when the handloader is careful to dump each charge into each case as similarly as is feasible.

Because the packing scheme and charge density both influence internal ballistics, the handloader must be careful to install charges as consistently as

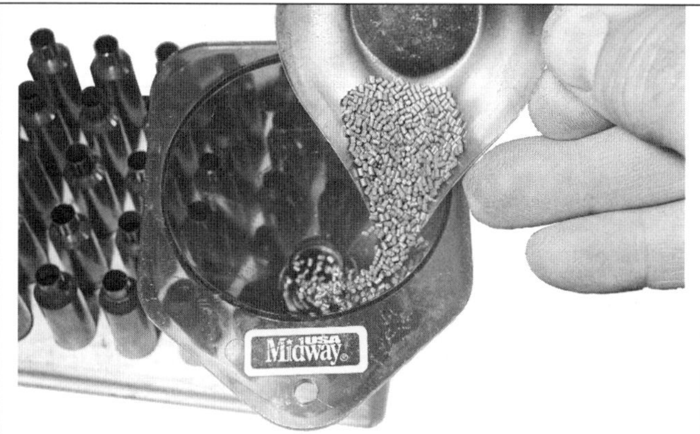

The swirl-charge technique is very easy to master. Some funnels work better than others. The midway funnel (shown here), while otherwise a fine tool, does not work as well for swirl charging as the RCBS funnel does.

is possible (identically, while impossible, would be ideal). This might sound a bit unusual, and this subject has received precious little attention, but the ballistic influence is real and it can be quite significant.

Many years ago, because I was curious about the importance of the packing scheme to ballistic uniformity, I charged forty match-prepped 30-30 cases with a nearly case-filling charge of VarGet (at that time, this was an untested load, so Hodgdon verified it for safety before I proceeded). I charged twenty cases by simply pouring the propellant through a standard propellant funnel in the standard manner—with the pan spout directed toward the funnel feed orifice (where the granules fall through and into the case neck). For the other twenty cases, I poured the propellant at the same rate, but I poured it so that the granules fell against the side of the funnel entrance cone—the pan spout was at the side of the funnel and pointing at a right angle to the direction between the end of the spout and the funnel orifice. In this instance, the charge swirled as it passed down through the funnel cone, and then through the orifice. (See picture on the bottom of page 181.)

This 270 Winchester with Speer 170-grain round-nose seated on 66.6 grains of H-570 (both are obsolete) represents about as much charge-compression as any handloader is apt to create in any rifle load.

I poured granules into the bottom (below card separator) of this six-inch test tube by using the swirl-charge technique; I poured granules above separator by using the standard technique. Note how many more granules in the bottom of tube are situated side-by-side and otherwise are neatly packed. This results in a significant increase in packing density (up to about 8 percent for uniform spherical granules; up to about 6 percent for typical extruded granules). As an added bonus, swirl-charged loads are usually more accurate and usually show significantly less velocity variation (after many dozens of tests over several decades, I have found one exception).

After dumping the charge from one of the above loads, only 14 granules (top row), out of approximately 1,400, were visibly damaged; each of these had been touching the bullet. For comparison: An equal number of undamaged granules (bottom row). Damage to 1 percent of the granules at the front of the charge will not measurably alter ballistics, if at all.

In both instances, the charge filled the case into the neck. I was pouring moderately fast in both instances, so there existed only a modest difference in packing density. Other than charging technique, I made every effort to make sure that the ammunition was as identical

The charge compression in the 270 load shown in the previous picture was sufficient to significantly deform this Speer Hot-Cor bullet! Interestingly, accuracy of this load is very good.

as possible. Seating the 150-grain bullets compressed every propellant charge substantially.

Test firing demonstrated a significant difference in the resulting cartridges. When chronographed, the non-swirl-charged group showed an 18.2 fps standard deviation whereas the swirl-charged group showed an 11.8 fps standard deviation. I was then, and continue to be, quite taken with this well-verified result. I have long since adopted the swirl-charge technique for all loads using pan-weighed propellant charges.

By combining the basic swirl-charge technique with a deliberately slow pouring rate, it is possible to increase charge density up to about 8 percent. (Surprisingly and interestingly, the greatest potential density improvement seems to occur with uniform spherical propellants.) If the charge requires further settling to allow bullet seating without undue difficulty, hold your thumb over the charged case mouth and lightly tap the case head downward against a hard surface. This will maximize settling.

Nothing is intrinsically wrong with using compressed charges. Many loads using highly compressed charges of relatively slow-burning propellants offer superior performance. If the load does not create unsafe pressure and so long as the handloader can seat the bullet on top of the propellant charge without deforming either the case or the bullet and without the charge pushing the bullet back out of the case, a compressed-charge load is perfectly safe. Often, such loads are particularly worthwhile, but these do require attention in the aforementioned areas, and one must take special care to make sure that consistent propellant settling exists.

The one glaring exception is cartridges used in revolvers that generate significant recoil. The classic example is the 454 Casull. In such a revolver, the use of a significantly compressed charge to generate full pressure (as with H110) is apt to result in bullets pulling out of unfired rounds in the cylinder during recoil. The propellant is pushing on the bullet, and this reduces the amount of bullet pull that remains to prevent the bullet from moving. The gun pulls the case rearward violently with only neck tension to hold the bullet in place (even an ideal crimp adds almost nothing to bullet pull). For such cartridges, avoid highly compressed charges at all costs—use a smaller charge of a faster propellant. Light charge compression, up to about 5 percent, is of little consequence in this regard and can be ignored—after bullet seating, the propellant soon relaxes and thereafter generates very little, if any, force on the bullet base.

To gain some understanding of the importance of the propellant-charging technique, consider this one fact: Benchrest competitors long ago stopped using scales to weigh propellant charges. Only one reason exists to explain this: Measured and dropped charges produce more consistent results than do carefully weighed charges. The weight variation of dumped charges of typical benchrest propellants is always greater than with weighed charges. Hence, something is more important than charge-weight consistency.

What could that be? The answer to that critical question is: Compared to weighed and pan-dumped charges, handloaders introduce dropped charges into cases with a greater level of consistency; therefore, dropped charges have less variation in the granule packing scheme. This proves unequivocally that a consistent granule-packing scheme is more important to the accuracy of benchrest cartridges than is any slight variation in charge mass. This fact has been proven thousands of times by match-winning benchrest competitors.

CHARGE CORRECTIONS—VARIATIONS IN CASE WEIGHT

The relationship between loading density and appropriate propellant charge adjustment, as necessary to compensate for variations in case weight and resulting case (boiler room) volume, should be obvious: If the case is heavier (less volume), reduce the propellant charge; if the case is lighter (more volume), increase the propellant charge.

In cartridges that use a nearly case-filling charge, adjust the propellant charge about six-tenths of a grain for each ten grains variation in case weight. For example, when using a five-grain-heavier case and a case-filling charge, reduce the charge by three-tenths grain to get nearly identical velocity and very similar pressure and barrel time. Similarly, in cartridges with 50 percent loading density, use a three-tenths-grain load adjustment for each ten-grain difference in case weight, etc. Refer to the associated table on this page for more precise charge-adjustment suggestions.

The surprising thing is that it does not matter what size the case is. The same correction works for the 22 Hornet, the 50 BMG, and everything between.

Of course, it is neither practical nor reasonable to make minute propellant charge adjustments. However, this table is always useful because it suggests approximately how much influence variations in case

Charge Corrections Required to Normalize Performance When Loading in Cases of Varying Weight

Case Weight Variation +/– Grains	Approximate Charge Adjustment to Maintain Similar Pressure and Velocity — Loading Density (Grains of Charge Used ÷ Grains of Water That Fills Case×100)					
	100%	87½%	75%	62½%	50%	37½%
	Approximate Charge Adjustment +/–Grains					
1	0.060	0.053	0.045	0.038	0.030	0.022
2	0.120	0.105	0.090	0.075	0.060	0.045
3	0.180	0.158	0.135	0.113	0.090	0.067
4	0.240	0.210	0.180	0.150	0.120	0.090
5	0.300	0.263	0.225	0.190	0.150	0.110
6	0.360	0.315	0.270	0.225	0.180	0.135
7	0.420	0.371	0.315	0.266	0.210	0.154
8	0.480	0.420	0.360	0.300	0.240	0.180
9	0.540	0.477	0.405	0.342	0.270	0.198
10	0.600	0.530	0.450	0.380	0.300	0.220
15	0.90	0.80	0.68	0.57	0.45	0.33
20	1.08	0.95	0.90	0.76	0.60	0.44
25	1.50	1.33	1.13	0.95	0.75	0.55

Unless you know that the cases you are loading are lighter than the cases used to prepare the load data you are using, NEVER exceed maximum charges listed in any manual.

weight have on the charge required to maintain similar velocity, pressure, and barrel time. This will also help the handloader estimate how much velocity variation will result from variations in case weight.

Compare the suggested charge adjustments to your load data. For example, consider a hypothetical charge that fills the available space with cases that vary by three grains in mass, from lightest to heaviest. According to the table on page 184, the suggested charge adjustment is 0.18 grain.

The load data you are using indicates that a 1-grain increase in propellant charge will increase muzzle velocity by 60 fps. Hence, lacking a correcting charge adjustment, a 3-grain variation in case weight will generate about an 11 fps difference in muzzle velocity between the lightest and heaviest cases in the group (60 x 0.18 = 10.8).

The table on page 184 suggests approximate compensating charge adjustments that should allow you to use cases of significantly different weights to create cartridges that generate similar muzzle velocity, peak chamber pressure, and barrel time. This will allow the use of different-mass cases to create cartridges that should shoot near the same point of impact at longer distances. An example of where this could be very valuable is cases of the 30-06 family—Winchester-made cases are often 20 grains lighter than Remington-made cases.

SOURCE FOR SPECIALTY TOOL REFERENCED IN THIS CHAPTER:

Quick Measure
c/o Johnson Design Specialties
4607 West Elderberry Avenue
Spokane, WA 99208
Telephone: 509-464-0697

At the range one cold day testing various loads in the Savage M40, 22 Hornet are Jim Williamson (learning how to bench test) and I (spotting his hits and trying to offer encouragement and useful advice). This rifle shoots several handloads with nearly ½ MOA accuracy at 100 yards. The Burris Fullfield II, 4½–14X is a wonderful choice for this and similar rifles. While it was a cold day, we had a great time.

Appropriate bullet choice depends upon relative cartridge performance, just as well as it depends upon intended usage. For example, the 300 Winchester Magnum, 7.62 Patriot, and 7mm Weatherby Magnum (above) require relatively tough bullets.

This is the jacket from the so-called "Premium" self-defense pistol bullet. In my testing, bullets of this particular brand demonstrated a disturbing propensity for jacket and core separations—100 percent! This jacket came from a 45-automatic loading that I fired into a saturated telephone book at 5 feet; this is typical performance for this brand, regardless of the particular loading. If your life depends upon it, you need to know that the bullet will hold together to get the job done.

The 44 Magnum (left) and the 475 Linebaugh (right) require relatively soft bullets.

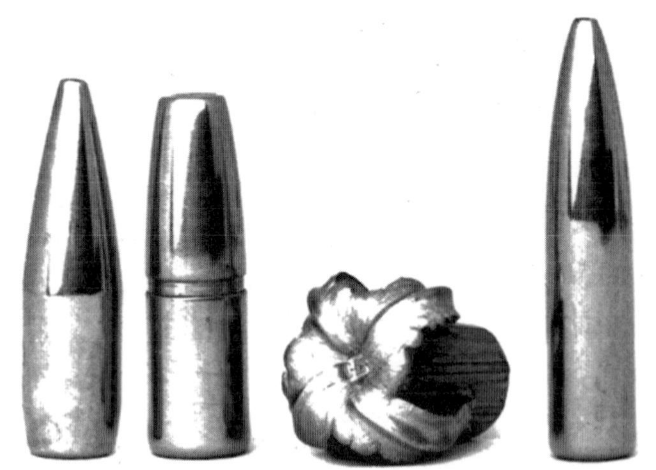

These various styles of Barnes X have wide application. Most shooters choose an entirely too heavy X. This style of bullet should be about 2/3 the mass of an ideal premium bullet of conventional style (e.g., Partition). To prevent "pressure excursions," make sure that the cartridge OAL provides at least 50/1000-inch bullet-to-rifling jump. Newer Barnes variants of the basic X (Triple Shock and others) are superior choices.

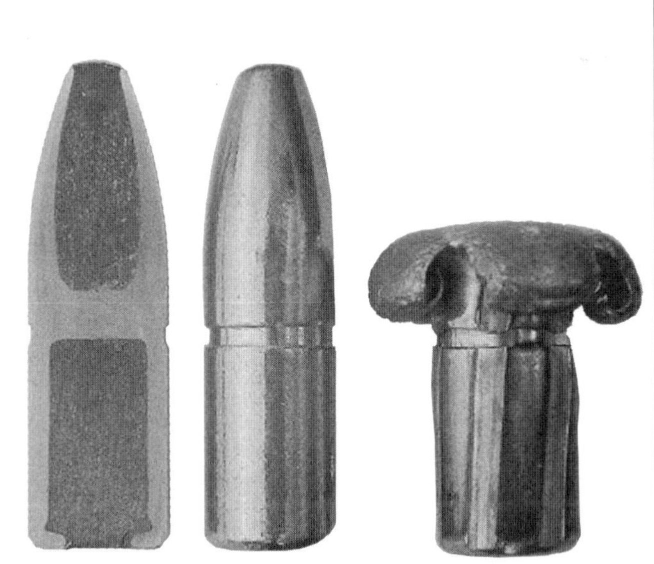

Swift A-Frame bullets combine a pure lead nose with a partitioned, pure copper jacket and a lead-base core. The nose core is soldered to the jacket (this anneals the jacket, providing maximum malleability). The jacket base is folded over the base core to maximize bullet integrity. Terminal performance is impressive and dependable.

The 230-grain, 45-caliber Speer Gold Dot on the left was fired at 850 fps into a saturated telephone book; the one on the right was fired at 800 fps into 10 percent laboratory ballistic gelatin. The single disadvantage of the Gold Dot is that each version is designed to expand optimally within a relatively narrow range of velocities. The Hornady XTP is far more forgiving in this regard.

On the left is a conventional bullet recovered from a trophy mule deer that I took in 1986. As in this example, when such a bullet hits the target at relatively high velocity, it will often lose more than 50 percent of its weight. Conversely, Barnes X-Bullet and similar bullets will expand effectively at relatively low remaining velocity (about 1,800 fps for the bullet in middle) and will still retain nearly 100 percent of its weight when impacting at relatively high velocity (bullet at right).

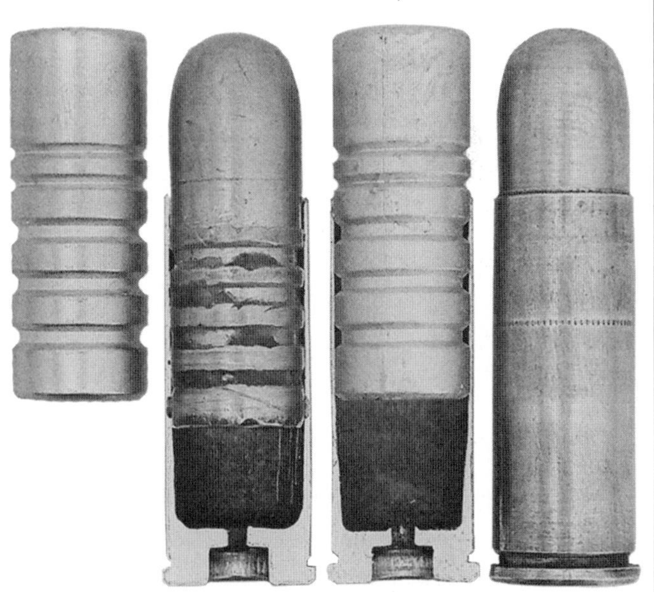

Design matters, even in nominally nonexpanding bullets. Left to right: 525-grain WC for the 45 Colt and the 454 Casull, 45 Colt cutaway with 500-grain RN, 45 Colt cutaway with 525-grain WC, 45 Colt 500-grain RN load. When launched at 900 fps, the RN achieves a 38-inch penetration in a saturated telephone book while the WC stops after 18 inches. The WC is, therefore, vastly more effective at transferring energy and is a proven elk killer.

The terminal performance (especially penetration) of X-style bullets is all out of proportion to weight. These bullets have many advantages for situations where significant penetration is needed.

Tinkering toward perfection (left-to-right) are the 6.5mm/60 SMc (ready to charge), the 62.5-grain Retumbo, and the 60-grain H1000. These charges were installed via the swirl-charge technique. The Retumbo is bulkier than the H1000. The Retumbo charge requires very slow and precise case filling, but the resulting cartridges are worth the effort.

These 380 ACP cases demonstrate the progressive result of using too much pressure in a case that is not fully supported: Eventually, increasing pressure will rupture the case wall.

This case shows evidence of neck turning before this loading. Thickening at base of neck reflects material moving from shoulder into neck as case stretched; thickening near case mouth is inexplicable.

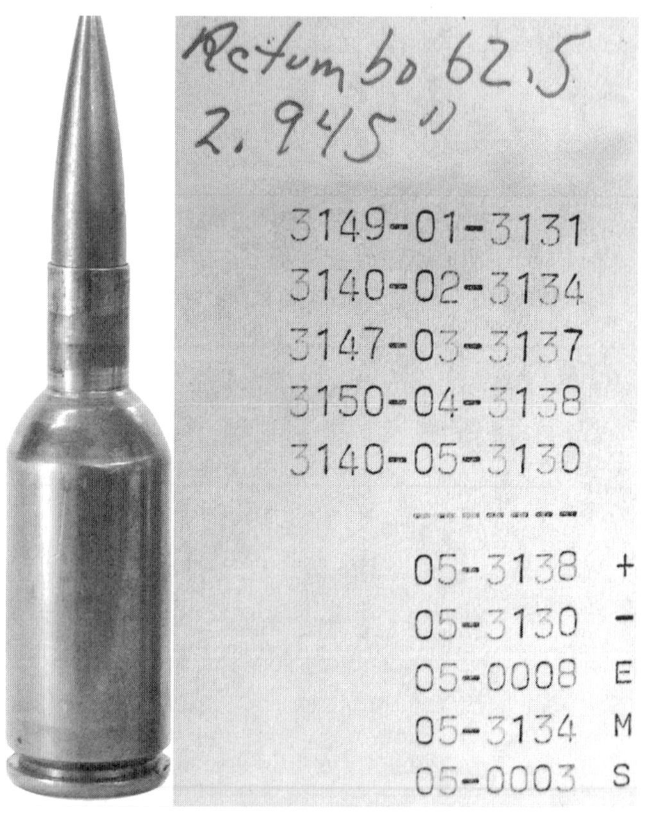

This load represents the last measure of precision. This string was consistent with five other test loads using this combination with the only variations in primer and seating depth. The cumulative standard deviation for all 6, 5-shot strings was 6 fps!

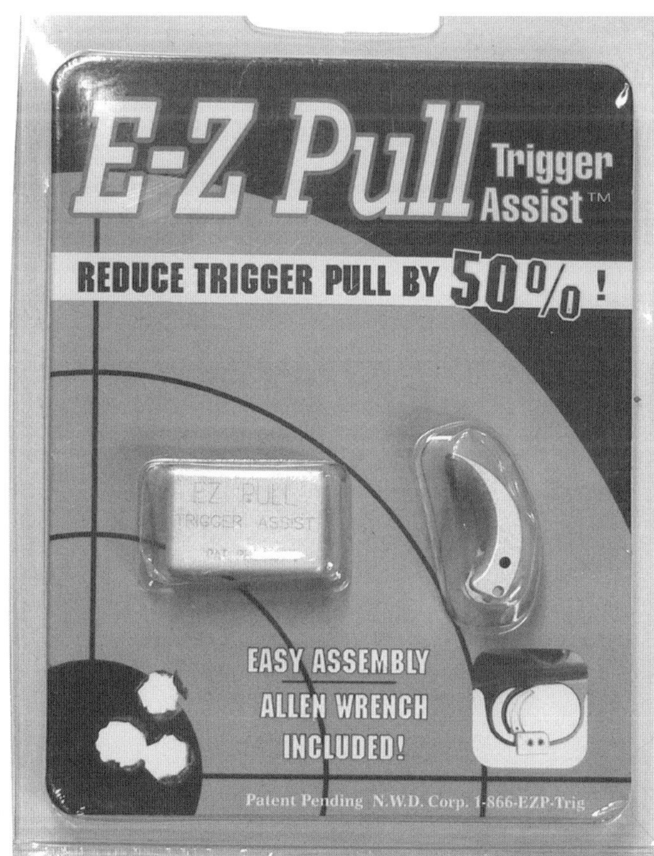

Regardless of ammunition, gun, and personal preparation, most of us can always do a better job of bench testing a gun and ammunition if the gun has a relatively light trigger let-off. The E-Z Pull trigger assist system is a handy companion for bench testing. It mounts easily on most rifles and is equally easy to remove. In most applications it reduces trigger let-off by more than 50 percent—on the M40 Savage, it reduced let-off fully 75 percent. When bench testing a rifle, I can handle (and do very much appreciate) an eight-ounce trigger let-off

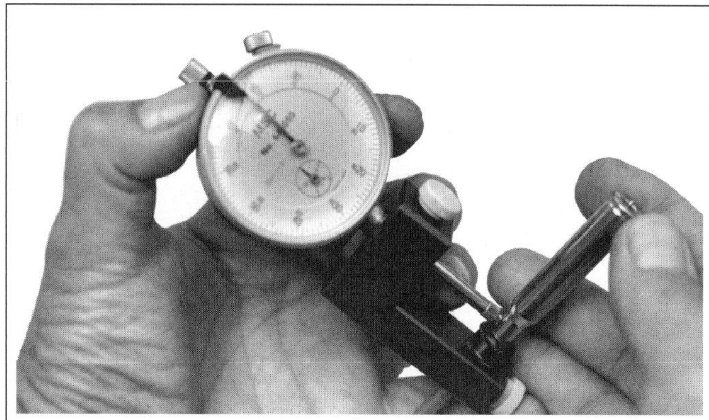

This Sinclair tool is used for measuring neck wall thickness and uniformity: Improving the case is a necessary first step for long-range accuracy; improving the bullet tip is an obvious final step.

When shooting cast bullets with relatively low-pressure loads that do not lead the bore significantly, propellant fouling is often the only problem we face. SharpShoot-R and others offer carbon removers that remove propellant fouling faster than other bore cleaners do because these are formulated to do nothing else. Many conventional bore cleaners loosen lead fouling. In extreme instances, Outers electrolytic lead remover is useful.

The M-16, and related guns, can tear weak (over-stretched) cases in two. When this happens, usually the case head ejects and the next round jams into the remaining portion of the case. Sometimes, working the bolt will remove the jammed-together cartridge and piece of case. Note the "worm tracks" on the case at left. This is an unusual and likely harmless manufacturing defect. Another rare defect is referred to as spindling, and results in thin layers of brass that peel off just as paper would from a roll (usually found in the case neck. Other rare defects, such as unpierced flash holes and flash hole material spindled into the case body area rather than piercing out cleanly, do occur.

Custom Marlins: Top, Model 1894 chambered in 50 M3, which uses the 50 AE case with loads to 1.9 inches overall length. Bottom, lightweight 44 Magnum (4¾ pounds).

Left and middle, 440 Cor-Bon loaded for use in similar Marlin 1894; at right, 50 AE.

INTERESTING PICTURES

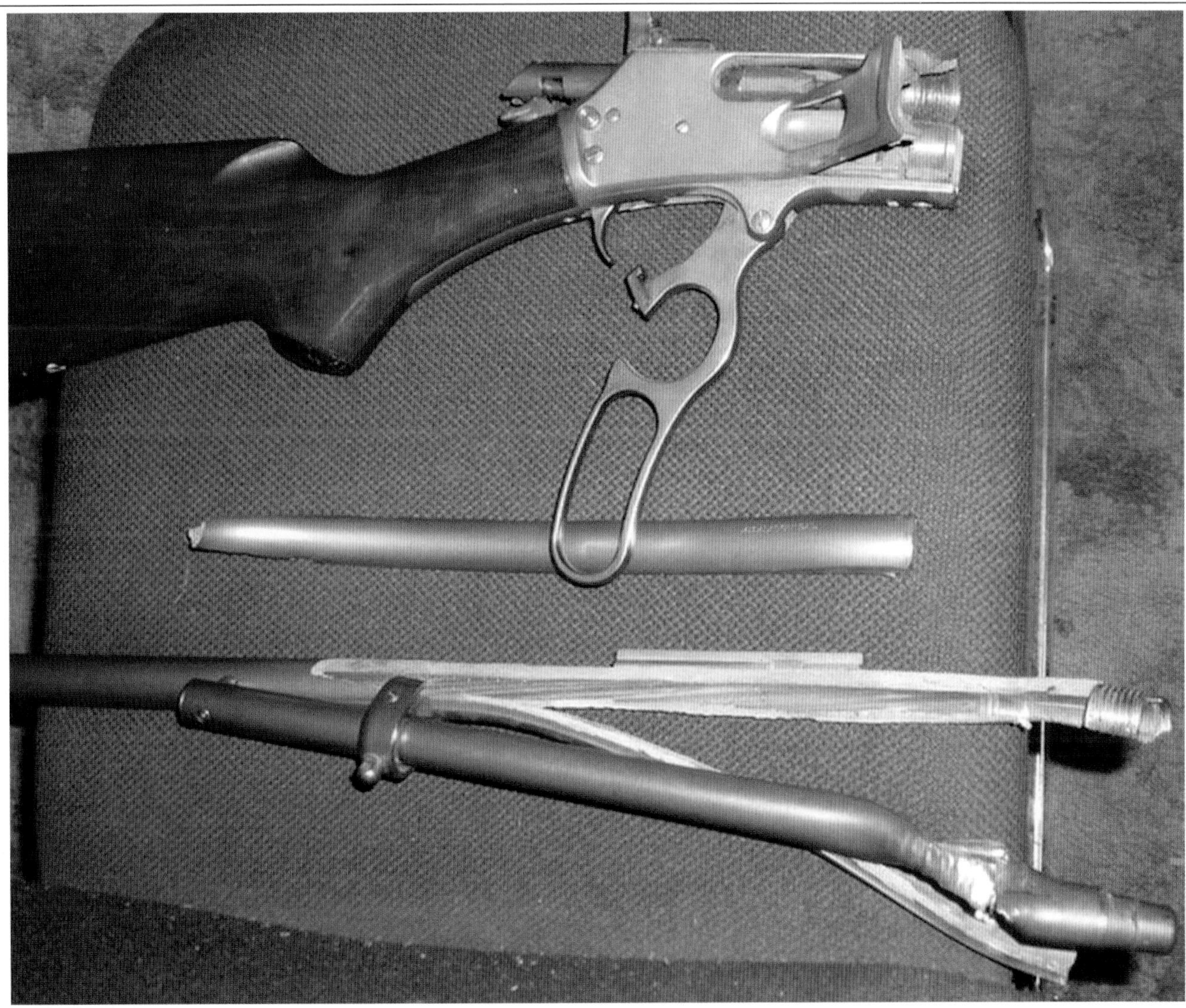

For complicated reasons, the combination of a relatively large case, a relatively hard-to-ignite propellant, and a relatively mild primer can lead to what ballisticians call a detonation. Except for the primer, the load that destroyed this fine custom Marlin was perfectly normal. It should have generated a relatively mild 30,000-psi peak chamber pressure. However, this handload used a too-mild pistol primer. After many normal shots, a partial-ignition occurred. Hot gas from the combustion of a small percentage of the charge compressed the remaining (unignited) charge into the front of the case and slowly heated that, en masse, until it reached kindling temperature. Then the entire unignited portion of the charge ignited and burned very rapidly as it and the bullet accelerated into the bore. The rate of gas generation and acceleration created a standing pressure wave near the chamber shoulder. The crest of this wave reached sufficient magnitude to overstress the steel. This demonstrated what the Krupp commission proved, circa 1888: Igniting a charge that is located at one end of a nearly cylindrical chamber always results in a standing wave. Under some circumstances, the peak pressure of this standing wave can reach catastrophic magnitude. Most, if not all, such detonations are the direct result of using a too-mild primer. But, the best ballistic uniformity results when we use the mildest primer that will reliably ignite the charge; hence, we face a strong temptation to substitute a milder primer. Whenever contemplating that approach, please keep a mental image of this costly pile of junk firmly in mind.

EVERYTHING HAS A LIMIT.
JUST BECAUSE YOU CAN LOAD IT, DOES NOT MEAN IT IS SAFE TO USE.

Above: It is hard to imagine anyone firing more than one such load, but here is the proof. Someone apparently continued to fire seriously overloaded 9x19mms in a Glock until he managed to destroy the gun.

Right: These 30 carbine cases demonstrate that one can sometimes get away with firing one dangerous overload. The first case held (left). The second case (right and middle) failed. We can only imagine what the release of an entire propellant charge at such pressure did to the shooter and gun.

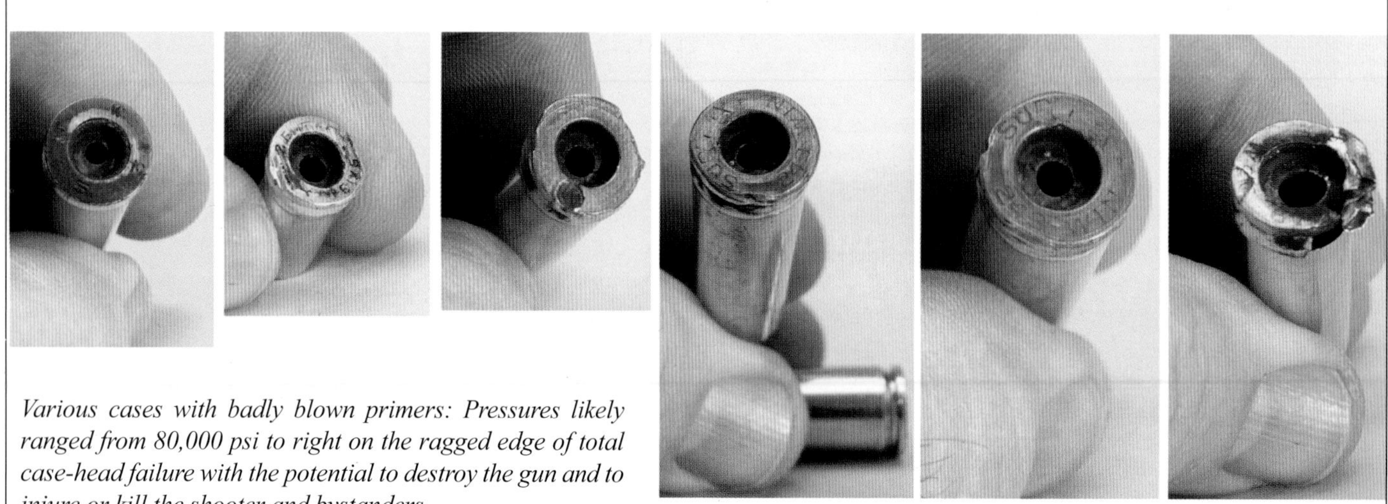

Various cases with badly blown primers: Pressures likely ranged from 80,000 psi to right on the ragged edge of total case-head failure with the potential to destroy the gun and to injure or kill the shooter and bystanders.

Left and middle: 243 Winchester cases. Right: a 270 Winchester case. These pressure-belted cases demonstrate what can happen when the load far exceeds what the case can support. Had the pressure been only slightly higher, the case head likely would have liquefied. This would have damaged or destroyed the gun and could have injured or killed the shooter and bystanders.

These 9x19mm cases show ample evidence of loads generating massively excessive pressure. Safety depends upon gun design. Had someone fired either of these in a gun with a relatively deep-feed ramp, case-wall failure and gun damage would have occurred.

More examples resulting from firing massively dangerous overloads. Firing any of these in a gun of less than massively excessive strength would have resulted in a catastrophe. Firing more than a few such loads in any gun will inevitably result in catastrophic failure.

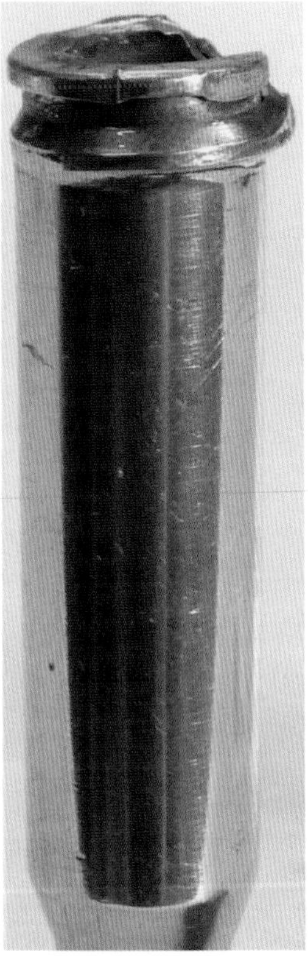

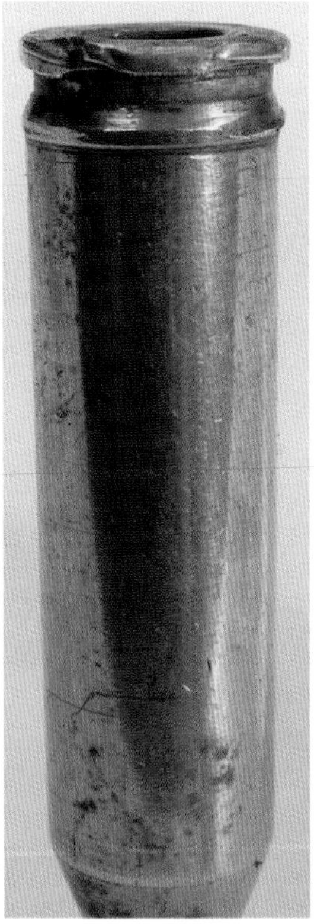

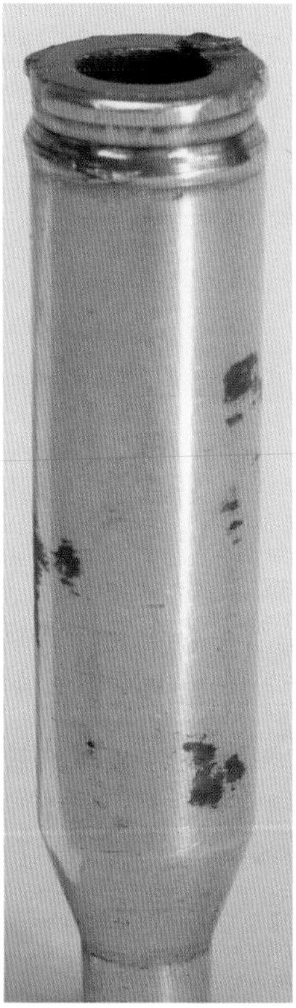

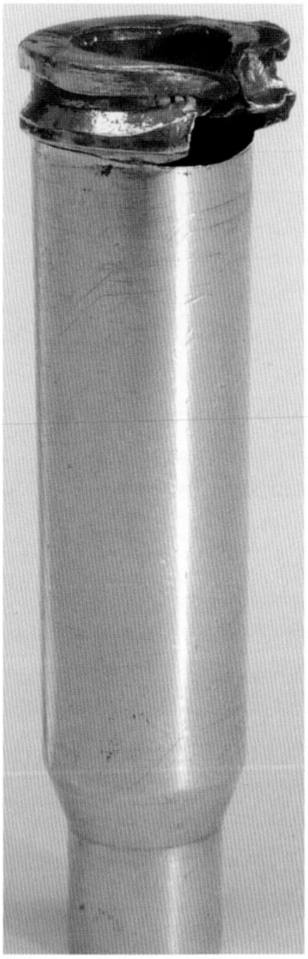

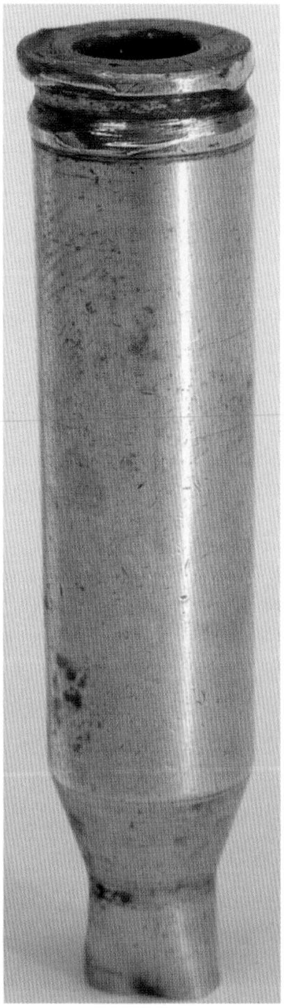

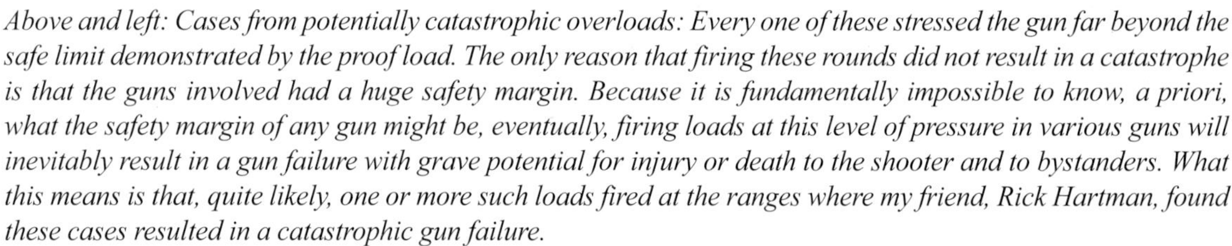

Above and left: Cases from potentially catastrophic overloads: Every one of these stressed the gun far beyond the safe limit demonstrated by the proof load. The only reason that firing these rounds did not result in a catastrophe is that the guns involved had a huge safety margin. Because it is fundamentally impossible to know, a priori, what the safety margin of any gun might be, eventually, firing loads at this level of pressure in various guns will inevitably result in a gun failure with grave potential for injury or death to the shooter and to bystanders. What this means is that, quite likely, one or more such loads fired at the ranges where my friend, Rick Hartman, found these cases resulted in a catastrophic gun failure.

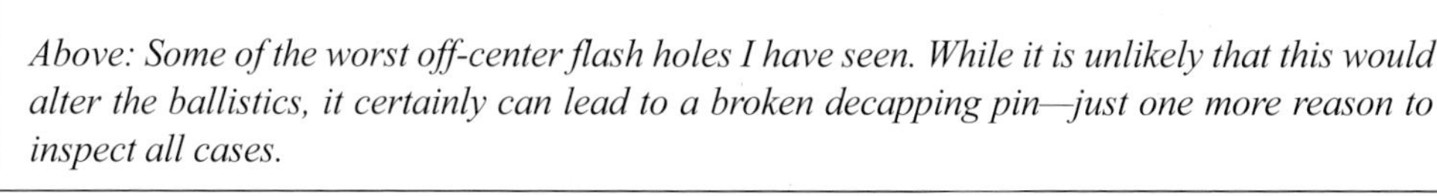

Above: Some of the worst off-center flash holes I have seen. While it is unlikely that this would alter the ballistics, it certainly can lead to a broken decapping pin—just one more reason to inspect all cases.

JUST BECAUSE YOU CAN FORCE IT INTO CHAMBER, DOES NOT MEAN YOU SHOULD USE IT! JUST BECAUSE IT WILL CHAMBER, DOES NOT MEAN THAT IT IS SAFE TO USE!

Top row, left to right: 223 fired in a 7.62x39mm; 6.5mm Jap fired in 6.5x55mm; 243 Winchester fired in 7x57mm; 308 Winchester fired in 30-06 Springfield; 308 Winchester fired in 8x57mm; 300 Savage fired in 30-06 Springfield; 7x57mm fired in 7.65x53mm; 303 Savage fired in 303 British; 243 Winchester fired in 308 Winchester; 7x57mm fired in 8x57mm; and, 7x57mm fired in 7mm Remington Magnum.

Top row, left to right: 9x19mm fired in 380 ACP; 9x19mm fired in 9mm Makarov; 9x19mm fired in 380 ACP; 9x19mm fired in 40 S&W; 9x19mm fired in 380 ACP; 40 S&W fired with a massive overload; 10mm Auto fired in 40 S&W; and, 45 Auto fired with gun out of battery. (It is a mystery to the author how this could have happened.) Bottom row, left to right: 30 Luger fired in 9x19mm; four 9x19mms fired in 40 S&W; 357 Sig fired in 40 S&W; and, two 40 S&Ws fired in 45 Auto.

A 16-gauge shotshell fired in a 12-gauge shotgun.

Left to right: a 222 Remington, a 222 Remington fired in a 223 Remington chamber, a 223 Remington, and another 222 Remington fired in a 223 chamber.

These factory 223s lack flash holes. Top, primer removed to show solid web; bottom, primer cup backed out as force from the primer blast drove the case into the chamber by setting the shoulder back.

EVEN FACTORY PRODUCERS CAN GET IT WRONG. FAULTY LOADS, CHAMBERS, AND COMPONENTS DO EXIST, AND CASES DO FAIL.

These various factory loads lack flash holes; the primers either blew out upon firing or fell out upon unchambering. The pressure generated inside a sealed primer pocket can be sufficient to swell the case head, and, thus, the primer can fall out.

Interesting primers in factory loads, left to right: A 223 with the primer installed backward; a 45 Auto with the anvil remaining after the primer was blown out because the reversed anvil almost sealed the flash hole as the round fired; and, a 303 British with the primer installed sideways.

These cases were fired in incorrectly reamed chambers.

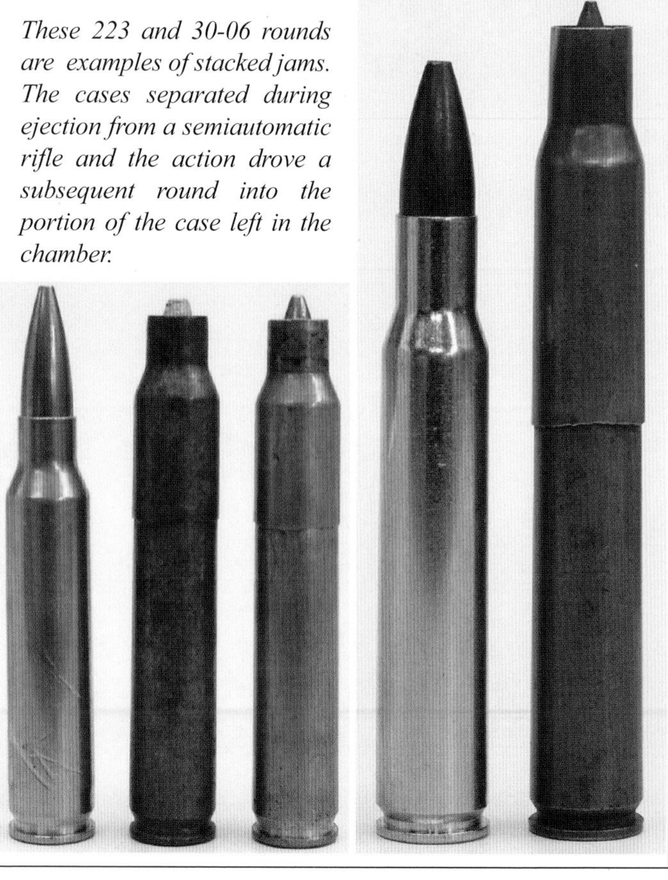

These 223 and 30-06 rounds are examples of stacked jams. The cases separated during ejection from a semiautomatic rifle and the action drove a subsequent round into the portion of the case left in the chamber.

These are various examples of separated cases and case heads recovered at various shooting ranges. Any such case separation has the potential to damage or destroy the gun, the shooter, and bystanders. While such bad results are rare, they do occur, which is all the more reason to be diligent about case inspection.

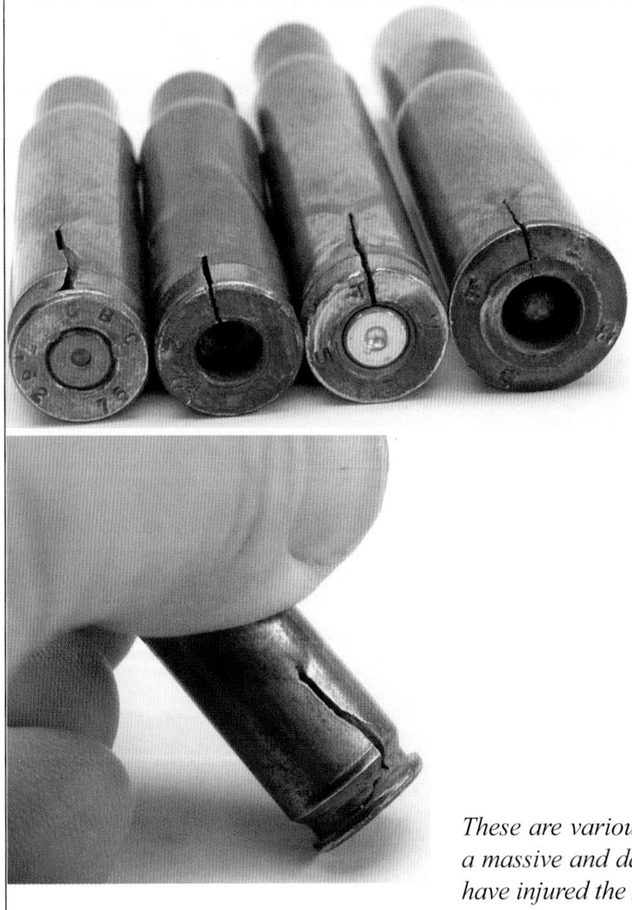

These are various examples of case splits at and near the base. Each of these generated a massive and dangerous gas leak that almost certainly damaged the gun and is likely to have injured the shooter.

Above: These interesting examples of case-head separations in semi-balloon-head cases show precisely why this type of case is no longer in use. Such separations leave no chance for the case head to seal the chamber, not even partially—VERY DANGEROUS.

Above: Hard to imagine how a loading machine could spit out these mangled rounds. Harder still to imagine this happening without destroying the machine or setting off a primer. Note headstamp, primer, and pocket engravement into bullet.

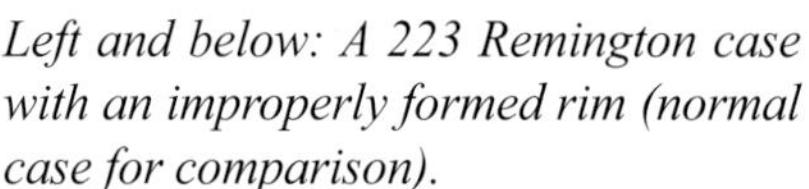

Left and below: A 223 Remington case with an improperly formed rim (normal case for comparison).

Right: Short 45 Auto Rim case and a 500 S&W Magnum case shipped with three rim cuts, two in the wrong location and one of those triple width.

Various case-wall cracks: At left is an enlargement of the 45 Winchester Magnum case showing more clearly the crack at the base of the case body. This case is otherwise perfectly normal. This is why inspecting a case is so important. When used, the leaking gas from such a crack could damage the gun or injure the shooter. The two bottlenecked cases with longitudinal cracks likely generated enough of a gas leak to damage the gun. The 223 nearly separated completely. Had it done so, it would have created a stacked jam.

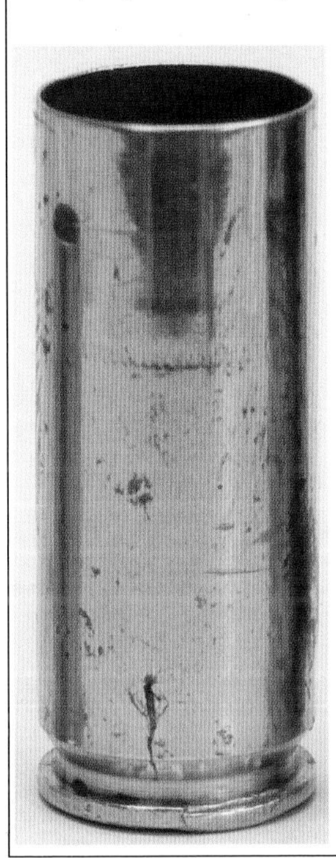

It is a bit hard to understand how this 30 carbine (third from left) managed to get through the loading process. This too-long 223 (fifth from left) generated massive pressure because it trapped the bullet.

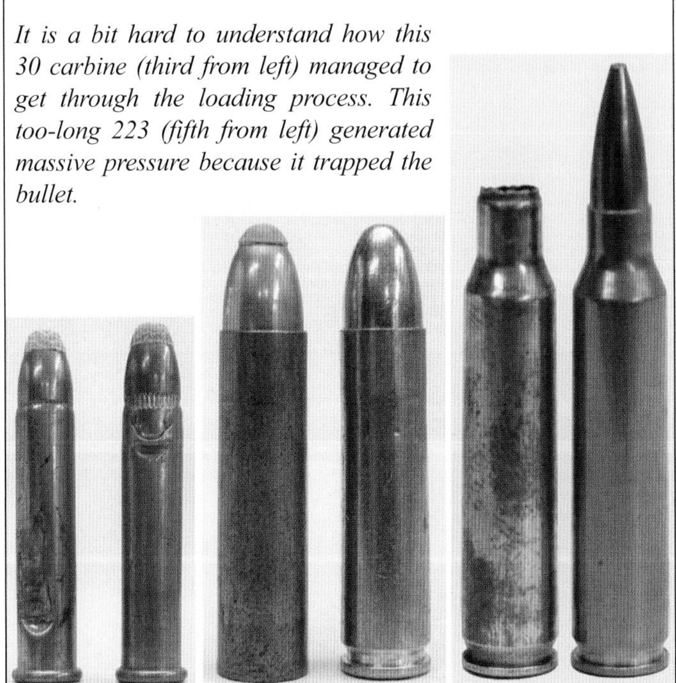

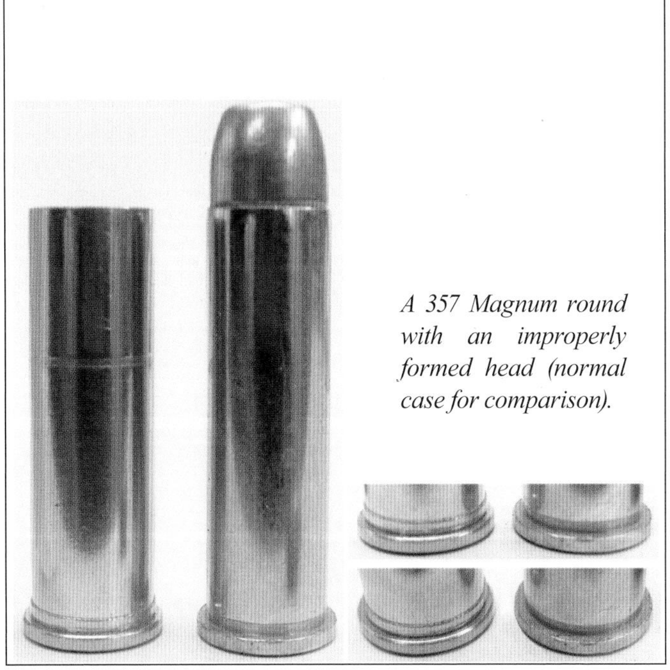

A 357 Magnum round with an improperly formed head (normal case for comparison).

WHILE RARE, FAULTY PRIMERS DO EXIST:

A manufacturer shipped this highly corroded primer along with perfectly normal primers (example at right).

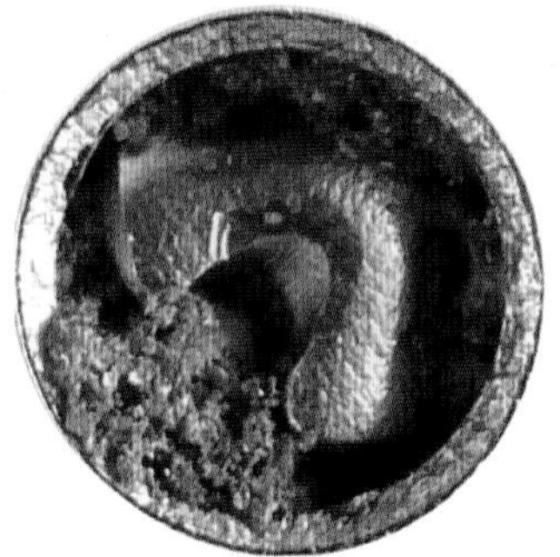
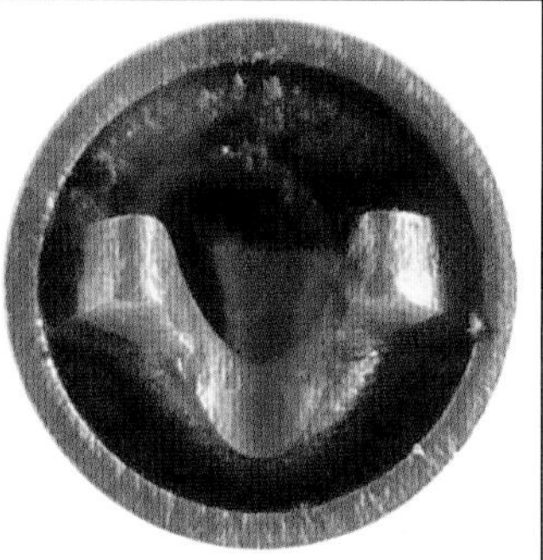

Above: Sideways anvils. It is unlikely that these primers would function. Primers with the anvil inserted backward also occur, and those can function (see picture of 45 Auto case in this section).

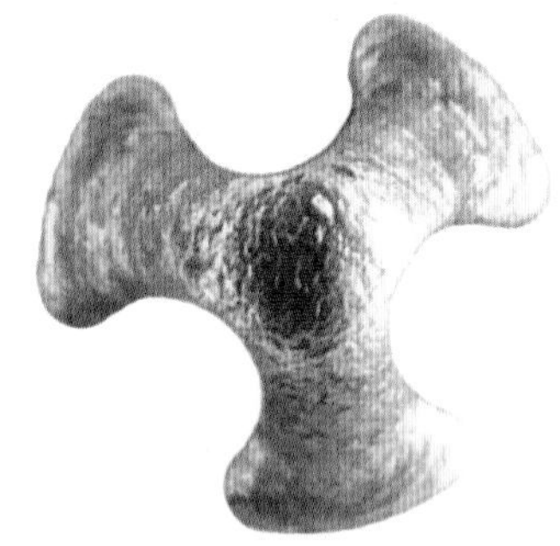
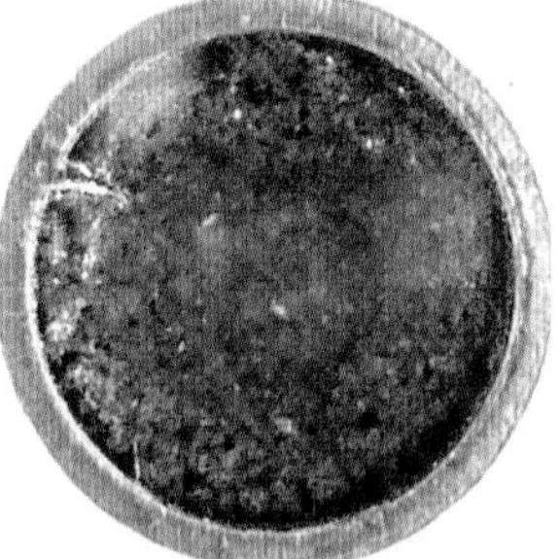
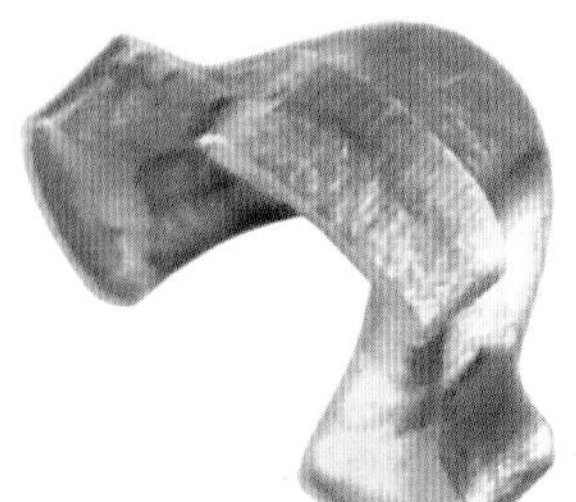
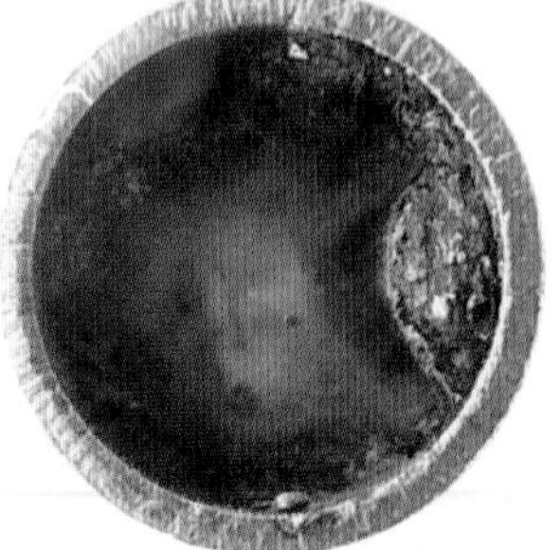

Above: Anvils do occasionally fall out of primers. Again, a very rare thing, but these examples, which shipped with other (perfectly normal) primers, prove that this does happen.

These primers with two anvils represent one-in-one-million events. If you look at enough primers, you will find one.

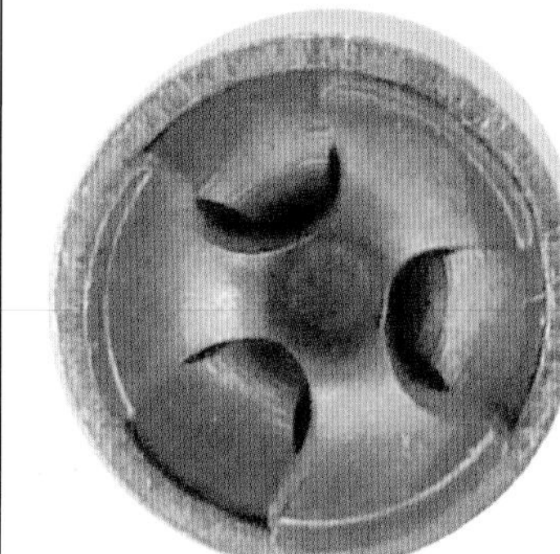

Below are views of a deformed and damaged cup. This primer would likely seat and function normally, but it is unlikely that it would properly seal the primer pocket.

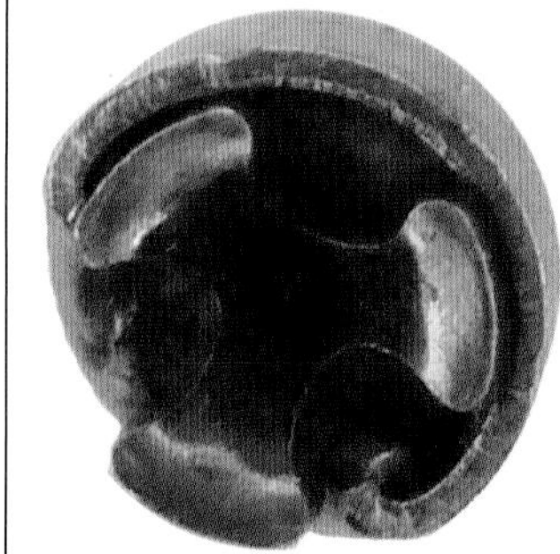
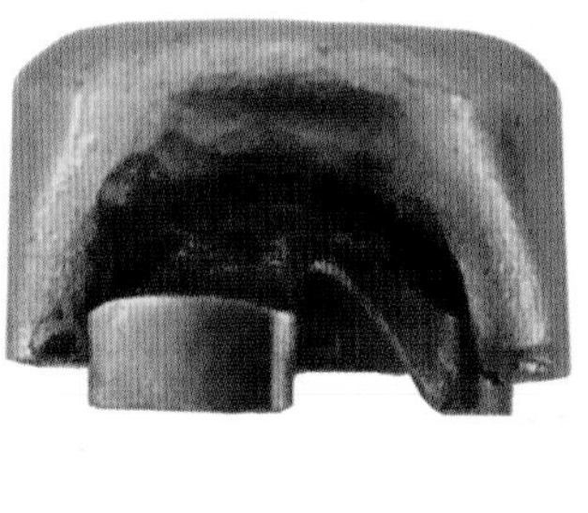

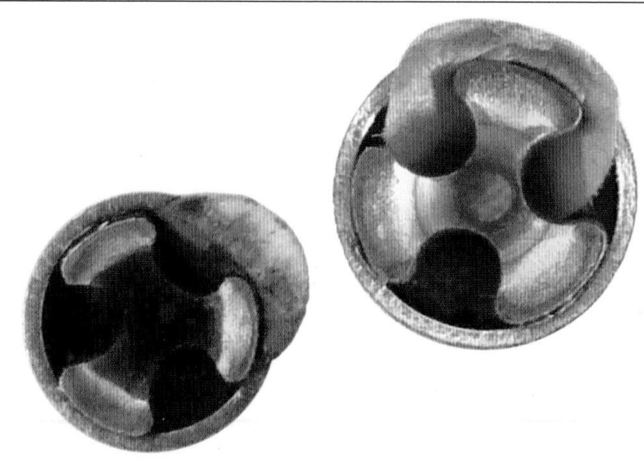

Another rare event is an out-of-place foil. While these examples would likely jam an automatic priming mechanism, both would likely function normally.

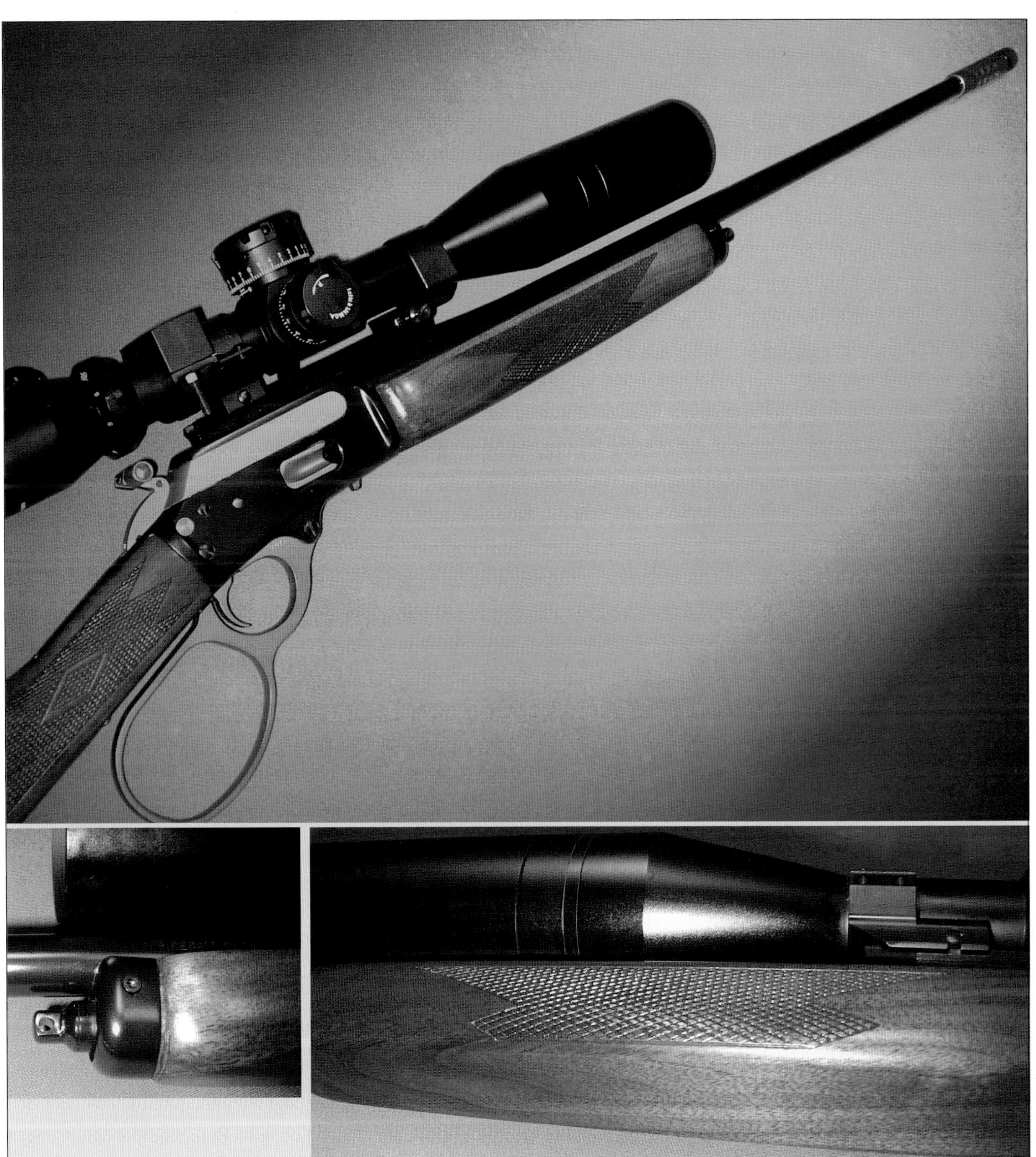

I built this 1894 Marlin chambered for the 17/23 SMc (improved 17 Fireball) for Tom Knight. This rifle includes various custom touches, including a Krieger barrel, a LAW muzzle brake, a magazine cap with built-in sling stud, and a flat-bottomed forearm. This lever-action gun is impressively accurate.

Barrel marking, as per Knight's request. This is one of two custom Marlins that Knight owns.

This rifle features many special design modifications, such as the special magazine follower represented here (which makes it perfectly safe to use with sharp-pointed bullets). Other modifications such as through-bolt buttstock attachment, special stock bedding, and lapping of locking lug engagement improve the accuracy potential. But most of the modifications were necessary to allow the gun to work safely with this high-pressure, high-performance varmint cartridge.

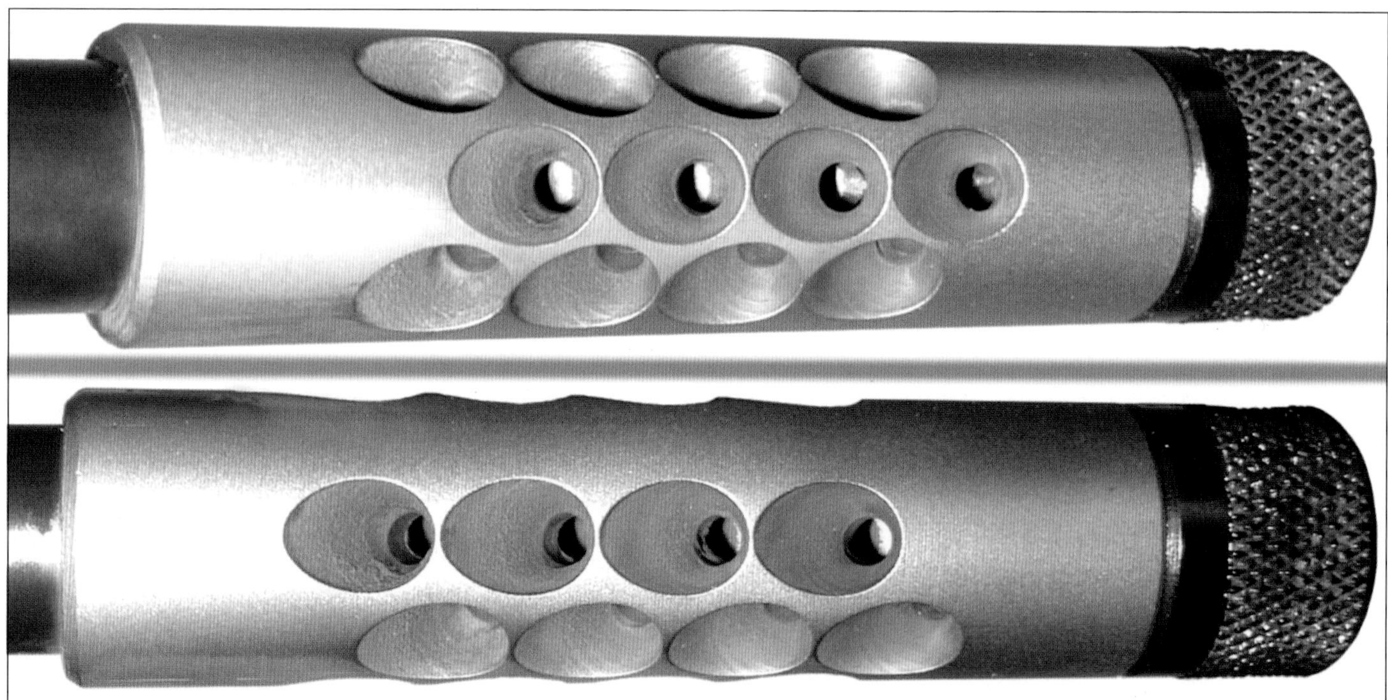

This custom LAW (Lightweight Air Working) muzzle brake has ports along the sides only so that when using the gun in a prone position the muzzle blast will not generate a significant dust signature. The special tapered port design reduces the noise so effectively that, amazing as this might seem to those who have experienced the added noise generated by poorly designed muzzle brakes, adding the LAW brake to the gun does not sensibly increase the muzzle blast. In testing on various guns, both the shooter and bystanders report that they cannot tell whether the gun is louder with or without the LAW brake installed. The ports are angled backward at 30 degrees so that the gas venting pulls the gun forward—in this application, recoil is reduced from about 1½ foot-pounds to essentially zero. This makes it possible to see the bullet hit the paper (or other target) because the recoil does not move the gun enough to matter—for varminting and target shooting, no such thing as "too little recoil" exists!

Knight has a very fine location to store his reloading supplies and to do his reloading. As he progresses further into this hobby, he likely will find the need for more storage space. (I sure did.)

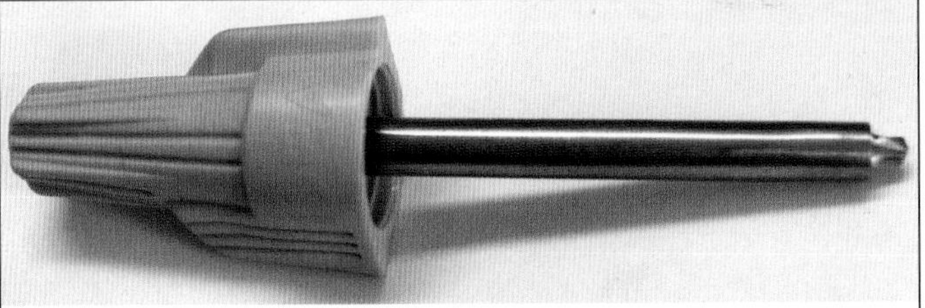

Knight uses this K&M flash hole uniforming tool to improve his 17/23 SM^{c} cases.

As do all cartridges that fall under the design parameters of Superior Ballistics patents, the 17/23 SM^{c} gives significantly better performance than do traditional case designs. While the usable capacity is significantly less than the usable capacity of the 17 Remington, the performance is essentially identical.

Knight uses the excellent K&M primer seater. His next case improvement steps will be to make the primer pockets uniform (using a K&M tool) and to make case necks uniform (using a K&M outside neck turning tool with the dreaded doughnut removing pilot). These steps are bound to improve the accuracy potential of his handloads. But, for a novice, as the pictures on the following page show, Knight is already doing quite well!

Knight, a novice handloader, has purchased this Lee Turret press (on my recommendation). I made this custom 17/23 SM^C die set to create cartridges that are a very close fit in the tight-neck chamber. This set includes a full-length die with a Redding Competition shellholder matched to the gun chamber so that properly resized cases fit freely and do not stretch significantly when fired; a collet neck sizing die; and, an RCBS Gold Medal seating die with the needed shellholder complete the set. (The Gold Medal is the premier die for seating small bullets.)

Knight is learning how to load benchrest-quality ammunition. Here he is charging the cases using the swirl-charge technique that significantly improves shot-to-shot ballistic uniformity.

While this load was entirely too hot for a gun lacking any camming force to extract a sticky case, a somewhat lighter charge launches the 20-grain V-Max in excess of 4,500 fps without any extraction difficulty and without overstressing the gun or the cases. So far, during much testing, the only problem Knight has encountered is that after many reloading and firing cycles, the case necks start cracking. (Annealing will solve this.)

Knight at his new shooting bench (located on his business property—how convenient). He is in the process of testing loads for his custom 1894 Marlin chambered in 17/23 SM^{C}. He is also in the process of gathering ballistic data. And, he is learning how to shoot a gun from the bench. As the associated pictures suggest, Knight is a quick study. (Bench testing any gun with a two-piece stock requires much more care and skillful manipulation than does testing a traditional bolt-action rifle.)

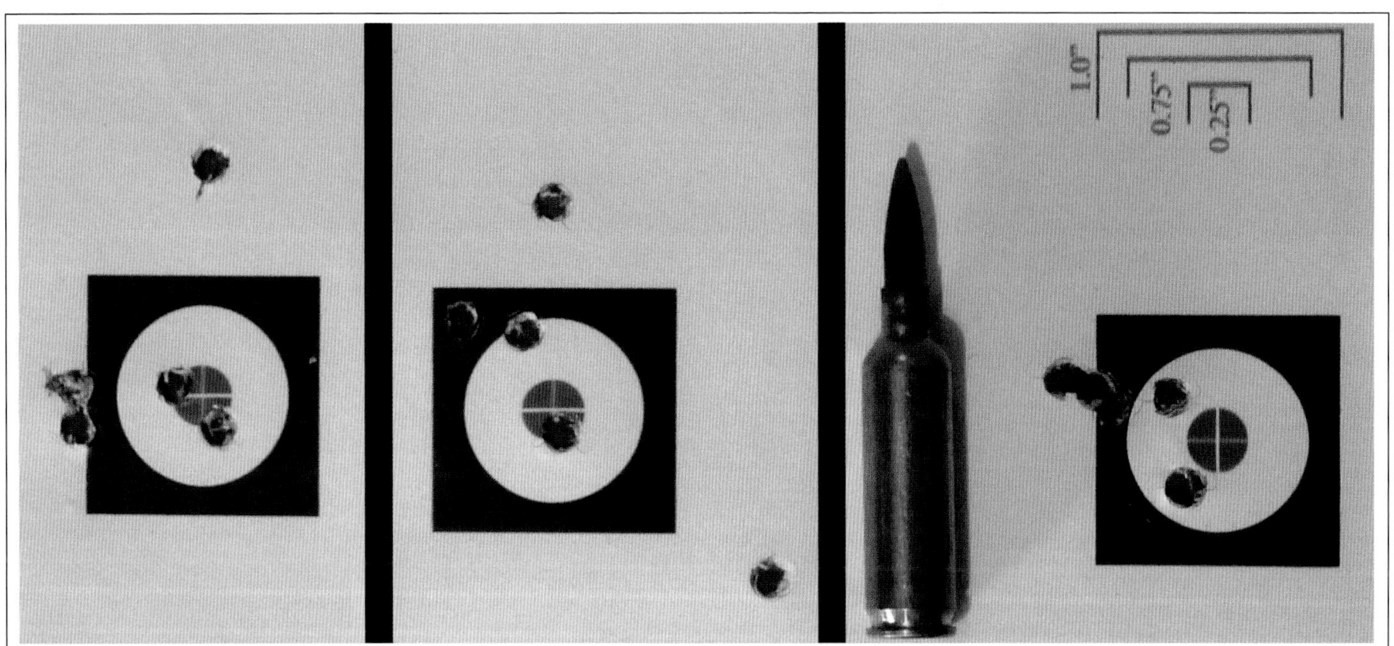

At my suggestion, Knight tested a specific load with all other factors held constant while changing the seating depth (overall length). This particular load showed an extreme sensitivity to bullet-to-rifling jump, as demonstrated here. Left to right are a 20/1000-, 15/1000-, and 10/1000-inch jump. Further testing verified that at a 10/1000-inch jump the load consistently shoots near ½-MOA groups.

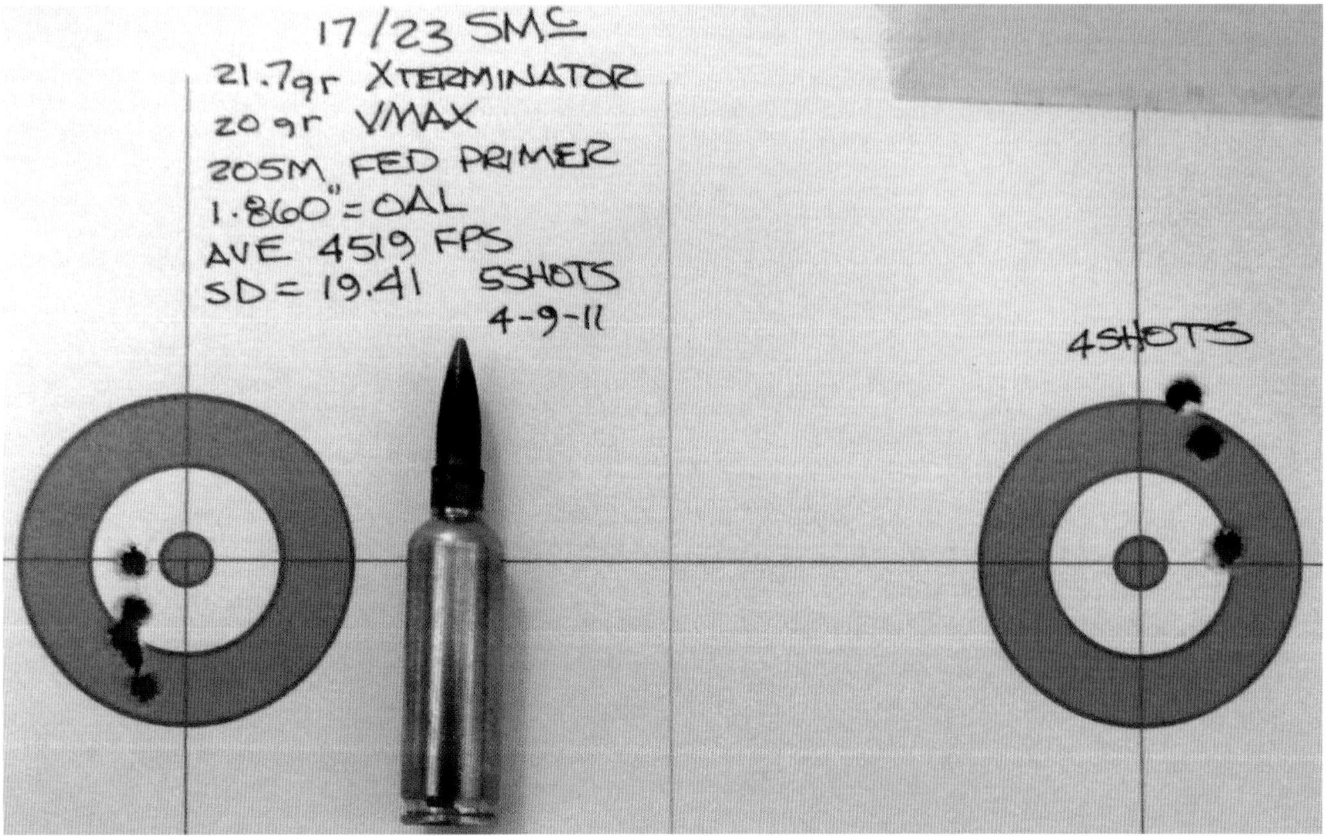

This load demonstrates similar vertical stringing with almost zero horizontal spread every time Knight tests it. While this is not the most accurate load tested, it is still rather impressive. More importantly, such stringing is harmless in a varminting load used against standing targets.

These life-size groups do a better job of indicating actual group size. The group at the right shows five shots with the 20-grain V-Max at 4,350 fps—now if Knight can only figure out how to keep the last two with the first three! The group at the left is from early testing with the 25-grain V-Max at 4,000 fps. (Knight has learned a lot more about loading and shooting target ammo, so we expect that when he revisits this load we will see smaller groups.) Note the larger hole in the scrap aluminum backing plate (an earlier shot from Knight's custom 45-70).

Knight has equipped this rifle for hunting varmints and predators at night. The battery pack has sufficient charge to run the light long enough for many hours of use. With the modest recoil generated by this gun, damage to scope, mount, or device is not a concern.

Top: Testing the 17 Hornet chambered Savage M-25. The single factory load launched the 20-grain V-Max at a consistent 3,675 fps from this 22-inch barrel with sufficient accuracy for any varminting with shots to about 200 yards. Inset: The first handload I tested with the 25-grain V-Max produced startling 100-yard accuracy, and, yes, the wind did gust as the trigger broke for the fourth shot and that did open this group, if only slightly.

Gunsmith Robin Martin holds the remains of a 7mm Remington Magnum chambered Savage that a careless shooter fired in an effort to clear out the mud that he had jammed into the barrel. Not surprisingly, firing both cleared that barrel plug and made some interesting modifications to the gun. When the barrel gave, it fractured with sufficient violence to split rearward to the chamber and it swelled enough to the rear end to deform the receiver ring.

Here I am at the Friends of Billy Dixon Range pointing to my winning hit. After zeroing the rifles, we took turns until someone hit steel. Shooting in the iron-sight, blackpowder equivalent class, I connected on my second shot for record. In the scoped-rifle class, By Smalley and the late Jim Ricord were using Smalley's rolling block 45-70 and his smokeless loads with his transonic bullet. Both made first-shot hits to become the first recipients of the Billy Dixon commemorative medals.

Far left: Testing various 35 Remington factory loads and handloads in an unusually fine Marlin 336. Top left: After publication of an article reporting my experiences with this rifle, Mr. Dikovic began to send me pictures of groups that he had fired using handloads in his similar Marlin. The three targets reproduced here represent only a few of the many similar 100-yard groups that Dikovic's handloads have produced.

Top left: Testing a custom 788 Remington chambered in 221 Fireball that I built for Jim Williamson. I designed the reamer to cut what I believe to be the ideal chamber for a varmint rifle. I used an almost new Savage 22-250 barrel by setting it back, threading, and rechambering it. Bottom left: Obviously, the reamer worked. These 100-yard groups with handloads (left and right) and the factory load (center) prove that this gun is a serious shooter. Right: Williamson warming up the barrel on his new custom rifle while varmint hunting in Wyoming.

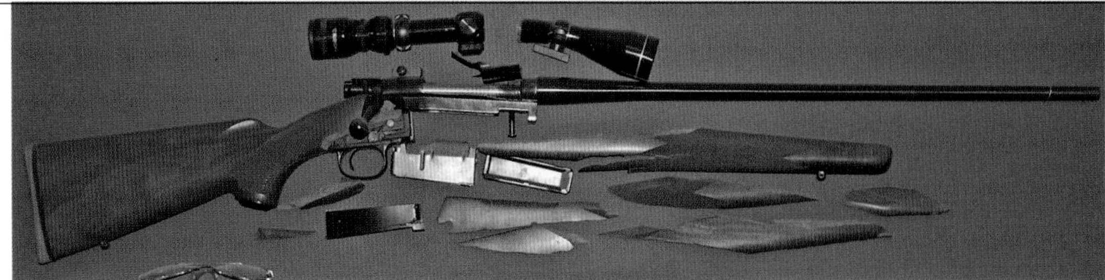

An M-70 Winchester destroyed by incautious handloading. As noted in the text, the use of the wrong propellant is akin to a coin toss. If the propellant that you actually use happens to burn significantly faster than the propellant that you intended to use (and for which the data had been developed), something similar to this is the likely result. Amazingly, when this gun failed—in response to a load that generated twice the standard working pressure—the shooter was not permanently injured. A piece of the receiver ring hit his safety glasses with sufficient energy and velocity to break one of the polycarbonate lenses. One shudders to think what might have happened had he not donned those.

Dave Torkelson, designer of the various targets at the Friends of Billy Dixon Range, at left, with our friends Deb and Bill Falin. As the target behind Torkelson shows, we had been hammering steel from the shooting line, 1,538 yards distant. Handloads are required for this type of target shooting using Sharps and related single-shot rifles. (June 2007)

Chris Keller (left) and Bill Tharp (right) exterminating vermin: Tharp cleared out targets to about 150 yards using his 17 HMR Savage, and then changed to a 5/35 SM^{C}. Keller was a novice who found that the 223 Remington handloads that he and Jim Williamson had created for this 700 Remington were completely adequate. The day after I took this picture, Keller was making hits on Richardson ground squirrels located well beyond 250 yards. (Spring 2012)

Martin Wanninger is testing handloads in the 17 Hornet chambered Savage M-25. We were doing a primer comparison study. We proved, among other things, that the Fed-100 is simply not up to the task of igniting Alliant 300-MP. In otherwise identical loads, where the Fed-200 had produced standard deviations of about 25 fps and far better than MOA accuracy at 100 yards, the Fed-100 gave the highest standard deviations I remember seeing with any handload and similarly dismal accuracy. Most tested combinations of charge and seating depth produced patterns rather than groups! Wanninger had the patience from long practice; consequently, the dismal results did not discourage him from giving each load combination a fair test. Because of his patience, we had an enjoyable day. Not every trip to the range can produce gold-medal groups, but almost every trip to the range can produce a red-letter day!

Top: Barry Taplin had this custom rifle built to use the 17/23 SM^{C} (an improved version of the 17 Fireball featuring the superior case design common to all SM^{C} cartridges). Bottom: The results of Taplin's load development testing suggest that this rifle has all the accuracy that he could ever need for varmint hunting. Subsequently, using about 20.5 grains of X-Terminator to launch the 25-grain Nosler Varmageddon at 4,000 fps, Taplin took many vermin at distances beyond 500 yards. In one string when the wind had entirely died away, Taplin made three solid hits, consecutively, on targets about 515 yards away. He did note that hits beyond about 350 yards did not produce spectacular results on larger prairie rats, which is not exactly surprising. In my opinion, except on the smallest of vermin, the 17s are not the best choice for shots beyond 350 yards.

Left: Here I was testing various 22 Hornet factory loads and a few handloads in the Savage M-25. Right: As it had been in two other Hornet rifles, a handload that combined the 30-grain Barnes Varmint Grenade, a full case of Lil'Gun, the Fed-100 primer, and Remington cases was a winner. In the varminting field, no factory load comes close to matching the performance of this bullet launched at 3,500 fps.

Left: Testing a custom Martini Cadet chambered for a 17-caliber wildcat based on a necked-down 357 magnum case. This gun was only partially finished but I needed to see if it would shoot. Right: This 100-yard test group was created while fireforming necked-down 22 Remington Jet cases. This load used the 20-grain Hornady V-Max ahead of 10 grains of H4227 and the Fed-100 primer. This load does a good job of fireforming the cases and launches this bullet at 3,500 fps, so it is certainly a useful varminting combination.

Earl Moore honored me by allowing me to shoot his 6mm Lee Navy rifle while I was testing the Krono-Beam II, Oehler 35P accessory system. I shot a few of the Buffalo Arms factory loads and handloads using the obsolete 105-grain Speer RN bullet. Winchester made this rifle the year my paternal grandfather was born. With handloads using cases from Buffalo Arms, Moore can now shoot this rare rifle affordably, which affords him the opportunity to enjoy a special bit of nostalgia. (2012)

As noted by my late friend Roger Johnston, the sum total of the accuracy equation depends upon the gun, sights, conditions, shooter, and ammunition. No matter how good the other components of this equation are, intrinsic accuracy potential of the gun will limit accuracy. For this reason, many serious shooters eventually own a custom rifle. When building such a gun, your gunsmith cannot go wrong with Manson tools, which are made to the highest level of precision, just as your best handloads are.

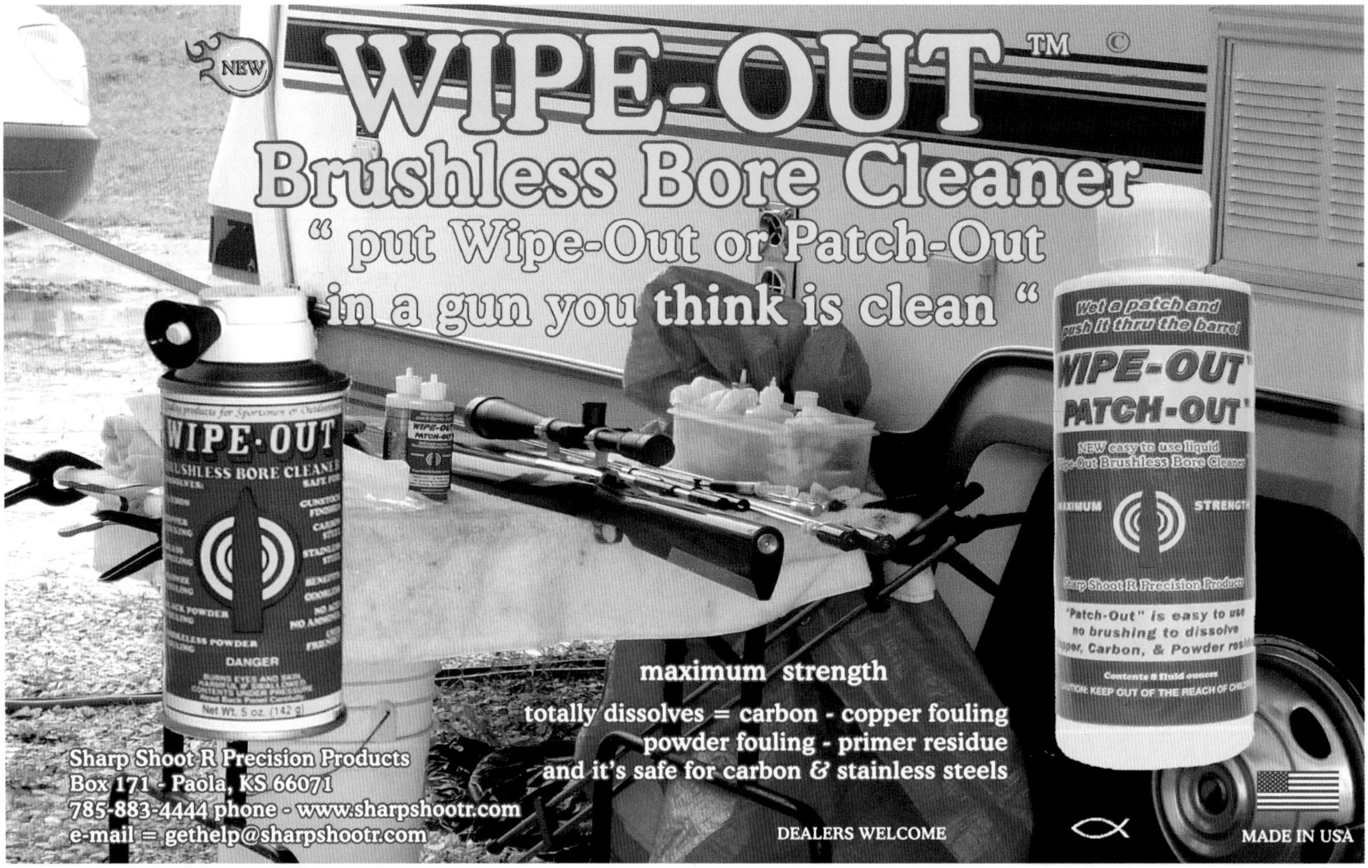
NEW
WIPE-OUT™ ©
Brushless Bore Cleaner
" put Wipe-Out or Patch-Out
in a gun you think is clean "
WIPE-OUT
WIPE-OUT
PATCH-OUT
maximum strength
totally dissolves = carbon - copper fouling
powder fouling - primer residue
and it's safe for carbon & stainless steels
Sharp Shoot R Precision Products
Box 171 - Paola, KS 66071
785-883-4444 phone - www.sharpshootr.com
e-mail = gethelp@sharpshootr.com
DEALERS WELCOME
MADE IN USA

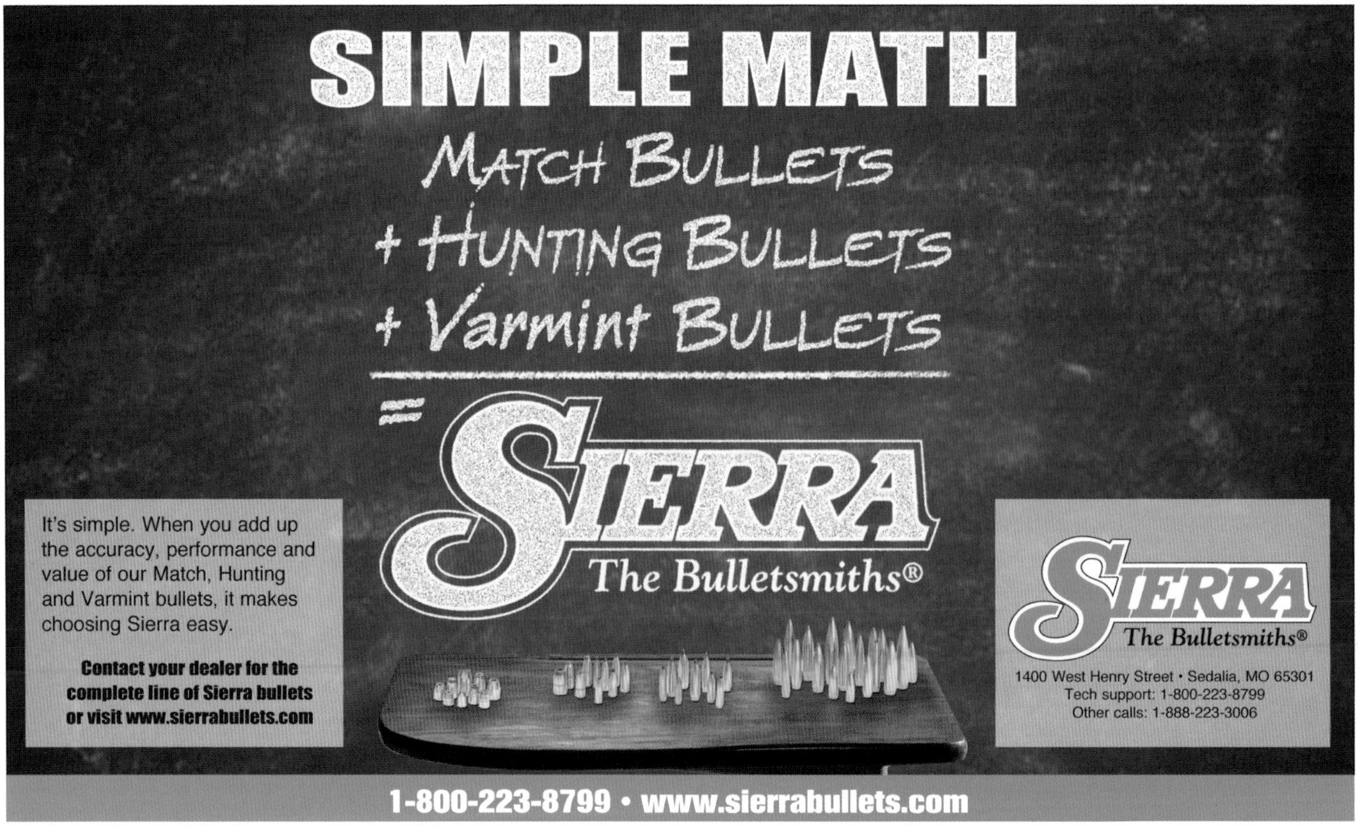
SIMPLE MATH
Match Bullets
+ Hunting Bullets
+ Varmint Bullets
= SIERRA
The Bulletsmiths®
It's simple. When you add up the accuracy, performance and value of our Match, Hunting and Varmint bullets, it makes choosing Sierra easy.
Contact your dealer for the complete line of Sierra bullets or visit www.sierrabullets.com
SIERRA
The Bulletsmiths®
1400 West Henry Street • Sedalia, MO 65301
Tech support: 1-800-223-8799
Other calls: 1-888-223-3006
1-800-223-8799 • www.sierrabullets.com

Precision tools facilitate precision handloading: K&M offers a wide selection.

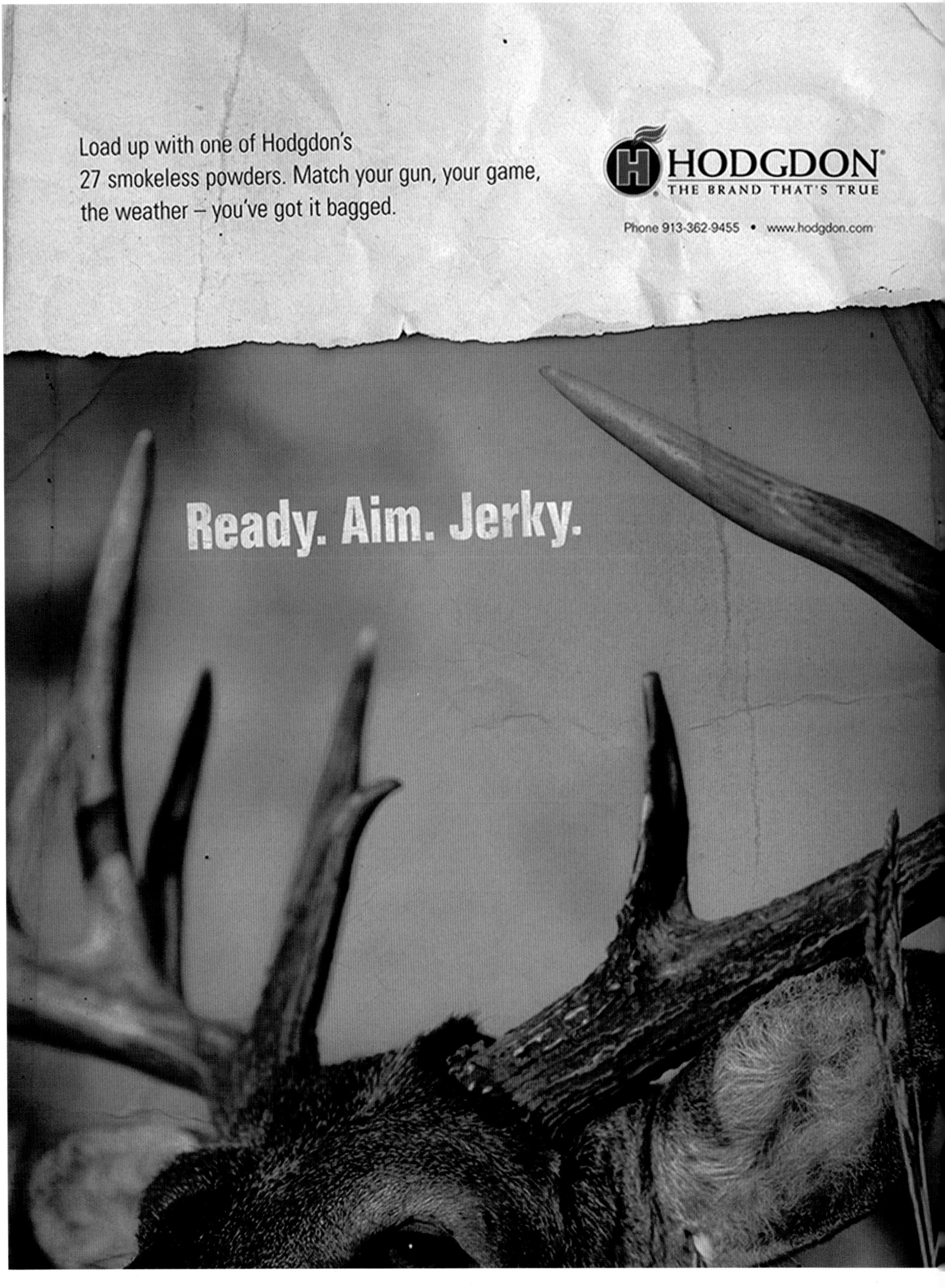
Load up with one of Hodgdon's
27 smokeless powders. Match your gun, your game,
the weather – you've got it bagged.
HODGDON
THE BRAND THAT'S TRUE
Phone 913-362-9455 • www.hodgdon.com
Ready. Aim. Jerky.

BULLETS

CHAPTER 10

INTRODUCTION

While many types of bullets are in common use, all share the same basic functions. First, all bullets (or an encompassing sabot) must seal the bore against chamber pressure. Second, to provide accuracy, bullets must be balanced and aerodynamically stable. Some designs are stable only for a limited time of flight and to a limited distance, and many designs lose accuracy while slowing through the transonic range, if that transition happens at extended distance. Third, to maintain accuracy, bullets must be strong enough to withstand the accelerating forces that engender muzzle velocity and rotation without undergoing significant asymmetric deformation. Finally, upon impact, bullets must perform appropriately.

To-scale representation of Speer SBT bullets: Left, 270, 150-grain and right, 7mm, 165-grain. Without measuring or weighing, these are difficult to distinguish. Many other visually similar pairs exist.

What happens to a bullet in the barrel is one aspect of the science that ballisticians commonly refer to as internal ballistics (for lack of a better term). While this is a misnomer, it is the only descriptive term available. External ballistics is the study of bullet performance between the instant the bullet leaves the barrel and the instant it reaches the target.

As to external ballistics, I will note here that bullets given a higher muzzle velocity and that have a higher ballistic coefficient (BC = aerodynamic efficiency) will shoot flatter, retain more energy at any given distance, and will deflect less in a cross wind (generally).

Terminal ballistics, another misnomer, is loosely the study of what happens to a bullet after it reaches the target. I will cover various aspects of terminal performance under "Terminal Ballistics—Testing Bullet Performance" in this chapter.

BULLETS—SAFETY

It is tempting to suspect that this section is unnecessary. However, despite mention elsewhere in this text, several things concerning bullets and safe handloading practices deserve reiteration. Foremost, always make sure that the bullet you are loading into a case is the bullet you intend to use.

As an example: Should you be so unlucky as to have a 270 Weatherby Magnum bullet seating die with a particularly loose neck section, and then find yourself accidentally loading a 7mm bullet into a 270 Weatherby Magnum case, you might not notice the increase in bullet seating resistance—new cases can have unusually soft necks. Such a combination could allow an oversize bullet to seat without undue resistance. Although things might seem normal, you could be creating the ingredients necessary to trigger an explosion.

Usually, such a cartridge would not properly chamber in a 270 Weatherby Magnum rifle. However, the unfortunate combination of a thin case neck and a loose chamber-throat could allow almost normal chambering of such a bastardized cartridge.

Chambering of such a round, if possible, is likely to squeeze the case neck sufficiently to trap the bullet. This will retard bullet acceleration when the round fires. This will result in skyrocketing pressure, perhaps to a gun-destroying level. Unfortunately, this exact scenario has happened. Other, similar-diameter pairs exist. All are more-or-less dangerous in this regard.

A concern that is more general in nature: Bullets are not interchangeable. Should you happen to think that all similarly designed, equal-weight bullets of any given diameter will generate similar pressure when used in any given load, you are very wrong.

Please study the load data in any modern manual and consider the ramifications of the data presented in the table on page 225. This table represents the results of a test that Bill Falin and I did at the Accurate Arms ballistic laboratory (Falin was then the chief ballistician at Accurate).

We compared thirteen commonly available 150-grain 0.277-inch bullets in a standard 270 Winchester load by firing those rounds in a 270 Winchester chambered pressure barrel. With otherwise identical loads, using cases that I had prepared to benchrest standards of uniformity, average pressure of the resulting loads varied from 54,700 psi to 72,400 psi, a difference of 32.4 percent! This approximates the difference separating standard factory cartridges and proof-load cartridges.

A small portion of the measured pressure variation resulted from differences in usable case capacity due to variations in bullet length. However, other differences, such as variations in bullet hardness, can exert a far more significant influence. For example, compare the nearly identical Speer Hot-Cor Spitzer to the Speer BT bullet—in this pair, core material, jacket material, and usable capacity are identical, but the Hot-Cor generated 12 percent greater peak pressure, a phenomenal difference.

Almost certainly, the annealing of the jacket and core that occurs as these bullets are heated accounts for this difference. This makes sense if we consider that the Hot-Cor bullet has less internal strength—it obturates (swells) more easily. Therefore, it generates more friction as it passes through the bore. Friction retards acceleration; greater friction retards acceleration more. Therefore, because it accelerates more slowly during the interval of propellant combustion that occurs before chamber pressure peaks, that peak reaches higher pressure. The bullet will not be as far down the bore (smaller boiler room) and more of the charge will have burned at the instant of peak pressure—more and hotter gas occupying less volume necessarily generates greater pressure.

Generally, if a specific load calls for a specific bullet, you cannot substitute any other bullet. Some data producers, such as Hodgdon, have attempted to handle this problem by choosing to do their testing with the bullet that evidently created the highest pressure among standard bullets of that weight and caliber. That fact explains the lack of bullet-specific requirements in some older data, all of which are now dangerously obsolete.

As producers of various handloading manuals have gained sophistication, this questionable practice has fallen into disfavor. Generally, you cannot be certain that the bullet chosen in developing such generic data was the one that will always develop the greatest pressure. It is entirely possible (in fact inevitable) that some (new) bullet will generate unsafe pressures when loaded using such data. Whenever it is feasible to do so, use only modern, bullet-specific data.

Never, for any reason, seat any Winchester Fail-Safe, Barnes X-Bullet, or any homogenous solid copper or copper alloy bullet so that bullet-to-rifling jump is less than 0.050 inch. Doing so can raise pressures drastically—such bullets require a running start to properly engrave into the rifling and to enter the bore smoothly.

Never use any homogenous copper or copper alloy bullet in any rifle with an unusually light barrel contour. Such barrels cannot withstand the down-barrel, obturation stress generated by such bullets. All conventional bullets obturate in response to maximum acceleration force. When a very tough bullet passes into the thin portion of the barrel, the bullet can stretch the bore (sometimes to the bursting point), rather than the bore swaging it smaller (to safely fit). This is particularly an issue with double-barrel rifles.

Manufacturers occasionally offer new bullets. Unless the manufacturer specifically states that it is safe to do so, do not use any preexisting data for handloading any new bullet. The only safe approach is to ask the manufacturer for load recommendations.

BULLETS—COMPOSITION, CONSTRUCTION, AND CHARACTERISTICS GENERAL CONSIDERATIONS

Bullets available to and used by handloaders are most often constructed of alloys of copper (gilding metal or brass) and lead (bullet metal). Most bullets are either

Comparison Study: Bullet Type versus Pressure and Velocity

Bullet versus Pressure: 270 Winchester, Accurate Arms Ballistics Laboratory

Bullet		Pressure			Velocity			Pressure	Velocity
Weight grains	Make and Style	Peak Pressure psi	Spread	Std. Dev.	fps	Spread	Std. Dev.	Difference from Lowest Pressure Load	
150	Barnes-X	72,400	8,900	3,000	2898	103	31	32.4%	1.5%
150	Speer Hot-Cor Sp	69,500	2,400	1,200	2917	47	14	27.1%	2.2%
150	Nosler BT	69,000	4,000	1,300	2923	35	10	26.1%	2.4%
150	**Speer GS**	**66,900**	**2,800**	**900**	**2930**	**34**	**11**	**22.3%**	**2.7%**
150	Hornady SP	66,200	3,700	1,200	2907	30	10	21.0%	1.9%
150	Sierra SBT	63,300	2,500	900	2887	76	21	15.7%	1.2%
150	Nosler Partition	62,600	1,600	600	2866	22	7	14.4%	0.4%
150	Speer BT	61,900	2,200	600	2907	20	6	13.2%	1.9%
150	Hornady RN	61,600	3,400	1,000	2866	29	8	12.6%	0.4%
150	**Sierra RN**	**57,600**	**2,900**	**1,300**	**2823**	**43**	**14**	**5.3%**	**-1.1%**
150	Barnes Solid	54,700	3,100	900	2854	38	13	0.0%	0.0%
140	Win. Fail-Safe	61,500	4,200	1,500	2927	52	17	12.4%	2.6%
160	Nosler Partition	63,100	3,100	900	2831	29	8	15.4%	-0.8%

Load details for this study: New 184-grain Frontier cases fully prepped via flash hole, primer pocket, case length, and case neck preparation using K&M and RCBS tools; CCI-BR2 primers seated precisely with K&M priming tool, to achieve 0.003-inch pellet preload; charge: 53.0 grains (plus or minus two granules). Accurate 4350; charges installed into cases using a consistent swirl-charging technique; and, all bullet types seated with RCBS Competition seating die at 3.25-inch overall length. Test gun: Universal receiver fitted with conformal transducer. Each test represents ten shots for record with each bullet; barrel cleaned before each string; fouling and warming shots fired before each string; and, barrel cooled to room temperature between strings.

Highlighted in bold font are bullets producing highest and lowest velocity; highlighted in italic font are exotic and non-150-grain bullets.

homogenous (composed entirely of one alloy), or have a thin copper-alloy jacket partially or totally enclosing a core made of bullet metal.

Two basic types of homogenous solid bullets are in relatively common use. The most common are lead-alloy bullets. The most prevalent type is a bullet simply cast or swaged from either pure lead or from an alloy composed chiefly of lead, antimony, and perhaps tin. Shooters have been using cast bullets for hundreds of years. Occasionally, manufacturers have also lathe-turned lead-alloy bullets. Less common are copper or copper-alloy bullets. Manufacturers swage, hammer-forge, or lathe-turn such bullets.

Most homogenous, hard lead-alloy, and hard copper-alloy bullets are of nonexpanding designs. Conversely, sophisticated design features allow the Barnes X and similar copper bullets to provide dependable, controlled expansion. Similarly, upon impact, hollowpoint bullets made from soft lead-alloy can expand. Bullets cast of common wheel-weight alloy and air cooled can expand to a useful degree. This will occur when impact velocity is between about 1,600 fps (minimum dependable expansion speed) and about 2,200 fps (maximum speed with dependable accuracy and without likely disintegration). This varies significantly, due to wide variations in bullet design, wheel-weight alloy, and casting techniques (melt, mold temperature, cooling rate, etc.).

Joe McPherson, my son, with his first elk. This 6x6-bull field dressed at 520 pounds. Proper placement of an appropriate 7mm Remington Magnum bullet did the job. (Joe's next two bulls were also 6x6s; more than a decade later, after more than 40 years of elk hunting, I finally got my first 6x6.)

Nonexpanding copper-alloy bullets and those with a tungsten carbide core are sufficiently tough to withstand impact dependably with almost any bone on any animal without deforming or fracturing. These bullets are also so tough as to be decidedly unsafe for use in thin-barrel rifles, such as British doubles. Firing such a bullet through the bore of such a rifle is almost certain to burst the barrel. DO NOT DO IT!

Various manufacturers offer expanding hunting bullets that are functionally made of pure copper. These include the Winchester Fail-Safe (FS), Barnes X-Bullet, Nosler TIP, and at least one European brand. These manufacturers design these bullets to provide controlled expansion. (The Winchester FS has a complicated base cavity containing steel, lead, and brass inserts, but none of these components directly influences terminal performance; Barnes has offered a similar bullet with a denser base core insert, and Nosler offers a bullet with a plastic nose insert.) Across a wide range of impact velocities, such bullets can deliver a unique combination of dependable expansion, essentially 100 percent weight retention, and deep penetration. Such performance suggests superior potential for use in big-game hunting.

Manufacturers include both design features and fabrication steps to control expansion characteristics of these bullets. A hollow cavity extends deeply into the bullet ogive. Four or more longitudinal cuts that almost reach the perimeter of the bullet radiate from this cavity. Upon impact, sections formed by these cuts begin to open, by folding outward. As each section (petal) bends, it tears the thin layer joining it to the petals on each side. Annealing of the nearly pure copper alloy used in these bullets maximizes malleability and, thereby, minimizes fragmentation potential. As with high-alloy copper solids, never use these bullets in any unusually thinly barreled gun such as a double rifle.

Cast bullets are widely available commercially from regional producers. With proper casting equipment, handloaders can easily produce cast bullets at home. This latter approach offers an essentially limitless variety of designs, using both ready-made and custom bullet molds. Affordability is the biggest advantage of cast bullets, but in many applications these are also among the most accurate of bullets.

Swaged-lead bullets are usually made of pure lead or of low-alloy bullet metal. Several regional and national bulletmakers offer swaged bullets, typically in target-pistol and blackpowder-rifle designs. With proper equipment and supplies, handloaders can swage both lead-alloy and jacketed bullets. Potential advantages of swaged bullets include low cost and superior accuracy.

Jacketed bullets also come in several varieties. Designs include nonexpanding, expansion controlling, and fragmenting bullets. Typical bullet jackets are a few hundredths of an inch thick. Producers control jacket thickness and other characteristics, as required, to achieve the desired level of accuracy and terminal-ballistic performance.

Usually, jacket material is gilding metal, an alloy of 95 percent copper and 5 percent zinc. This highly malleable and relatively inexpensive metal limits bullet-to-barrel friction. It also limits metallic bore fouling.

Several bulletmakers use pure copper jackets in high-performance expanding bullets. Compared to gilding metal, copper is more ductile and is, therefore, more resistant to fragmentation. However, copper generates considerably more bullet-to-bore friction and much more metallic bore fouling. Manufacturers also sometimes use different copper alloys, mild steel, or aluminum for bullet jackets.

Nonexpanding jacketed bullets often use a very thick copper-alloy or copper-clad steel jacket. This latter construction allows a strong steel jacket to support a weak lead core without subjecting the bore of the gun to the abrasiveness of a steel jacket.

Nonexpanding jacketed bullets fall into two categories: Those where terminal performance is not a consideration (chiefly for target and plinking use) and those where the bullet must withstand the stresses of impact without suffering significant deformation (chiefly for use against dangerous game). In the former instance, the jacket is usually comparatively thin and of gilding metal. The jacket of these bullets is either closed at the front and open at the back (hunting), or closed at the back and open at the front (target).

We commonly call a bullet with the jacket closed at the front a full-metal jacket (FMJ), despite the jacket opening at the bullet base. When constructed using a thick copper, gilding metal, or copper-clad steel jacket, these FMJ designs are very robust against deformation after impact. Usually, such bullets have a very hard lead-alloy core. Often, producers fold the jacket base to cover the bullet base partially, thereby locking core and jacket together.

Controlled-expansion bullets are typically gilding metal jacketed with an opening in the jacket at the bullet point. Some have an exposed bullet-metal tip and some have a plastic or metal insert in the point (Nosler Ballistic Tip, Hornady V-Max, and similar designs). Exposed lead facilitates expansion through hydraulic deformation. The various inserts resist deformation that might result from the stresses of recoil and mishandling. In some instances, inserts also facilitate expansion. Controlled expansion is a desirable characteristic in most bullets intended for big-game hunting and self-defense. Producers use various jacket features to control the expansion rate and the total degree of expansion.

Fragmenting bullets usually have thin gilding metal jackets, usually with an open jacket tip. These, too, sometimes feature a plastic nose insert (e.g., Nosler Ballistic Tip, Hornady V-Max, and Sierra BlitzKing). Tip inserts facilitate fragmentation at lower impact velocity, compared to conventional lead-tipped or hollowpoint bullets. Because fragmenting bullets essentially eliminate the potential for dangerous ricochets so long as impact velocity is high enough, these are particularly desirable for varmint hunting.

Producers most commonly use lead alloy for the core of bullets because it is affordable, ductile, and dense. Use of this material in bullet manufacture is so common that bullet metal has been the familiar name of this alloy for centuries. Alloy composition ranges are usually 91 percent to 98½ percent lead, 1½ percent to 6 percent antimony (increasing antimony content increases hardness), and up to 3 percent tin (improves bullet castability). Though rarely done owing to expense, adding about 1 percent silver to bullet metal dramatically improves castability—the melt is more fluid. Producers make the cores of most commercial jacketed bullets by swaging sections parted from extruded lead-alloy wire.

Producers can alter terminal bullet performance by adjusting various bullet-core characteristics. Alloy composition influences core hardness and ductility, as do heat treating, hollow pointing, and precutting.

Pure lead is the core material of choice for most high-performance, controlled-expansion bullets. Compared to bullet metal, pure lead is more ductile—it is less apt to fragment. Often such bullets have pure copper jackets. Compared to gilding metal (copper alloy), pure copper is more ductile—it is less apt to fragment. In these bullets, to assure that the relatively tough jacket supports the otherwise too-weak lead core, producers often bond core and jacket. Soldering is a common bonding method.

For example, in its A-Frame bullet, Swift inserts the nose core into a cavity in the front end of the pure copper jacket. It then heats this assembly with a propane flame. This melts the core, which spontaneously solders to the cleaned-and-fluxed jacket. This process also anneals both core and jacket, assuring maximum malleability and, thereby, minimizing fragmentation potential. Norma uses similar materials and techniques to make its fine Oryx bullets.

Nonexpanding, totally jacketed bullets are growing in popularity. Combined with the use of lead-free primers, these can eliminate airborne lead contamination at indoor target ranges. Manufacturers produce these bullets by electroplating a lead core with copper or a copper alloy. Plating is typically about 0.010-inch thick and covers the entire bullet surface.

BULLETS—SHAPE

Manufacturers offer bullets in several basic shapes. We can classify most bullets as either blunt-nosed or sharp-nosed. These include special short-range target designs, long-range target designs, shapes intended to function properly through certain types of guns, and several specific designs that are specialized for hunting and self-defense purposes.

Blunt bullets come in several styles. Made of either pure lead or low-alloy bullet metal, the wadcutter (WC) is a flat-pointed bullet used for short-range handgun target competition and practice. When the sharp edge at the nose of such a bullet hits a typical paper target, it cuts out a bullet-diameter circular paper wad, whence the name. At shorter distances, this creates an easily visible impact hole. Generally, WC bullets are designed for target use and for relatively low velocities, so expansion characteristics are not a design consideration.

The lead alloy semiwadcutter (SWC) is a related blunt bullet style. These are very popular for handgun hunting, target shooting, and target practice. Semiwadcutters combine a sharp, full-diameter shoulder with a truncated-cone nose section. These bullets also produce easily visible impacts on paper targets and

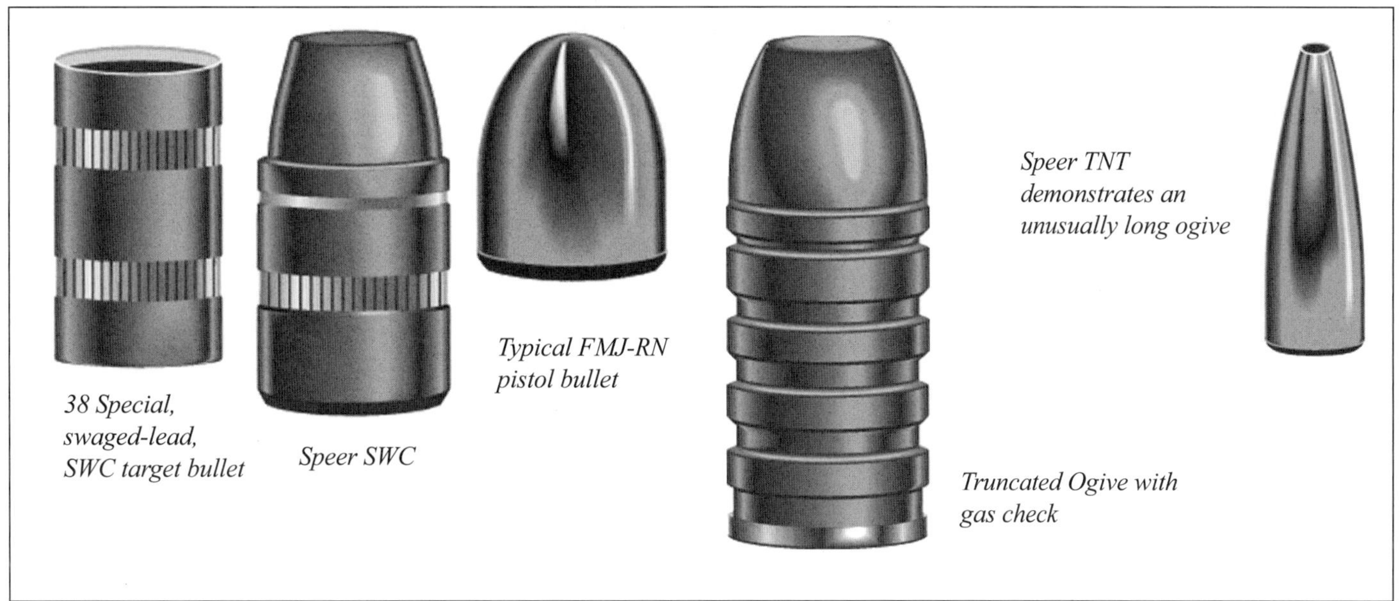

have the advantages of working in semiautomatics and shooting accurately at long distances. Popularized by Elmer Keith, the SWC is a particularly effective bullet design for handgun hunting.

Typically, such cartridges generate comparatively high chamber pressures, and, typically, SWC bullets for use in such applications are cast from a relatively hard alloy (too hard to swage). Ideally, such bullets feature both a gas check and one or more lubricant-filled grooves that are at least twice as deep as the rifling. Usually, producers do not intend lead SWC bullets to expand; however, producers have offered jacketed bullets of similar shape that will expand.

A third type of blunt bullet, which is growing in popularity, includes the truncated cone (TC) and the truncated ogive (TO) flat-point designs. The former is a simple cone with a flat nose. The latter has a spitzer-style ogive and a flat nose. In both instances, the diameter of the meplat is about two-thirds of the diameter of the bullet. The ideal meplat surface area is near one-half of the bullet's cross-sectional area; hence, the meplat diameter should be 0.7 times the bullet's diameter.

Both of these styles are unusually easy to cast and are, therefore, popular with home and commercial bullet casters. These designs are popular for use in both handguns and rifles and can be either cast or jacketed. The relatively large flat nose delivers impressive terminal performance on game.

When used in semiautomatic pistols, TC and TO bullets can match the superior feeding characteristics of round-nosed bullets but with superior terminal performance. The jacketed TC is an ideal choice for a self-defense, semiautomatic pistol that will not function correctly with lead or jacketed hollowpoint bullets. This design is also useful for hunting with a relatively low-powered pistol.

Usually, unlike SWCs, TCs and related designs do not shoot accurately at unusually long distances. Testing has also proven that these designs will not penetrate nearly as far as will otherwise similar SWC bullets.

Particularly for use in semiautomatic pistols, the round-nosed (RN) bullet is common. In these guns, this bullet style can provide superior functioning and dependability. Typical construction is lead, lead alloy (variously RNL or LRN), or lead-core jacketed (FMJ-RN). Usually, producers do not intend lead RN bullets to expand; however, many producers offer similarly shaped jacketed softpoint (JSP) expanding bullets.

Pointed bullets fill a variety of applications. Manufacturers usually design varmint and big-game hunting bullets to combine several features. Important considerations include:

- Dependable expansion
- High retained energy
- Relatively flat trajectory
- Minimum wind drift

Typically, hunting bullets are jacketed designs with a sharp point (spitzer or spire-point) and, often, with a flattened tapered base (boattail). Numerous pointed bullet styles are available.

The spitzer is the most common. The ogive (pointed-nose) of a spitzer follows a tangent radius. This means that the point simply rounds over, beginning at the end of the cylindrical portion (shank) of the bullet. Another popular design is the spire point; in this, the ogive follows a secant radius. This means that the point begins with a sudden onset at the front end of the shank, rather than with the gentle transition of a spitzer design. Both styles often have a pointed exposed-lead tip but are sometimes hollow-pointed, flat-nosed, or include a plastic or metal-nose insert.

Jacquelyn Copeland, with her first bear (her father, Dave, at right, and Paul Palmer). When a well-placed 150-grain bullet from a 7mm-08 hit this 275-pound bear, it dropped, then jumped up, but ran only 50 yards before piling up. The previous year, at age 12, Jacquelyn took a buck deer and a big cow elk (one shot, 253 yards). Jacquelyn was comfortable using a modest chambering to hunt bear because of the prescience of what her dad and grandfather (Loren Anderson) have passed along: A properly placed shot is what does the job; it's a matter of marksmanship, not a bigger gun. I could not agree more.

Increasing the weight of the bullet, reducing the meplat diameter (blunt portion of nose), sharpening the point, and adding a boattail are methods to reduce velocity loss as the bullet passes through the air, which is generally beneficial. The technical term for the measure of ballistic efficiency is ballistic coefficient (BC). This is merely a comparative measure of how much velocity a bullet will lose as it travels through the air to reach a distant target. All else being equal, a bullet with a higher BC will lose less velocity with any given initial velocity. Increasing the BC has several advantages:

- Bullets reach the target sooner (less time of flight)
- Reduces necessary lead on a moving target
- Bullets are traveling faster at target
- Increases delivered energy and momentum

BULLETS—SELECTION

Appropriate potential bullet choices depend very much upon the use for the intended ammunition. Obvious categories include:

- Cowboy Action
- Formal target (competitive)
- Informal target (plinking)
- Varmint hunting
- Big-game hunting
- Small-game hunting
- Dangerous game (either for hunting or protection)
- Self-defense

Each of these categories has unique priorities and is worth considering in some detail. I discuss hunting and self-defense bullets later in this chapter.

BULLETS—COMPETITION

With formal target shooting, as noted in the propellant chapter, accuracy is of ultimate importance. In these games, when considering two otherwise similar bullets, the more accurate is the better choice. However, in long-range events, questions of bullet weight and profile are a different matter; longer, more-streamlined bullets can deliver an advantage, despite a relative deficit in potential accuracy.

If you are contemplating involvement in any competitive target shooting sport, ask your future competitors what components they use. Advice thus solicited will generally be most valuable. Another source of good information is bullet producers. Those companies certainly know what sells. What sells for a given application is what works therein.

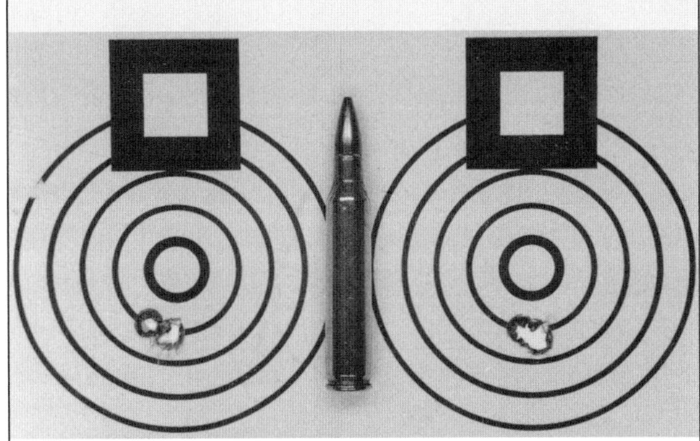

Factory, Remington 223 chambered rifle, first ten shots fired—no break-in. Range: 200 yards; ammunition: Black Hills reloads! Shooter: Dr. Richard Maretzo, president of Precision Shooting Publications and noted benchrest competitor. This was a witnessed event. Good luck to those who believe that they can haphazardly throw together a batch of reloads and thereby surpass the performance of (the best) factory ammo!

RIFLE TARGET SHOOTING—BEST BENCH TECHNIQUE

Generally, when shooting any dedicated benchrest gun, to the extent that doing so is feasible, the shooter always achieves the best accuracy by lining up the sights and then not touching the gun other than to pull the trigger. Shooters and experimenters have demonstrated this result both theoretically and empirically. However, some disciplines require the shooter to control the gun solidly in order to get the shots fired rapidly or for other reasons. If you must interact with the gun, work to do so as consistently as is humanly possible.

TARGET BULLETS—LONG-RANGE ACCURACY

In any game combining high-velocity bullets and long-range targets, avoid combinations where bullet velocity drops to near the speed of sound before the bullet reaches the target. In such a combination, the bullet can demonstrate a significant accuracy loss after the velocity drops below the speed of sound (about 1,120 fps), and differences in atmospheric conditions (a cold dry day, for example) could cause this to happen before the bullet reaches the target. (Cold air is denser than hot air, and dry air is denser than humid air.)

Conversely, bullets dropping below the speed of sound near the gun muzzle show little, if any, loss in accuracy. This significant difference has to do with the magnitude of the forces acting upon the bullet. In spinning (gyroscopically stabilized) bullets, forward velocity slows much faster than the spin rate slows. Destabilizing forces are approximately proportional to the square of forward velocity; stabilizing forces are proportional to the square of the spin rate. Hence, as any bullet travels downrange, it rapidly becomes progressively more able to resist destabilizing aerodynamic forces.

However, as the bullet travels downrange, it also falls through the air progressively faster. Therefore, the wind force against the bottom of the bullet grows progressively stronger. This bottom wind and other forces ultimately generate a tipping-moment force on the bullet. In small arms, this force always keeps the bullet tipped into the flight path with almost exact precision.

Because this tipping force depends upon wind from the bottom acting on the bullet, which increases according to the time of flight squared (resulting from the gravitational constant), the magnitude of this force is proportional to the time of flight squared. Hence, because the spin rate is not slowing significantly, both the relative stabilizing force and the tipping force continuously increase and do so at similar rates. Inevitably, with certain bullet designs at extended distance, the magnitude of these competing forces can become sufficient to destabilize the bullet partially. When this happens, the bullet begins to exhibit significant yaw. This might not destroy accuracy, but it is never beneficial.

Moreover, the buffeting generated by the collapsing supersonic shock waves occurring as a bullet slows through the sonic barrier can compound the existing yaw (some degree of yaw always exists). Experience proves that when the sonic transition occurs after about one second of flight, it can introduce dramatic yaw. Such a bullet can begin a wild oscillation that resembles tumbling, although the bullet never actually turns end-for-end. What actually happens is that bullet tipping (yaw) repeatedly cycles from nearly a point-on flight to nearly a 45-degree angle of flight and back to nearly a point-on flight, and it does so at a characteristic frequency. Once this type of yaw begins to occur, the bullet is monumentally inaccurate. Moreover, once established, such yaw continues unabated until the bullet reaches the terminal distance.

TARGET BULLETS—COWBOY ACTION

In traditional Cowboy Action Events, competitors are shooting at metal targets from a close distance. For safety reasons, the Single Action Shooting Society (SASS) and other organizations, which sponsor official events, allow only a plain-base cast or swaged bullets. Safety concerns also cover muzzle velocity, which is limited to 900 fps. However, because any hit counts the same as any other hit, and these are all timed events, recoil considerations are critical; therefore, winning competitors typically use relatively light bullets loaded at low velocity—much slower than the 900 fps statutory limit.

In certain stages of many events, it is necessary to reload revolvers and tubular-magazine rifles. Hence, the bullet's shape is also a consideration, and truncated cone and round-nosed bullets are the most popular styles.

Soft cast or swaged bullets work best. Several companies offer swaged-lead bullets specifically designed for use in this game. Bear Creek Supply (BCS) offers cast bullets with a unique, baked-on rosin coating that it has saturated with molybdenum-disulfide; hence, BCS bullets do not require traditional grease lube. BCS bullets work particularly well across an unusually wide velocity and pressure range with minimal leading and are, by many orders of magnitude, the cleanest cast bullets to handle and to shoot.

TARGET BULLETS—TRADITIONAL BULLSEYE TARGET PISTOL

Bullseye pistol competitors are concerned with barrel time, recoil, and accuracy. As a practical matter, load choice boils down to a combination of components that works for the shooter in his gun.

If you follow the lead of experienced competitors, you will not go far wrong. Load tinkering is often of more value than is spending a great deal of time working to find a bullet that no one else has discovered.

If possible, test loads that are used by one or more fellow shooters who are competing well with guns similar to yours; by doing so, you might well find the right combination for your gun without doing any load testing. The next-best approach is to test different loads using the same bullet. You should soon find a suitably accurate load by testing a few combinations with likely propellant, primer, and loading variations (seating depth, neck tension, and crimp style and degree). If not, it is likely time to engage the services of a good pistolsmith. Similarly, judicious pistolsmithing will usually allow any given semiautomatic pistol to function properly with such cartridges.

For this game, light- to medium-weight wadcutter or semiwadcutter bullets are good choices. However, where recoil is not a problem (even light recoil is fatiguing to those who are trying to do their best precise shooting), heavier traditional lead, round-nosed designs might be the most accurate bullets ever created. Look for an affordable combination that is consistent and that has the necessary intrinsic accuracy to shoot inside the ten-ring when you do your part. Testing from a sandbag rest can be helpful in this determination.

TARGET BULLETS—ACTION PISTOL (IPSC) AND SIMILAR GAMES

The Action Pistol game is somewhat different. Here, competitors are always looking for anything that reduces recoil—to reduce shot-to-shot recovery time—while maintaining that all-important major power factor. If the bullet mass times the velocity does not meet a specific requirement, officials adjust the shooter's score downward. As a practical matter, it is essentially impossible to win a match when shooting any load that falls below the major power factor.

Formerly, the line separating major from minor was 185—bullet mass (in grains) times velocity (in fps) divided by 1,000; e.g., 115 grains x 1,609 fps (1,000 = 185.035 = Major. In any given gun, a lighter bullet generates less recoil when making major; hence, competitors prefer light bullets. Conversely, lighter bullets generate higher pressure when achieving any given power factor. These competing facts led many competitors to use unusually light bullets at unusually high pressures. This led to the creation of an entire culture of special guns and customized loads, and to large piles of broken equipment—gun failures were inevitable.

The recent popularity of the 40 S&W chambering has prompted IPSC to ratchet down the requirement for major. This is now set at 165 units, which dramatically reduces the pressure required to put any given bullet into the major category. Generally, most 45-caliber and 40-caliber pistols, and many 9mm chamberings, will safely reach the current major requirement without the necessity of using loads that generate excessive pressures.

Many competitors prefer jacketed bullets. These are slicker and can feed faster. This minimizes the potential for anything to retard the gun from functioning. Look for a bullet that provides adequate accuracy and that works properly in the gun—careful pistolsmithing will usually solve functioning problems.

TARGET BULLETS—SILHOUETTE

The silhouette game is yet another different animal. Here, the goal is to dislodge (knock over) a steel target. The wide base of these targets rests on a steel rail. A hit that slides the target back a few inches or one that rotates the top or bottom of the target beyond the balance point will result in a toppled target. Bullet momentum (mass times velocity) is what topples a target, and momentum is the only thing that topples a target.

As far as scoring a hit goes, it makes no difference where the bullet hits the target—even a bullet that ricochets into a target can count so long as the target falls (good luck). For this reason, two distinct considerations exist:

- Overall accuracy of shooter and load
- Bullet momentum at target

Competitors, necessarily, must choose a bullet and chambering that will deliver sufficient momentum at the target to assure toppling with any good hit. At the same time, the load should minimize recoil and provide sufficient accuracy so that it does not limit the shooter's ability to make the hit. This sounds simple enough, in theory; in practice, we might never solve the vagaries of what constitutes the ideal silhouette combination. Worse, a combination that works perfectly for one shooter might not get the job done for another (effectiveness depends upon where any given shooter's shots routinely hit the target).

Regarding recoil, bullet weight generally is a nonissue. Compared to some base load, a bullet that is twice as heavy and that hits the target with one-half the velocity will generate identical target-toppling momentum. However, ballistic efficiency (BC) is an issue. Because—all other things being equal—heavier bullets have higher BCs, those can be a better choice. Conversely, owing to barrel-time considerations, most folks can shoot lighter bullets more accurately because increasing the amount of time that the bullet is moving through the barrel increases the influence of inevitable variations in the shooter's hold.

With a heavier (higher BC) bullet, any given cross wind will have less influence; however, as the bullet travels from muzzle to target, more time will exist for wind changes to occur within the flight path—to foul the shot. Hence, on a day with relatively steady winds, a heavier bullet might have the edge (once the shooter has dialed-in the proper drift correction); conversely, on a day with wildly gusting winds when the shooter is necessarily making wind corrections for each shot, a lighter bullet might have the edge—for bullets of similar weight, the one with the highest BC has the edge.

TARGET BULLETS—BENCHREST

For those shooting in traditional (short-range) benchrest competition, minor variations in ballistic coefficient (BC) are of little consequence. However, when distances stretch significantly beyond one hundred yards, influences such as wind drift progressively increase the importance of BC.

Although it is true that benchresters are only moderately concerned with the exact aerodynamic efficiency (BC) of a particular bullet, an important consideration that is independent of intrinsic accuracy still exists. That question has to do with barrel time. Ideally, all target shooters would prefer the bullet to exit the muzzle instantly upon beginning to accelerate through the bore; this is because, the greater the barrel time, the greater the opportunity for variations in interactions between the gun and shooter and the gun and rest, and all these can alter the bullet's flight. (Of course, Mr. Newton, long ago, and forever thereafter, dashed any hope of achieving this zero-barrel-time goal.)

Because the gun can interact with the shooter and will always interact with the shooting bags upon which it rests, each microsecond that the bullet is in the bore is one more microsecond for something to go wrong (for the bullet to react differently from other bullets in the group). In addition, note that heavier bullets elicit greater recoil. For this reason, heavier bullets move the gun proportionally farther before leaving the bore, even when barrel times are identical, and, normally, heavier bullets have a longer barrel time, so this difference is quite significant.

It works out that, given ideal loads at similar pressure, recoil interaction is approximately proportional to relative bullet mass. For example, a bullet that is twice as heavy generates about twice the variation in response to any given variation in shooter hold or bag interaction.

For example, theoretical calculations for the 6mm PPC fired in a 9-pound gun with identical charges of ideal propellants for 65-grain and theoretical 130-grain bullets are as follows. Barrel times from the instant that each bullet begins to move until the instant that it exits the muzzle: 0.8144 MS versus 1.1002 MS (time); recoil momentum at the instant that a bullet exits the muzzle: 36.40 pound feet per second and 49.36 pound feet per second (force). Taking the ratios, we get 1.351 (time) and 1.356 (force). Multiplying these (total effect equals time, times force), we get 1.83. Hence, in this example, variations in gun-to-shooter and gun-to-bag interactions will result in 1.83 times the accuracy loss with a bullet that is twice as heavy.

Even for a more realistic difference in relative bullet mass, such as between a 70-grain bullet and a 77-grain bullet, this is a critical consideration. In this instance, these interactions would lead to about an 8 percent difference in accuracy potential.

For these reasons, benchrest shooters working at distances up to about two hundred yards generally choose comparatively lightweight bullets. For the benchrest competitor, barrel-time considerations explain why heavier bullets that have an absolute intrinsic accuracy advantage are very apt to demonstrate a practical accuracy disadvantage.

Recently, Berger and custom bullets have won most benchrest matches. Comparatively small shops swage such bullets to the highest possible level of precision using the best jackets made.

TARGET BULLETS—HUNTER BENCH

This game requires the use of a case that has no less capacity than the 30-30 Winchester case. Most winning competitors use shortened, wildcat 30-caliber cases based upon the 308 Winchester or the 284 Winchester.

Most competitors use custom-made, 30-caliber match bullets weighing between 110 and 150 grains. As these events involve relatively short-range shooting, BC is not a critical issue—accuracy is king. Nevertheless, all else being equal, the bullet with the higher BC will have the edge due to the complication of wind drift. Generally, the same issues that apply to traditional benchrest apply to this game; see previous section.

TARGET BULLETS—LONG RANGE

This too, is a unique game. One can either read the wind and fire shots only when the conditions seem similar or fire shots as fast as possible when the wind seems stable. The latter method has produced most record and match winning groups. These competitors must control recoil with their bodies. Barrel-time considerations are important but so is wind drift. Just as serious pistol shooters recognize the importance of a consistent hold, winning long-range shooters must develop the ability to repeat every facet of their hold for every shot consistently.

Nevertheless, not one of my acquaintances is perfect. Relevant human imperfections most certainly show up when the bullet path provides 1,000 yards to amplify the influences of a heartbeat or a muscle twitch. For this reason and because of the general reduction in battering associated with lighter bullets, long-range competitors will sometimes choose a lighter bullet, thereby trading off a measure of reduced wind-drift error for a combination that is easier to shoot accurately.

Another problem crops up for high-power competitors who shoot the 223 Remington or the 308 Winchester at 1,000 yards. In these applications, bullet weight and profile (BC) are critical. If the bullet is too heavy or if it does not have a sufficiently high BC, it will be impossible to load the cartridge safely to launch the bullet fast enough to maintain supersonic velocity to the target. If the bullet does not remain supersonic, it loses accuracy. Refer to "Target Bullets—Long-Range Accuracy."

Consider that NRA high-power shooters are shooting at concentric circles with the goal of making the smallest possible group and centering that group within those circles. For this reason, paradoxically, bullet drop variations associated with shot-to-shot velocity differences can suggest an advantage for a lighter bullet. Given the same degree of human error in wind doping and the same degree of muzzle velocity variation, a lighter bullet might develop a one-inch greater windage error. However, it might shoot with two inches less vertical impact error. In that situation, the lighter bullet will be more apt to fall within the next smaller circle, thus keeping the group as small as possible, and scoring higher.

The reason this happens is that lighter bullets reach the target faster. Gravity has less time to accelerate those and less time to amplify minor muzzle-velocity variations into major variations in bullet drop. This is one reason that long-range target shooters seldom choose to use the heaviest available target bullets.

Another reason that lighter bullets can have an edge is equally paradoxical. Although these will have a lower BC, the higher available muzzle velocity means that total time of flight can be less. If the shooter has correctly doped the wind and if the wind is steady, either bullet will shoot to the horizontal center of the target. Conversely, if the shooter has correctly doped the wind, but a wind change occurs at any point as the bullet passes toward the target, the bullet will not hit the horizontal center. Because the lighter bullet reaches the target sooner, less time exists when such an unpredictable wind change can occur; hence, the lighter bullet will be more apt to hit closer to the horizontal center.

Conversely, because it is impossible for anyone to judge any wind correction precisely (the best shooters often come so close that their performance is intimidating and seems supernatural), all bullets will miss the horizontal center by some distance—the higher the bullet BC, the less this error.

The combined consequences of the potential for gusts and the reality of wind doping errors combine to create a reality wherein most winning shooters usually shoot bullets near the middle of the available weight range. Exceptions have occurred but those are rare.

Finally, so long as the nose profile and the base design are equal and if each bullet is loaded near the maximum feasible velocity, middleweight match bullets always have the least wind drift across 1,000 yards.

TARGET BULLETS—INFORMAL (PLINKING)

Loading requirements for informal target shooting are purely subjective. My handloads and reloads have run the gambit from ammunition handloaded to the highest possible level of consistency using expensive target-grade bullets to ammunition loaded with a scoop-measured charge of recovered military rifle propellant behind home-cast bullets made from scrap lead. Both extremes, and everything in between, have served the intended purpose and often quite impressively.

Generally, informal target shooting serves two functions: improving the shooter's familiarity with the gun at hand and providing a bit of relaxation. For these purposes, ammunition quality plays a distant second-fiddle to cost and ease of production, at least in my opinion.

If appropriate-diameter, commercially cast bullets are available, such as those offered by Bear Creek Supply, those will be hard to beat for cost. Typically, the handloader can use these bullets to load any of the 30-, 35-, 40-, 41-, 44- or 45-caliber rifle cartridges and all common pistol and revolver chamberings. Where available, commercially cast bullets can reduce the cost of handloaded plinking cartridges to less than one-half of what is possible when using any jacketed bullet. The only less expensive bullets are home-cast ones using scrap lead or wheel weights; however, even if such bullet metal is free, home-cast bullets take time and electricity to produce. In the end, these save very little when compared to commercially cast bullets. However, in many applications commercially cast bullets are unavailable or are available only in an alloy hardness that is unsuitable to the chamber pressure of the load you wish to use; hence, the serious handloader must cast such bullets. Furthermore, bullet casting can be a rewarding and enjoyable hobby.

Commercially cast bullets are, generally, of very high quality. Almost invariably we can use these for all informal target and practice shooting applications. Winning competitors often use these in the most intense of target matches. As a salient example consider Terry Labbe, a top ranking national Bullseye pistol competitor. Labbe competes with Magnus Bullet Company, commercially cast bullets, and he just happens to own the company. He and his partners set the civilian national record for the Outdoor Pistol, Four-Member Team on 11 May 1991. Their score was 1170-46X out of a possible 1200-120X. And, yes, they did use run-of-the-mill Magnus bullets, and, no, they did not attribute any lost points to bad bullets.

Consider several of my favorite plinking combinations. In the 45-70 Marlin, cast bullets from various producers have proven adequate. A good, all-purpose load consists of 40 grains of IMR4895, H4895, A2495, or IMR4064 behind any 300- to 405-grain standard-cast bullet of typical modern commercial production—pressure is too low to properly obturate typical hardened cast bullets. The velocity is around 1,200 fps, and the pressure is quite mild. A surprisingly accurate load is 15 grains of Accurate No. 7 behind a 300-grain cast-lead bullet with a magnum rifle primer. The velocity is consistent at 1,000 fps, and the recoil is extremely mild—this load violates practically every accuracy protocol, but it still works. Another charming load combines 8.0 grains of N310 and the Remington 2½ primer behind the 405-grain Bear Creek Supply bullet. The velocity is nearly 800 fps, and the accuracy is nearly one inch at 100 yards. The recoil is extremely light, as is the muzzle blast.

In the 38-55, each of the following pet loads serves a specific purpose. Each uses the relatively soft Bear Creek Supply 255-grain bullet, sized at 0.377 or 0.378 inch (depending upon the gun chamber and the case neck thickness—use the largest diameter bullet that allows free chambering). The Remington 2½ primer gives best results. Either use redrawn Buffalo Arms cases (2.13-inch length) or use the new Starline 2.125-inch cases. These match the chamber better than standard commercial cases, which are universally too short, except for the new, thinner-necked Starline case, which also allows use of 0.380-inch bullets. Ideally for this load, fully anneal the case mouth. Use an expander that matches the bullet diameter and apply sufficient case mouth belling to assure a smooth bullet seating.

The "funnest" load to shoot is 5½ grains of N310 for 750 fps, with an unusually mild report; 7½ grains of Unique generates 1,020 fps and, therefore, duplicates modern factory cartridges; and, 11½ grains of BlueDot generates 1,320 fps and, therefore, duplicates original factory loads. Each of these combinations routinely produces three-shot, 100-yard groups near one inch in a modern Marlin or the modern 1885 Browning. Firing any number of any of these cartridges leaves the gun clean, inside and out. After firing more than 1,000 N310 loads in my Marlin, I found the bore remained shiny, spotless, and clean!

For the 45 Automatic, available 155-grain target bullets are most useful. When loaded to moderate velocity, many loads using these bullets reliably cycle the action of a typical gun. Such cartridges have worked flawlessly in two 1911 Colts and an AMT 45 Backup. The biggest advantage these bullets offer is a vast recoil reduction compared to typical 185-, 200- or 230-grain loads. Recoil matters, especially when plinking with the 23-ounce AMT Backup, or any relatively lightweight gun.

For those rifle cartridges for which less-expensive cast bullets either are unavailable or have a muzzle velocity exceeding about 2,000 fps, which is about the maximum velocity for accurate cast-bullet cartridges, we can shop only for bargain-priced jacketed bullets. The possibilities include the occasional factory-second offerings (an important source is Sierra), quantity purchases, and bullets from regional producers.

Although you or a compatriot will have to go to the Sierra factory, it usually has a wide assortment of seconds, all of which it sells on a price-per-pound basis and will often reduce total consumable cartridge component costs by about half.

In many calibers, those who do not want to use commercial or home-cast bullets can use jacketed pistol bullets. Because these are typically lighter in weight and easier to manufacture, jacketed pistol bullets are often considerably less expensive than are jacketed rifle bullets. If all the shooter is doing is practicing gun-handling and action manipulation, or just simply relaxing, a 125-grain pistol bullet will offer just as much pleasure when fired from a 35 Whelen as will a 250-grain rifle bullet. Considering the recoil issue, the lighter bullet might well offer significantly more pleasure. In this instance, assuming the same muzzle velocity, use of the lighter bullet will cut recoil energy to about one-fourth.

For such lighter-bullet cartridges, choose the fastest extruded propellant listed for the lightest jacketed rifle bullet shown with that cartridge (this is the propellant using the smallest charge for a maximum load). Choose a charge weight near the bottom of the listed range. Such a load will be a good starting point and will usually provide the necessary accuracy for plinking.

When loading plinking ammunition, remember your purpose. Try to minimize costs, recoil, noise, and general wear and tear on yourself and on the gun. If cast bullets do not appeal, look for a bargain on jacketed bullets.

For this type of shooting, you must determine the required accuracy level. I have one criterion: If I can hit what I am aiming at, the load serves its purpose.

HUNTING AND SELF-DEFENSE BULLETS—SPECIAL CONSIDERATIONS

Unlike bullets used in any kind of target shooting, hunting and self-defense bullets must perform properly after impact. Here terminal performance is critical. Although target or match-style bullets will often deliver significantly more energy to a distant target, will shoot flatter, and will be more accurate, such bullets are usually a poor choice for big-game hunting due to unpredictable and generally poor terminal performance. Conversely, most match bullets work very well for varmint hunting. Nevertheless, the best approach is to ascertain that the manufacturer has designed the specific bullet for the specific application of interest. Seek and heed manufacturer recommendations. Obviously, this admonition also well applies to self-defense ammunition.

It is possible for the average hunter to test bullets, whether handloaded or factory loaded, to measure both accuracy and the characteristics of the bullet's terminal performance. The serious hunter should perform both tests. Again, this applies to cartridges that you might use for self-defense. Interested readers should review the following section in this chapter, "Terminal Ballistics—Testing Bullet Performance."

For hunters, accuracy is only the beginning of the story. Of critical importance is functionality—how the cartridge performs in the field. This includes many important facets: how robust the cartridge is; how well it cycles through the action; how much accuracy the load delivers in that gun; how much energy the bullet can deliver to the target; and how the bullet performs after reaching the target. We will consider each of these factors. Keep in mind that your specific needs will depend upon your specific goals, but certain factors are always important.

Expanding jacketed bullets come in many types and styles. Many features and characteristics of both jacket and core influence expansion. Generally, the following jacket properties tend to increase expansion rate:

- Thinner
- Cut or fluted
- Longitudinal folds
- Work-hardened (A harder jacket is more apt to tear rather than to stretch, and tearing takes less energy than stretching takes.)
- Larger nose opening

Generally, the following core features tend to increase expansion rate:

- Increased exposure forward of jacket
- Softer alloy
- Annealed (not work-hardened)
- Longitudinal cuts into nose
- Hollow point (progressively with larger and deeper hollow cavity)
- Larger meplat (progressively with larger exposed portion of lead at bullet nose)
- Generally, any resilient nose insert (commonly plastic)

Finally, terminal performance depends upon impact velocity and the characteristics of the impact medium. Generally, bullets that strike with progressively more velocity or that strike a progressively harder material will expand progressively more rapidly.

In the real world, the potential for an expanding bullet to penetrate also depends upon the impact velocity and the impact medium, but, as it works out, generally, so long as the bullet remains essentially intact, maximum penetration will occur at some intermediate impact velocity. Either increasing the impact velocity above or reducing the impact velocity below that optimum value always results in reduced penetration.

Because the handloader has little chance of correctly predicting terminal performance, a priori, I will not further qualify the matter here. To gain some insight into likely terminal bullet performance in the field, refer to the manufacturer's recommendations. To actually see how a bullet is apt to perform, do terminal performance testing. Refer to end of this chapter, "Terminal Ballistics—Testing Bullet Performance."

HUNTING BULLETS—TYPES

Various manufacturers offer many types of hunting bullets. Hunters can choose bullets specially made for

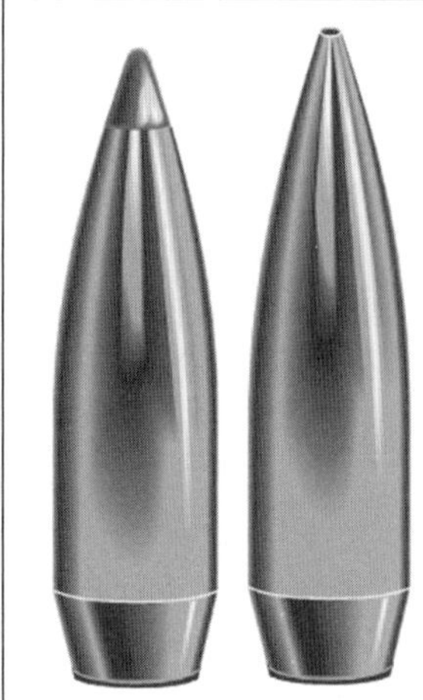

To the hunter, bullet selection makes all the difference. Any slight advantage in BC or in accuracy afforded by the use of a conventional Match bullet (right) will never offset any disadvantage resulting from poor terminal performance. The single exception is Berger, which specifically rates its VLD line of match bullets for big-game hunting.

varmint, light game, heavy game, thin-skinned dangerous game, or thick-skinned dangerous game. Each bullet type is specialized and such specialization can "all the difference" make. Generally, each hunting bullet type performs properly only when used in the appropriate application, which is no real surprise. To a certain extent, the more specialized a bullet is toward one application, the less likely it is that it will perform acceptably across a wide range of applications. As an obvious example, one cannot count upon target bullets for use in big-game hunting.

HUNTING BULLETS—VARMINTING

Varminting bullets are, conceptually, the easiest hunting bullet to understand. Such bullets are relatively easy to make. The manufacturer has only two goals. His first objective is to make sure that the bullet is strong enough to hold together when fired at the maximum rated velocity—manufacturers specifically proscribe certain varmint bullets for use at velocities exceeding some absolute number. The second objective is for maximum feasible accuracy.

The basic idea behind a varmint bullet is to deliver maximum energy into the target—designing the bullet to disintegrate as rapidly as possible after impact is the best way to achieve this goal. At any reasonable distance, most varmint bullets disintegrate upon impact.

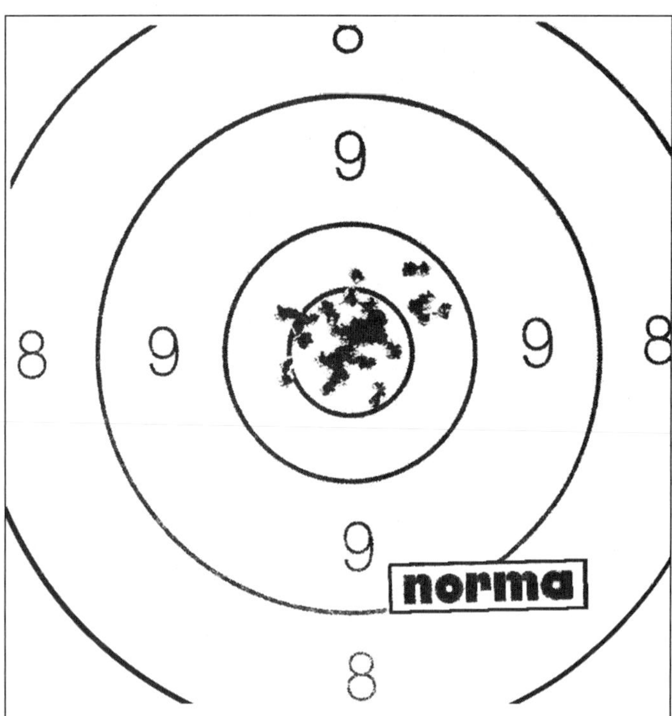

Shooter: Christer Larsson, chief ballistician for Norma Precision; chambering: 6mm Norma BR; ammunition: Norma 6mm BR Diamond Line. This represents the sort of multishot string that the handloading varmint hunter seeks—a 60-shot, 1.8-inch group fired at 328 yards.

This characteristic prevents most ricochets, provided that shooters fire only at targets where the first bullet impact is with either the target or with the ground. If, before it hits something, a conventionally constructed bullet travels far enough so that the velocity drops below about 2,000 fps, it can ricochet intact; such a bullet can carry dangerous energy for several hundred yards. Some bullet types, such as the Barnes Varmint Grenade, will fully disintegrate upon any impact with anything more substantial than perhaps a blade of grass. Even at much lower impact velocity, these are safer against the hazard of ricochet.

Formerly, choosing the ideal varminting bullet required consideration of the maximum rated velocity along with the barrel twist rate. (A faster twist reduces the maximum feasible velocity with any given frangible varminting bullet.) All major bulletmakers at one time produced two versions of practically every style and weight of varminting bullet in the product line. In each such pair, the manufacturer designed a lighter-jacketed version that was intended to provide dependable fragmentation when used in guns of moderate ballistic potential, e.g., up to about 222 Remington performance. The otherwise similar heavier-jacketed version would usually withstand the velocity and the twist rate generated in any chambering. When available, such bullets are still useful and are often less expensive than the newer plastic-tipped varminting designs and are, thus, worth considering. However, Nosler started a revolution with the introduction of the Ballistic Tip (BT) varminting bullet—a better idea.

The BT combines a thick, solid base with a sharp and durable plastic tip. This combination allows Nosler to offer unusually light bullets with very efficient nose profiles and a boattail and yet to maintain sufficient bullet shank length to ensure good accuracy potential. The thick, solid base provides a significant added advantage—Nosler BT bullets tend to be very forgiving of vagaries in chambering alignment and bullet jump. Compared to other plastic-tipped varminting bullets, developing accuracy loads is easier with the BT—due, likely, to the solid base—however, BTs are often more expensive than and are not as explosive as similar bullets from Sierra and Hornady.

For general varminting, the bullet offering the flattest trajectory across the usable hunting range usually has the edge. Generally, where the shooter prefers to see a spectacular, instantaneous kill, impact velocity above 2,000 fps is preferred.

Formerly, experts held that bullet weight and case capacity went hand in hand—larger cases best utilized heavier bullets. Before the advent of plastic-tipped varminting bullets, that contention held significant merit. However, the Nosler BT changed things. Due to the plastic tip and the solid base, these bullets are longer than similar conventional bullets; this allows Nosler to make the bullet nose long

Regardless of the game hunted, the chambering used, or the conditions encountered, modern bullets offer an ideal option for practically any application. Here, Ron Coburn (CEO, Savage Arms) on the left and I pose with his then new Predator rifle and his first kill using that new gun. On this hunt, I took eight coyotes, including two doubles. Having the right equipment and skilled guides made all the difference. Our contribution to the local ranching economy was well appreciated.

enough to maintain a high BC while still keeping the shank long enough to produce good accuracy without the bullet being too finicky during load development.

The 22-caliber Nosler BTs, in 40- and 55-grain weights, have essentially the same base and nose profiles—only the weight and shank-length differ. Hence, ballistic efficiency mirrors the difference in mass. If we consider optimum loads (highest feasible velocity) with each of these bullets in various feasible chamberings from the 22 Hornet to the wildcat 22-243 and use 2,000 fps retained velocity as a useful limit for the maximum range, we discover some interesting things.

First, the 40-grain BT shoots significantly flatter across the useful range regardless of chambering. Second, although the lighter bullet exhibits more wind drift across the useful range, the difference is not particularly significant—distance estimation errors are far more apt to result in a miss than are windage estimation errors. Third, the lighter bullet generates sufficiently less recoil, so the shooter can see hits at much closer distances. Therefore, where the target is a relatively small varmint, the 40-grain BT might be the ideal 22-caliber choice; similarly, the 55-grain BT in 6mm and the new 32-grain BT in 20-caliber have similar characteristics.

The same criterion that guides 1,000-yard target shooters is the best guide for those interested in truly long-range varminting. Such shooters should keep in mind that spectacular long-range kills are impossible with any load used in any feasible chambering.

Those who are hunting larger vermin might well need to look to slightly heavier varminting bullets to be assured of adequate penetration—the solid base of the BT series allows these bullets to shine in this application. However, some guns and chamberings might not work well with the BT, and other bullet brands and types are sometimes significantly less expensive, so other options are often a better choice for specific needs.

Historically, errors in determining range were a major consideration for varminters. Because of this, varminters placed a significant premium on muzzle velocity. With the advent of affordable, portable, and accurate laser rangefinders, things have changed, but velocity remains king. Anyone who can afford to spend nearly $1,000 on a proper long-range varmint-hunting rig will likely find little problem spending a few hundred dollars on a device that can report exact target distance. (No doubt, the same will be true for many big-game hunters.) Good distance information combined with accurate external ballistics data can virtually eliminate holdover errors.

To judge the varminting accuracy of any given bullet, go to the range on a calm day and fire a series of groups on paper at 300 yards. Keep firing shots until your results convince you that the load can deliver almost every shot into a group that measures no larger than 1 to 1½ minutes of angle. As explained below, occasional fliers are meaningless. A reasonable test group would include no fewer than 20 shots.

What should one look for in these groups? Think of it this way: Would you rather use a load that prints 20 bullets inside four inches at 300 yards with a uniform pattern density, or would you want an otherwise similar load that prints 18 out of 20 shots inside 2½ inches at 300 yards with two fliers that open the group to six inches? Remember that you are trying to maximize your percentage of solid hits. Also, remember that misses are practically inevitable—hold, wind, and ranging errors will occur. For me, the latter combination would be preferable, but to each his own.

The varmint hunter is a different breed. Commonly, a shooter will fire hundreds of rounds through a prized rifle in one afternoon. While he might know that he should stop shooting to clean the bore (to improve accuracy) or to let the barrel cool (to prevent excessive wear), often he is likely to do neither. Hence, varmint hunters should consider fire lapping because this process can monumentally reduce fouling buildup, and it can dramatically improve the accuracy potential of a typical factory barrel. Similarly, it sometimes can rejuvenate a well-worn barrel by polishing away the sharp edges of the bore in the damaged area of the leade where bullet damage is most apt to occur. David Tubb, many times national NRA high-power champion, offers firelapping products through his company, Superior Shooting Systems Inc.

Should you choose to perform terminal ballistics testing with varmint bullets, look for complete bullet disintegration, with no more than about four inches penetration; for smaller species, less penetration is better. (Refer to "Terminal Ballistics—Testing Bullet Performance" covered toward the end of this chapter.) The only reliable method is to test full-power loads at the distance of your longest anticipated shots. Bullets should fully disintegrate, even when impacting at long distance. The results of short-range testing with reduced loads are unreliable—the lower spin rate and reduced bullet temperature create a radically different disintegration scenario.

HUNTING BULLETS—BIG GAME

Hypothetically, consider a small group of elk hunters sitting around a campfire the night before the big hunt. Ask each of these nimrods (hunters) what chambering he considers the minimum for elk and what bullet weight he recommends. Unless a fight breaks out in the meantime, you are likely to eventually get as many answers as there are faces staring back at you. Believe me, considering the nature of such a faux pas, those you ask are apt to stare, and considering that each is apt to have a strong and unique opinion, tension could run high.

I have an opinion too. Having witnessed far more than one hundred kills, perhaps my opinion has merit. When considering what constitutes adequate delivered energy and proper bullet choice for hunting other big game, opinions might not vary so much and hunters might not feel the need to back their opinions quite so vehemently. Nevertheless, rest assured, opinions about hunting bullets and chamberings will always vary. Nevertheless, in considering this subject I cannot ignore one thing. This is a fundamental tenet that all-too-many, so-called experts all-too-often completely disregard, or at least seriously underplay: No amount of BIGGER GUN can possibly substitute for adequate shot placement.

A POORLY PLACED SHOT
IS
A POORLY PLACED SHOT
IS
A POORLY PLACED SHOT!

Chamberings promising more power lure all too many hunters—many of whom simply do not have

My friend, Sören Gindahl, is obviously pleased after taking an unusually large Swedish moose in 2003. His rifle was a new custom gun chambered in 358 Norma Magnum, a gift from our mutual friend, Torbjörn Lindskog (Norma CEO). Gindahl's lifetime moose harvest exceeds 25. With the first shot fired at a game animal using this rifle, Gindahl killed the biggest moose he had seen in more than twenty years of hard hunting. The Norma Oryx bullet did the job, instantly. Gindahl's admirable hunting motto is, "Ett skott, en träff" *(one round, one hit). The implication of a humane kill is lost in the Swedish-to-English translation.*

the necessary marksmanship skills to take advantage of what such chamberings can offer. Shooters who can handle the recoil generated by a more powerful cartridge might find benefit from carrying such a rifle; those who cannot handle the recoil are thereby taking a significant step—in the wrong direction.

Never forget this fact: Any hunter's first priority—some consider this an obligation—is to place any shot fired where intended. To put this very bluntly, it is a stone cold fact that a 60-grain Hornady HP launched from a 22-250 and fired into the lungs of the biggest bull elk that ever lived, broadside at 300 yards, will absolutely bag that animal and will do so more humanely than will any 500-grain round-nose fired from a 460 Weatherby Magnum, broadside through the guts of the same animal.

As a matter of fact, not theory, I know that a 40-grain JHP fired from a 22 magnum rifle into the lungs of a full-grown cow elk at 400 yards will result in a very dead cow elk, which will have expired rapidly. (No, I did not do this, but I do know who did, and while he will freely admit that it was an ill-advised stunt, he might add that his family needed the meat and that it was good eating.) I also know of a man who during the Great Depression when folks were desperately in need of meat (or any other food) killed two spike elk in the wilds of Colorado with three precisely placed shots from his trusty 25-20 WCF. Shot placement matters.

ON A SCALE FROM ONE TO TEN, EFFECTIVENESS OF ANY GIVEN SHOT ON A GAME ANIMAL IS DETERMINED BY:

EFFECTIVE SHOT PLACEMENT—10
PROPER TERMINAL BULLET PERFORMANCE—7
ADEQUATE DELIVERED ENERGY—3

As to the question of accuracy: For the big-game hunter, the best method of accuracy testing is to fire three-shot groups. Choose a calm day for your test. Next, decide at what distance you want to know what the load will do—this should reflect your skills, ballistics of the chambering and the load that you are using, and the maximum distance at which you are willing to take shots at the intended target. If you often hunt where long shots are possible, you should try to find a place to set up targets at 300 yards, or at an appropriate greater distance. You should:

- Fire many three-shot groups from a cold barrel.
- Fire a few three-shot groups from a warm barrel.
- Fire a few three-shot groups from a clean, cold barrel and a few three-shot groups from a barrel that has had a dozen rounds through it, without cleaning.
- Fire three-shot groups in the crisp, early morning air.
- Fire three-shot groups in the warm afternoon, after the gun has been resting in the sun for a while.

The compilation of these results will suggest what you can expect of your rifle and your load in the real hunting world. Who cares what a hunting load and gun will do when firing ten-shot groups? If you have the time to fire five (or ten!) shots at a game animal, you certainly will have had the time to have properly placed one of your first few shots.

HUNTING BULLETS—THIN-SKINNED GAME

For those hunting lighter, nondangerous, thin-skinned big game, the arguments are very much the same as for the varmint hunter. First, consider the intended application. As this is among the most popular types of hunting, every major and many custom bullet producers cater to this application.

Excepting for use in large-caliber handguns, nonexpanding bullets are a poor choice—many jurisdictions also proscribe use of nonexpanding solids for big-game hunting, regardless of chambering. To provide dependably quick kills, nonexpanding bullets require shots into the brain or spine. Equally, one cannot count on varmint bullets to anchor big game unless the shot directly enters the rib cage, where such bullets can be unusually effective, often rendering instantaneous kills. Regardless of this, varmint bullets are inappropriate for big-game hunting because few hunters can guarantee the required level of shot-placement precision. The same prohibition holds for many types of target bullets, which can fragment, expand too violently, or fail to expand.

Hunters hold wildly varying opinions about what constitutes a proper big-game chambering and bullet. One reason for such disparity in and vehemence of these views has to do with the variability of big-game hunting habitats. Consider the following setting: thick bush in heavy timber. In such a place, while a potential trophy moves through a clearing, the hunter might only have one or two seconds to assess the animal, take aim, and make the shot. Moreover, in such an area, locating an animal that travels only a few dozen yards before succumbing to a fatal wound can become a living nightmare. There, the hunter will certainly want a cannon-class rifle that delivers a heavy bullet that will absolutely break heavy bones and that will achieve full penetration and leave a gaping exit wound. With any well-placed shot, such a combination is almost certain to generate an adequate blood trail and will prevent any well-hit animal from traveling far.

Under that blanket of snow is a typical 42-month bull elk. Bob McPherson, my father, took this bull with two perfectly placed shots from a Remington Pump chambered in 270 Winchester. His handload used the 150-grain Sierra SBT at 2,850 fps MV. Both bullets stopped under the hide on the far side, after expending 100 percent of delivered energy, mostly within the thorax—ideal performance. The second shot was unnecessary, albeit cheap, insurance.

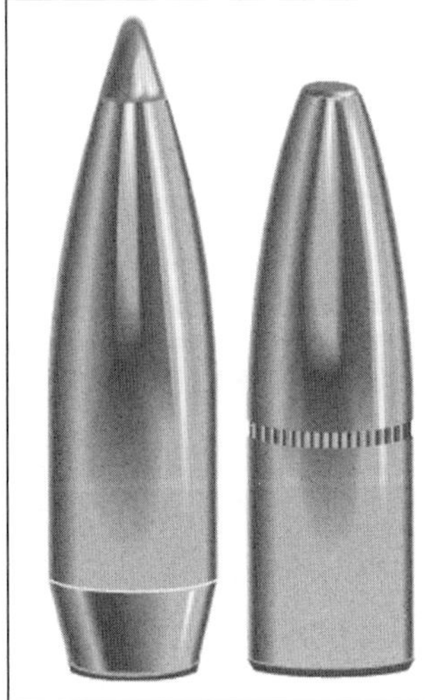

Comparing the Speer Spitzer Boat Tail with the Speer Grand Slam illustrates the importance of BC. When equal weight examples are launched at the same velocity, energy delivered to 300 yards is about 15 percent greater with the SBT. At 500 yards, the difference reaches 30 percent. To the long-range hunter, this matters. The Grand Slam was designed for use at closer ranges and shines in that application.

We can speculate that this type of hunting was behind Elmer Keith's famous arguments for just such a gun and load. No doubt, the conditions he encountered in the areas that he habitually hunted had a lot to do with his beliefs about what constituted a proper elk rifle and cartridge. As nearly as I can determine, based upon what he wrote and upon our correspondence, Keith believed that the 338-378 Weatherby Magnum, a cartridge capable of launching a 300-grain bullet at nearly 3,000 fps, was just about right for mule-deer hunting! (Among other things that are important to serious shooters, Keith was one of only a few persons behind standardization of the 44 Magnum, and he designed and popularized the most effective semiwadcutter bullets ever made.)

My friend, Norm Nelson, a noted outdoor writer, hunts elk in the same heavily timbered and underbrush infested habitat that Keith once haunted. Interestingly, Norm complains that he would like to be able to get more velocity out of his 340 Weatherby Magnum. Having seen pictures of the country where Norm hunts, I can understand why. Were I hunting there, I would want a gun and a load that would kill, gut, skin, quarter, and hang the elk with one simple squeeze of the trigger. Further, if I could arrange this, it would be handy if the bullet impact also transported the carcass to the hunting rig and then loaded it on board!

Elk are big, tough, animals, but when hunted in relatively open terrain as shown here, any high-power rifle bullet that performs properly and that is delivered to the thorax will do the job. Typically, the animal will succumb before traveling more than about 200 yards; conversely, when hunting in dense cover, without a good blood trail to follow, an animal that travels 20 yards can be very difficult to locate (see photograph at left).

For hunting where brush and timber is so heavy, Norm Nelson wanted as much gun as he could carry. When the first (premium) 358 Winchester bullet failed to expand despite a good hit at 30 yards, only a quick follow-up shot saved him from a long, hard day of tracking. His Savage M99 was the ideal gun.

Conversely, if you are hunting in open parklands and sparse aspen groves (such as we often find in western Colorado) where I usually hunt elk and where you can watch a shot animal until it succumbs, you might feel completely confident using a 270 Winchester and shooting properly constructed 130-grain bullets. I know three hunters who have collectively taken more than 100 animals with similar load combinations and who have yet to lose a single shot animal. What is necessary to get the job done properly is largely a function of the hunter's skill and of the terrain and vegetation where he hunts.

This likely explains why Jack O'Connor, a noted outdoorsman, outdoor writer, and rival authority to Keith on ballistics and hunting, felt perfectly confident when taking elk with his 270 Winchester. His favorite load was a 130-grain bullet in front of a stiff charge of H4831, whereas Keith made no secret of his dislike of using that or any similarly puny chambering on elk.

This was the basis of a decades-long war of words. The ongoing controversy sold copious copy for both men and their respective publishers.

O'Connor normally practiced an entirely different style of hunting (in open country), compared to what Keith practiced. In their day, folks generally viewed this controversy as a question of personality. However, I believe that the type of hunting each man practiced had more to do with their opinions of what constituted a proper gun and load than any other factor. Certainly each man was an expert hunter, and each man humanely collected more than his fair share of game animals using his personal choice of equipment—viewed from that perspective, both men were right.

As to what constitutes proper terminal performance, that depends. If you are hunting Keith style, you had better choose a bullet that will positively achieve 100 percent penetration; this increases the chances of the wound creating a good blood trail. If you are hunting O'Connor style, a bullet that will deliver 100 percent of the impact energy into the target vitals will likely serve you better because it will generate a quicker kill. You must determine your needs and proceed from there.

The best approach is to choose the most powerful gun you can properly handle and with which you can practice without developing a terminal case of flinching (plinking loads help here). Choose a bullet with an appropriate terminal performance, taking into consideration the hunted species and the conditions in the hunted area. Generally, lighter and more ballistically efficient bullets are a better choice, provided those have the necessary terminal performance. Lighter premium bullets will shoot flatter, generate less recoil, and yet deliver superior terminal performance.

Having chosen the proper bullet type, consider general bullet quality with regard to terminal performance characteristics. Significant differences do exist. Those concerned with taking their best shot will often choose a more expensive, premium-grade, hunting bullet, such as those offered by Speer, Nosler, Barnes, Winchester, and Swift. A premium bullet can deliver significantly better terminal performance and usually costs only a few pennies (or nickels) more than a conventional hunting bullet. Compared to the cost of a hunt, this added expense is unworthy of consideration.

A slight increase in terminal performance might make all the difference in the instance of a bad hit or of a shot taken from a bad angle. This argument is especially pertinent when one considers species larger than mule deer. Here, delivered bullet energy per pound of animal is significantly limited. This fact suggests that the use of an appropriate premium-grade bullet makes especially good sense.

However, these bullets are generally not necessary for lighter big-game species where it is possible to deliver substantial (per pound) energy. In addition, certain premium-grade bullets have a lower BC compared to typical big-game bullets. This is a significant consideration for those anticipating shots at longer distances.

I should also note that pronghorn hunters have special needs. First, owing to the extended distances often encountered, these hunters should choose a bullet that can deliver the flattest possible trajectory. Second, because these are relatively small animals, impact resistance is always limited, and, because of the potentially long distances involved (which considerably compromise impact velocity), look for a rapidly expanding bullet that can quickly transfer a great deal of energy. Finally, energy delivered is not particularly important; pronghorns are neither very big nor particularly hard to anchor. Further, these animals dwell in open country. Tracking one that makes a short death-run is not a particular problem. Lighter and softer bullets designed to expand faster are in order.

Lee Wynkoop, my cousin, in November 2002 with his first deer. As you can tell, he is a very happy nimrod (mighty hunter). During the same hunt, I took a bull elk using a 50-90 Sharps, thereby fulfilling my own lifetime dream.

Obviously, the appropriate bullet weight depends upon the species hunted, but many pundits have vastly overrated this factor. For example, when using the 270 Winchester, I have long preferred the Sierra 150-grain SBT for hunting both mule deer and elk. Compared to the 130-grain Sierra SBT, the 150 SBT destroys much less meat on deer and seems to be a better choice on elk. The long-range trajectory is very similar, and the delivered energy at extreme usable distance is significantly higher with the heavier bullet. However, when hunting pronghorns or the smallest species of deer, it is important not to choose a too-tough bullet—in such applications, the Sierra 150-grain SBT would likely be a poor choice when using the 270 Winchester.

Once you have established a group of bullets that you feel will provide acceptable terminal performance, consider the ballistic coefficient (BC) ratings. Most experts consider this a critically important characteristic in any long-range shooting. All other things being equal, regardless of distance, a bullet with a higher BC is always preferable because it generates a flatter trajectory (thereby reducing ranging holdover and target lead errors), reduces wind drift (thereby reducing windage correction errors), and delivers more energy (thereby potentially doing the job faster).

However, generally, if shots will never exceed a few hundred yards, you can generally ignore BC—most bullets of similar shape are sufficiently similar in this regard. Exceptions do exist. For example, the choice between the highest BC 30-30 bullets and lowest BC 30-30 bullets can monumentally alter delivered energy at the far end of useful 30-30 range. At 200 yards, the best of the lot (Speer) has an amazing 40 percent energy advantage over most others.

Unlike the varmint hunter, big-game hunters are concerned with delivered energy. It is often desirable to forgo a measure of trajectory flatness in order to deliver more energy at long distance. Obviously, a bullet that can deliver 20 percent more energy at the reasonable maximum distance at which the hunter might shoot would be a far superior choice, even if it required a few inches greater holdover.

It is worthwhile to see if the selected bullet delivers the necessary accuracy for your needs. I prefer three-shot groups consistently smaller than one inch at 100 yards for big-game hunting. Given the opportunity, I prefer to test accuracy at 300 yards. For normal hunting, a load that routinely places three shots inside about 4½ inches at 300 yards is not limiting my ability to place the shot properly for deer or elk. When I am hunting inside this distance, my favorite hunting rifle can deliver the bullet with enough velocity to create acceptable expansion. For long-range hunting, I have different, much stricter, accuracy criteria.

Should you perform terminal ballistics testing of controlled-expansion hunting bullets, refer to "Terminal Ballistics—Testing Bullet Performance" in this chapter. Look for penetration from about 12 inches to about 18 inches—less is acceptable for hunting pronghorn and smaller species of deer. You can expect bullets that penetrate only about 12 inches to deliver more energy into the vitals while those reaching the upper limit will likely produce an exit wound. Weight retention near 60 percent is desirable (premium bullets often approach 100 percent). The expanded bullet diameter should exceed 1½ times the original bullet diameter; typically, the diameter will almost double.

Winchester Fail-Safe, Barnes X-Bullet, and related bullets are capable of penetration that is all out of proportion to weight. For this reason, hunters who are unfamiliar with the terminal performance characteristics of these bullets tend to choose versions that are entirely too heavy for the job at hand. Regardless of impact velocity, the weight retention of these bullets is virtually 100 percent. Hence, such bullets generally penetrate farther than either typical or premium-quality jacketed bullets that weighed 50 percent more before impact. For example, among 30-caliber bullets, my experience demonstrates that the 140-grain Barnes X-Bullet will penetrate farther than will the 200-grain Nosler Partition.

HUNTING BULLETS—HEAVY, NONDANGEROUS GAME

Even though this category seems badly named to me, I could think of no other way to separate these species from those of similar size that are traditionally recognized as dangerous. I do not, however, consider all game in this category to be nondangerous. I say this after having been charged by a wounded mule deer buck and after having considered the number of hunters and others who are mauled each year by various animals from species that are not listed within the dangerous-game classification.

Those hunting heavier species of nondangerous game—elk and especially bison and moose in North America—are well advised to consider using Barnes X, Winchester Fail-Safe, or heavier premium-grade, controlled-expansion bullets. Most mere mortals are unable to carry and properly shoot a gun that is capable of routinely delivering sufficient energy to stop one of these big critters in its tracks (excepting with a brain or a spine shot). These animals are simply too massive.

Consider a comparison based upon energy delivered per pound of animal weight. This reasonably assesses the capability of a bullet to stop an animal with any given hit. For example, compare the 30-30 Winchester used on mule deer with the 460 Weatherby Magnum used on elk: Assuming that each bullet stops inside the

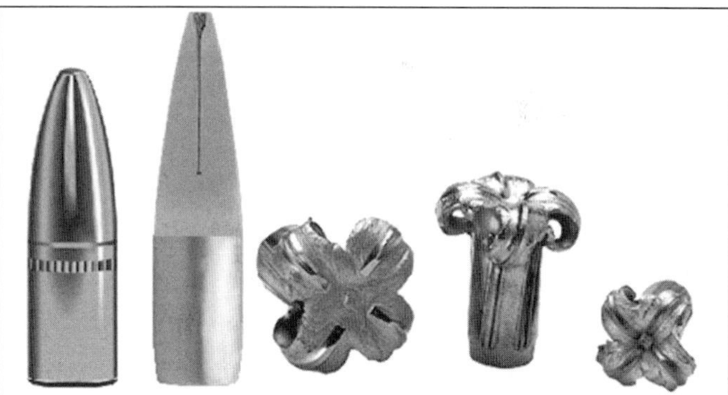

Examples of premium big-game hunting bullets: Speer Grand Slam (left) offers performance that is similar to the legendary Nosler Partition. Cutaway of Barnes X (next to left) only shows part of the secret of this solid-copper bullet. The deep hole in the point is produced by a fluted punch when the bullet is still cylindrical. This punch creates four cuts that extend almost to the perimeter of the bullet, which is then formed into its final shape. Hence, X-Bullet expansion requires only a slight tearing and subsequent bending of each petal. X-Bullet expansion is dependable across a wide velocity range, as indicated by the tested bullets at right. Expanded bullets tested in a saturated telephone book have an impact velocity (fps) of, left to right: 2,500, 2,200, and 1,900. The weight retention of "X-Bullets" usually exceeds 95 percent.

animal (hence it delivers 100 percent of impact energy), the energy delivered per pound of critter is quite similar. The 460 WM is about four times as powerful as the 30-30, and elk are about four times as heavy as mule deer.

Regardless of the gun he might use (up to and including the 460 Weatherby Magnum), a hunter who shoots a particularly big North American moose is in a situation somewhat similar to a hunter taking an average southern whitetail with a 22 Winchester Magnum Rimfire. Certainly, a properly placed shot will get the job done, but anything other than a brain or spine shot will certainly not bowl the animal over. Moose hunters cannot deliver truly devastating energy to such a large target with any gun that they could reasonably carry and shoot. (On the other hand, moose are relatively easy to stop.)

The solution is to choose a solidly constructed bullet, preferably one that offers superior weight retention and penetration potential and to learn to be able to place that bullet well. Considerations of delivered energy and the limitations that impact velocity can place on bullet performance suggest against taking long shots at any of the larger species.

I strongly advise terminal ballistics testing for any cartridge used in this type of hunting. Refer to "Terminal Ballistics—Testing Bullet Performance" covered toward end of this chapter. For moose, look for a minimum penetration of 15 inches. Again, premium bullets demonstrating at least 75 percent weight retention at realistic impact velocities are preferable. An expanded bullet diameter should be between 1½ and 2 times the original bullet diameter.

Again, note that the penetration of Winchester Fail-Safe bullets and Barnes X-Bullets is all out of proportion to weight. Refer to text toward end of previous section.

HUNTING BULLETS—THICK-SKIN DANGEROUS GAME

Hunting thick-skinned, dangerous game (elephant, rhino, Cape buffalo, hippo, alligator, and crocodile) presents a different set of bullet-choice problems. First, the hunter should never take a shot unless he can guarantee proper shot placement—his life might well depend upon that. Wind, target distance, and target motion are all considerations. Second, as with moose, these thick-skinned, dangerous animals are often very large. No mortal can possibly carry and use any gun that is powerful enough to deliver substantial per-pound energy to larger animals in this category.

The great white hunters of yore often used truly outsized guns in this endeavor; many died very young with various maladies stemming from the brain damage incurred each time they pulled the trigger. Some of those guns developed recoil levels in the hundreds of foot-pounds range (similar to the energy that a 22 Long Rifle bullet generates at the muzzle). Typically, after firing the gun, those intrepid souls would find blood seeping from one or both ears, their nose and, perhaps, one or both eye sockets. Despite the extraordinary muzzle energy and correspondingly obscene recoil levels generated, just as with modern

From left to right are the cross sections of progressively tougher bullets: Hornady Interbond (note jacket protrusion into core below cannelure), Nosler Partition, Swift A-Frame (bonded core), Barnes X, Winchester Fail-Safe, Barnes Brass Solid. Each has its place in big-game hunting applications—no single bullet is ideal for all hunting situations.

guns, instant stops were always a matter of proper shot placement. Imagine that.

For example, when used against a small elephant, the vaunted 700 Nitro Express (or any of the proprietary maximum chamberings, which all produce about 9,000 foot pounds of muzzle energy) would deliver about one foot-pound of energy per pound of animal. On a pound-per-pound basis, that is just about what the 17 Remington would deliver to a good-sized bull elk at point-blank range. To achieve the per-pound energy typically accepted as required for effective big-game performance, the elephant hunter would have to more than triple the energy of the 700 Nitro—about double the muzzle energy of the 50 BMG. Within acceptable recoil limits, such a gun would be too heavy to carry into the field, and few among us could possibly bring it to bear when presented with the opportunity to use it.

As most animals in this class can easily survive long enough after a heart or lung shot to travel more than one mile, the wisdom of such a shot is highly questionable, at best. The only safe course with most of these species is to target the brain, spine, or heavy bone.

Another important consideration is the thick-skin issue. These animals have very tough and unusually heavy hide, perhaps thick fat, thick and dense muscles, and heavy bone structures. Because of these characteristics and even with perfect shot placement, the hunter cannot count upon a conventional expanding bullet penetrating into the vitals. Even when expanding bullets do reach the vitals, these seldom retain sufficient energy to get the job done with any expedience. For these reasons, some professional dangerous-game hunters and guides exclusively favor nonexpanding bullets for use against any such game—monolithic solids offer maximum performance.

Perhaps the ideal design is the flat-pointed brass solid. Such bullets will deliver more energy to the target faster and can break heavy bone without as much deflection as is exhibited by round-nose solids.

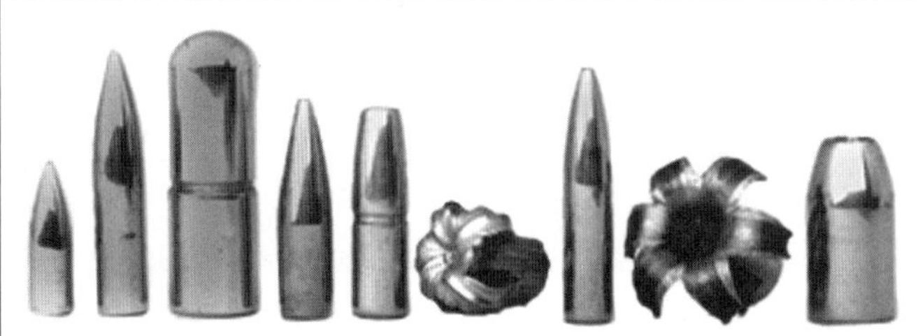

Barnes offers an entire suite of bullets, both expanding and non-expanding types. These have gained a reputation for achieving superior penetration.

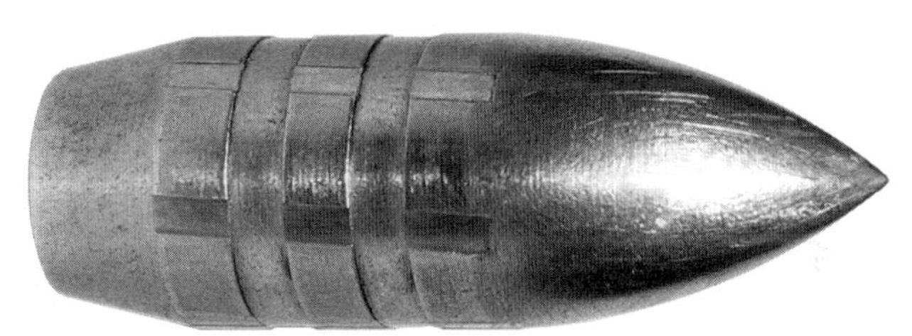

Smalley 45-caliber, 362-grain, Transonic solid: Recovered after 950-fps impact into weathered shale at 1,540 yards. Made from leaded brass, this bullet is certainly a tough enough solid. However, the nose shape is wrong for hunting. This bullet is designed for extreme accuracy at extreme distances when launched at 2,000 fps, and it delivers.

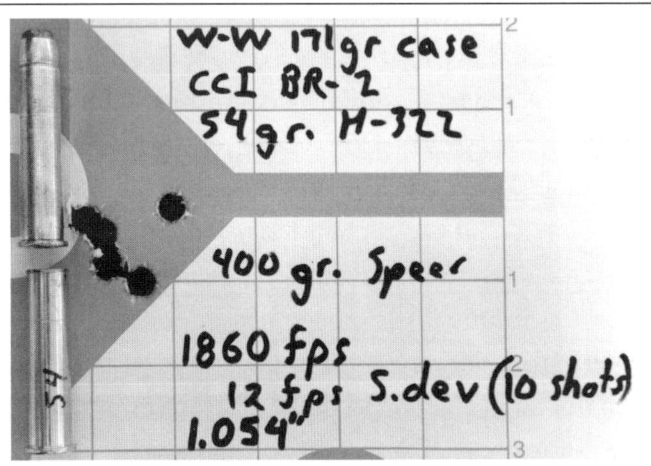

This is a classic example of a load that has plenty of energy and accuracy but lacks terminal performance. This Speer bullet was developed for use at much lower velocity. When used as shown here, it is apt to disintegrate partially and penetrate poorly. The Remington 405-grain FNSP has a much harder core and works perfectly at this velocity.

Trophy Bonded, Woodleigh, and Belt Mountain offer such bullets.

Do not use monolithic solids in any thin-barrel, double-type rifle. An investigation has linked this practice with catastrophic barrel failures on many such rifles. Evidently those bullets simply overstress the thin portion of the barrel; this results in a catastrophic barrel rupture, typically beginning about eight inches from the breech.

Accuracy is no less important when hunting dangerous, thick-skinned game than it is for a varmint hunter. The target area might be very small and a shot that misses the proper target can be more than just a little embarrassing—such critters are reported to exhibit an extreme dislike of loud noises that give them a headache. Professional guides report that these animals have a propensity for stomping two-legged animate objects into pancake-shaped inanimate objects when given the chance—especially when those two-legged animate objects are responsible for giving them said headache.

Test three-shot groups fired from a clean and then a dirty ambient-temperature barrel. It would seem odd to deliberately attempt to bag one of these critters immediately after using one's elephant rifle to blaze away at a wildebeest or some such animal, but you never know. One-inch, 3-shot, 50-yard benchrest tested groups are more than adequate. Generally, the important consideration is how closely the first shot fired from a cold barrel comes to the point of aim.

Again, terminal ballistics testing is advisable. However, in this instance, the test is pure simplicity and requires nothing more than to fire bullets into stacks of dry telephone books. The bullet either deforms or it does not deform—uncomplicated. Ideally, solids should not deform at all. If a recovered bullet shows significant evidence of deformation, performance is suspect. Premium expanding bullets should demonstrate at least 75 percent weight retention. Test at least three bullets of any given type.

WHEN FIRING INTO STACKED PAPER

THIS TYPE OF BULLET COULD PENETRATE SEVERAL FEET OF DRY PAPER. THESE BULLETS CAN ALSO DISRUPT THE STACK SIGNIFICANTLY. IF IMPACT DIRECTION IS NOT VERY CLOSE TO SQUARE TO THE FACE OF THE STACK, OR IF THE BULLET HITS TOO CLOSELY TO THE EDGE OF THE STACK, IT IS QUITE APT TO EXIT THE SIDE OF THE STACK, AT A SIGNIFICANT ANGLE TO THE DIRECTION OF FIRE. FIRE ONLY ONE SHOT PER STACK, AND FIRE THAT SQUARELY INTO THE CENTER OF EACH STACK. USE EXTREME CAUTION AND HAVE AN ADEQUATE BACKSTOP.

HUNTING BULLETS— THIN-SKINNED DANGEROUS GAME

Here we are considering the bigger species of cats, bears, and wild boar. Smaller species can certainly be dangerous but, for those species, any reasonably powerful gun loaded with a controlled-expansion bullet of reasonable weight will do the job, given proper shot placement.

Even when concerned with the biggest of cats or wild boar, one can often carry a sufficiently powerful gun to deliver a fatal shock almost instantaneously, even with shots that do not directly hit the brain or spine. However, wounded cats have mauled or killed many an otherwise cautious hunter because he used the wrong bullet. In several well-studied cases, it appears that the first hit would have anchored the cat had the shooter only used any properly constructed expanding bullet.

Consider the accounts of four instances where an African lion seriously mauled a hunter. Three of those occurred after the hunter had wounded the cat with a nonexpanding bullet. The fourth occurred after the hunter had made a poor hit with an expanding bullet that failed to hold together properly. As always, what matters is shot placement, bullet performance, and (least) delivered energy. No doubt a similar argument would hold for wild boar. Similarly, feral hogs are very tough and can be quite dangerous.

For hunting these species, the use of anything other than a premium-quality, controlled-expansion bullet seems truly foolish. A fundamental difference separates a ruined hunt, caused by a failed bullet and resulting in a lost trophy, and what could happen if that trophy were to take a hankering toward biting back. Believe me, having been charged by a big, wounded mule deer buck—I foolishly used the wrong bullet—I, for one, want no part of any charging predator, wounded or not.

As noted above, for thin-skinned dangerous species, nonexpanding solids are usually a bad choice. A 500-grain, 45-caliber solid delivered broadside through the lungs of a big cat or boar delivers precious little energy. For that shot, such a bullet will do much less damage than a controlled-expansion, 150-grain, 30-06 bullet will do. For myself, I would much rather take on any lion or boar while carrying a 30-06 loaded

Barnes X-Bullet is one tough expanding bullet. Weight retention usually exceeds 95 percent. Expansion is dependable across a wide range of impact velocities. This bullet will break heavy bones and keep on penetrating. It is an ideal choice for heavy game. See the text for bullet-weight suggestions and for handloading precautions.

Barnes X (two examples at left), Nosler Partition (thee examples in middle), and Hornady InterBond (two examples at right) are relatively tough bullets for use against thin-skinned game. The Partition is perhaps the most versatile of these. In my opinion the X is not the best choice for lighter species, but it can be effective. A problem with the X is that folks insist on treating it as if it were a conventional bullet. With essentially 100 percent weight retention, the lightest available X in each caliber always penetrates farther than the heaviest available Partition or conventional bullet. Except when hunting heavy African game, always use the lightest X.

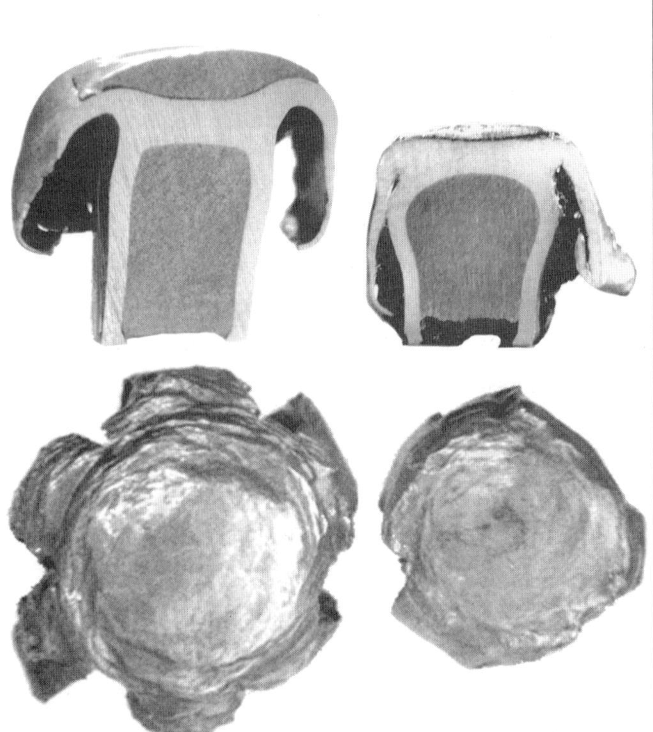

Cross sections and frontal views of similarly expanded Nosler Partition bullets: The one on the left represents typical results with impacts at intermediate velocity; the one on the right represents typical results with impacts at higher velocity or into heavy bone. This is one of the all-time great bullets for many big-game hunting applications, worldwide.

with heavy, expanding, premium-grade bullets than with any rifle loaded with solids. However, the better choice is a gun launching a big, heavy, controlled-expansion bullet that the shooter delivers properly to break heavy bones. Even if such a bullet misses a heavy bone, one would expect disabling damage and delivery of a devastating blow. Here, the most powerful gun that one can handle is none too big.

Again, I strongly advise testing. Refer to "Terminal Ballistics—Testing Bullet Performance" covered toward end of this chapter. Exceptionally deep penetration is not particularly critical. (It is a rare lion that weighs 500 pounds and very few boars are anywhere nearly that big.) Look for about eighteen inches of penetration. However, these animals are tough to stop; for this reason, premium bullets that demonstrate more than 75 percent weight retention at realistic impact velocities are a superior choice. Additionally, the hunter should test bullet integrity. Fire bullets into stacks of dry telephone books—consider only bullets that do not fully disintegrate when tested in this manner.

When we consider the biggest of bears, we have new rules. As is true with thick-skinned species, when hunting these bruins it is simply impossible for a mere mortal to carry enough gun to deliver a devastating blow that will instantly stop a fight unless the animal is hit in the brain or spine. Here, bullet weight and the ability of a bullet to hold together are even more critical.

There is no doubt that a properly placed 130-grain, 270 Winchester bullet (broadside into the lungs) will dispatch the largest of bears. Jack O'Connor, among others, demonstrated this many times. The question becomes: How long will it take that mortally wounded bear to realize it is dead? When you consider that a grizzly can cover rough, fallen-tree-covered ground as fast as a thoroughbred can negotiate Churchill Downs, and that it would only take one blow from any big bear to dispatch you, do you really want to play games just to learn how little energy will do the job? On the other hand, remember that unless you hit the brain or spine, the chances of instantly stopping any big bear are virtually zero, regardless of the chambering or bullet used. Again, to stop the fight instantly, you will have to hit the brain or spine, or break large heavy bones.

Again, I highly recommend testing. Refer to "Terminal Ballistics—Testing Bullet Performance" covered toward the end of this chapter. The biggest bears can weigh far more than 1,000 pounds and are exceptionally sturdy. Look for no less than 21 inches of penetration. I strongly recommend premium bullets demonstrating more than 75 percent weight retention at realistic impact velocities. Also, test the integrity of the bullet by firing into stacks of dry telephone books. Consider only bullets that never completely disintegrate in that test.

For those hunting thin-skinned dangerous game, accuracy is no less important than for those hunting non-dangerous big game. Vital shot placement is even more critical. Test three-shot groups from a clean barrel and from a dirty barrel—one might get a shot after bagging another game animal. How close the first shot comes to where it should hit is the critical issue in this analysis. However, because it seems truly foolish to consider shots at a big bear or any other animal of this class at long-range, accuracy need not be all that startling, so loads that will shoot into 2–3 MOA are certainly adequate.

SELF-DEFENSE BULLETS—SPECIAL CONSIDERATIONS

Consider the situation of a bear versus an outdoorsman armed with a handgun only. Historically the outcome in a duel such as this has been rather grim for the human. Barring a hit to the brain or spine, the most powerful rifle is not up to the task of instantly stopping such an attack; obviously any necessarily far-less-powerful handgun will be even less apt to deliver an instant stop. Hence, if such an encounter is your concern, handload the heaviest hard-cast semiwadcutter bullet that you can find to the maximum velocity that you can safely achieve and that you can handle. Be ready to place your shots into the brain or into the upper spinal column—that is your only chance. Against the biggest of cats, using the same handgun, cartridge, and shot placement is sound practice.

When your concern is two-legged predators and guns appropriate for concealed-carry use, different criteria apply. With sophisticated designs and improved metallurgy, the best modern jacketed hollowpoint (JHP) bullets offer dependable expansion at the modest velocities typical of cartridges appropriate for self-defense handguns. Controlled-expansion is desirable. An expanding bullet can transfer energy faster and do more damage without achieving full penetration and, thereby, potentially becoming a hazard to bystanders. Such bullets are essentially useless against bear or big cat.

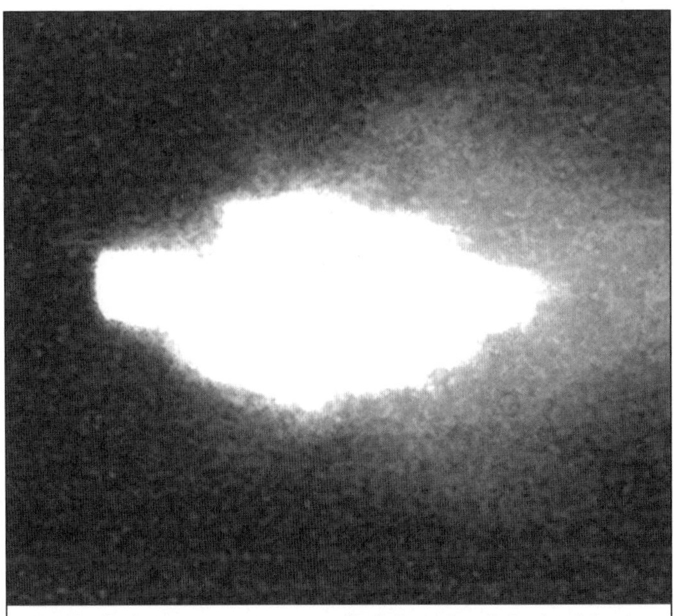

Muzzle flash is an issue in any self-defense load. Such a blinding flash as is demonstrated here is unacceptable.

Elsewhere in this text, I cover certain legal considerations—just remember that the only reason you use handloads for self-defense is that you are a handloader. A critical further consideration is that any ammunition (factory or handload) intended for self-defense must be thoroughly dependable and proven to work in the gun used—semiautomatic pistols are notorious for not working dependably with certain bullets and with some types of loads. Handload and test as if your life depended upon it, because it might.

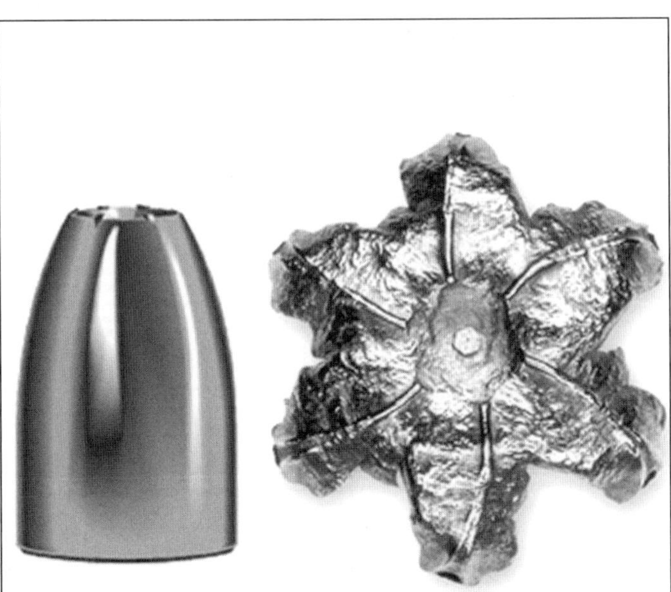

Speer Gold Dot is the premier self-defense bullet. Many design characteristics lead to maximum performance. Hornady XTP and the even better new Hornady self-defense bullet (not shown) are also fine choices.

Appropriate concealed-carry handguns deliver very limited energy. Most authorities deem any cartridge and gun that generates less energy than full-power 357 Magnum cartridges to be marginal at best. Lacking a hit to the brain or spine, you simply cannot count on any such load to produce instant fight-stopping results.

The Speer Gold Dot JHP offers unique advantages in such chamberings. This bullet nose is precut, so expansion is generally more dependable, and expansion also consumes far less energy, leaving more energy to do the necessary work (stopping the fight). Because Speer electroplates the jacket onto the core, jacket separation is impossible. Gold Dot bullets will hold together, to achieve sufficient penetration, while doing maximum possible damage; this also means that these bullets are far superior when it comes to penetrating laminated glass, which is a significant consideration because those intent upon violence commonly use an automobile as a weapon.

When you can use a relatively powerful gun, choose a modern premium-expanding bullet of moderate weight. My handloading favorites are the Hornady XTP and the Speer Gold Dot. The XTP is generally preferable because it is more forgiving as to impact velocity, and it offers impressive terminal performance across a wide range of velocities. However, the Gold Dot, when loaded within the relatively narrow design-velocity range, is a better choice—the new Hornady self-defense bullet with a rubber tip is even better than the XTP.

Determining the correct load needed to achieve ideal Gold Dot expansion requires both chronographing and testing. I cover the latter under "Terminal Ballistics—Testing Bullet Performance" toward the end of this chapter. Look for penetration between about 6 and 9 inches. Weight retention of about 75 percent is certainly acceptable. The expanded bullet diameter should exceed 1½ times the original diameter.

As I covered in chapter 8 entitled "Smokeless—Self-Defense," the handloader should consider one additional aspect of any cartridge he might use for self-defense: muzzle flash.

Accuracy is a fine goal in any cartridge, but here the most important measure is entirely different. Intrinsic accuracy of both gun and load is of little consequence in a typical self-defense encounter—target distance is typically seven feet or less. The critical question is: Can you control the gun, as necessary, to deliver more than one well-placed shot quickly? Therefore, recoil is a consideration.

In any given chambering, lighter bullets generate significantly less recoil. Consider a lightweight, concealed-carry 38 Special. Compare two likely self-defense loads in such a gun: maximum loads with 158-grain bullets and maximum loads with 125-grain bullets. The former generates about 13 percent more recoil than the latter does. Therefore, using the heavier bullet, it will take significantly longer to recover from recoil and to place each subsequent shot properly.

A PERSISTENT MYTH—BUSH BUSTER BULLETS AND CHAMBERINGS

Forced to review only one of the many enduring misconceptions among otherwise well-informed hunters, I would choose the concept of the bush buster. To put this bluntly: Contrary to the intuition of many folks, no such thing as a bush-buster chambering or bullet type exists or will ever exist. "The bush buster" is nothing more than useless, potentially harmful folklore.

Should an intervening branch or twig get in the way, a high-velocity spitzer has exactly the same chance of penetrating to reach the intended target as does a low-

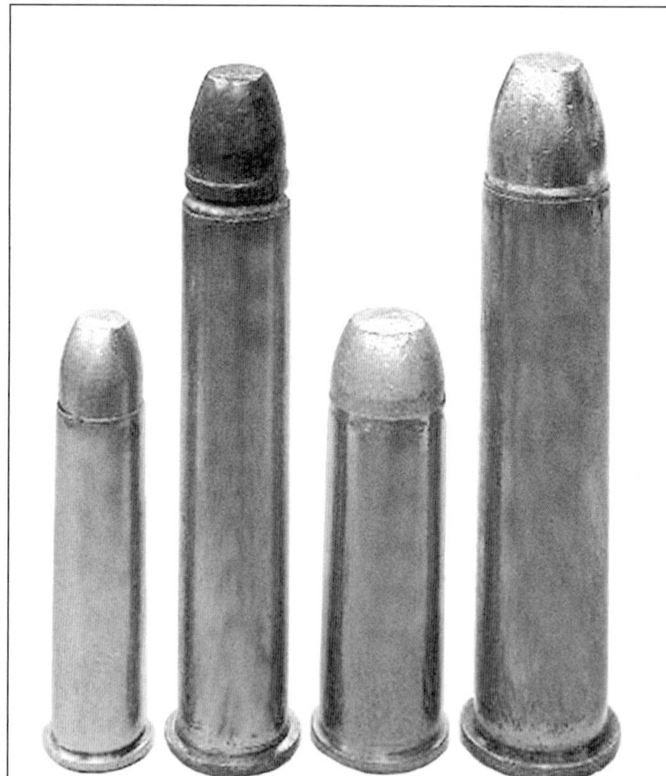

If any of these cast-bullet loads has any "brush busting" advantage over any other sporting load of any kind, that is only because these bullets are hard enough as to not deform when hitting such an obstacle at the normal velocity at which we load such bullets. Regardless of the cartridge or bullet used, hitting any target located beyond any intervening brush is a matter of chance. Deliberately attempting to do so is unsporting, at best.

velocity round-nose bullet. Regardless of folklore to the contrary, the 243 Winchester is just as unlikely to get the job done as the 45-70 Government is. Serious testing has repeatedly proven that for every example where the large, low-velocity, round-nose bullet penetrated to the intended target and the high-velocity spitzer failed to reach the intended target, a counter-example exists, where the high-velocity spitzer penetrated to the target and the low-velocity, round-nose deflected and, thereby, failed to reach the target.

Certain bullet shapes might possibly have a comparative advantage for certain types of impacts with certain types of obstacles. For example, a grazing impact with the edge of a small branch might deflect a round-nose bullet less than it would deflect a sharp-pointed one, while an impact more nearly centered on a somewhat larger branch might deflect a sharp-pointed bullet less than it would deflect a round-nose bullet.

In the real world, any intervening branch (or branches!) might be of any size, shape, and hardness; bullet impact on that branch might be centered, or grazing, or anywhere in between, and that impact might be perpendicular or oblique to the length of the branch. Therefore, for any shot fired through any random maze of branches, it would be impossible to guess a priori which bullet shape might be deflected least.

Most importantly, unless the intended target is very close behind an intervening twig or branch, I can state unequivocally that any bullet that first hits a twig or branch is almost certain to deflect enough to ensure that it will almost certainly miss the intended target. Even if it does not miss, it is apt to hit in the wrong place. Even if it does not hit in the wrong place, it is apt to hit while going partially sideways and therefore not expand and penetrate as it should. In any case, it is not apt to result in a humane kill.

Only one result seems constant in such tests: Compared to bullets that are more frangible, heavily constructed bullets tend to deflect less. This is not exactly a surprise, but it does suggest a surprising prediction: As a so-called bush buster, a 270 Winchester shooting the relatively tough Barnes 130-grain X would likely be a better choice than a 30-30, 308 Winchester, or a 300 Magnum loaded with any conventional round-nose bullet.

The important point here is that the bush buster simply does not exist; nevertheless, this nonsense simply will not go away. Just today, as I was reviewing this text, I received a magazine with an article expounding the virtues of the 450 Marlin as a "brush buster." Regardless of any such hype, reality proves that it makes no sense to choose a hunting bullet based upon any such misconception.

Of the three loads represented here—(left-to-right) 45-70 Springfield 405-grain SP, 6mm Remington 90-grain X, and 30-30 Winchester, 170-grain Silvertip—the 6mm load likely comes closest to being a "brush buster" because that relatively hard bullet is less apt to deform significantly upon hitting any intervening twig. However, none of these nor any other sporting cartridge combination is in any meaningful sense a "brush buster." Among feasible sporting cartridges, such a combination simply does not exist.

Having said this, I am, no doubt, destined to incur the wrath of many who simply know better. Hence, I will restate the fact that experimenters have done these tests. If you do not trust that, please set up your own tests. With a few weeks of dedicated study and with considerable expense, you should be able to prove this fact to your satisfaction—the bush buster is a fantasy.

REGARDLESS OF HOW ROMANTIC THE NOTION MIGHT BE, THE BUSH BUSTER SPORTING CARTRIDGE SIMPLY DOES NOT EXIST.

BULLET SEATING—ACCURACY CONSIDERATIONS

Many typical loads in bottlenecked cases place the bullet shank (cylindrical full-diameter portion of bullet) fully to the bottom or beyond the bottom of the case neck—see the related sketches on page 259. Persuasive arguments suggest that, ideally, for maximum accuracy and efficiency, chamber design and cartridge length should position the base of a flat-base bullet (or, with boattail bullets, the base of the bullet shank) very near the neck-to-shoulder junction.

The following sketches demonstrate why placing the base of the bullet shank flush with the base of the case neck is apt to result in more consistent propellant packing during charging and compression (as happens during the ignition phase). Regardless of how tiny any real-world difference might be, that difference might matter.

Unfortunately, it is not feasible to design any chamber that will allow for an ideal seating when using bullets of significantly varying lengths. If seating depth and bullet jump are simultaneously correct for a bullet of one length, then a longer bullet will protrude into the case body and a shorter bullet will either not be close to the rifling or it will not be seated to the ideal (base-of-neck) depth.

The best solution to this quandary is to design cases with sufficiently long necks so that the neck holds all bullets squarely and securely, despite possible shallow seating (with light bullets). Short case necks present other problems. Ballisticians and serious shooters alike have long recognized that cases with unusually short necks create chamberings with unusually short barrel life, e.g., 223 WSSM, 243 Winchester, 264 Winchester Magnum, 300 Winchester Magnum, and so on. I cover one possible reason behind this characteristic in chapter 13.

IN EXPLAINING WHY CHAMBER DESIGNS REQUIRING DEEPLY SEATED BULLETS ARE NOT CONDUCIVE TO ACCURACY, THE FOLLOWING ARE ONLY THEORIES.

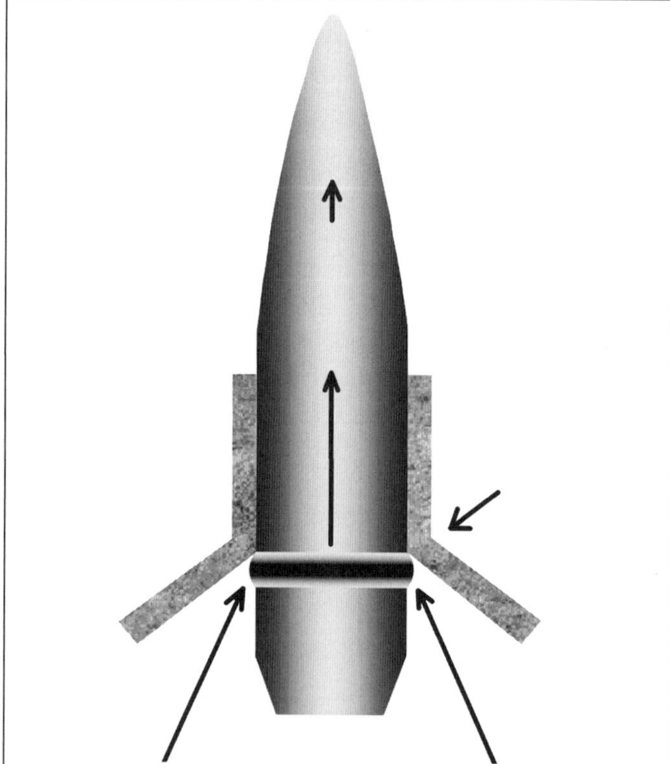

This is a representation of a pressure wave generated by the impact of a primer shock wave on an exposed bullet base. The wave bounces between the ends of the bullet and causes a slight swelling as it passes any given area. Bullet-to-neck friction increases as this shock wave swelling passes through the case neck. This periodically retards bullet acceleration. The lengths of the vertical arrows suggest relative velocity after the bullet begins to move: The bullet velocity is indicated by the shorter arrow and the pressure wave velocity by the longer arrow. The actual bullet velocity is always orders of magnitude slower than the shock wave velocity—this wave will pass through the case neck many times before the bullet clears the neck.

Representation of Normal and Abnormal Pressure Curves
Depending upon Location of Bullet Base
(Near Base of Neck or Extending Well below Base of Neck)

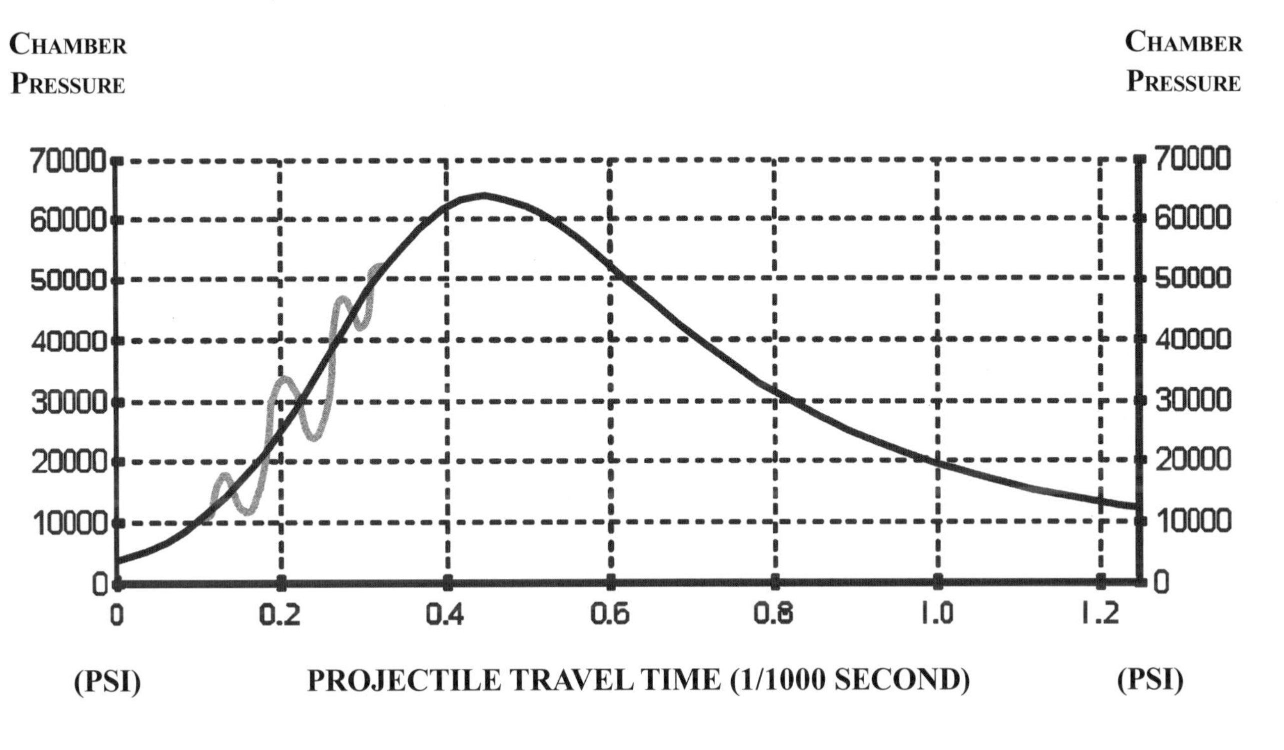

Ideal versus Imperfect Bullet Seating Depths

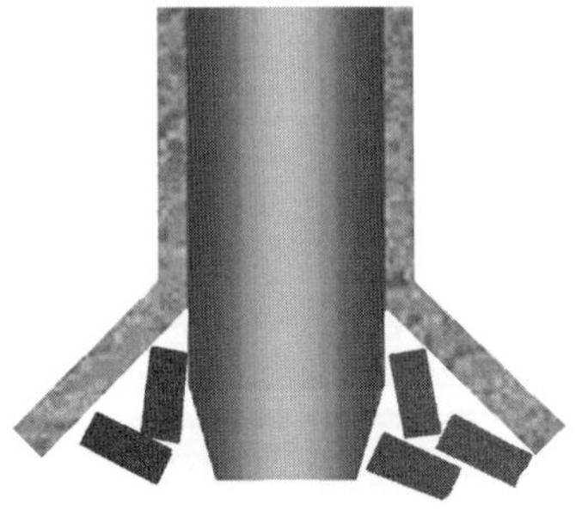

TOO DEEP
Bullet protrudes into propellant chamber, thus reducing performance and degrading accuracy

IDEAL DEPTH
Granules fill similarly around the bullet base, regardless of orientation

TOO SHALLOW
Granules filling around the bullet base depends upon random granule orientation

FAR TOO SHALLOW
Very short bullet with ideal bullet-to-rifling jump is not well supported by the case neck

BULLET SEATING—ANOTHER POSSIBLE ACCURACY ISSUE

Seating the bullet shank deeper than the base of the case neck sets up a situation where shock waves traveling end-to-end through the bullet can create a periodic increase in friction between the bullet shank and case neck. This results because of the dynamic swelling of the unsupported bullet base, which is in response to the impact of the shock wave from the primer blast onto the bullet base. See cartoon on page 258.

This phenomenon might explain why loads using deeply seated bullets sometimes show numerous pressure spikes along the rise side of the pressure curve—a consequence seldom seen with otherwise similar loads in which the bullet shank is seated at-or-above the neck-to-shoulder junction. (See sketches on bottom of page 259.) Regardless, when designing a cartridge and chamber, it seems advisable to design the chamber throat so that the base of the bullet shank comes as nearly as is feasible to lining up with the neck-to-shoulder junction of the case.

A shock wave induced by the primer blast travels up and down the bullet. This shock wave produces an increase in the bullet diameter as it passes any given section of the bullet. This shock wave reflects off each end of the bullet and, therefore, repeatedly passes back and forth along the length of the bullet. As this pressure wave passes through the unsupported portion of the bullet shank, a modest increase in the bullet diameter occurs (as suggested by the stippled area in the cartoon on page 258). If a significant length of the bullet shank extends below the base of the case neck, wave velocity is sufficient to bring the swelled zone into contact with the base of the case neck several times before the bullet moves sufficiently so that the entire shank is within the case neck. The impact of this swelled zone with the case neck (as suggested at the point indicated by the diagonal arrows on page 258) causes a significant periodic increase in bullet-to-neck friction. This can result in periodic temporary reductions in bullet acceleration, which can result in periodic pressure spikes and subsequent temporary decreases in pressure.

This is just a theory. Regardless, something is happening because cartridges with deep-seated bullets do often show such a pressure-curve response and are often less accurate.

TERMINAL BALLISTICS—TESTING BULLET PERFORMANCE

Shooters who are particularly interested in terminal performance should collect used telephone books. My erudite friend, Ed Wosika, refers to these as a

Note how little of the bullet shank is engaged by the case neck, with the shallow seating of a boattail bullet (example at right). Note how far the bullet extends into body of case with the optimum seating depth (example at left). Such seating is often a necessity when combining bullets with long boattails and cases with short necks. This is one reason that case designs with relatively long necks are superior; other reasons exist, which I discuss elsewhere.

ballistic laminar attenuation medium, or BLAM. He suggests, and I agree, that this moniker should render the importance of this pursuit a bit easier to remember. Contrary to intuition, this material is one of the best substances available for this purpose. My acquaintance, the late Finn Aagaard, who promoted the type of bullet testing proposed in this section, deserves the honor for promoting this valuable method.

Always do any such testing only with a proper backstop and with the target located so that an errant bullet will neither ricochet nor find an unintended downrange target. The best practice is to place the target on a table so that you can shoot directly into it, as if you were shooting a conventional target. Always shoot squarely into the face of the stack so that bullets do not escape from the perimeter. Always use a thick enough stack to stop all bullets—if in doubt, place about twelve inches of dry books behind the saturated stack.

Terminal ballistics testing involves the evaluation of bullet performance when firing into any given substance, at any given angle, and at any particular impact velocity. Those working in ballistics laboratories report that many variables complicate any such testing. When measuring overall bullet performance, ballisticians must often evaluate the consequences of these various types of impacts with more than one substance.

These studies can include tests where various amounts and types of intervening materials are placed between the gun and the ultimate target. These materials can include various combinations of glass (standard, tempered, or laminated), sheet metal, sheetrock, wood, paperboard, armor plating (both soft and hard), fabric, and other substances. Ballisticians must also consider bullet impacts that are not at a 90-degree angle to the surface.

When a bullet fails to penetrate the intervening materials, the ballistician evaluates the apparatus and records what it was that the bullet did do. When a bullet achieves penetration, the tester might measure the retained velocity. The apparatus might include a water tank in order to capture the bullet without creating further deformation. Bullet evaluation factors would include deformation and weight retention.

Easy to obtain telephone books are an ideal expansion-test medium.

Conversely, assuming the bullet penetrated any intervening material, it might then enter a block of ballistic gelatin. Ballistic gelatin is the laboratory standard for evaluating the anticipated bullet performance in living flesh. The tester could measure and record the penetration into this block and record the bullet's expansion, weight retention, final orientation, and any unusual characteristics of the bullet or of the developed "wound" channel. The simplest testing involves firing bullets straight into naked gelatin.

Although ballistics laboratories use gelatin for all standard terminal ballistics comparisons intended to suggest bullet performance in flesh, gelatin is not necessarily the best substance for this purpose. Certainly, the handloader has a better choice. We can use exactly two substances to answer all our terminal performance questions with sufficient accuracy for any need:

- Dry newspaper or telephone book
- Saturated newspaper or telephone book

Telephone book paper is the preferred material (avoid shiny pages). We observe the penetration, expansion, and weight retention of bullets that we have fired into both the wet and the dry versions. Relative bullet-to-bullet performance comparisons are likely the most revealing aspect of such testing. Additionally, a comparison of the performance of a given bullet at various impact velocities is useful.

Saturated telephone books contain water, cellulose, and clay in proportions that reasonably simulate living flesh, especially with regard to how this substance interacts with a bullet. No such substance is an ideal substitute for living flesh and blood and bone, but this particular substance comes much closer to the mark than does ballistic gelatin, clay, or any other substance that is readily available. Because all telephone book paper (excepting shiny paper) is essentially identical, this material provides repeatable results. Furthermore, shooters can easily obtain used telephone books. Finally, almost anyone interested in terminal ballistics can prepare and use this substance. That is not true of ballistic gelatin; even the most careful ballisticians have considerable trouble obtaining consistent results with gelatin.

To mimic heavy bone, Mr. Aagaard suggested placing about one inch of saturated phone book in front of about four inches of dry phone book followed by another eighteen-inch thickness of saturated phone book. This mimics impacts into the heavy shoulder bones of large big-game animals. This is a useful method for testing the ultimate reliability of a bullet. However, a simple stack of saturated phone books satisfies most needs.

If you are concerned about bullet integrity (toughness), shoot bullets into a stack of dry telephone books that is at least twelve inches thick—for deep penetrating solids, back this up with another twelve inches of dry paper. Any expanding bullet that can hold together at all in this test is apt to fair well even against the most solid of bones; any solid that does not significantly deform in this test is apt to retain the full integrity of shape and mass even after hitting the most solid of bones. This test also provides a handy performance comparison of the potential integrity of different expanding bullets.

For standard (wet) tests, remove all shiny pages and make a stack of books that is about nine inches thick. Place this in deep water—a large trash can is handy for this. Allow twenty-four hours to fully saturate the stack. The thickness of the stack will reach about thirteen inches.

Remove the saturated stack from its water bath and press it until you have reduced the stack's thickness to about twelve inches. To do this, place the stack face up on a handy flat surface, cover it with a dry, thick telephone book or a similarly rigid object, and press on that with about fifty pounds of force for about thirty seconds. Using heavy monofilament fishing line, tie the stack together across the center from both sides and ends. Keep the ties in the same location for all stacks and do not shoot through the strings. Perhaps amazingly, hitting a tie string thoroughly fouls test results.

An initial test requires firing into the face of a stack at close range—the bullet's impact should always be at a 90-degree angle. For most cartridges up to 30-06 class and using full-size telephone books, you can use each stack for six shots. When testing low-power handgun (and similar) cartridges, with well-placed shots you can fire nine shots into one stack. However, with too many shots, it does become difficult to keep the wound channels sorted out. For powerful cartridges, four shots per stack is about maximum; center the shots in each of the four quadrants produced by visually dissecting the height and width of the page. For testing expanding bullets in the most powerful cartridges, two shots might be all that will work well; when testing solids in dry paper, one shot per stack might be all that works. As noted, be certain to fire all shots squarely into the stack so that a bullet does not exit the perimeter and fire all shots parallel so that bullet paths do not intersect.

Bullets intended for thin-skinned hunting applications should achieve about twelve inches of wet-stack penetration. For heavier species, eighteen inches of penetration is usually sufficient. For self-defense loads, where the shooter might encounter vermin of the two-legged variety, six inches of penetration is reasonable. Any bullet that fails to maintain significant integrity in this test is a poor choice for anything except varmint hunting. I define significant integrity as 60 percent or greater weight retention.

Big-game hunters can mimic but not duplicate long-range shots using reduced loads at point-blank range. These are worthwhile tests whenever the hunter considers using a new bullet. Use published data to estimate the impact velocity of the bullet at the far end of the useful hunting distance for that chambering, shooter, and load. Develop a load that launches the bullet at that velocity. Then test that load, as described here.

However, for several reasons note that the terminal performance of a bullet launched at reduced velocity into an expansion medium at close distance fails to duplicate precisely the performance of the same type of bullet launched by a full-power load into an expansion medium at long distance.

First, at impact, the reduced-load bullet will not be spinning as fast as will a full-power bullet impacting at long-range. When launched faster from the same barrel, the bullet is necessarily spinning faster, and the spin rate slows very little as the bullet moves downrange. Bullets fired with reduced loads are less stable after impact (are more apt to turn) and have less rotational stress (will expand slightly less). Second, during firing reduced loads do not stress the bullet as much as full-power loads do (the jacket could end up being stronger). Finally, a bullet fired with a reduced load is cooler when it hits the target—it was heated less during firing, and it is heated less by friction as it passes through the air (which makes it harder). These variations influence terminal results, perhaps considerably. (With fragmenting varmint bullets, these differences render the reduced-load test essentially meaningless.)

To mimic actual long-range results properly, the best method is to set up the saturated stacks of telephone book at the distance in question and fire shots into those stacks using your actual hunting load. This takes some work, but the results are most interesting and are certainly worthwhile. If a bullet fails to expand properly in the saturated telephone books at any given distance, you can be certain that it is a poor hunting choice for shots at that distance.

Examining the recovered bullet and measuring the distance penetrated provide good information. Although no such measurement proves anything about real-world hunting effectiveness of any bullet, the hunter can use the measured results to compare the performance of various bullets. Such results are suggestive of actual relative hunting performance. The most important considerations are:

- The percentage of original weight retained:
  - » For varmint hunting of small critters, the bullet should disintegrate.
  - » For expanding hunting bullets, a greater percentage of retained weight is better
- Final diameter:
  - » For expanding hunting bullets, about 1½ to 2½ times original diameter is good
  - » For nonexpanding bullets, the nose diameter should not increase more than about 5 percent
- Distance penetrated by bullet or bullet fragments:
  - » Small varmint—about 4 inches

» Large varmint—about 6 inches
» Self-defense—about 6 to 9 inches
» Smaller big-game species about 9 to 12 inches (antelope, small whitetail)
» Medium big-game species about 12 to 15 inches (mule deer, medium black bear)
» Large big game about 15 to 18 inches (elk, moose, large black bear)
» Very large big game about 18 to 24 inches (large grizzly species and similar size African species)
» Solids intended to give maximum penetration—at least 48 inches.

I provided specific penetration recommendations in the previous sections of this chapter that cover specific bullet recommendations for specific types of hunting. Comparison of similar bullets will readily suggest which ones offer the greatest chance of providing the best terminal performance for the intended purpose.

As a demonstration of just how worthwhile this simple method can be, consider that some ballisticians who routinely use ballistic gelatin at work prefer to use saturated telephone books for personal bullet testing. This is chiefly because this medium provides a superior representation of the potential performance of a hunting bullet.

FRICTION-PROOF BULLETS—GENERAL CONSIDERATIONS

Because of the extended shot strings involved, varmint hunters and NRA high-power competitors find benefits in the use of friction-proofed bullets, which reduce bullet-to-bore friction and thereby reduce bore fouling. Norma, Berger, Sierra, Hornady, and Barnes have offered such bullets. Often, the use of such bullets requires special cartridge loading and barrel cleaning techniques.

My late friend Roger Johnston had several prescient comments about guns, accuracy, and newfangled devices and methods. He was one of the original investigators of bullets that were plated with molybdenum-disulfide, so folks often asked him if he believed that "moly" would eventually prove its worth and thereby gain wide acceptance. He always replied with a thin smile and a veiled message, "We shall see."

Because Johnston developed and promoted moly plating for one purpose only—to reduce bore fouling—it is perhaps surprising that so much misunderstanding and controversy surrounds this substance regarding its potential value to shooters and its correct use.

Molybdenum-disulfide (hereafter, moly) has indeed proven its worth. However, in order to achieve the maximum benefit from using moly-plated bullets, shooters must consider and attend to each of the following:

- Proper application of pure material to correctly prepared bullets
- Use of properly prepared cases
- Use of the right primer and the correct charge of correct propellant
- Careful barrel cleaning, prior to initial use
- Proper barrel break-in
- Proper barrel maintenance

To use moly-plated bullets to the best advantage, shooters must consider many things. Many who have had bad experiences with moly have used impure moly or some so-called equivalent material or have otherwise failed to use common sense and to attend to the above-listed criteria.

WHY MOLYBDENUM-DISULFIDE IS BENEFICIAL AND THE NEED FOR BARREL CLEANING

Technically, what we call moly is a simple chemical (MoS_2, known to geologists as the mineral molybdenite). This material has useful physical and chemical properties; pertinent to this discussion are the following:

- Physical affinity for metallic alloys
- Low coefficient of friction
- High sheer strength
- Low chemical reactivity
- Nontoxicity

Beginning with a properly cleaned bullet (lead alloy, copper, brass, or gilding metal), moly will easily and spontaneously bond onto the surface and infiltrate into any porosity. Moly is a world-class friction-reducing agent. Producers add moly to high-performance lubricants intended for use under extremes of both heat and pressure. The coefficient of friction is so low that, compared to conventional bullets, moly-plated bullets engrave into the rifling and slide through the barrel with dramatically less resistance. This accounts for much of the reported barrel life increase associated with use of moly.

Very briefly, because moly-plated bullets slide through a barrel more easily, these also pass through the barrel without creating as much swelling (obturation). These also slide through the barrel without pulling so hard on individual metallic crystals, which temporarily expose intercrystalline boundaries to corrosive gases.

When we fire a shot and during much of the acceleration of the bullet through the bore, the acceleration force exceeds the bullet's strength. When this is true, the bullet will swell (obturate) and thereby stretch the bore until the resistance of the barrel to further stretching exactly balances the stress applied by the swelling bullet.

Obturation increases bullet-to-bore contact pressure until that exactly matches the force acting to swell the bullet (force on the bullet base minus the internal bullet strength). Increasing the obturation force directly increases the bullet-to-bore friction and resulting bore-interior friction, stress, and heating. Increasing the stress increases the corrosion rate. Contrary to intuition and folklore, corrosion (not erosion) is the chief culprit that wears out most sporting-rifle barrels.

Because moly reduces barrel stress, it also reduces barrel corrosion—the barrel is apt to last longer. This advantage probably diminishes as the relative case capacity increases, becoming of little importance in the super-magnum chamberings. This is likely true because erosion in those guns significantly limits barrel life. However, in most typical chamberings, the increase

The RCBS Inertial Bullet Puller is the "handloader's crowbar and eraser in one tool." It provides a handy method of pulling bullets. If you handload, sooner of later, you will find that you need an inertial bullet puller.

This bullet was pulled using an inertial hammer: Significant jacket damage occurred as the improperly prepared case mouth cut deeply into the jacket—just as would happen when the round was fired. If you never pull a bullet, you cannot know if this sort of damage is occurring. This type of damage is common, especially with cast and swaged bullets, and it will limit accuracy.

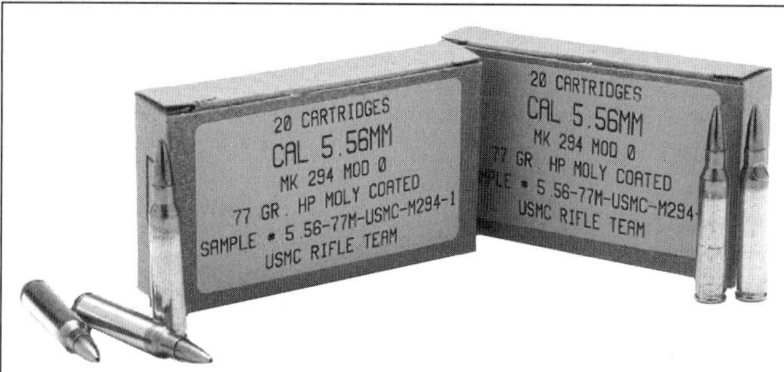

Those who do not believe in the benefits of moly plating should discuss the matter with expert military marksmen who choose to use Black Hills moly-plated ammunition when placing their lives on the line.

The bullet on the left shows significant damage from seating into an improperly prepared case—burs on the inside of the case mouth have cut into the bullet jacket. The bullet at right demonstrates what happens when one attempts to apply moly to a bullet that is not properly cleaned—the moly is merely coated onto the bullet; it will not adhere. This is a useless enterprise—moly only plates onto properly cleaned bullets.

in barrel life is significant—exclusive use of moly can more than double accurate barrel life.

Moly easily withstands the physical and chemical abuses associated with firing a cartridge. As a bullet accelerates through the bore, some moly stays on the bullet, some transfers to the bore. This explains why the first few moly-plated bullets fired through a clean barrel will tend to show variable ballistics and might not shoot to the same point of aim as subsequent bullets do. However, barrels vary widely in this regard. Some shoot normally from the first shot using moly; others require dozens of shots before settling down. A good practice is to pretreat a just-cleaned barrel with a thin coating of a moly-saturated grease—this might eliminate the need for such a break-in. After applying moly grease, run at least one dry patch through the bore several times to remove any excess grease.

Bore adaptation to moly also partly explains the need to clean the bore properly before initially using moly. Obviously, in a fouled bore, moly cannot reach the steel surface. However, another reason exists: Bore fouling will cut through the minute layer of moly that plates the bullet surface and into the underlying metal. Preexisting fouling tears away pieces of the plated bullet. Some percentage of this abraded material directly bonds to existing bore fouling. The remainder entrains into the propellant cloud. Some of the entrained metallic material vaporizes and some of that condenses onto cooler bore surfaces (chiefly in bottoms of grooves) toward the muzzle.

This process leads to a continuing buildup of bore fouling. We have seen evidence that shooting moly-plated bullets through a fouled bore can significantly increase the fouling rate. Completely clean any barrel before beginning to use moly-plated bullets. Not to belabor the point, but clean means clean—it does not mean that you think you have it clean. It means that you have used plenty of elbow grease with an abrasive cleaner, followed by a chemical cleaner (to check for remaining traces of copper).

I believe the best way to remove heavy fouling is to use a patch that is saturated with an abrasive cleaner, such as Iosso Paste. A patch wrapped around a worn-out bore bush, or one that is one size smaller than bore size, is an effective tool.

Moly is not chemically inert. In the presence of humidity and oxygen, moly will react chemically. In the presence of moisture and when in contact with metal (the bullet or the bore), it can react to form molybdenum trioxide and sulfuric acid—(MoS_2 + 5[H_2O] + 3O_2 MoO_3 + 2[H_2SO_4] + 3[H_2]).

While molybdenum trioxide (MoO_3) is a good lubricant, sulfuric acid (H_2SO_4) is rather corrosive. While other reactions are possible, the reaction always creates some type of acid. After several years of storage in a humid environment, moly-plated copper (or copper alloy) bullets can show this effect—evidenced as a bluish iridescent sheen. The use of bullets showing this effect evidently creates no problems.

The conversion of molybdenum disulfide into molybdenum trioxide can also occur when reactive propellant gases attack it. This conversion can produce minute quantities of free sulfur that can react to form acids. Under normal circumstances, it seems unlikely that such sulfurous traces will do significant harm unless the barrel is stored in a humid environment without cleaning. Some shooters have reported a reaction between steel and moly, but this is most likely the result of the conversion of moly into molybdenum trioxide and sulfuric acid, as noted above.

These folks have reported evidence of a minute etching at the surface of moly-coated steel after long-term storage. We know that salt and humidity exacerbate this effect and might, in fact, be completely responsible for any such reaction. In any case, the blame for any resulting damage rests entirely on the careless gun owner who did not properly clean and oil the gun before storage.

DO NOT PLACE A MOLY-FOULED BARREL IN LONG-TERM STORAGE! CLEAN IT, AND THEN LIGHTLY OIL IT, JUST AS YOU WOULD ANY OTHER BARREL.

Finally, with regard to toxicity, while no one advocates eating it—although this fine black powder will get on everything in the area—moly is perfectly safe to handle.

On a related subject, any barrel with metallic fouling in it is subject to the electrolytic reaction known as the battery couple. In the presence of significant atmospheric humidity and especially in areas where salt air exists (near the ocean), the two metals will spontaneously react to generate oxidized metal, acid, and an electric current. Hence, cleaning and oiling any barrel before placing it in long-term storage is always the best practice.

MOLY-PLATED BULLETS—LOADING AND USING

Companies offer kits that allow the handloader to apply moly at home. Use only the best; per-bullet cost

This is a premium factory load using a properly moly-plated match bullet. When properly applied, moly has a steel-gray color and a metallic sheen.

is so minuscule as to make the kit price irrelevant. If you do not get the bullet clean, you cannot properly plate it with moly. Full-strength Dawn Ultra (liquid dishwashing detergent) does a fine job here.

Place bullets in a small container, squirt about one tablespoonful of Dawn on bullets, and mix those until the detergent fully coats each. Wait five to ten minutes (fifteen to twenty minutes for Barnes and Speer bullets) and rinse thoroughly with hot water. (Leaving this mildly corrosive soap on bullets too long could result in the potentially damaging etching of the bullet surfaces.)

The addition of water to the moly, to create a slurry, is extremely beneficial. The water will evaporate as plating progresses. After the water has fully evaporated, bullet plating will be perfect.

The perfectly plated bullet, at left, has a uniform metallic gray sheen; the imperfectly plated bullet, at right, has tiny patches of excess moly that create a mottled surface—when underlying moly is properly plated onto the bullet it will have the same metallic gray sheen as a perfectly plated bullet. This mottling harms nothing but the appearance.

For handloaders, the use of moly-plated bullets requires several additional loading steps and careful attention to detail in several other steps. Often, the handloader must increase the propellant charge. This is necessary to keep the resulting load at the same velocity (when fired through a barrel that is properly broken-in with moly). Sometimes (as when the charge of the original load was significantly compressed), this can require the use of a different (slightly faster) propellant.

Note that once the barrel is properly mollied, it will stay that way, despite any normal cleaning operations. Do not try to remove every trace of moly from the bore. That is both impossible and counterproductive. (Firing enough unplated bullets through the bore will eventually strip out the moly.)

Often, owing to the relatively reduced bullet-to-case friction that occurs when using moly-plated bullets, the primer blast can move the bullet. Because primer-induced bullet movement is likely to vary from one shot to the next, this can destroy ballistic uniformity and, hence, accuracy. To keep the bullet in place against the primer blast, it is necessary to use more case-neck tension than when using conventional bullets.

For the same reason, it is sometimes necessary to use a milder primer. Where a magnum primer gave good results when using a conventional bullet, with moly it is sometimes necessary to switch to a standard primer. (Note that, generally, Winchester rifle primers are very powerful and generate more impulse to dislodge the bullet than other rifle primers generate.)

When loading with moly, it is critical to know that the case neck is properly prepared so that bullet seating does not significantly damage the thin and fragile plating. (Seating and then pulling a bullet is the only way to know.) A necessary step is the proper deburring and polishing of the interior of the case neck. Not only must you remove any burs (as are created with trimming), but you must also polish the case mouth interior to eliminate sharp edges, which are certain to cut through the moly. To test for this potentiality, use an inertial bullet puller to remove a seated bullet from a fully prepped case. If the moly is not 100 percent intact along the bullet shank, you have a problem. When using moly-plated bullets, bullet surface scarring degrades performance; this will lead to excessive bore fouling. (Often the seating operation will have scuffed the moly at the bullet base enough for the bullet to show through; this is not a significant problem.)

FRICTION PROOFED BULLETS—USAGE AND POTENTIAL BENEFITS

In a rifle with a decent barrel, moly-plated bullets can dramatically reduce fouling—varminters and competitive NRA high-power shooters who use moly can fire hundreds of rounds between barrel cleanings without any measurable accuracy degradation. The Late Eunice Berger won the national benchrest championships using moly-plated bullets.

A moly-coated bore interior provides precious little purchase for propellant fouling. In addition, moly is interposed between the bullet and bore. This reduces metallic fouling. Finally, as noted in the previous section, moly-plated bullets swell less in the bore and thereby reduce bullet-to-bore friction and the resultant corrosion. Finally, in similarly performing loads, moly-plated bullets generate less barrel heating, chiefly because these bullets do not deform the barrel as much—contrary to common misconception, the primary source of barrel heating is barrel deformation, not friction or hot gas.

Experience proves that moly-plated bullets might or might not produce better accuracy in any given rifle and load. Any accuracy improvement likely stems from two sources. First, because a moly-plated bullet has less friction, it swells less while accelerating through the barrel. A bullet that swells less will deform less; therefore, it stays closer to the original shape and might retain superior balance. If so, it will be more accurate.

Second, the moly-related fouling reduction means that the barrel stays cleaner during any extended shot string. It seems obvious that a reduction of fouling buildup must correspond to a reduction of accuracy

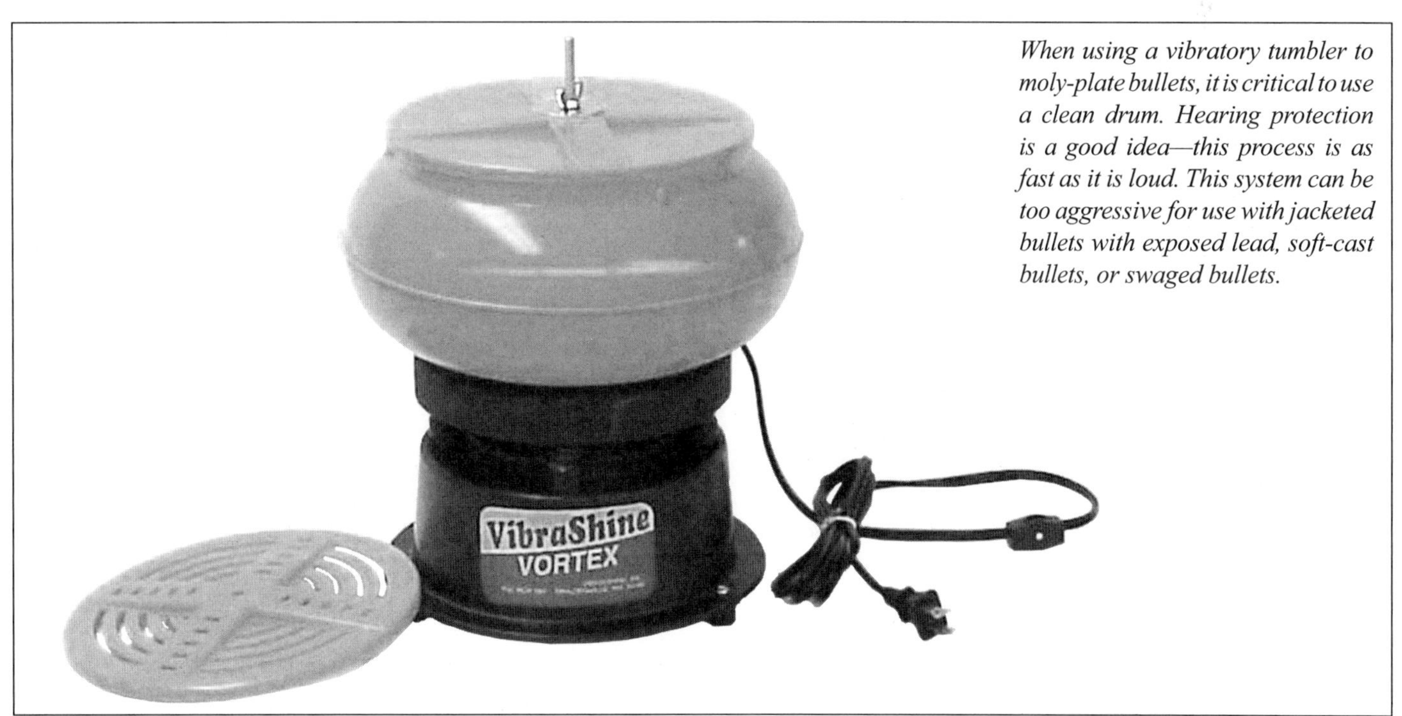

When using a vibratory tumbler to moly-plate bullets, it is critical to use a clean drum. Hearing protection is a good idea—this process is as fast as it is loud. This system can be too aggressive for use with jacketed bullets with exposed lead, soft-cast bullets, or swaged bullets.

Tumbling is the method used by Berger and Norma to apply world-class moly plating to their bullets.

loss: If fouling did not degrade accuracy, why would we ever clean a barrel?

Finally, we have evidence that properly moly-plating a bullet can increase the effective ballistic efficiency. Long-range shooters sometimes see moly-plated bullets shoot noticeably flatter, compared to unplated bullets launched at the same velocity. Most of this effect probably reflects reduced deformation during obturation—the bullet remains slightly more streamlined.

FRICTION-PROOF BULLETS—LIMITATIONS AND POTENTIAL PROBLEMS

Factory ammunition using moly-plated bullets is not apt to perform up to the maximum velocity potential. The producers of factory-loaded cartridges cannot assume that every barrel in which customers might use ammunition with moly-plated bullets has been properly broken in (with moly). Therefore, most such ammunition is generally loaded to produce somewhat less than full pressure when fired from a bore that has been exposed to moly; hence, such loads cannot exceed the ballistics of otherwise similar conventional cartridges. This is only one of the reasons that ballisticians tend to have a negatively biased opinion of the potential benefits of using properly moly-plated bullets.

SOURCES FOR SPECIALTY TOOLS REFERENCED IN THIS CHAPTER:

Bear Creek Supply
P.O. Box 177
Waterford, CA 95386
Telephone: 209-874-4322

Belt Mountain Enterprises Inc.
Box 353, Belgrade, MT 59714
Telephone: 406-388-1396
www.beltmountain.com

Buffalo Arms Company
660 Vermeer Court
Ponderay, ID 83852
Telephone: 208-263-6953
bufarms@netw.com

Magnus Bullets
Telephone: 256-420-8360

Superior Shooting Systems
800 N. Second St.
Canadian, TX 79014
Telephone: 806-323-9483

By Smalley holds a custom Rolling Block, which he built. Chambered in 45-70, this rifle has proven to be particularly effective when launching Smalley's 362-grain Transonic brass bullet at the main Friends of Billy Dixon Target. Using this combination, Smalley has made four consecutive hits (a record that stands as I write this). Note that the scope is mounted at an extreme angle to the barrel; this is necessary when launching bullets at a target that is 1,538 yards distant. Smalley accomplished this significant mounting bias using modified Burris Signature Zee rings and a much taller rear base.

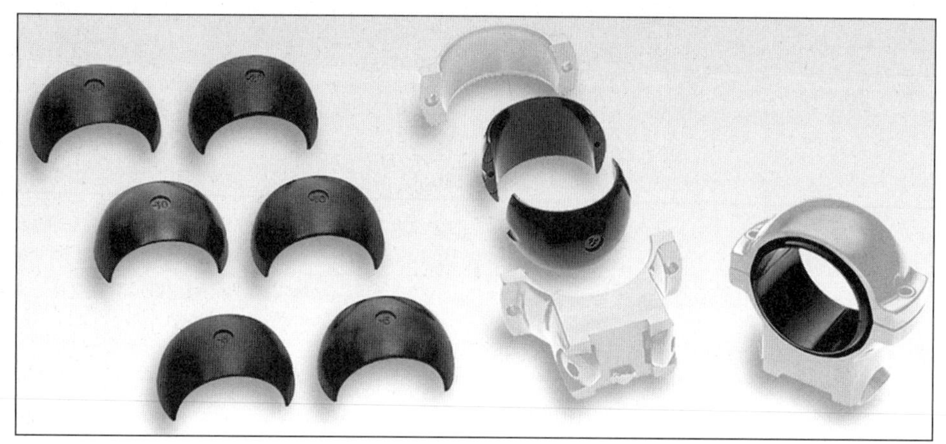

Burris Signature Zee Rings with offset inserts provide up to 30 minutes of angle bias between the axis of the scope and the axis of the bore. By using a taller rear base (see previous picture on page 271) it is possible to achieve many minutes of angle bias. More importantly, this system eliminates the need to lap the scope rings while eliminating the stress between the scope and rifle.

Many die manufacturers offer dedicated case-mouth expanders of various types. Sometimes, it is quite useful to expand the mouth of a bottlenecked case slightly before seating a bullet. When using cast bullets, this is necessary; when seating moly-plated bullets into a case with a significant amount of neck tension, this can mitigate, or eliminate, plating damage. Some producers offer a stepped expander that enlarges a small length of the end of the case mouth to slightly more than the bullet's diameter—such a die is particularly useful for easing the bullet seating, and it will minimize bullet damage during seating.

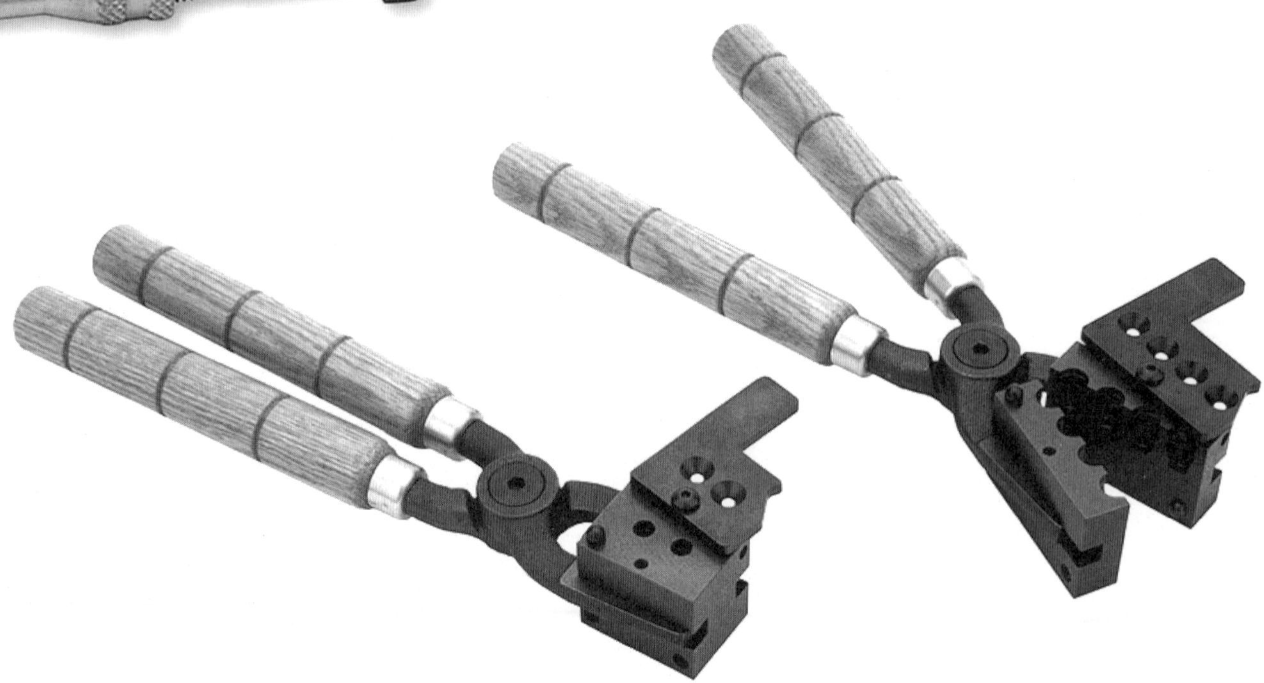

Cast bullets, discussed in a later chapter, offer serious handloaders practically unlimited opportunities to make affordable bullets at home and to create a specific type of cast bullet—to fulfill some real or perceived need.

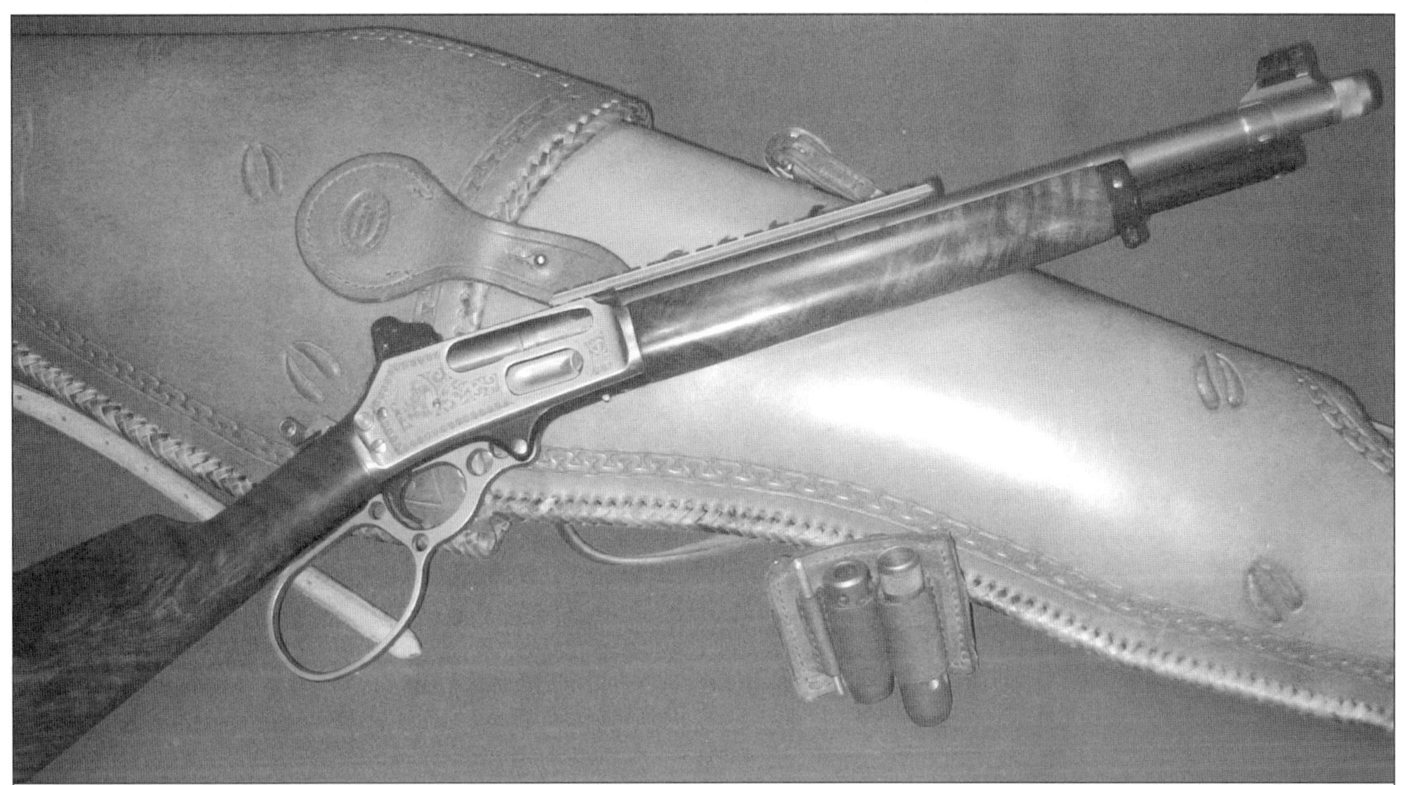

This custom lightweight 45-70 Marlin carbine belongs to Tom Knight. This rifle weighs less than seven pounds, even with an optional Scout scope mounted on the XS Systems rail with QD rings. It features premium wood, optional LAW muzzle brakes, premium sights, WWG's finger-lever, and a significant action tuning to allow the use of rounds up to 2.73 inches long.

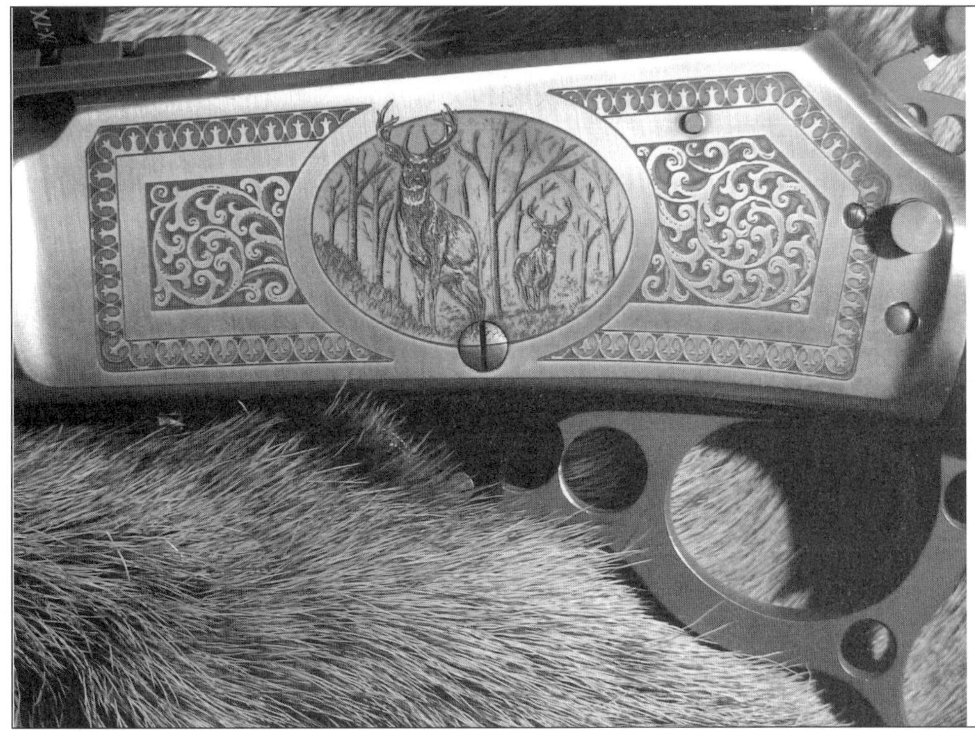

Knight began with a rifle from a special run that Davidson's had made. Fine machine engraving on both sides of the receiver adds considerably to the appearance of this special rifle. The addition of a Krieger barrel with custom match-grade chambering and various alterations and modifications adds greatly to the uniqueness and appeal. The biased LAW (Lightweight Air Working) muzzle brake cuts felt recoil in half. Knight reports that after testing this gun twice without the brake he will never do so again.

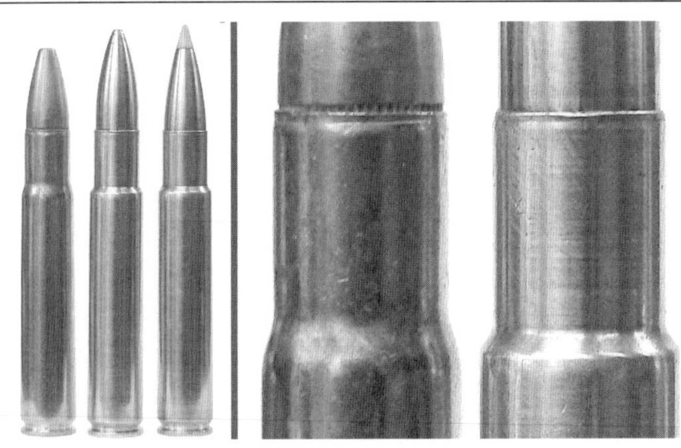

On the left are Factory 35 Whelen and 35 Whelen Ackley Improved handloads with Nosler 225-grain bullets (Partition and Ballistic Tip). On the right is a close-up view of a standard 35 Whelen and a 35 Whelen Ackley Improved shoulder. Owing to the wider and sharper shoulder, the improved version has more than four times the headspace control and is otherwise superior. While the 35 Whelen is a fine chambering, the improved version is universally superior. Without handloading, it is impossible to take advantage of the Ackley-Improved design.

Barrel marking on custom Remington Pump. I built this gun for Len Roman as a project to resurrect his original hunting rifle. Roman purchased this rifle as a 30-06 in the early 1960s. He had always wanted a 35 Whelen and, as the original barrel was well worn, this gun was the perfect platform for that project. The improved version of the Whelen chambering was an obvious upgrade. With RoBar NP3 plating, this gun is unusually attractive, slick to operate, and unusually corrosion resistant.

Bench testing a fully customized Remington 760 Pump chambered in 35 Whelen Ackley Improved: Contrary to the belief of many bolt-action aficionados, the Remington Pump is one of the finest hunting-rifle designs ever created. This improved 35 Whelen easily launches 225-grain Nosler bullets at 2,700 fps or 310-grain Woodleigh FMJ or JSP bullets at 2,300 fps with sub-MOA accuracy.

For many years, I had heard of cases (usually belted designs) cracking far forward on the body. Recently, when I began working with the 17 Ackley Hornet, I witnessed this firsthand. The case at left almost separated at the obvious bright line; the case at right stretched and cracked near the head, and it stretched at the same location nearer the shoulder.

SEATING BULLETS

CHAPTER 11

INTRODUCTION

In this chapter, we will consider various aspects of bullet seating, neck tension, and crimping. Our particular perspective is how each of these relates to the following: Functioning, how the cartridge interacts with the gun; accuracy, how the length and neck-to-bullet tension of a loaded round influences accuracy; and dependability, various bullet-loading characteristics that can improve or compromise the integrity of a cartridge. We will also consider bullet-seating tools and techniques. To a considerable extent, I am chiefly addressing hunting and self-defense ammunition, but many of these concepts also apply to target and plinking ammunition.

LOADING BULLETS—FUNCTIONALITY AND DEPENDABILITY

Typically, with conventional seating dies that include a crimping feature, one achieves the best seating results by adjusting the die body about one-half turn up from the point where the die body begins to apply a crimp to the case. With seating dies that do not include a crimping feature, the best results are achieved by adjusting the die so that the fully raised shellholder solidly abuts the die. The most sophisticated bullet seating dies that are available, as covered later in this chapter, do not include a crimping option and require different initial adjustments. For these, refer to the instructions provided by the manufacturer.

Using one die and one die adjustment to seat and crimp the bullet in one operation can complicate this process. (When you are not crimping, you must adjust the die body differently.) Because it is always best to use a seating die to seat bullets and a crimping die to crimp bullets in separate operations, I will assume that method and, therefore, assume that you have adjusted the seating die so that it does not apply any crimp to the case mouth. I cover crimping operations and associated die adjustments in this chapter under "Loading Bullets—Crimping."

LOADING BULLETS—DETERMINING MAXIMUM USABLE CARTRIDGE LENGTH

In many types of cartridges, static parameters tightly control either the bullet seating depth (how deep we seat the bullet into the case) or cartridge OAL (overall length). The former include bullets intended for typical revolver and tubular-magazine rifle cartridges. Such bullets have a built-in crimping groove (cannelure). In creating this type of cartridge, the handloader

The folks at MTM are serious about handloading, which leads to useful products. The MTM die box is one of those, a handy asset.

usually has no choice but to seat bullet into the case until the cannelure lines up with the case mouth and then to apply a correct crimp (neither too little nor too much). Beyond this, little room exists for adjustment or accuracy improvement.

(Correctly adjusting neck tension during the case sizing operation is necessary to get best results. I cover that in chapter 5.)

When using the Lee rifle-style Factory Crimp Die (FCD), we do have some leeway in the seating depth. On reasonably soft bullets (lead or jacketed) that do not have a crimping cannelure or when bullet seating does not align the cannelure to the case mouth, the FCD will impress a crimp into the bullet shank. For this and many other reasons, this is a superior handloading tool. This die uses a superior crimping method and, in many applications, it applies a superior crimp.

In many guns, bolt travel, box magazine length, ejection port length, or other features limit the maximum OAL. For this reason, the handloader might not be able to adjust the seating depth sufficiently to alter accuracy or performance significantly. Generally, seat the bullet only deep enough so that the cartridge is short enough to fit into and function through the magazine and action. At the same time there must be an adequate amount of bullet shank within the case neck to assure functionality and so that the bullet will not impinge the rifling (which rarely happens in guns with standard chambers). I cover this later in this chapter.

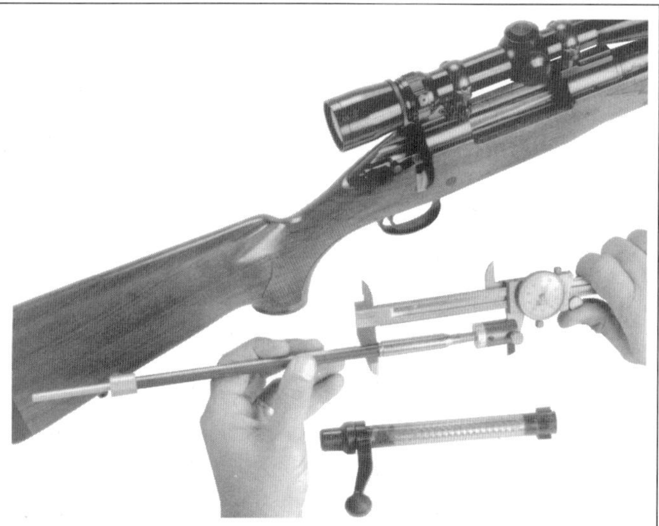

The Stoney Point OAL Gauge is one of the handier tools for the advanced handloader. It is easy to understand and to use. It measures length and location where any given bullet touches the rifling. This gives the handloader a reference. Using the same tool to measure loaded rounds makes it easy to set OAL, to provide a specific bullet-to-rifling jump, and to make precise length changes. This seems to be the fastest and easiest tool to use when tinkering with OAL to improve accuracy.

Conversely, with some bullets used in some custom-chambered guns (and a few guns with standard chambers), only the chamber's design limits the maximum OAL. A classic example is a single-shot rifle, but some bolt-action chamberings share this feature. Here, handloaders can tinker with the bullet-seating depth so as to exceed the listed maximum OAL significantly. Sometimes, they can tinker until the bullet comes very close to touching the rifling. This can dramatically improve accuracy. When OAL places the bullet close to touching the rifling, OAL changes of about 0.005 inch can dramatically alter accuracy.

Handloaders have several useful OAL gauges. With any of these tools in hand, we can accurately assess the cartridge OAL where the bullet touches the rifling. The Stony Point Chamber-All OAL Gauge is my favorite for this application. This tool is simple to use and provides accurate results.

In conventional guns using typical bullets, we usually get the best accuracy with about a 0.020-inch bullet-to-rifling jump; hunting cartridges using solids, Barnes X, Winchester Fail-Safe, and similar bullets should never have less than about 0.050-inch bullet-to-rifling clearance. In such loads—where the bullet is significantly far from touching the rifling—measurement errors of a few-thousandths-inch are insignificant. Conversely, target shooters and varmint hunters often seat bullets to provide little or no bullet-to-rifling jump; in such loads, the precision of the OAL measurement is quite critical.

The Redding Instant Indicator provides OAL data and information on other important load variables. This tool might be the ultimate option for the most serious of handloaders. As with all Redding tools, this is a precision instrument.

In either instance, an OAL tool is a handy way to determine the OAL starting point—the cartridge length with the bullet of interest, where the bullet's ogive just touches the rifling leade in the chamber of interest. Always begin with the minimum recommended propellant charge when testing cartridges with the bullet seated against, or very close to touching, the rifling.

The handy, easy to use, and affordable Stony Point Chamber-All OAL Gauge features a specially modified cartridge case that approximately fits the gun chamber. An attachment with a sliding rod screws into the base of this modified case. The handloader assembles this attachment to the special case and inserts a bullet into the case mouth. (Stoney Point sizes this case neck to provide just enough clearance so that any bullet of the proper diameter will freely enter and slide through the neck without significant friction.)

Insert and slide this assembly into the gun chamber. Then, while holding the case fully into the chamber, gently push the sliding rod through the attachment. This pushes the bullet forward until the ogive touches the rifling leade. Then, without moving the case or sliding the rod, snug the set screw against the sliding rod, just enough to keep that from easily moving in the housing.

Insert a hardwood dowel through the gun muzzle until it touches the bullet. Then, as you slowly pull the assembly from the chamber, gently tap the dowel against the bullet tip to dislodge it from the rifling. Then, use the dowel to push the entire assembly from the chamber while allowing the assembly to move freely. In this manner, ideally the bullet will be in the case when this assembly comes free. (In many factory-chambered guns, the throating is so long that the bullet will not touch the rifling until after the bullet base is outside the case mouth.) To keep the bullet in the case, tip the tool to point the bullet upward during handling.

With the bullet in this assembly, measure the OAL using a dial caliper and the special Stoney Point OAL attachment. This piece attaches to one jaw of the caliper and includes an insert with a hole that has been sized to mimic the rifling leade. (Inserts are available for every common caliber.) The measured SPL (Stoney Point Length) provides a dependable reference length; when a cartridge is loaded with that bullet, seated to give the same SPL reading (with the Stony Point attachment on the caliper), the bullet will be touching the rifling in the tested rifle. This becomes a baseline measurement to compare with any test cartridge loaded for use in the same gun with the same bullet. The difference between this baseline SPL and the measured SPL for a loaded cartridge represents how far the bullet will move before it hits the rifling (or, conversely, how far chambering the round will drive the bullet into the rifling).

When using electronic calipers, fit the Stoney Point bullet adapter onto one jaw. Insert the dummy SPL test round into the calipers. Insert the bullet tip into the adapter and fully close the jaws onto the test round. Then turn the caliper on. On some calipers, the resulting readout will be 0.000; if not, press the "zero" button so that the readout changes to 0.000. Next, insert the loaded round. The new reading on the display will represent the bullet offset (from the leade-touch position). For example, if the reading is -0.020 (minus 0.020), the bullet is 0.020 inch from touching the rifling—very handy.

Generally, seat the bullet deep enough so that a portion of the shank equaling a minimum of one-half of bullet diameter is within the case neck. For example, for a 22-caliber bullet, insert at least 0.11 inch of the shank into the neck. Cartridges with less seating depth might not be dependable for normal use. For dangerous-game hunting ammunition and for ammunition used in rifles that generate significant recoil, make sure that the shank is in the case neck a minimum of two-thirds the diameter of the bullet. Seat the bullet deeply enough into the case to assure that it functions through the gun and that the neck securely holds the bullet. Provide about 0.035-inch clearance in a box magazine.

An old favorite method of testing for the maximum chamber OAL requires no special tools. This method is inexpensive and is certainly adequately precise for hunting cartridges, but it is time consuming. Load a dummy round (a sized case with no propellant or primer) that will have about a 0.035-inch endwise clearance in the magazine. Turn the dummy while holding the bullet's ogive in a candle flame. This will almost instantly deposit black soot. Gently chamber this dummy. (Be cautious to avoid marring this delicate candle black during handling and chambering.)

If the gun is a controlled-feed style, carefully insert the dummy into the magazine and then begin to close the bolt. If the gun is not a controlled-feed action, simply insert the dummy into the chamber and begin to close the bolt. In the latter instance, when the bolt stops moving freely, use just enough force to snap the extractor over the case rim. In any instance, do not force the bolt shut, only push it hard enough to assure that the dummy round is fully chambered (or that the bullet has come up against the rifling). Gentle is the watchword here.

In many factory rifles, this magazine-length dummy (hereafter, MLD) will not be long enough for the bullet to reach the rifling. If so, the bolt will freely close, and the bullet will show no rifling marking. When this happens, further testing is still required because the bullet might be very close to touching the rifling. Use an inertial puller to pull the bullet partially and then seat it to create a cartridge that is about 0.020-inch longer (we can call this test round the MLD+20) and test again. If this MLD+20 round does not touch the rifling, then the MLD represents the longest feasible OAL with that bullet. If the MLD+20 round does touch the rifling, proceed as described below to determine the maximum OAL.

If this round is sufficiently shorter than the magazine so that all such rounds freely cycle through the action, all is well. If not, it will not be possible to load rounds at or very close to the SPL. But, after doing this test, you will know what situation holds with that bullet in that gun.

This MLD might be too long to allow the bolt to travel far enough to engage the locking lugs. Should this be the situation, remove the MLD and observe the bullet. You should see shiny marks where the rifling leade touched the bullet and marred the candle black—the shiny bullet surface will show through. Seat the bullet about 0.005-inch deeper, then reblacken the ogive and repeat this test.

After you have shortened the round sufficiently, through this trial-and-error process, so that it allows the bolt to begin to engage the locking lugs, proceed very carefully. At this point, the bolt camming force is sufficient to allow you to fully close the bolt easily, whether or not the bullet is hitting the rifling. As you gently lower the bolt handle toward the fully locked position, feel for any increase in resistance. Such an increase suggests a bullet-to-rifling impingement.

Guns having spring-loaded ejector plungers present additional difficulties. This plunger can make it hard to judge whether the resistance noted is from the case pushing against the ejector spring or from the bullet jamming against the rifling. Refer to chapter 5.

Continue shortening the round and reblacking the bullet until the bolt fully and freely closes—without any evidence of increased resistance. When this happens, the bullet's ogive should exhibit no shiny marks from the rifling leade. Pull that bullet and insert a new one using the same die setting. (The test process is likely to have damaged the old bullet; if so, it can no longer give precise results.) Candle blacken this new bullet and chamber the dummy. Extract the dummy and carefully examine the ogive. If that shows only a slight marring from the rifling, this OAL is close enough to give an acceptable MLD measurement.

If you see pronounced marring, adjust the seating stem slightly deeper and repeat the test. When carefully done, this measurement can be sufficiently precise for any application.

If the new bullet shows no marring, adjust the seating stem to increase the OAL about 0.002 inch. Use an inertial puller to pull the bullet slightly from the case. Usually one or two moderate taps will do the job. Reseat the bullet to the slightly longer length; reblacken the ogive and rechamber. The bullet should now show a slight marring where the rifling touches the ogive. If not, progressively lengthen the dummy and repeat the test.

Regardless of the method used—with the Redding tool, the Stoney Point tool, or the candle-black method—when you are satisfied with the maximum OAL measurement, you are almost ready to test the finished dummy round for proper and consistent fit and functioning in the rifle magazine, through the rifle action, and for free ejection from the gun. If the resulting round does not fit in the magazine, you can only use it for single loading. If it fits the magazine with very little endwise clearance, keep in mind that the shape of individual bullet tips vary enough so that even with an identical SPL measurement the actual cartridge OAL can vary by at least 0.015 inch—a minimum magazine clearance of about 0.035 inch seems prudent.

In some guns, even when a maximum OAL dummy fits into the magazine and freely passes fully into the chamber, the round might not eject from the action. For this reason, before testing the maximum OAL dummy, test a dummy round with that bullet loaded to the industry maximum OAL for that chambering and measure (or estimate) the bullet-to-ejection port clearance as the round comes free of the action. Add this distance to the length of the industry OAL dummy to determine the maximum cartridge length the gun will eject. If this is less than the length of the maximum OAL dummy, it might not be possible to use cartridges that place the bullet close to rifling, as required to provide maximum accuracy. In this instance, a modest gun alteration might solve the problem—for suggested action alterations, refer to my book, *Accurizing the Factory Rifle,* available through Brownells.

If all is well with regard to fit and functioning, measure the maximum OAL and write all pertinent information on the case body using a fine-point permanent marker. This information should include:

- Gun tested
- Bullet
  - » Make
  - » Style
  - » Weight
- OAL or SPL

The Sanford Sharpie Fine Point marker is ideal for this job.

With this dummy sample in hand, it is a simple matter to adjust the seating stem to provide any specific bullet-to-rifling clearance.

Regardless of the method employed to determine the maximum OAL (the cartridge length where a particular bullet touches the rifling in a particular gun), a marked dummy round makes a useful record. Where feasible, storing such dummy rounds in a die box is handy. In an instance where you end up with too many dummy rounds to fit all of those within the reloading die box, use an empty die box with a label that includes the words "OAL gauges" along with the chambering and rifle information. It is most convenient to store that box with the reloading die box. (All die manufacturers sell empty die boxes, and it is most convenient if the box used to store the dummies matches the associated die box.)

LOADING BULLETS—ADJUSTING SEATING STEM TO ALTER CARTRIDGE LENGTH

Before using any dummy round to obtain a given amount of bullet-to-rifling jump for a new load, screw the seating die into press. Then back the seating stem far enough out of die so that it cannot touch the bullet in the dummy round. Insert the dummy in the shellholder and carefully raise the ram to push the dummy fully into the seating die.

Then, carefully adjust the seating stem until it just touches the bullet. Depending upon the amount of neck tension in the dummy round, a threaded seating stem can make it all too easy to drive the bullet into the case by turning the stem with too much force. It is better to leave the stem adjusted so that the bullet will initially seat a few thousandths longer than the measured SPL than to turn the stem too hard and thereby ruin a valuable gauging tool. (To add robustness to the dummy rounds, consider applying Loctite to the interior of the case neck to lock the seated bullet solidly at a specific seating depth.)

Then, when loading the cartridges, use the Stoney Point (or Redding) tool to determine the final seating-stem adjustment needed to provide the desired bullet-to-rifling jump. With conventional bullets, this is usually about 0.020-inch shorter than the measured maximum OAL, with Barnes X, Winchester Fail-Safe, or any similar bullet, this will be between 0.050- and about 0.075-inch shorter than the measured maximum OAL.

If you are using a seating die that has a micrometer on the seating stem (as are offered by most manufactures), the OAL adjustments are a simple matter of counting thousandth-inch clicks, or gradations, as you turn the stem or die cap. With a conventional die, stem travel per turn depends upon the thread pitch (tpi). The pitch depends upon the die manufacturer and the style of the die. It is easy enough to measure the thread pitch using a thread pitch gauge (as are supplied with tap and die sets) or by other means. If, for example, the stem has 20 threads per inch (20 tpi), then each full revolution of the stem will raise or lower the seating head 1/20 inch, which is 0.050 inch. See the following table.

TABLE OF COMMON SEATING STEM THREAD PITCHES WITH CORRESPONDING STEM TRAVEL

		ROTATION OF SEATING STEM (TURN OR PARTIAL TURN)								
		1	7/8	3/4	5/8	1/2	3/8	1/4	1/8	1/16
DIE MAKE AND TYPE	TPI	APPROX. CHANGE IN CARTRIDGE OVERALL LENGTH (1/1000")								
HORNADY NEW DIMENSION LEE PRECISION REDDING LARGE STEM	18	56	49	42	35	28	21	14	7	3½
REDDING SMALL STEM	20	50	45	37½	31	25	19	12½	6	3 1/10
FORSTER (LARGE) AND RCBS	28	36	31	27	22	18	13	9	4½	2 2/10
FORSTER (SMALL)	32	31	27	24	20	16	12	8	4	2

With the seating die stem set to match the dummy round approximately and with a known seating-stem thread pitch, it is a simple matter to adjust the seating stem to provide any approximate bullet-to-rifling jump. For example, if you are using a die with a small seating stem (like most Redding rifle dies) to provide 0.020-inch bullet-to-rifling clearance, simply turn the stem 3/8-turn deeper into the die.

When using the Stoney Point tool, it is very easy to fine tune the seating stem adjustment to achieve a precise amount of bullet-to-rifling jump in your cartridges. Sans that, or a similar tool, the adjustment will be close enough for practical purposes—it really does not matter if the jump is 0.018, 0.020, or 0.022 inch. What matters is that you can then fine tune the actual jump, whatever that might be, until you get the best accuracy.

Switching to a different type of bullet will usually require a seating-stem adjustment—different bullets seldom give the same jump with the same seating die adjustment. Hence, repeat the above process for each type of bullet that you use for that cartridge and thereby create corresponding reference dummy rounds as needed. These provide a reference OAL (or SPL) so that you can quickly adjust the seating die for use with any given bullet.

RCBS Gold Medal seating die with bullets (30-caliber and 5mm) and a 5mm/35 SMc cartridge case for comparison: A sliding, case-alignment body retains the bullet, so the handloader can insert a bullet at any time. This die also has a floating bullet-seating stem. This feature increases precision and reduces the potential to bend a case shoulder during bullet seating. The RCBS Gold Medal seating die is particularly useful when loading large batches of cartridges using short, small-caliber bullets.

LOADING BULLETS—ACCURACY—ADJUSTING BULLET-TO-RIFLING JUMP

(For practical purposes, altering the bullet-seating depth might not significantly improve the accuracy of cartridges used in free-bored rifles, such as guns chambered for Weatherby cartridges. In such guns, the bullet-to-rifling jump is sufficient so that any slight seating-depth alteration is unlikely to bring about any significant improvement in accuracy, except due to a resulting variation in barrel time. However, such guns might be particularly sensitive to variations in case neck tension and crimping. Seat the bullet deep enough to maximize the bullet pull and to be assured of dependable functionality, as discussed throughout the remainder of this chapter. Then tinker the OAL with 0.005-inch adjustments to improve accuracy by tuning the barrel time of the load to match the barrel vibrations optimally.)

Once you have determined the maximum OAL for a gun and bullet, you can look toward adjusting the seating depth as a method of improving accuracy. Minor iteration of a bullet-to-rifling jump can profoundly influence accuracy. The primary reasons are:

- How the bullet moves (if it does) in response to the primer blast (before propellant combustion generates enough gas pressure to begin to accelerate the bullet)
- How fast the bullet is traveling when it hits the rifling (after it starts accelerating, in response to gas pressure)
- Barrel time (as covered elsewhere in this text, this is critical to accuracy—all else being equal, altering the OAL alters the barrel time)

A full analysis of these issues is beyond the scope of this chapter. I will simply note the well-demonstrated fact that, often, the load that is the most accurate, for any given combination of rifle, case, primer, propellant and charge, bullet, and neck tension, will have a specific bullet-to-rifling jump. When this is true, increasing or decreasing the OAL (altering bullet-to-rifling jump) will have a moderately to profoundly negative influence on accuracy. For most hunting rifles and bullets, the optimum bullet-to-rifling jump is usually near 20/1000 inch; for target cartridges used in target-chambered guns, the ideal jump can be near zero.

Before considering adjusting the bullet-to-rifling jump, memorize the following facts:

- Hunters, and most target shooters, require cartridges that function properly through the magazine and action of a repeating rifle or pistol, or that fit in the cylinder of a revolver.
- In hunting cartridges, accuracy is always subordinate to functionality.
- Chamber pressure depends upon the OAL—usually, less jump (longer OAL) results in greater pressure.

As a specific example, I own a Remington 7600 Pump-Action rifle chambered in 280 Remington. In this gun, loading the Barnes 130-grain XBT with a 0.070-inch bullet-to-rifling jump provides wonderful accuracy in a powerful and effective elk load. The trouble is that these loaded rounds will not eject from a factory-stock Model-7600! This represents a serious concern for all shooters—be certain the cartridge you intend to use (factory loaded or handloaded) will function through the gun, and will do so under every condition. As a practical matter, you might have to sacrifice a bit of accuracy to make sure that your handloads meet this necessary requirement.

With that background, let us now consider adjusting the seating depth to improve accuracy where feasible and desirable. In the previous sections, I covered the seating die adjustment (to determine the zero-point bullet-to-rifling jump OAL) and adjusting the seating die (to alter the bullet-to-rifling jump).

For locking the position of any threaded die, Lee Precision locking rings are a superior design. These work with a rubber O-ring. When the ring is finger tightened against the press, this rubber ring allows the die body to wiggle in the press; conversely, the mechanical lock provided by standard die locking rings prevents the die from moving sideways or tipping in the press. With the Lee lock ring, if the die does not align with the ram (a common condition) it can freely do so when the case and then the shellholder push against it. Conversely, with a conventional locking ring, if the tightened-down die does not align with the ram, it is not apt to ever do so, regardless of the case or shellholder forces. Misalignment between the ram (shellholder) and die cannot contribute to the accuracy of resulting cartridges.

When using the Lee locking ring, or an O-ring under a conventional locking ring, it is convenient to create scribe marks on the press and on the locking ring and die body so that you can install the die in the same orientation each time.

Similarly, install an O-ring between the die body and the seating-stem lock nut. This allows the seating stem to freely align with the case. This reduces the chance of bending the case shoulder during bullet seating. If, for any reason, the seating stem does not align with the case and if it is locked in place, the bullet will necessarily align with the stem. If misalignment is sufficient, this could result in a bent case shoulder, with degradation of accuracy potential of the loaded round. If the stem is free to wiggle sideways, far less chance will exist for this to happen—as far as possible the bullet will push the stem into alignment with the case. This method also facilitates finger adjustments of the seating depth. The same O-ring system is also beneficial with the neck expander stem on a resizing die.

Before beginning this test, refer to chapter 12. Using that method (or some other accuracy-load-development method), determine a safe and accurate load when the bullet is about 0.040 inch (conventional bullets) or 0.075 inch (X-style bullets) from touching rifling.

After establishing a safe load (that fulfills your needs) and a maximum OAL for that load in your gun, it is time to explore the accuracy consequences of varying the bullet-seating depth. Load the sets of cartridges at different OAL settings. Generally, five or ten rounds at each setting will suffice.

Adjust the seating depth in 0.005-inch increments. With conventional bullets, test for accuracy with otherwise identical loads while seating the bullets so that the bullet-to-rifling jump is in the range from about 0.040 inch to about 0.010 inch. Exact values are not critical. With hunting bullets, do not reduce bullet jump below about 0.010 inch. Doing so can raise the pressure. It can lead to a bullet hanging in the chamber leade and, thereby, creating a mess when you eject the unfired case—leaving the bullet and much of the charge in the gun. This can happen because the bullet profiles vary within any given batch and, more so, from lot to lot.

THE MEASURED MAXIMUM SPL WITH ANY GIVEN BULLET IS NOT A PRECISE MEASURE OF THE MAXIMUM OAL OR OF THE BULLET-TO-RIFLING JUMP EVEN FOR A BULLET OF THE SAME MAKE AND TYPE AND EVEN FOR BULLETS WITHIN ONE PRODUCTION LOT.

THE BULLET-TO-BULLET AND LOT-TO-LOT PRODUCTION VARIATIONS ARE CERTAIN TO ALTER THE ACTUAL BULLET-TO-RIFLING JUMP SIGNIFICANTLY.

However, generally, you can safely seat swaged or soft- to medium-hardness cast bullets close to, or even somewhat driven into, the rifling. Similarly, often, seating properly moly-plated jacketed bullets against the rifling seems to cause no problems.

For hunting cartridges using solid copper or a copper-alloy, Winchester Fail-Safe, or similar bullets, test loads only in the 0.075-inch to 0.050-inch bullet-to-rifling jump range. Loads with less bullet jump can, and occasionally do, generate dangerous pressure. Further, these bullets generally require a significant jump to achieve optimum accuracy. While moly-plating seems to mitigate pressure spikes associated with seating this type of bullet closer to the rifling, it seems prudent to avoid close seating and, as we have no evidence that close seating improves accuracy with these bullets, please take no such chances.

NEVER USE ANY CARTRIDGE WITH A BARNES X-BULLET, WINCHESTER FAIL-SAFE, OR A SIMILAR BULLET THAT IS SEATED SO THAT THE BULLET-TO-RIFLING JUMP IS LESS THAN 0.050 INCH.

In target guns with special chambers, typical testing begins with a jacketed bullet almost touching the rifling, and with progressively longer cartridges until the bullet is solidly jammed into the rifling. However, no data listed in any manual are appropriate for such loads, which can create significant pressure increases compared to loads with typical bullet-to-rifling jump.

If you are loading for such a rifle, consider the advice of experts loading for that target chambering and begin your load development with the starting charge they suggest, or their working charge minus 10 percent, whichever is less. Largely, in that situation, you are on your own. Learn to recognize and interpret pressure signs and pay particular attention to those signs any time you are adjusting any load parameter.

The next step is to bench test the accuracy of your loads of various lengths. In this evaluation, five-shot groups are appropriate. Begin with the shortest load. Often, as you try progressively longer loads, accuracy will initially improve, and it might degrade as you reach the shortest loads. After testing all such loads, if one OAL shows a clear accuracy advantage, it might be worthwhile to test loads near that OAL. Often differences as small as 0.005 inch can measurably alter the sizes of the group, and it is possible that the lengths that you have happened to test bracket the best possible length. However, further refinement beyond that point is seldom of any value. If no accuracy advantage is apparent in this initial OAL test, use the OAL giving the best ballistic uniformity according to chronograph results.

Should you find that the most accurate load tested was also the shortest load tested, you should test shorter loads. In rare instances, to get the right barrel time for the best accuracy, a conventional jacketed-bullet load will require more than about a 0.030-inch bullet-to-rifling jump. When this happens, it is likely that a load using a different primer or propellant would give better results with less bullet jump.

Advanced seating dies—as available from Forster, Hornady, RCBS, and Redding—allow simple and precise OAL adjustments in one-thousandth-inch increments. Any such die allows effortless, precise, and repeatable seating-depth adjustments.

Those who are developing loads for varmint or target rifles might find accuracy improvements by further reducing the bullet jump, perhaps even to the point where the bullet solidly impinges the rifling. This is problematical: We cannot know, or predict, the pressure consequences of seating a bullet close to, against, or into the rifling. This will usually increase the pressure but it can reduce the pressure, or it can make no difference in the pressure.

Consider a test that Christer Larsson (chief ballistician at Norma) and I did at the Norma ballistics laboratory. We compared four 308 Winchester load variations using the N201 propellant, WLR primers, and the 168-grain Sierra MatchKing bullets. Our test goal was to see what would happen to the pressure when the only load change was to reduce the bullet-to-rifling jump from 0.020 inch to zero. With unplated bullets, this increased the pressure about 3 percent; with moly-plated bullets, this decreased the pressure by 15 percent!

Because seating the bullet against the rifling can increase the chamber pressure, I cannot condone this practice; however, because it can sometimes improve accuracy, I certainly understand the motivation behind it. I can offer one tidbit in this regard: Generally, if velocity increases, pressure increases. If you have a chronograph, you can make a fair guess as to the reduction of the propellant charge that might be necessary to keep the chamber pressure within the normal range when seating bullets very close to or against the rifling. However, this cannot be a particularly accurate guess. Moreover, as the aforementioned Norma test proved, under these circumstances, pressure and velocity might not be well correlated—in the moly-plated test, the longer load generated much less pressure but almost identical velocity. I cannot explain that result.

Consider a hypothetical load "X" for your 22-250 chambered rifle. Assume that you have worked up load X using current data. Assume that load X shows no signs of excessive pressure. Further, suppose that load X chronographs at 3,600 fps when the OAL allows a 0.020-inch bullet-to-rifling jump. Suppose that you test a 5 percent reduction in the propellant charge with the bullet seated to just touch the rifling; call this load X+20. Suppose that the X+20 load also chronographs at 3,600 fps.

Because the velocity of the X and the X+20 loads are identical, you might be tempted to assume that the pressure is also similar, and it might be. However, the longer load might generate significantly greater pressure.

First, the very fact that 5 percent less propellant generates the same velocity suggests that the peak pressure might be higher. This is analogous to using a 5 percent faster propellant to achieve the same velocity in an otherwise identical load. Often, a load using a faster propellant to launch any given bullet to the same velocity will create greater peak pressure. (The pressure curve is narrower because less gas is generated.)

Second, accelerating a bullet and engraving the rifling simultaneously will likely increase the initial bullet-to-bore friction. Increasing the bullet-to-bore friction increases barrel heating. In order to generate more barrel heating and equal muzzle velocity, the propellant will necessarily have created more energy. The only way for less of the same propellant to create more energy is for it to burn at a higher temperature (greater pressure). This fact comes directly from the fundamental laws of thermodynamics. However, refer to the above aside on the Norma testing—without pressure testing we cannot know.

The important point of the forgoing, dramatically incomplete analysis, is this: It is impossible to guess the pressure consequences of seating a bullet very close to, against, or into the rifling. Eventually, those who believe otherwise are likely to be surprised. In target, varmint, and other high-grade guns, the handloader can often achieve the best accuracy by locating the bullet nearer to the rifling rather than farther from it; hence, the temptation to seat a bullet against the rifling is strong. Generally, unless you understand how to compare fired cases to estimate pressure accurately, this is a temptation better denied. As with target shooters using special cartridges in special guns, if you follow this practice you are doing so on your own and at your own risk.

Laboratory testing seems to indicate that properly moly-plated bullets are far less sensitive overall in this regard. The seating depth has less influence on the pressure, and seating the bullet against or solidly into the rifling might not alter pressure significantly, and, as noted above, this might well reduce pressure. However, this generality is neither dependable nor predictable.

To reiterate, most benchrest guns, the occasional commercial rifle, and many custom rifles achieve the best accuracy when the cartridge OAL places the bullet very close to or against the rifling, at least with some loads. However, it is unusual for a typical hunting rifle and cartridge to achieve a worthwhile accuracy improvement with an OAL where the bullet-to-rifling jump is much less than about 0.020 inch.

Hypothetically, let us imagine loading 100 rounds of hunting ammunition. I will assume the use of standard loading dies and a standard press. Suppose that we have chosen a bullet with desirable external ballistic and terminal performance characteristics and because that bullet has performed well in a similar rifle.

Based upon a typical and erroneous philosophy, we make the following bogus assumption: "If seating the bullet a little closer to the rifling improves accuracy a little, then seating the bullet a lot closer to the rifling must improve accuracy a lot." Therefore, we set the OAL of our load so that the bullets almost touch the rifling, or so we think. This scenario is a recipe for an accuracy disaster because this type of bullet, our loading equipment, and our loading procedures are not consistent enough to provide the necessary level of precision that is required by this approach. (For this hypothetical consideration, we will ignore the little matter of the potentially dangerous chamber pressure that such a load might create.)

Slight variations in the bullet-to-bullet ogive will alter the precise location of that part of the bullet that first contacts the rifling. Also, slight variations in propellant compression forces (in a compressed-charge load) and case neck tension will combine to add a tiny amount of variation to the flexing of both the press and die and to the case shoulder during bullet seating. Hence, the resulting bullet-to-rifling jump will vary from one round to the next. Typically, such variation is at least 0.006 inch.

If our hypothetical gun, load, and sizing-die combination produce a uniform effective headspace of 0.004 inch, in our batch of 100 cartridges, we might find the following number of cartridges with the following actual bullet-to-rifling jumps:

- 2 @ -0.002 inch: Locking the bolt pushes the bullet against the rifling. This holds the case back and thereby removes slack from the system. This reduces the cartridge-to-chamber clearance, bolt-end play, and bolt-to-case clearance; alternatively, the bullet might simply engrave into the rifling enough to eliminate some or all of the reduction in case-end play. A spring-loaded ejector plunger might or might not provide enough force to engrave the bullet slightly. The striker fall and the primer explosion would certainly drive the case forward. This could seat the bullet deeper, or (more likely) it could drive the bullet up to 0.006 inch into the rifling, or it could do some of each.

- 15 @ 0 inch: In taking up the existing cartridge-to-chamber clearance, the plunger ejector or the striker impact and primer explosion would drive the bullet about 0.004 inch into the rifling, or it might reseat the bullet to some degree and thereby engrave the bullet less.

- 67 @ +0.001 inch to +0.002 inch: In taking up the existing cartridge-to-chamber clearance, the plunger ejector or the striker impact and primer explosion would drive the case forward, pushing the bullet 0.002 to 0.003 inch into the rifling.

- 15 @ +0.003 inch: In taking up the existing cartridge-to-chamber clearance, the plunger ejector or the striker impact and primer explosion would drive the case forward and seat the bullet 0.001 inch into the rifling.

- 1 @ +0.004 inch: In taking up the existing cartridge-to-chamber clearance, the plunger ejector or the striker impact and primer explosion would drive the case forward, leaving the bullet just touching the rifling.

Beyond the shot-to-shot variations in the gun and barrel vibration that will inevitably result from the use of such ammunition, any load that exhibits such a mismatch of variables at the instant of firing cannot possibly generate consistent pressure and velocity—this is not theory; this is well-demonstrated fact. Intrinsic accuracy variables will differ dramatically. It would be nothing short of pure good luck if the shots with such cartridges, randomly chambered and fired, produced decent groups.

In the above analysis, we ignored the very real issue of effective headspace variations. In resized cases, shoulder placement typically varies by several thousandths of an inch. This exacerbates the problem, creating even greater variation in the bullet-to-rifling jump from one round to the next.

Consider one example of this exact scenario. In that instance, a hapless handloader discovered a load combination that showed promise. He loaded a batch of 7mm Remington Magnum ammunition, where the bullet-to-rifling jump was about 0.005 inch. To his delight, accuracy was wonderful.

He tinkered with primers and made minor propellant-charge adjustments. Finally, he settled on a combination that gave simply marvelous ballistics and accuracy. However, when he had finished his load development, he had also used up all the bullets he had on hand. Therefore, for his hunting cartridges, he purchased another box of what were nominally the same bullets. However, as luck would have it, those were from a different production lot.

He loaded 100 cartridges and headed to the range to do a final sight-in with his elk rifle. He wanted a 300-yard zero, so he set up a target at that distance and proceeded to fire shots. When he tried to make a group, his world melted down around him. His formerly proven ½-MOA wonder load was shooting 2 MOA with persistent fliers opening groups to 3 MOA—his best 5-shot, 300-yard groups were nearly ten inches. What had gone wrong?

Our hypothetical scenario described it well. His new box of bullets was from a different production lot. Evidently, before beginning that new production run, the manufacturer had changed the final bullet-forming die. This change resulted in a slight alteration of the bullet profile along the ogive. Compared to the old version, the area where the ogive met the rifling on the new bullets was several-thousandths-inch closer to the bullet nose. When using these newer bullets, our hapless handloader's carefully concocted loads featured bullets that were sometimes touching the rifling and were sometimes not touching the rifling.

After he called me and we discussed the problem, Ol' Hapless simply adjusted his seating die to reseat all the bullets in his remaining cartridges about 0.018 inch deeper. With those shorter cartridges, accuracy was again ½-MOA (a fortunate outcome).

The critical point here is that for hunting ammunition, when considering all the variables involved, it is best to maintain a judicious amount of bullet-to-rifling jump. This is good practice even in instances where doing so precludes achieving that last tiny measure of accuracy improvement.

LOADING BULLETS—SEATING CAST BULLETS INTO THE RIFLING

With most cartridges using conventional cast bullets, the situation is different. Usually, cast bullets are much less resistant to rifling engravement. Moreover, usually, such cartridges do not work at relatively high pressure—this leaves a significant safety cushion so that load variables that might raise the resulting chamber pressure are less apt to lead to a potentially dangerous situation. Exceptions to the latter point do exist. Perfectly normal cartridges loaded with hard-cast bullets and fired in any rifle designed for a relatively low-pressure chambering (where peak chamber pressure is below about 30,000 psi) might well generate chamber pressure that is too near the safe maximum for one's comfort.

Cast bullet cartridges often use a charge that gives relatively low loading density. For this reason, it is

Relative Force Required to Seat a Typical Cast Bullet into Rifling Sufficiently to Seal Bore

Bullet	Approximate Bullet Diameter (Caliber)				
Hardness (Brinell Scale)	**22**	**28**	**34**	**40**	**46**
Pure Lead	1	1¼	1½	1¾	2
5% to 10% Tin in Lead	2	2½	3	3½	4
Soft Wheelweight Alloy	1½	1⅞	2¼	2⅝	3
Hard Wheelweight Alloy	2½	3⅛	3¾	4⅜	5
Linotype	4	5	6	7	8
Heat-Treated Wheelweight	6	7½	9	10½	12

possible that before the chamber pressure can obturate the bullet, hot gases can begin to escape between the bullet shank and the case neck or chamber leade. In these instances, seating the bullet so that the driving band firmly abuts the rifling can be particularly beneficial toward both improving accuracy and minimizing barrel leading. Usually, such hardcast bullet seating is a perfectly safe practice.

With blunt-nosed, cast bullets, a useful method of determining a good depth to seal the bore is to push the bullet into the chamber with a hardwood dowel that is close to the bore's diameter. Then push on the dowel hard enough to firmly seat the bullet into the rifling—with care, you can feel when the bullet stops moving easily. Pushing significantly harder will begin to drive the bullet into the rifling, which is not the goal.

The following table suggests the relative degree of force required for this test, based upon the bullet's diameter and hardness. I include the following table only to provide a relative comparison. The actual required force is critically dependent upon the bullet and leade design and upon the bullet's hardness. What is required to seat the bullet into the rifling when a sharp driving band shoulder on a bullet comes up against a low-angle leade in the barrel might be an order of magnitude less than the force required when a sloping ogive on a bullet comes up against a high-angle leade taper in a barrel.

Generally, cast bullets have a blunt point. Therefore, the handloader can easily determine the cartridge OAL that will correspond to this tamped-in (into the leade) setting. Carefully insert a similar (longer) section of a hardwood dowel into the muzzle until the dowel touches the bullet. Then scribe a fine line on the dowel that precisely aligns with the muzzle. Use this dowel to tamp the bullet free of the bore.

Then, close the action and insert the dowel until it touches the bolt face. Scribe a fine line on the dowel that precisely aligns with the gun muzzle. The distance between the resulting scribed marks is the required cartridge OAL.

It might be necessary to use a dowel to remove any chambered (unfired) cartridge so loaded. Otherwise, opening the action and ejecting the unfired round might leave the bullet stuck in the bore, with attendant spilled propellant. Always use extreme caution when tapping on a dowel to remove such a round—remain clear of the muzzle and the chamber and keep both ends of the bore pointed in a safe direction. Finally, after removing the round, be sure to remove the dowel from the bore!

In one instance, two men working with a modern bolt-action rifle and a high-pressure chambering managed to stick a cartridge in the chamber—the round would neither fully chamber nor come free. In attempting to open the action and free the offending case, one man was standing behind the gun and holding it while the other man was standing in front of the gun, hammering a brass rod against the bullet. For whatever reason, the round fired (which is really not much of a surprise). To facilitate the removal of the round, they had unlocked the action, and, therefore, both the bolt and brass rod blew out. This killed both men. Always use extreme caution whenever handling any jammed gun.

In another instance, a nascent benchrest competitor had problems closing the bolt on a round during a match. He had to use a brass rod to remove the stuck cartridge. Running out of time to complete his string, he hurried to chamber the next round and fire the shot, but he had not removed the rod from the barrel. When he pulled the trigger, the action failed. The resulting explosion killed him.

LOADING BULLETS—SEATING

For typical hunting cartridges, the bullet seating consists of simply inserting a bullet into a sized, primed, and charged case, inserting that into the shellholder, and fully raising the ram with the properly adjusted seating die installed in the press. Many otherwise serious handloaders never give the intricacies of this operation a second thought.

Serious target shooters use different methods and can achieve superior control of a finished cartridge's overall length and concentricity. An in-between system exists where any handloader can achieve superior results using relatively conventional tools and techniques. This is one area where serious hunters and informal target shooters can easily improve their handloaded ammunition.

Several manufacturers offer dies that can provide improved bullet seating when used with a conventional press. For example, Redding offers the Competition seating die, Forster offers the similar Benchrest die. These dies feature specific advantages that are worth noting.

Competition and Benchrest seating dies have a sliding (spring-loaded) case alignment body. As the shellholder pushes the bullet and case into the die, the sliding sleeve fully supports and centers the case body as it centers the bullet shank over the case mouth. As the ram continues upward, a separate, floating seating stem centers and supports the bullet nose. Hence, precisely centered sliding bodies support both the case and bullet before the seating stem reaches a stop that prevents it from moving farther into the die. The spring-loaded chamber (that is responsible for positive case alignment) allows the ram to continue pushing the case upward until the seating stem has fully seated the bullet. This design virtually eliminates lateral forces on the bullet or case neck. This minimizes the potential to bend the case shoulder during bullet seating. (Hornady uses a less sophisticated but quite effective system in its modern seating dies.)

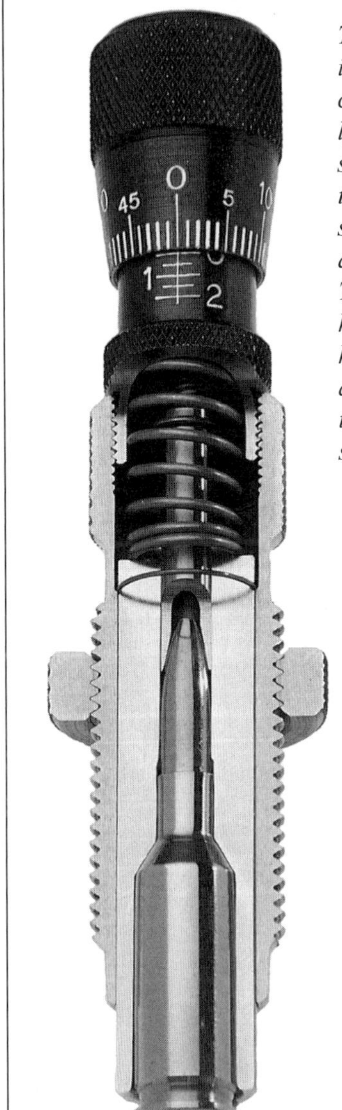

The Redding Competition Seating Die is phenomenally precise, every tolerance is minutely controlled. A spring-loaded sliding body centers and aligns the case to a floating bullet seating stem that centers and aligns the bullet with the die. The micrometer seating cap has a zero-set feature, so the handloader can set a basic die adjustment with a zero bullet-to-rifling jump at "0" on the scale—a handy reference.

The RCBS Gold Medal Die set is a great tool. Varminting handloaders will find the windowed seating die to be particularly valuable—no more pinched fingers, damaged bullets, dropped bullets, damaged case mouths, etc. Just drop the bullet through the large window, base downward, at any time—the sliding body catches the bullet and holds it until seating begins.

For anything but the most serious of target ammunition, these Forster and Redding seating dies might well provide the best promise of concentric and undamaged cartridges. These dies include a micrometer that allows the handloader to apply precise seating-depth adjustments; micrometer calibration is in 1/1000 of an inch increments.

The RCBS Gold Medal Seating Die is equally special. The functioning of this die is similar to that of the Forster Benchrest and the Redding Competition dies, except that it includes a large bullet insertion window in the case body. When installed in the press, this window is above the top of the press. (When loading unusually short cartridges, the use of an extended shellholder is a necessity.)

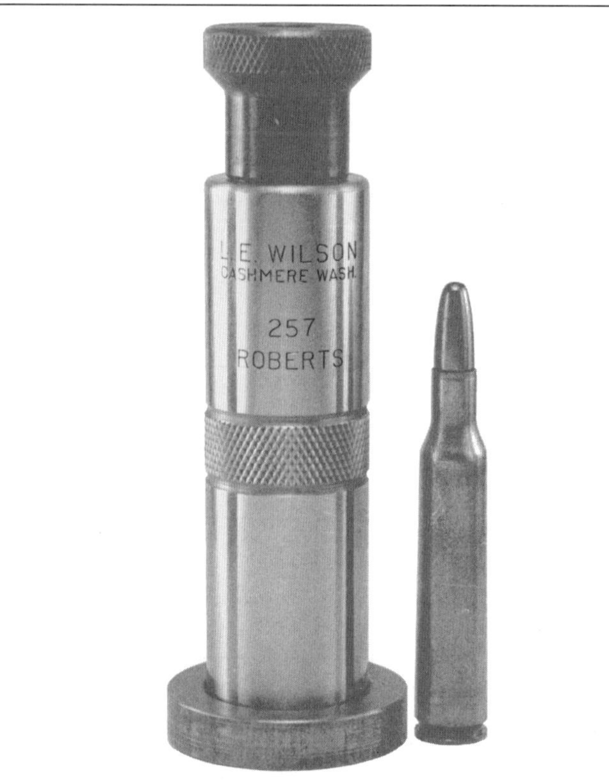

Custom die makers offer in-line seating dies. These are most useful for benchrest competitors who create cartridges immediately prior to use (between relays). Such loads usually have only enough neck tension to keep the bullet in place during careful handling. Generally, such loads are designed so that the bullet is pushed against the rifling as the round is chambered and then is pushed farther into the case as the action is fully closed and locked. In match guns, this type of load can provide phenomenal accuracy, but such cartridges generally are not sufficiently robust for any other type of use.

When using an arbor press and an in-line, bullet-seating die, the handloader starts the bullet into a sized, primed, and charged case by hand. He then places the seating die over the case. When the die body fully covers the case, the seating stem protrudes from the die body. Sliding this assembly under the ram and pulling the press handle drives the seating stem into the die and thereby seats the bullet.

Once the Gold Medal seating die body is properly adjusted, the handloader drops a bullet (base downward) into the window. The tool design forces the bullet into alignment with the die's axis. An O-ring holds a steel roller-pin in a slot in the sliding case-alignment body. This steel roller-pin retains the bullet in the sliding body. Raising the ram pushes the case into the sliding body, thereby assuring alignment between the case and die. Raising the ram farther lifts the case, sliding body, and bullet until the bullet's tip enters the floating seating stem. Continuing to raise the ram pushes the stem into contact with a micrometer stop; thereafter, bullet seating begins. The critical advantages of the RCBS Gold Medal die are twofold:

First, during the entire seating operation, the bullet remains perfectly aligned with the case neck. This can

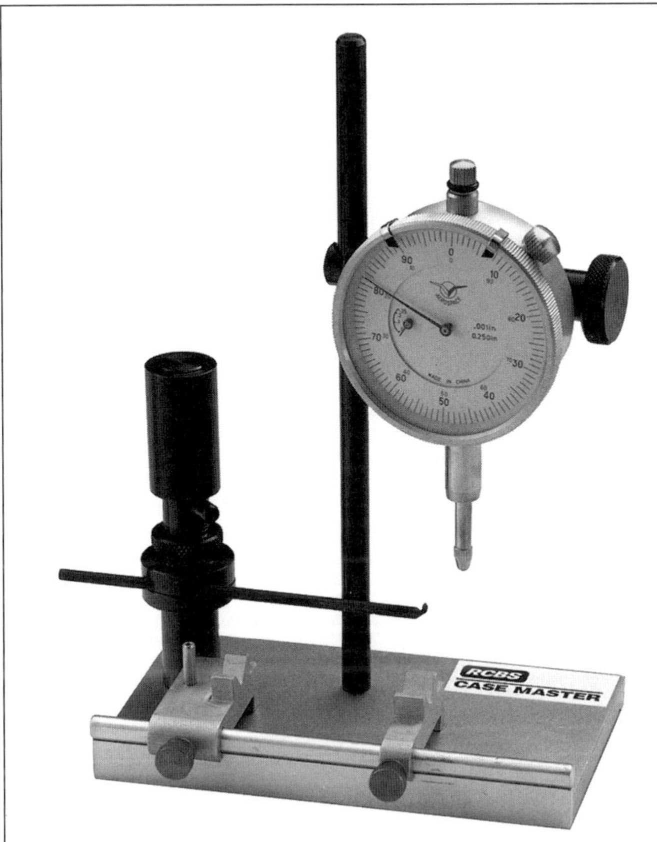

With the RCBS Case Master, you can compare runout between the case neck and the case body, before and after the bullet's seating. Thereby, you can determine whether your seating die or seating procedure is contributing to significant case shoulder bending. Set up the tool (as described in instructions) to measure the runout near the case mouth, then compare each case before and after seating the bullet—less change is better.

be important when loading cartridges using very short bullets—as is common in varminting combinations. When seating such bullets with a conventional die (or even with other premium dies), the bullet can tip in the neck so that the bullet tip follows the contour of the interior of the die, as the case pushes the bullet into the die. In that instance, when the tip reaches the die's shoulder, as the shoulder of the die forces the bullet to rotate into alignment with the case, the bullet's base begins to push the neck of the case sideways. The magnitude of this sideways force depends upon the relative bullet length and case diameter, shoulder angle, bullet base design, and details of the case mouth interior at the opening.

While unlikely, the resulting stress could damage either the bullet or the case mouth, or it could bend the case shoulder. Such damage is most likely to occur with short delicate bullets (typical varminting types), flat-based bullets, case designs with a relatively sharp shoulder, and in instances where the case body diameter is significantly larger than the case neck diameter (Modern short-fat cases with sharp case shoulders are particularly susceptible.)

The second advantage of the RCBS Gold Medal seating die is that bullet insertion is simple and insertion timing is uncritical. When using a conventional seating die, the handloader must make sure that the bullet base stays on the case neck and that the bullet tip enters the die opening. With short, flat-based, small-caliber bullets, this can be a finger-pinching nuisance, at best—most of us have pinched or will pinch fingers and damaged bullets and cases while seating such bullets using any die other than the RCBS Gold Medal.

Various specialty manufacturers, such as Meacham Tool and Hardware, offer dies with similar features. These tools provide precise control over the depth of bullet seating, and these reduce the chance of bullet distortion or case shoulder bending during bullet seating. Such tools are worth considering, and most are extremely easy to adjust and to use. (Meacham designed and intends his dies specifically for use with large cast bullets in traditional blackpowder cartridges.) Some of these special dies are designed for use with an arbor press.

NEVER USE A CONVENTIONAL ARBOR PRESS FOR FULL-LENGTH CASE RESIZING.

LOADING BULLETS—CASE OR BULLET DAMAGE DURING SEATING

If, for any reason, the seating operation either bends the case shoulder or significantly deforms the bullet, accuracy will be degraded. One example that can lead to the former is a bullet-seating die for a bottlenecked case where the seating stem is not well centered with the rest of the die. With such a die, as you seat the bullet, the die body holds the case as the seating stem forces the bullet nose sideways. If this stem-push is of sufficient magnitude, the case shoulder will bend beyond the elastic limit. When this happens, the case neck (and, hence, the bullet) will no longer align with the case body. When one chambers such rounds, the bullets will not align with the bore's axis. This degrades accuracy. When such bending occurs in some but not all the rounds in any given batch, the load might shoot otherwise tight groups but with occasional fliers.

FAULTY SEATING DIES ARE RARE, BUT IF YOU HAVE ONE, YOU MIGHT FIND THIS TO BE ONE OF THE MOST DIFFICULT ACCURACY PROBLEMS BECAUSE, OFTEN, THE CASE OR BULLET WILL NOT DEFORM, WHICH MEANS THAT MOST OF THE CARTRIDGES WILL SHOOT JUST FINE; OCCASIONAL EXCEPTIONS WILL CAUSE FLIERS. OCCASIONAL FLIERS ARE ONE OF THE MOST FRUSTRATING ACCURACY ISSUES THAT ANY HANDLOADER FACES.

An example of a seating die problem that can result in bullet damage is the same situation where the handloader is seating soft, swaged-lead bullets (most commonly in a cylindrical case). The soft bullet is apt to bend or deform—bending the shank, deforming the nose, or deforming the heel (base).

LOADING BULLETS—BULLET-TO-NECK TENSION (BULLET PULL)

Before beginning this section, note that we have good evidence that unusually cold ammunition storage can sometimes dramatically reduce neck tension. Ammunition loaded with minimal neck tension, through a lack of sufficient interference fit between the bullet and the case neck, can demonstrate a functionality failure after being subjected to a temperature significantly below zero—a common example is a shipment of ammunition in the cargo hold of an airliner.

In chapter 5 (and other places within this text), we explore the importance of consistent case neck tension (bullet pull) in some detail. Both benchrest competitors and serious varmint hunters often tinker with case neck tension, as a final means of finding a measure of improved accuracy.

Often, the slight additional delay in initial bullet movement that results from increasing the bullet pull will improve accuracy. Perhaps, the bullet obturates to fit the bore diameter sooner. If the chamber pressure is higher when the bullet starts moving, the pressure will reach the level necessary to obturate the bullet before the bullet moves as far into the bore. This can improve the bullet-to-bore alignment and thereby reduce the accuracy-degrading asymmetric bullet deformation that can occur when the bullet is not properly aligned as it enters the bore.

Handloaders can use several methods to adjust the case neck tension. When using neck-sizing dies with interchangeable inserts, we can use incrementally smaller inserts to size the neck accordingly smaller. Within reasonable limits, a 1/1000-inch reduction in neck size significantly increases bullet pull. When using neck-bushing dies, if sizing the neck 1/1000-inch smaller increases bullet pull too much, the handloader can adjust the die to size less of the case neck length. Thus, very fine adjustments in bullet pull are feasible.

Redding and others also offer full-length, neck-bushing sizing dies. Handloaders can use these dies to load hunting ammunition with an ideal bullet pull and without overworking the case neck. As covered in chapter 5 on neck tension, those using standard dies can easily increase case neck tension by modifying the expander diameter.

Should a load with very little case neck tension prove to provide the best accuracy, those shooters

Cracks in case necks can be subtle as seen on this 30-30 cartridge (left). This round had been loaded for several decades, and stress on the overworked brass eventually resulted in failure. Often this occurs upon firing, but it can occur during storage, as happened here. Conversely, cracking can occur at the time of loading as happened with this nickel-plated 45-70 case on the right.

most interested in extreme accuracy will use it. They can get away with this because they can handle their ammunition with due caution and feed single cartridges into the chamber. This practice minimizes the potential to dislodge a seated bullet. For that type of ammunition, accuracy is the only criterion for determining the ideal neck tension.

Big-game hunters and those carrying a gun for self-defense have different needs. A jammed gun, caused by a bullet that dislodged from or pushed into the case might be of little consequence when one is shooting at paper or vermin. However, as all too many African hunters have learned the hard way, a jammed gun can be a life-threatening hazard when hunting dangerous game. Similarly, proper functioning is critical with self-defense cartridges and guns.

Assuming that you have properly sized the case body, that you have properly seated the primer (always below flush), and that the load is otherwise safe, one pertinent outstanding question remains: the integrity of the bullet-to-case bond. Two factors are important here. Foremost, is neck-to-bullet friction, which results from an interference fit created when the handloader forces a bullet of one diameter into an elastic case neck of a slightly smaller internal diameter. Second is the application of a proper crimp in those cartridges where a crimp is appropriate. Refer to "Loading Bullets—Crimping" later in this chapter.

The degree of neck-to-bullet friction depends upon several factors. The first is the existence of or lack of lubrication between the case and the bullet. Lubrication can decrease the force required to dislodge a bullet. For most (low-recoil) hunting ammunition, a small amount of graphite, white mica (as sold by Midway), or molybdenum-disulfide in the case neck is of little concern. However, any such lubrication should be uniform from round-to-round and should be kept to a minimum. For absolute security with dangerous-game cartridges used in high-recoiling guns, both the case neck interior and the bullet must be scrupulously free from any form of lubrication.

As noted above, we have some evidence that cartridges that are otherwise perfectly usable will have loose bullets after having been shipped. Perhaps the extreme cold to which ammunition is stored in the cargo hold of an airliner can stress-relieve the case neck, thereby allowing it to release the bullet. Increasing the degree of interference fit can eliminate this potentiality. Keep in mind that unless you deform the bullet or the case during bullet seating, it is simply impossible to create too much neck-to-bullet friction

SUGGESTED APPROXIMATE EXPANDER AND BUSHING DIAMETERS FOR VARIOUS BULLETS OF VARIOUS SIZES

(THIS TABLE IS MOST USEFUL AS A RELATIVE COMPARISON CHART; ACTUAL VALUES WILL VARY.)

<table>
<tr><th colspan="11">BULLET DIAMETER IN CALIBERS (1/100 INCH)</th></tr>
<tr><td><20</td><td>20–23</td><td>23–26</td><td>26–29</td><td>29–32</td><td>32–35</td><td>35–38</td><td>38–41</td><td>41–44</td><td>44–47</td><td>>47</td></tr>
<tr><th colspan="11">BEST EXPANDER (LEFT) AND NECK BUSHING (RIGHT) DIAMETER EQUALS: MULTIPLY 0.001-INCH BY THE APPROPRIATE FOLLOWING VALUE: SUBTRACT THAT RESULT FROM BULLET DIAMETER</th></tr>
<tr><th colspan="11">SOFT BULLETS (SWAGED LEAD)</th></tr>
<tr><td><⅛ | ¾</td><td>⅛ | 1</td><td><¼ | 1⅛</td><td>¼ | 1⅜</td><td><⅜ | 1½</td><td><⅜ | 1⅝</td><td><½ | 1⅞</td><td>½ | 2⅛</td><td><⅝ | 2¼</td><td>⅝ | 2½</td><td><¾ | 2⅝</td></tr>
<tr><th colspan="11">SOFT CAST BULLETS</th></tr>
<tr><td>>⅜ | 1⅛</td><td>½ | 1⅛</td><td><⅝ | 1½</td><td>>⅝ | 1¾</td><td>¾ | 2</td><td><⅞ | 2⅛</td><td>>⅞ | 2⅜</td><td>1 | 2⅝</td><td><1⅛ | 2¾</td><td>>1⅛ | 3</td><td>1¼ | 3¼</td></tr>
<tr><th colspan="11">MEDIUM CAST AND SOFT JACKETED BULLETS</th></tr>
<tr><td>⅝ | 1⅜</td><td>¾ | 1⅝</td><td>⅞ | 1⅞</td><td>1 | 2⅛</td><td>1⅛ | 2⅜</td><td>1¼ | 2⅝</td><td>1⅜ | 2⅞</td><td>1½ | 3⅛</td><td>1⅝ | 3⅜</td><td>1¾ | 3⅝</td><td>1⅞ | 3⅞</td></tr>
<tr><th colspan="11">HARD CAST AND CONVENTIONAL JACKETED BULLETS</th></tr>
<tr><td>¾ | 1½</td><td>1 | 1⅞</td><td>1⅛ | 2⅛</td><td>1⅜ | 2¼</td><td>1½ | 2¾</td><td>1⅝ | 3</td><td>1⅞ | 3⅜</td><td>2 | 3⅝</td><td>2⅛ | 3⅞</td><td>2⅜ | 4¼</td><td>2½ | 4½</td></tr>
</table>

NOTE: The marking on the neck bushing might not reflect the actual inside diameter of the bushing.

by simply increasing the amount of interference fit between the case and bullet. For standard cartridges used in standard guns, experience has proven that the best accuracy always results from using the greatest feasible deformation-free interference fit.

Ultimately, bullet hardness, case neck thickness and hardness, and the shape of the bullet base limit the possible neck-to-bullet tension. An undersized, thick, and hard case neck can deform a very soft bullet during seating; similarly, as chamber pressure forces a soft bullet from such a case, any significant crimp will deform (swage) the bullet.

Sometimes, case necks can be either too soft or too hard. After repeated reloading cycles, case necks get very hard. The handloader will notice a progressive increase in the effort required during neck expansion and bullet seating. As noted, high neck tension for hunting ammunition is quite desirable. However, an excessively work-hardened case neck might spontaneously split at any time between seating the bullet and firing the round. Obviously, a split case neck cannot properly hold a bullet.

To eliminate this eventuality, either discard such cases or anneal the necks. I cover annealing in chapter 3. Annealing softens case necks, eases resizing, and extends the life of the case. If the primer pockets are still tight and the case body has not thinned unduly near the web-to-body junction, no reason exists to discard the cases just because the necks have become too hard—anneal those necks and save those cases. This practice makes particularly good sense for the handloader who might have fully prepped a batch of cases; having spent hours getting a few boxes of cases into a state of near perfection, he will appreciate any opportunity to extend the useful life of those cases.

Should you suspect that your freshly annealed case necks or the necks of factory-fresh cases are not providing sufficient neck tension to keep the bullets in place under the stresses associated with recoil, or if you suspect that increasing case neck tension might improve ballistic uniformity, you can easily work-harden any case neck. Properly lubricate both the neck's exterior and interior (either or both are unnecessary when using a carbide expander or a TiN, or similarly plated bushing), then run the case fully into a full-length resizing die. This will resize the neck. Then withdraw the case. This will expand the neck.

Cycling each case a specific number of times into and out of the die will provide a consistent amount of work-hardening to each case neck. You will have to experiment to achieve the desired degree of hardening. The result can be worth the effort. Using this method, handloaders can work-harden case necks of a large batch of cases quite rapidly, especially with the use of a raised expander button in the resizing die. Refer to chapter 5. When using such a die, the handloader need only raise and lower the ram a bit more than the length of the case neck for each cycle.

Deliberately hardening the case necks adds measurably to the force required to move a bullet deeper into or farther out of a case. This force relates to cartridge dependability. Several classes of ammunition warrant consideration in this regard. This includes ammunition that:

- Is intended for dangerous-game hunting
- Generates unusually heavy recoil
- Is used in
    - » magazine-fed guns
    - » double rifles
    - » tubular magazine guns
    - » revolvers
    - » semiautomatic guns

As an example of a rifle cartridge where increasing bullet pull might be particularly worthwhile, or even necessary, consider the 358 Winchester. Many factors suggest the potential of functionality problems with this particular cartridge. These include:

- Many propellant charges that produce optimum ballistics are highly compressed
- For proper functioning in most guns, handloaders must seat normal hunting bullets deep into the case
- Similar bullet and propellant-column diameter
- Propellant column is relatively short
- Recoil is relatively high

Propellant granules are both elastic and plastic; therefore, when a volume of propellant is significantly compressed, it can store a significant amount of elastic energy. Hence, in 358 Winchester cartridges where bullet seating results in significant charge compression (and in loads using highly compressed charges in similarly shaped cartridges), the propellant pushes on the bullet with considerable force. If the compressed propellant is pushing against a large bullet base, the neck tension might be insufficient—elastic forces within the propellant can drive the bullet somewhat out of the case.

Experience shows that otherwise normal 358 Winchester charges will spontaneously move the bullet out of a case a small amount as the handloader withdraws the cartridge from the seating die. When this is happening, it is quite impossible to produce cartridges with consistent OAL. Worse, rounds with this sort of propellant compression can spontaneously lengthen at any time, for example, in the gun magazine, in response to the battering associated with recoil. Such lengthening can jam the gun; my friend, Norm Nelson, has seen this.

If your luck is similar to mine, such an event will occur after you shoot at the biggest bull elk that ever walked the earth and you manage to hit an intervening tree limb, consequently creating a clean miss. As you stand helplessly, trying to chamber the next round out of the magazine, that elk will stop, dead in his tracks, and stare at you in apparent disbelief.

After an eternity of fighting with the gun, while trying to chamber a round for a follow-up shot, you will notice that the round in the top of the magazine has mysteriously lengthened—either that or the magazine has shortened! That round is now hopelessly jammed and will not move into the chamber. In desperation, you will drop the magazine and begin digging in your pocket for a loose round. Of course, just as you begin to close the action on the cartridge that you finally freed from your keys, Swiss Army Knife, can opener, bottle top, and whatever else might have been in the same pocket, Mr. Bull will decide that he has seen enough and will mosey on over the ridge, unmolested.

What could have happened to cause such a circus maximus at your expense? Recoil from the first shot drove the front of magazine into the bullet. That shock was just enough to break the frictional bond between the bullet and the case. With the bonds of friction thus broken, the elastic force within the propellant's column pushed the bullet from the case until it hit the front of the magazine. When the bolt moved out of the way, the magazine spring pushed on the case, but now the cartridge was just as long as the magazine, so the bullet hung up and would not slide upward. The resulting tipping as the base of the case slid upward only served to tighten the jam. Pushing the bolt against the rim of the case only drove the bullet against the front of the magazine. No chance that round would come free of the trap thus created. If you are wondering, yes, this has happened.

If post-seating bullet movement is a concern, consider these additional steps. Be certain that both the bullet and the case-neck-interior are free of lubricant. Settle any compressed charge as much as is feasible before seating the bullet. Refer to chapter 9. To maximize neck tension, create a smaller expander button, as explained in chapter 5. That step along with expander polishing can considerably increase the tension in the case neck and the resultant bullet pull. Before loading dangerous-game cartridges, vibratory tumbling in a clean corncob medium to remove any traces of lubricant from both the cases and bullets is a very good idea.

LOADING BULLETS—SEALING

The application of a small dab of George & Roy's primer sealer at the junction of the case mouth and bullet is cheap insurance against infiltration of moisture, oils, or other contaminants—anything can happen in the field. Lacking that fine product, a small dab of a bright red, enamel-based fingernail polish does an acceptable job. Wipe the excess off using a clean rag. (Apply the polish fully around the junction. Cap the bullet with a rag and give the case a twist while withdrawing the rag.) Properly done, this leaves a thin line of red polish at the bullet-to-case intersection and little or none anywhere else. These materials cure without infiltrating significantly into this joint and, hence, will not significantly alter the ballistics. (Similarly, George & Roy's primer sealer is the best product for sealing primers, but fingernail polish will do that job also.)

LOADING BULLETS—CRIMPING

If ever there existed an ill-understood facet of handloading, it would have to be what a crimp can do and what it cannot do. For example, in a revolver that generates heavy recoil, a heavy crimp alone will never hold a bullet in the case. Those who think a crimp will do so are welcome to reprime a batch of fired 44 Magnum cases without resizing these, drop in their favorite heavy charge of Hercules 2400, seat a bullet, and apply the heaviest crimp possible with any crimping tool made. That done, they should take these cartridges to the range, load a cylinder full, and start shooting. After one or two shots, the gun will jam with the bullets protruding from the cylinder. The bullet-to-case friction, not a crimp, is what holds a bullet in place.

A similar experiment with a normally prepared 44 Magnum case loaded without any crimp will prove the point. Such cartridges work just fine. A proper crimp can modestly increase bullet pull. However, when improperly done, a crimp will always decrease the bonding between the bullet and the case—an improper crimp always reduces bullet pull.

The purpose of a proper crimp is to add a measure of security to the cartridge's dependability. That much

As with primers, it is useful to seal the case mouth on ammunition that might be used for dangerous-game hunting or where handling is suspect and where contamination with any fluid or vapor might occur.

crimping can do but only if done properly. Crimping can also improve ballistic uniformity in revolver cartridges. For rifle cartridges, a significant roll crimp into a deep cannelure can mechanically lock the bullet against deeper seating despite insufficient neck-to-bullet tension. When neck tension is insufficient, recoil forces acting on cartridges within a rifle magazine (particularly a tubular magazine) can drive the bullets deeper into the case.

For this reason, in ammunition used in tubular magazine guns, preferable loads develop normal pressures with a significantly compressed charge. In this manner, the propellant's compression effectively prevents the recoil from driving the bullet farther into the case. However, the application of a good crimp can still be beneficial because this adds a mechanical lock, and it prevents the case mouth from impinging against the rear face of the chamber, and thereby it smoothes the cartridge's chambering.

Ammunition used in many types of guns can benefit from, or will require, a proper crimp. A proper crimp in most types of cartridges is a roll crimp into the bullet cannelure. The profile crimp is an alternative that can provide similar results. For cases that headspace on the case mouth, a taper crimp is appropriate. Examples of situations where a crimp can help or might be critical include:

- High-recoil box-magazine guns
- Double rifles
- Tubular magazine rifles
- Revolvers
- Semiautomatic pistols

However, never imagine that any crimp can do the job by itself—it cannot. Refer to the preceding section, "Loading Bullets—Bullet-to-Neck Tension" (Bullet Pull).

This Redding Taper Crimp Die is precisely engineered to produce the proper amount of crimping on 45 Automatic loads. Redding and others offer similar dies for all cartridges designed to headspace on the case mouth.

The Redding Profile Crimp Die is designed to mimic a factory, collet-style crimp. In some instances, this crimping style can improve the cartridge's functionality.

The rifle-chambering version of the Lee Factory Crimp Die (FCD) is a particularly handy tool. The handgun-chambering version is also useful, but due to case-length limitations, that die cannot incorporate the superior collet crimping system. However, if we could persuade Lee to offer extended shellholders, this limitation would no longer apply. I have used that approach to create both FCD- and Neck Collet–die systems for several very short cartridges.

When using a noncannelured bullet, consider the possibility of using either a taper crimp die or the Lee Factory Crimp die (FCD) to crimp the case mouth slightly into the bullet. With soft-jacketed bullets, handloaders can often use the FCD to swage a crimping groove into the bullet while effectively crimping the case mouth. The FCD does this without damaging the case. Finally, consider deliberately work-hardening the case necks. Refer to the preceding section, "Loading Bullets—Bullet-to-Neck Tension" (Bullet Pull).

In loads where you have belled the case mouths to facilitate bullet seating, such as is required with cast-bullet loads and with most pistol and revolver loads, you usually need to turn the case mouth back straight. This is necessary to guarantee free chambering. Crimping automatically accomplishes this task.

However, with blackpowder cartridges and particularly with any load using a very soft bullet, it is often desirable to eliminate the crimp. Moreover, it is often worthwhile to leave the case mouth slightly belled so that fully chambering the round requires a bit of a push. Benefits of this approach include:

- Prevents bullet deformation—forcing a soft bullet from a crimped case, especially if the case mouth is particularly hard, will swage the bullet under size.
- Seals the chamber and thereby significantly reduces the amount of smoke infiltrating back along the case, thereby keeping both the case exterior and the chamber cleaner.
- Centers the front end of the case, thereby improving the alignment of the cartridge and bullet.

Many standard bullet-seating dies allow the option of crimping the case into a groove on the bullet. These dies can apply a roll crimp during the bullet seating operation. However, it is always best to apply any crimp in a separate operation.

Handloaders should never use a roll crimp on ammunition used in the 30 carbine and various semiautomatic pistols where headspacing occurs on the case mouth. For these chamberings, a taper crimp is required. This process involves a taper-crimp die that simply pushes the case mouth against the bullet in a separate step after bullet seating.

Handloaders can adjust the taper crimp die to push the case mouth slightly into the bullet and, thereby, lock the bullet against deeper seating, which can occur in semiautomatic guns when the battering force (that occurs as the slide slams the bullet against the magazine and the feed ramp during action cycling) exceeds bullet pull. However, any taper crimp will always result in a reduction in bullet pull because the case mouth will spring back from the bullet.

The only advantage is that if applied with sufficient force, a taper crimp will create a matching tapered section on the bullet shank. The front end of that section will include a relatively sharp shoulder, and because the diameter of the inside edge of the case mouth is smaller than the outside edge of this shoulder on the bullet, subsequent deeper bullet seating requires significant force (usually far greater than will ever exist during normal handling and action cycling).

At best, a crimp can improve functionality, but it cannot add significantly to bullet pull; at worst, a crimp can significantly reduce bullet pull or render the cartridge unusable.

Taper crimping can be beneficial and does not normally significantly degrade intrinsic accuracy. Experiment and see what happens. As noted, never use roll or profile crimping dies for cartridges that headspace on the case mouth. A properly designed taper-crimp die should not reduce the case mouth diameter sufficiently to interfere with headspace control.

Two things can contribute to bullets pulling out of cases when firing revolver cartridges. First, is the obvious influence of inertia. As the gun accelerates backward in recoil, the cylinder pulls the cartridge back. To get some idea of the magnitude of the force involved, consider this: When you fire a typical 44 Magnum cartridge, the gun accelerates to about 23 fps in less than 1/1000 of a second. The maximum acceleration force is 1,600 times the force of gravity; hence, resulting bullet pull is equal to what would occur if the cartridge were held rigidly with the bullet pointing straight down with a 55-pound weight attached. Meanwhile, as the gun and cartridges accelerate violently rearward, the only things pulling the bullets back are neck tension and the crimp. The real surprise is that the case can hold the bullet at all.

The Lee Factory Crimp Rifle Die produces an excellent crimp that is as good as it gets for the hand-loader. FCD offers many advantages. Case length is not critical; weak cases will not collapse or malform, and the case mouth is not turned into the bullet, so no sharp edge exists at the end of the case to damage the bullet as it exits the case.

Second, when present, a compressed propellant charge always pushes on the bullet. In certain magnum revolver loads using highly compressed charges, this pushing force can exceed 100 pounds. Obviously, this can vastly reduce the recoil force necessary to dislodge the bullet. Furthermore, once a bullet begins to slip out of a case, a highly compressed propellant charge tends to keep it moving.

Some pundits have denigrated crimping as always detrimental to accuracy in rifle ammunition, but this is not necessarily so. When properly applied to cases of uniform length, a crimp can be accuracy neutral. In some instances, the slight added bullet pull of an ideal crimp could improve ballistic uniformity. The Lee Factory Crimp Die (FCD) really shines for this and other reasons. This is a useful last loading step for any ammunition intended for use in any tubular magazine rifle. For most rifle loads, the FCD provides a superior crimp compared to any roll-crimping die. It offers the added advantage of not leaving the case mouth turned toward the bullet. Hence, as chamber pressure forces the bullet to move, the case mouth is less apt to scar the bullet's surface.

Here the photographer (Allan Jones) ideally captured before-and-after images as I fired a full-house 454 Casull load. Decades of practice and significant upper body strength allow unusually good control of the momentous recoil. (This load generates fully twice the muzzle energy of a factory 44 Magnum load, and many shooters find the gun muzzle recoiling far past vertical during recoil.) This degree of force easily pulls the bullets from the cases, particularly when the handloader uses less than ideal loading practices or when the die parameters are imperfect.

Left: a factory load with inadequate neck tension. Revolver recoil pulled bullet. Right: a factory round with plenty of neck tension but inadequate belling before the bullet seating. The case cut into the bullet during seating and ruined the load.

A significant advantage of the FCD is that it is not particularly sensitive to case length. Conversely, as the case length increases from too short to too long, a standard crimping die will progressively apply: no crimp, an insufficient crimp, a perfect crimp, and too much crimp (and thereby mangle the case). Worse, cartridges with fragile and springy case shoulders, such as the 30-30, are almost impossible to crimp properly using a conventional die (even when the handloader has carefully trimmed

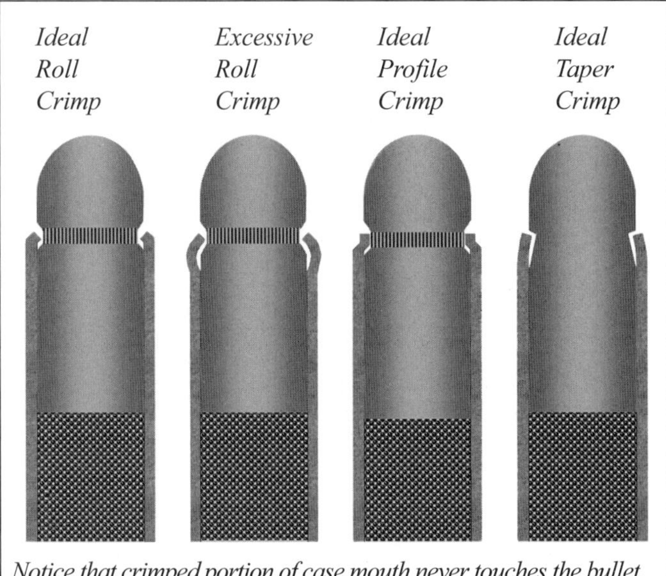

Notice that crimped portion of case mouth never touches the bullet.

Midway offers handy Maximum Cartridge Gauges for revolver and pistol chamberings. If a round freely enters this gauge, without either the bullet or the case head protruding, it will fit in any properly chambered gun.

all cases to a uniform length). This problem reflects variations in seating resistance that induce variations in the flexing of the case body and the shoulder during seating. Hence, as one applies the crimps and despite having trimmed the cases to identical lengths, the case mouths will not align similarly or properly with the bullet cannelures. The Lee FCD solves this problem.

When using a standard bullet-seating die to apply a crimp, keep the following things in mind:

- You cannot achieve best results without trimming the cases to a uniform length.
- If you apply the crimp in a separate step (after bullet seating), you will achieve better and more uniform crimping.
- Seat the bullet to an OAL that places the case mouth very close to the front end of the cannelure.
- Generally, combining seating and crimping into one operation is frustrating, at best.
- Simultaneous seating and crimping is feasible when loading cases with heavy neck walls; however, when loading cases with thin neck walls, doing so is exceedingly difficult, at best.

TIPPING HOLLOWPOINT MATCH BULLETS

Most hollowpoint match bullet tips show noticeable imperfections and significant bullet-to-bullet variations. These things are obvious when you view these bullets using significant magnification. The reason these bullets do not have a uniform tip is related to the fact that, unlike lead, gilding metal (an alloy composed of 95 percent copper and 5 percent zinc) is live, in the sense that it has significant elastic strength. When the forming die creates the tiny meplat typical of long-range match bullets, the gilding metal at each portion of the tip is forced to deform sufficiently so that when the bullet is withdrawn from the forming die the tip will inevitably rebound—it will open back up, if only a tiny amount. The degree of rebound opening depends upon the jacket's hardness and thickness and upon how small the die sizes the tip. It is also important to note that polishing or moly plating can also generate flared or peened tips on hollowpoint bullets.

Because bullet jackets are never precisely uniform, this rebound varies around the tip's perimeter and from bullet to bullet. As the die squeezes the bullet tip from full diameter to typically less than 25 percent of full diameter (during bullet forming), tiny variations in the thickness of the jacket wall, the alloy, and the annealing will compound—the tip will never size down with precise uniformity. Hence, the jacket material at the tip will seldom be of uniform length or thickness—one side is usually longer and the opposite side will usually rebound more. The profiles of individual bullet tips can never be identical.

Close examination demonstrates that the tip profile of hollowpoint match bullets typically shows an inordinate degree of variation. This characteristic is detrimental to long-range accuracy for two reasons. First, each bullet will have a slightly different BC, which increases vertical stringing. Second, the coning induced yaw of each bullet in ballistic flight will generate varying degrees of turbulence and steering push, which will enlarge the resulting groups. It is infeasible to sort bullets according to tip profile, if for no other reason than the fact that one would only be guessing as to what tip shapes might generate similar variations.

David Tubb, through his company Superior Shooting Systems, has addressed this issue. He has designed and is marketing a bullet-tipping tool called the Ballistic Meplat Uniformer (BMU). This tool is relatively easy to use, and it does a very good job of uniforming tips of hollowpoint match bullets.

At the heart of this tool is a simple cutter that shortens the bullet tip, as necessary, to form a uniform

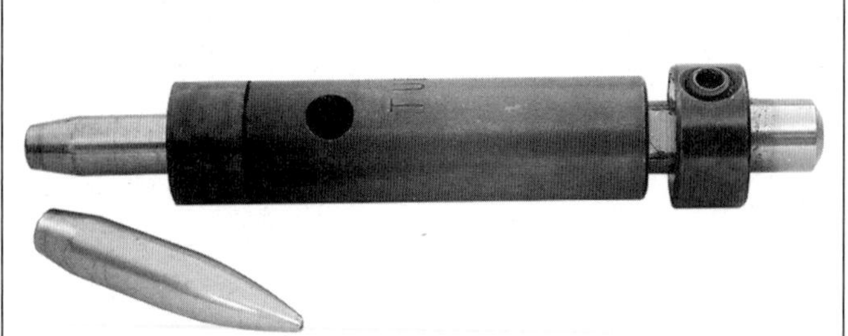

This is a 30-caliber BMU with sample match bullet and a bullet in the working position. I suspect that this is a useful alteration for any bullet fired beyond about 600 yards, but it might help at shorter ranges, and, when properly done, it cannot hurt.

The Lee Three-Jaw Chuck is most useful for many case alteration operations. It chucks into a power hand drill and provides a quick means of clamping onto cases.

ogive and a flat, square meplat. A tube that extends to include a caliber-specific collar houses this cutter. This centers and somewhat squares the bullet while limiting bullet entry depth. The cutter shaft is fitted with an adjustable collar. This collar limits the distance the cutter can enter into the tube; thus, the handloader can set the amount of tip that this tool will remove.

Tool adjustment is simple. Loosen the set screw in the sliding collar, move the shaft slightly, and retighten the set screw. With a micrometer or feeler gauge set, the user can make precise adjustments. After establishing a crude collar setting so that an unaltered bullet tip just touches the cutter, adjust the collar. This will allow the shaft to enter the tube sufficiently deeper so that it can remove the entire nonuniform portion of the bullet tip—typically less than about 0.010 inch of length. This is easy to do when using a feeler gauge, which will allow you to create a specific gap between the cutter shaft collar and the tool housing. When the

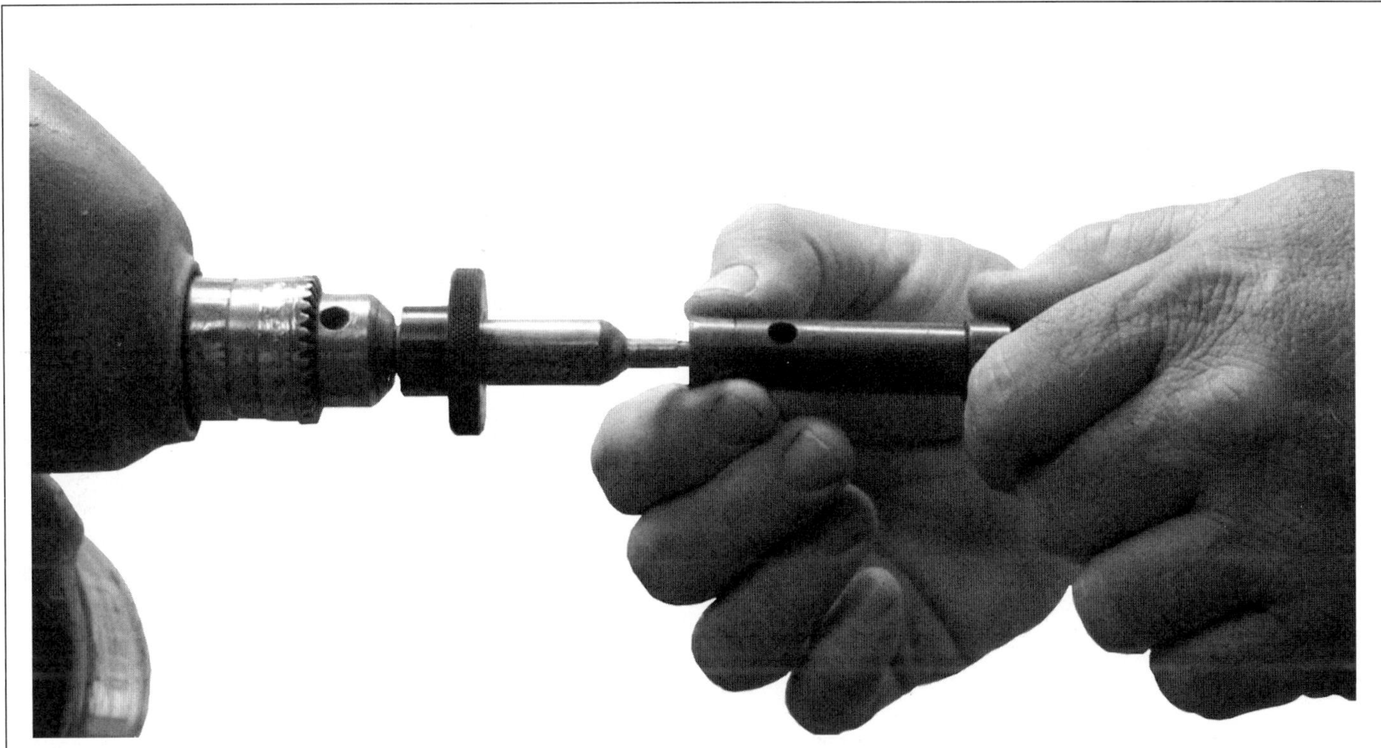

This view shows one possible setup for using the Ballistic Meplat Uniformer (BMU). Here a hand drill is vised in a bench vise; the Lee Three-Jaw Chuck is chucked into that; and, a 6.5/60 SM^C round is installed in that. The best application of the BMU uses two hands, as shown. This operation takes seconds, including a final bullet-tip polish with four-aught steel wool.

cutter is just touching the unaltered bullet, you then tighten the collar. Alternatively, one could use a caliper to measure the shaft's protrusion from the collar and adjust the tool accordingly.

Due to use of good materials and proper design, the bullet collar limits bullet entry while tending to keep the bullet square in the tool. It does so without marring the bullet surface, even with moly plating.

After trimming the bullet tips using this tool, it is necessary to dress each with four-aught steel wool in order to remove 100 percent of the inevitable burs. Tumbling the tipped bullets in corncob might do the same job, but steel wool is a more certain method.

Generally, the handloader needs a loupe, at least a 10X, to see just how much tip must be removed to assure uniformity on any given bullet type. (An Opti-Visor—available from Brownells—fitted with a high-magnification lens works well.) As noted above, the tips often have various types of imperfections. Remove only sufficient material (length) to leave a flat tip and a uniform ogive, with no flaring. While it is important not to trim unnecessarily as doing so progressively reduces BC, it is more critical to trim sufficiently so that all the bullets have a uniformly flat tip without any flaring.

The farther one is shooting, the more important tipping will be. However, it is worth noting that those who are shooting unusually light match bullets, such as are used in the Hunter Bench game, might also benefit from tipping, even when shooting at intermediate ranges.

Walt Berger, founder of Berger Bullets, and I have discussed this issue. We agree that the nonuniform flared tip of match bullets is apt to result in a BC that is actually less than the rated value (if that value is based upon anything other than actual firing tests). We also

Note the gilding metal chips on this Ballistic Meplat Uniformer (BMU) cutting head. These cuttings used to be part of the nonuniform protrusions at the tips of long-range match bullets. Minute variations in the shape of unaltered bullet tips can be the tiny detail that makes all the difference in long-range accuracy. I suspect that this is a useful alteration for any bullet fired beyond about 600 yards, but it might help at shorter ranges, and, when properly done, it cannot hurt.

suspect that such a nonuniform meplat could result in a steering push that would increase the group size.

Bob McCoy was perhaps the most knowledgeable modern authority on the subject of bullets in flight. Shortly before his premature death, he and I discussed this steering-push issue. He agreed that a nonuniform bullet tip that was significantly biased into the air stream due to bullet yaw could well explain why match bullets having tiny meplats tend to be less accurate than otherwise similar bullets having a somewhat larger meplat. If this steering push theory reflects reality, the value of making long-range match bullet tips uniform is obvious: Tipped bullets should generate less tip turbulence, hence less steering push, and should, therefore, generate smaller groups at extended distances. And, as if to prove the point, tipped bullets have won many recent matches and are setting new records.

USING THE TUBB BALLISTIC MEPLAT UNIFORMER

Tubb designed the Ballistic Meplat Uniformer (BMU) so the handloader can use it by hand (slow and painful when doing hundreds of bullets) or with power tools, in various ways. (Those using a power tool should apply a dab of moly grease to each friction surface of the tool.) One can either modify naked bullets or modify bullets in loaded cartridges.

The use of a power tool is well worthwhile. I tested chucking the cutting shaft into a vised hand drill and tipping the bullets in cartridges. Most handloaders will find that, as a matter of dexterity, working on cartridges is easier than working on bullets.

A far easier method is available to those owning a lathe. Chuck loaded rounds into the lathe and run the BMU by hand. This proves to be very fast and to produce very precise results. This also eases and speeds the deburring operation. The handy Lee Precision three-jaw cartridge chuck, used in a vised hand drill, also proved to be a worthwhile tipping adjunct.

This is a close-up of the BMU uniformed bullet tip: Berger, 6.5mm, 140-grain VLD. The lighter shaded concentric rings are those areas where tip deburring has scarred or removed the moly-plating. This harms nothing other than appearance because this is restricted to the tip area where moly does nothing. Note that the bullet tip is precisely square and uniform.

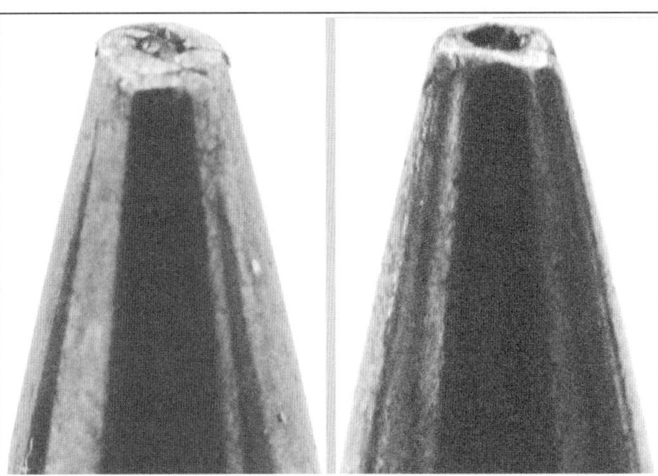

These are random examples of 30-caliber, 190-grain Berger VLDs, as produced and shipped. These show modest tip irregularity and flaring. Unaltered 6.5mm, 140-grain Berger VLDs exhibited significantly more tip flaring.

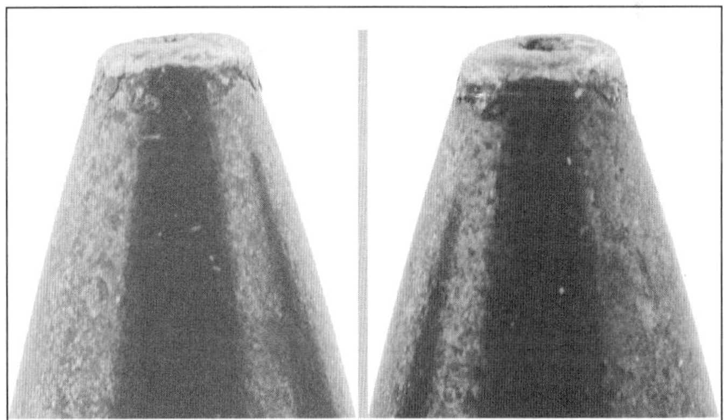

Random samples of 30-caliber Sierra MatchKings: Note that while these tips are comparatively square, there exists significant and variable tip flaring (partly due to moly-plating).

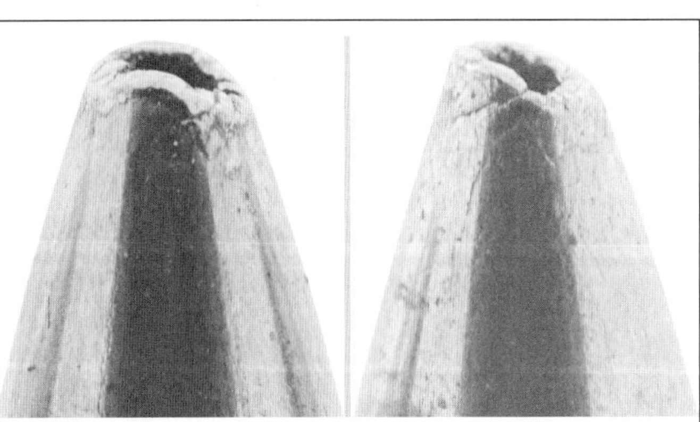

Compare these MatchKings, from a different production lot, to the previous pictured pair. Note the minimal tip flaring but significant tip irregularity.

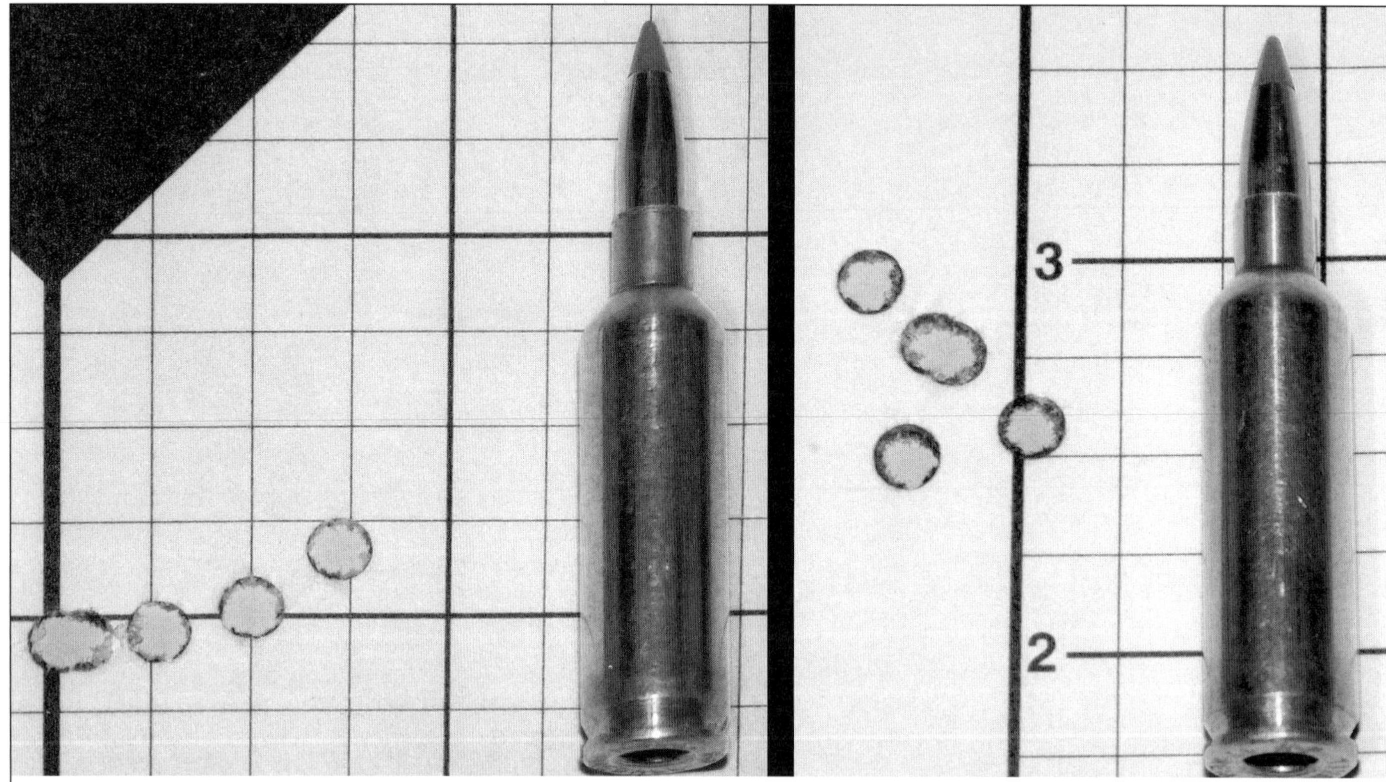

While tinkering with this load (by adjusting the seating depth), I first noted significant fliers (group at right). This could be an indication of bent cases or bent case shoulders, which could indicate a problem with case quality or loading die quality. (See chapter 4.) However, as I tested longer versions of the same load, the fliers disappeared and stringing developed (example group at left). As I further lengthened the rounds to place the bullet progressively closer to the rifling, the orientation of the stringing rotated from nearly horizontal to nearly vertical. Evidently, this accuracy problem was related to barrel time. (See chapter 12.) Because I was only interested in near-maximum loads, adjusting the charge (to change the barrel time) was not an option. To get this gun to shoot accurately with this bullet, I had to use a different propellant.

SOURCES FOR SPECIALTY PRODUCTS AND TOOLS REFERENCED IN THIS CHAPTER:

George and Roy's
2950 NW 29th
Portland, OR 97210
Telephone: 800-553-3022

Meacham Tool & Hardware Inc.
1070 Angel Ridge Road
Peck, ID 83545
Telephone: 208-486-7171

Superior Shooting Systems Inc.
800 N. Second Street
Canadian, TX 79014
Telephone: 806-323-9483

ACCURACY LOAD DEVELOPMENT

CHAPTER 12

INTRODUCTION

Ultimately, most handloaders want to know how accurate their ammunition is. Unlike functionality, which is rather easy to test—it either works or it does not work—at best, determining the relative accuracy of any given load requires considerable effort, patience, and skill. In this chapter, I offer some pointers toward the goal of accuracy testing any given load in any given gun, and I hope to make sense of the results of that testing. For many of us, this is a relaxing, enjoyable, and fulfilling pursuit.

Quality rests and bags are critical for target shooting, hardly less so for the serious handloader who is interested in developing accurate loads. A good front rest, such as this Sinclair unit, soon pays for itself in saved time and components—the dividend is increased confidence, which leads to the self-fulfilling reality: If you believe that you can shoot better, you can shoot better!

BENCH TESTING—GENERAL CONSIDERATIONS

Ultimately, the only way I know to tell if some particular load is more accurate than some other (similar) load is to sit down at a bench, rest the gun properly, and fire shots carefully, through paper, to create comparative groups.

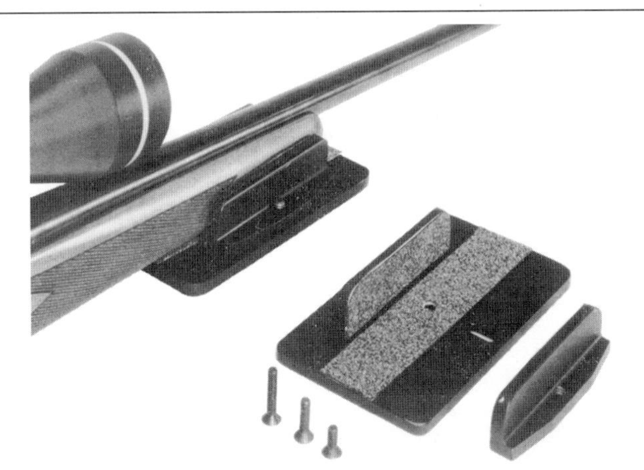

The R. W. Hart Accuracy Asset is a valuable aid for those shooting any rifle that does not have a wide and flat forearm (all typical hunting and most other rifles). Attachment and removal are simple operations that take about one minute. With this unit, it is reasonably easy to shoot over a simple set of sandbags with good results.

Although dedicated rests and bags are unnecessary, these do speed and ease the bench-testing process while increasing one's confidence in the results. Most likely, such tools will allow you to obtain better results. Ultimately, almost any serious shooter will find that using proper rests eventually saves enough time and money to justify the expense.

Bench testing is the definitive method used to measure the accuracy of any load and gun, regardless of the gun type or the type of shooting involved. The goal is to minimize variables. As an example, if you are shooting a hunting rifle, equip it with a good enough

Bill Falin at the defunct Accurate Arms Range, circa 1995. As I took this picture, Falin was firing a 5-shot, 300-yard group with his 45-70, C. Sharps. His load combined his cast bullets with 5744 and Remington 2½ primers. All five shots fell well inside a three-inch circle, impressive shooting with an iron-sighted gun. Lacking quality cartridges that were tuned to a quality gun, firing one such group would have been nothing more than an accident. Falin usually does better.

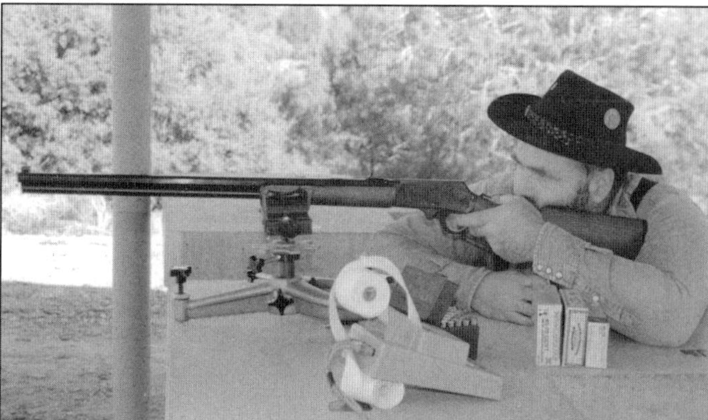

Here I am chronographing and accuracy testing the Marlin 45-70 cowboy rifle. On this day, this gun (with a scope installed) produced a 1¼-inch, 8-shot, 100-yard group using a cast bullet handload. Federal ammunition produced the best 3-shot group using the factory iron sights—inside ¾-inch, on-centers. Barrel time matters. In every other Marlin I had previously tested (at least ten 22-inch and 18½-inch barreled guns), the Winchester factory load was always extremely accurate; in this gun, that load shot 3-inch patterns!

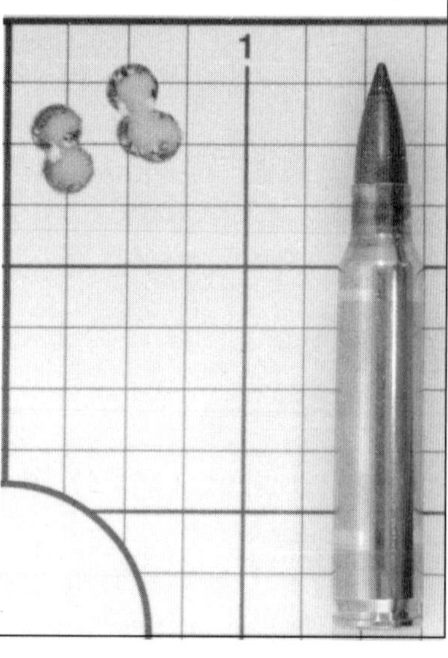

One of 4, 5-shot, 100-yard groups fired with a Bushmaster using Black Hills Factory ammunition. This level of accuracy was typical of this load in this gun. Such consistent accuracy requires precision ammunition.

riflescope so that your ability to see does not limit your ability to aim—generally, we cannot hit what we cannot see (although, paradoxically, skilled and well-trained target shooters do just that, routinely). Then, rest the gun on some sort of cradle that will support it while providing a steady platform so that you do not have to hold the rifle on target. Make sure that you rest and hold the gun in the same way for each shot, and that you rest your cheek on the stock in the same way and with the same amount of pressure—every variable matters so try to replicate each shot in an identical manner. Then, after centering the cross hairs, gently increase the pressure on the trigger until the gun fires. By repeated testing with an empty chamber, make sure that you can break loose the sear without disturbing the alignment of the gun on the target.

Although I prefer the 8½-25 Leupold VX-III LR, this Bushnell 4200 worked on this gun. With it, this short-barreled Bushmaster produced 4, 5-shot, 100-yard groups that were each smaller than ½-inch!

Be sure that your shooting ability and technique is not limiting your ability to measure the intrinsic accuracy of the gun and load—remember that measuring intrinsic accuracy is your goal. The results of sloppy or incautious target shooting usually prove nothing. Equally, if the wind is gusting (any significant change in direction or velocity), the resulting test groups will be of much less value unless you are skilled at doping the wind.

I know of no way to quantify this latter point easily. Generally, unless or until you have acquired significant skills at reading the wind so that you can fire shots only when conditions are significantly similar or so that you can compensate accurately for the conditions that prevail as you fire each shot, testing loads for accuracy on a windy day is a waste of time and ammunition. About the only thing it will do is give you some feeling for just how far any given cross wind will blow a bullet off course—useful but not the goal under discussion here.

ACCURACY TESTING—SIGHTS

Another point, not previously stressed, is the issue of sight quality and repeatability. Few shooters realize just how often a so-called quality riflescope can exhibit significant shot-to-shot zero error. Just because you have installed a new, high-dollar scope does not mean that you can assume that it works correctly—about 30 percent of all riflescopes do not.

Experience has taught us that as many as three out of ten name-brand scopes will not maintain shot-to-shot zero. This is not the place to fully address a solution to this problem, but it seems obvious that a shooter with a scope, rifle, and load combination that produces exemplary accuracy might want to test each new scope on that gun and, conversely, use the known good scope on each new gun during load development.

I present a detailed scope-mounting seminar in *Accurizing the Factory Rifle,* available through Brownells.

Scope testing is a simple process. Once the scope is properly mounted, go to the range and zero the gun at 100 yards. Then, using a clean target and while always aiming at the center of the same bull's-eye, fire one shot after each of the following scope adjustments:

- Three minutes (or inches) left and three minutes (or inches) down
- Six minutes (or inches) up
- Six minutes (or inches) right
- Six minutes (or inches) down

Setting up to test loads in a 5mm/35 SMC chambered Savage M12 at the shooting bench. The 30-grain Berger generates greater than 4,800 fps in this Pac-Nor 1:16 Twist, 28-inch-barrel rifle, and does so with consistent sub-½-MOA accuracy.

Testing a 225 Winchester chambered Meacham 1885 reproduction. With the best handloads and bench technique, this gun consistently shot fantastic 5-shot groups–usually 3 bullets through one tiny hole and 2 through a different tiny hole. These 2 holes were usually about ½ inch apart. A subsequent examination revealed a faulty scope mount. After fixing that problem, this gun produced consistent ¼-inch, 100-yard groups with the Nosler 40-grain BT at 4,250 fps. And, practically every time anyone showed up at the range while I was testing this gun, I found that no gun I have ever tested has elicited more admiration.

This should create holes at each corner of a six-inch box (rectangle). Repeat the above process, beginning with adjusting the scope six minutes left to bring the impact point back to the lower left corner of this box. Fire at least two, preferably three, shots with each corner adjustment. Then, finally, adjust the scope to center the group in the box, and fire at least five shots to see if, or how soon, the scope settles after the final adjustment.

Ideally, each individual group should be as close as you, the gun, and the load are likely to place shots. The group centers should be located where the scope adjustments should have located those. Often, the corner groups will be dismally large. If so, and the center group demonstrates that the scope requires one or more shots to settle down after an adjustment (you observed that the first few shots created a relatively large group and then the remaining shots all went into a very small area), the scope is still useful. (Significant testing has proven that the oft'-quoted technique of rapping on the scope with a screwdriver handle, or a similar tool, to settle the reticle after any adjustment, simply does not work—the only way to settle a scope that requires settling is to fire shots.)

ACCURACY LOAD DEVELOPMENT—THE TRADITIONAL METHOD

If accuracy is your sole criterion, all that remains is to fire each load on a target. Once you have demonstrated that the load produces safe pressures, test various charges of the selected propellant while holding all other variables as constant as possible. The safe charge that gives the smallest group is the obvious choice.

It is an interesting study to watch a group change in character as you vary charge weight in say, ½-grain increments. Back in 1974, I worked up a load in a Remington Pump chambered in 270 Winchester, using the Nosler 160-grain Partition Bullet and surplus H4831 with Remington 9½M primers. As I incrementally increased the charge in ½-grain steps, my 100-yard, 3-shot groups changed from 1½-inch vertical strings to 1½-inch horizontal strings to 1-inch vertical strings and, finally, to sub-¾-inch clusters. Happily, this group tightening occurred very near the maximum load. This was a perfect—and fortuitous—hunting-load result.

Similar results are common in hunting rifles. Shot stringing results from complex barrel vibrations. The secret to good accuracy is to find a combination where each bullet comes free from the muzzle when the barrel is in the same orientation. To achieve this goal, the end of the barrel must be near the end of a vibrational arc (where it is stopping to change directions) just as each bullet exits. As in the above example, it is a happy occurrence when this accuracy-maximizing situation happens to coincide with a near-maximum safe load.

For long-range hunting cartridges, this requirement can necessitate either a change to a propellant that does not deliver quite as much velocity with maximum safe loads, or a slight charge reduction with the preferred

Accuracy testing can be simple or complicated. Here, I am testing various load combinations for accuracy, ballistic uniformity, and velocity for a major article for The VARMINT HUNTER Magazine. *I prefer not to do this sort of testing when it is cold enough to warrant a jacket because I seldom shoot good groups on such days. This day was an exception. My 17 Ackley Hornet Contender carbine proved to be exceptionally accurate with many tested loads. My Oehler 35P, shown as I use it here, has been in dependable service for more than twenty years.*

propellant. For many excellent examples, refer to *Nosler Reloading Guide 3.* Therein, you will find dozens of instances where the most accurate propellant they tested in the test gun could not deliver the most velocity and where that propellant also delivered the best accuracy with the minimum listed charge. Similarly, you can find examples where the propellant offering the highest potential velocity gave the best accuracy with the minimum listed charge. In such a situation, a propellant that offers neither the best velocity nor the best accuracy might, nevertheless, be the best overall choice for a particular hunting load.

Likely, that was the situation with my aforementioned 270 Winchester load. I am certain I could have achieved more velocity with N205, and I suspect that H414 or IMR4350 might have delivered smaller groups. However, it is unlikely that any of those propellants could have matched the combination of velocity and accuracy I was getting with H4831. I sacrificed a small degree of potential accuracy and perhaps 50 fps of velocity to achieve overall superiority for a hunting load.

Almost every combination of propellant, bullet, case, and primer has several propellant-charge sweet spots. Even after the handloader has settled upon a propellant, he might find that tinkering with charge and bullet seating depth are worthwhile. Generally, it does not help much to test charge increments smaller than about ½ percent of the nominal charge. Dogma holds that a handloader who sees some sort of magic change in his groups as a result of altering the charge by one- or two-tenths grain is almost certainly seeing the result of some other loading or shooting factor that he is not controlling properly. Often, this is the simple consequence of the shooter not properly considering the variability associated with typical sample sizes. To get a decent statistical value, at least twenty shots are required and even with twenty-shot sample strings you eventually will get bad data. I covered one possible example in chapter 9.

ACCURACY LOAD DEVELOPMENT— THE AUDETTE METHOD

Many years ago, Creighton Audette popularized a shortcut for developing an accuracy load. Audette was a well-known and effective benchrest competitor. Considering the power of this method, it is difficult to understand why knowledge of this technique has spread so slowly within the shooting fraternity.

Developing any accuracy handload is a potentially complex task. With regard to the load, the handloader must consider each of the following: bullet quality, type, seating depth, and neck tension; propellant type, charge, and charging method; primer choice and seating method; and overall case quality and various case-preparation steps. Shooters who alter these variables one at a time and then test a single five-shot group for accuracy (admittedly inadequate) could still spend weeks at the range. Any shooter working with a modern high-performance cartridge would certainly destroy the barrel long before exhausting the likely primer and propellant combinations with only one bullet type.

Before explaining the Audette method, I must give some background that will help explain why it works. Here, we must consider barrel vibrations and barrel time, which are related phenomena, and how those influence accuracy. In all guns, the barrel vibrates as the bullet accelerates through the bore. This vibration causes the last increment of the barrel to point in an ever-changing direction as the bullet moves toward the muzzle.

Hereafter, we will designate the direction in which the bore axis of the final barrel increment points as MPD (muzzle-pointing direction). In a conventional barrel, MPD changes continuously in response to barrel vibrations. In some guns with attached barrel extensions, devices known as bloop tubes, it is possible that the end of the muzzle is located at a vibrational node (the goal). In that situation, MPD does not change significantly; however, transverse (side-to-side or up-and-down) velocity of the muzzle does change. Transverse muzzle velocity results in the same kind of accuracy loss as is explained in the following text, albeit to a significantly smaller extent. The bullet leaves the muzzle while drifting with some modest transverse velocity but while the muzzle is pointing in the correct direction. Compare this to the following situation.

If the muzzle is not at a vibrational node (all conventional barrels), MPD (at the instant the bullet escapes and, therefore, the direction the bullet travels as it comes free of the bore) depends upon barrel time (how long the bullet was in the bore as the barrel vibrated). Although barrel vibrations are quite complex and poorly understood, the important accuracy consideration is simple to state: During some periods, MPD changes comparatively slowly; during other periods MPD changes relatively rapidly.

Consider the following thought experiment. Imagine yourself riding in a child's swing. As the swing moves toward the end of the arc, it slows, stops, and changes direction; this is where it moves the slowest. Conversely, as it moves through the center of the arc, it moves the fastest. Assume that someone places identical buckets beside and under the center and forward end of the arc. You have a handful of BBs. Your goal is to drop one BB in a bucket each time the swing reaches one of the two buckets. Your choices are: 1) drop a BB when the swing stops moving forward and 2) time your release precisely as the swing moves toward the centered bucket. Which bucket will be easiest to hit?

It would be impossible to release BBs at precisely the same relative instant of the swing's path on each pass, but no matter which bucket you choose to try to hit, your error in BB release timing will be the same. Any given error will be magnified when you try to hit the centered bucket because you are moving faster as you pass over it. To look at this in another way, hitting the centered bucket requires that you release BBs more precisely. This is analogous to the relationship between a gun and shot-to-shot variations in barrel time and how that relates to accuracy for any given group of shots.

> SHOT PLACEMENT IS ALWAYS FAR MORE IMPORTANT THAN DELIVERED ENERGY OR TERMINAL BULLET PERFORMANCE.

HOW THE AUDETTE METHOD APPLIES TO AMMUNITION AND ACCURACY

Perfection is nonexistent. With regard to perfect accuracy, consider the following fact: Shot-to-shot variations in barrel time always exist. Those variations are precisely analogous to your inability to release every BB at precisely the same relative instant on that imaginary swing. You can hit a smaller bucket at the end of the arc. Similarly, loads that produce bullets from the muzzle as it passes through the end of the arc (where it slows and changes direction) will produce smaller groups; conversely, loads that produce bullets from the muzzle as it is moving fastest (near the center of vibrational arc) will produce larger groups. Relative timing is everything.

Historically, many of us have used chronographs to look for promising loads. That method is simple. We adjust various parameters (primer, propellant, charge, bullet seating depth, neck tension, etc.) while measuring ballistic uniformity. Our belief is that loads having a superior level of ballistic uniformity will probably also exhibit greater barrel time uniformity. Although this is usually true of itself, this says nothing about whether that particular barrel time is apt to match the characteristics of the barrel vibrations in that particular rifle as is necessary for the load to produce good accuracy.

For example, consider two similar loads that differ only in the charge mass. In such loads, velocity and barrel time will differ. For whatever reason, it is demonstrated that load A generates only one-third the velocity variation of load B. It would seem that load A ought to be more accurate than load B. However, it just so happens that, on average, load A produces bullets from the gun muzzle when the barrel is near the center of its vibrational arc. This is where (when) the muzzle-pointing direction (MPD) changes fastest; conversely, load B just happens to produce bullets from the gun muzzle when the barrel is passing near the end of the vibrational arc. This is where (when) the MPD changes slowest.

If we used mirrors attached near the muzzle and laser beams to measure muzzle movement (as is done, routinely, on artillery), testing might show that during the interval when bullets from load A exit the muzzle, MPD is changing ten times as quickly as it does when bullets from load B are exiting the muzzle. We could test this more easily simply by firing each load at a reasonably short distance, 100 yards for example. If we found that groups generated by load A were about three times as large as groups generated by load B, we could conclude that the barrel time of load A was ill-suited to the gun. In that instance, a fine goal would be to look for ways to improve the uniformity of load B without altering the mean barrel time of load B.

When fired in a particular gun, some particular load that is unusually consistent might well be unusually inaccurate because the barrel time is wrong. Chronographing alone can never tell the entire accuracy story.

It is critical to understand that long-range accuracy depends upon consistent muzzle velocity and correct barrel time. When shooting at extended distances, regardless of any other factor, loads with significant variations in muzzle velocity cannot shoot to the same point of impact (except by coincidence or by pure accident). Therefore, we might find a load that was a tack-driver at 200 yards, only so-so at 600 yards, and completely useless at 1,000 yards. (Actually, such loads are common.)

For short-range accuracy, the correct barrel time is the critical consideration; conversely, for long-range accuracy, consistent velocity and correct barrel time are both necessary. This is easy to understand. At short distances, there will not be time for differences in muzzle velocity to alter the drop and wind drift of any given bullet significantly; conversely, as the distance to the target progressively increases, differences in muzzle velocity will progressively increase differences in drop and wind drift.

Enter the Audette method. Given any gun and combination of handloading components, this method will demonstrate the propellant charge needed to produce loads with optimal barrel time. It will work for any potentially accurate gun, and it will work every time. The amazing thing about the Audette test is that it requires less than thirty shots.

This method does have limitations. First, it will not work unless both the gun and load are capable of reasonably good accuracy—minute of angle (MOA) or better. Second, it requires relatively consistent wind conditions and a shooting range where the shooter can fire at 200 yards—300 yards might be better. Third, the shooter must have a quality benchrest and sighting system and possess the skills necessary to fire shots consistently—the shooter's goal is to test each shot, not his benchrest shooting ability. Equally, the shooter must have the skill and confidence to call those shots where something was wrong when the gun fired—a legitimate called flier causes little harm, not calling a legitimate flier can ruin any such test.

So, here is the routine. Begin by settling upon a bullet, propellant, and primer. It is probably best to do this testing with new, top-quality cases. (Upon firing, poor quality cases can bend and thereafter will never place the bullet squarely in the chamber throat. This complication reduces the potential for accuracy and can corrupt test results.) Any case preparation steps that you accomplish are likely to improve overall test results.

Let us consider a specific example—the basic procedure for any other combination of cartridge, bullet, primer, and propellant is, essentially, identical. Hypothetically, I have a new rifle chambered in 308 Winchester. I have mounted a target scope of proven quality on this rifle (about 30 percent of all new scopes are, in some way, faulty). I have fired several factory loads for 100-yard accuracy, a few of those shot particularly well; the Black Hills, Diamond Line load printed two, 10-shot, ½-inch groups—obviously, the gun will shoot.

I want to establish an accuracy handload using the unique 80-grain JRP varmint bullet. (JRP bullets use a tin core, so this bullet is the same length as a conventional 110-grain JHP). I would prefer to load the bullet so that it will be about 0.020-inch from touching the rifling; however, for durability and functionality, I want my field ammunition to have at least one-half-caliber (0.154-inch) of bullet shank within the case neck. With my Stoney Point tool, I determine that seating this comparatively short bullet in my gun so that the ogive is about 0.020 inch of the rifling is not feasible. Therefore, to achieve my one-half-caliber functionality requirement, I load to an OAL of 2.70 inches.

Because I intend to use moly-plated bullets, I will use significant neck tension, and I will polish the case mouths. For the same reason, I will use a relatively mild primer (which is less apt to move the bullet before propellant burning begins). Because the CCI BR-2 is a mild, large rifle primer, I will test that primer first.

Reviewing suggested loads from JRP, I note that Ramshot TAC shows promise. Hypothetically, 52.5 grains should develop about 44,700 psi, and 55.5 grains should give about 55,000 psi (about 3,600 fps muzzle velocity). These are well within reasonable minimum and maximum useful pressures for this cartridge.

I load TAC and the 80-grain JRP into new, primed, and fully prepped Norma cases as follows: 11 rounds at 51.4 grains and, starting at 51.6 grains, incrementally one round at each 0.2-grain greater charge up to 55.2 grains. This gives me 10 rounds (51.4-grain charges) to foul the thoroughly cleaned barrel and to zero the scope, leaving one 51.4-grain load and 19 loads with 0.2-grain incrementally greater propellant charges, as required to perform a 20-shot Audette test. Using my Oehler 35P chronograph, I will record the velocity of each shot. I will observe the fired case appearance and the bolt opening resistance for signs of pressure. In my notes, I will record these facts and anything unusual about any of the shots.

Using a bit of math, if I want to, I can develop a standardized ballistic uniformity result based upon the recorded velocity of these incremental shots. This will help me determine the relative consistency of the load. For a 20-shot, incremental charge string, the following (simplified) formula determines the approximate expected velocity difference for each incremental (0.2 grain in this case) charge deference (V18 indicates recorded velocity of shot 18 and similarly):

((V18 + V19 + V20) . . . (V2 + V3 + V4)) / 48

To do the Audette test, I will need a bench with a good rest and a good spotting scope. In addition, I will need to post sufficiently large targets (18 inches wide by 24 inches high should be adequate) side-by-side at 300 yards (200 yards will work for loads using bullets launched significantly slower or having a significantly lower BC). I will set up my chronograph and position a duplicate target on the bench, or otherwise, where it is handy. Now, I will fire fouling shots while making scope adjustments, as necessary.

Because I am shooting such a light bullet, I begin with two shots at 25 yards. I then adjust the scope, as needed, to place the impact about one inch low; I then fire two shots at 100 yards and adjust the scope again to place the impact about center; I then fire two shots at 300 yards and adjust the scope to put the impacts about six inches below the bull's-eye. After firing a few more shots to verify the scope adjustment, I begin the Audette test.

Aiming at the bull's-eye of the clean 300-yard target, I fire the remaining 51.4-grain load, noting the shot number, charge mass, and impact point on the duplicate target at the shooting bench. (Obviously, I must be able to see the bullet hole—this is one valid reason to shoot at less than 300 yards.) Then, using the same bull's-eye and scope setting, I fire the 51.6-grain load and repeat the associated paperwork.

I continue firing the progressively heavier-charge loads, using the same bull's-eye hold, until one of two things happens:

- I run out of test ammunition.
- I note some sign suggesting that pressure of the last round fired exceeded what I am comfortable using.

Now, if I have chosen the starting load well, I will have fired twenty incrementally loaded rounds while recording the velocity and impact point for each shot. Examining the target, I will note one of three things:

- All shots formed one reasonably small group—very unlikely because the higher velocity generated by rounds with heavier propellant charges are bound to result in higher impacts at such an extended distance;
- No set of consecutive shots formed any sort of cluster. I see just one big scattered group—a sufficient demonstration that the chosen component combination will never shoot well in that gun, regardless of any further load development that I might do; or
- A relatively vertical string of shots with several clusters of four to six consecutive shots, separated by approximately vertical strings of individual shots.

This last is the desired goal and is what happens, commonly.

Such shot clusters represent charges where barrel time matches the needed accuracy barrel-time interval of the gun—bullets from these shots produced from the muzzle when the muzzle-pointing direction was changing slowly and (possibly) the slower shot happened to come free of the bore when the muzzle was pointing a bit higher, and conversely.

Hypothetically, let us say that the average charge of shots in the last fired cluster is 53.9 grains. *Voila,* I have an accuracy load for that bullet, propellant, and primer. This does not mean that this particular load is the most accurate for that combination; for example, I might find improved accuracy by tinkering with bullet seating depth or neck tension.

In addition, I can estimate from the recorded velocity data if this particular load seems to show good promise for ballistic uniformity. Considering the small charge increments used, I might not see each subsequent shot manage the predicted velocity increase

(15 fps in this instance). However, I should see a general velocity progression. If velocities were wildly scattered, I probably would not have seen the desired shot clustering.

If I require absolute accuracy, I can repeat this test while tinkering with the seating depth or with other propellants or primers. By doing so, I could find several candidate loads to compare by firing three-, five-, or ten-shot groups for accuracy. In this manner, I can find three or four likely loads and compare those for absolute accuracy—and, I can do all this without firing two hundred shots.

SOURCES FOR SPECIALTY TOOLS OR COMPONENTS REFERENCED IN THIS CHAPTER:

JRP Bullets
Telephone: 518-282-0084

R. W. Hart & Son, Inc.
401 Montgomery Street
Nescopeck, PA 18635
Telephone: 717-752-3655

FULFILLMENT OF A LIFETIME DREAM

My brother, Stan McPherson (left), collected this fine bull elk in 2003 while hunting on public lands in Colorado. I was able to accompany him on this hunt. We saw six smaller, 6x6 bulls in the few days before he took this one—you can bet that he used ammunition that he loaded and you can bet that doing so added to his enjoyment of the moment and the fondness of the memory. Stan dropped this huge bull in its tracks using one well-placed shot from a 280 Remington.

Barrel Vibrates as Bullet Accelerates toward Muzzle

Hypothetical Target: Audette Method

20) 55.2
19) 55.0
18) 54.8
17) 54.6
16) 54.4
15) 54.2
14) 54.0
13) 53.8
12) 53.6
11) 53.4
10) 53.2
9) 53.0
8) 52.8
6) 52.4
7) 52.6
4) 52.0
5) 52.2
3) 51.8
2) 51.6
1) 51.4

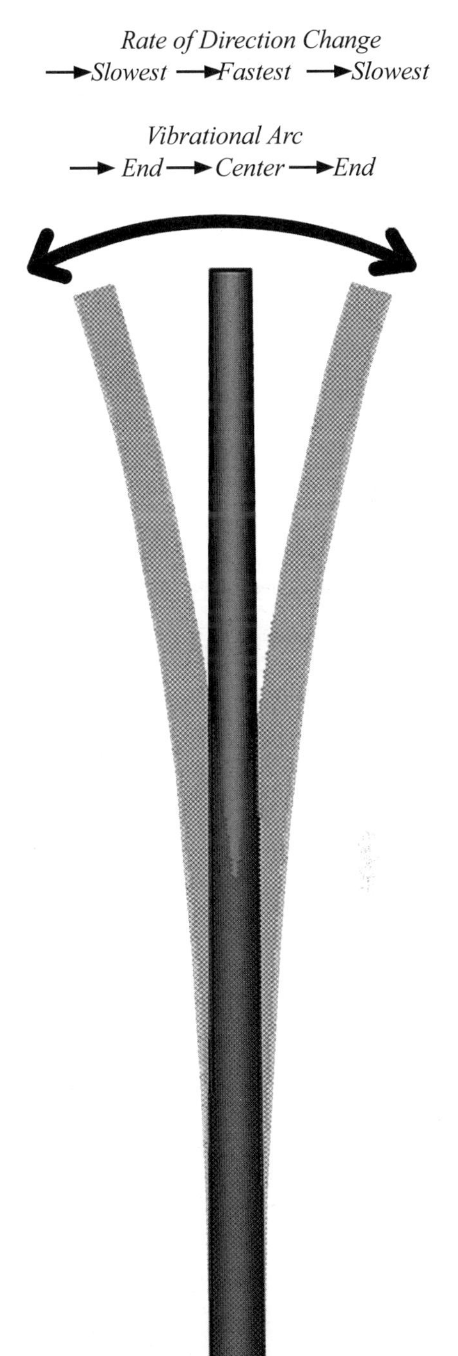

Exaggerated Representation of Barrel Vibrations:
Muzzle moves sideways and changes pointing direction fastest near center of arc
Muzzle moves sideways and changes pointing direction slowest near ends of arc

GATEWAY, COLORADO, BIANNUAL DYNAMITE SHOOT

Here, I was preparing to fire on a Big-Dog target. These are 4½ inches of pop can filled with blasting jell, located about ½ mile away — two shots and back to the end of the line.

Left of center offhand target (about 150 yards) an instant after being hit: Never any arguments about the score in this game. The Gateway Dynamite shoot is a charitable blast.

View of Big-Dog target area at Gateway, Colorado, Dynamite Shoot: Targets are near center of hillside, centered and straight ahead in this view. When the target is 4½ inches of pop can located about ½ mile distant and you only get two shots per turn, load development is critical.

My son Jody and me at the Spring 2007 Dynamite shoot. Jody has taken more Big-Dog targets than any other shooter and he is the only shooter to ever make consecutive hits—with such targets at varying, unknown distances, that feat might never be matched. He has also taken the largest and smallest "pots" ever—on a windy day he hit the first of those two cans when he and the rest of us had fired 275 shots at it; that emptied the pot, so his second hit won him the "I hit the Dynamite" hat that he is sporting in this picture.

Left: By Smalley at the 2010 Dynamite shoot preparing to fire on the Super-Big-Dog target—1,000 yards distant.

TROPHY-WALL STORIES

Those who decry long-range hunting as unsporting or inhumane might want to consider the following generalization: Of every 10,000 big-game animals wounded by poor marksmanship, 9,000 are shot at 50 yards or less, 900 are shot between 50 yards and 100 yards, 90 are shot between 100 yards and 200 yards, and 9 are shot between 200 and 300 yards. Anyone shooting at a big-game animal at an extreme distance either has the skill and equipment to make the shot cleanly or he does not; in which case he is most likely to miss the animal completely.

Jody and Joe McPherson, my sons, with a fine bull elk that Jody took cleanly at 962 yards, dropping it where it stood. He used a Sako TRG-41 chambered in 338 Lapua, fitted with an 8½–25 power Leupold VX-III. Such marksmanship requires the right equipment, ideal conditions (no wind), precise knowledge of target distance and angle of fire, and precise zero correction information (which requires adequate planning, preparation, and preliminary testing). A spotter is also mandatory, just in case something goes wrong. A few days prior to this hunt, Jody had fired a five-shot group at 1,000 yards that measured less than five inches, on-centers; hence, he knew that his equipment was up to the task and he was confident that he could place the shot with adequate precision to make a clean and humane kill, as he did.

Joe, my son, glassing two bull elk that are feeding in the area highlighted by the circle, near the upper-center of this picture. Two days earlier, Jody, my other son, had taken a fine 6x7 bull as it fed near where these two are feeding. Jody's perfect kill shot was 962 yards. Soon after I took this picture, Joe took the nearer of these two bulls with a perfect shot at 860 yards. Ten seconds later, I took the other bull; our hunt was over and the work began. As with any hunting, taking elk at long range requires ideal circumstances (no wind and a stationary target at a known distance), skill, and the right equipment. Jody's Sako TRG-41 chambered in 338 Lapua with Leupold 8½–25 VX-III did the job for us.

Another shot of the fine bull Jody McPherson took the second day of our 2006 hunt. He is justifiably proud of this bull.

Torb Lindskog, CEO of Norma Precision, and his mountain zebra. As always, Lindskog used the combination of a well-placed shot with a properly performing bullet fired from his 300 Winchester Magnum.

Esie Monserud's first elk: She took this fine bull with a steady offhand shot at about 120 yards using her favorite hunting rifle, a Savage 99, and a load selected by Norm Nelson.

INTERNAL BALLISTICS

CHAPTER 13

INTRODUCTION

Correctly, the term ballistics can only be applied to the study of projectiles in flight. However, modern parlance has incorporated two additional and related fields under this moniker:

- Internal ballistics: what happens after striker falls but before bullet leaves bore of gun
- Terminal ballistics: what happens after the bullet strikes the target but before the bullet stops moving

This case shows ample evidence of use with a dangerous overload. This includes the brass extruded into the ejector plunger hole (left side), the primer pocket enlarged, and the rim damage that occurred during extraction. This load was on the ragged edge of generating a catastrophic total case failure. Besides destroying the gun, such a failure could injure or kill the shooter.

Although both terms are technically misnomers, each has entered the general shooting parlance, and because we have no better descriptive terms, I will use these.

In this chapter, I will concentrate on internal ballistics; I will touch upon external ballistics in chapter 14; and I have already covered terminal ballistics in chapter 10. Peak chamber pressure is the only critical internal ballistics concern for handloaders. We have considered an entire host of other internal ballistic influences throughout the preceding chapters. Those factors include everything that happens to the shooter, gun, and cartridge (and each of its components), after the striker hits the primer and before the conclusion of propellant gas venting (after the bullet leaves the barrel). Here I will explore, in detail, the process of a shot being fired.

INTERNAL BALLISTICS—SAFETY—THE WEAK LINK

For handloaders, I can express the most important aspect of internal ballistics in one word: SAFETY! Notice that I did not write *pressure* or even *safe pressure.* Pressure is what makes a gun work; without pressure these useful tools would not exist. In this sense, pressure is very much our friend.

Controlling pressure is the issue. When pressure is properly controlled, placing one's face a few inches from a chamber containing, perhaps, 65,000 psi poses no danger whatsoever. Typical rifle shooters do this with every trigger squeeze. Conversely, without control, chamber pressure can turn a barreled-action into a bomb. Controlled pressure allows the production of effective ballistics, so my goal here is to help shooters understand what it is that repeatedly and dependably contains chamber pressure within any given gun.

In every cartridge gun, a chain of safety exists; this chain separates the shooter and bystanders from injury. As with any other chain, this chain always has a weakest link. With guns, the weakest link is not always the same thing—various gun types and chamberings have different weakest links.

In most modern bolt-action rifles, the weak link is the cartridge case. In some lever-action and other rear-locking rifles, the action is indirectly the weak link. In many revolvers, the cylinder is the weak link. In some pistols, the feed ramp in the barrel is a weak link (where it leaves part of the hollow case body unsupported). In other pistols, the barrel or locking lugs in the frame might be the weak link.

I will make no effort to analyze the weak link in every chambering in every gun ever made, but I will try to highlight and to consider most of the important generalizations.

In modern rifles, in which the locking lugs are located at the front end of the bolt, the gun is usually sufficiently strong and rigid to control any pressure that the cartridge case can withstand—at least for any reasonable number of shots. However, refer to the analysis of proof testing in the following section before you assume that any particular load is always safe to use repeatedly in any particular gun.

In modern front-locking, bolt-action guns, if the striker properly fits the striker hole in the bolt, the hardness of the case head, and nothing else, controls how much pressure the system will safely contain for any one shot.

Some shooters believe that a thicker or larger-diameter case head is a stronger case head. Bluntly, this is not necessarily true. However, a harder case head is usually a stronger case head. This is true, even if the softer case head is twice as thick but only slightly softer. In modern solid-head cases, case head hardness is the most significant factor behind how much pressure a case can withstand before the head enters the plastic deformation regime. Case safety depends primarily upon case-head hardness, not thickness. (See drawing, page xi.)

Regardless of the thickness of the case head, when the chamber pressure exceeds the elastic pressure limit of the case, the case head will begin to deform. In this instance, the brass will react in a familiar manner. It will flow as if it were made of bubble gum. It will swell, perhaps expanding into the cavities in the bolt face. This deformation will be permanent. Should the pressure remain sufficiently high for enough time and should the case head find sufficient room to expand (before the bolt and chamber begin to provide support), the primer-to-case seal can fail.

The resulting gas leak will involve a considerable volume of extremely high-pressure gas. Once released, the incandescent cloud will proceed at a frightful rate through all available avenues of escape. Significant gun damage and shooter injury are likely results.

At higher pressures, the brass case will eventually liquefy. Again, it will act, as does water, another familiar substance. The gas pressure (greater than 100,000 psi) pushing on this fluid brass will blow it through any minute action openings. Obviously, nothing but the action itself will exist to slow this release of high-pressure gas. The resulting tempest will likely destroy the gun and is apt to injure or kill the shooter.

Only a very fortunate shooter can survive such a high-pressure-encounter-of-the-worst-kind unscathed. Nevertheless, serious related injuries are rare, but only because most guns are so strong and are so well designed.

Even with normal cartridges, case-head failure can occur. In a case that has been exposed to temperatures exceeding about 400 degrees F (≈200 degrees C) for enough time, the head will be sufficiently annealed so that it will no longer withstand normal chamber pressure. This is true for any modern cartridge. If loaded and fired, such a case will catastrophically deform. For this reason, if you cannot verify that the case head has sufficient hardness, never use any case of unknown history. Refer to chapter 2. Similarly, hot loads that do not cause case-head expansion in one brand or production lot of cases can cause failure in other softer, although perfectly normal, cases.

INTERNAL BALLISTICS—SAFETY—PROOF TESTING

The historical view, often unwritten, has been that if the cases can hold the pressure, the load is perfectly safe for use in front-locking guns; however, this is not necessarily correct. Continual use of hot loads in particularly hard (strong) cases is demonstrably imprudent. Such loads might be stressing the action past, or dangerously too close to, the knee of the life-cycle curve—see associated graph on page 326. This is an important safety concept that I will cover in some detail.

Steel has an interesting property. If a piece of steel can withstand a specific stress level one time without failing catastrophically (breakage), it is automatically proven that the part can withstand one-half that level of stress many, many tens of thousands of times, without failure.

At the Friends of Billy Dixon range in 2008, Bill Falin and I were testing the trajectory of various Sharps loads at 100-yard increments out to 1,800 yards. This work led to Down Range Data, *a complete guide to zeroing any Sharps rifle for targets out to 2,025 yards. While three of us watched, Falin fired this 1.3-inch, 3-shot group at 300 yards. He downplayed this as an accident, but I have seen him repeat such "accidents" too many times to believe that. Keep in mind that this was a smokeless, blackpowder-equivalent, cast-bullet load fired from a Sharps rifle with iron sights! Hot loads are not necessary for extreme accuracy.*

A performance curve exists for any type of steel, regardless of alloy or heat treatment. This curve relates the stress level to the number of stress-and-release cycles that a new piece can withstand before failure occurs. This curve has a characteristic shape. Applied stress that causes a catastrophic failure on the first cycle represents the ultimate-failure stress load for that part. The amount of stress that causes failure on a nominally identical new part on the second cycle will be considerably less. Similarly, the amount of stress that causes failure of a different new part on the third cycle will be considerably less still. This process continues.

These stress-cycle failure points initially form a more-or-less straight line. (Refer to graph on page 326.) However, long before the applied stress (during each cycle) on a new part drops below one-half of the stress that would cause failure on the first cycle, a wonderful thing happens: The incremental decrease in stress needed to double the number of cycles (before failure occurs) begins to decrease dramatically. Effectively, the curve flattens. Very small decreases in applied stress lead to very large increases in the number of stress cycles the part can endure before failure occurs. (Refer to the graph on page 326.)

Another characteristic of all properly heat-treated steels is that they will undergo significant permanent deformation at a significantly lower (first time) stress than is required to produce catastrophic failure. This depends upon the type of steel (chiefly stainless-versus-conventional) and upon the type of heat treating, but this deformation-versus-failure relationship is always greater than about 15 percent—if the applied test stress did not permanently deform the new part, then that stress was at least 15 percent less than the failure-point stress.

These characteristics of steel are the basis of all proper proof testing. Compared to the stress imposed by a standard load, a proof load stresses the gun sufficiently so that if the gun survives intact and without permanent deformation we automatically know that it will safely withstand firing an almost unlimited number of cartridges that generate normal pressure. Necessarily, cartridges generating normal pressure produce no more than some specified percentage of the pressure generated by proof loads.

This relationship between the pressure created by industry proof-load cartridges and the pressure created by normal factory ammunition explains the safety concerns involved with habitually using hot handloads. When cartridges (handloads) that are routinely fired in a gun significantly exceed the pressure of standard (factory) loads, the shooter can no longer assume that the gun will safely endure a sufficient number of stress cycles (shots) before it fails, that is, one more shot than will ever be fired in the gun!—it might survive intact, yet it might not.

All too often, the pressure of hot handloads is essentially equivalent to the pressure of industry proof loads. Firing such cartridges nullifies any margin of safety provided by proof testing—thc shooter cannot know how many cycles the gun will endure before the steel becomes sufficiently fatigued to fail catastrophically. This fatigue will happen without the steel deforming in the slightest—hence, the fatigue and resulting catastrophic failure are hidden until it is too late.

As was once demonstrated by an IPSC competitive shooter who was using very hot 38 Super Automatic handloads (to make major power factor under the old specifications, while using particularly light bullets—to minimize recoil), you do not want to be around when an overstressed and fatigued gun finally lets go. Although that shooter suffered no permanent damage or disfigurement of any consequence, those who saw him immediately after the gun disintegrated in his hand report his general appearance as rather tattered. This little event could very easily have killed him. Should that untethered slide have struck two inches lower, he would certainly have lost one eye, at the very least. For your health and well-being, please:

AVOID THE ROUTINE USE OF HOT LOADS.

In rear-locking actions, the cartridge case might not be the weak link in the safety chain. In these guns, when a cartridge fires, the case head pushes against and compresses the steel within much of the length of the bolt. At the same time, the bolt pushes against the locking lugs (located toward the rear of the action) compressing those. These lugs then push against the receiver, stretching that. (This situation also occurs in front-locking guns; however, in those guns, the total resulting bolt face movement is insufficient to cause any safety issue during any one shot.)

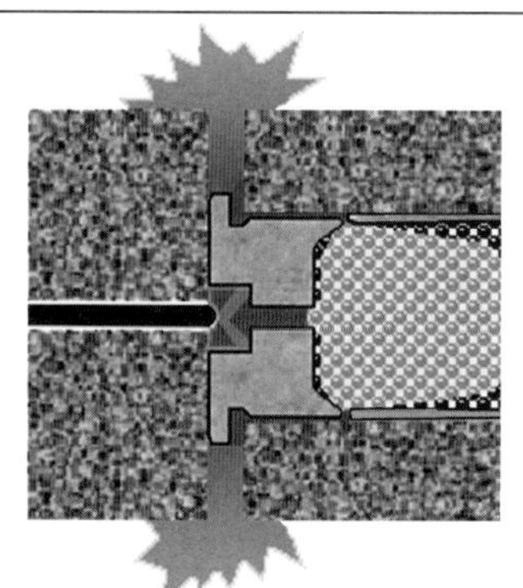

Thin-wall cases can separate with relatively little stretching. This can allow a dangerous gas to leak.

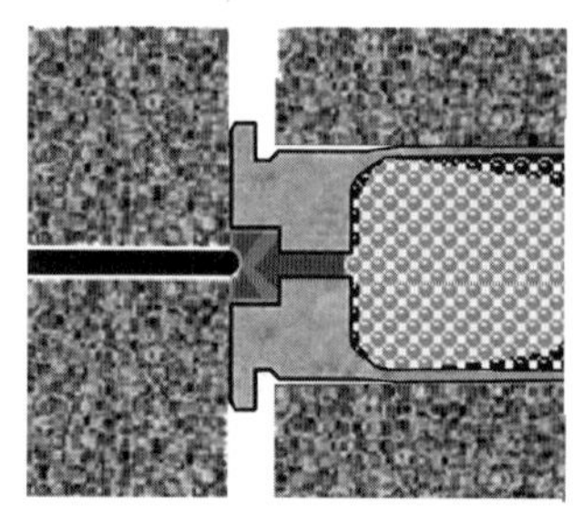

A thicker case wall is safer but will separate after loading and firing several times—stretching cumulatively thins the case wall.

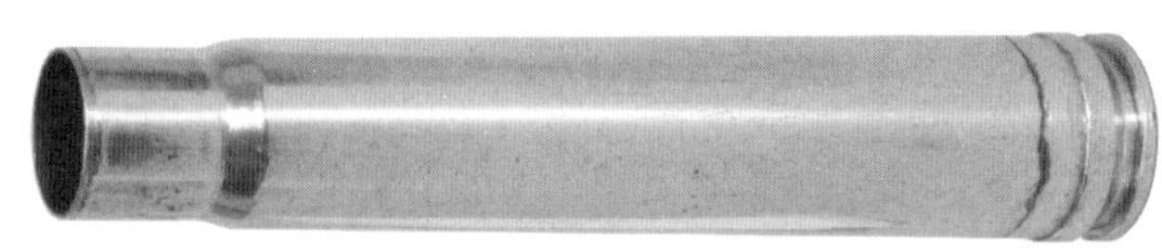

This case is cracked near the belt, and it occurred when the last round was fired. This crack could have generated a dangerous gas leak. Always check cases for excessive thinning before use.

This tarnished case has a visible bright line near the web. This handy RCBS Case Gauge provides verification that the case wall has thinned to only about 0.020 inch at that point—this case is no longer safe to use.

When a cartridge fires in a rear-locking action, the chamber pressure locks the case body to the chamber wall and the case head moves back as the case head pushes the bolt rearward. At some level of chamber pressure, the case head will force the bolt face sufficiently rearward to allow (force) the case head to separate from the case body. Among the places you do not want to be is hovered over a rifle action when this happens. In the worst-case scenario, such a case head separation can lead to a dramatic loss of chamber pressure control. This generates a massive release of high-pressure gas into the shooter's face. Such a failure is almost certain to destroy the gun and to ruin the shooter's day—at the very least!

In rear-locking rifles, a load that shows none of the classic pressure signs—primer flattening, case-head expansion, difficult extraction—can, nevertheless, cause this sort of catastrophic failure. This sort of failure is not the fault of the case. A stronger case, in the sense that the head is harder, will not help here. Conversely, a case with walls that are thicker back near the body-to-web junction can provide additional safety because such a case can stretch more before it separates.

When you are handloading for a rear-locking gun and, generally, if your handloads produce more per-shot case stretching than is exhibited by factory cartridges, very likely, the pressure is too high. In that instance, you should reduce the charge until the case stretching is similar to what occurs when firing factory cartridges.

As noted, if separation occurs while significant chamber pressure exists, gas containment can fail. If so, the resulting leakage can destroy both the gun and shooter. However, due to inertial effects, such separations often occur only after the bullet exits the muzzle; inertia can continue to stretch the case after the chamber pressure stops increasing; hence, before the case fails, chamber pressure has plummeted to an insignificant level. It is also likely that the case wall behind the separation can swell sufficiently against the chamber wall to provide a continuing seal against the chamber pressure. Please do not let such a possibility lead you into a false sense of security. As likely as not, the next separation will occur before the chamber pressure peaks, and the seal will fail. You do not want to be there.

All high-pressure loads with normal headspace stretch the case with every firing, regardless of the action type. This stretching thins the case wall at a point near the junction of the solid web and hollow body. With repeated reloadings, such thinning will eventually result in the separation of the case head from the case body.

Examine cases during each reloading cycle. Destroy and discard any cases that show significant thinning at the body-to-web junction. While you can use a bent paper clip to locate such a thin zone, the RCBS case gauge gives better data. This tool shows exactly how thick the case body is at any point. It is prudent to destroy and discard any case where the thinned zone has become less than about two-thirds the thickness immediately forward of that zone.

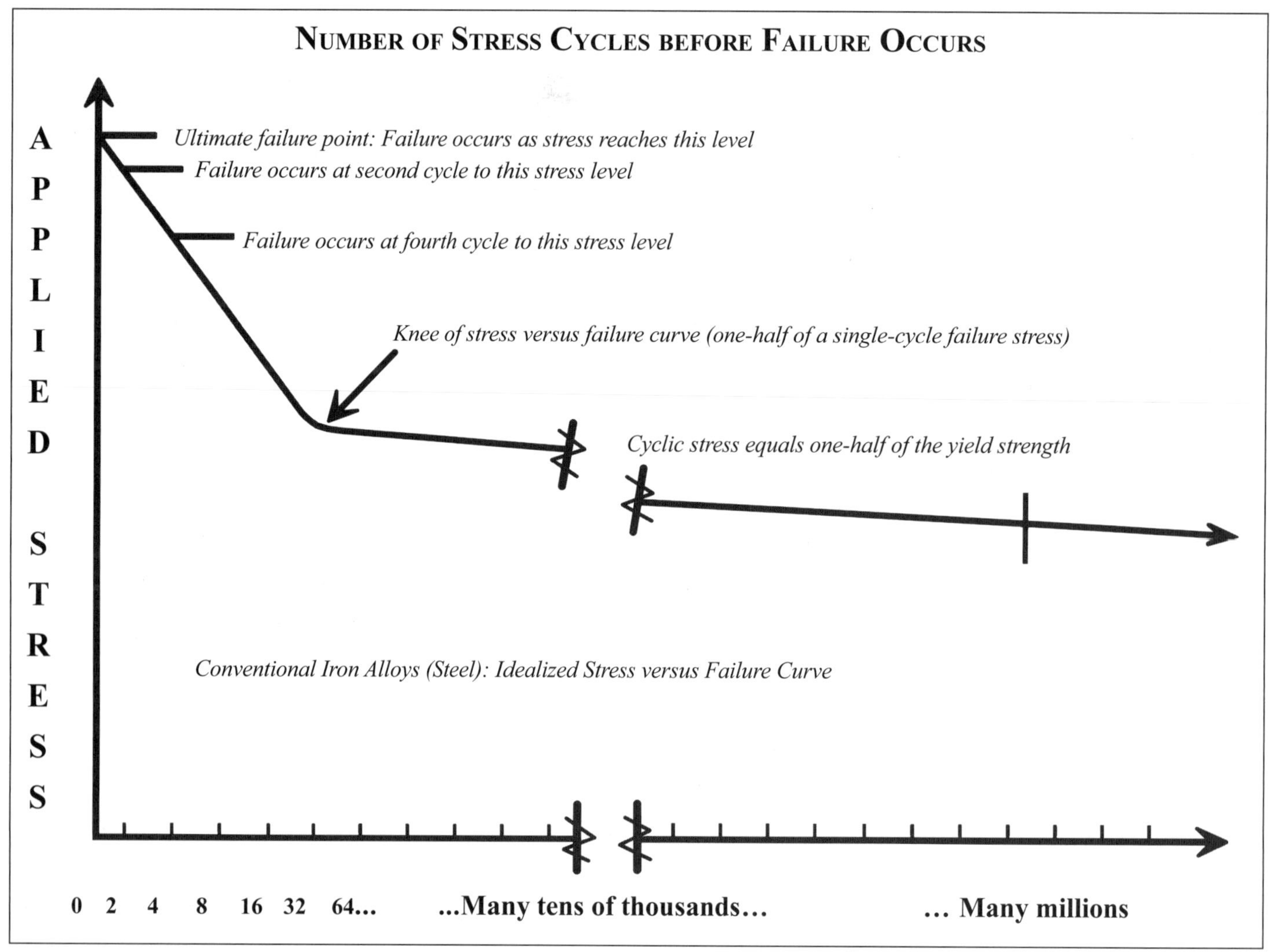

The classic symptom of excess thinning is a shiny ring around the case body. This will be visible just forward of the web. This remains a useful indicator, but it certainly lacks precision. Any case showing such a bright band is suspect. If you cannot measure the actual degree of thinning, the only safe course is to destroy and discard any such case.

In some pistol chambers, a portion of the case near the rear of the body wall is unsupported. This is the area where the feed ramp leads into the chamber. This is common in 45 Automatic pistols. The geometry of pistol feed ramps includes significant gun-to-gun variations. In addition, the thickness of the case web (front to rear) and the thickness of the case wall vary from lot-to-lot. Therefore, some individual gun and cartridge combinations can leave a significant portion of the hollow case body unsupported. Depending upon the load pressure and the case wall thickness, this might or might not represent a potentially dangerous situation.

Generally, this is unpredictable. Pressure containment in an unsupported case relies entirely upon the case-wall strength near the junction of the case web and body. Case strength in that zone can be significant; often it is more than adequate to withstand the pressure generated by standard pistol loads.

However, a significant danger here is that some enthusiastic handloader might work up a "hot" load for such a gun and then find himself unknowingly using a case with thinner walls near the web or with a shorter web, or he might switch to a gun with a longer feed ramp, or he might have the feed ramp of the existing gun polished and, thereby, deepened. Such a situation could result in a ruptured case. The typical result is a swelled grip frame with the grip panels blown off and the magazine destroyed and violently ejected. When this happens, the shooter's opportunity for serious injury is rather significant.

Further, just as with rifles, such hot loads might be stressing the action sufficiently to nullify the proof testing. Such loads could cause a catastrophic failure after a relatively small number of shots. (We define small as the number of shots that any given gun might fire during its useful lifetime.) Holding such a bomb when it finally explodes is not likely to be conducive to good health or to calm nerves.

Someone fired this 9x19mm (9mm Luger) in a 9x18mm Tokarev. The result is identical to what can happen when firing a high-pressure round in a gun with a too deep feed ramp.

Hornady and Federal offer many loads using superior propellants, which have only recently become available to handloaders (through Alliant and Hodgdon). These loads typically generate about 100 fps greater velocity than standard loads. In some instances, even using the new High-Energy numbers, it might be impossible when handloading to duplicate the performance of these factory cartridges safely.

Revolvers pose a different set of problems. Many, but not all, have critically weak cylinders. Long before the pressure reaches a level that would swell the case head or stretch the gun frame sufficiently to allow the case head to separate from the case body, the cylinder is apt to fail. The classic result is a splitting at the top of the cylinder over the fired chamber, shearing through the webs that separate that chamber from adjacent chambers, and the breaking of the cylinder over both adjacent chambers.

This violently rupturing cylinder often shears the revolver top strap completely from the frame. When this happens, three or more rapidly moving pieces, along with various scraps of the offending cartridge case and perhaps the adjacent cartridges, follow independent ballistic trajectories. Evidence proves that these pieces usually fly in a safe direction. The number of shooters

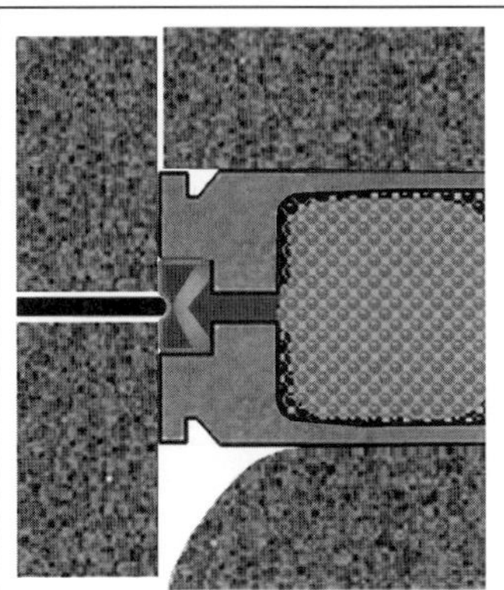

Semiautomatic pistol chambers usually include a significant feed ramp. This feature facilitates design compactness and a dependable operation.

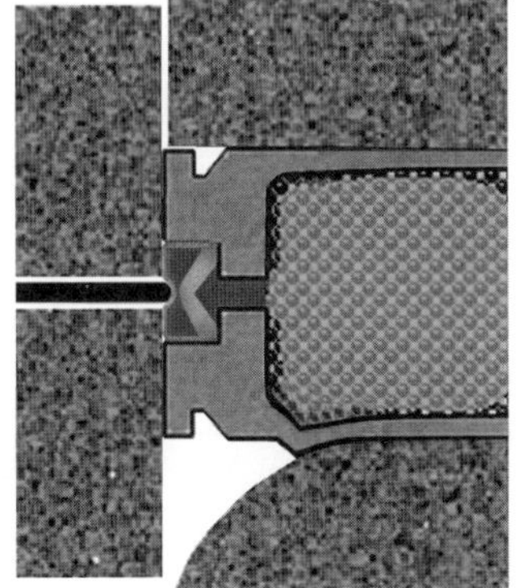

With a deeper feed ramp or a thinner case web, a significant portion of the case body is unsupported. In this situation, a chamber pressure that would be perfectly safe in a chamber that fully supported the case body can rupture the case.

who experience such catastrophic revolver failures without incurring any permanent physical injury is a source of continuing amazement. However, the opportunity to imbed one of these loose pieces in one's forehead seems ample cause for significant prudence in avoiding firing any overload in any revolver.

The classic revolver overload is a double charge where a case gets two charges of a fast, dense smokeless propellant. Such a load creates about four times the intended pressure. (Peak pressure is similar to charge mass squared.) Very few revolvers can withstand such a genuinely massive overload.

The point here is that limited cylinder strength constrains loading in many revolvers, and the handloader has no good method of determining when the pressure generated by any given load might be pushing the cylinder past the pressure limit that it will survive in the long term. Hot loads can work fine in such a gun many times (perhaps thousands). However, a catastrophic failure is inevitable. Hotter overloads lead to failure after fewer shots. The hotter the load when the failure does occur, the more violent the resulting failure.

My goal here is to explain why it is always prudent to avoid using hot handloads. Regardless of the action type, such loads are likely to nullify the safety value of any proof-load testing performed with that gun. This leaves the shooter at the mercy of one rather important unknown variable—just how many rounds of the shooter's hot handloads will the gun withstand before it violently disintegrates?

All handloaders have a responsibility to try to identify and understand the weak link in the chain of safety of the guns they are loading. Specifically, situations occur where factory ammo or otherwise prudent handloads might be dangerous in a gun because of some problem in the chamber or barrel. I have witnessed this. Shooters who do not understand how to judge pressure by looking at primers, to measure case-head expansion, or even just to note the effort of extraction, can endanger themselves and bystanders.

WHAT IS THE INEVITABLE RESULT OF USING HOT HANDLOADS? SOONER OR LATER, SOMETHING BAD WILL HAPPEN. USUALLY, THAT "LATER" WILL BE AFTER MORE SHOTS THAN ANYONE COULD HOPE TO FIRE FROM ANY GIVEN GUN. USUALLY.

About 1974, an acquaintance was interested in learning to handload. He owned a European-manufactured 243 Winchester–chambered rifle. He had been shooting 80-grain Remington factory ammunition with acceptable results. We loaded up several boxes of handloads using his once-fired cases. Some of our reloads used the 85-grain Sierra JHP; others used the Sierra 100-grain Spitzer. We loaded the 85-grain bullet to about the same cartridge OAL as the 80-grain factory cartridge, and the 100-grain bullets to approximately the maximum OAL for the 243, as listed in my handloading manual. Ultimately, the safety issue was that those 100-grain handloads were significantly longer than the 80-grain factory cartridges.

Because he only had a few boxes of once-fired cases, he also purchased for our testing one box of 100-grain Remington factory cartridges. My chosen loads for both bullets should have been mild, and the two loads should have generated similar pressures.

We started our range testing by firing groups with our 85-grain handloads and the remaining few 80-grain factory loads. I was pleased to see the Sierra bullet shooting smaller groups than the factory load did. Everything seemed completely normal. Both loads grouped acceptably, and we saw no evidence of any untoward pressure signs.

Then we switched to the 100-grain handloads. The gun owner did this test shooting. The report of the first shot was normal, but something caught my eye (smoke emanating from the action), and the bolt would not open freely. When I asked what was happening as he pried on the bolt handle (eventually getting it open), he reported that, indeed, opening the bolt was difficult.

I suggested that he stop shooting those loads. We switched to the 100-grain factory cartridges. I stood there, staring at the head of that 100-grain handloaded case, which clearly indicated that the load had generated significant excessive pressure. I was scratching my chin and trying to comprehend what could possibly have gone wrong with my carefully concocted handload. Then he touched off one of the 100-grain factory cartridges. Even though I was not looking directly at the gun, I saw smoke roll out of the action again—lots of smoke.

This failure did not harm either the shooter or the gun, but the case head had opened sufficiently to allow considerable gas leakage. Because he could not open the bolt without help, we both knew enough to suspend that project.

What had happened? It took some sorting out, but we finally ascertained that both the bore and the groove diameters of that barrel were unusually tight. Moreover, the leade was tapered and extremely short. The 80-grain factory and 85-grain handloads worked safely because those bullets had a running start at the rifling. Conversely, chambering a round in both the factory and handloaded 100-grain cartridges jammed the bullet hard into the tapered leade.

KNOW THE GUN AND ALWAYS LOOK FOR INDICATIONS OF EXCESSIVE PRESSURE, REGARDLESS OF THE AMMUNITION USED.

Revolvers and other low-pressure guns present what is potentially the worst problem in this regard. How can a shooter know if the pressure is safe when even a proof-load might not visibly alter the primer, swell the case head, or cause any extraction difficulty? The only answer I can offer is to consider the velocity of the handload. If, for any reason, your handload using a good propellant for that load achieves a velocity that is significantly higher than the velocity produced by similar factory cartridges or if your load produces more velocity than modern loading data suggest it should produce, the chamber pressure could well be significantly too high for safety, especially with continued use of that load.

ALL ELSE BEING EQUAL, THE ONLY WAY TO INCREASE VELOCITY IS TO INCREASE PRESSURE.

This is a classic example of the prudence of using only recently published data. Unfortunately, I must add the word *recently* because some formerly published data included potentially dangerous overloads. For your safety, never use such data to create handloads.

ONE REASON MODERN MANUALS HAVE TAKEN A MORE PRUDENT STANCE ON MAXIMUM LOADING PRESSURE IS THAT EARLIER SUGGESTED LOADS HAVE DESTROYED GUNS AND HURT PEOPLE.

INTERNAL BALLISTICS—CARTRIDGE BASICS

A conventional modern metallic cartridge consists of a case, projectile, propellant charge, and primer. The case houses the charge, primer, and projectile. Pressing the primer and projectile into the case seals the cartridge. When the cartridge fires, the case neck swells and thereby seals the gun chamber.

We refer to the bore diameter as the caliber. In modern terms, the caliber correctly means 1/100 inch; hence, 30 caliber means 30/100 inch and ".30 caliber" is either a misnomer or an exceedingly tiny bore (0.003 inch!). Moreover, any English sentence with a leading decimal point in any number is grammatically incorrect.

In rifled barrels, we measure a caliber across the lands (bore diameter). In some instances, we use the groove diameter; this is especially common in British English-language regions. Such naming uses the projectile's diameter (groove's diameter) in thousandths of an inch or in millimeters, e.g., 308 Winchester, 375 H&H, 7mm Mauser, etc. However, a cartridge name is just that—a

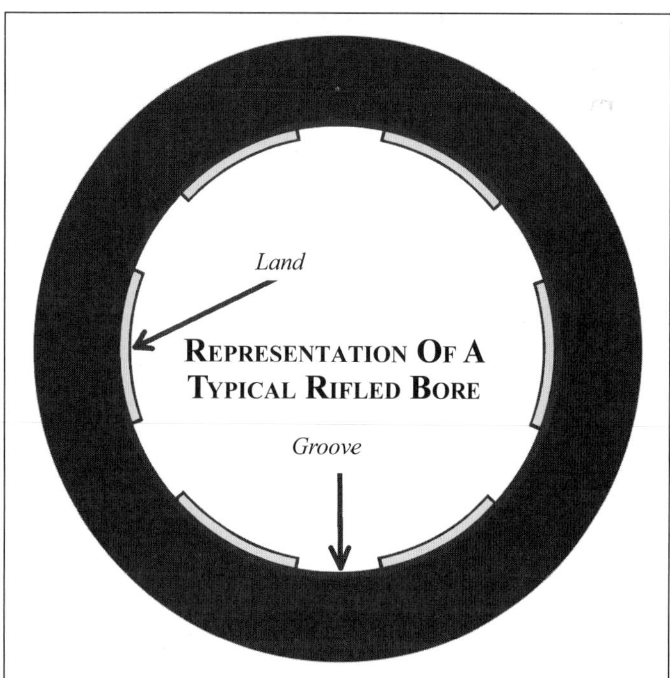

Cross-sectional representation of a typical sporting rifle barrel (depth of groove somewhat exaggerated compared to typical examples).

name. The digits and other verbiage used are generally meaningless—e.g., 218 Bee stands for nothing except a cartridge designation; it is just a name.

The use of a leading decimal in cartridge naming is a longstanding erroneous construction. This seems to have originated within the U.S. Military Ordnance Department sometime in the late 1800s. That error has been widely parroted. A related and equally obnoxious error is to speak of the caliber of a gun when one means the chambering. Many gunwriters routinely make this error. When someone asks you what caliber your (30-06-chambered) rifle is, one correct response is, "What caliber? It is a 30-caliber, just as are my 30-30 Winchester, my 308 Winchester, and my 300 Savage; only this one happens to be chambered for the 30-06 Springfield!" An alternative, correct, answer is, "Thirty." Concise communication is difficult enough without this sort of careless, needless, obfuscation through use of loose and careless verbiage.

A cartridge fits in the chamber, which is an enlargement at the rear end of the barrel. The case interior forms the combustion chamber. The case head forms the back end of the combustion chamber, and the bolt (or breechblock) supports the case head.

A cylindrical section between the chamber end and the beginning of the rifled bore is variously called freebore or throat. The throat diameter can be either constant (equal to the groove diameter), or it can be slightly tapered from a few-thousandths inch larger than the groove diameter. It can be of any length from zero to several inches. (When longer than about one-half inch, it is referred to as freebore.)

Forward of this is the tapered leade. The leade starts at the front of the throat and extends to the point where the lands are full depth. Modern chamber designs usually use a relatively shallow leade angle—¾ of a degree is the standard for benchrest chamberings; something near 1½ degrees is common in commercial chamberings. Some older designs have a much sharper lead angle—the throat-to-bore transition is much shorter.

In conventional revolvers, the front end of the cylinder forms a relatively long throat that leads to a funnel at the rear end of the barrel that we call the forcing cone.

Normal small-arms bullets cannot support the acceleration force created by propellant gases; hence, the bullet obturates (swells) and stretches the barrel. Obturation forms a tight bore seal. After the bullet engraves the rifling, it rotates progressively faster during acceleration through the bore.

In small arms, the rifling twist is normally constant, but useful gain-twist barrels are available. The number of rifling grooves depends upon the barrel make and type. Both right- and left-hand twist barrels exist. We often express twist rate in terms of the units of barrel length per complete turn—as in, 1 in 12 (meaning 1 turn in 12 inches of barrel length). We can also describe this as a 12-inch twist, and, often, we abbreviate it with a colon-based construction—for example, 1:12. Or, we simply can say a 12-twist barrel.

Imparted spin gyroscopically stabilizes a bullet during atmospheric flight. Gunmakers choose a twist rate according to various characteristics of the intended projectile. These include:

- Length—most important
- Shape—important
- Location of longitudinal centers of gravity and aerodynamic force—a significant factor in long-range stability
- Expected muzzle velocity—least important, except for loads launching long bullets near the speed of sound, which often require a much faster twist (for complicated reasons that I will not entertain here).

A theoretical optimum twist exists for any given bullet launched at any given muzzle velocity. For proper stabilization (accuracy), longer projectiles require a faster twist than shorter projectiles require. Many small-arms projectiles leaving the muzzle traveling faster than about 2,000 fps will not remain accurate beyond that distance where velocity drops below the speed of sound. With such bullets, as velocity becomes subsonic, the buffeting from collapsing shock waves initiate wild yaw fluctuations that continue until the bullet stops. Such wild yawing destroys accuracy.

INTERNAL BALLISTICS—EFFICIENCY—WHY CASE SHAPE MATTERS

Although this has taken more than 150 years, modern shooters can now begin to realize the benefits of cartridges designed for maximum efficiency. These advantages include increased barrel life, superior accuracy, reduced felt recoil, and reduced barrel heating. My partner and I, as Superior Ballistics Inc., have identified the reasons why case design makes such a large difference, and, therefore, we know how to optimize case design. We also now know that doing so is relatively simple. The question is, "Why did this take so long to figure out?"

Consider a conventional sporting, centerfire cartridge. Experienced shooters know instinctively that for any given bore size a cartridge using an optimum propellant and generating greater chamber pressure generates greater muzzle velocity. Similarly, they expect that a larger case will launch any given bullet at greater velocity. However, what most do not understand is that case design affects cartridge efficiency—the case capacity and the charge required to achieve any given velocity at any given maximum chamber pressure. The details of the shape of the case affect barrel life, barrel heating, recoil, and accuracy potential.

INTERNAL BALLISTICS—THE SEQUENCE OF EVENTS WHEN A CARTRIDGE FIRES

Here, I will review a somewhat simplified version of the events that occur after the firing pin strikes the primer. First, as the primer cup crushes the pellet, the pellet ignites. The pyrotechnic primer pellet burns very rapidly, explosively releasing hot gases and particles. These still-reacting components stream through the flash hole and into the combustion chamber and thereby begin to ignite propellant granules that happen to be located near the flash hole. (Testing has proven that in normal rifle cartridges the primer plume does not directly ignite any propellant granules that were originally located more than about one-half inch forward of the flash hole.)

Simultaneously, as the primer blast hits the base of the charge and as those granules begin to burn, developing gas compresses the remaining charge toward the front of the case, behind the case shoulder (in a bottlenecked case), and the bullet. This charge compression results from two factors. First, the primer shock wave hammers into the base of the charge and thereby transfers significant momentum; second, inchoate propellant combustion and continuing primer pellet combustion generate a high-pressure gas pocket near the flash hole.

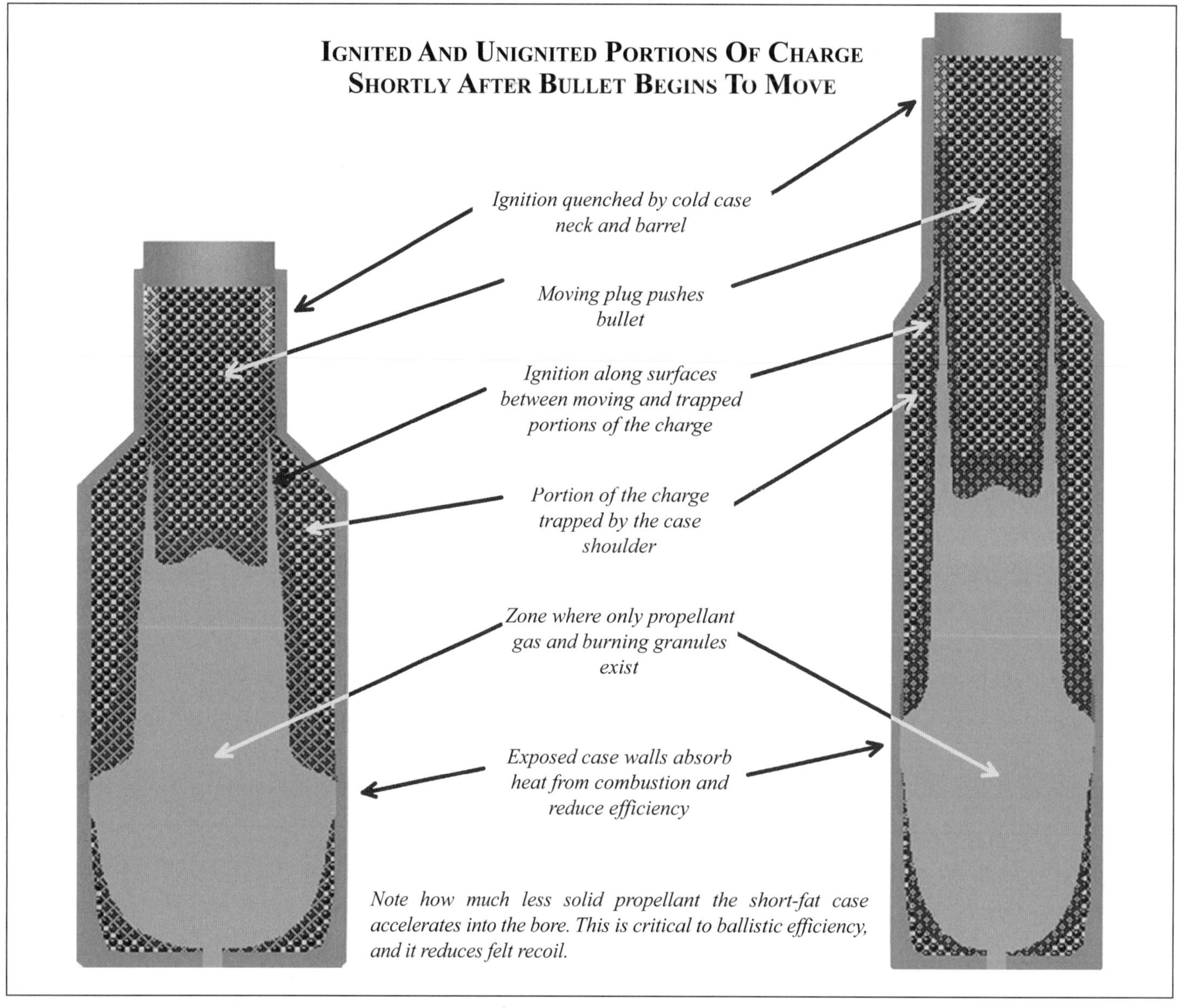

The bullet seals the case neck, preventing free passage of the gas through the charge. Furthermore, although the charge is initially both porous (filled with voids) and permeable (which allows gas to flow into the charge in response to any pressure differential), the permeable conduits in the compressed propellant mass are both tiny and convoluted and, hence, retard gas flow. Given that the entire combustion event typically completes within about 1/1000 second, gas pressure simply does not have time to equalize throughout the charge. The only way that pressure can equilibrate throughout the chamber volume is for the propellant mass to compress until the trapped gas within that mass is at the same pressure as the gas between the flash hole and the compressing mass. However, this cannot happen due to the intrinsic strength of the propellant granules, which resist the degree of deformation necessary to achieve that result. Moreover, because this is not a static system—the process of the charge burning is dynamic—an equilibrium condition (in which all components reach and remain at a stable and balanced condition) can never occur.

Furthermore, the volume behind the propellant mass contains various gases (carbon dioxide, water vapor, and others), ignited propellant granules, incandescent reacting primer particles and vaporized solids, and areas of higher and lower pressure—the ignition process occurs far too fast to allow gas pressure to equilibrate throughout the available space.

As burning generates more gas at the rear end of the propellant mass, the gas pressure remains highest there, and because plastic granules deform, the pressure progressively compresses the unignited mass toward the front of the case. This is a self-supporting progression. As compression increases, it becomes progressively more difficult for gas to enter the unignited charge (conduits become ever tinier and ever more convoluted). Very quickly, any remaining unignited mass becomes essentially impervious to continued gas infiltration. Thereafter, no significant hot gas infiltrates this mass. Subsequent ignition and combustion can occur only in granules that the primer initially ignited, in adjacent granules sufficiently heated before gas infiltration ceased, and along exposed surfaces of the compressed, unignited mass.

INTERNAL BALLISTICS—CYLINDRICAL VERSUS BOTTLENECKED

Compare the 284 Winchester and the 45-70 Springfield. In each, the primer plume will penetrate and carry enough heat to ignite granules to a depth of about one-half inch. This amounts to about one-third of the granules in a normal charge. Before compression can seal the remaining charge, secondary ignition into the rearward zone of the unignited mass will penetrate sufficiently so that, perhaps, another one-sixth of the granules of the total charge will ignite. Hence, about one-half of the charge will become individual, ignited granules; the remaining one-half will be a more-or-less solid chunk that is progressively compressed while burning only on the rearward surface.

As chamber pressure continues to build, the pressure acting through this unignited propellant mass eventually becomes sufficient to begin to force the bullet from the case and into the bore. To do so in the 45-70, all that is required is that the total force on the bullet base (the force on the base of the charge mass minus the friction between the charge mass and the case walls) exceeds the force required to push the bullet from the case.

Conversely, in the 284, because the case shoulder prevents the perimeter of the propellant mass from moving forward, the pressure differential must be sufficient to shear a plug through this unignited propellant mass before the bullet can begin to move. Hence, in this bottlenecked case, chamber pressure will be significantly greater before bullet movement begins—when compared to an otherwise-similar, straight-walled case (the 45-70); before the bullet begins to move, more granules will have ignited (more time will have elapsed since primer ignition).

In the 284, as a plug shears free of the trapped cylinder, it accelerates and forces the bullet from the case; the case shoulder traps and retains the remaining unignited cylindrical portion of the charge. As the shear line creating the propellant plug develops, line-of-sight ignition occurs along the shearing surface between the plug and cylinder. This significantly increases the total burning surface, compared to the situation in the 45-70 (where the entire unignited mass simply accelerates into the bore while burning only along the rearward face. Because brass absorbs so much heat so rapidly, the case wall quenches ignition along the perimeter of the plug).

INTERNAL BALLISTICS—FELT RECOIL IS A FUNCTION OF MASS AND ACCELERATION RATE

Tests prove that initially in the 45-70, a considerable charge mass accelerates into the bore behind the bullet. In a typical modern load, this could amount to about 30 grains of propellant. Conversely, in the 284, this charge plug contains only about 8 grains of propellant; the remaining 22 grains of unignited propellant stays in a cylindrical mass trapped behind the case shoulder.

Now, compare the 300 Winchester Magnum and the 300 Winchester Short Magnum. These, same-caliber, bottlenecked cases have a similar capacity and use charges of similar mass. In each instance, the primer will ignite the charges to a similar distance from the flash hole. The propellant chamber in the 300 Win Mag is about 2 inches long; the propellant chamber in the 300 WSM is about 1½ inches long. Hence, the plug created in the 300 Winchester Magnum will be about 50 percent longer and will therefore contain about 50 percent more mass. The total initial accelerating mass will be significantly greater in the 300 Winchester Magnum. Because the initial bullet acceleration rate is similar in these chamberings, the initial rearward gun acceleration is greater in the 300 Winchester Magnum.

Under such conditions, initially, the 300 WSM gun accelerates more slowly into the shooter's shoulder, which means that it generates less felt recoil. Moreover, because less unignited propellant accelerates into the bore, the accelerated mass does less total work on the barrel; therefore, the barrel heats less. Because this design uses less energy to heat the barrel, it will do more work on the bullet, which means that it will generate more bullet velocity. When compared to the 300 Winchester Magnum, this explains why the 300 WSM yields similar performance but generates noticeably less felt recoil.

Any shooter who has done a side-by-side comparison of otherwise nominally identical guns chambered in 300 Winchester Magnum and 300 WSM will agree that the WSM does, indeed, generate noticeably less felt recoil, despite these two chamberings producing essentially identical ballistics. As noted above, the 300 WSM accelerates far less unburned propellant into the bore.

We are not breaking Newton's law here. The total recoil might be similar, but with the shorter case the rate of initial rearward gun acceleration will be milder. This is what the shooter is most sensitive to; this is what he feels. Also, muzzle pressure will be lower in the more efficient design, so gas venting will generate less recoil, so the actual recoil will indeed be less.

This explains why case design influences felt recoil. As the ultimate example, consider a very fat and very short 30-caliber bottlenecked case. No such case is readily available, but we could certainly create a case with just as much case volume as the 300 WSM but with a propellant column only about one-half inch long. In such a cartridge, primer-induced ignition would reach the bullet base. In that instance, as the pressure became sufficient to dislodge the bullet, no solid propellant plug would follow the bullet into the bore; therefore, such a design would minimize the initially accelerating mass and it would minimize felt recoil.

Now to the crux of the matter. The energy consumed by the act of accelerating the solid propellant into the bore cannot contribute to bullet acceleration; hence, case designs that accelerate less solid propellant into the bore accelerate bullets more efficiently—all else being equal, those designs will generate greater bullet velocity.

Hence, in general, when considering cases with identical usable capacity, bottlenecked cases are vastly more efficient than cylindrical cases and, among bottlenecked cases, progressively shorter cases are progressively more efficient. Modern designs are simply getting closer to the ideal where the case body is sufficiently short so that very little unignited propellant follows the bullet into the bore.

INTERNAL BALLISTICS—BARREL LIFE CONSIDERATIONS

The reasonable desire for a long barrel life introduces a complication. To understand this, compare the 243 Winchester to the 6mm Remington cases. The base diameters are identical; shoulder diameter and shoulder angle are very similar. However, in the 6mm, both the body and neck are significantly longer. Also, the 6mm has a significantly higher working pressure.

Experts agree that the 243 should have the barrel-life edge because it has about 4 percent less usable capacity, and it works with about 8 percent less pressure. However, evidently, the shorter neck of the 243 makes a difference—a considerable difference. Ballisticians who routinely work with these two chamberings have long recognized two significant distinctions.

First, the 6mm is always well behaved—no surprises; conversely, the 243 is notorious for generating unexpected results, including unexplained pressure spikes (excursions, in the parlance of ballisticians).

Second, the 6mm's barrel life is always significantly greater than is the barrel life of the 243. The only reasonable explanation for the latter fact (which might also indirectly explain the former quandary) is that the long neck of the 6mm somehow protects the barrel throat. How could this be?

Brass absorbs heat about 420 times faster than smokeless propellant and twice as fast as steel, so cool brass is extremely effective at delaying ignition and slowing burning of any smokeless propellant granule that is pressed against it. Cool brass can extinguish contacting granule surfaces that are exhibiting inchoate combustion (beginning to burn).

Left to right are a 204 Ruger, 5mm/35 SMc, and 22-250 Remington. The left and the right are examples of old-school designs; the center represents state-of-the-art technology and performance.

As the propellant plug passes into and through the case neck, the brass saps heat out of the perimeter of that plug. If the case neck is long enough, it can extract enough heat from the plug to quench burning, at least along the front end of the plug. When this happens, a significant length of unignited propellant follows the bullet into the leade (beginning of rifling).

In the 6mm Remington, as the pressure peaks, the passing bullet dramatically heats the bore's interior through deformation and friction—friction only heats the surface layer, but it heats that by hundreds of degrees. The subsequent passage of the unignited portion of the plug allows the bore's surface to cool, if for only an instant, before that surface is assailed by the full brunt of high-temperature, corrosive propellant gases. The critical issue is that because the frictional heating was only at the bore surface, the total heat added is minuscule and heat transfer into the cool barrel interior will rapidly reduce bore-surface temperature.

Conversely, in the 243, the short case neck cannot always cool the surface of the charge plug sufficiently to quench the burning along any length of the perimeter; hence, as the plug passes into the barrel, the exterior can be burning entirely to the bullet base. Therefore, as the (burning) plug passes, rather than allowing the bore surface to cool for an instant, this plug further heats and corrosively damages the bore surface. Occasional variations in how the plug perimeter continues to burn as it passes through the short case neck could explain the widely reported 243 Winchester pressure excursions.

Chamberings with short case necks are notorious for giving short barrel life (223 WSSM, 243 Winchester, 264 Winchester Magnum, 300 Winchester Magnum, etc.). Evidently, a long case neck adds life to the barrel because such a design allows for a short protective plug of unignited propellant to follow the bullet through the leade, where the damage to the bore is usually greatest. If this explanation is accurate, then not only is a long case neck desirable, but we also do not want to use a too-short case, else no (throat-protecting) propellant plug can exist.

The above hypothesis might not be precisely the correct explanation, but something must explain why cases with unusually short necks are notorious for creating a short barrel life. At least it seems fair to conjecture that a long neck is beneficial to barrel life, as the 243 versus 6mm example suggests. While I will not debunk those here, rest assured, nothing exists to support the so-called "turbulence" or "crossing point" ideas.

INTERNAL BALLISTICS—OPTIMUM CASE DESIGN

My partner, By Smalley, and I have done exhaustive analysis, both from first principles and in the laboratory, and have demonstrated that an ideal case design does exist. Such a case has a propellant column (behind the case shoulder) about 2.15 times bullet diameter and uses an elliptical case shoulder. This case design is patented and protected under the SM^C (pronounced *smick*) moniker. For any given case volume, these parametric design characteristics provide optimized performance while minimizing barrel heating and wear.

Compare the characteristics and performance of the 300 Weatherby Magnum, 30/100 SM^C, and 30-378 Weatherby Magnum. The peak pressure is essentially identical for all three. The usable capacity is nearly identical for the 300 Weatherby Magnum and the 30/100 SM^C; however, with the best loads used in each, the 30/100 SM^C generates 10 percent more velocity than the 300 Weatherby—it duplicates 30-378 Weatherby performance despite having 33 percent less usable capacity. However, no current mainstream action will handle the unusually fat case that is necessary for the 30/100 SM^C.

IDEALIZED SM^C CARTRIDGE

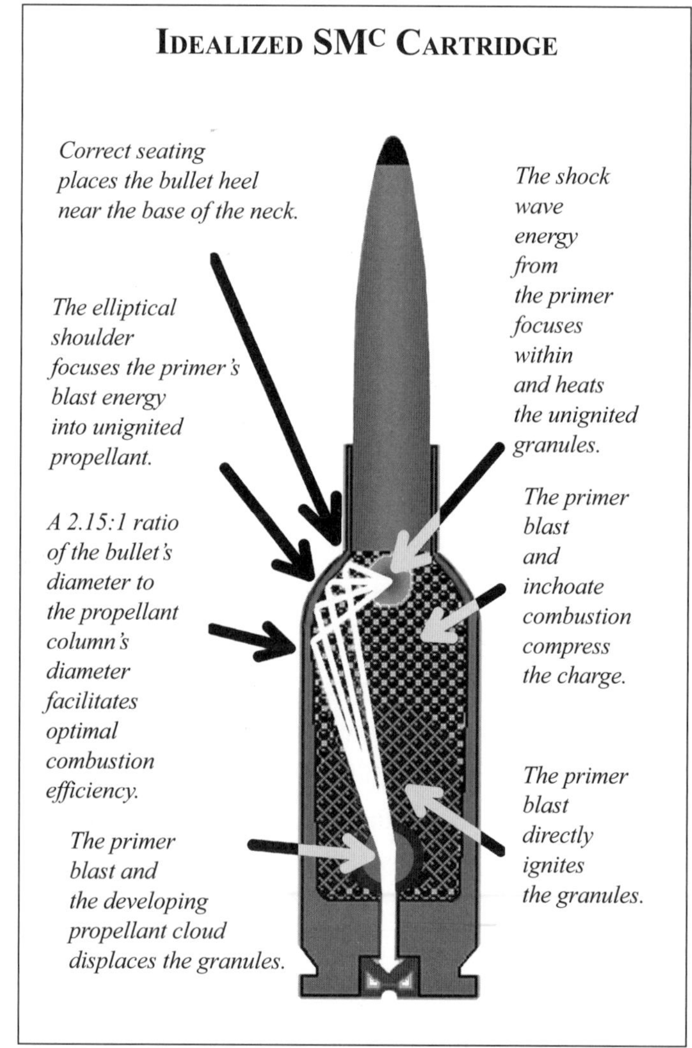

5/35 SMC 30gr Berger
34.0 BenchMark
BR-4
1.645" SRL.

4697-01-4692
4686-02-4674
4653-03-4648
4670-04-4660
4694-05-4689

05-4692 +
05-4648 -
05-0044 E
05-4672 M
05-0018 S

For such a small case, the 5mm/35 SM^C generates impressive ballistics. With a 26-inch, 1:12 twist, and Savage barrel, a maximum BenchMark load accelerates 30-grain Berger HP to 4,700 fps muzzle velocity!

Through its Custom Shop, Savage offers the 5mm/35 SM^C, and this chambering is CIP certified. The 5/35 SM^C is a 20-caliber varminting number that does just about anything that the 220 Swift will do and does so without heating the barrel any more than the 223 Remington does. The 5/35 SM^C surpasses the performance of the 204 Ruger by 300 fps without generating significantly greater barrel heating—efficiency matters.

My best 22-250 loads with 40 BT reach 4,400 fps, far short of the 4,700 fps generated by the 32 BK 5/35 SM^C load. The recoil generated by this 5/35 load is only about one-half of that generated by a 40-grain, 22-250 load. The lighter recoil makes it easier to observe impacts, especially on close-in targets. Finally, when shooting is good, the relatively reduced barrel heating of the 5/35 SM^C allows firing of more than twice as many shots in any given period while heating the barrel to the same temperature.

With a 28-inch, 1:16 Twist, Pac-Nor barrel, a maximum charge of TAC accelerates the 30-grain Berger bullet to a muzzle velocity of 4,850 fps. With the same length barrel, the new high-energy propellants from Hodgdon and Alliant will safely launch the 26-grain Barnes Varmint Grenade faster than one mile per second at the muzzle with quarter-minute accuracy.

With time, we expect to see other commercial SM^C chamberings. Ideal SM^C designs up to about 6.5mm will work in existing actions; for 7mm and above, a larger action is required.

INTERNAL BALLISTICS—MEASURING CHAMBER PRESSURE

Sir Alfred Nobel—benefactor of the Nobel Prize—invented the first commercially successful method of measuring chamber pressures in firearms. His system used a simple arrangement of a movable piston fitted to a hole drilled through the gun chamber. When the chamber pressure pushed on one end of this piston, the other end pushed on one end of a lead cylinder. A relatively rigid anvil attached to the barrel supported the other end of the lead cylinder. By adjusting the size of the pressure piston and lead cylinder, Nobel used

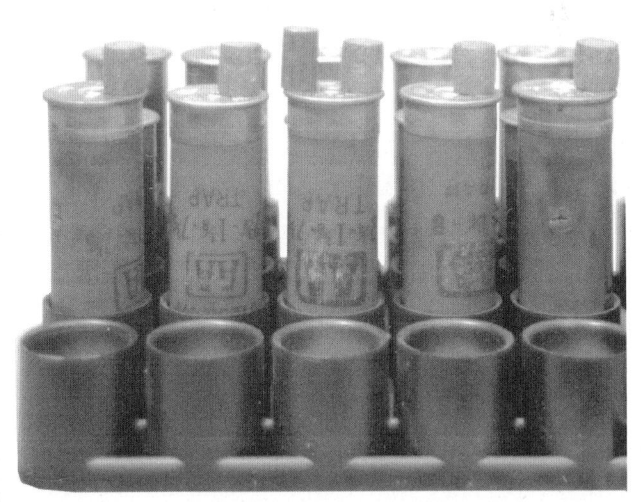

Sitting atop these fired shotshell cases are lead crusher pistons. Note the case in the middle: On that, at left, is an unused crusher; all other pistons are used and thereby shortened. The testing of higher-pressure metallic chamberings use copper-crusher pistons, but the system is identical and the degree of crushing is similar.

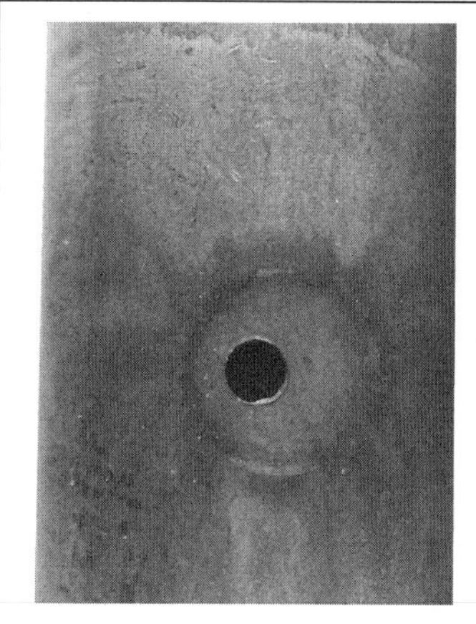
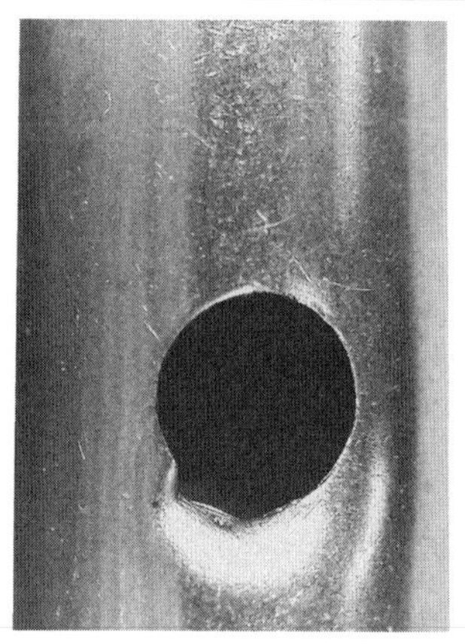

Cases used in CUP testing are drilled on the left and undrilled on the right (blanked upon firing). The same load gives different pressure readings, depending upon the testing technique used.

this system to interpret pressures within the normal blackpowder range.

However, this system was not particularly useful for comparing pressures normal to smokeless cartridges. The substitution of pure copper cylinders for pure lead cylinders solved that problem. When properly annealed, pure copper proved to be useful for comparing pressures from smokeless proof-load cartridges.

Crusher systems suffer from significant errors resulting from inertia. (Inertia is the measure of mass in motion.) I will return to this subject. The other problem with these systems is that this technique requires considerable finesse. Different operators can, and often do, get substantially different readings when measuring identical loads fired in the same barrel and using the same crusher system. (No two operators ever get statistically identical results.)

Ballisticians applied this pressure measuring method to muzzleloading guns and then to cartridge guns. For many decades, laboratory testing procedures for cartridge pressure called for drilling a hole in the case so that the chamber pressure would have direct access to the pressure piston. With the adoption of copper for higher-pressure smokeless loads, laboratories continued to use this procedure. However, because case drilling was time consuming and nerve wracking, U.S. ballistics laboratories eventually omitted this step. However, European ballisticians continued this practice—a prescient decision.

Evidently, some ballisticians assumed that omitting the case-drilling step would make little difference when testing cartridges generating sufficient chamber pressure to easily rupture the case wall. Perhaps they assumed that once the case wall had ruptured, full chamber pressure would press against the piston and the piston would therefore crush the copper just as it would have crushed it had they used a drilled case. The problem was that this analysis ignored some rather significant inertial influences.

A cartridge case wall can support thousands of pounds of chamber pressure before it fails. Therefore, when it does rupture, the force generated by many thousands of pounds of pressure almost instantaneously hammers against the piston. For this reason, with identical cartridges a drilled case generally flattens a crusher piston less than an undrilled case does.

Worse, depending upon the load variables, two loads that showed identical pressures with drilled cases often showed vastly different pressures with undrilled cases. This was a significant clue that the readings taken with this system did not accurately reflect actual chamber pressure. Inertia was significantly corrupting all such

This case was used in a conformal transducer (psi) test. Note the circular patch near the top of the case body, toward the right side. This area was under a conformal piston in the chamber wall when the round was fired. The inside of the end of that piston matches the shape of the chamber wall (conforming to it—whence the name). The piston compresses a trapped piezo transducer. This generates voltage. A computer converts that into data that represent real-time chamber pressure.

data, regardless of whether or not the cases were drilled. Hence, ballisticians could only count on these results for comparing pressures generated by different loads in the most general of ways.

Today we have a far better system. This new standard for measuring pressure relies upon computers and sophisticated electronics, but it gives a very close approximation of the progress of the chamber pressure in real time. Ballisticians now refer to the numbers generated by this newer system as psi (pounds per square inch); they now refer to the old crusher method as CUP or LUP (copper units of pressure or lead units of pressure). An important consideration is that no proper conversion from one system to the other exists. A usefully accurate formula-based conversion of data between these systems is simply impossible.

CUP is still in use but the less expensive and more accurate psi method is rapidly replacing it. (For use with obsolete cartridges, the CUP and LUP systems should continue in use indefinitely because we can never evaluate a proper psi standard pressure because all we have is the old CUP or LUP measurements, and no reference ammunition exists.) The British have a unique pressure measuring method and, in some instances, Europeans still use the drilled CUP pressure measuring method.

The psi method uses a conformal transducer to measure the force of the case body pushing out on the chamber wall. A portion of this gauge replaces the chamber wall—it conforms to the chamber wall contour, whence the name. As the case pushes on the conformal portion of the gauge, that piston compresses a piezoelectric cell. That compression generates an electrical signal.

Electronics connected to this gauge measure this signal. Through a calibration correction, a computer thereby records chamber pressure in a continuous, real-time, basis. This system provides an opportunity to examine a representation of chamber pressure that includes the entire pressure history after chamber pressure is high enough to expand the case wall to touch the transducer piston (3,000–12,000 psi).

Conformal transducer systems can be extremely accurate. The use and maintenance of these systems is comparatively simple.

Ballisticians must calibrate each lot of cases for use with the conformal transducer system. (See previous picture and caption.) They do this by hydraulically pressurizing sample cases in a special test fixture until the transducer registers the case expansion.

As noted, transducer systems give a very close approximation of the actual chamber pressure. However, because no system can measure pressure without any movement of anything and because chamber-pressure is dynamic, it is fundamentally impossible to measure the exact pressure at any given instant. Nevertheless, assuming a properly calibrated piezo system, the difference between the actual peak pressure and the measured peak pressure is inconsequential.

INTERNAL BALLISTICS—BASIC PRESSURE MEASURING TOOLS AND METHODS FOR THE HANDLOADER

Most handloaders do not have access to any official, standardized system of pressure measurement. However, we can, and should, observe various pressure manifestations. This is all about SAFETY. Understanding how to observe pressure signs and what those pressure signs can mean is most important in this regard.

Beginning at the low end of the pressure scale, let us consider a revolver shooter. Excepting higher-pressure magnums and a few other high-pressure numbers, revolver cartridges do not generate enough pressure to create any signs of pressure on the case or on the primer. Exceptions include the 357 Magnum, 357 Maximum, 375 Supermag, 41 Magnum, 44 Magnum, 445 Supermag, 454 Casull, 460 S&W (possibly), 480 Ruger, and 475 Linebaugh,

500 S&W Magnum (only when loaded with pistol primers), and similar chamberings. Even these high-pressure revolver numbers offer precious little in the way of pressure clues. Therefore, handloaders have very little to observe that will be of any value toward evaluating the chamber pressure.

In some instances, low-pressure revolver cartridges exceeding normal pressures might exhibit modest case extraction resistance. However, one cannot rely upon this. In these low-pressure chamberings, the handloader's only option is to stay within the limitations imposed by the loads recommended in a recently published loading manual (older manuals sometimes listed dangerously hot overloads).

Should any such load combination generate any signs of difficult extraction, immediately discontinue using that load. If chambers are clean and unless those have an unusually rough finish, any level of resistance to the extraction of the fired case is ample reason for concern regarding excess pressure. However, chambers with a particularly rough surface combined with soft case bodies can cause a difficult extraction, even with perfectly normal cartridges that generate normal (relatively low) pressure.

I once tested a Colt-replica revolver chambered in 38-40 Winchester. In that gun, certain factory cartridges produced a surprisingly difficult extraction. The reamer used to cut the chambers in that cylinder had been in very bad repair. The chambers exhibited visible grooves and ridges. Polishing away the tops of the high spots solved the extraction problem.

If you suspect that rough chambers are causing difficulty in extraction, have a competent gunsmith examine the gun. If necessary, a simple job of polishing the chambers will improve function. If the chambers are well polished and clean, difficulty in extraction is almost certainly indicative of excessive pressure.

The aforementioned high-pressure revolver chamberings work at pressures exceeding twice the pressure at which cartridges such as the 38 Special function. Nevertheless, even in the hottest of magnums, the only sign of excess pressure one can rely upon is difficulty in extraction and even that sign can be lacking in guns with highly burnished (polished) chambers and with some (unusually hard) cases.

A few revolver chamberings, such as the 454 Casull (pronounced *kah-sool),* work at pressures that generally show notable primer flattening. As the handloader works up a 454 Casull load, he can sometimes see the primer getting flatter and flatter. With certain types of primers, this might also be manifest in other high-

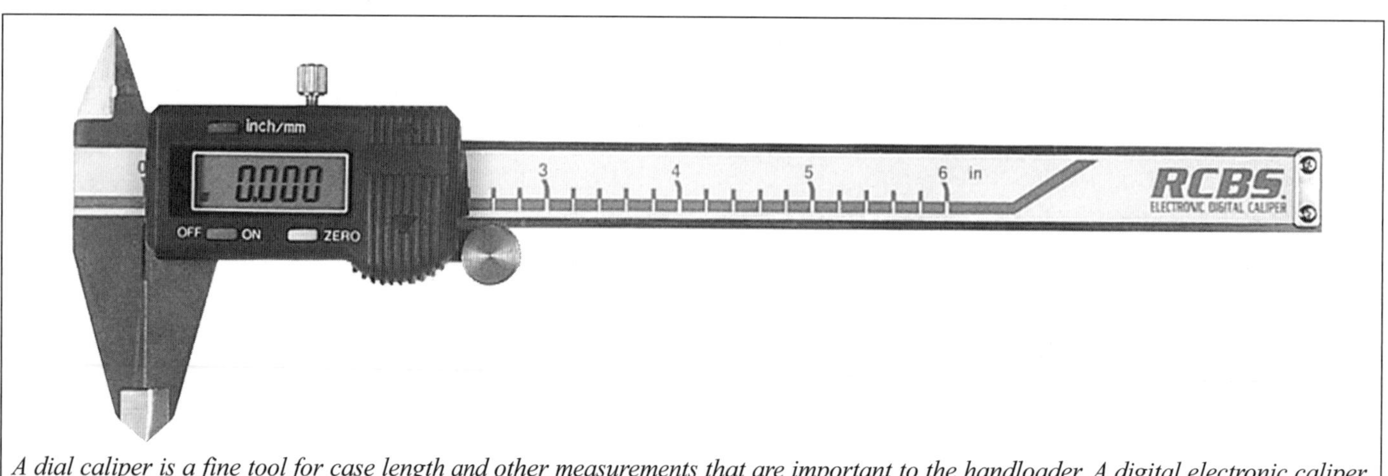

A dial caliper is a fine tool for case length and other measurements that are important to the handloader. A digital electronic caliper, however, has significant advantages in many applications.

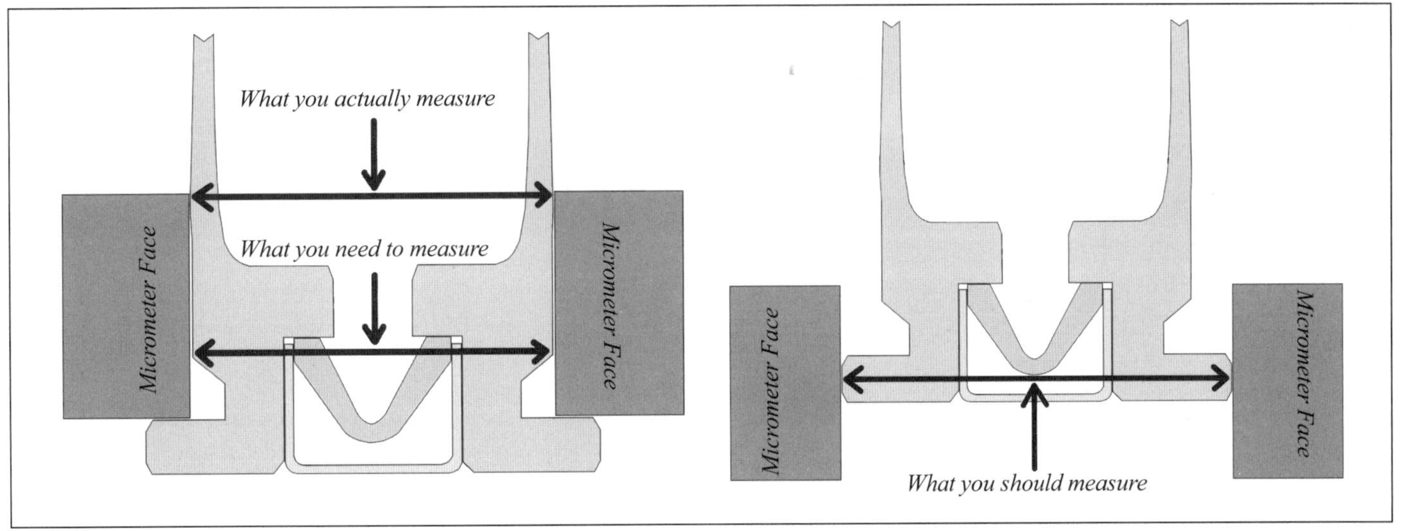

pressure revolver chamberings, but you cannot count upon this happening.

Again, as with revolver chamberings that work at low pressure, a difficult extraction is ample cause to interrupt any load development, pending investigation of the gun for unusually rough chambers. If you find that the chambers are properly finished, the difficult extraction suggests that the load generates more pressure than the gun can reliably handle. It can also suggest that the load generates pressure that exceeds the nominal specifications for that chambering. For your safety, do not continue to use any such load.

Most pistol cartridges, just as do most revolver cartridges, work in a pressure regime that leaves absolutely no objective evidence. The only advice that I can give is to stick with the loads recommended in modern manuals. Should such a load produce any indication of excessive pressure, discontinue use and consult a gunsmith. Chamber roughness or other mechanical gun problems can cause difficulties, such as bent or torn rims or scratched cases, even with loads generating normal pressures.

Rifle cartridges come in two basic pressure categories—those that can create evidence of excessive pressures and those that do not. Many old, relatively low-pressure cartridges, such as the 30-30 Winchester, exhibit no signs of pressure variations that one could use to differentiate perfectly normal loads from patently dangerous overloads. In such designs, long before the pressure generated by a load reaches a level that would cause primer flattening, case-head expansion, or difficult extraction, it will generally have exceeded the safe working limit of the gun and cartridge system.

In guns chambered for low-pressure cartridges, generally found in rear-locking, lever-action rifles, the exhibition of primer flattening, case-head expansion, or difficult extraction is ample reason to discontinue using the load. The best course is to use only those loads suggested in modern loading manuals and data guides.

Case stretching offers one means of comparing pressures on rear-locking guns that is reasonably reliable. In these guns, cartridges working at normal pressures generally cause the case to stretch a few thousandths of an inch with each firing. Top-end loads often exceed 0.010-inch case stretching on each shot (depending upon the headspace of the gun and other variables). On rimmed cartridges, handloaders can establish a reasonable baseline amount of stretching by comparing the handload to factory loads using the same brand of case.

Measure the case length of several factory cartridges and fire those clean and unlubricated cases in a clean and unlubricated chamber. Then resize and measure the case length again. You can use the average lengthening in that group of cases as a baseline. If your handload in the same brand of new cases generates similar case stretching (after firing and resizing), then that load is generating similar pressure and should, therefore, be safe.

Of course, both the reloads and the gun chamber must be clean and unlubricated. This brings us back to one particularly important point that I have covered previously several times—potential case separations.

Prudent handloaders will not reload cases that are used in a rear-locking gun as many times as they will reload cases that are used in a front-locking gun. Typically, rear-locking actions allow cases to stretch enough to warrant trimming after each reloading (or use of the RCBS X FL sizing die).

Handloaders should maintain careful records of the number of reloading cycles that each batch of cases has been through. Upon seeing any signs of significant thinning at the web-to-body junction, destroy and discard those cases—the RCBS case gauge is useful for accurately measuring the relative thinning of the case wall. Once any case in a group shows excessive thinning, all cases in that group are suspect, so check each carefully. (Excessive thinning of a case occurs when the thinnest spot of the body wall has thinned to about two-thirds the thickness of the thickest portion of the case wall immediately toward the case mouth from that thin zone.)

Generally, it is advisable that handloaders working with high-pressure, large-diameter cartridges in the Savage Model 99 discard cases after the third or fourth firing. Cases from lower-pressure cartridges, such as the 30-30 Winchester, are usually good for at least five or six reloadings in the Model 99. Marlin and Winchester lever actions are a bit more rigid, but it is still prudent to discard cases after a similar number of reloading and firing cycles. Discarding overworked cases is good insurance; this protects the gun and your health and peace of mind.

In modern, high-pressure cartridges used in strong, front-locking guns, the case is always the limiting factor in containing chamber pressure. These combinations will show several signs of excessive pressure that are useful to handloaders.

Typically, the degree of primer flattening increases as peak chamber pressure increases. Eventually, the fired primer has a large flat surface with very little area between the rounded surface of the perimeter of the cup and the flat surface of the case head. If you use the same primer brand, type, and lot number, the total area of the flat surface can be a reasonably good indicator of the relative pressure. However, vast differences in cup hardness exist between primer brands; differences in cup hardness from one lot to the next are significant; and primer cups do age-

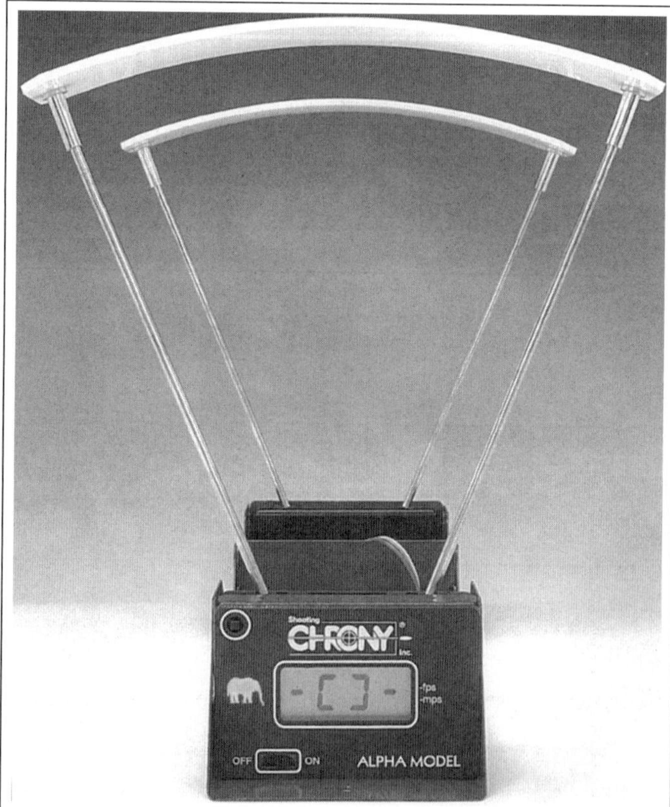

Shooting Chrony offers several chronograph models. Each is equally effective, accurate, and easy to use. This is the baseline model. It costs about as much as a few boxes of premium hunting bullets. In my opinion, no serious handloader can afford not to own a chronograph! For indoor use, Chrony also offers a lighted skyscreen system.

harden. Furthermore, headspace and other variables can significantly alter the appearance of fired primers, even when load pressures are identical.

A good example of the variation in fired primer appearance comes from a comparison of the older two-leg-anvil style Remington rifle primers and CCI rifle primers used in 7mm Remington Magnum cartridges. Pressures that would greatly flatten CCI primers and that were, in fact, excessive, would hardly alter the appearance of the old Remington primers (at least that is true of one batch that I have on hand). If you do use the appearance of the primer as a measure of the relative pressure, keep these considerations firmly in mind. Comparing the pressure of your handload to some other handload or to factory ammunition based solely upon the appearance of the fired primer is generally meaningless and can be downright dangerous.

Another means of comparing pressure is to measure the expansion of the case head. If your handloads in new cases generate case-head expansion similar to that produced by factory-load cartridges fired in the same gun and using the same brand of cases, you can reasonably assume that the two cartridges probably generate very similar pressure. This holds especially true when the cartridges use similar weight bullets and have similar burning rate propellants, and when the case heads actually are similarly hard (which is not necessarily always the situation).

Measuring the expansion of the case head is very simple. The best results occur when you take this measurement on the case web, directly ahead of the rim cut. However, doing that requires the use of a blade micrometer that is capable of accurately measuring and reading to one-ten-thousandth inch. The micrometer must be capable of measuring across the narrow, solid-web portion of the case, in front of the rim and behind the hollow portion of the case body. (On belted-magnum cases you can use a standard micrometer to measure on the belt, just forward of the rim cut.) Measure from a point aligned with the first letter in the brand stamp (as the "R" in R-P) to the opposite side—the important point is to be certain to measure across the same diameter, both before and after firing the cartridge and to avoid measuring where any scars on the case body or rim might interfere.

On other case types, if you do not have a blade micrometer, use a conventional micrometer to measure across the rim. Be very careful to avoid any extractor mark or other scars on the rim. The resulting data are acceptably accurate to be quite useful.

After firing the cartridge and allowing the case to return to ambient temperature, measure the distance across the same diameter of the case. On new cases, it is common for modern high-pressure rifle loads to cause between 0.001- and 0.0015 thousandths-inch expansion of the case head. This expansion is greatest in the most intense chamberings—these include the 220 Swift, 6mm Remington, 25-06, 270 Winchester, and most magnum, super magnum, and similar rifle chamberings. In these, case-head expansion with factory loads can sometimes approach 0.002 inch.

Handloads in new cases that produce expansion that is similar to factory loads will generally fall within industry pressure guidelines. Further, when repeatedly used with similar loads, case-head expansion will not occur or will be minimal, and the primer pockets will not significantly loosen with the repeated reuse of the case at that pressure level. Most importantly, you can be reasonably certain that such handloads do not exceed the safe pressure limit for the chambering. However, in no instance should you use a lack of a case-head expansion as justification for exceeding published loads—cases can work-harden with each full-pressure use, and some cases come from the factory with unusually hard heads.

Should your handloads cause the primer pockets to loosen after repeated reloadings, the pressure is too high for those cases, and it might exceed the acceptable limit for the gun. Should this occur, the safe course is to reduce the load a few percent. The increased safety factor will

GENERALLY, A LOAD THAT IS STRESSING CASES BEYOND THE ELASTIC LIMIT WILL ALSO IMPOSE VARIABLE STRESSES ON THE GUN. THE CASES WILL RESPOND PLASTICALLY TO THE CHAMBER PRESSURE. THE DEGREE OF PLASTIC RESPONSE WILL VARY FROM CASE TO CASE; THIS DEPENDS UPON THE PRESSURE GENERATED BY THE INDIVIDUAL CARTRIDGE AND UPON THE HARDNESS OF THE INDIVIDUAL CASE HEAD. BOTH VARY FROM SHOT TO SHOT. SUCH VARIATIONS IN CASE HEAD RESPONSE USUALLY RESULT IN INCONSISTENT BARREL VIBRATIONS AND A LOSS OF ACCURACY.

more than compensate for the modest sacrifice in velocity. You might also see an improvement in accuracy.

Above all, regardless of the chambering or type of gun that you are using, it is up to you to use good sense in determining what is a prudent and safe handload. If you see any unusual pressure signs with your handloads, stop what you are doing and try to figure out what you are seeing. If you cannot sort things out, seek expert advice.

Obvious signs that something might be wrong include, but are not limited to: handloads exceeding the maximum charge listed in a current reputable manual, hard bolt lift, sticky case extraction, excessive case stretching, visible primer flattening, partial primer blanking (cratering), blanking (disk of primer cup under striker sheared free of the cup and extruded into the striker hole in the bolt), primer leaks, continued case-head expansion (with each use), and visible case-head damage.

Always use reputable, currently recommended loading data. Always begin load development with a charge that is at or near the minimum suggested load. Always watch for any obvious pressure signs. Never exceed the maximum listed load. Never assume that any data suggested by anyone else (as from an Internet forum) will generate safe loads. If you have a chronograph, use it.

If your handload produces unusually high velocity, consider that fact as a sign that you might have done something wrong. Most of us find it less than impossible to make mistakes. Examples of related errors include using the wrong propellant, wrong scale setting, wrong bullet, or wrong primer. Furthermore, it is perfectly possible for a perfectly normal load (factory or handmade) to generate excessive pressure when used in a perfectly normal gun. Such combinations do occur (rarely), which is just one more reason to use common sense and to maintain constant vigilance. You should always work up to a maximum safe load in your gun using caution.

INTERNAL BALLISTICS—ADVANCED PRESSURE TOOLS FOR THE HANDLOADER / OEHLER PERSONAL BALLISTICS LABORATORY, M-43; RECREATIONAL SOFTWARE PRESSURE TRACE

The serious handloader can measure the relative pressure of any given load in his gun and can do so without permanently altering the gun. The Oehler Model-43 Ballistic Laboratory and the Recreational Software Pressure Trace are affordable systems that will give real-time pressure data for almost any load fired from almost any type of rifle or rifle-type handgun. These systems are not suited to revolvers or semiautomatic guns with moving barrel shrouds—such as is typical in pistols. However, the tinkerer can adapt these to almost any other kind of gun.

Although it is relatively expensive, the Oehler system, which has more useful features than the Recreational Research system has, is within the reach of most serious shooters. (Chiefly, the M-43 includes downrange acoustic targets that measure groups and display hits on the computer screen at the shooting bench; the Recreational Research system lacks this feature.) The cost of the M-43 is similar to a typical high-performance rifle and riflescope setup. This system provides information that was unavailable, even in sophisticated ballistics laboratories, as late as the 1980s.

Conversely, pressure readouts produced with the Recreational Research system offer a level of precision and resolution that is unavailable with the Model-43. This system uses advanced electronics and software and allows the user to follow the pressure course while tracking the passage of the bullet through the bore, and to do so with impressive precision.

The use of either unit requires a computer. Generally, a portable computer is necessary. Few shooters are so fortunate as to have 110 volts available at their local range or to have a range in their basement—the rest of us envy those who do.

Both systems determine a chamber's pressure by measuring the strain imposed on the gun chamber when a cartridge is fired. In steel, stress (chamber pressure) and strain (chamber stretching) are linearly related—a load that generates twice the chamber pressure also generates twice the chamber stretching.

These systems do not require drilling holes or otherwise compromising the gun chamber. A special strain gage [that is how the gauge maker spells it] is glued over the chamber, and the system measures the change in electrical properties as this gauge stretches (along with the chamber) when the cartridge fires.

The 5mm, 32-grain Sierra BK (left) and the 22-caliber, 40-grain Nosler BT (right) are rated as having similar BCs. One suspects that the Nosler BT might have a real edge, but for the varmint hunter that cannot make up for a significant difference in initial velocity.

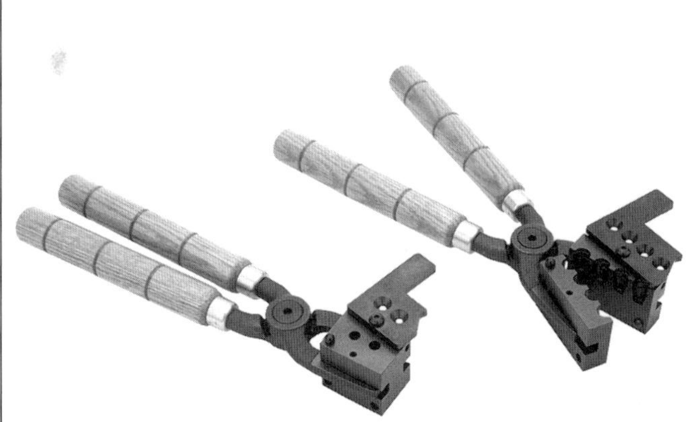

Cast bullets, discussed in a later chapter, offer serious handloaders practically unlimited opportunities to make affordable bullets at home and to create a specific type of cast bullet—to fulfill some real or perceived need.

These systems do not measure the actual chamber pressure, but they do accurately compare the pressure generated by various loads fired in the same chamber. The simple expedient of comparing handloads to conventional factory loads allows the handloader to be assured that his loads fall within industry standards. For this reason, these are the only systems that can absolutely guarantee the relative safety of any given handload in any given gun. The real-time pressure curve printouts produced demonstrate the relative consistency of any particular load.

For many chamberings, Oehler sells industry reference ammunition. This allows the users to compare their handloads to precise standard ammunition. (Testing reference ammunition in a standard pressure barrel provides a pressure-calibration reference.)

The current version of the Recreational Research Pressure Trace records only the relative chamber pressure, but the Oehler Model-43 combines chamber pressure data with chronograph results and downrange acoustical target data. This allows the shooter to measure and record all important load parameters simultaneously, without leaving the shooting bench. The model-43 system automatically records the following data for every shot:

- Pressure curve
  - » shape
  - » time
  - » peak
- Bullet
  - » muzzle velocity
  - » velocity at target
  - » ballistic coefficient
- Target;
  - » impact for each shot
  - » group size

On the other hand, the Recreational Research system offers significantly greater precision with regard to the resolution of the pressure curve—those interested primarily in internal ballistics might find this system more useful. If you are serious about handloading, consider one of these systems. Both offer dedicated handloaders, target shooters, and hunters unprecedented information.

INTERNAL BALLISTICS—WHAT ACTUALLY HEATS A BARREL

Contrary to what would seem to be common sense and what is the common popular belief, incandescent heating (from propellant gases) and friction (from the passage of the bullet and propellant) are actually only minor contributors to barrel heating. Anyone who has ever rapidly and repeatedly bent a piece of bailing wire knows exactly what is responsible for the majority of barrel heating—elastic deformation of the barrel steel, in response to the rise and fall of pressure within the barrel. Other sources include, more or less, in order of magnitude:

- Condensation heating, as propellant gases and vaporized carbon and bullet material condense onto the bore interior (a significant factor in blackpowder loads)
- Friction of the bullet and propellant's passage through the bore
- Incandescent heating.

Proof that deformation is the primary factor includes the following demonstrated facts:

- Heating of the barrel exterior occurs instantly as the bullet passes;
- Heating is essentially independent of bullet mass;
- Heating progressively increases in the last fraction of an inch toward the muzzle, where the last increments of the bore can deform progressively faster because those are not tied to the mass and strength of the bore equally rearward and forward (less mass / equal stress / greater deformation rate).

Having stated this, it might be necessary to explain why barrel bore damage occurs almost entirely at the chamber end despite the fact that barrel heating is usually greatest right at the muzzle and is usually similar along the entire length of the bore, up to the muzzle. As the bullet passes toward the muzzle, deformation is progressively reduced but the deformation rate is progressively increased. The explanation is simple: In conventional chamberings, the damage to the barrel is almost entirely the result of corrosion, which is greatest where the chamber pressure is greatest, which is at the chamber end. In large and very large chamberings, barrel damage is a combination of corrosion and erosion, and erosion is greatest where flame temperature is highest, which is also at the chamber end.

SOURCES FOR SPECIALTY TOOLS REFERENCED IN THIS CHAPTER:

Recreational Software Inc.
1343 Navajo Drive
Cottonwood, AZ 86323
Tele: 928-634-8028
www.shootingsoftware.com

Oehler Research
P.O. Box 9135
Austin, TX 78766
Tele: 800-531-5125

Superior Ballistics Inc.:
www.superiorballistics.com

MORE TROPHY WALL STORIES

Jill Anderson took her first elk with a 7-08 Remington, which was more than adequate for this task. As always, her skills in placing the shot allowed her to fill her tag humanely and to put meat in the freezer. Sitting next to Jill is her proud father, Loren.

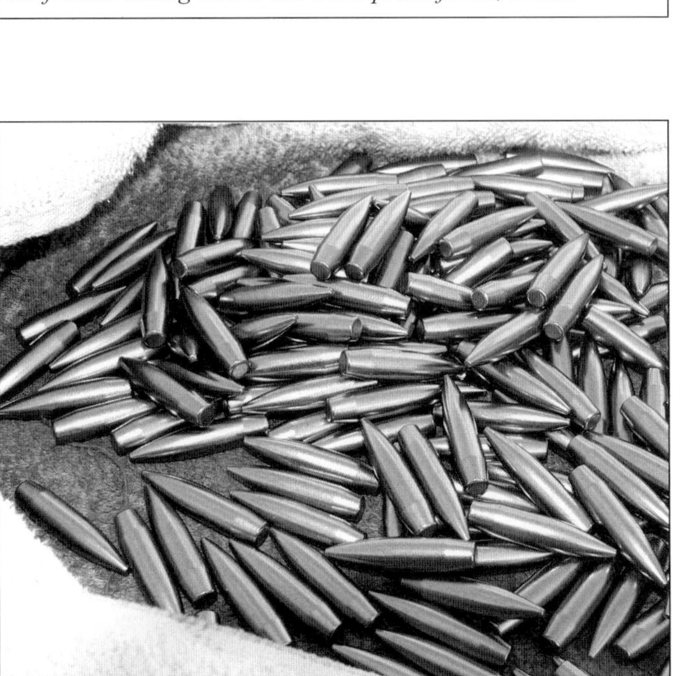

In a good year, I improve my chances of a successful hunt by converting a large pile of new bullets into a large number of used bullets while plinking, varmint hunting, and target shooting. Shown here are about two hundred 30-caliber, 200-grain Sierra MatchKings just after molyplating and polishing with a towel (to remove moly dust). Some folks seem to be naturals when it comes to accuracy; I need practice to hone what skills I do have.

Stan McPherson in 1965 with his first trophy.

This is Stan McPherson in 1995 with the antlers from his first trophy—in every respect a phenomenal mule deer buck.

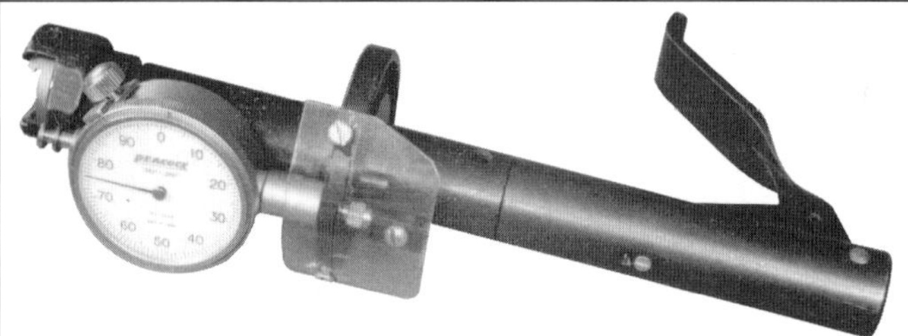

Uniform primer seating improves ballistic uniformity and was critical to quality of results of the primer substitution study (tables in chapter 7). Because the premium K&M precision primer-seating tool is the most precise tool available, I used it for priming all cases used in those tests.

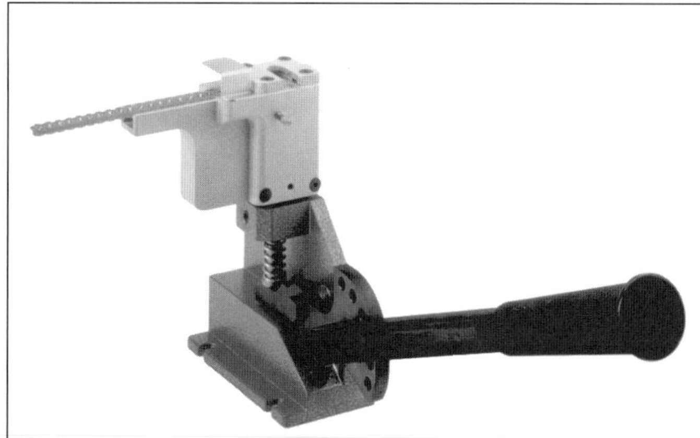

Seating hundreds of primers with the time-consuming method required with the K&M tool was onerous. This RCBS bench-mounted APS unit would have been almost as precise and would have been far easier and faster to use.

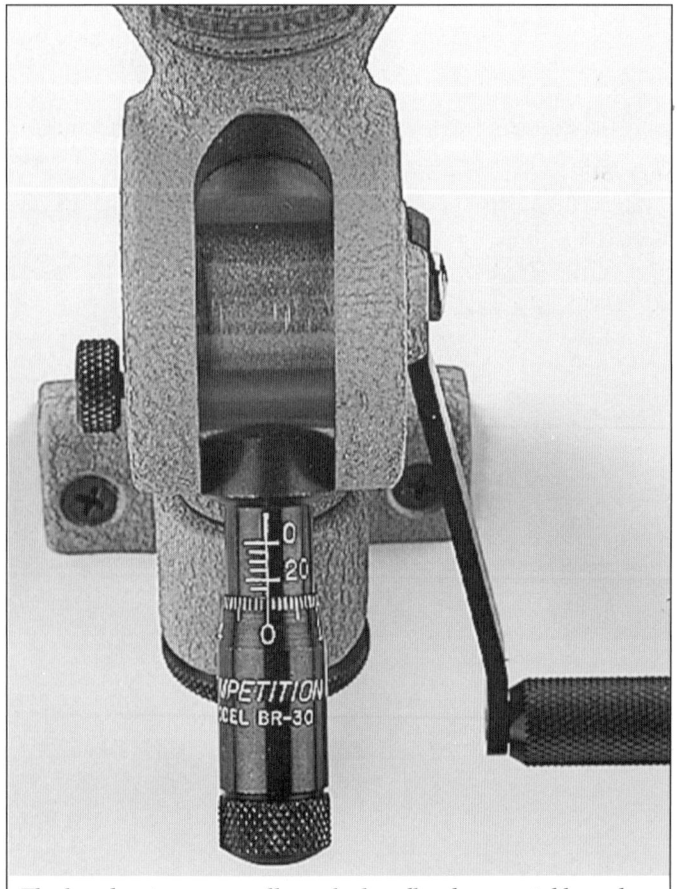

The handy micrometer allows the handloader to quickly and accurately return the Redding BR-30 to a specific charge setting. This is quite convenient.

Regardless of whatever else you might do to assure the best possible accuracy with your handloads in your gun, careful, proper, and diligent bore cleaning and preservation are necessary for best results.

EXTERNAL BALLISTICS

CHAPTER 14

INTRODUCTION

Ballisticians have scientifically studied external ballistics since Galileo, who seems to have been first in this pursuit. Amazingly, before Galileo's studies were accepted, many so-called scientists held that cannon balls traveled in a straight line until reaching terminal distance, at which point those projectiles simply fell out of the sky. Galileo knew that the standing dogma of his day was nonsense, just as did anyone who had bothered to observe a thrown rock, and he set out to prove the reality; this led to the understanding of the ballistic parabola.

Understanding how bullets react in flight is crucial to understanding how to make well-placed hits at long range. Understanding how bullets react in flight also requires knowledge of bullet design and muzzle velocity. Manufacturers provide data on the former; chronographs provide data on the latter.

The chronograph is the handloader's speedometer, thermometer, and quality monitor, all rolled into one handy device. While it is perfectly feasible to handload quality ammunition without using a chronograph, having such a device generally improves the handloader's enjoyment of his hobby, at the very least. Affordable, quality chronographs now cost less than $100, so it is hard to justify not owning one.

For the serious shooter developing accuracy loads, the chronograph is apt to pay for itself within a few sessions at the range—analysis of chronograph data can eliminate (wasted) testing by alerting the handloader that a particular load simply does not perform, either in terms of velocity or in terms of ballistic uniformity.

UNDERSTANDING EXTERNAL BALLISTICS

Although the study of ballistics covers many aspects of projectiles in free flight, only a few of those concern the average handloader. A bullet's path beyond the gun muzzle depends primarily upon muzzle velocity (which depends upon internal ballistics) and upon how rapidly the bullet loses velocity (which depends upon wind resistance). For sporting projectiles, in most applications, the only significant additional complication results from a cross wind.

In order to estimate bullet drop, energy, and wind drift at any given distance, the shooter must know only two things about the bullet:

- Muzzle velocity
- Rate of velocity loss

In addition, to judge the correct lead on a moving target accurately, the shooter must know these facts about the target:

- Distance
- Speed and angle of movement

Affordable chronographs now allow serious shooters to measure the bullet's velocity at almost any distance and to do so with accuracy that is far better than one part per thousand. Shooters can estimate bullet velocity loss using the published ballistic coefficient (BC) and ballistic tables. Every major bulletmaker publishes BC values for every bullet in its product line. Ballistic coefficient deserves a bit of explanation. The following is an idealized, first-order, approximation of the very-complicated real story.

Early in the modern study of ballistics, which began to mature in the latter decades of the 1800s, ballisticians recognized that the adoption of standard references would make their lives dramatically less complicated. Their idea was to establish a standard measure of ballistic efficiency and to then use that to compare all bullets. This is similar to having any other standard—for example, the inch or the meter. This realization presaged development of the standard bullet. Ballisticians designed and adopted such a bullet and then measured the ballistic properties of their invention. Specifically, they determined the rate of velocity loss for a bullet with a specific size, mass (weight), and shape as it moved through air at a specific velocity.

This one quantity, velocity loss, was comparatively easy to measure, even in the days before electronic wizardry. Ballisticians could accurately measure bullet velocity by firing into a ballistic pendulum. In this device, a bob-weight attached to a string stops the bullet. The bullet's momentum transfers to the bob, which swings in a pendulum arc. Given a specific bob and bullet weight, the height to which the bob raises during the resulting swing provides all the data necessary to calculate the impact velocity of the bullet precisely.

This simple equation is based upon a fundamental characteristic of physics: conservation of momentum. The pendulum must acquire precisely the velocity necessary so that the new pendulum weight (bob-weight plus bullet weight) times pendulum velocity exactly equals bullet weight times bullet impact velocity. Because the value of gravitational acceleration is well established, it is relatively simple to use the height to which the pendulum swings to back-calculate initial pendulum velocity and, from that, to determine the bullet's impact velocity.

Toward the end of that era, ballisticians had developed sophisticated chronographs, and measurement of bullet velocity became routine. However, modern chronographs have the advantages of being far easier to use and of measuring bullet velocity without interfering with ballistic flight.

For any given bullet, the rate of velocity loss (deceleration rate) depends upon the bullet velocity. To ascertain the deceleration rate of the standard bullet at any given velocity, ballisticians fired many standard bullets, loaded to as constant a muzzle velocity as was practical, into pendulums or through chronographs at various distances. The average velocity calculated for many shots at each distance gave a very close estimate to the average bullet velocity at that distance.

Consider two target distances, say, 100 yards and 200 yards. Subtracting the average velocity measured at 200 yards from the average velocity measured at 100 yards gave the velocity loss rate for the standard bullet across 100 yards (within the specific velocity range tested). If the standard bullet reached 100 yards with 2,585 fps velocity and 200 yards with 2,515 fps velocity, it lost about 70 fps while traveling 100 yards at an average velocity near 2,550 fps. With tests made at many distances and at many muzzle velocities, experimenters measured velocity loss for the standard bullet across a surprisingly wide velocity range (everything between about 500 fps and about 4,500 fps).

Significant complications exist. Chiefly, this regards the rate of velocity loss within different velocity ranges. Few real bullets match the standard bullet. Compared to the standard bullet, a particular bullet design might hold its velocity better at high velocity but lose velocity faster at low velocity. This is a common situation. The shape of the bullet nose, shank, and base each matter in this regard, as does the character of the nose-to-shank transition. For this reason, in an effort to cover most basic bullet shapes using fewer corrections more accurately, ballisticians eventually adopted several standards. The modern alternative is to apply the needed corrections—computers make this feasible and simple.

Well, now that we have a standard bullet for comparison, what do we do? First, we assign the standard bullet a ballistic coefficient (BC) of unity, or one (standard bullet BC = 1). Thereafter, we can calculate the relative ballistic properties of any other (tested) bullet by making one comparison: the rate of velocity loss of the tested bullet, compared to the known rate of velocity loss of the standard bullet. Then we can publish the resulting data in tables.

Consider bullets launched with identical muzzle velocity. If the standard bullet (BC = 1.00) lost 100 fps while covering 100 yards, a bullet that traveled only 50 yards before losing 100 fps would have a BC rating of one-half (BC = 0.50). Similarly, a bullet that traveled 200 yards before losing 100 fps would have a BC rating of two (BC = 2.00). Therefore, a higher BC means the bullet will lose less velocity while traveling any given distance. As a practical matter, most sporting bullets have BCs in the range from about 0.10 to about 0.70 (the standard bullet was an unusually heavy (long) round-nose design).

Given a choice of equal-mass bullets for any given muzzle velocity, the bullet with the highest BC will deliver the most energy to a distant target, will have the flattest trajectory, and will have the least wind drift. The bullet with the higher BC also gets to a distant target sooner, and, therefore, it requires less lead on a moving target.

Amazingly, the amount of deflection exhibited by a bullet in a cross wind is more closely related to how much velocity it loses in reaching the target than it is to how long it takes the bullet to reach that target. This is a well proven, if counterintuitive, fact.

The best demonstration of this fact is with the 22 Long Rifle. For target ammunition, manufacturers load a round-nose bullet at a muzzle velocity of about 1,050 fps; conversely, for high-speed ammunition, producers load the same bullet at a muzzle velocity of about 1,250 fps. Obviously, bullets from the high-speed loads take less time to reach any given distance. However, the high-speed bullets remain supersonic to about 50 yards (the speed of sound is about 1,120 fps) and the deceleration rate of a bullet is significantly greater when it is supersonic than when it is subsonic. Air cannot as easily move around a supersonic bullet; hence, the bullet constantly passes through a high-pressure zone (denser air) while dragging along a low-pressure zone. Effectively, a supersonic bullet feels more resistance—it decelerates faster.

Consequently, in crossing the first 100 yards, a high-speed 22 RF bullet loses about 240 fps, while an otherwise identical target (subsonic) 22 RF bullet loses only about 150 fps. Under these circumstances, the effective BC of the slower bullet is significantly higher. As a result, in a 10 mph cross wind the high-speed bullet deflects about 5.5 inches whereas the subsonic bullet deflects only about 4.1 inches. This result occurs despite the fact that the high-speed bullet covers the 100 yards 10 percent faster (0.27 seconds versus 0.30 seconds) and is, therefore, subjected to less total time of sideward push. This paradox holds for all bullets and all velocities. A slower bullet with a higher BC can exhibit less wind drift despite taking longer to reach the target.

The trajectory consequences of shooting at relatively steep uphill or downhill angles at a relatively distant target are far more complicated than has commonly been reported. You cannot calculate precise holdover by using any simple formula.

Several factors confuse this issue; the most important is the following: First, gravity only acts in the vertical direction, so it does not deflect a bullet that is fired at an uphill or downhill angle as much as it deflects a bullet that is fired level. Second, the sights (on conventional guns) are above the axis of the bore, and the gun is almost certainly sighted so that the bullet initially launches with an upward angle to the line of sight. For a scoped, 30-06 shooting level with 150-grain bullets, the bullet might cross the line of sight at 30 yards (on the way up) and again at about

200 yards (on the way down). When fired uphill or downhill, the bullet is subjected to less gravitational influence during each period of its flight. Therefore, it travels farther before dropping back to cross the line of sight the second time.

Hence—for those of us who are not seriously mathematically inclined—when we are firing at a distant target and shooting at a steep angle, the only feasible way to know with significant precision where to hold is to use computer software to develop trajectory charts for various angles of fire. If you expect to make such shots on game, get the needed software and develop range tables covering likely scenarios with your gun and load.

EXTERNAL BALLISTICS—CHRONOGRAPHS

Serious handloaders should own a chronograph. Even the least expensive units provide a degree of accuracy far beyond what most handloaders require. Chronographs measure the bullet's velocity for each shot, which is obvious. What is not so obvious is that a handloader can learn about the quality and potential long-range accuracy of any particular load by chronographing a string of shots from that load.

Generally, loads with a particularly low shot-to-shot velocity variation are good candidates for further accuracy development. Though exceptions do occur, loads with relatively high velocity variation do not generally shoot accurately, even at a short distance—100 to 300 yards. Such loads never perform particularly well at longer distances—beyond, perhaps, 500 yards.

A chronograph can indicate the potential problems with a load. Be very suspect of any load where the mean velocity is significantly above published ballistics for that recipe or of similar conventional factory loads. The only way to increase the velocity of any given bullet substantially is to push on it harder or longer. Therefore, any load that generates unexpectedly high velocity, most likely generates unusually high pressure. Equally, any gun that always produces velocities that are significantly lower than normal might have a problem, such as a markedly worn throat.

A chronograph is an important tool; with proper record keeping, it can become an integral part of any trip to the range. This also gives shooters a means of independently evaluating progressive bore deterioration—generally, as damage to the bore progresses, any load will generate a progressively lower velocity.

Reintroduced in 2010, the Oehler 35P is the most precise chronograph ever offered to the hobbyist. I have chronographed tens of thousands of shots with a 35P, purchased in the 1980s, with absolute satisfaction.

However, please keep in mind that typical guns do not generate the same velocity as typical pressure-test barrels do. Often, the velocity difference is significant. Hence, most load combinations fired in sporting guns generate less pressure than is reported for that recipe when fired in a test barrel; hence, when fired in a sporting gun, a load that matches the velocity obtained with the test barrel might also exceed normal pressure—this adage is quite apropos:
"There Are No Free Lunches."

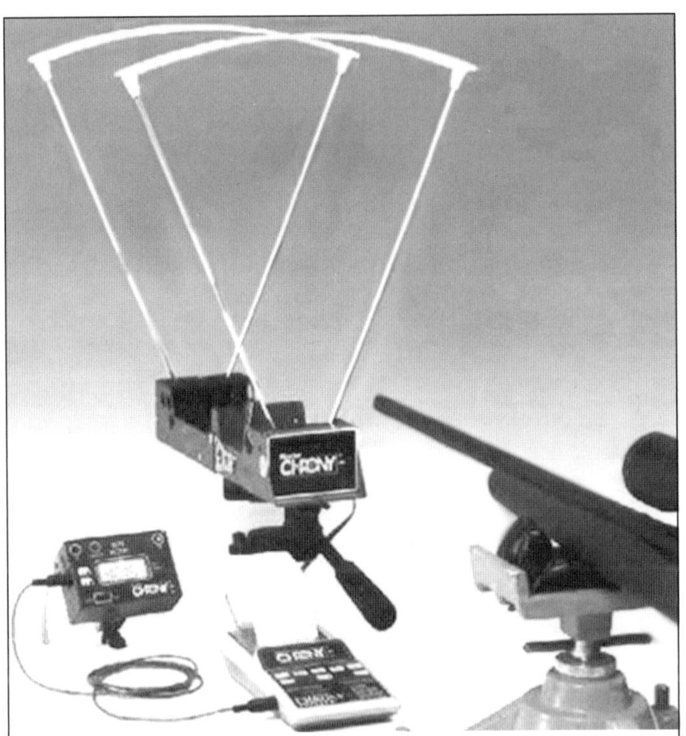

This mock-up with the top-of-the-line Chrony demonstrates several useful features. These include a printer (lower center) to create a permanent record, a remote display (lower-left corner) for easy reading, and long cables for the handy placement of the printer and display. Not evident is the associated computer software and interfaces that allow the user to transfer data to a computer almost instantly and to then manipulate that data easily. The other hidden feature is the huge amount of permanent (erasable) memory—one can shoot all day without filling the memory!

My friend, Duane Erkman, with whom I began my reloading career when he was 13 and I was 14, reports that his standard hunting load, a combination he developed in about 1974, fired in his Parker Hale, 7mm Remington Magnum rifle now generates fully 10 percent (300 fps) less velocity than it originally did. The only thing that has changed is the condition of the bore in that gun.

Through the intervening years, Erkman has killed many elk with that rifle. He has also fired quite a few target groups—a skilled hunter always wants to know how he and his gun are performing. You can rest assured that this has paid off. Erkman's shots have been well placed, and some of those at a rather long distance. His elk rifle has served him well, and it deserves a new barrel.

The Oehler 35P is the premier personal chronograph. Fortunately, as of 2010, Oehler has resolved component supply issues, and the 35P is once again available. (Oehler had discontinued the 35P around 2007.) This chronograph offers an unmatched level of precision and repeatability. As with any chronograph that includes a printer (such as the top-of-the-line Chrony model), the shooter can set up this unit, and then proceed to shoot at targets without the interruptions that might otherwise be necessary for immediate record keeping.

Shooting Chrony, Inc., offers an inexpensive line of useful, accurate, and dependable units. These are ideal for shooters requiring simple setup and uncomplicated use. All Chrony units deliver sufficient precision. Top-end units also feature erasable permanent memory. Shooters can connect these to a personal computer for further load analysis, without the need to enter data manually.

Setting up a Chrony takes only minutes. A sturdy tripod is the best method for locating and positioning the Chrony Skyscreens. As with the Oehler 35P, the Chrony Skyscreen window is large enough to allow the user to shoot at several targets without repositioning either the gun or the screens. Top-end Chrony units include a remote button that allows the shooter to review shot-group data and to switch to a new group without leaving the shooting bench—this is most convenient. As noted, the top-of-the-line model now includes a printer; it also has a bench-located readout for maximum convenience. Due to the relatively short Skyscreen spacing, ultimate accuracy is not as good as that provided by the Oehler 35P, but it is generally adequate and the results are eminently repeatable.

Most chronographs provide built-in, shot-string statistical analysis. The values typically reported for a shot string include individual shot velocity, extreme spread (fastest minus slowest), standard deviation, average velocity, and the number of shots recorded.

EXTERNAL BALLISTICS—COMPUTER PROGRAMS (SOFTWARE)

6.5MM, 140-GRAIN BERGER VLD:

(Standard sea-level conditions, 10 mph cross wind)

YARDS	fps	FOOT POUNDS	DROP INCHES	DRIFT INCHES
0	3,070	2,930	-1.7	0.0
100	2,914	2,639	+1.2	0.4
200	2,763	2,373	0.0	1.9
300	2,617	2,130	-5.8	4.4
400	2,476	1,906	-16.5	7.8
500	2,340	1,701	-32.9	12.5
600	2,207	1,514	-55.9	18.6

A basic trajectory table provides useful information for those contemplating long-range targets.

The advent of (affordable) personal computers has given shooters the opportunity to include external ballistics programs in their handloading repertoire. Several companies offer useful software. These programs allow shooters to compare the downrange performance of various loads easily.

These and other programs are more-or-less user-friendly, and they allow shooters to learn more about their pet loads than they could hope to know, based upon any reasonable amount of shooting.

Examples of the uses for these programs run the gamut of almost all types of serious shooting. Varmint hunters can easily compare various potential loads (particularly bullet weights) to see which might be best for any particular shooting conditions (winds and differing elevations). Hunters can see what happens to the trajectory of a given load with significant changes in shooting elevation—a rifle properly sighted to zero at 300 yards when near sea level will shoot considerably differently when fired at 9,000 feet. Target shooters can prepare for rezeroing a rifle at a different distance and elevation, instead of having to rezero the gun on the fly, which is never convenient.

The documentation features of these programs are significant. These programs record all the important handloading data, internal and external ballistics data, and accuracy results all in one place. The graphic printouts are of no small consequence. Shooters can carry these in the field and use this information to

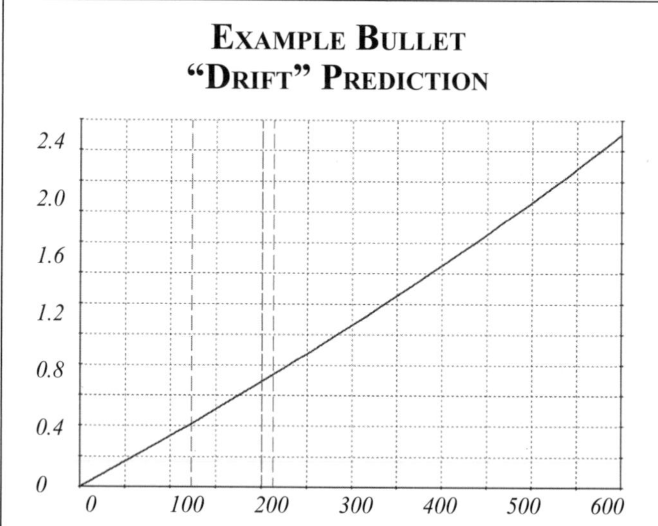

The required target lead in yards out to 600 yards: 140 Berger VLD, 3,070 fps muzzle velocity, with the target crossing at 10 miles per hour.

estimate external ballistics at the locale of the hunt or target match.

Nevertheless, for myriad reasons, no ballistics program can substitute for actual shooting. First, the shooter cannot know the precise BC of any bullet by any means other than by firing that bullet and then measuring the actual performance. Second, firing will alter the bullet's shape so that the in-flight BC will be a function of the gun used (variations in rifling deformation on the bullet jacket and variations in bore diameter, for example). Third, no ballistics program can exactly account for all real-world variables.

When all is said and done, even the big boys measure BC by testing. This applies to bullets and space shuttles alike. Nevertheless, because ballistics programs can provide a reasonably accurate, first-approximation estimate of actual performance, such a computer program is an extremely useful adjunct to handloading.

Modern external ballistics software provides all manner of information. Generally, if the shooter can think of a germane question, the software will answer it with useful accuracy.

SOURCES FOR SPECIALTY TOOLS REFERENCED IN THIS CHAPTER:

Oehler Research
P.O. Box 9135
Austin, TX 78766
Telephone: 800-531-5125

Shooting Chrony Inc.
3840 Robinson Road PMB#298
Amherst, NY 14228
Tele: 800-385-3161

MEACHAM CUSTOM SEATING DIE

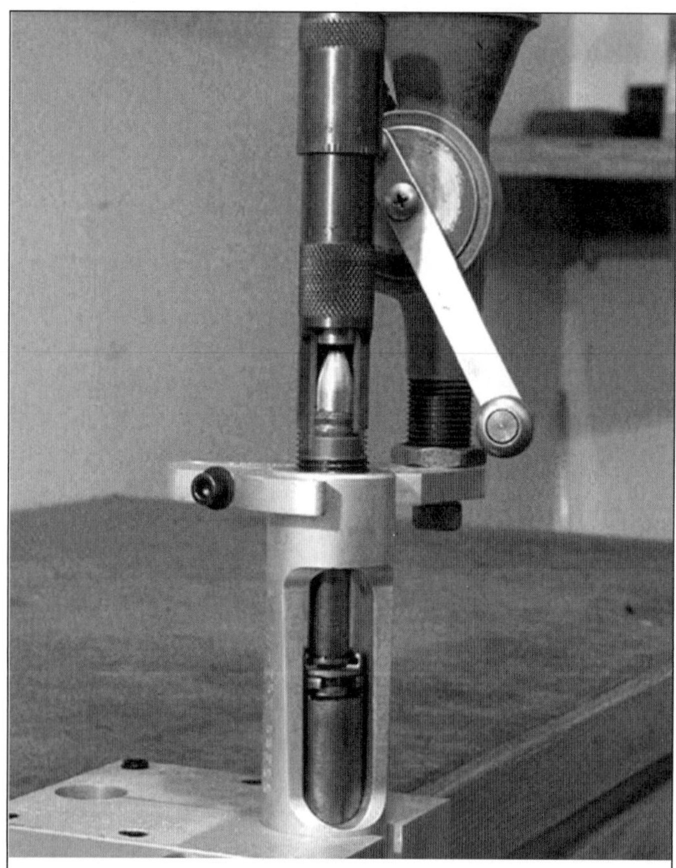

Here the ram is pushing the case toward bullet. Notice the handy adapter for mounting a powder measure. This press and base system are specifically intended for field use. Handloaders can mount this system almost anywhere with nothing more complicated than a C-clamp. For serious blackpowder shooters and others who shoot relatively low-pressure cartridges and who might need to handload while at the range, this is an ideal system.

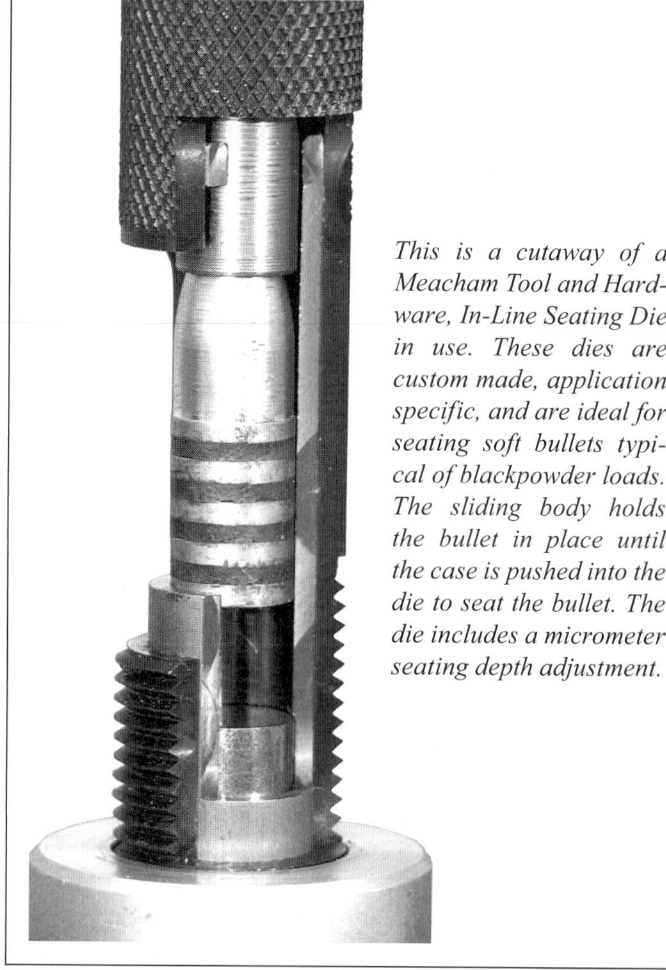

This is a cutaway of a Meacham Tool and Hardware, In-Line Seating Die in use. These dies are custom made, application specific, and are ideal for seating soft bullets typical of blackpowder loads. The sliding body holds the bullet in place until the case is pushed into the die to seat the bullet. The die includes a micrometer seating depth adjustment.

Left to right are a 32, 32 case (fired in a 380), and a 380 case. A case rupture such as this can damage or destroy the gun, and it can cause injury.

Bullet casting (and swaging) allows the handloader the opportunity to experiment with a vast variety of bullets in any given cartridge. Pictured is a tiny fraction of likely cast bullet options for 45-caliber handgun cartridges—cases from left to right are 454 Casull, 45 Colt, and 45 S&W. These bullets run the gamut from 155-grain SWC (a target design) to 300-grain TC (a hunting design).

BULLET MAKING

CHAPTER 15

INTRODUCTION

Unlike other ammunition components that are essentially impossible to manufacture effectively at home, handloaders can readily make their own bullets. We can control almost every aspect of homemade cast or swaged bullets. In both systems, lead or lead alloy is the material of choice for the core. However, these two systems are distinct in almost every other way.

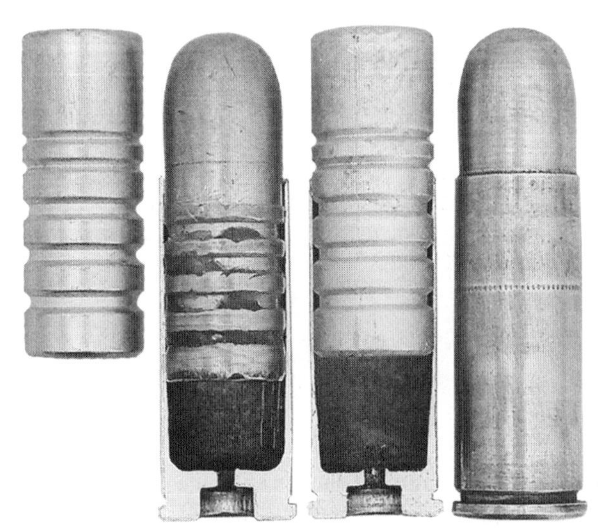

Those who want something radically different, such as this 525-grain wadcutter or a 500-grain round-nose for the 45 Colt and 454 Casull, will not likely find it as a commercial offering. A custom bullet mold is the answer—if it is feasible, it can be made. The purpose of this WC bullet is to hunt elk without having to don hearing protection and without suffering significant hearing damage resulting from firing normal full-power 454 loads without hearing protection (while hunting, donning hearing protection before firing is usually difficult, at best). When launched at 1,050 fps from the 454, this bullet delivers as much energy at 100 yards as any conventional 454 load and smacks an elk as if it were poleaxed. In terms of loudness, it is more similar to a factory 45 Colt load than it is to a typical 454 load. The round-nose load is accurate at extreme range and delivers more than 38 inches of penetration in a saturated telephone book.

Generally, handloaders view casting as a means of generating inexpensive homemade bullets. Most of us have several goals when casting bullets. These might include:

- Creation of a useful bullet that is not commercially available
- Duplication of a commercially available cast bullet but with the required hardness for a specific application
- Saving money

For example, I cast an unusually heavy full wadcutter for use in the 45 Colt and the 454 Casull. This is an effective elk-hunting bullet that does not generate hearing-destroying noise, whereas equally effective conventional 454 hunting cartridges do.

Swaging bullets at home is generally a purely esoteric endeavor. Equipment costs are so high that for most shooters the only real justification for bullet swaging is the satisfaction of one's ego. Nothing is wrong with this, and I admire individuals with such incentive and drive.

Bullet casting involves various equipment to heat and handle bullet metal (various alloys of lead, antimony, tin, and—rarely—silver, usually with a trace of arsenic) and to transfer the molten bullet metal into a bullet mold. Other equipment can include bullet-sizing and lubricating tools and supplies. When hardening cast bullets, a kitchen oven is also useful.

The basic process involves the following: melting the bullet metal, pouring that into a bullet-shaped mold, sizing the resulting bullet so that it properly fits the gun bore (not always required), and lubricating the bullet to minimize barrel leading.

Making one's own bullets is nostalgic, and it adds a bit of satisfaction, extending the "making your own" aspect of handloading.

BULLET MAKING—CAST BULLETS GENERAL CONSIDERATIONS

Observe all safety warnings included with all bullet-casting equipment. Bullet casting can expose you and others to heat, burn, and fire hazards, and potentially to toxic fumes. Never heat bullet metal above 850 degrees F. When heated to or beyond about 850 degrees F, lead alloys can generate a significant amount of toxic fumes that are both invisible and odorless. No reason exists to ever heat bullet metal anywhere nearly this hot—temperatures below 800 degrees F are always adequate.

Before I proceed with this discussion, I want to note that bullet casting is very much an art. Do not expect to learn how to make perfect cast bullets in one afternoon. Perfect practice makes perfect.

Read and follow the instructions that come with the equipment you use. Never be afraid to ask for advice from those with more experience—very likely you will need it. For example, before I tried to cast 525-grain wadcutters, I thought I was reasonably adept at the art of bullet casting. Each type of mold has unique idiosyncrasies that require different practices for proper use and to get good results.

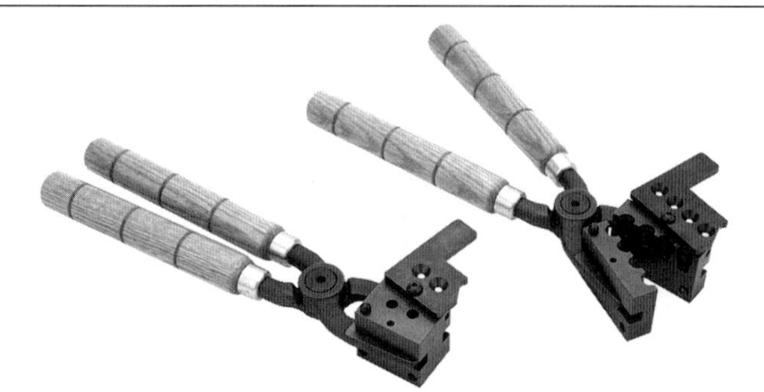

Modern bullet molds, such as these examples from Saeco, often come with two or four cavities. Such molds speed the casting process and have other advantages, but these also have potential disadvantages. Those looking for the last measure of accuracy will usually prefer single-cavity molds.

Bullet casting harks to the earliest days of shooting when all guns were custom muzzleloaders. During, and long after the end of that era, gunmakers always included one or more bullet molds with any new gun. Without these accessories, shooters had no means of procuring proper bullets for any gun; in those early days, no standards existed. Each barrel was unique and therefore required matching bullets.

Modern bullet casters choose to cast bullets because they have more time than money, because they want to shoot a particular type of bullet that is unavailable commercially, or because they want the satisfaction of creating and using their own bullets. Mr. William Falin, former chief ballistician at Accurate Arms Company, provides a classic example. Falin casts a particular 44 Magnum bullet using the Lyman #429650 mold. Although listed as a 300-grain bullet mold, these bullets typically weigh about 325 grains when he uses his (not-too-hard) alloy. The as-cast diameter of this SWC is large enough to fill the somewhat oversize cylinder throats in his S&W Model 29 revolver properly. No commercially available bullet combines these features.

Falin loads those bullets over 16.8 to 17.0 grains of Accurate No. 9 with a CCI-300 primer. The long-range accuracy of this load is nothing less than astounding. Moreover, as a big-game hunting load, this combination is hard to beat.

For an excellent review of techniques required to produce match-grade cast bullets, refer to the *Precision Shooting Reloading Guide,* Precision Shooting Publications. Mr. Clouser's article, pages 237 through 261, represents a tour de force in the art of making precision cast bullets.

Those who do not believe that cast bullets can be accurate should refer to the 1,000-yard records of the 1880s and the 200-yard records of the early 1900s, all established with cast bullets. In many instances, the best jacketed-bullet cartridges failed to eclipse those records for more than fifty years. This is not to diminish what current modern target shooters are doing but to point out that one should never underestimate the accuracy potential of cast bullets (or of blackpowder, for that matter).

BULLET MAKING—ALLOY, HARDNESS, AND HEAT TREATING

By altering the alloy, a bullet caster can change the pressure range within which his cast bullets properly work. Purer lead produces a softer alloy. It is possible to harden alloys containing lead, tin, antimony, and a smidgen of arsenic (a necessary ingredient) significantly through heat treating.

CAST BULLETS—WHAT CAUSES LEADING

As acceleration force progressively increases beyond internal cast-bullet strength, obturation swelling and bullet-to-bore friction progressively increase. At some point, friction generates heat so fast that the bullet surface melts because the bullet and barrel cannot carry heat away fast enough to keep the bullet surface below the melting-point temperature. Conversely, if the load does not create enough pressure (force), the bullet will not obturate sufficiently to seal the bore; hot gases escaping past the bullet can then melt the bullet surface. Either situation creates leading with a progressive loss of accuracy.

The amount of pressure required to create proper obturation depends upon the bullet's hardness. For any given load, bullets that are either too soft or are too hard will have limited accuracy and will lead the bore; therefore, the handloader must adjust the load parameters to match the bullet's hardness.

If a cast bullet shoots properly with one particular load (standard) and leads when tested with a slightly heavier charge, the bullet is too soft for use with a load that generates significantly more pressure than the standard load. In such a situation, if the goal is to launch the bullet faster, the handloader must use a slower propellant (to achieve increased velocity without significantly altering peak chamber pressure), or he must add antimony to the bullet's metal (to harden the resulting bullets), or he could harden the bullets through heat treating—by dropping the bullets directly from the mold into water or by using the oven method (see below).

Conversely, a very mild load that creates significant barrel leading most likely does not generate enough pressure to obturate the bullet adequately. If so, try using a faster-burning propellant (to generate more pressure and the same velocity) or add lead to the bullet metal (to soften it). The biggest problem in the understanding of cast-bullet hardness seems to be that so many novice casters just know that barrel leading is indisputable evidence of a too-soft bullet. (Bevel-based bullets tend to exacerbate this problem because those require greater pressure to create an effective obturation seal.)

This belief is understandable because experts have been preaching this for decades. However, with the high quality of modern commercial cast bullets and the good casting alloys now commonly available, barrel leading is more often indicative of a too-hard bullet or of too-little pressure rather than of a too-soft bullet or of too-much pressure.

CAST BULLETS—TERMINAL PERFORMANCE

As noted in chapter 10, in order to see how your loads perform, fire bullets into a stack of saturated telephone books. A twelve-inch stack will stop most pistol bullets, but to reliably stop the deep penetrators one should back up the saturated stack with a twelve-inch stack of dry books. Always test with the stacks of paper located at a safe distance and with a safe backstop.

The shank of a too-soft bullet will exhibit melting—the grooves will show smearing. A too-hard bullet will show gas cutting—the lands will have worn tracks.

CAST BULLETS—MEASURING HARDNESS

Determining the necessary adjustment in bullet hardness is something of a trial-and-error process. Fortunately, most bullets cast of typical alloys will work properly in some useful load that is usually easy to determine. Exceptions exist and those exceptions can cause difficulty for handloaders. Nevertheless, with a little thought the handloader can generally figure out why a bullet and load is causing excessive leading.

A tiny amount of leading is almost inevitable when shooting lead-alloy bullets from most guns. However, one should be able to fire hundreds of shots before leading measurably interferes with accuracy (if it ever does). Obviously, a rougher bore results in a faster baseline leading buildup. A perfectly wonderful method of removing minor barrel leading is simply to fire a few jacketed bullet loads through the bore—never do this when significant leading exists.

Saeco (Redding) offers a hardness tester for serious bullet casters. This simple, albeit precise and affordable, device allows bullet casters to compare the hardness of any lead alloy bullet or piece of bullet metal easily to a standard. The Saeco Hardness Tester reports hardness on a vernier scale. Most bullet alloys measure between 5 and 13. Saeco includes a chart that relates Saeco hardness to Brinell hardness (Bh). Bh is an industry standard used for measuring the relative hardness of soft metals.

The Saeco hardness tester uses a vernier scale and a sophisticated system that combines one spring-loaded plunger and one spring-loaded probe. This tool determines the bullet's hardness by measuring the amount of force required to create an indentation of a specific depth. When used carefully on the end of the bullet opposite the sprue, the results are accurate and repeatable.

CAST BULLETS—ACCURACY AND LEADING

Handloaders who happen to know the approximate peak pressure of the load in use can easily calculate the maximum Brinell hardness (Bh) that will allow proper bullet obturation. Conversely, if you know the Bh of the bullet, you can estimate the pressure required for good accuracy. To estimate the minimum chamber pressure required to achieve adequate obturation, multiply the Bh by 1,500. (In the pressure range typical of cast bullet loads, CUP and psi are sufficiently similar that we can use these pressure units interchangeably for this purpose.)

For example, assume that you are loading for a 30-30 Winchester using a slow-burning propellant and a 173-grain cast bullet. Published data suggest that your load generates about 30,000 psi peak chamber pressure. Therefore, maximum bullet hardness will be about 30,000/1,500 or 20 Bh. (A Bh of 20 corresponds to a Saeco hardness of about 9.5.)

What this means is that if your bullets measure 10 on the Saeco scale (Bh=22), obturation is suspect and both barrel leading and accuracy problems are likely to occur. For such a bullet, use a higher-pressure load (where safely feasible). Conversely, when using plain-based cast bullets, you will find loads that generate peak pressure exceeding about 2,000 psi per Bh unit are apt to generate barrel leading due to excessive frictional heating. So, for our example, bullets measuring less than about 8½ on the Saeco scale (Bh=15) would be suspect. (To use a softer bullet, choose a lower-pressure load.) In this instance, an ideal Saeco hardness would be near 9 (Bh=18)—such a bullet should work well.

CAST BULLETS—GAS CHECKS

Gas checks usually allow the use of higher pressures with any given bullet-metal alloy. Hence, where the gas check shines is with loads at the top end of useful cast-bullet pressures.

As peak chamber pressure increases, the window of correct hardness, wherein obturation is complete and frictional melting does not occur, gets progressively narrower. Eventually, this window has a negative width. When working with progressively harder bullets, progressively more pressure is required to obturate the bullet to fit the bore fully and to overcome the bridging strength within the bullet. The latter tends to prevent the bullet from swelling into the bottoms of the grooves in order to seal the bore (as is necessary to prevent gas cutting). Hence, with a sufficiently hard bullet, any load that generates enough pressure to obturate the bullet adequately will also generate enough bullet expansion force so that bullet-to-bore friction is so great that frictional bullet melting will occur. In other words, when using cast bullets, there exists an upper end to the velocity that we can achieve with accuracy and without significant leading.

Fortunately, that upper end (around 2,200 fps, typically) is sufficient to allow full-power loads in magnum revolver chamberings and milder midbore rifle chamberings, such as the 30-30 Winchester and 35 Remington. To maximize cast-bullet results in higher-performance rifle chamberings, use heavier bullets with loads at less than maximum pressure.

Gas checks mitigate this velocity limitation in several ways. When properly sized, these tend to form a good gas seal, independent of bullet obturation. Gas checks also strengthen the bullet base so that casting weaknesses near the base do not result in higher local bullet-to-bore friction. Gas checks will also scrape away a small amount of bore leading. Generally, when compared to otherwise similar plain-based bullets, with ideal loads we can shoot gas-checked bullets about 200 fps faster, about 10 percent, before leading or a loss of accuracy occurs.

CAST BULLETS—ADJUSTING ALLOY HARDNESS

By adding more antimony and tin to the basic alloy, the caster can make harder bullets. Here we are considering antimony in the range from about 1 percent to about 6 percent. Increasing the antimony content 1 percent will typically harden the bullet alloy about two Saeco points. The degree of hardening resulting from each 1 percent increase in the antimony content decreases as the antimony content increases. The standard method of increasing the antimony content is to mix a harder alloy into a too-soft mix until the desired hardness is reached.

Adding around 1 percent tin to a common wheel-weight alloy makes it far easier to cast. However, take care that the tin content never exceeds the antimony content; it is a little-known fact that such excess-tin alloys develop hard and soft spots in random patterns, which will potentially play hob with the accuracy of the bullet. For a 10-pound pot of wheel weight alloy, add 0.1 pound (1.6 ounces) of tin, and you will have an ideal alloy for most purposes.

Bullet casters can also use the melting point of alloys of lead, antimony, and tin as a first-order guess of the resulting bullet hardness. (See the following section.) Unless you are using a quantified alloy mix, this approach is only approximate because with most bullet-metal alloys you cannot know the actual percentage content of each alloying agent.

BULLET METAL—TEMPERATURE OF TOTAL LIQUIDITY FOR ESSENTIALLY PURE ALLOYS OF LEAD, ANTIMONY, AND TIN

With an essentially pure alloy of lead, antimony, and tin, we can estimate the composition by measuring the temperature when complete melting occurs, if we know the percent by weight of tin, antimony, or lead.

Refer to the chart on page 364. For alloy estimations based upon known tin or antimony content, find the row (tin) or column (antimony) that matches the known tin or antimony content, then follow that row or column until you find the cell listing the closest temperature when total melting occurred. The percentage heading at the top of that column (antimony), or at the left of that row (tin), is the approximate percentage of the other alloying element.

For example, consider a 3 percent tin alloy that fully melts at 589 degrees F. The closest listed temperature in the 3 percent tin row is 591 degrees F at 2 percent antimony (approximate lead, antimony, and tin percent composition is therefore 95/2/3). Such an alloy will not cast good bullets because it has more tin than antimony. To make sure that the alloy has more antimony than tin, add about 1½ percent antimony. This will make a relatively hard alloy. To make a softer alloy, add lead. (Or just add wheel-weight metal, which will add antimony and lead.)

For estimations based upon a known percentage of lead, an example will best illustrate the procedure. Consider an alloy known to contain 90 percent lead, alloyed only with tin and antimony. Measure the melting point temperature; then locate the cell where the total alloy content is 10 percent and the melting temperature is closest to the measured temperature. Consider examples of alloys that first fully melt at:

- 520º F—8% antimony, 2% tin;
- 530º F—7% antimony, 3% tin; and,
- 540º F—6% antimony, 4% tin.

Note that this chart is only approximate and that interpolation will commonly be necessary because few unknown alloys happen to contain an exact integer percentage of each alloying agent. Further, low-tin alloys show very little temperature effect from significant variations in tin content. Nonetheless, with a good thermometer, this chart is useful.

Adding 1 to 3 percent tin to lead adds a small measure of hardness, but tin chiefly improves castability and is necessary for good bullet casting when using high-antimony alloys—all alloys containing more than about 3 percent antimony. However, as tin is comparatively expensive, bullet casters try to keep the tin content to the minimum level that still provides good castability.

If testing suggests that the resulting bullets are too hard, mix pure lead or a softer alloy into the casting mix. As a starting point, try mixing one part pure lead with three parts of the original bullet metal. On the other hand, if the bullets are too soft, then it is necessary to add antimony or to mix in a harder alloy.

Alloys containing 1 percent silver are particularly fluid and tend to cast extremely good bullets. Silver in such an alloy adds one-to-two cents to the cost of a typical bullet (circa 2000 prices).

BULLET CASTING—HEAT TREATING

Because many lead alloys contain traces of arsenic, heat-treating cast bullets becomes a useful process

A lead thermometer is an invaluable asset to the bullet caster. This affordable tool can make all the difference when you try to duplicate a specific bullet—as when the last batch that you cast was the best you had ever made.

for enhancing hardness. The easiest method, where safely feasible, is to drop the new bullets directly from the mold into water. Alternatively, heat cast and sized bullets at 450 degrees F for about fifteen minutes, then quench, as described below.

To establish accuracy of and a correction factor for the thermostat readings on your oven, use Tempilaq 450 degrees F. This is available from Brownells (as is the useful thinner). Set the oven at 425 degrees F and allow it to heat to a stable temperature. Then, mark a test bullet with Tempilaq—just a dab on the bullet tip will do.

Then stand the bullet in a pan and place that in the oven, on a middle rack, and located above a pie sheet or some other metal piece that will prevent incandescent heating from the element or burner from directly heating the pan upon which the bullet rests. Periodically check the bullet for about fifteen minutes.

Unless the thermostat on your oven is very badly out of calibration, the Tempilaq will not melt to the clear, reacted appearance. If the Tempilaq does melt, reduce the temperature of the oven by 5 degrees F, allow oven to cool slightly, and try again with a new test bullet. Repeat this test, adjust, and retest until it takes several minutes for the Tempilaq to melt and clarify.

More likely, the Tempilaq will not melt within about fifteen minutes with the original (425 degrees F) temperature setting. If so, increase the oven temperature setting by 5 degrees F and wait fifteen minutes to see if the Tempilaq melts; repeatedly increase the temperature and wait. When the Tempilaq melts, whatever temperature setting the oven thermostat is set at represents an actual oven temperature between about 450 degrees F and about 455 degrees F. This is close enough to the needed 450 degrees F for bullet hardening. Note or permanently mark this thermostat setting for future reference.

Heating to 450 degrees F, followed by proper quenching will harden a typical wheel weight plus tin alloy bullet to between 26 and 30 Bh. This is certainly hard enough for most applications.

Setting the oven at progressively lower temperatures produces less hardened bullets. Quenching after heating to less than about 380 degrees F will not result in measurable hardening.

Progressively harder bullets are possible through heating to higher temperature. However, if the oven temperature exceeds 464 degrees F, bullets will soften, slump, and be ruined. Because we can gain very little hardness by heating above 450 degrees F, the best approach is to work with oven temperatures between about 400 degrees F and about 455 degrees F, depending upon the desired bullet hardness.

Ready-made accessories for the oven hardening of cast bullets are not available; hence, you must fabricate several devices. The basic idea is to have a pan that will fit in your oven and that will allow you to stand bullets on their bases and not touching each other. This pan must have a perforated bottom. When placing this pan in the oven, you should also position it above a solid pan, as noted above. (This will prevent radiant heat from the burner or electric element from overheating and melting the bullets.)

Note: Never allow any lead to remain in any oven used for food preparation. This second pan will also act as a trap in the unfortunate event of a melted bullet. Never use the top element to heat an oven that contains bullets. If the bullets require sizing, always perform the sizing operation before heat treating.

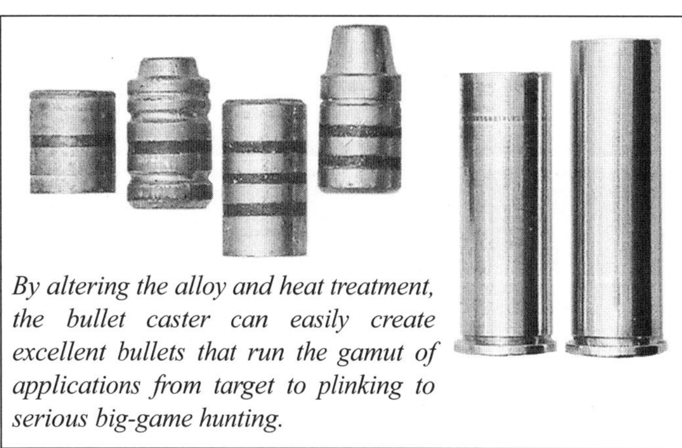

By altering the alloy and heat treatment, the bullet caster can easily create excellent bullets that run the gamut of applications from target to plinking to serious big-game hunting.

Approximate Temperature (Degree F) at Liquidus for Lead, Antimony, Tin Alloys Where Bullet-Metal Alloys Become Fully Liquefied

% TIN	% ANTIMONY 0	1	2	3	4	5	6	7	8	9	10
0	621	608	595	581	567	555	544	532	521	511	498
1	620	606	594	579	566	553	544	531	520	508	495
2	618	603	593	578	565	551	543	530	519	507	493
3	612	601	591	576	563	549	542	530	518	506	492
4	608	600	588	573	561	548	540	529	517	504	491
5	606	594	582	570	558	547	536	526	514	501	490
6	600	588	576	565	553	541	530	521	510	498	487
7	594	581	570	556	548	535	524	514	505	496	484
8	587	575	563	551	542	529	518	509	501	490	480
9	580	568	558	546	537	522	513	505	497	485	476
10	574	561	553	542	532	518	510	501	493	481	473

Bullet Metal Alloy Characteristics (from the RCBS Cast Bullet Manual)

Material	Alloy	Brinell Hardness Number	Suggested Casting Temperature
Lead	Pure	5	700°F
	5% Tin	10	700°F
	10% Tin	11	700°F
Wheel Weights	As Cast*	8–13	775°F
	Heat Treated*	25–35	775°F
Linotype	84% Lead, 12% Antimony, 4% Tin	22	775°F

**Most producers maintain good lot-to-lot uniformity; but, alloys vary among producers.*

Alloy Percentages versus Temperature (Degree F) of Fully Liquid Melt (from the RCBS Cast Bullet Manual)

% Antimony	%Tin 0	2	4	6	8	10	12	14
0	621							
2	550	525			Region of			
4	484	470	468			Soft Spot		
6	484	471	464	470			Formation	
8	484	471	464	466	473			
10	484	471	464	464	468	473		
12	484	472	464	464	466	470	471	
14	484	472	464	464	464	467	471	470
16	484	472	464	464	464	465	469	472
18	484	472	464	464	464	464	467	468
20	484	472	464	464	464	464	465	468

The perforated bullet pan should also have a handle with which you can pick it up and carry it. (Of course, use a potholder when removing the bullet carrier from the oven!) A second necessary device is a pot that is large enough to accept this bullet carrier pan. Fill this second pot with sufficient cold water (ice water is ideal) to cover the bullets fully.

Let the unlubricated bullets stand in an oven at the desired temperature for thirty minutes or longer. Remove the bullets and immediately (sooner is better—instantly would be ideal!) quench the batch in cold water. After you have fully submerged all the bullets, you should repeatedly agitate the carrier pan by lifting and lowering it a few inches at a time and at a reasonably fast rate. You are thereby keeping the coolest possible water in contact with the bullets. Do not remove quenched bullets too soon. Lead is not a particularly good heat conductor. Allow a slow count of five for the water to cool the bullets to the core. Lubricate the hardened bullets after thoroughly drying.

Depending upon the size and shape of your bullets, other methods might work adequately. The goal is to heat each bullet thoroughly and to then cool it as rapidly and uniformly as is feasible. The harder you want to make a bullet, the hotter you must heat it (higher oven temperature) and the faster you must cool it (lower water temperature).

This custom, 3-cavity mold produces 525-grain full-wadcutter bullets for the 454 Casull. The bullet caster who is willing to pay for a custom mold is hardly constrained, other than by imagination.

Commercially heat-treated bullets are widely offered. These can provide serious performance for hunting dangerous game.

Sizing heat-treated bullets will return the surface to pre-heat-treating hardness, or nearly so! The same deformational softening occurs when you shoot heat-treated bullets. However, deformation-related softening occurs over a period of several minutes, so this is not a problem during firing.

After quenching, heat-treated bullets continue to harden for several days. The duration of the continued hardening depends upon the alloy, impurities, heating time, cooling rate, and subsequent storage temperature. Generally, the bullets will be almost fully hardened after about eight hours, but full hardening can take much longer.

Depending upon the alloy you use and the quality of your heat-treating operation, oven hardening can harden bullets to between about two times and about three times the as-cast hardness. With the correct heat treating, bullets of a proper alloy (up to about 3 percent antimony) will be substantially harder than bullets simply cast from the hardest feasible alloy of bullet metal.

If you use a heat-treatable alloy (any bullet metal containing antimony and a trace of arsenic), all cast bullets are hardened to some degree through the process of heat treating. The determining characteristic of this natural hardening is the cooling rate. Bullets cool very slowly in the mold and moderately fast when removed from the mold. We can create the hardest possible cast bullets by dumping the bullet from the mold directly into ice water immediately after cutting the sprue. When done as soon as possible, the bullet core is still molten when the bullet hits the water.

Some commercial bullet casting companies use this method with great success. However, for those of us who cast bullets by hand, this method is inconsistent because we cannot easily dump all the bullets from the mold and into the water when the bullet temperature is the same. This method is also hazardous. We must not ignore the potential of getting water in the lead pot—which is extremely dangerous. Finally, in order to use this method to good effect, we must cast the bullets at almost exactly the needed diameter to minimize the softening due to sizing.

After casting, bullets made of a heat-treatable alloy will spontaneously harden after casting over a period of several months. Additional hardening occurs whether or not bullets are deliberately heat treated in a separate step. However, when stored at room temperature, heat-treated bullets eventually will begin to soften spontaneously and progressively.

After about five years (perhaps sooner) and if stored at room temperature, a deliberately heat-treated bullet will be about 20 percent harder than if the bullet had not been heat treated. However, heat-treated bullets will maintain essentially full hardness for many years if stored in a home freezer. When kept at minus 20 degrees F, heat-treated cast bullets will maintain practically full hardness for many decades.

Beginning on page 60 of the January 1995 issue of *Precision Shooting Magazine,* my late friend Mr. Roger Johnston explored bullet heat-treating in some detail. I highly recommend his excellent article for detailed information on this subject.

BULLET MAKING—
PAPER PATCHED BULLETS

Buffalo hunters and target shooters of the 1800s often used paper-patched bullets. This design includes a cast or swaged lead-alloy bullet with a cylindrical shank portion and, usually, a slightly hollow base. Specially treated and sized paper is wrapped around the bullet shank and folded over a flat base or into a concave base. Paper patched bullets are still in use. Molds and special paper are commercially available. Paper-patched bullets were once very popular and are still in use because these bullets can work amazingly well.

Originally, paper-patched bullets were used because patching eliminated barrel leading and reduced propellant fouling, which was a significant issue when blackpowder was the only option. Shooters soon learned that paper-patched bullets also offered distinct accuracy and long-range trajectory advantages.

A paper-patched bullet is far more aerodynamic than an otherwise similar grooved and greased bullet. Firing stresses are also less apt to deform such a bullet asymmetrically. Finally, these bullets can achieve extremely high velocities without creating barrel leading. Modern shooters have exceeded 3,000 fps with smokeless loads using paper-patched bullets, with zero metallic barrel fouling—a feat that no lead or jacketed bullet can ever match.

For blackpowder shooters, paper-patched bullets can deliver more energy to long distance targets and shoot flatter, while providing extended shot strings without the necessity of frequent bore cleaning. This was something that buffalo-market hunters appreciated. Because it is less susceptible to fouling, this design can provide superior accuracy.

Paper-patch-bullet molds are available from various makers. Custom molds are available in almost any imaginable length and nose profile. These often include very heavy spitzer designs. One must cast these bullets appropriately smaller than the bore's diameter to compensate for patch thickness, minus patch compression in the loaded round. Paper-patched bullets do not require sizing, provided the mold size is correct and both the alloy composition and the casting temperature are correct.

As a general rule, for blackpowder cartridge loading, use a soft bullet that is up to about 0.009 inch smaller than bore diameter and wrap either two or three layers of patching so that the final diameter is about 0.002- to 0.004 inch smaller than the groove diameter. Adjust the final diameter by using a thicker or thinner paper or by sizing the bullet core differently.

When chambered, the majority of the bullet extends into the rifling, with the paper patch pinched between the land tops. Upon firing, the bullet obturates to seal the bore and to engage the rifling, but it will ride over the fouling (which is heaviest in the throat area). This swelling locks the core into the jacket and centers the bullet in the bore.

For use with smokeless powder, the shank portion of the bullet should be between about 0.001 inch and 0.002 inch smaller than the groove diameter. Alloy hardness should be less than one Bh point for each 1,500 psi of peak chamber pressure. The wrapped diameter will be anywhere from the groove diameter up to several-thousandths inch greater than the groove diameter. Upon firing, the core will obturate but relatively more slowly than with a blackpowder load. Due to this relative slow core expansion, it is generally more difficult to obtain good results with smokeless powder when using paper-patched bullets.

Optimum paper patches are made from 100 percent rag paper. Yesteryear Armory and Supply has recently offered precut and treated paper patches for 40- and 45-caliber guns. Handloaders can easily make patches from any high-quality, thin rag paper.

The basic process involves wrapping the bullet shank with the needed number of wraps of paper of the correct thickness to achieve the desired final diameter. Leave an excess length of paper extending over the bullet base. The paper should extend only slightly more than one-half of the bullet diameter. Fold this material against the flat or concave bullet base. Then dip it in hot wax to seal the paper in place. This process sounds a bit daunting, but it is actually rather easy to master.

Our forebearers used to do this entire process in the field, both when hunting and at the target range. For a taste of nostalgia and for surprisingly good results, I encourage interested shooters to try paper-patched bullets.

BULLET MAKING—SWAGED BULLETS

Bullet swaging involves using pressure to form cold bullet metal into a specific shape. This step begins with swaging a lead-alloy wire to the proper diameter and then cutting that wire to the proper length. This cylinder of bullet metal is then converted into a finished bullet by swaging to a final shape in a forming die. Rolling such a

The 38-55 WCF is an ideal candidate for use with cast bullets. While this circa 1883 chambering works OK with jacketed bullets, it was designed for paper-patched bullets. With modern cases, as offered by Starline, it can deliver impressive performance, and it can be equally fun with light loads using relatively soft cast bullets. The variation in case length is significant, as shown here. Uniquely, until Starline offered its thinner-necked and correct-length case (at left), it was never possible to load any conventional bullet of the correct diameter in any standard 38-55 case to create a round that would chamber correctly in a standard chamber. As noted, the 38-55 was designed for paper-patched bullets, and those are always undersized. Therefore, historically, the only way to get maximum accuracy from the 38-55 was to use paper-patched bullets, and that required either casting or swaging. Manson now offers a custom reamer that is designed to give a benchrest-quality chamber using the new thin-necked, 2 1/8-inch-long Starline case.

bullet between special rollers is the preferred method of creating lube grooves or a crimping groove. You could also swage such a core to the correct finished size and shape, to make a paper patch bullet. Respectively, this would be a finished bullet or a ready-to-wrap bullet.

Often, however, a bullet swagerer inserts the lead-alloy cylinder into a commercially produced, semi-finished, gilding-metal jacket. Additional processing involves swaging-up the core so that it stretches the jacket. This is necessary because this is the only way to maintain an intimate contact bond between the elastic bullet jacket and the ductile core, which is necessary for accuracy.

After the various shape-forming steps to create the desired nose and base contours, the bullet is final sized to a slightly smaller outside diameter. Alternatively, shape forming and final sizing are done in one operation.

The tools and materials for swaging jacketed bullets are expensive as are the tools required to produce quality jackets. Even the most dedicated shooter would have a hard time justifying taking up that hobby. Further, the best standard and custom commercial bullets offer a level of quality that would be difficult or impossible for any hobbyist to match. Nevertheless, swaging does have a certain appeal to those interested in doing it for themselves or in doing as much of it as is feasible for themselves. These are the only shooters generally interested in bullet swaging.

However, the tools and supplies are available. Those willing to invest the price of a very good rifle can set themselves up in the bullet swaging business. We must note that each new style of bullet that one wants to swage requires a considerable additional investment for dies. Nevertheless, just as with casting, swaging offers considerable latitude in bullet design. Custom forming dies are available. If you simply must have a 300-grain 30-caliber spitzer boattail to shoot from your 1-in-6-inch twist, custom-barrel, super-varmint-special rifle, swaging is the only game in town.

Swaging tools are well represented on the Internet, and the fine folks at Corbin Manufacturing & Supply, Inc., among others, are always willing to offer advice and references.

Field-testing a Marlin 38-55 Cowboy Action rifle: Note the high-magnification Trijicon scope and quality rests. With good loads, this gun routinely shoots sub-MOA. Without proper test equipment, it is impossible to evaluate the intrinsic accuracy of various loads in any gun. With any gun having a two-piece stock, the bag technique is unusually critical. The method shown is the best I have found for testing traditional lever-action guns. Keep the front rest near the front of the forearm, apply only rearward pressure with each hand, and either apply as little cheek pressure as is possible or diligently apply the same cheek pressure for each shot.

SOURCES FOR SPECIALTY TOOLS REFERENCED IN THIS CHAPTER:

Corbin Manufacturing & Supply, Inc
P.O. Box 2659
White City, Oregon 97503
Telephone: 541-826-5211
www.corbins.com
sales@corbins.com

Yesteryear Armory and Supply
P.O. Box 408
Carthage, TN 37030

SSRJ (Single Shot Rifle Journal)
10608 Summer Mountain Court
Knoxville, TN 37922
www.assra.com

BULLET CASTING

CHAPTER 16

INTRODUCTION

The process of bullet casting and its associated equipment has changed little over the centuries. Perhaps the most significant change is that, while our ancestors had to use fire to heat the bullet metal, we can now use an electric element. Another relatively recent improvement toward easing this operation is the addition of insulating wood handles to mold blocks. We now have accurate and affordable thermometers to report the melt temperature, and we can buy bullet metal alloys of specific compositions. Finally, modern bullet sizing and lubricating equipment is more sophisticated than what was readily available to the individual as recently as one century ago. However, none of these advancements in any way alters these basic processes. Casting is done as follows:

- Heat the bullet metal to proper temperature
- Transfer the melted alloy into a heated mold (the process heats the mold; the caster simply returns the first few, imperfect bullets to the melt)
- Wait for the casting to cool sufficiently to solidify
- Cut off the sprue (protrusion from alloy filling the conduit into the mold)
- Open mold and dump bullet

Sizing and lubricating is usually done as follows:

- Force bullet into a die of specific internal diameter
- Inject lubricant into bullet grooves via hydraulic pressure
- Push sized and lubed bullet out of sizer

For the home bullet caster, few functional alternatives are available for the casting operation, but sizing and lubing can involve several alternative approaches. Nevertheless, the goals are always the same—create a solid casting of the bullet metal that is the proper shape and size and fill the grease grooves with lubricant (a solid, waxy material).

I could have included the discussion of bullet heat treating and the associated equipment in this chapter, rather than in the preceding chapter, but such equipment is rather limited and is generally homemade, so I covered that discussion in chapter 15.

BULLET CASTING—BASIC EQUIPMENT

One can spend a little or a lot on basic casting equipment. The Lee Pro-20 bottom-pour lead pot is quite affordable. For a shooter who might only need to cast a few thousand bullets annually, this unit is a fine choice. For those interested in a top-of-the-line unit, RCBS offers a fine bottom-pour lead pot that will last a lifetime, even for the most serious home bullet caster.

An alternative, superior but slower, method is the bottom-draw ladle, as produced by Rowell. This tool has several advantages. When using the Rowel Ladle, hold the mold over the lead pot and pour the alloy from the ladle into the mold until it overflows—when the melt puddle over the sprue stops flowing or drawing into the mold, the mold is full. Then refill the ladle and let that rest in the lead pot. Later, return the solidified sprue cut-off to the lead pot.

While it is possible to fill a mold similarly using a bottom-pour pot, the excess melt creates a mess and that method is a bit more likely to result in the spilled melt causing a hazard. A bottom-draw ladle introduces less air into the mold and therefore is less apt to result in bullets with significant cavities or porosity. With a bottom-pour pot, the flow rate depends upon how full the pot is; with the ladle, the flow rate is always the same.

The bottom-draw ladle design keeps trash out of the alloy stream. The ladle method allows the use of a conventional (non-bottom-pour) lead pot to achieve this goal. These lead pots are usually a bit less expensive. Bill Ferguson offers bottom-pour ladles in various sizes.

Molds are commonly available in iron alloy, aluminum alloy, and copper alloy (brass). Each alloy has advantages. Aluminum blocks are a bit easier to use, a characteristic that many novice bullet casters appreciate. Iron blocks are somewhat more robust and are less susceptible to damage from handling and hard use but do require more casting skill. Brass is slightly less robust but heats far more uniformly. You can find lead alloy sources on the Internet.

Lee Precision offers a wide variety of high-quality bullet casting equipment.

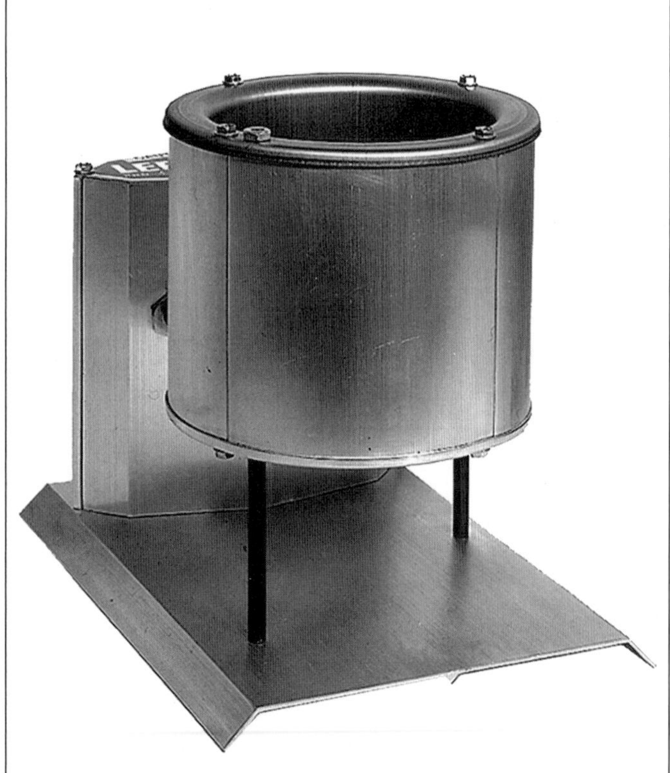

The modern lead pot uses an electric element. This Lee Precision model is intended for use with a ladle, a method that many serious bullet casters prefer.

The variety of available commercial molds is staggering. Custom molds are available in any feasible design. Refer to the Internet for active makers.

The pertinent difference between iron and aluminum bullet casting molds revolves around one fact. Users can preheat aluminum molds by simply positioning one corner of the closed mold blocks into the molten bullet metal for a couple of minutes; conversely, the only safe way to bring the iron mold blocks up to the proper casting temperature is to cast bullets. This process requires a few minutes, and those bullets cast before the mold is properly heated are unusable—carefully return all such bullets to the lead pot.

A thermometer is a good addition to any casting kit. You will discover other useful casting accessories, but this covers the basics required to get the bullet metal into the proper condition for casting and into the mold. This is a place to start. You can produce potentially useful bullets with no additional accouterments.

For those who simply want to cast bullets from available lead alloy scrap, such as wheel weights, a mold that casts a bullet similar in style and weight to an original factory round-nose, flat point, or semiwadcutter is always a good choice. Such molds are available from Lee Precision, RCBS, Saeco, and others. Generally, spitzer-style (sharply pointed) cast bullets are difficult to cast, harder to find accurate loads with, and almost certain to perform inadequately on game.

By using a bullet mold that casts a bullet of a typical weight for the application, the handloader can usually make bullets that shoot very accurately and that do so without generating significant barrel leading. As covered in the previous chapter, simply choose the appropriate propellant and velocity level that is necessary to match the hardness of the bullet to the pressure generated by the load.

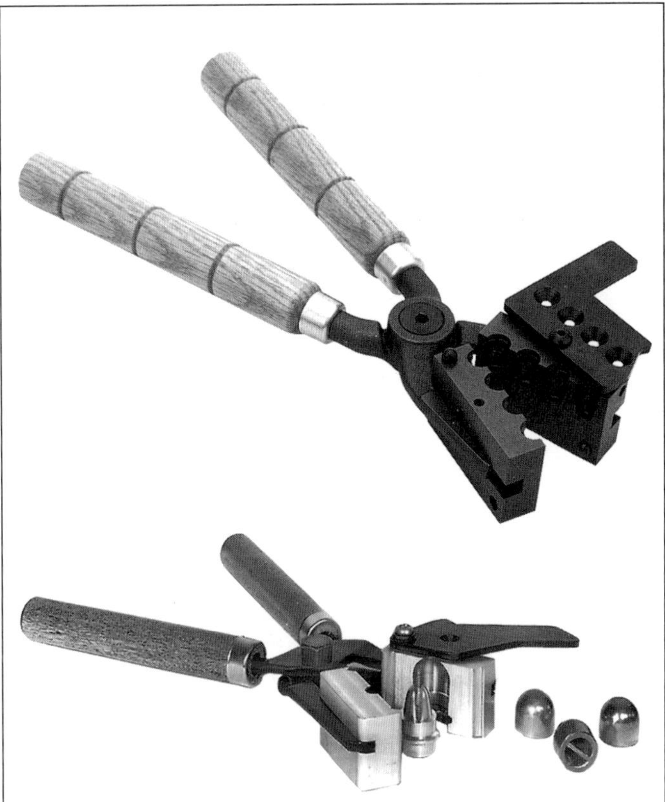

The Saeco mold (top) is an extremely robust, high-precision tool that appeals to experienced, high-volume bullet casters. The Lee Precision mold (bottom) uses aluminum for the mold cavities. Aluminum has the advantage of being easy to preheat. Such molds are generally easy to learn to use and are a good choice for economy-minded bullet casters.

If you are using a high-power chambering and must load to somewhat less pressure to avoid exceeding the typical 2,200 fps upper velocity limit for gas-checked cast bullets, choose a heavy-for-the-caliber cast bullet. In this way, you retain downrange punch despite the relatively limited muzzle velocity.

For many years, I cast usable bullets without using a lead thermometer. However, I never knew from one session to the next exactly how to set the heater control on the lead pot. Now I know what temperature works for each mold and alloy. For this and other reasons, no bullet caster should do without a casting thermometer.

The secret here is to use an accurate bullet-hardness tester. The Saeco hardness tester is a quality tool, useful for testing the hardness of any cast bullet. When you switch to a different bullet metal, test the hardness of a few bullets (always test on the end opposite the sprue), then adjust the alloy as needed (soften or harden it) to match the hardness that has proven to work well with your established load. Refer to chapter 15. This makes it easy to use inexpensive scrap alloys to make useful bullets.

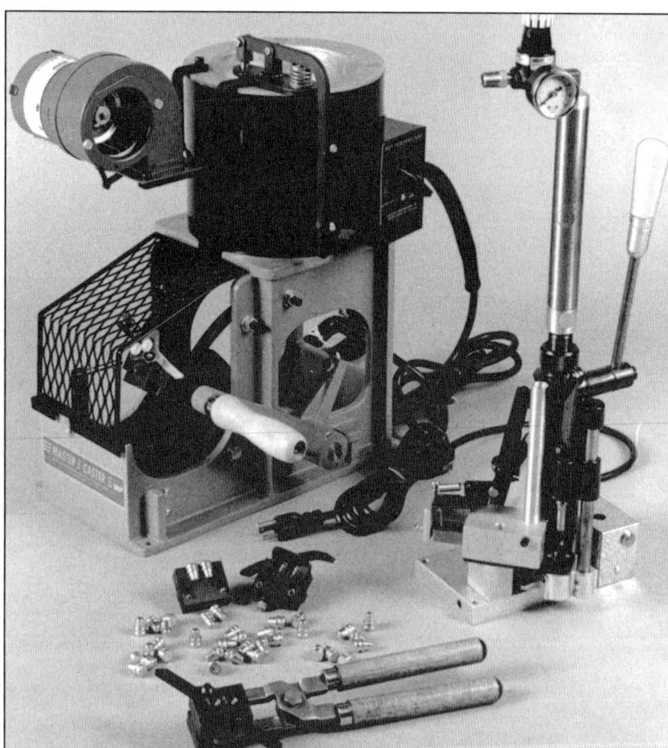

The Magma Master Caster (left) and the Magma accessorized Star Sizer (right) allow hobbyists to produce finished, top-quality bullets at an overall rate of nearly 600 per hour and to do so without breaking a sweat.

The casting process is pure simplicity. Heat the bullet metal to the proper temperature, and then pour the molten bullet metal into a bullet mold until the mold overflows. Modern molds include a cover plate (called a sprue plate) with a fill hole. Pour the alloy through that hole and fill the cavity until a large dollop of the bullet metal accumulates on the cover plate—more is better.

When the bullet has cooled sufficiently so that the perimeter has fully solidified, tap the cover plate to break the sprue and rotate the plate out of the way. Open the mold handles to separate the mold block halves, then dump the bullet free of the mold halves, either onto a soft cloth or into your quench water. It is helpful to use a short section of a broom handle to tap the sprue cover open and then to rap on the hinge of the handles, as required, to rattle the bullet free of the molds. The difficulties are in the details:

- What is the proper melt temperature?
- How fast should you pour the melt into thc mold?
- How much excess alloy should you pour on top of the sprue plate?
- How long does it take the bullet to solidify sufficiently so that you can dump it from the mold without damaging it?
- How long should you wait to allow the mold blocks to cool before filling the mold for the next bullet?

I can only offer the most basic of guidelines here. If the alloy fills the properly warmed-up mold fully and forms good, sharp corners on the bullets, it is hot enough. Hotter than necessary is undesirable. Such bullets will have a frosted surface, and while some degree of frosting is usually OK, less is usually better. The sprue plate should have sufficient excess alloy covering it so that the bullet does not exhibit a hollow cavity or significant porosity at the sprue-cut-off surface. You should pour the melt as fast as the hole in the sprue plate will allow, without an undue amount of melt running off the plate. If, as you cut the sprue, the sprue plate wipes lead across the top of the mold blocks, you must allow the casting more time to solidify.

Applying a controlled amount of water to the sprue puddle is a handy way to cool the sprue. This also allows for faster bullet dumping into the water (to provide a Bh between about 16 and about 20 with a typical wheel weight alloy), or to simply speed production. As soon as the sprue puddle begins to solidify, turn the mold over and place the sprue mound lightly against the top of a wet sponge and hold it there for about one to three seconds. Alternatively, with a misting water bottle, simply spray the sprue area one or more times with a very fine mist spray (one spray is usually sufficient).

If the bullets begin to exhibit a frosted surface appearance, you should allow the mold to cool longer before refilling it, or you should reduce the alloy melt temperature (the latter is the preferable choice, when possible). When casting particularly heavy bullets and when using multicavity molds, this will not work well; the best solution is to cool the top of the mold with a wet sponge or a mist of water. It is helpful to use more than one mold, allowing one or more to cool in turn.

By trial and error, almost anyone can learn to cast good bullets in a matter of hours. However, the operator must have a good understanding of the basic principles. The best time to get at least some of that understanding is before starting. Becoming an expert bullet caster might take years, decades, or a lifetime and some of us might never reach that lofty pinnacle, but most of us can become sufficiently proficient to cast perfectly useful bullets. A good source of advanced bullet casting information is the Cast Bullet Association. Interested readers with Internet access might want to visit www.castbulletassoc.org.

Those interested in casting large numbers of high-quality bullets in one afternoon should consider the Master Caster from the Magma Engineering Company. This machine is reasonably affordable and offers production rates of about 600 bullets per hour. In only a few hours each week, this unit, combined with the Magma accessorized Star Sizer, allows even the most dedicated of shooters to cast, size, and lube more bullets than they could ever shoot. (See picture on page 372.) This tool serves small clubs and shooting teams well. However, the most significant advantage of using such a tool is not speed; rather, it is the consistency of the bullets produced.

When it only takes a few seconds to cast a bullet, the bulletmaker can be very critical about rejecting bullets of questionable appearance or those that do not weigh close to the normal weight, and he can do so painlessly. These tools make it easier to achieve one important thing: consistent bullet quality.

BULLET CASTING—KEEPING IT CLEAN

Cover the melt with about one-quarter inch of unscented clay-based kitty litter (not the fancy, expensive stuff!). This prevents oxidation, thereby keeping the alloy fluxed. It also provides a safety cushion when you reintroduce cut-off sprues and rejected bullets into the melt.

Change this covering at the beginning of each session. As soon as the alloy melts, spoon out most of the black, dusty, used material. Then cover the melt with a new layer of granular kitty litter. Then vigorously stir the melt for a few seconds to flux it. Fluxing is purification through removal of oxygen—the kitty litter oxidizes (burns) and thereby removes (scavenges) oxygen from oxidized molecules within the melt.

The flux causes no problems when using either a bottom-pour pot or a bottom-draw ladle. With the former, the floating litter stays on top of the melt. For the latter, merely slide the ladle against the off side of the pot, point the pour spout upward, and push the rear portion of the ladle down into the melt. This method excludes the floating kitty litter from entering the ladle as it fills with alloy. While some litter might enter the ladle, that material floats and does not contribute to the pour, which comes from the bottom of the pool in the ladle.

As with sorting by weight (next section), it is entirely possible to cast perfectly useful plinking-class bullets without ever thinking about fluxing the melt. But, when accuracy matters, fluxing is critical.

BULLET CASTING—SORTING

Finding faulty cast bullets (a relatively high percentage) and faulty swaged bullets (a very low percentage) is a two-fold operation. First, a visual examination will disclose bullets that are obviously faulty to any given degree. For example, with the optical assistance of a loupe, the caster might separate bullets into three categories:

- Visually perfect, perhaps for use in the most serious of target shooting applications
- Visually almost perfect, for general plinking use
- Visually imperfect, for remelting

The degree of perfection and the number of possible categories and uses for the sorted bullets is a matter for each craftsman to decide. For all but the most demanding of uses, it is very easy to overdo this. Providing a bullet does not contain a significant void, if it looks good, it will shoot well enough for almost any use, even if it does not look perfect.

The second step is to sort bullets by weight to find those with significant voids. The size of a void that is apt to alter accuracy significantly depends upon the bullet weight and design, the distance at which you intend to shoot, and where the void is located. Voids near the bullet axis are least harmful and those near the perimeter are most harmful. For progressively greater target distances, any given flaw will influence accuracy greater. The following table might provide useful guidance, but I do not intend these data to represent a hard and fast rule. Each caster will have to determine what level of perfection is adequate for his needs.

Regardless of the visual appearance, return all bullets that are too light to meet your criteria to the lead pot. Depending upon the tightness of the sorting criteria, this practice will progressively reduce the occurrence of fliers. Because all that is usually required is to find any too-light bullets, this requires very little time and is certainly worthwhile. So long as the melt and mold temperature remains relatively constant, too heavy bullets can only occur when you did not properly close the mold block, which usually occurs only when some sort of debris interposes the block halves. Usually, such a situation is obvious during the casting process and this often is a one-time occurrence.

Even when we use the best techniques and equipment, about 10 percent of our cast bullets will look perfect but will contain a significant void. Generally, both tiny bullets and very large bullets are harder to cast perfectly. Mold design matters—some designs cast near-perfect bullets easily, others not so easily, and some are practically impossible to use.

Weigh a few randomly chosen sample bullets from the batch to determine the maximum nominal bullet weight. With a beam balance, set the scale at the maximum, minus your desired deviation threshold (or as suggested in the table). Bullets that do not immediately lift the beam pointer above the centerline are suspect. In a few seconds, the beam will settle sufficiently to allow either selection or rejection, as appropriate. A digital scale makes this process far faster and easier, especially when working with particularly heavy bullets.

Suggested Sorting Criteria for Cast and Swaged Bullets
(+/– Grains from Nominal Average Bullet Weight)

		Bullet Weight (grains)				
Application		<100	100–200	200–300	300–400	>400
	Plinking	1	1½	2	3	4
	Hunting	¾	1⅛	1½	2¼	3
Target Distance	Short	½	¾	1	1½	2
	Long	¼	⅜	½	¾	

Each handloader must decide what level of precision he needs. As we gain expertise, we tend to become more critical of bullets used in our most serious applications and less concerned otherwise.

BULLET CASTING—LUBRICATING AND SIZING

Here I must mention that sizing a cast bullet also softens the bullet. Sizing can also distort the bullet base, thereby destroying accuracy potential. If bullets come out of the mold more than about 0.002 inch larger than necessary—generally, groove diameter to 0.001 inch larger—consider adjusting the alloy or casting temperature, as required, to get the bullets to cast closer to groove diameter. A reduction of the tin and antimony content will allow the bullet to shrink more as it cools; also, casting at a higher temperature will (usually) result in smaller as-cast bullets.

Lubrication and sizing runs the gamut. If as-cast bullets are close to the proper diameter, which is typically from the barrel groove diameter to about 0.001 inch larger, the caster can lubricate and use the bullets as cast. For this method, Lee Liquid Alox bullet lube works very well.

Another handy method is to stand the bullets in a shallow pan. Melt the necessary amount of a favorite bullet lube and add that to the pan. After the lube cools fully, punch the bullets individually out of the sheet of lube. This will leave the lube in the grease grooves.

Lee Precision offers die bodies and matching rams to allow easy sizing of cast bullets using any conventional reloading press. This method works best when using Lee Liquid Alox lube, but it also works with pan-lubed bullets.

The Saeco Lubrisizer is the only truly heavy-duty bullet-sizing tool available to hobbyists. It is the preferred choice of those interested in working with two-diameter bullets (nose riders) and for those who intend to size particularly large bullets and any bullet cast of a linotype or a similar alloy.

Bullets cast to fit the gun properly without sizing are generally more accurate. Sizing distorts and softens cast bullets. However, in some instances, it is infeasible to cast bullets at proper diameter; in those instances, sizing is necessary.

Handloaders can size bullets very inexpensively using the Lee Press-Mounted Lube and Sizing Kit. This unit is very fast to operate and the results are most impressive. The only limitation is that standard bullet

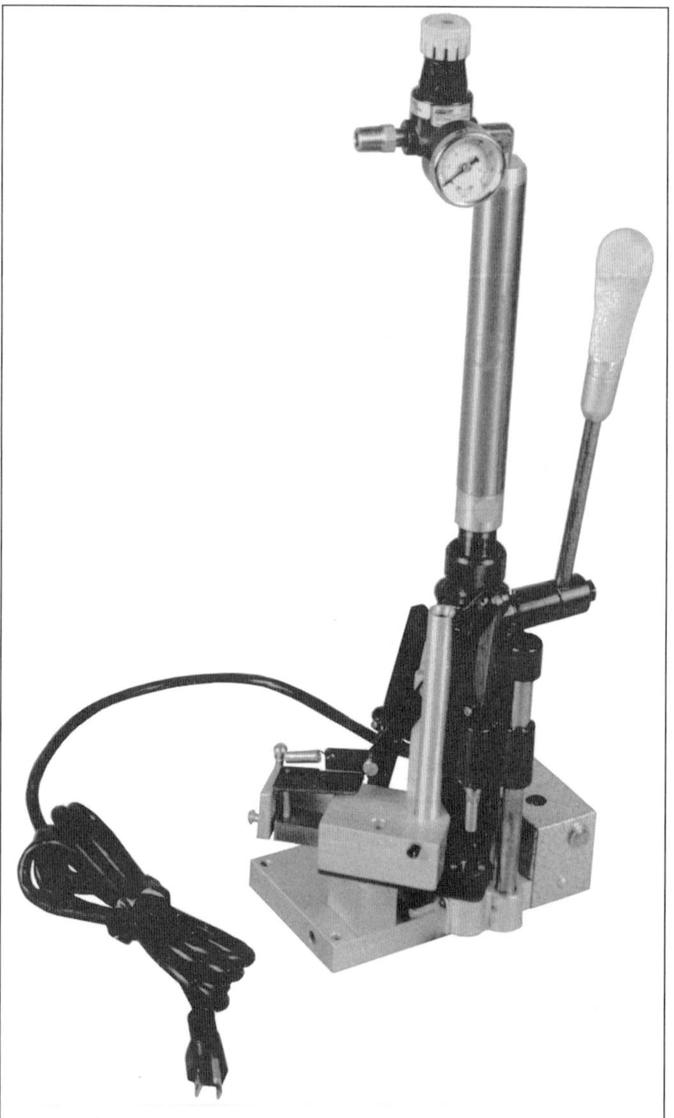

With a few auxiliary hookups (compressed air and electricity), the Magma accessorized Star Lubrisizer becomes a high-volume cast-bullet finishing machine; many large-scale casting houses use this very combination.

After pulling a bullet (Lyman 458125) from a loaded round, I shortened the butt end to create a template for a similar but significantly shorter bullet. In that process, I exposed a significant cavity. This is why we cull lighter-than-normal cast bullets from use in our most serious loads.

lubes are harder to use. With plain-based bullets, you can use the above-mentioned pan-lube method before the sizing step; with gas checked bullets this is best done after sizing. Alternatively, you can use liquid Alox lube, which does a fine job but it leaves the bullets a bit messy to handle.

Standard lubricator sizers, available from RCBS and Saeco, are easy to use. Each does a fine job of properly lubricating and sizing bullets. These units provide a means of attaching a gas check to the base of bullets designed to accept a gas check. Copper gas checks allow increased velocity, help reduce leading, and can improve accuracy.

The ultimate manual lubricator, sizer, and gas checker is the Star Machine Works Auto Lubricator and Sizer. Unlike the aforementioned units, the Star uses a push-through mechanism and is ideal for bullets sized to a single shank diameter. However, many bullets used in target rifles include a bore-riding nose section. With such bullets, it is necessary to size at one diameter on the nose and at a larger diameter on the shank. The Star will not properly size such bullets.

Conversely, when sizing single-diameter bullets, the Star is ideal. All that is necessary is to place a bullet in the top of the sizing die and to stroke the handle. The sized and lubricated bullet falls out the bottom—into a padded container located under the unit. Raise the handle, position a new bullet under the ram, and repeat the process. Every stroke yields a sized and lubed bullet, and you only have to handle each bullet once.

The Magma Star Helper automatically feeds and aligns bullets under the ram with each handle stroke. The operator must only stroke the handle, fill the feed tube—which he can do with one hand while articulating the handle with the other hand—and periodically turn the lube reservoir handle (to keep enough pre-feed lube pressure in the reservoir to assure proper lubing). The sizing of plain-based bullets is amazingly fast.

Gas checked bullets take longer. You must place a gas check on the ram before placing the bullet on the base of the bullet that is under the ram, during the proper portion of the cycle. This causes little interruption. For those serious about casting a mountain of bullets at home, a Magma accessorized Star sizer is the ideal tool.

For sizing two-diameter bullets, or for bumping up the diameter of the nose-riding section of a two-diameter bullet, the Saeco lubrisizer is the best available tool. To bump up a bullet, simply insert it fully into the die and then lean on the tool handle, as necessary to slightly swell the bore-riding section of the bullet nose. I do not recommend this practice with other lubrisizers.

For the utmost in precision with two-diameter bullets, begin with a bore-diameter die and a flat punch. Drive the bullet nose into the die, to size only the bore riding section, before lifting the handle, to push the bullet back up and out of the sizing die. After all bullets in the batch are nose sized, install the correct sizer and nose punch to work the bullet shank. If you must first bump up the nose-riding section, reverse the sequence.

All lubricator sizers use stick lubes, which are available from many suppliers. Find one that you like; I cannot possibly make any specific recommendation. The one that works best for your purpose might not work best for the next person. This involves too many variables. Harder lubes are preferable for smokeless loads. Bullets lubed with these are cleaner to handle. Also, these lubes are not apt to melt in a loaded round that might get particularly warm, as when the cartridge is exposed to the sun. (Note that the temperature of ammunition left in the desert sun in metal ammo cans or see-through plastic boxes can easily exceed 160° F!) Melted lube can infiltrate the propellant. This can alter ballistics or even kill the primer!

Hard lubes require heating. Thermostatically controlled electric units that bolt under the lubricator sizer are easily adjusted, as needed, to heat the sizer to the proper temperature for any lube. Judicious use of a hair dryer or a propane torch from time to time during your lubrisizing operation can provide a similar effect at low cost.

Finally, I should note that special blackpowder-specific lubes are available. Such lubes offer distinct advantages for those shooting blackpowder metallic cartridges.

SOURCES FOR SPECIALTY TOOLS REFERENCED IN THIS CHAPTER:

Bill Ferguson
PO Box 1238
Sierra Vista, AZ 85636
Telephone: 520-458-5321

Old West Bullet Molds
1175 17¼ Road
Fruita, CO 81521
Telephone: 970-858-1449

Regardless of the ballistics software used, a chronograph is necessary to obtain the needed input data. Even the least expensive units provide indispensable data for those interested in long-range shooting. When targets are beyond about 500 yards and without knowing actual muzzle velocity and ballistic uniformity, long-range shooters cannot predict either the accuracy potential of the load or the correct sight adjustments for long-range zeros.

MORE PICTURES OF TOM KNIGHT'S CUSTOM 45-70 MARLIN

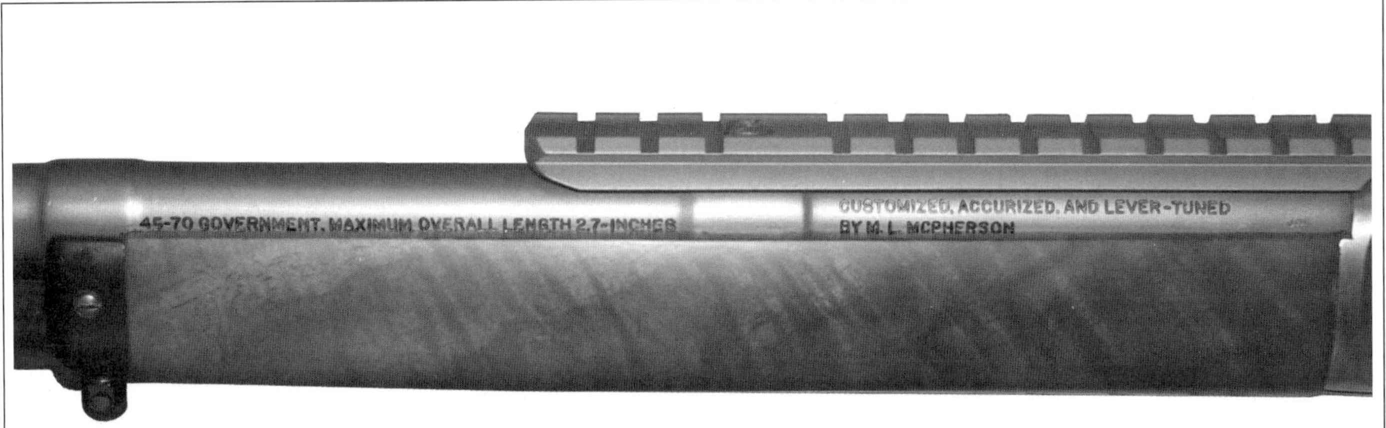

Barrel marking indicates who built this rifle and also that it will handle cartridges up to 2.7 inches. Note that the barrel is smaller between the dovetail locations. Turning most of the barrel to a significantly smaller diameter and skeletonizing the stocks and various action parts allowed me to remove more than 2 pounds from the original weight, making this a very handy hunting rifle.

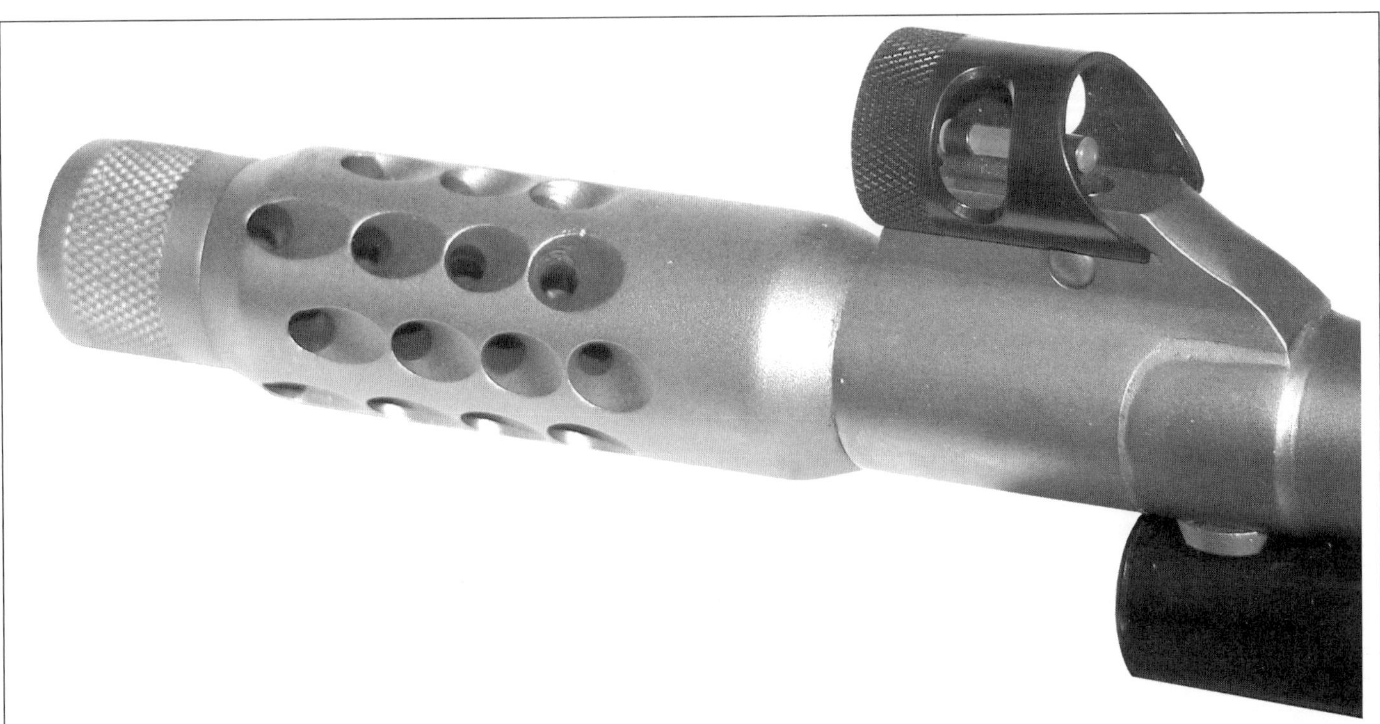

This view shows radically progressive porting of the custom LAW (Lightweight Air Working) muzzle brake. Both the size and the rearward angle of the ports increase with each forward set. This significantly reduces recoil because the jetting propellant gases pull the gun forward. The rocket-nozzle port design significantly reduces noise. We have tested it. No one at or near the shooting line, including the shooter, could tell that the gun is louder with the brake installed—design matters! The knurled portion at the front is a built-in thread protector. (If you want to use the gun without the brake, you will have the thread protector handy.) The LAW brake has other superior design features that allow it to function far better than any other brake on the market.

TROPHIES AND ONCE-IN-A-LIFETIME EXPERIENCES

Joe dropped this 5x6 bull with a perfect shot at 860 yards. This is Joe's third bull and the first that was not a full 6x6.

While this bull, taken in 2006, is not the biggest I have taken in a fair-chase hunt on public lands, this was my most fulfilling hunt because my sons and I all filled our tags. This day I carried this custom 475 Linebaugh Marlin super carbine, but I used my son's 338 Lapua for an 875-yard kill.

Here I am heading out with antlers and a packful of what proved to be excellent meat from the elk that my son (Jody) took in 2006. Elk often inhabit rough country, and this was no exception. We faced a serious climb just to reach the top of the ridge (about 500 feet above us), and then we had about a 1½-mile hike to the rigs.

Three generations of McPherson hunters. While Dad can no longer join us in the hills, he does enjoy the camaraderie of the hunt. This portrait, taken by Sierra (daughter of Jody and Malea), recalls a lifetime of memories. We took these trophies hunting in the same hills where Dad took me on many hunts, starting when I was ten.

THE LOADING PRESS

CHAPTER 17

INTRODUCTION

Throughout this text, I have reviewed various tools that experienced handloaders might want to consider adding to their loading bench. One subject I have not specifically covered is the reloading press. Handloaders can now choose from more than fifty handloading presses; these include:

- Affordable single-stage presses (for simplicity)
- Compound-leverage presses (for rock-crushing leverage)
- Portable presses (for loading in the field)
- Progressive presses (for loading hundreds of rounds of quality ammunition each hour)
- Power driven progressive presses (useful for a small gun club or a shooting team)
- Arbor presses (for loading the most precise ammunition possible, using special dies and special techniques—never use any arbor press for conventional full-length case sizing)

To be comfortable while handloading, most of us need a special area dedicated to our hobby; this can be a small space or a large area, and the related equipment can be either simple or sophisticated (which usually means complicated).

THE LOADING PRESS—SINGLE-STAGE

The common, single-stage handloading press is a simple mechanical device. The dies screw into the press body. The shellholders slip into the ram. A lever actuates the ram—usually through compound linkage. Although handloading presses are simple devices, some types are better than others; design matters.

The ideal single-stage press will have a large opening in the front or at both sides to allow the operator to easily insert and remove cases. It will also be designed and constructed so that under the stress of loading cartridges, the die and ram will remain in alignment. Finally, it will provide ample ram travel and leverage to allow for the loading of any typical sporting cartridge without the need of any undue effort. The ram of some compact presses (and some other models) does not have enough travel to work with longer rifle cartridges. (Several manufacturers offer presses specifically designed to load 50 BMG cartridges—no other sporting cartridge requires such a massive press, and few presses will handle the 50 BMG.)

Many presses include various attachments that allow primer seating and other operations. Excepting the Forster Co-Ax, the built-in primer-seating adapter on any single-stage press is a poor substitute for a good hand-priming tool.

A single-stage press is a good place for any handloader to start, and even the least expensive single-stage is adequate for most handloading tasks. Several manufacturers offer inexpensive but functional beginner presses. Few handloaders will ever give up this basic press, even after obtaining several advanced presses.

THE LOADING PRESS—PROGRESSIVE

Most handloaders started with a single-stage press, and many have stepped up to a progressive unit. While a progressive can add considerably to handloading and shooting enjoyment, these are not necessarily

All these tools and accessories are handy to have when loading, so a bench with plenty of room is useful. However, as long as the system you use provides adequate convenience, it will do. As a college student, I loaded thousands of revolver cartridges with a press mounted on a simple shelf inside a very small closet where I, necessarily, had to store everything.

appropriate for loading ammunition used in all types of shooting. Generally, handloaders can do a better job of loading the largest rifle cartridges when using a single-stage press. Serious handloaders still need a quality, heavy-duty press, such as the Redding UltraMag. Such a press is most useful for case forming and other heavy-duty operations. However, for loading classic handgun cartridges and rifle cartridges up to at least 30-06 size, a progressive press is a joy to own and use.

Several manufacturers offer perfectly useful units, but several stand out from the crowd. Lee prices the LoadMaster affordably. This sophisticated press offers five positions, automatic indexing, automatic case feeding, automatic bullet feeding, and a simple but generally functional primer feeding system.

The Lee LoadMaster does require a bit of patience to set up properly. Further, I cannot recommend this press for those who might be intimidated by sophisticated mechanisms. When using this press, handloaders should limit their primer choice to the CCI brand and then only those CCI primers produced since about 1990. In my experience, these are the only primers that will work dependably, safely, and properly.

The best application for this press is loading conventional pistol and revolver cartridges. However, it does a fine job with rifle cartridges through 30-06 size. But, it will not automatically feed cases or bullets for rifle cartridges. Handloaders who are not afraid to do a bit of tinkering to get this machine working perfectly and who want to load a mountain of handgun ammunition in a hurry will find this press a joy to own and to use. The quick-change removable tool heads and shell plates allow for conversions in about one minute.

Hornady's Lock-n-Load is conceptually on the other side of the aisle. While the basic version of this press does not come with all the bells and whistles offered in the Lee Load Master, it does offer five positions, automatic indexing, automatic priming, and the options of automatic propellant dispensing and automatic case feeding. With all these options implemented, the operator must only feed bullets, work the handle, and keep supplies (cases, primers, and propellant) stocked in the various feed systems.

The Lock-n-Load uses individual quick-change die holders that allow for a rapid cartridge changeover. In total, the only place where this press is lacking in sophistication is the primer feed system. This requires filling and changing the primer tubes every one hundred loads. This is a significant handicap, which dramatically slows the overall production rate. Positive and correct priming is the biggest problem with any progressive press and, although the Hornady system

This handloading cabinet takes up surprisingly little space when closed, yet provides ample storage for the needs of most hobbyist handloaders.

works, filling and changing the tubes reduces productivity. Hornady builds the Lock-n-Load to standards of fit and quality that are astounding. Using this press is a genuine pleasure. A skilled operator can easily turn out top-quality metallic cartridges for practically any typical chambering using the Lock-n-Load.

The Dillon 550B is fully capable of loading quality handgun ammunition. By design, manual shellholder indexing is required. This allows the operator to advance the shellholder at his leisure, which can be beneficial. However, this does add to the opportunity for error. To prevent double charges, always make certain that you turn the shellholder after charging a case. In reality, manual indexing is not much of a handicap. The operator has time to advance the shellholder while bringing a new case to position one. This press is both fast and dependable, but as with the Hornady press, it uses primer tubes, which are a nuisance at best. Dillon now offers an automatic case feeder for this press and an automatic primer tube loading system that dramatically eases and speeds that chore.

Dillon's XL 650 offers five die stations and adds auto-indexing. The fifth die position is a boon. This enables the installation of a propellant level alarm (available from Dillon) without forgoing the separate bullet seating and crimping stages. This alarm produces a piercing audible warning when any case not charged with the proper amount of propellant reaches that position. The auto-indexing feature is most useful when one equips the XL 650 with the optional electric pistol case feeder. With this option, the operator must only work the handle, feed bullets, and keep the basic

Opening the facing doors turns on a fluorescent light and provides ample access to considerable storage within easy reach. The reinforced shelf at standard height provides ample support to a handloading press, even for the most arduous of handloading operations. The next higher shelf supports a press that is not being used (a progressive press in this instance), along with a scale and measure that are located at eye level for easy use. My article in the October 1993 issue of American Rifleman *covered the design and construction of this corner-standing handloading cabinet.*

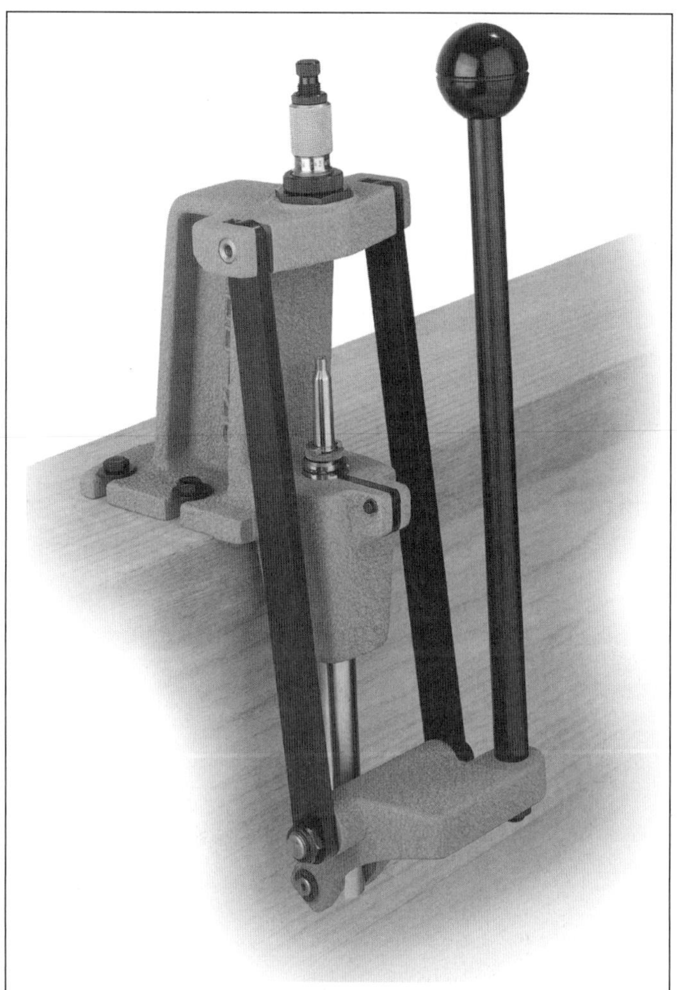

Redding UltraMag is an extremely heavy-duty press of unique design. The connection of the compound linkage between the handle pivot and the top of the press provides alignment advantages—regardless of the amount of stress applied, the die remains aligned with the ram.

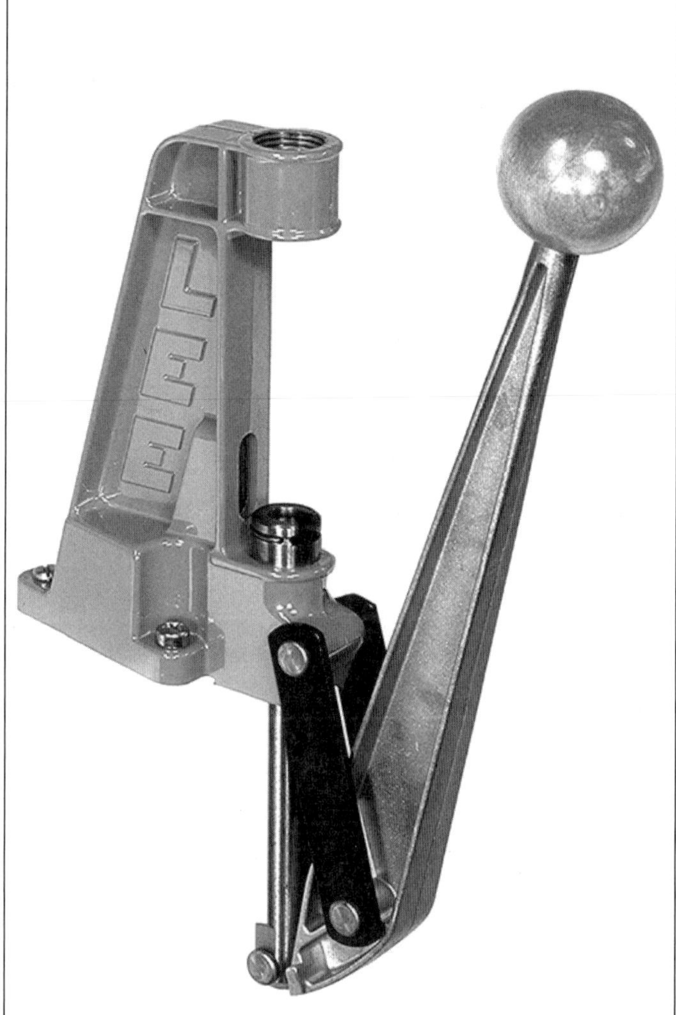

The Lee Precision Reloader press is an affordable option for beginning handloaders. It will produce perfectly good pistol and revolver ammunition. Although it will load rifle ammunition, it is not an ideal choice for that purpose.

supplies stocked. The production rate is most impressive. This press will process most common handgun and rifle cartridges.

The Dillon RL-1050 is an altogether different system. Rather than detail everything the RL 1050 will do, I will just note that it includes eight die stations and automatic case feeding. Additional die stations allow special case processing (for example, swaging out the military primer pocket crimp). With proper conversion kits, this machine will load all common handgun cartridges and 223 and 7.62x39 rifle cartridges. Small-scale ammunition makers often use this press to produce tens of thousands of rounds of high quality ammunition every week. Enough said?

My personal favorite progressive press is the RCBS Pro-2000. This progressive features a die plate that changes four of the five die positions—the propellant measure stays in the press during die changes, which is desirable. This press uses manual indexing but this does not particularly slow the operation or production rate (an auto-indexing feature is now offered as a retrofitable option).

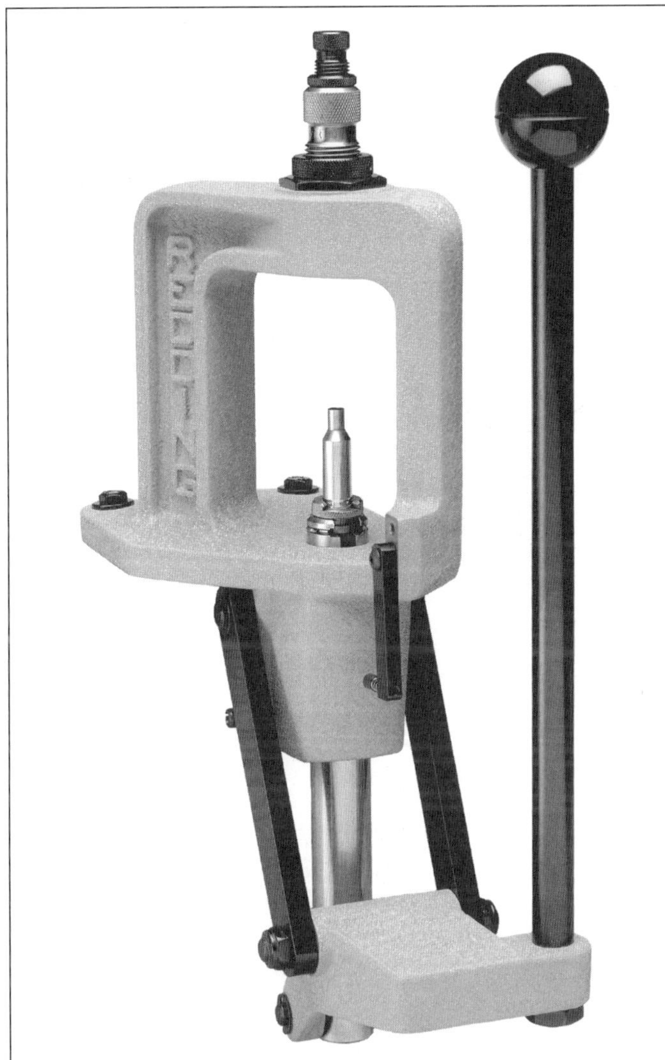

The Redding Big Boss is a massive press. It is most useful for loading unusually large cartridges and for heavy case-forming and bullet-swaging operations.

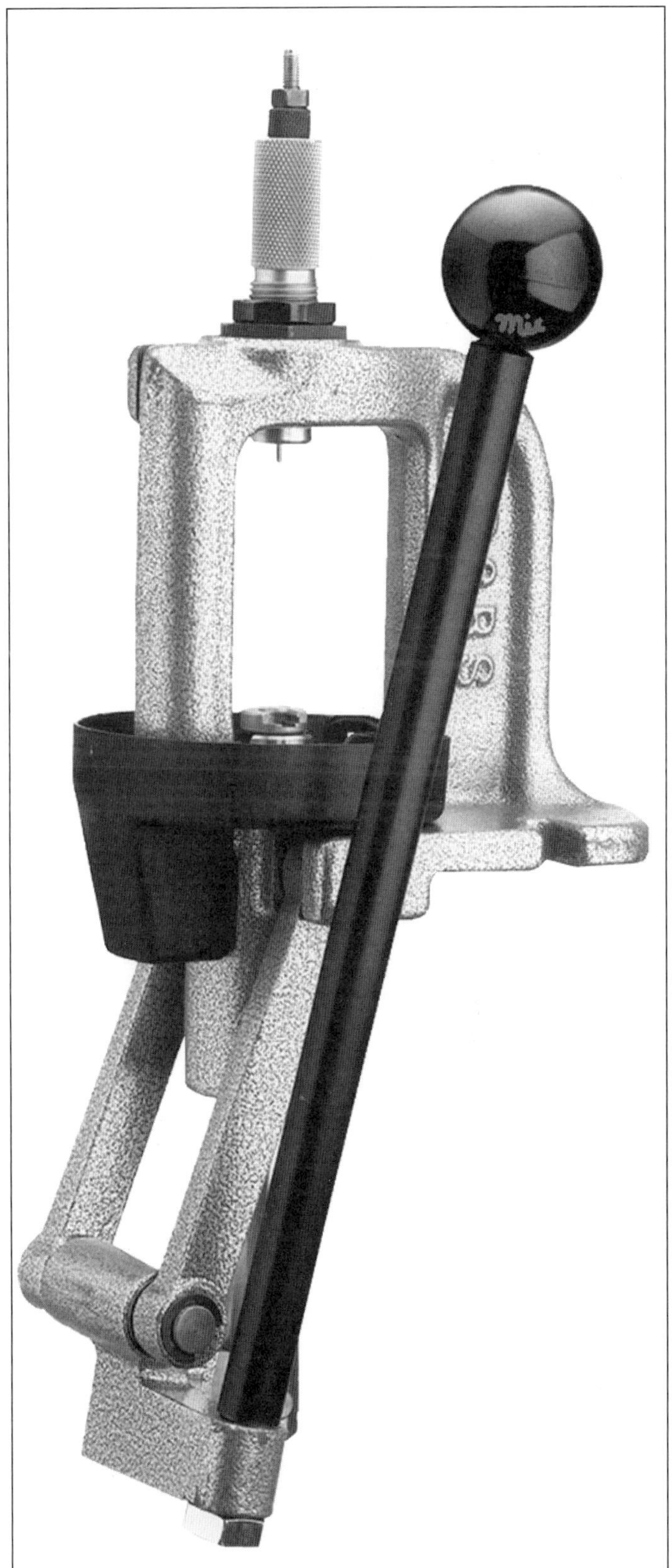

The Rockchucker from RCBS is a conventional "O"-frame press with decades of proven performance. It is capable for any likely application, and it will last a lifetime. All major makers of handloading tools now offer similar single-stage presses.

The main reason this press is so desirable is that it uses the RCBS APS primer feed. This system uses plastic strips that hold twenty-five primers and that clip together. Primer feeding is simply flawless. All that is necessary for continuous press operation is to pause to clip another strip onto the last-installed strip (when the working strip is down to the last few primers). The handloader never has to touch a primer, and these strips are perfectly safe to handle and to use. Moreover, the handloader can use a strip-loading tool to install any type of primer very rapidly into these reusable strips.

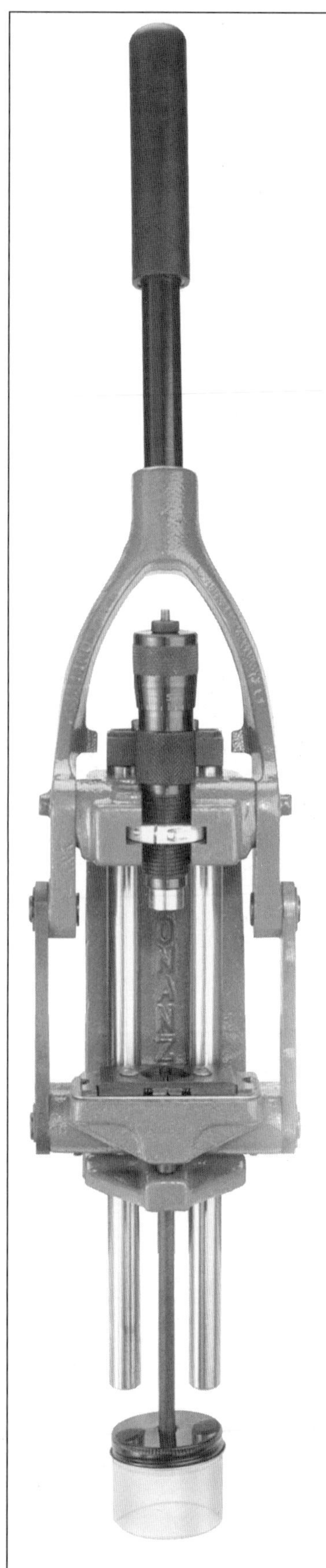

The Forster Co-Ax is a unique single-stage press. The list of superior features is quite long, so I will only note a few here: slip-in quick-change for dies, automatic universal shellholder (two sizes cover all likely applications), monumental leverage, ambidextrous design, and the die and ram remain aligned (regardless of applied sizing stress). Most handloaders who get to work with a Co-Ax press soon learn to love it. The folks at the prestigious Norma ballistics laboratory, who can have and use any press made anywhere, prefer this press for their work. They load tens of thousands of test cartridges annually. When Forster adds special shims that will allow a headspace adjustment, the Co-Ax will be the premier single-stage loading press without any compromises.

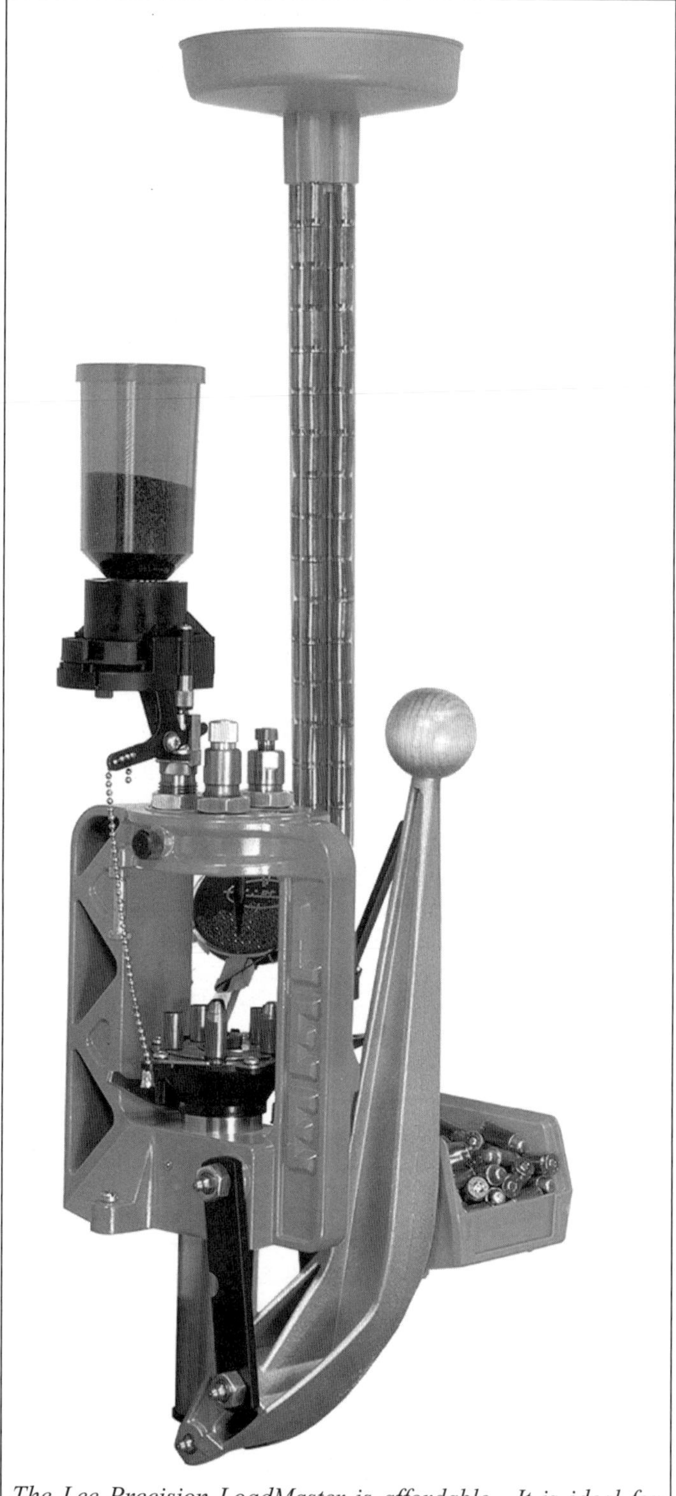

The Lee Precision LoadMaster is affordable. It is ideal for loading large quantities of handgun ammunition. Built-in case feeder and collator systems work very well. For the tinker who is not afraid to tune a tool and who is not intimidated by a sophisticated mechanism, this is an ideal choice. Priming system is the fastest to fill of any progressive press and production rate far exceeds that of any other hobby handloading press.

Autumn, my daughter, is producing 45-70 cartridges using an RCBS Pro-2000: Mostly because of the APS priming system, which renders reliable priming, the Pro-2000 is my favorite progressive. (This prototype press produced more than ten thousand rounds before the first failure; that was a broken part, which RCBS had already upgraded.)

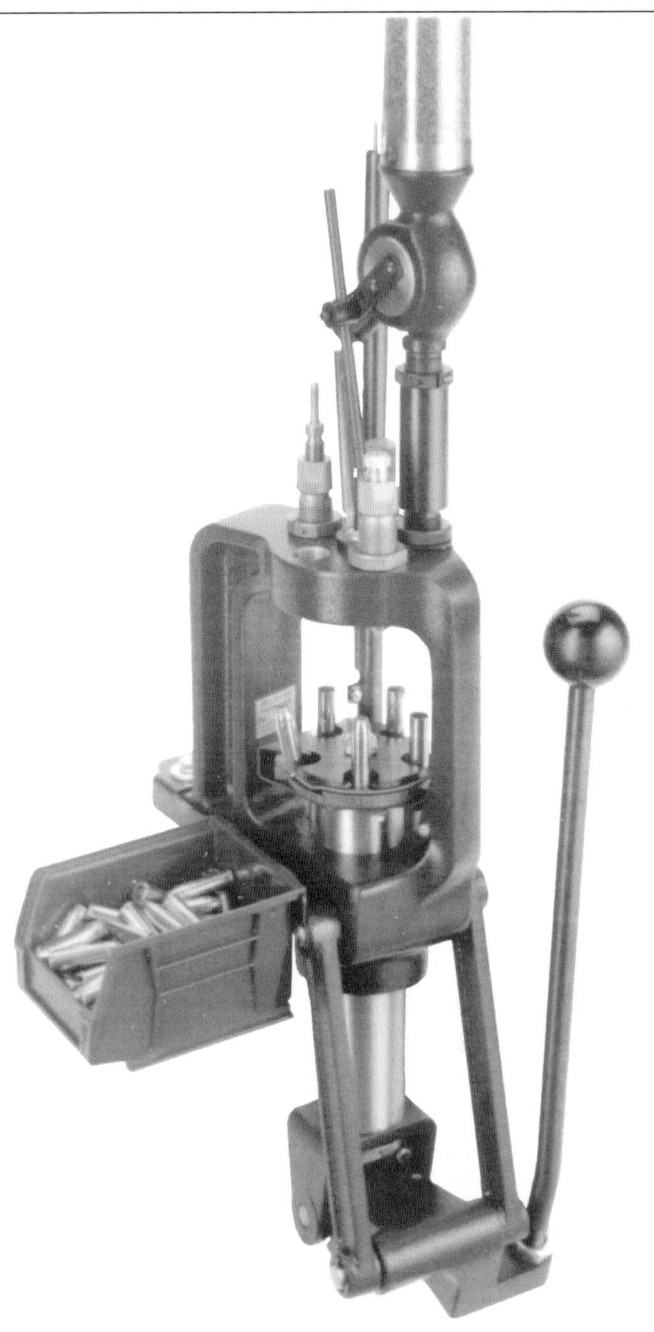

If the priming system were not such a nuisance, the Hornady Lock-n-Load would be my favorite progressive for loading rifle ammunition. (This primer system is no worse than the system on most other presses—only the RCBS Pro-2000 has a decent system because it uses APS strips.) On presses that use a primer tube, it is necessary to interrupt the loading process after each 100 rounds in order to remove and refill the tube and then replace it. At best, this is frustrating and disruptive. Tolerances are unusually tight and the auto-indexing system is the best now available from any manufacturer. Pictured here is an older version. The new version features quick-change die positions, improved case ejection, case-activated propellant charging, and other improvements.

Most of these presses are fully capable for loading any standard rifle cartridge. About the only limitation is that achieving a good dropped-charge consistency requires the use of a ball-type propellant or one of the extruded numbers that will meter consistently. This is a limitation that all progressive presses share with regard to rifle cartridges. However, after raising the case through the tool head at an open location, the handloader can simply omit the automatic dispensing of the propellant and charge the sized and primed case with a weighed charge. This will slow the loading process somewhat, but it is not a major limitation. Combining the RCBS

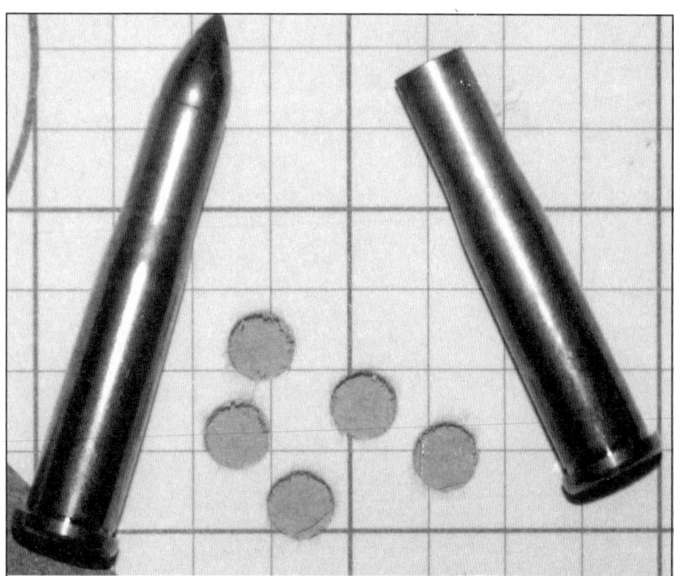

It is not only feasible but it is also entirely worthwhile to produce many rifle loads using a progressive press—the 22 Hornet is a natural. When loading hundreds, or thousands, of varminting cartridges in one session, a progressive press makes all the difference.

ChargeMaster propellant dispensing system with the use of a progressive press, handloaders can produce any rifle cartridge at an overall rate approaching two hundred rounds per hour. (Prelubricating cases and removing the case lube after loading takes time, so the overall production rate is somewhat less but is still sufficient for any reasonable hobby application.)

Compared to using a single-stage press, with which most handloaders are most familiar, using a progressive press differs in several important ways. First, when using a progressive press, handloaders do not have to handle each case to accomplish each separate loading operation. With a single-stage press, handloaders must install the case into the shellholder, then lower and raise the press handle and, finally, take the case back out of the shellholder to accomplish any single task.

The handloader must install the sizing die into the press. He then inserts a case into the shellholder, lowers and raises the press handle, and, finally, takes the sized case out. He can prime the case in the sizing step but it is better to prime the case separately using a hand tool.

For a case requiring a separate neck expansion step (all straight-walled cases), he must then change to the expanding and bellmouthing die. Then he must insert the case into the shellholder, lower and raise the press handle, and, finally, take the bell-mouthed case back out of the shellholder.

He must then charge the case. And then install the bullet-seating die into the press. Then, he must insert the sized, bellmouthed, primed, and charged case into the shellholder, set a bullet on top of the case mouth, lower and raise the press handle, and, finally, remove the loaded cartridge.

If the load and process requires separate crimping, he must install the crimping die and perform that operation. Only then will he have completed one reloaded cartridge.

In reality, handloaders do these operations in batches—often up to hundreds of cases at a time. By this means, changing dies does not become a significant issue. However, no matter what method is used, the handloader must insert the case, raise and lower the ram, and remove the case for each operation.

Conversely, when using a progressive press (here I will use the RCBS Pro-2000 as an example), the handloader simply inserts the cases into the shellholder plate at position one and the bullets at position four.

Once the operation is in full swing, when the handloader lowers and raises the press handle, the following things happen automatically:

- Position one
    - » Case full-length resized and decapped during upstroke
    - » Case primed, at end of downstroke
- Position two
    - » Case neck expanding and bellmouthing (if necessary)
- Position three
    - » Measured propellant charge installed
- Position four
    - » Bullet seated in case

- Position five
  - » Case mouth crimping (if desired), during upstroke
  - » Case ejected at end of downstroke.

Obviously, compared to a single-stage press, both the handling of the case and the number of press-handle strokes required per loaded round are drastically reduced.

The opportunities for error are entirely different when using these two basic reloading approaches. The use of a progressive press obviously reduces the opportunity for errors related to handling, but it equally increases the opportunity for errors related to processing. As an example of a most serious processing error, it is quite possible to stop the ram stroke partway down and then to return the ram to the top. With automatic propellant dispensing, this act could result in the installation of a double charge in the case located at the propellant-charging position.

The safe use of any progressive press requires that the operator maintain great concentration. When using such a press, he should religiously observe one cardinal safety rule: Once he starts the ram moving either upward or downward, he must always complete that stroke without changing directions. If some problem prevents him from doing so, he must make sure that the incomplete action does not result in a double-charged case, a case with no propellant, a case with no primer, or a case (or cartridge) that is in any other way defective (or incomplete).

Note that conventional (single-stage) loading is by no means necessarily safer. Handling errors can, and all too often do, result in cartridges without any charge and cartridges with a double charge. Whatever loading system the handloader uses is only as safe as he is careful.

LOADING PRESS—TURRET

The turret press is an old design. While not a progressive press, the turret press allows quick die changes. This is useful for those who do not want the complication of a progressive press but who do want their loading to go a bit faster, without so many distractions.

Turret presses also feature quick-change, interchangeable tool heads. The Redding Turret Press tool head holds seven dies. This allows the handloader to load several types of cartridges without any interruption for die changes. The extra turrets provide a convenient place to store properly adjusted dies for loading other cartridges.

Using a turret press is no different from using a single-stage press, except that you can choose to load ammunition sequentially. For example, size and prime a case, then turn the tool head and charge it, then turn the tool head and seat a bullet in it. While this process is possible, it is not the best approach, except during load development work where you load only a few rounds with each component combination. However, for that purpose, the turret press is particularly handy. You can mount a measure in one turret position and use it for standard manual case charging. This is a convenient method because it simultaneously keeps the measure handy and out of the way.

Lee offers an interesting variation. The Lee Turret press includes a quick-change die turret and the option of automatic turret indexing. This compact unit is

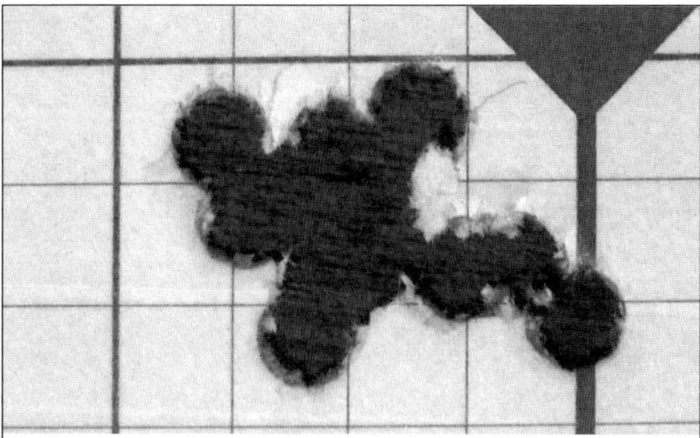

A 22 Hornet and a 20-shot group: Finding a varminting load that shoots this accurately is a treat. It is no problem to load quality varminting ammunition using a turret press, such as the Redding T-7.

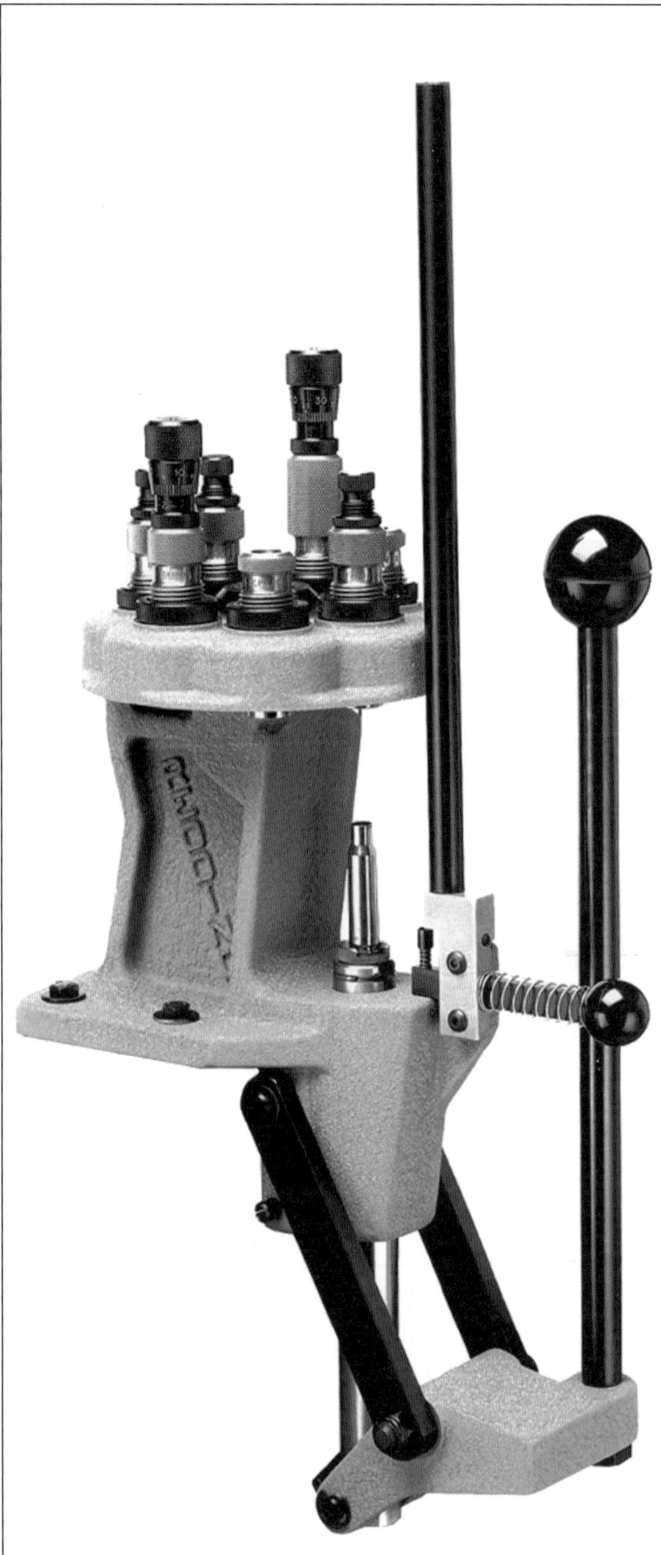

The heavy-duty Redding T-7 is a turret press that is built to an outstanding level of strength and precision, as is true of all Redding tools. This press has one of the better tube-fed priming systems available. Those interested in a turret press will be hard pressed to find a better option.

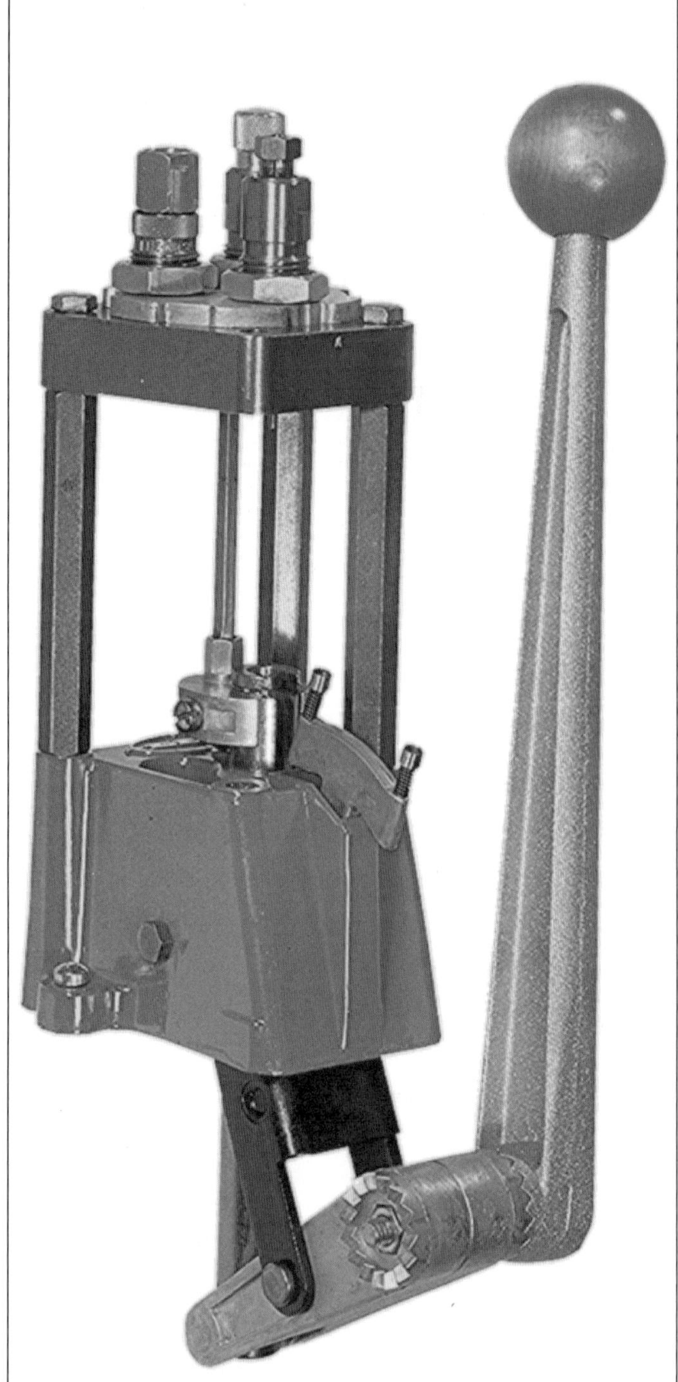

The Lee Turret press is a different sort of press. A removable rod rotates the die plate with each handle upstroke. Hence, this press can operate either as a conventional turret or as a semiprogressive. The affordable quick-change die heads allow quick and handy changes between cartridge types; automatic indexing allows the handloader to load a finished cartridge with only a few handle strokes and without handling the case between strokes. As a college student, I used this press to load thousands of very accurate 44 Special and 45 Automatic cartridges.

The K&M Arbor Press seems to be one of the better designs among this genre. The height adjustment is simple, and this unit delivers plenty of leverage for the intended purpose.

reasonably portable and is a wonderful press to take to the range for load development. I have one attached to a small plank.

With that and a couple of large C-clamps, I am ready for load development work at the range. With the automatic-indexing cam installed, loading with this press is also much quicker than with any single-stage press, and it can be safer. It is relatively difficult to make a mistake.

THE LOADING PRESS—ARBOR

Several makers offer arbor presses for use with various makes of hand dies. Manufacturers offer three basic types of arbor presses. Lightweight models are easy to transport and are appropriate for neck sizing and bullet seating. Standard models are not as easy to transport but have greater mechanical advantage and rigidity and are, therefore, a bit more precise. Heavy-duty models have the rigidity, durability, and gearing required for full-length resizing of small rifle cartridge cases.

Besides portability, arbor presses provide a simple means of neck sizing cases and of seating bullets. The use of these presses requires special dies, and these tools are most appropriate to benchrest shooting, where loading is often done at the shooting bench between relays.

Using these dies does not necessarily require an arbor press, but such a press certainly does ease this chore. An arbor press is a good investment for those interested in loading the most precise ammunition possible.

To neck size a case, insert the case into the open end of die, then set the die in the die base with the case head up and position that assembly under the ram. Next, crank the handle to lower the ram until you drive the case fully into the die. On most models, the crank is spring-loaded, so releasing the handle automatically raises the ram. Turn the die over, insert the decapping rod into the case mouth, and place the die in the base. Crank the handle to deprime the case and drive it from the die. Prime the case using a hand-priming tool. Charge the case. Then seat the bullet using a special die and this press.

SOURCE FOR SPECIALTY TOOLS REFERENCED IN THIS CHAPTER:

K&M Precision Shooting Products LLC
6852 Lakeshore Drive
West Olive, MI 49460
Telephone: 616-399-7894

A relaxing day at the range with my friend, Jim Williamson: We were testing various loads in his custom M12 Savage, 17/23 SM^{C} and his 5-pound, 10-ounce Marlin 357. We had a great day.

THE BASIC HANDLOADING PROCESS

CHAPTER 18

I have used the following photographs courtesy of Redding Reloading. These selected photographs are intended only to represent a general outline of the typical process used in handloading; these do not necessarily represent the only methods that are valid or recommended. Similarly, I have not illustrated all necessary steps.

To minimize variations in the effective headspace of bottlenecked cases, adjust the full-length resizing die so that when you lower the handle until the ram reaches the top of its travel, the shellholder abuts solidly against the die body. If the shellholder does not abut against the die, variations in case lubrication, case toughness, and the speed that you work the press will increase inevitable variations in case headspace length. Use Redding Competition Shellholders to adjust the headspace effectively. With other dies, this setting is unnecessary but it is good practice to use this approach with all dies when feasible.

After trimming the case, it is necessary to debur the inside of the case mouth. Some factory-loaded cases and some brands of new cases require inside neck deburring before handloading.

The only conventional dies that you cannot adjust in this manner are combination bullet seating and crimping dies. The handloader must adjust these dies according to the case length and depending upon how much crimp he intends to apply, if any.

When using a single-stage press for normal loading, the best practice is to work the cases in batches. Clean and lube (as necessary) all the cases in the batch, then resize and decap, then prime (a hand priming tool is the best method), then bellmouth (when necessary), then charge, then seat bullets, then crimp (if necessary), and, finally, wipe off any lubricant. Loading blocks are useful in some or all of these operations.

When working with large batches of cases, a vibratory cleaner loaded with a clean corncob medium is a faster method. In any instance, it is always im-

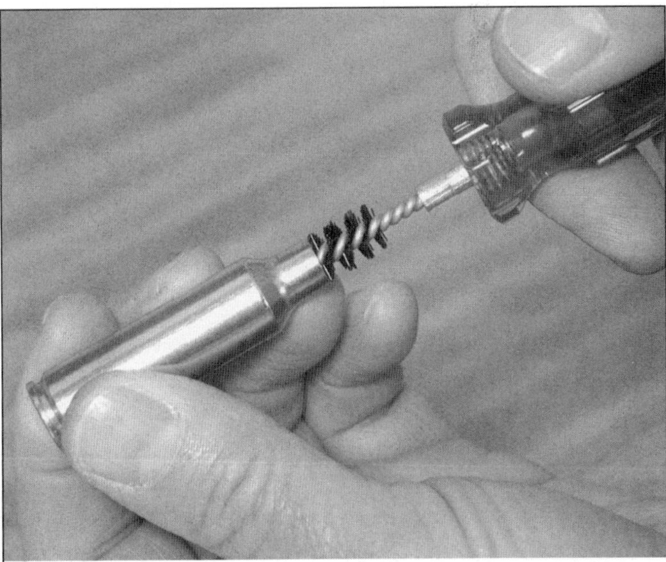

A neck brush is useful for removing excessive propellant residue. Such a brush is also useful for applying dry lube to the interior of the neck. For more aggressive inside neck cleaning and to remove the wire edge that is created by inside deburring, use a bronze bore brush.

portant to clean the lubricant from cases after full-length resizing.

The degree of belling illustrated is typical. To increase case life, use only enough belling to prevent damage to the bullet or case during bullet seating.

Always double-check to see that the scale setting is the intended scale setting. A quality electronic scale has the edge in this regard because it continuously provides readout feedback.

Refer to the section of the text on swirl charging, for a complete discussion of just how critical it is that you consistently pour the charge from the pan in the same way for each case in each batch. The method demonstrated here is not apt to give the best results.

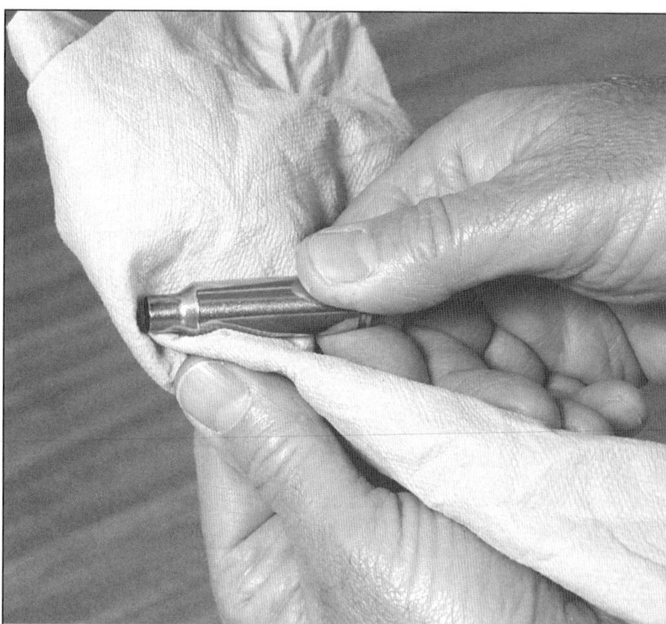

The difficulty of removing case lubricant from the cases depends upon the type of lubricant used. Lanolin-based lubricants are particularly handy in this regard. These clean cases and wipe off with little effort.

On modern single-stage presses, swapping out the shellholder is a simple matter. A spring holds the shellholder in place. On progressive presses, this operation is more difficult and, on most types, requires a wrench. The best practice is to have a dedicated shellholder for each set of dies and sometimes for each gun in each chambering. Refer to the text discussion on Redding Competition Shellholders.

With a single-stage press, it is necessary to swap the dies after completing each operation on each batch of cases.

Refer to the section on swirl charging for a photograph and description of a method that usually results in improved ballistic uniformity and that will allow you to install a charge easily that would, otherwise, overflow the case. (See page 181.)

All that remains is bullet seating and crimping. Normally, these are relatively straightforward procedures. (I strongly recommend.) If you must crimp the case, that you do so in a separate operation. It is seldom possible to combine seating and crimping into a single operation without compromising the quality of the finished product.

Charging a primer tube is potentially dangerous. Never use excessive force and always wear safety glasses. CCI APS strips and associated tools are far handier and safer to use.

When loading flat-base, cast bullets and when working with cases that have very thin necks, it is necessary to flare the case mouth (bellmouth) to prevent damage to the bullet or destruction of the case. With most pistol and revolver cases, bellmouthing is a useful step regardless of the bullet type.

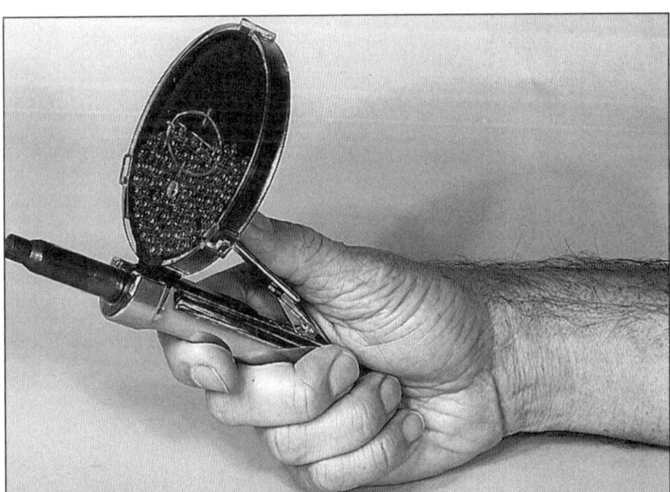

Most handloaders will prefer some sort of dedicated priming tool, such as the Lee Auto-Prime.

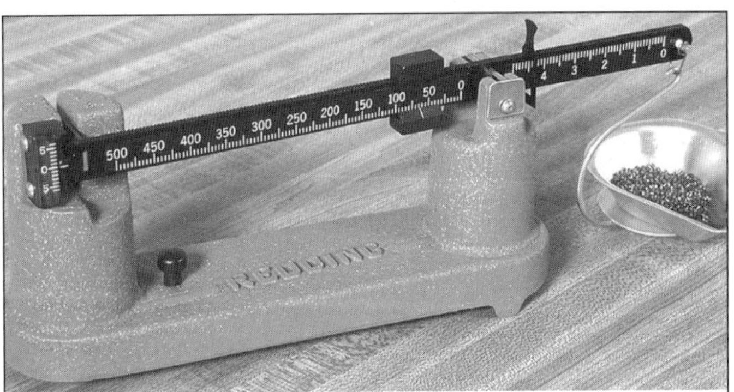

When feasible, locate the scale at eye level and on a separate table so that loading operations will not disturb the scale.

Pouring the charge from the pan through the funnel and into the case is not dead simple. It turns out that this is a step where many handloaders lose a considerable percentage of the potential quality of any handload; refer to "Swirl Charging—Consistently Installing Dumped Charges" on page 181.

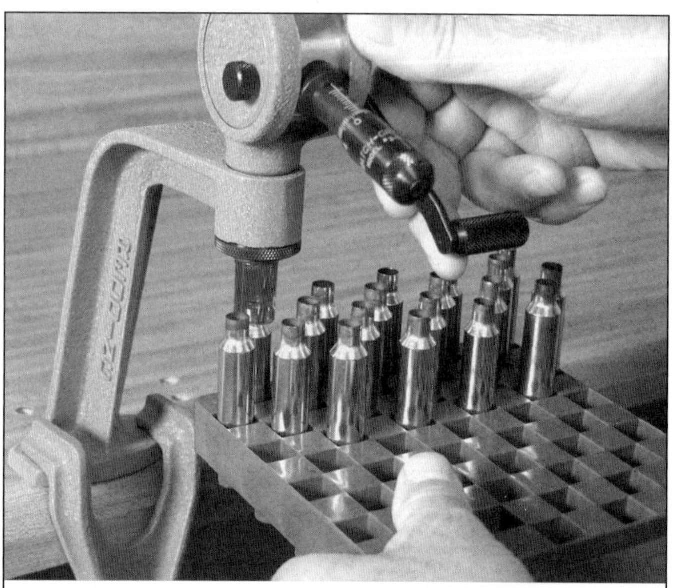

When using most propellants, the handloader who is willing to practice and use a consistent technique usually achieves superior load-to-load ballistic uniformity when charging cases with a measure, rather than with a pan-poured scale charge. Paradoxically, even when dumped charges vary by several tenths of a grain, the variation in velocity is often less than it is with carefully weighed charges that are pan poured into cases. Behind this incongruity is the issue of the granule-packing scheme; measure-dumped charges usually have a more consistent packing scheme than do hand-poured charges. The packing scheme significantly influences internal ballistics. A careful swirl charging technique can eliminate the poured-charge disadvantage; refer to "Swirl Charging—Consistently Installing Dumped Charges" on page 181.

After charging the case, all that remains to complete the cartridge is bullet seating (and optional crimping, where appropriate). A windowed RCBS seating die is particularly handy when loading small-caliber cases—such bullets are difficult to handle when using any conventional seating die.

GLOSSARY

APPENDIX A

The following are common words used in shooting and handloading, and words specific to these pursuits.

ACCURACY: Intrinsic characteristics of gun, cartridge, sights, rest, and shooter. Each of these, and Mother Nature, help determine the size of any group fired and how close to the desired point of impact any given bullet will come.

ACKLEY IMPROVED (AI): The modification to standard case designs developed by Parker O. Ackley, who standardized a 40-degree shoulder angle and a modest body taper (about 0.009-inch total taper, per 1 inch of body length) and applied his design to many factory chamberings. Since Ackley's time, other wildcatters have applied the Ackley modification to newer standardized factory designs.

When correctly cut, rimless AI chambers are nominally 0.006 inch shorter at the neck-to-shoulder junction so that standard cartridges are a tight fit and will fireform (to properly fit the new chamber) without undue case body stretching; this requires setting the barrel back before rechambering and is a critical step that all too many so-called gunsmiths skip.

ACKLEY, PARKER O.: One of the most influential gunsmiths and wildcatters of the modern era. While anyone can hypothesize, Ackley experimented. The results of his experiments proved most interesting.

ACTION: Gun parts involved in loading, locking, firing, and unloading the gun chamber.

ADSORPTION: Term used to distinguish the type of assimilation where osmotic pressure forces a dissolved chemical into a solid material. Adsorption is similar to what happens when one applies oil-based stain to wood. Adsorbed chemicals occupy intermolecular spaces. The distinction between adsorption and absorption is important. A sponge absorbs water, into voids; it is easy to squeeze the water out because relatively large, easily deformable, spaces contain it. It is not possible to squeeze adsorbed chemicals out of the adsorbent because those occupy microscopic, relatively undeformable, intermolecular voids.

AIR (WIND) RESISTANCE: The effects of air on bullets in ballistic flight.

AGE-HARDENING: A change in metal hardness due to the passage of time and most notable when metal is under stress; important in cartridges where the case neck can, eventually, harden sufficiently so that it spontaneously splits during storage or upon firing—see *Annealing.*

ANNEALING: Heating the brass case neck and shoulder area, often necessary to soften work-hardened brass and thereby to prevent it from becoming so brittle that it will crack during loading, storage, or firing.

ANTIMONY: Element that hardens lead alloys.

ANVIL: Portion of primer that provides a relatively rigid and fixed point against which the priming mixture is compressed as the firing pin deforms the primer cup.

BALL: Early term for a bullet, regardless of shape—this was likely the origin of the current word usage ball, as in baseball.

BALL POWDER: The name for double-based smokeless propellants developed by Olin, Inc. The term ball-type is preferable as it avoids trademark infringements. Ball-type granules are either spherical or flattened-spherical shapes.

BALLISTICS: Strictly the science and study of a body freely moving through a gravitational field. In modern parlance, for lack of better terms, we divide ballistics into phases of bullet motion:

- Interior ballistics—primer ignition to muzzle exit
- Exterior ballistics—muzzle to target
- Terminal ballistics—deceleration, deformation, and disintegration at impact

BALLISTIC COEFFICIENT (BC): Efficiency of a bullet in overcoming air resistance. Across any given distance, a more efficient bullet (higher BC) will retain more velocity (kinetic energy), demonstrate less deflection (in any given cross wind), and shoot closer to the line of sight.

BARREL-TO-CYLINDER GAP: Necessary gap between the revolver barrel and cylinder of a revolver.

BARREL HEATING: An increase in the barrel temperature resulting from firing a cartridge. Contrary to folk wisdom, in a typical gun the vast majority (usually more than about 85 percent) of barrel heating results from elastic barrel deformation as the round is fired and the bullet moves toward the muzzle; friction and incandescence contribute only minor heating. When using blackpowder, the condensation of hot particulates onto the bore's interior contributes significantly to barrel heating (perhaps more than one-half of the total heating!); when using smokeless powder, much less material condenses onto the bore's interior, so much less heating results from this source (never more than a tiny percentage of the increase in total temperature).

BEARING SURFACE: The portion of the bullet that touches the bore, as the bullet passes through the barrel.

BEDDING: The method and materials used in connecting the riflestock to the barreled-action. Pillars do not bed an action; hence, the term pillar bedding is erroneous.

BELL: Expand case mouth—to seat the bullet more easily, without damage to the case or bullet. Belling is most commonly needed when using cast bullets.

BELTED CASE: Design with an unusually thick (front-to-rear) rim and an extraction groove cut in it. Just as with any other rimmed case, the rim (belt) on this type of case nominally controls the headspace—compare to rimmed, rimless, semirimmed, and rebated-rimless.

BERDAN: Primer system using no primer-mounted anvil; instead, an anvil is formed in the bottom of the primer pocket. Named after a United States Army officer, Col. Hiram Berdan who invented the system; commonly used everywhere but the United States! Generally, when compared to Boxer-primed ammunition, Berdan-primed ammunition produces superior ballistic uniformity—see *Boxer.*

BENCHREST (BENCH REST): Table, or bench, used to support a gun during accuracy testing. Benchrest target shooting is an important sport, where the smallest group wins, regardless of the location on the target. Modern benchrest guns, shooters, and cartridges routinely generate 10-shot, 100-yard groups much smaller than 0.1 inch, on centers.

BLANKED PRIMER: A primer with a portion of the cup driven into the firing-pin hole in the bolt. Always caused by a defective firing pin, too-light firing pin, too-weak firing-pin spring, excessive clearance between the firing pin and firing pin hole in the bolt, or by a too-large firing pin. Substituting primers with thicker cups (Remington rifle) can eliminate blanking, in otherwise identical cartridges. Federal primers seem to be most prone to blanking but are also most easily ignited and, partly for that reason, often give the best ballistic uniformity and accuracy.

BLACKPOWDER: Physical mixture of powdered (and subsequently recrystalized) potassium nitrate (saltpeter [KNO3]), charcoal (carbon [C] and sometimes hydrocarbons [HxCx), and sulfur [S]. The original propellant still commonly used in muzzleloaders and antique cartridge guns.

BOATTAIL (BOAT TAIL): Name given to bullet with tapered heel (base).

BOILER ROOM: Informally, the volume inside a case not occupied by the bullet.

BODY (OF CASE): The section of the case between the front of the solid web (at head) and the shoulder where the charge is contained—generally represents the boiler room.

BOLT: The locking and case-head-supporting mechanism of the firearm that usually operates in-line with the bore's axis. The bolt can or does carry the:

- Firing pin
- Firing pin spring
- Extractor
- Ejector

BOLT THRUST: Force on the bolt face (or firearm breech) caused by the pressure of propellant gases pushing against the inside of the case head and primer.

BORE: The hole through the barrel's interior. In rifled arms, the bore size is the diameter of the hole through the barrel before cutting or swaging grooves to create the rifling. Another way of saying this is to measure the diameter of a barrel from land to land.

BORE SIGHT: To align the firearm sights with the target by sighting through the bore.

BOXER: The primer system invented by British Army officer Col. Edward Boxer. This is the standard primer type used in the United States. Boxer primers have built-in anvils—see *Primer* and *Berdan.*

BRASS: An alloy of copper and zinc, of which cartridge cases are often made. Often erroneously applied to cases—all cases are cases but not all cases are brass and not all brass is a case; in fact, most brass is not a case! Ideally, cartridge brass is 70 percent copper and 30 percent zinc, with minimal impurities—see *Case.*

BRIDGING STRENGTH: The resistance of a malleable substance against filling a void completely. Bullets have enough internal strength so that these never fully seal the corners at the bottoms of the rifling grooves—the bullet simply cannot deform into full contact at that location. This is important to those shooting cast bullets, for the resulting gas leak can lead to leading if the bullet does not obturate enough to almost seal these gaps.

BRISANCE: Relative explosive shattering power.

BULLET: The portion of the cartridge that when fired becomes the projectile. A bullet is not a cartridge and a cartridge is not a bullet. Terminology matters. The aspiring actor Brandon Lee died because the fools he was working with did not understand the difference between a bullet and a cartridge—see *Ball.*

BULLET PATH: A track followed by a bullet in ballistic flight. We describe this path in terms of distance above (+) or below (–) line-of-sight at any given distance.

BULLET PULL: The force required to extract a bullet from a loaded cartridge. Ammunition producers measure bullet pull to verify the neck tension and crimp quality. (Contrary to common belief, crimping NEVER significantly increases bullet pull, but when done badly, a crimp can significantly reduce bullet pull.)

BULLET PULLER: A tool for extracting bullets from loaded cartridges; types include:

- Collet
- Inertial
- Spring

BURNING RATE: Term used to indicate the relative burning speed of a given propellant. Common smokeless propellants for handloading sporting cartridges vary in absolute burning rate by a factor of about twelve.

CALIBER: Correctly, caliber refers to the bore's diameter in multiples of 1/100 of an inch. The common construction ".30 caliber" is simply ridiculous. First, it is grammatically wrong—in English, it is never correct to use a leading decimal point (not preceded by a digit—a zero would be required in this example) because the reader must ask: "Was a digit omitted and if so, which one?" Second, it is technically incorrect; the diameter of such a bullet would be 3/1000 inch (0.30 ÷ 0.01 inch = 0.003 inch).

This nonsense evidently originated with some stubborn, illiterate purchasing agent in the United States military in the 1890s. Before that, Winchester catalogs never used a preceding decimal point in any cartridge designation. Evidently, some ordnance officer insisted that ammunition manufacturers include a preceding decimal point in the designation for the 30 Army (30-40 Krag).

Perhaps for uniformity, many manufacturers eventually adopted this same incorrect system for all cartridge names, as listed in catalogs. The persistence of this nonsense in modern printed usage is simply phenomenal. Note that according to SAAMI and CIP, no cartridge name includes a leading decimal point. And, when was the last time that you heard someone say, "I was just out shooting my decimal-point forty-five Colt?"

CALIPER: A precision measuring tool. Three common types include:

- Vernier, robust but hard to read accurately
- Dial, has been more popular because it is easier and faster to read accurately
- Electronic, digital readout, the best type for many reasons—more robust, zeroing feature allows fast measurement comparisons, greater accuracy

CANNELURE: Circumferential groove around a bullet or case. Used for identification, to hold the lubricant, or to allow for easy crimping.

CANISTER (GRADE) PROPELLANT: Because handloaders generally lack the facilities and equipment required to determine the characteristics of any given propellant safely and accurately, manufacturers offer propellants that are held to rigid specifications. Each lot of canister-grade propellant is made, or is blended, as necessary to meet the specification requirements for that product in terms of burn rate, energy, and density. With canister-grade propellants, handloaders can expect relatively consistent results regardless of production lot.

Conversely, commercial ammunition manufacturers usually have laboratory facilities to determine the relative performance of bulk propellants, which can have enough lot-to-lot variation to produce dangerous loads if used with standard data. When using bulk propellants, producers adjust the charge, as required, to achieve the desired performance.

CAP: Original name for primer, because it capped the nipple.

CARTRIDGE: Assembled and complete unit of metallic ammunition, which includes the following components:

- Case
- Propellant
- Primer
- Bullet

CASE OR CASING: Abbreviations for cartridge casing, paper, metal, plastic, or composite container that holds other cartridge components.

CASE FORMING: An alteration or modification of one case to work in a chamber that was designed for a differently shaped case; often, only the neck diameter differs—see *Wildcat.*

CASE SEPARATION: A break usually near the case head; can allow gas to escape, always potentially dangerous—see *Partial Separation.*

CASE TRIMMING: Shortening the case neck.

CAST BULLET: Formed from molten lead or lead-alloy using a mold—see *Mold Blocks.*

CENTERFIRE (CENTER-FIRE, CF): Refers to cartridges with a primer inserted into the center of the base of the case. Most centerfire cartridges are reloadable—compare to rimfire.

CENTRAL IGNITION: Cartridge where an incandescent primer flash is delivered to the entire longitudinal center of a propellant charge through a perforated metal tube, very common in artillery rounds.

CHAMBER: The portion of the breech end of the bore formed to accept and support a cartridge. In a revolver, multiple chambers are located in a separate cylinder that also acts as a magazine.

CHAMBER CAST: By sealing the bore with a paper or rag placed just forward of the leade and filling the chamber with a molten casting agent, one can create a mirror image of the chamber. This makes it easy to measure a chamber's shape and condition. Materials used include sulfur, low melting-point metal, and paraffin wax.

CHAMFER: To ream a taper inside a case mouth—facilitates bullet seating, which is always necessary after case trimming and is sometimes necessary on new cases.

CHARGE: A weighed or measured propellant inserted into a cartridge case during cartridge loading.

CHOKED BORE: The modest constriction of the bore as it tapers from the chamber's end to the muzzle's end; highly desirable for maximum accuracy in any rifled gun and necessary for maximum accuracy with 22 rimfire and other relatively small-cased chamberings.

CHRONOGRAPH: Device that measures a projectile's velocity.

CIP: European counterpart to SAAMI.

CLIP: Common abbreviation for a stripper clip, a device designed to hold cartridges and to load a magazine. A clip is not a magazine.

COMBUSTION: Burning: In firearms, the chemical process that converts a solid propellant into a hot gas. Very rapid burning is called deflagration.

COMPENSATOR: A device fitted to a gun muzzle to reduce recoil, muzzle rise, and sometimes gun rotation. This term is usually restricted to devices fitted to handguns and shotguns—see *Muzzle Brake.*

COMPRESSED CHARGE: A propellant charge compacted by the bullet's seating. When using the right propellant, compressed charges often create the best possible loads. Such loads are particularly beneficial for cartridges used in guns with tubular magazines because the compressed charge helps keep the battering from recoil from driving the bullet of a cartridge within the magazine into the case.

COMPONENTS: In a metallic cartridge these include:

- Primer
- Propellant
- Bullet
- Case

COPPER CRUSHER: A copper cylinder used to measure the chamber's pressure and used with a specially fitted pressure gun—see *Pressure Gun.*

CORE: The interior of a jacketed bullet; usually a lead alloy.

CORDITE: The trade name for an obsolete propellant that was usually used as long tubular granules. Cordite was double based (made with both nitrocellulose and nitroglycerine) and included a significant percentage of petroleum jelly.

Cordite was one of the earliest, highly successful smokeless propellants and was used mainly by Great Britain. When used in rifle cases, cordite granules were usually the same length as the boiler room; when used in bottlenecked cases, cordite granules were inserted before the bottleneck was formed; when used in very small cases, cordite was cut into granules that resembled modern extruded smokeless propellants.

CORROSION: The damage to a bore's interior resulting from stress, heat, and reactive gases generated when a cartridge fires. Corrosion is a chemical alteration of steel; it results from rusting, chemical etching (salts, from propellants and primers, and reaction products of bore cleaners and bore fouling), and electrochemical action (electrolysis between barrel steel and metallic bullet fouling). Corrosion weakens the steel and creates open cracks between crystal boundaries. Salts or acids can also corrode cases. Most sporting gun barrels wear out because of corrosion, not erosion.

CORROSIVE PRIMER: A primer that generates hygroscopic salt residues (such substances attract and absorb moisture). Until such residue is removed, it rapidly rusts or corrodes the bore. Primers made in the United States since about 1950 are noncorrosive.

CRIMP: Bending a case mouth inward to facilitate chambering. The best crimp adds very little, if any, to bullet pull, and most crimps reduce the bullet pull. Two main crimp types exist:

- Roll crimp, bending or rolling a case mouth into bullet crimping groove (cannelure);
- Taper crimp, pressing case mouth into bullet body, creating a short, gentle taper at end of case mouth.

CRIMPED PRIMER: A case with the brass crimped inward over the edge of the primer; prevents the primer setback and hardens the case head. Usually found only on military cartridges intended for use in machine guns. Unless the primer crimp is removed after depriming—either by swaging or by reaming—repriming is difficult or impossible.

CROWN: Carefully prepared barrel muzzle contour at the bore's opening to ensure a concentric exit of the bullet.

DEBURRING: The removal of burs from the outside edge of the case mouth after trimming—see *Chamfer.*

DECAP OR DEPRIME: To remove the (spent) primer from the case, usually done by a decapping pin in a case-sizing or neck-expanding die.

DETERRENT: An inert chemical adsorbed into propellant granule surfaces; retards initial energy release during combustion.

DETONATION (TO DETONATE): A chemical reaction where the conversion of a substance into energy and new substances occurs faster than the speed of sound through that substance. High explosives detonate. Normally propellants do not detonate.

DIE: A tool used to form or reform cases or bullets, to seat bullets, or to apply a crimp.

DOUBLE-BASED: Nitrocellulose propellant (NC) with added nitroglycerine (NG) to increase energy, reduce propensity of granules to adsorb humidity, and mitigate granule degradation due to oxidation from residual acids. (NG wets NC and thereby protects it from ever-present residual acids.)—see *Single-Based.*

DRAG: See Air Resistance.

DRIFT: In exterior ballistics, the deviation of a projectile from the line of departure due to the rotation of the Earth and the projectile—commonly (incorrectly) applied to wind influences—see *Wind Deflection.*

DROP: The distance a projectile falls due to gravity. Drop is measured, or is calculated, from the line of departure. Drop must be corrected for the difference between the line of sight and the line of departure. Drop is normally reported for shots fired from a horizontal barrel—see *Path.*

DUPLEX LOAD: The use of two types of propellant in loading a single cartridge; offers little ballistic advantage in sporting loads. Duplex loads can be unpredictably dangerous.

ELEVATION (ZEROING): The vertical adjustment of sights to bring the point of aim into coincidence with the point of impact at a specific distance.

ENERGY: A common abbreviation in ballistics for Kinetic Energy.

ENGRAVING: The marks on a bullet created by the rifling as the bullet is forced into the rifled bore.

EROSION: The wearing away of the bore's surface due to friction from the projectile and the action of the propellant gases and primer residues. In most chamberings, erosion is so minor as to be a nonissue; the cracking that results from corrosion, which results from firing cartridges, causes the bore's interior to grow shut faster than erosion causes the bore to enlarge. Chamberings using cases that are unusually large for the bore size are exceptions; in those, erosion can be dramatic and can wipe away any indication of rifling for many inches forward of the chamber after only a few dozen shots.

EXPANDER BALL OR BUTTON: The part of the die that expands the sized case neck to the needed diameter to hold the bullet firmly—expanders are often larger and sometimes smaller than is ideal for the best accuracy and cartridge functionality.

EXPANSION RATIO: The ratio of the boiler room to the overall bore volume plus the chamber volume at the instant the bullet's base exits the bore.

EXPLOSION: The rapid, almost instantaneous release of stored energy. When a balloon breaks, it explodes; bombs explode; propellants do not explode.

EXTRACTION CANNELURE: A swaged or cut groove forward of the rim; exposes a surface for the extractor to grip (front edge of rim).

EXTRUDED PRIMER: A primer that, after firing, has produced metal from the cup into the firing pin hole in the bolt but with the extruded part still attached to the primer cup. Shooters often, erroneously, refer to this as a cratered primer. Usually, this is a gun problem and not a sign of excessive pressure—see *Blanked Primer.*

EXTRUSION: Forcing malleable material through an opening—used in the manufacture of bullet jackets and cores and in tubular and some flake propellants.

EXTRUDED TUBULAR PROPELLANT: A cylindrical propellant formed by forcing the propellant dough through a die, allowing the resultant strands to cure (through evaporation of volatile solvents), and cutting those strands into granules of a desired length. Extruded propellants used in sporting cartridges usually have one centered longitudinal hole formed by a pin that passes from the working side through the extrusion hole in the die plate.

FEET PER SECOND (fps, feet/second, ft/sec, f/s)**:** U.S. English measure of velocity.

FIREFORM: Using the pressure of normal firing to shape a case, as needed, to fit a chamber that (usually) has less taper along the case body, a sharper shoulder, and (on rimmed cases) a shorter neck.

FIRING PIN: The part of the gun mechanism that strikes the primer and thereby initiates the ignition—also called a striker or a striker pin.

FLAKE PROPELLANT: Smokeless propellant characterized by thin, disc-shaped granules.

FLASH HOLE: A vent between the primer pocket and the case body—carries the primer flash to the propellant.

FOOT-POUND: English unit of kinetic energy. Defined as the work required to lift one pound one foot against the gravity of the Earth.

FORCING CONE: In a revolver, the bevel at the barrel's entrance—see *Taylor Throating.*

FREEBORE: Upon firing, the distance, if any, a bullet travels before reaching the beginning of the leade (beginning of rifling).

FRONTAL IGNITION: The cartridge where an incandescent primer flash is delivered to the front end of a propellant charge, usually through a metal tube, sometimes used in military cartridges larger than about 50-caliber.

FULL METAL JACKET (FMJ): Also Full Patched (FP) or Metal Cased (MC); jacket opening is at base.

FUNCTIONAL HEADSPACE: Distance a chambered cartridge can freely move (forward and backward) in chamber when the action is closed and locked.

GALLING: Damage due to friction between any two pieces of material that move past each other, exacerbated by the lack of lubrication and the presence of grit. Galling can occur on gun locking lugs and mating surfaces and in cases and sizing dies. Galling scratches cases and dies, and it deposits brass in die.

GAS: Hot (energetic) gas produced by burning the propellant; generates pressure that produces the force on the bullet's base and accelerates the bullet through the bore.

GAS CHECK: Device to mitigate two effects that commonly lead to barrel leading:

- Gas cutting, as hot gas escapes past the bullet
- Frictional heating, as the bullet passes through the bore.

When sufficient, either effect can melt the surface of a lead-alloy bullet. As the bullet moves forward, any resulting molten lead will subsequently freeze onto the cooler surface of the bore.

A gas check can be made of copper, brass, plastic, paper, fabric, or other material and is located between the bullet and charge. A copper or brass cup attached to the bullet's base absorbs heat much faster than lead; hence, any gas escaping past such a gas check is cooled before reaching the bullet alloy and is, therefore, less apt to melt the bullet's surface. During the interval before the bullet obturates, all properly designed gas checks seal the bore better than a naked lead-alloy bullet can. These characteristics reduce, or eliminate, gas cutting, thereby reducing the leading with all loads, but especially with low-pressure loads.

An attached copper or brass gas check has one advantage over any other type: As it passes through the bore, it tends to scrape out any minor lead deposits. Due to this scraping of the bore and to the fact that the bullet's base (where obturation swelling is maximum) is protected, traditional gas checks allow the use of any given lead-alloy bullet at higher pressure without undue bore leading.

GILDING METAL: A copper-zinc alloy used for bullet jackets. By definition, gilding metal is 95 percent copper and 5 percent zinc. Alloys with more zinc have been used but are more fragile.

GRAIN: A recognized unit of mass worldwide. This term originated with the fact that seeds of a certain Egyptian grain crop were a convenient standard for comparing light masses. Eventually, a grain was standardized such that 7,000 grains equals one pound (avoirdupois).

Some handloaders sometimes incorrectly use the term grain when referring to a propellant granule (an individual propellant particle). When we refer to a certain number of grains of propellant, we should always mean a measure of mass (weight).

GRANULE: An individual piece of smokeless propellant.

GRANULATION: Refers to the size and shape of granules that make up the propellant.

GREASE GROOVE: Lubricating groove. On a lead bullet, it's the circumferential groove that can hold lubricant.

GROOVES: Spiral cuts or impressions in the bore, the larger diameter portion of the rifling; compare to lands.

GROUP: The pattern made at the target by all bullets fired with one aiming point and sight setting. Shooters usually measure the group's size as the center-to-center separation of the most distant two holes.

GUNPOWDER (GUN POWDER): A propellant used in small arms. When used in cartridges, propellants burn; these materials normally neither detonate nor explode.

HALF-JACKET: A jacketed bullet where some portion of the bullet's core (before it tapers) is exposed. Similar to a long gas check but used on swaged bullets.

HANDLOADING: Loading small arms ammunition using hand-powered equipment—see *Reloading.*

HAND-PRIMING TOOL: A specialized, hand-held tool, designed specifically to prime cases. Some such tools are designed to decap and to prime—see *Primer Tool.*

HANGFIRE: Informal term identifying the firing of a cartridge when a perceptible delay between the trigger pull and firing occurs. Two types exist:

- Mechanical—something prevents or delays striker from falling until something else happens (such as when the shooter begins to open the bolt!)
- Chemical—something delays ignition and propellant burn

A mechanical hangfire can extend for any period, between the trigger let-off and the removal of the cartridge from the chamber.

Chemical hangfires are very rare in modern ammunition. These can result from a problem with the primer or propellant or can result from a mechanical problem (light striker fall that does not correctly ignite the primer). Typically, such hangfires delay ignition less than 0.3 second; however, much longer delays are possible—Elmer Keith reported a hangfire of about one-half hour!

HEADSPACE: Indicates specific surfaces and datum in the gun and on the case that control rear-to-front clearance between the case and chamber. Important to handloaders in order to adjust functional headspace and to thereby produce dependable, safe, and accurate ammunition with an improved case life.

HEEL: Edge of bullet's base.

HOLDOVER: When firing at a target beyond the zeroed distance of the gun, it is the distance above the target that the shooter must aim in order to hit the desired point of impact—see *Zero.*

HOLLOWPOINT (HP): A bullet with an axial hole in the nose.

HOT-COR: Speer registered trademark for the exclusive process of manufacturing flat-based rifle bullets. A molten lead alloy is poured into a clinically clean jacket and the bullet is immediately swaged into shape, with a resulting tight bond between the core and jacket. Generally, this bond is not quite as good as the bond that results with soldering, but it is far superior to what occurs in a conventional bullet where (other than mechanical tension) no bonding exists between the core and jacket.

IGNITION: The process of igniting a propellant; the primer provides the necessary heat and incandescent materials. (Striker compression of the primer pellet adiabatically heats trapped gas within microscopic pockets inside the pellet; this heating is sufficient to ignite adjacent pellet surfaces, thereby igniting the pellet)

IMPROVED: A standardized cartridge altered by fire forming usually to reduce the taper of the case body and to increase the shoulder angle; also descriptive of a gun so chambered. Improving a case increases the capacity and often provides significantly better headspace control against a striker blow and primer explosion. Improved case designs can also improve the internal ballistic efficiency by keeping more unignited propellant trapped within the cartridge chamber.

IMR: Abbreviation for Improved Military Rifle, trademark of DuPont (now IMR Powder Company, now owned by Hodgdon Powder Company). IMR propellants are single-based rifle types containing less tin than the predecessor DuPont Military Rifle (MR) types (tin scavenges copper fouling from bore).

INGALLS TABLES: Ballistic tables computed by Col. James M. Ingalls, first published in 1918. The most widely used ballistic tables in the United States, used to determine ballistic coefficients of most sporting bullets.

JACKET: Bullet covering; United States producers usually use gilding metal; elsewhere, copper-clad steel and mild steel are commonly used—see Gilding Metal, Cupro-nickel, Paper Patch, and Half-Jacket.

K (PREFIX): Applied to cartridge case improvements developed by experimenter Lysle Kilbourn, similar to Ackley-Improved designs—example: 22 K-Hornet.

KINETIC ENERGY (KE): Energy of a mass in motion. Commonly, shooters abbreviate kinetic energy as energy. Represents the amount of work a moving projectile can do. Proportional to impact velocity squared, times bullet mass—expressed in foot-pounds (in the English system).

KEYHOLE: A bullet's imprint on a target showing that the bullet was not traveling point-on. Such bullets were not tumbling (in the sense of turning end-over-end), which never happens in gyroscopically stabilized bullets. But a keyholing bullet does have significant yaw, just as does a spinning top, before it settles down.

LANDS: The remaining, spiraling, raised portion of a hole bored through a barrel after grooves have been cut or swaged.

LEADE: The portion of the bore where a transition occurs from the end of the groove diameter section (throat) to the beginning of the full-depth rifling. Leade is always tapered; the angle of this taper is usually about 1½ degrees from the axis of the bore (on each side) but steeper and gentler leade angles are used—see *Throat* or *Freebore.*

LEADING: The deposit in a bore from lead or lead-alloy bullets; results either from excessive frictional heating or from gas cutting. Minor leading is common; when excessive, leading increases pressure and reduces accuracy.

LINE OF DEPARTURE: The line at which a bullet leaves a gun muzzle; matches the axis of the bore at the instant a bullet clears the barrel. When fired in a gravitational field, the bullet immediately begins to accelerate away from the line of departure (vertically downward).

LINE OF SIGHT (LOS): Line through the sights of the gun to the target.

LOADING BLOCK: Tray, with rows and columns of holes that hold cartridge cases; very useful when charging cases using a measure and when working cases in batches.

LOADING DENSITY: The ratio of propellant volume to available case volume—see *Boiler Room.*

LOADING PRESS: A tool used to load ammunition. Press designs usually provide significant mechanical advantage to reduce significantly the force required to resize or reform cases. Modern manufacturers offer presses in many basic types.

LOCKING LUG OR LUGS: Devices that lock the bolt to a receiver when the action is closed (often protrusions on the bolt). A locking lug prevents a bolt from freely moving in a receiver when a gun fires. Excepting blowback guns that use the inertia of a relatively heavy bolt to retard the action from opening, all conventional guns have one or more locking lugs.

LOCK TIME: The period between sear release and the instant that the firing pin hits the primer.

LUBRICANT: Case-sizing lubricant is used to reduce friction when sizing cartridge cases; bullet lubricant is used to minimize leading with lead-alloy bullets.

LUBRICATOR-SIZER: A tool used to simultaneously size and lubricate cast bullets.

LUBRISIZER: The common name of or the contraction for a lubricator-sizer.

MAGNUM: Originally applied to large bottlenecked cartridges that had the same basic shape as a magnum (large) wine bottle. This term has been so abused that it now signifies absolutely nothing; any cartridge can be a magnum so long as it is so named!

MASS: The technical term for what we commonly refer to as weight. In the Earth's gravitational field, by definition mass and weight are equal.

MAXIMUM ORDINATE: The highest vertical distance a bullet reaches above the line of sight along a path from a gun to a target. Always occurs when the bullet is about 60 percent of the distance to the target; hence, the common term for midrange trajectory is a misnomer.

McPHERSON'S LAW OF GUN SCOPE ENTROPY: All gun scopes fall into one of two categories:

- Those that have already failed
- Those that will soon fail

Corollary:

- Gun scope failures are most apt to occur at the worst possible moment.

MEPLAT: The relatively flat portion of the bullet nose. Meplat derives from the French and is correctly pronounced *meh-pla,* with the first syllable accented.

MEPLAT DIAMETER: The size of the flat or blunt end of a bullet's nose—see *Meplat.*

METAL FOULING: The bullet material deposited in a bore due to friction, abrasion, and heat. Generally, cartridges that generate higher velocity engender more fouling. To prevent electrolytic (galvanic) bore corrosion between the fouling (copper, zinc, or lead) and the steel of the barrel, always remove the fouling and lubricate the bore as soon as is feasible after use.

MICROMETER: A measuring instrument with a fine, precise, screw-in-screw adjustment system allowing accurate, repeatable distance measurements. In the United States, micrometers are calibrated and marked for either 1/1000- or 1/10,000-inch readouts. Electronic micrometers are routinely calibrated to provide readouts in 5/100,000-inch increments (one-half of one-ten-thousandths inch!).

MIDRANGE TRAJECTORY (MRT): Midrange trajectory is a misnomer because it always occurs when the bullet is about 60 percent of the distance to the target. MRT is correctly called the maximum ordinate.

MINUTE-OF-ANGLE (MOA): The unit of angular measurement equal to 1/60th of 1 degree. Although usually approximated as 1 inch at 100 yards, the actual value is close to 1.047 inches.

MISFIRE: The failure of a cartridge to discharge after the firing pin strikes the primer. Most commonly, misfires result from loading error or a mechanical gun problem. Common loading errors include the failure to seat the primer properly and the failure to charge the case; less commonly, a misfire occurs from the contamination of the primer or charge. Common mechanical problems are dried-out grease gumming the firing pin and an excessive reduction of striker-spring tension—common in highly tuned guns as used in competition.

MOLD BLOCKS: Mirror-twin pieces of metal, each with a hemispherical half of a bullet-shaped cavity. Used to cast bullets from a molten lead-alloy.

MUSHROOM: The common result of the impact of an expanding bullet; term derived from the ideal shape of a bullet after expansion.

MUZZLE: The front end of the barrel. What you do not want to look into!

MUZZLE BLAST: The consequence of high-pressure propellant gases jetting from a gun muzzle and, often, subsequently detonating.

MUZZLE BRAKE: A propellant gas diverter attached to a gun muzzle; designed to deflect the propellant gases sideways or backward; used to reduce recoil by redirecting the gases that would otherwise jet forward after the bullet exits the bore—see *Compensator.*

MUZZLE ENERGY (ME): The kinetic energy of a bullet at the muzzle where velocity (and therefore kinetic energy) is highest. Often abbreviated as Energy.

MUZZLE PRESSURE: Gas pressure acting on a bullet base at the instant the bullet exits the bore. Due to the Bernoulli effect, muzzle pressure is always lower than chamber pressure at that instant (typical difference is nearly 15 percent). (From the instant the bullet begins to move, pressure on the bullet base is always less than chamber pressure—the difference in pressure depends upon cartridge parameters but is usually in the 10 percent to 20 percent range.)

MUZZLE VELOCITY (MV): Bullet velocity at the muzzle—see *Velocity.*

NECK: The portion of a case that grips a bullet. In bottlenecked cases, the portion forward of the case shoulder.

NECK DOWN OR NECK UP: To alter the case neck diameter significantly during case forming; this is distinct from the normal operation of sizing that slightly reduces the neck diameter, as required, to hold a same-caliber bullet properly. Necking is the alteration of a case to accept and hold a bullet of a different caliber properly.

NECK EXPANSION: The act of expanding a sized case neck by forcing it over an expander plug or button; what occurs when firing the round—when the force of the pressure of the chamber exceeds the strength of the case neck, the neck expands until supported by the chamber.

NECK REAMING: Reducing the thickness of a case neck by removing material from the inside. Formerly common after forming a short case from a longer case, such as when converting 30-06 Springfield cases to work in a 243 Winchester chamber. Today, outside neck turning is the preferred method of achieving this goal.

NECK SIZE: To resize part or all of a case neck, leaving the case body relatively or completely unchanged.

NECK TURNING: Reducing the thickness of a case neck by cutting material from the outside. The preferred method used to create necks with a uniform, desired thickness—see *Neck Reaming.*

NIMROD: A great hunter. (Contrary to what many folks seem to believe, this is not a pejorative term—I am quite proud that both of my sons are nimrods.)

NONCORROSIVE: Priming mixtures free of compounds capable of causing bore corrosion. Modern primers made in the United States are noncorrosive. Ammunition manufacturers outside the United States still commonly use corrosive priming mixes. Bore cleaning, immediately after shooting, prevents damage from the use of corrosive primers.

NRA: National Rifle Association of America—the only reason you are reading this book! If you are not a member, you should be. If you are a member, consider also joining and supporting Rocky Mountain Gun Owners (RMGO) or one of its state affiliates in your area. When it comes to protecting your freedom, this organization is effective all out of proportion to its membership roll. Other organizations such as GOA (Gun Owners of America) and JPFO (Jews for the Preservation of Firearms Ownership) are unusually effective at educating the masses about why guns are critical to our freedom and safety, but that has proven to be a generally useless enterprise.

Your freedom and your very life depend upon the protections that guns give you. Since 1900, governments have murdered more than 100,000,000 of their own citizens because those poor souls did not have the right to keep and bear arms. Only a fool would believe ". . . such a thing could never happen here"—it already has! Tens of thousands of innocent United States citizens have been murdered because their various local and state governments refused to acknowledge their God-given and Constitutional right to self-defense, forcing these people to remain defenseless against criminals. What the government can do to any, it can do to all. It can happen to you! Constitutional protection is meaningless without the political clout to enforce it.

NRMA: National Reloading Manufacturers' Association.

NSSF: National Shooting Sports Foundation.

OBTURATION: Bullet swelling to seal the bore; occurs when the force of acceleration exceeds the strength of the bullet, which always happens with all conventional bullets in any conventional loading.

OGIVE: The curved portion of a bullet, forward of the shank. Also, the radius of the curve forming that ogive—usually expressed in calibers (multiples of the bore diameter). French in origin, ogive is pronounced *oh-jive*, with both syllables accented.

OIL (HYDRAULIC) DENTS: Deformations in the cartridge case or bullet resulting from excessive lubricant during sizing; usually found on a case shoulder or bullet ogive.

ON-CENTERS: The term used to indicate the size of a target group and the spread between the centers of the most-distant pair of bullet holes.

OVERBORE (OVERBORE CAPACITY): Common but unscientific term indicating a cartridge case having too much boiler room for the volume of the bore. Technically, every case is overbore when using relatively fast propellants. Generally, the term *overbore* is applied when the case design is so large in relation to the bore's diameter that only the very slowest burning propellants give satisfactory performance and when none of those fill the boiler room with a charge that generates full normal working pressure.

Fundamentally, as the boiler room increases, it becomes more difficult to create a smokeless propellant that both fills the boiler room and generates a safe maximum chamber pressure; at some point this becomes impossible. Nothing can be done about this—this is a fundamental characteristic of internal ballistics; hence, a maximum useful capacity always exists for any bore size. The largest super-magnum chamberings are quite close to this maximum; any further increase in relative capacity will provide very little increase in velocity potential and will monumentally increase recoil (due to increased gas venting) with a massive reduction of barrel life (to the point where it would be impossible to develop a good load before ruining the barrel!).

PAPER-PATCHED (PATCHED) BULLET: A bullet wrapped with paper, commonly used in blackpowder cartridges. The patch was derived from a cloth patch as was used to wrap a round ball when used in a muzzleloader. Patches help seal the bore and eliminate bore leading. Paper patching serves the same function as a metal jacket; when used in guns designed for patched ammunition, accuracy can be extremely good, even by modern standards.

PARALLAX: In telescopic sights, a condition that exists when a reticle does not lie exactly on one of the optical image planes. Excessive parallax makes eye position critical for repeated accuracy—radial eye movement about the centerline of the axis of the scope significantly alters apparent reticle position on the target. Most relatively low-power scopes are designed to be parallax free at either 100 or 200 yards; most high-magnification scopes have an adjustment that allows the elimination of parallax at any desired distance beyond about 50 yards; many scopes made for 22 rimfire guns are parallax free at 50 yards.

PARTIAL SEPARATION: A case crack near the head; can allow gas to escape; always potentially dangerous.

PATH: Apparent projectile path in ballistic flight—divergence from the line of sight.

PIERCED PRIMER: Common misnomer; correct term is blanked primer.

PLINKING: Informal target practice, commonly at targets of convenience—target shooting simply for the fun of it and for practice.

POINT OF AIM: The point where a shooter aligns the sights; except when shooting at a zeroed distance, the point of aim will always be above or below the point of impact and in a cross wind it will be windward of the impact.

PORT PRESSURE: In a gas-operated firearm, the pressure at the port in the barrel when a bullet passes that opening—the force of vented gas actuates the action.

PORTING: Creating holes in a barrel; intended and designed to deflect propellant gases, usually radially, sideways and upward, or backward. Such porting is usually used to reduce recoil by redirecting gases that would otherwise jet forward after a bullet exits a bore. In handguns and shotguns, such porting is most often called compensating—see *Compensator.*

POWDER: Misnomer indicating a solid propellant—it is not a powder!—see *Propellant.*

POWDER (PROPELLANT) BRIDGING: Condition that can occur at the mouth of a charging funnel or within the drop tube of a powder measure. Propellant granules interlock and wedge together, thereby blocking the propellant's passage—a propellant logjam; most commonly occurs when using long, cylindrical propellant granules.

POWDER (PROPELLANT) MEASURE: A mechanical device used to meter propellant charges by volume. Always much faster than weighing charges and usually produces ammunition that is far more accurate because it results in more uniform granule packing schemes within resulting charged cases.

POWDER (PROPELLANT) SCALE: A sensitive measuring device used to weigh propellant charges; designed expressly for cartridge loading; usually graduated to permit weighing with 1/10-grain accuracy (1/70,000 pound).

POWDER (PROPELLANT) TRICKLER: A mechanical accessory that dribbles propellant granules, a few at a time; used with a powder scale.

PRESSURE: The force exerted by burning a propellant within a gun chamber. Pressure is normally reported in terms of peak pressure—pounds per square inch (psi) or copper units of pressure (cup), depending upon test equipment used.

PRESSURE GUN: A device for measuring the pressure within a chamber generated by a cartridge. Usually, a crusher type or an electronic transducer type. However, many laboratories now routinely use a strain gauge, which is not approved by SAAMI or CIP but which is, nonetheless, quite useful, when properly used.

PRESSURE-TO-VELOCITY RATIO: A numerical comparison of velocity-to-pressure in a specific cartridge with a given primer, bullet (and OAL), propellant and charge, and loading techniques. Ballisticians often use this as a statistical measure of propellant consistency (or dependability) when the charge is varied but with all other loading and firing variables held constant. Ideally, when a pressure-to-velocity ratio for various charges does not form a reasonably straight line, the propellant should be considered undependable for use in combinations with those components. A dangerous situation is too apt to occur when the handloader uses components from different production lots with different handloading techniques and tools and when fired in different guns.

PRIMER: Also called a cap, derived from percussion caps used with relatively modern muzzleloading guns. In a centerfire cartridge, the metal cup contains an exploding mixture that generates an incandescent plume that ignites the propellant. The primer is seated in a pocket in the base of a case. Boxer primers, the standard United States type, contain an anvil. In a rimfire cartridge, the priming mixture is contained within a fold inside the case rim.

PRIMER FLIPPER: A two-piece metal or plastic tray for orienting and turning primers; facilitates loading primer tubes that are used with some loading presses.

PRIMER INDENT: A depression made in a primer cup by the impact of the firing pin.

PRIMER LEAK: When propellant gas escapes between a primer cup and the wall of a primer pocket. Usually indicates a damaged primer pocket, either due to excessive chamber pressure (during firing) or to a burred primer-pocket-forming tool (during case manufacture).

PRIMER POCKET: A cavity in the base of a centerfire cartridge case designed to hold, seal, and support a primer.

PRIMER POCKET REAMING OR SWAGING: Methods for removing the crimp from military-case primer pockets.

PRIMER PUNCH: The tool part that inserts primers.

PRIMING TOOL: A tool designed specifically to prime cases—see *Hand-Priming Tool.*

PROGRESSIVE: Often used to indicate two separate propellant characteristics. First, by design, most smokeless propellants burn, initially, at a relatively increasing rate during the progress of combustion; this results from the inclusion of inert (deterrent) chemicals into the surface layers of granules. Second, it is the nature of any propellant to burn at a progressively faster rate as the confining pressure (temperature) increases. In the latter sense, all propellants are progressive—smokeless more so than blackpowder.

PROJECTILE: A bullet, or any other object, projected by force and continuing in inertial motion. Note that a bullet is not normally considered a projectile until it is launched from a gun muzzle.

PROOF CARTRIDGE: A specially loaded cartridge, used to test a new or repaired firearm for strength and safety. Usually, such cartridges are loaded to generate about 25 percent greater peak chamber pressure than normal cartridges of the same type.

PROPELLANT: The correct term for energetic chemicals used in cartridges—see *Powder.*

PROTRUDING PRIMER: A primer partially backed out of a primer pocket upon firing and not reseated by the chamber pressure driving the case head back against the bolt, usually indicative of unusually low peak chamber pressure.

RAM: The driving shaft of a reloading press that holds a shellholder.

RANGE: Two common meanings:

- Location where shooting is conducted, usually formal
- Projectile travel—distance between a muzzle and a target

REBATED RIMLESS: A case where the rim is noticeably smaller than the body. Examples include 50 Action Express and 284 Winchester.

RECOIL: The backward thrust (or kick) of a gun due to inertia: For every action, an equal and opposite reaction occurs. Three distinct things generate recoil:

- Acceleration of air column, forward of bullet within bore
- Acceleration of bullet and propellant gases through the bore
- Propellant gas jetting, after bullet clears bore

In most guns, the first is essentially meaningless. In guns chambered for unusually large cases and with cartridges using unusually heavy charges, the last generates far more recoil than does the second—this is why an effective muzzle brake can often reduce recoil to far less than one-half.

RECOIL BUFFER: A cushioning device installed in a gun action and used to reduce the battering between the action parts; most commonly seen in semiautomatic firearms.

RELOADING: Cartridge loading when reusing a case—see *Handloading.*

RELOADING PRESS: See *Loading Press.*

REMAINING ENERGY: The kinetic energy (foot-pounds) delivered by a projectile at the target.

REMAINING VELOCITY: The projectile's velocity at the target.

RETICLE: An aiming indicator in a telescopic gun sight. Can have straight or tapered lines (cross hairs), dots, posts, or some combination of those and markings of other shapes. Some reticles include auxiliary marks for estimating distance and sometimes for correcting for windage. Some are optionally lighted by fiber optics, tritium, or an electric light source.

RIFLING: Spiral grooves cut or impressed into a gun bore to force the bullet to rotate as it passes through the bore; this generates gyroscopic stability in ballistic flight—see Grooves and Lands. In conventional guns shooting conventional bullets, such stability improves the potential for accuracy by many orders of magnitude.

RIM: The feature at the base of most cartridge cases that an extractor can engage in order to extract a fired case from the chamber—see Rimless and Rimmed.

RIMFIRE (RF): Cartridges containing priming mixture within a folded rim. Reloading rimmed cases is impractical—compare to centerfire.

RIMLESS: A misnomer, a case type where the diameter of a rim equals the diameter of a case forward of the extractor cannelure (groove). Standardized in 1888, the 8mm Mauser was the original rimless case design.

RIMMED: Case type where a rim diameter is larger than the diameter of a case body. As the original self-contained cartridge, circa 1840, the 22 Short is the oldest recognizable example.

ROUND: One complete cartridge.

ROUND-NOSE: A bullet design with a blunt, rounded, hemispherical, or hemielliptical nose shape.

SAAMI: The Sporting Arms and Ammunition Manufacturer's Institute establishes gun and ammunition-related standards in the United States. Some of these standards were badly chosen, and many are inexplicitly and all too often routinely ignored. CIP is the related European organization. Unlike CIP, which involves government controls and all the attending inefficiencies that those entail, SAAMI is voluntary. Industry members established this organization explicitly as a means of limiting government interference in free enterprise. Specifications established by SAAMI cover cartridges, gun chambers, and gun designs. All cartridges generated within SAAMI specifications will work in all guns of the same chambering that are also produced according to SAAMI specifications—universal functionality.

SABOT: French for shoe. In small arms usage, a (lightweight) carrier or shoe in which a subcaliber projectile is centered. A sabot permits firing a bullet from a significantly larger-caliber bore; thereby, it allows the generation of a much greater muzzle velocity. Sabots usually fall away from a bullet at the muzzle. Correctly pronounced, *sah-bow,* with both syllables accented.

SEATING DEPTH: In a loaded cartridge, depth of bullet base below case mouth.

SECTIONAL DENSITY (SD): A bullet's weight in pounds, divided by the square of the diameter in inches. A perfectly useless concept to all shooters and handloaders. Within normal ranges, SD means very little to ballistic efficiency (BC)—the shape of the bullet nose and the base are vastly more important. SD means almost nothing to terminal ballistics—materials and design are more important. Hence, this is the single place you will find SD mentioned in this text.

SEMIRIMMED CASE: A case having a rim that is only slightly larger than the body. Examples: 32 Automatic, 38 Automatic, and 220 Swift.

SHANK: The cylindrical section of a bullet, behind the ogive and forward of the base radius (or boattail)—the length of the portion of the bullet that is equal to the maximum bullet diameter.

SHELLHOLDER (SHELL HOLDER): A tool that holds the head of a case during handloading; usually found on a press ram but also used in other case-modification tools and in hand-priming tools.

SHOCK: The disruption of the nervous system, through whatever means, by a bullet's impact.

SHOCK WAVE: A compression wave formed whenever a projectile's velocity exceeds the speed of sound in a material through which the projectile is passing. In shooting, this is most important when considering the consequences of air resistance on a supersonic projectile.

SHOULDER: A sloping or radiused part of a bottlenecked case—an area between the body of the case and the case neck.

SIGHTING IN: Carefully firing a rifle or pistol at a target and adjusting the sights to align the point of impact with the point of aim, or at some specific distance above or below the point of aim. For example, for most nimrods, an elk hunting rifle should be zeroed so that the bullet hits about three inches above the point of aim at 100 yards. With this setting, bullets from properly aimed shots (dead center in kill zone) will hit within the kill zone out to the longest possible distance and will not rise above the kill zone at shorter distances; this allows the hunter to take any reasonable shot without holding over or holding under the center of the kill zone.

SINGLE-BASED: A propellant with nitrocellulose (NC) as the only energetic component—see *Double-Based.*

SIZING: Also resizing. Reducing the diameter and body length of a fired case to allow for easy chambering and so that the case neck will properly hold the bullet. Sizing may be full-length, partial, or neck only. Cast bullets are also sized to reduce the diameter by forcing the bullet through a bullet-sizing die, usually in a dedicated tool (a lubrisizer) but sometimes with a die mounted on a loading press.

SM[c]: An abbreviation for Smalley-McPherson, the trademark of Superior Ballistics Incorporated, owner of various parametric patents covering optimum cartridge and gun chamber designs to provide maximum efficiency, including the mathematical algorithm behind the solution of what it is that constitutes the most efficient cartridge design. Here, maximum efficiency is defined as the generation of any given muzzle velocity with the least barrel heating, longest barrel life, and least recoil (both felt and absolute) when constrained by any given peak chamber pressure.

SMOKELESS POWDER (a double misnomer—modern propellants are neither smokeless nor powder)**:** Usually refers to a propellant that is composed mostly of nitrocellulose, often with a significant admixture of nitroglycerine. Such propellants generate noncorrosive residues.

The term *smokeless propellent* comes from the fact that these propellants generate so much less smoke than does blackpowder. The term *powder* is a holdover from when blackpowder was produced in the field of battle immediately before use, by mixing three powdered materials—that practice ended centuries ago! What we call blackpowder has not been a powder since then, but the name persists. Somehow, it has carried over to modern propellants that at no time during manufacture contained anything that could be correctly defined as a powder!

SOFTPOINT (SP): A bullet design feature where a portion of the lead-alloy core extends forward of the jacket.

SPENT: A used cartridge component.

SPHERICAL POWDER®: The registered trademark of the Hodgdon Powder Company and used to describe propellants composed of spherical or flattened-spherical granules—see Ball Powder. The term Ball-Type is preferable as it avoids trademark infringements.

SPIN: The rotation of a projectile, initiated by the barrel's rifling. At the muzzle, a spin can exceed 400,000 revolutions per minute. Doubling the spin rate quadruples the gyroscopic stability; it also quadruples the rotational bullet stress; an unnecessarily fast spin (rifling rate) degrades accuracy.

SPIRE POINT: A conical pointed bullet. The line from the shank to the ogive generates a relatively distinct shoulder—see *Tangent Ogive.*

SPITZER: A bullet design feature indicating a sharp nose; derives from the German word for point.

SR: Abbreviation for Sporting Rifle, applied to three single-based DuPont propellants (now IMR Powder Company, now owned by Hodgdon Powder Company).

Dick Casull (inventor of the 454 Casull and myriad gun designs) in 2009 showing off one of the most innovative rifles ever built. Unfortunately, fear of unwarranted litigation killed the project at the last minute, which is too bad. This rifle launches a 6.5mm, 155-grain bullet at 3,300 fps using loads that generated perfectly normal pressures. The case design, while unique in many respects, is similar to SM^C designs because it uses a very short and fat case and a very long neck. Casull is a craftsman and design genius of the first order.

STABILIZE: To spin a projectile around its longitudinal axis rapidly enough to generate sufficient gyroscopic stability to keep it point-on in flight, despite aerodynamic overturning forces.

STRIKER: Part of gun mechanism that strikes the primer and thereby initiates cartridge ignition, also called a firing pin.

STRIPPER CLIP: Abbreviated as clip. The device designed to load a magazine. A clip is not a magazine.

SWAGE: Forming something into a different shape by forcing it into, or through, a die. Swage rhymes with page.

TANGENT OGIVE: A pointed bullet where the shank rolls smoothly into the ogive; the transition from the shank to the ogive generates no sharp shoulder—see *Spire Point.*

TAYLOR THROATING: The system invented by the late Allan Taylor to freebore revolver barrels sufficiently so that a bullet can fully enter a barrel without touching the rifling. Compared to the traditional forcing cone, this is a vastly superior system because the bullet is fully supported when engraving occurs. In the conventional system, engraving occurs as the entire rearward portion of the bullet is within or is passing through the forcing cone and the cylinder-to-barrel gap. This results in monumental, accuracy-harming bullet deformation. Taylor revolver throating has no disadvantages.

THROAT: The cylindrical portion of a bore immediately ahead of the chamber neck (sometimes slightly tapered) and is sometimes slightly greater than the groove's (bullet's) diameter, compared to the leade.

TIME OF FLIGHT (TOF): The time (in seconds) of a bullet's flight, from the muzzle exit to any given distance.

TRAJECTORY: A projectile's path in ballistic flight, usually compared to the line of sight.

TRANSDUCER: A quartz-based device that develops voltage in direct proportion to applied force. A modern system used to measure the chamber pressure.

TWIST: The angle of rifling, in relation to the bore's axis. The twist is usually measured in terms of the length of the barrel required to rotate a bullet one complete turn and is represented as, 1:12 for 1 turn in 12 inches.

UPSET: There are two distinct meanings:

- Tendency for a bullet to become shorter and more cylindrical as it obturates into the bore, as happens when an acceleration force acting upon the bullet base exceeds the bullet strength.
- Expansion of a hunting bullet upon impact with the target (see mushroom).

VARMINT: A variation of the word *vermin*; an animal or bird considered a pest, usually not covered by hunting regulations.

VELOCITY: A projectile's speed, usually measured and reported in feet per second (fps or f/s) in the United States.

WADCUTTER (WAD CUTTER): A cylindrical, sharp-shouldered bullet designed to cut a clean, round hole in a paper target. WC holes are more visible and larger, so the use of these bullets can increase a score in competition.

WCF: Winchester Center Fire. The proprietary name applied to various cartridges developed by the Winchester Company, especially in the 1800s.

WEB: The part of a cartridge case between the bottom of the primer pocket and the hollow portion of the case body.

WEIGHT: A common term used when we actually mean *mass*. By definition, in the normal gravitational field of the Earth, these two are equal.

WILDCAT: A cartridge or chamber formed by altering an existing commercial case or chamber to a style not generally commercially available. Wildcats lack agreed-upon dimensional and pressure standards.

WINDAGE: Sight correction, left or right, applied to compensate for a projectile's deflection at any given target distance and with any given wind conditions.

WIND DEFLECTION: Lateral change in projectile path, due to cross-wind effects—see *Drift.*

WORK-HARDENING: A change in metal hardness due to repeated flexing or stress. In reloading, continued sizing and firing can work harden a case until it cracks, usually at the neck—see *Annealing* and *Age Hardening.*

WORKING-UP: There are two meanings in handloading and shooting:

- Process of developing a safe (maximum) load, by testing propellant charges with progressive increases.
- Step-wise accuracy testing of known safe loads while varying other load parameters.

YAW: The situation where a bullet wobbles on its longitudinal axis at a small angle to the line of flight. A significant initial yaw is created as the gun's muzzle kicks the bullet base sideways when the bullet comes free of the bore—the muzzle is always accelerating sideways as the bullet exits the bore. The bullet's spin quickly dampens the initial excessive yaw into generally a stable flight; however, no spinning bullet is ever completely free of yaw. Yaw has two components:

- Large, slow-changing component—precession
- Small, fast-changing component—nutation

Each cycles from maximum to minimum in such a way that when precession is maximum, nutation is minimum and vice versa. Violent collapsing shock waves that occur as a high-velocity spitzer bullet slows to subsonic flight often generate sufficient buffeting to initiate massive yaw, which destroys accuracy and normally persists to a bullet's terminal distance.

ZERO: More correctly, Zero Sight Adjustment. That adjustment setting of a gun sight that in the absence of wind will bring a properly aimed shot to the desired point of impact at some specific distance with a given load—the basis from which subsequent sight adjustments are made.

ZERO RANGE: In the absence of wind, the distance at which the nominal bullet path exactly coincides with the line of sight (LOS). Each gun and load combination actually has two zero distances—one nearer the muzzle (as the bullet rises through the LOS) and another at some greater distance (where the bullet descends through the LOS). Normally, we are only concerned with this second zero-distance.

SOURCES FOR REFERENCED SPECIALTY TOOLS AND COMPONENTS

APPENDIX B

Bear Creek Supply
P.O. Box 177
Waterford, CA 95386
Telephone: 209-874-4322

Belt Mountain Enterprises Inc.
Box 353, Belgrade, MT 59714
Telephone: 406-388-1396
www.beltmountain.com

BERSIN GmbH
30 St. Jakobs-Strasse, CH-4002
Basel, Switzerland
www.bersin.info
bersin@bersin.info

Buffalo Arms Company
660 Vermeer Court
Ponderay, ID 83852
Telephone: 208-263-6953
bufarms@netw.com
Champion's Brand
(case cleaner and polish)
www.championsbrand.com

Corbin Manufacturing & Supply, Inc
P.O. Box 2659
White City, Oregon 97503
Telephone: 541-826-5211
www.corbins.com
sales@corbins.com

George and Roy's
2950 NW 29th
Portland, OR 97210
Telephone: 800-553-3022

JRP Bullets
Telephone: 518-282-0084

K&M Precision Shooting Products
6852 Lakeshore Drive
West Olive, Michigan 49460
Telephone: 616-399-7894
www.kmshooting.com

Magnus Bullets
Telephone: 256-420-8360

Meacham
Tool & Hardware Inc.
1070 Angel Ridge Road
Peck, ID 83545
Telephone: 208-486-7171

Oehler Research
P.O. Box 9135
Austin, TX 78766
Tele: 800-531-5125

Old West Bullet Moulds
1175 17¼ Road
Fruita, CO 81521
Telephone: 970-858-1449

Quick Measure
c/o Johnson Design Specialties
4607 West Elderberry Avenue
Spokane, WA 99208
Telephone: 509-464-0697

R. W. Hart & Son, Inc.
401 Montgomery Street
Nescopeck, PA 18635
Telephone: 717-752-3655

Recreational Software Inc.
1343 Navajo Drive
Cottonwood, AZ 86323
Telephone: 928-634-8028
www.shootingsoftware.com

SharpShoot-R Inc.
Box 171
Paola, KS 66071
Telephone: 785-883-4444
e-mail: grtinfo@sharpshootr.com
www.sharpshootr.com

Shooting Chrony Inc.
3840 Robinson Road PMB #298
Amherst, NY 14228
Telephone: 800-385-3161

Sinclair International
2330 Wayne Haven Street
Fort Wayne, IN 46803
Telephone: 800-717-8211

Superior Ballistics Inc.
www.superiorballistics.com

Superior Shooting Systems
800 N. Second Street
Canadian, Texas 79014
Telephone: 806-323-9483

SSRJ (Single Shot Rifle Journal)
10608 Summer Mountain Court
Knoxville, TN 37922
www.assra.com

Yesteryear Armory and Supply
P.O. Box 408
Carthage, TN 37030

Bill Ferguson
PO Box 1238
Sierra Vista, AZ 85636
Telephone: 520-458-5321

MAJOR HANDLOADING EQUIPMENT MANUFACTURERS

Dillon Precision Products
8009 E. Dillon's Way
Scottsdale, AZ 85260
Telephone: 800-762-3845

Forster Products
82 E. Lanark Avenue
Lanark, IL 61046
Telephone: 815-493-6360

Hornady Manufacturing
P.O. Box 1848
Grand Island, NE 68802
Telephone: 800-338-3220

Lee Precision
4275 Hwy U
Hartford, WI 53027
Telephone: 262-673-3075

Lyman Products
475 Smith Street
Middleton, CT 06457
Telephone: 860-632-2020

Midway
5875 W. Van Horn Tavern Rd.
Columbia, MO 65203
Telephone: 800-243-3220

RCBS
605 Oro Dam Blvd.
Oroville, CA 95965
Telephone: 530-533-5191

Redding
1089 Star Road
Cortland, NY 13045
Telephone: 607-753-3331

INTERESTING RIFLESCOPE TEST RESULTS

APPENDIX C

Readers might find the following results interesting. These are a few of the results garnered from a study of typical scopes when used on a typical 50 BMG chambered target rifle. The test consisted of mounting each scope on that gun, firing 20 shots, and then moving the scope to a 22-250 Savage for further evaluation. Only the scopes that survived the 50 BMG battering are considered in these tables.

A full review of this extensive riflescope testing is outside the purpose of this manual, but readers might be interested to know that, in this test, 8 of the 19 scopes submitted for evaluation either failed during testing (5) or were faulty before testing began (3)! The salient point here is this:

EVERY SCOPE WILL FAIL; IT IS NOT A QUESTION OF "IF" BUT A QUESTION OF "WHEN." IF YOU ARE HAVING AN ACCURACY PROBLEM, ALWAYS ASSUME THE SCOPE IS FAULTY UNTIL YOU PROVE OTHERWISE.

CALIBRATION ACCURACY: WINDAGE AND ELEVATION ADJUSTMENTS

MAKE	MODEL	5-SHOT, 100-YARD GROUP: WITHOUT SETTLING	5-SHOT, 100-YARD GROUP: AFTER SETTLING	NUMBER OF SHOTS REQUIRED BEFORE SETTLING
Nikon	5½–16½	0.75	0.33	0
Tasco	9–40	1.06	0.36	0
Weaver	4½–14	0.66	0.41	0
Kahles	3–9	0.75	0.43	0
Shepherd	6–18	1.36	0.59	0
Burris	6–24	1.07	0.28	3
Bushnell	4–16	1.09	0.29	2
Nikon	3½–10	0.75	0.39	2
Pentax	8½–32	0.79	0.60	2
Springfield	4–14	1.00	0.68	2
Swarovski	3–12	1.08	0.71	2
Shepherd	3–10	0.89	0.88	3
Millet	4–16	0.87	0.49	0

Without settling: Groups were fired by adjusting the reticle to move the impact to each corner of a square, one shot was fired after each adjustment, and this process was repeated until a five-shot group existed at each corner. After settling: group fired by adjusting reticle to move group to point of aim and firing shots without adjustment. If the final group showed evidence of reticle settling, I continued to fire shots until settling evidently ended and I had a five-shot group inside a larger group that contained settling fliers. Confusing as this might be, it shows that how the reticle settles depends upon how it is adjusted. Bringing the point of aim to the center of the square required adjustment of both elevation and windage, which evidently often settled the reticle when either adjustment alone (as occurred when firing shots at the corners of the square) did not. As this data suggest, many scopes require settling after any reticle adjustment. My conclusion is that, in general, the only way to settle the reticle of any given scope after an elevation or windage adjustment is to fire the gun.

Claimed Reticle Adjustment versus Actual Reticle Adjustment, as Measured

Make	Model	Windage	Elevation
Shepherd	3–10	101%	101%
BSA	6–24	98%	98%
Weaver	4½–14	103%	103%
Kahles	3–9	96%	96%
Swarovski	3–12	95%	95%
Nikon	3½–10	94%	94%
Nikon	5½–16½	93%	93%
Bushnell	4–16	112%	112%
Tasco	9–40	84%	84%
Burris	6–24	84%	84%
Shepherd	6–18	80%	100%
Pentax	8½–32	91%	118%
Springfield	4–14	134%	106%
Millet	4–16	101%	101%

Calibration errors less than about 5 percent are not apt to cause most shooters much problem in most situations. Calibration errors of 10 percent or more are likely to cause almost any serious shooter grief. Calibration errors as great as some of these scopes demonstrated are something else.

Here Casull is firing his 800-rpm, gas operated, 22 WMR prototype. This machine gun fires from an open bolt. It features a 300-round, gas actuated, drum magazine. The function is flawless.

Dick Casull and P.O. Ackley created this simple assembly in the 1950s. With it they launched relatively light steel and copper-alloy bullets at velocities near 10,000 fps! Steel bullets began to burn after about 20 feet of travel and never reached 25 feet of travel. Copper alloy bullets vaporized near 25 feet of travel.

RIFLESCOPES ARE NOT CREATED EQUAL—CONSIDER THE FOLLOWING TEST RESULTS

The following data represent the comparative accuracy of a particular custom 22-250, Black Hills Ammunition load (using a Starke bullet) when fired from a stock Savage Model-12, fitted with the riflescope indicated. This rifle and load combination routinely generates 3-shot, 100-yard groups near ¼-inch, on-centers when fitted with my best target riflescopes.

I trust these data, but I must caution the reader that this table represents the results of testing only one scope of each type; this might, therefore, be of no value because scope-to-scope and lot-to-lot variations are likely to be significant. Furthermore, some data presented here might be indicative of a scope that has already begun to fail—I had previously subjected these scopes to a torture test consisting of mounting on a typical 50 BMG target rifle, through the firing of 20 rounds of typical 50-BMG ammunition. Nevertheless, these data are interesting.

A faulty riflescope can thwart your best efforts toward tuning a rifle and ammunition combination. This problem is so common that serious shooters recognize it as a routine part of life—so far, I have had at least eight scopes fail while in use; I expect to see more failures.

Measured Eye Relief (Inches)

Make	Model	Minimum	Maximum
Shepherd	6–18	1.8	2.1
Shepherd	3–10	1.7	2.1
Springfield	4–14	1.6	2.5
Bushnell	4–16	1.4	2.2
Weaver	4½–14	1.3	2.1
Burris	6–24	1.1	2.2
Nikon	3½–10	1.1	2.2
Tasco	8–40	1.1	1.8
BSA	6–24	1.5	1.7
Kahles	3–9	1.5	1.7
Pentax	8½–32	1.1	1.4
Swarovski	3–12	1.4	1.4
Millet	4–16	1.1	2.2

Riflescope Accuracy Test Results (Typical 100-Yard, 3-Shot Groups)

Make	Model	MOA
Burris	6–24	0.28
Bushnell	4–16	0.29
Nikon	5½–16½	0.33
Tasco	9–40	0.36
Nikon	3½–10	0.39
Weaver	4½–14	0.41
Kahles	3–9	0.43
Millet	4–16	0.49
Shepherd	6–18	0.59
Pentax	8½–32	0.60
Springfield	4–14	0.68
Swarovski	3–12	0.71
Shepherd	3–10	0.88

Average of several groups.

Useful Elevation and Windage Adjustment Range

Make	Model	(MOA)
Springfield	4–14	30
Burris	6–24	29
Kahles	3–9	28
Nikon	3½–10	23
Bushnell	4–16	22
Weaver	4½–14	22
Pentax	8½–32	21
Sightron	4–16	20
BSA	6–24	18
Swarovski	3–12	17
Shepherd	3–10	11
Tasco	8–40	6
Shepherd	6–18	4
Millet	4–16	31

Left to right: Dick Casull, Dave Torkelson, and Andy Tuttle. We were visiting the Casulls (Dick and Teri) at their home in September 2009. Here, we were testing various one-of-a-kind Casull-built guns. The gas-operated semiautomatic that Torkelson is holding is chambered for the 38 Casull, a high-pressure version of the necked-down 45 Automatic. It launches 150-grain bullets at 2,100 fps. Tuttle is holding a 300-round, gas-operated 22 WMR, 800 rounds-per-minute machine gun.

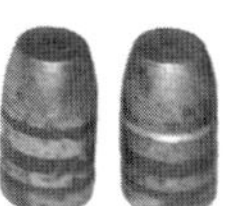

Gunsmiths can make custom loading dies to match any chambering. Such dies allow us to venture beyond standard chamberings. This set includes: full-length sizing, bellmouth expanding, seating, and Lee FCD. Note that it also includes a dedicated shellholder. I learned years ago that whenever feasible it is easiest to have a shellholder for each die set and to keep those together.

Above: Perhaps only a handloader would think of demonstrating the muzzle flash of a particular load on a pitch-black night. Here, Andy Tuttle demonstrates the flash generated by his 460 S&W load when fired from his matching, ported S&W revolver with a 2¾-inch barrel. To say that 38 grains of H110 lit up the night might be hyperbole in understatement. About 20 of us had just completed a night-fighting training seminar at the 2010 Shootists' Holiday and this demonstration was a highlight of the evening for all present (shooters, coaches, and observers alike).

Left: My late friend, Roger Hazlewood. I would like to dedicate this book to Hazlewood, who was an inspiration to all like-minded people who knew him. He was one of those rare souls who knew how to even-handedly justify his opinions with logic and facts. He was a serious shooter and handloader. He and I shared many, but all too few, red-letter days at the shooting range, in the field, and teaching concealed carry classes to about 1,000 people.

VERY LONG-RANGE SHOOTING

APPENDIX D

In an effort to simulate the conditions that Medal of Honor recipient, Billy Dixon, encountered at the Battle of Adobe Walls, Bill Falin, my father and mother (Bob and Joyce), and I created a cardboard cutout that resembled a mounted warrior. Falin and I erected this on a hillside, almost seven-eights of a mile from our shooting location.

Bill Falin preparing to fire at a life-size silhouette of a man on horseback located 1,538 yards distant.

View of target from about 200 yards.

Second Billy Dixon Shoot target: Harvey Watt and Paul Armbruster did most of the shooting: 7½ feet by 15 feet cardboard target nailed to ground with 10-inch spikes.

Crossed sticks; C-Sharps (40-65 Falin—necked-down 444 Marlin); Montana Precision, long-range sights. Handloads: RCBS 400-grain bullet, A5744 to duplicate blackpowder velocity. Falin's cheek is several inches above stock; despite this difficultly, this combination proved effective. In one string of 16 shots, I managed several hits on the target with all misses either passing just over and falling behind the target or very close, at the sides.

Falin posing as if he were ready to fire. Gun is stable. With tiny adjustments of his left fist, Falin can raise, lower, or move gun butt slightly sideways, as needed, to bring the sights on target.

Although the sights are not aligned perfectly with the target (arrow), this view gives some sense of the distance involved. Dixon was shooting at a group of about fifteen riders huddled on a hillside.

THE HUNT

I looked down off the rocky ledge, at the canyon far below,
that glistened bright, just dusted white, from an early autumn snow.
And soon the sun would burn it off, other colors to unfold,
of oak leaves turning reddish brown, and aspen leaves of gold.
I looked with pride, for by my side, my sons had joined the hunt.
To have them there, tradition share, was all that I could want.
Time passes by so quickly, and in my happiness was sad.
It seems like only yesterday, I'd hunted here with Dad.
But in my hands held history that helped make this hunt great.
I'd brought Grandfather's rifle, made in nineteen hundred eight.
For he too had walked these trails, nature's heaven he had found,
and breathed in God's creation, that somehow's lost in town.
For hunting's not a lonesome thing, it's shared with those you love.
Can't help but feel, Gramps with me still, looking down from up above.
And maybe it was just the wind, then again, well maybe not,
but I thought I heard him chuckle, saying, "Now don't you miss this shot!"
But the trail is mine today to walk, Grandfather, Dad, now me.
And tomorrow it will be my sons'; I'll be their memory.
And perhaps they'll pack my rifle, and with pride call it their own,
and as they walk this mountain path, they'll never be alone.

D. J. Wynkoop,
Fruita, Colorado, 2006

(Written by my cousin, D.J., after I told him of my first hunt with my sons in an area that I had not hunted for decades. The hills where my father had first taken me when I was a mere child. Where Dad and I had trekked many times during my childhood. Not only did my grandfather hunt in those same hills but so did three of my paternal grandmother's brothers—quite a family tradition.)

NOTES

NOTES

NOTES